AMERICAN WORK

AMERICAN WORK

Four Centuries of Black and White Labor

JACQUELINE JONES

W. W. NORTON & COMPANY

NEW YORK • LONDON

For information about permission to reproduce selections from this book,
write to Permissions, W. W. Norton & Company, Inc., 500 Fifth Avenue,
New York, NY 10110

The text of this book is composed in Dante
with the display set in Copperplate
Desktop Composition by Gina Webster
Manufacturing by Quebecor Printing, Fairfield Inc.
Book design by Chris Welch

Library of Congress Cataloging-in-Publication Data
Jones, Jacqueline, 1948–
American work : four centuries of black and white labor / Jacqueline Jones.
p.   cm.
Includes bibliographical references and index.
ISBN 0-393-04561-7
1. Afro-Americans—Economic conditions. 2. Afro-Americans—
Employment—History. 3. United States—Race relations. 4. Race discrimina-
tion—United States—History. I. Title.
E185.8.J767   1998
331.6'396073—DC21   97–20337
                                              CIP

W. W. Norton & Company, Inc., 500 Fifth Avenue, New York, N.Y. 10110
http://www.wwnorton.com

W. W. Norton & Company Ltd., 10 Coptic Street, London WC1A 1PU
1 2 3 4 5 6 7 8 9 0

FOR SARAH AND ANNA

CONTENTS

PART II

WORKERS AND OVERWORKERS:
BLACK AND WHITE LABOR IN
THE ERA OF SLAVERY

PART III

THE RISE AND DECLINE OF THE RACIALIZED
MACHINE:
TECHNOLOGICAL AND POLITICAL CHANGE
IN THE WORKPLACE

Acknowledgments

First and foremost, I owe several debts of gratitude to various groups and individuals within the Brandeis University community. Since I came to Brandeis six years ago, I have received invaluable support from four of my colleagues in the History Department in particular—Morton Keller, David Hackett Fischer, James Kloppenberg, and Jane Kamensky—all of whom have inspired me with the excellence of their own American work. In the classroom, my students, both undergraduate and graduate, helped me to explore interlocking systems of black and white labor; the first-year students I taught in a university seminar in the fall of 1994 prodded me to consider when race mattered, and when it did not, in the creation of regional labor forces throughout American history. A number of current and former graduate students helped with research and bibliographical work; I appreciate the assistance of Ann Marie Plane, Brian Kelly, Christian Warren, and Darra Mulderry. In the History Department office, Ina Malaguti and Judy Brown were always willing to respond to my pleas for help, some more frantic than others. My friend and colleague Ibrahim Sundiata graciously allowed me to use his photograph, taken by Brandeis chief photographer Julian Brown, in the book. The Brandeis Provost's and Dean's Offices provided me with financial support to complete this project during a year of sabbatical leave. The reference, interlibrary loan, and circulation staffs of the Brandeis Library were unfailingly generous with their time, and patient with my queries and requests. And finally, in chapters scattered throughout the United States, members of the Brandeis National Women's

Committee have helped to build and sustain a truly impressive library collection of books, periodicals, and microfilms in the field of American history; I am grateful for their hard work on behalf of Brandeis students and
faculty over the years.

In its earliest form, this book was a series of long working papers, and I
greatly benefited from the suggestions of several historians who helped me
to sharpen the argument and strengthen the narrative line. I especially
appreciate the substantive and editorial comments of Jack E. Davis,
Thomas Dublin, Ellen Fitzpatrick, Eric Foner, Steve Fraser, James Horton,
Lois Horton, Jane Kamensky, Michael Katz, Morton Keller, Brian Kelly,
Elizabeth Pleck, and Joe William Trotter, Jr. Darlene Clark Hine encouraged me in writing this book; her support has meant a great deal to me over
the years.

The American Council of Learned Societies provided me with a fellowship that helped to fund a year of research and writing. Also, I had the
opportunity to give several presentations and take away from the ensuing
discussions a number of ideas that I subsequently incorporated into the
book. Members of the Brown University Latin American Studies Gender
Workshop, the W. E. B. Du Bois's *The Philadelphia Negro* Centenary Reappraisal working group (organized by Michael Katz and Thomas Sugrue), an
American Antiquarian Society seminar, and the Massachusetts Historical
Society, as well as participants in the W. E. B. Du Bois Institute's Fiftieth
Anniversary Conference on Myrdal's *American Dilemma*, offered helpful criti-
cisms and suggestions.

I would like to thank Christine Jacobson Carter for her research in the
Georgia State Archives, Jack E. Davis and Brian Kelly for several relevant
documents and references, and Chad Cover for a copy of the Dunlop Commission Report. Richard Steven Street, a fellow historian and award-winning
photographer, allowed me to use two of his evocative photographs of Mexican immigrant workers in California, and Coreen Simpson granted me permission to reproduce her 1980 photograph of Harlem service workers on
strike. Chris Steele, Curator of Photographs at the Massachusetts Historical
Society; Georgia B. Barnhill, Andrew W. Mellon Curator of Graphic Arts at
the American Antiquarian Society; Jim Huffman of the Photographs and
Prints Division of the Schomburg Center for Research in Black Culture; and
Rutha Dicks of the Still Picture Branch of the National Archives at College
Park, Maryland, helped me to locate and then arranged for the efficient
reproduction of a number of photographs.

I was fortunate to have Alane Salierno Mason of W. W. Norton as my editor; she offered me guidance that was thorough, exacting, and ever attentive

to the shape of this book as a story as well as a work of history. I have learned a good deal from Alane, and consider it a privilege to have worked with her.

I belong to two extended families—the Joneses and the Abramsons, and draw strength from both of them. In particular, my mother, Sylvia Phelps Jones, and my in-laws, Rose and Al Abramson, provided me with unconditional love and encouraged me in this project (though I too often appeared on their doorsteps encumbered with notes, books, and papers). My father, Albert H. Jones, Jr., did not live to see the completion of this book, but I am thankful that he derived so much satisfaction from his own life's (unwaged) work on behalf of all of the public school children of Delaware; he was a firm believer in the transcendent power of education.

As always, my husband Jeffrey Abramson served as my most demanding critic. His support ranged from the sublime—urging me to think about larger issues of class and social transformation with precision and clarity— to the mundane—coaching and coaxing me through more computer crises than either one of us wants to remember. I have profited from his example as a scholar and a writer uncompromising in his passion for justice.

The names of two young avid readers grace the dedication page of this book. The aspirations of my daughters, Sarah Jones Abramson and Anna Jones Abramson, have made all the more compelling to me the story that unfolds in the following pages—the story of countless Americans thwarted in their attempts to seek out and find jobs commensurate with their talents and with their desire to provide decently for themselves and their families.

INTRODUCTION

J
obs are never just jobs; they are social markers of great real and symbolic value. The abolitionist Frederick Douglass recognized that work matters when he warned his fellow free people of color in 1853: "Men are not valued in this country, or in any country, for what they *are*; they are valued for what they can do." (And if white ladies of leisure were any indication, then women were also valued for what they did *not* do.) At stake was not work alone—slaves for example never lacked for jobs—but the legal and social status of workers. Douglass further understood that irregular and poorly paid employment could render even free men and women dependent, "at the mercy of the oppressor to become his debased slaves." The work that people did, and the terms and conditions under which they did it, revealed both their place and their possibilities within American society.[1]

This book tells the story of the jobs performed by Africans and their descendants in America, and in the process tells a larger story about the "racial" conflicts that remain the moral burden of this country's history. This story was not foreordained; rather, each generation of whites defined and redefined themselves in relation to black workers, and each generation of blacks struggled to resist the demands imposed upon them, whether by slaveowners, landlords, or employers. In devising political strategies to retain their economic advantages over blacks, whites drew upon various ideologies of racial superiority. Indeed, racism was not a primal prejudice but rather a fluid set of rationalizations, always shifting in response to considerations related to military defense, labor supply and demand, and technological innovation. Consequently, black people's work outside their own homes and communities in large part reflected the self-interests of groups of whites, and those interests varied from place to place and changed over time.

Most people will acknowledge that in the history of American work, blacks have suffered disproportionately and received unequal rewards compared to their white counterparts; and most people believe this fact to be the result of racially discriminatory employment practices which, according to some, are no longer a decisive factor in shaping the late twentieth-century workforce. They are both right and wrong. "Racial discrimination," understood as barring blacks from certain kinds of work, cannot explain (for example) the fact that blacks performed a wide variety of skilled jobs under slavery. Too, at times black people as free men and women were preferred for specific jobs on the assumption that they worked more cheaply and endured harsh conditions more easily compared to poor whites. Indeed, white people who utilized black labor almost always considered the relative value of different kinds of workers—in the antebellum South, for example, bound and free, male and female, black and white, child and adult—and reckoned that value not only in economic but also in political terms.

An emphasis on employer discrimination downplays the role of the state in shaping regional workforces. From the earliest colonial settlements, public policies have provided certain kinds of workers with advantages over others. Colonial courts facilitated the extensive use of bound laborers—slaves, servants, apprentices, and orphans—and later, municipal licensing boards favored white tradesmen over their black counterparts. The late twentieth-century national political economy, which encourages business consolidation, technological innovation, and international free trade, has been responsible for the displacement of hundreds of thousands of manufacturing workers since the 1950s. Just as the federal government began to dismantle state-sanctioned all-white workplaces, then, global economic forces wrought devastation on American workers at the lowest echelons of the labor force, a trend that harmed blacks disproportionately.

Moreover, an exclusive emphasis on racial discrimination does not help us to distinguish between instances where employers believed that black people were incapable of performing a particular task, and instances where fellow white workers, government officials, consumers, or some combination of all these groups expressed their opinion that black people regardless of their skills should not be allowed to perform a particular task under any circumstances. In the antebellum North, textile mills did not hire black people as machine operatives; in contrast, in the antebellum South, mill owners used slave men, women, and children extensively in those same jobs. By the late nineteenth century, factory work throughout the United States was reserved for whites; thereafter emerged an insidious new idea—that black people were incapable of working with machines. In itself, the fact that antebellum northerners "discriminated" against blacks in textile production and southerners at the same time did not offers little insight into the complicated political forces that shaped these respective regional economies. In the twentieth century, more and more employers could claim they eschewed racial discrimination in hiring altogether, favoring applicants on the basis of their formal credentials, not their race. This disclaimer masked the historical fact that by that time, significant numbers of black people were clustered in poor neighborhoods, without access to the good schools and specialized training that would provide them with a competitive edge in the labor market.

Racial ideologies are fluid, and reflective of shifting power relations over time. These ideologies in fact constitute strategies deployed for specific reasons; rhetoric more often than not follows function. By focusing on the idea of racial difference as one among any number of political weapons, it is possible to outline at least three (admittedly broad) historical contexts in which it has been used. First, groups of relatively powerful people have claimed "racial" superiority over other groups in order to enforce a certain kind of labor upon them. Second, people who perform the same kinds of work as people labeled "racially" inferior have seized upon racial ideologies to distance themselves from the targeted group. For example, at certain times these ideologies proved useful to southern white sharecroppers and tenants, people who shared with blacks certain jobs, as well as a similarly lowly material standard of living, and feared that historic forces of economic inequality would condemn them to continue to work alongside blacks in the future. These specific, strategic uses of racial ideologies remind us that emerging classes of whites have often used blacks as a counter-reference group, defining themselves as a unified group (of wage earners or housewives, voters or union members) not just on the basis of who they are, but also on the basis of who they are not—that is, "blacks."

And too, in certain instances, other racial ideologies (those invoking difference but not inequality) have also been used by members of oppressed groups as rhetorical tactics of liberation, a source of strength and collective resistance to injustice. Nevertheless, while notions of "blackness" might function as a force for political cohesion among African descendants living in the United States, these notions might also expose fault lines within the group itself—for example, when men proclaimed that only they were able to speak on behalf of the "race," or when middle-class persons proved reluctant to acknowledge the forces of class stratification within their own communities.[2]

The constant negotiation of "whiteness" over the generations—that is, the way whites defined themselves as English colonists, American revolutionaries, or free laborers in relation to the black workers in their midst— produced no single "racial division of labor" throughout American history. In seeking to defend precarious colonial outposts within a highly volatile Atlantic world, early English settlers saw African servants and slaves, English indentured servants, and Indian hirelings as equally dangerous and undisciplined. It was not until the late eighteenth century that white elites began to stress the distinctiveness of Africans and their descendants, and to describe that distinctiveness in "racial" (not just ethnocentric) terms.

Around the time of the Civil War, German and Irish workers began to replace northern blacks in service and manual labor jobs; noted Frederick Douglass, "a few years ago, and a *white* barber would have been a curiosity—now their poles stand on every street." Labor patterns shifted perceptibly as immigrants, "whose hunger and whose color are thought to give [them] a better title to the place," did not hesitate to take "black" jobs.[3] In federal office buildings in Washington, D.C., black men found employment as custodians and sweepers, but in the Great Depression they were replaced by white men desperate for work. Indeed, within particular places throughout the generations, few menial jobs have been reserved exclusively for black people; even in the slave South, some poor whites worked stooped over in the cotton fields with slaves. On the other hand, the realm of good jobs— defined progressively as those that offered a worker some independence from a master or employer, or those that paid well, or came with Social Security or unemployment benefits, or provided safe working conditions and health care and paid vacations—remained the province of whites, at least outside the narrow confines of black-owned businesses.

Too, it is misleading to single out a "racial division of labor" characteristic of American history because racial ideologies have been invoked to justify the legal subordination of a number of groups of wage earners, and not just blacks. In nineteenth-century California, Anglos might at times identify Mexicans and Asians as members of distinct "races," but these whites also took pains to distinguish among social classes of Spanish-speaking peoples, and between Chinese and Japanese immigrants. By the mid-1870s, anti-Chinese sentiment in particular had emerged as a major political movement in California, and rhetoric emanating from that movement bore a striking resemblance to anti-black prejudice in the East during the antebellum period. Many white men blamed Chinese workers for their own economic misfortune within an unstable regional economy, and these whites claimed that the Chinese as a group possessed certain "racial" characteristics—a predisposition to crime, for example—that made them unworthy of American citizenship. In fact, most Chinese were "gap fillers," taking jobs that white men (and women) did not want or were unavailable to do; and it was the railroad, bringing cheap goods from the East Coast, rather than degraded Chinese "coolie" labor, that pushed manufacturing wages low and eventually killed off a number of fledgling local industries, including shoes and cigars. Throughout this process, then, the "cultural" proclivities of Chinese immigrants counted for less than the unique contours of the California political economy. The result was a distinct social division of labor that eventually limited Chinese immigrants to work as laundry owners and agricultural workers.[4]

Where other studies have explored the historic development of free labor, and the persistent efforts of workers to retain some autonomy within the workplace, this one follows forced labor as a subtext illustrative of the historic forces shaping the entire American workforce. Until 1800 or so, the vast majority of American workers were unfree, bound to masters or dependent on fathers or husbands. People were assigned jobs on the basis of their status at birth; they did not apply for or aspire to jobs as much as they tried to resist the particular demands of the jobs they were forced to do. Even after emancipation, peonage continued in one form or another in rural southern timber and turpentine camps, in sweatshops and on truck farms and in other industries marked by ruthless competition, hazardous working conditions, and small profit margins. The Vietnamese and Chinese sweatshop workers smuggled into the United States in the 1990s and beholden to ship captains for their passage served as a reminder that a high-technology, so-called postindustrial economy was not inconsistent with the use of bound labor. Too, colonial state-sponsored "pauper auctions" and workhouses are not so removed from the late twentieth century, when increasing numbers of young black men are remanded to prison, there to bust rocks or engage in other forms of work (productive or otherwise).[5]

American Work focuses on the history of specific jobs, but in many cases the social context of a job mattered more than the routine nature of the work itself. In the humid tobacco fields of the seventeenth-century Chesapeake, on any one day in the early fall, groups of workers performed identical tasks, and yet those tasks were imbued with different social meanings. Indians working on their ancestral grounds, now enslaved by white captors; English servants numb with homesickness; servants and slaves of African heritage thrust violently into a Christian, English-speaking world; the white children of a father-landowner, and the white wife of a husband-landowner, all labored to harvest a crop that was alien to them, a crop that promised, or threatened, strikingly different futures for them according to their legal status. Similarly, in the antebellum South, the simple act of cooking a meal became a chore or a celebration, depending whether the black woman worker was catering to the exacting tastes of a well-to-do white family, caring for her own family members after they had spent a long day picking cotton, or preparing food to hawk on a city street in order to earn money to purchase the freedom of a loved one in bondage. After the federal government delegated substantial social welfare responsibilities to large private employers in the 1930s, workers judged their own well-being not only according to the job they performed but also according to the benefits and security attached to the job. The temporary or contract worker might share the same workplace with a union member guaranteed health benefits and paid vacations; but the two would necessarily approach their tasks in ways that reflected their dissimilar statuses.

Throughout American history, black people have pushed hard against the circumscribed nature of their employment, and against their exclusion from all but the most menial of tasks. In the twentieth century, their struggles to secure for themselves decent jobs have ranged from legal test cases sponsored by the National Association for the Advancement of Colored People (NAACP), and moral suasion exerted on employers by the National Urban League, to grass-roots boycotts of all-white workplaces within neighborhood department stores and grocery stores, and skilled workers' protests against the policies of racially discriminatory labor unions. When they migrated in search of better jobs up north during World War I or out west during World War II, southern black people collectively defied the caste system that condemned them to work only as field hands and domestics. Together, integrationists and black nationalists alike hailed black communities that offered a relative range of employment opportunities for their residents. Velma Dolphin Ashley, a schoolteacher in the all-black town of Boley, Oklahoma (founded in 1904), observed that she managed to avoid a work life "in which white people would expect her to clean and cook but not, for example, to teach Shakespeare."[6]

This study draws upon the recent secondary literature in the "new labor history"—a body of scholarship that stresses the social and demographic characteristics of specific groups of workers. In synthesizing this literature, I have attempted to place the history of African Americans within a larger conceptual framework in order to understand both the uniqueness of their historical experience and, in particular instances, the fate they shared with certain groups of whites. Over the generations, classes of working people have figured and reconfigured themselves in response to perceived threats and opportunities, both real and imagined. As individuals and as groups, workers upheld exclusive racial, religious, or ethnic loyalties one day, and in some instances acted upon more inclusive, class-based interests the next. Black wives and mothers shared certain family obligations with their white counterparts of a similar status; but together with their menfolk, black women encountered uniquely constricted options in the larger world of paid labor. Hamstrung by a variety of Black Codes designed to limit their political rights and economic opportunities, black farm workers in the pre–Civil War Midwest suffered from unique liabilities compared to white men in similar jobs; but members of both races faced an uncertain future with the consolidation of landholdings and the introduction of agricultural technology.

Emancipated from slavery with little in the way of material resources, most black men and women in the postrevolutionary North represented the vanguard of "free labor," workers released from their masters but persistently poor and subject to the vagaries of the marketplace. They were "free" to be hired at the lowest wages, and "free" to be fired at a moment's notice. Compared to the persistent plight of black workers, the tribulations associated with white male artisans undergoing enforced deskilling in the early nineteenth century, or with white women workers limited to clerical or retail positions in the early 1900s, appear purely relative; urban black workers always aspired to indoor jobs that paid cash wages. In the cities, African Americans enjoyed little of the intergenerational upward mobility (or residential mobility) that immigrant groups came to take for granted; indeed, the occupational success of those groups over time rested squarely on the shoulders of black men, women, and children who continued to scrounge for daywork and scrub floors and wash clothes. Whites exclusively (although not all whites) benefited from an expanding job structure; yet African Americans through the generations, regardless of ideology or political affiliation, shared the conviction that equal access to employment, like the right to vote, was a cornerstone of the fight for civil rights.

At the end of the twentieth century, debates over affirmative action policies evoke the turbulence of the antebellum period, when immigrants vied for the jobs of blacks, and whites in general charged that, for each black person hired, a white person would have to be fired, or not hired. Despite their poverty and their small numbers, free people of color in the antebellum North spoke in a unified voice to insist that access to decent jobs be linked to political rights. Nevertheless, whites of the laboring classes, anxious about their own job security within an industrializing economy, saw black protest as only a ploy in a zero-sum game calculated to reduce white families to beggary. In nineteenth-century parlance, these whites feared that the "elevation of the blacks" (into good jobs) would necessarily mean the "degradation of the whites" (into poverty). The political and "racial" ideology that portrayed black men and women as ruthless predators on the job market had little connection with the material reality of their everyday lives. Indeed, the rhetoric of racial prejudice merely served to rationalize ongoing efforts to subordinate black people to whites. Of blacks, James Freeman Clarke, a white man active in the abolitionist cause at the time, observed, "We dislike them because we are unjust to them." By this he meant that injustice preceded the ideology that sought to justify it.[7]

Historically, the same whites who decried free men and women of color as rapacious job seekers also denounced all black people as lazy and unwilling to work. By the 1980s and 1990s these mutually exclusive, contradictory stereotypes had found renewed expression in debates over the rights of, on the one hand, black women recipients of Aid to Families with Dependent Children (AFDC), considered to be "shiftless" in a way that white middle-class women who stayed home with their children were not, and, on the other, black beneficiaries of affirmative action policies, considered to be unprincipled in their attempts to gain access to good schools and jobs at the expense of white people. Meanwhile, debates over affirmative action (narrowly defined) deflected public attention away from longstanding inequities in housing and education, and from the global economic forces that were producing multi-ethnic, multi-racial distressed communities throughout the country.

To gauge the current state of American civic life, then, we must understand the labor systems that assign certain groups to certain kinds of jobs, and then explore the way those jobs are organized. Within each worksite is embedded a history of social transformation, a history that illuminates our collective sense of power and justice. As a society, we are what we do at work, and we remain the sum of our radically divergent workplaces.

PART I

INSUBORDINATES

Servants and Slaves in a

Militarized Age

CHAPTER ONE

PLACES OF LABOR'S "HARD USAGE" IN THE SOUTH BEFORE SLAVERY

In the eyes of Captain John Smith, early seventeenth-century Virginia offered up a perverse paradise of sorts, a bountiful Eden where, nevertheless, English men, women, and children could earn their bread—and a dry coarse cornbread at that—only by the sweat of their brow. Here was a place that abounded in the promise of "incredible pleasure, profit and plenty," and yet yielded only the noxious plant called tobacco; a place, moreover, where native "savages" indulged in "hunting and fowling," the sport of the English aristocracy, while Christian men and women were "rooting in the ground about Tobacco like Swine." Colonization mandated work that the settlers found both arduous and unfamiliar; to extract a living from the ground, all available hands must first clear brush and cut down trees, though "strange were these pleasures to their [former] conditions." High-born Englishmen "blistered their tender fingers" with the felling ax, and "poore Gentlemen, Tradesmen, Serving men, libertines, and such like" together found themselves reduced to the common lot of working in dirt.[1]

Future generations would glorify the place of Jamestown in history as the first permanent settlement in British North America; but Captain Smith understood his mission as only the most recent in a bloody, century-long series of attempts to conquer southeastern territory, and to extract riches from it. At Jamestown, the tightly intertwined tasks of conquest and commercialization impelled early colonial officials to harness a workforce of Europeans, Native Indians, and Africans, all the while lamenting a "want of skillfull husbandmen." The labor of English

planters in particular consisted of guarding against the Indians in the forest and the traitors in their midst, and they toiled in the fields as if under
siege, forced "to watch vigilantly, and work painfully," at once workers
and soldiers. After the massacre of 1622, which claimed 347 English lives
at 31 sites scattered throughout the colony, Captain Smith and his men
determined to "inforce the Salvages to leave their Country or bring them
in . . . fear and subjection." In the process whites also aimed to appropriate native crop fields, saving themselves the trouble of "cleering the
ground of great Timber."[2]

In those "New World" mainland colonies governed by England and built
on a foundation of tobacco, rice, cattle, timber, Indian corn, and peas,
human labor was the key to wealth. Modeled after Barbados, South Carolina (founded in 1670) immediately institutionalized the system of black
slavery, first within a "frontier" economy based on cattle and lumber products, and later, by the early eighteenth century, within a staple-crop economy based on indigo and rice. In contrast, the Chesapeake tobacco colonies
of Virginia (founded 1607) and Maryland (1634) produced tobacco with a
predominantly white workforce until the latter part of the seventeenth century; and the "barrier colony" of Georgia (1733) developed a relatively diversified economy without black labor until both rice cultivation and slaves
were introduced almost two decades after its founding. In these labor-intensive agricultural systems, physical strength and endurance served as the hall-
marks of the workforce. These colonies needed "lusty labouring men . . .
capable of hard labour, and that can bear and undergo heat and cold, any
one who is but able to inure himself to the Ax and the Howe. . . ." A Georgia
settler put the case in appropriately neutral terms according to gender,
racial, and ethnic classifications: he called for "strong robust people, fit for
our plantation work."[3]

Native groups shaped patterns of colonial labor in the pre-slave South
not as workers so much as warriors hostile to the planters and their designs
on the land. The earliest Chesapeake settlers unwittingly set down roots in
the midst of the powerful Powhatan Confederacy, an extensive network of
thirty tribes, all part of the Algonquian language group.[4] More than a century later, white men in Georgia attempted to carve out a place for themselves wedged between the slave society of South Carolina to the north,
and St. Augustine, an enclave of Spaniards, Indians, and runaway slaves, to
the south. Colonization depended upon military security; and persistent
threats to the integrity of English settlements throughout the 1600s meant
that field workers could be called upon to use their guns against foes as
likely as use their hoes in the ground. In 1623, Virginia officials set out to

humiliate Captain Richard Quaile, guilty of some unspecified offense, when they decreed that he was to be "ignominiously degraded from his degree of Capt his sword broken and sent out o[f] the port of James Citty with an ax on his shoulder. . . ."; his title of captain was to be replaced by that of carpenter. Yet by the mid-1620s, colonists in the Chesapeake were refusing to draw such an explicit line between soldiering and laboring. A century later, the Georgia Trustees took pains to link the tasks of planting and defending the colony through tail-male, an ancient land tenure system that ensured all freeholders would be soldiers by forbidding daughters to inherit land. Field laborers doubled as defenders and conquerors, as the times demanded.[5]

White men might hope someday literally to outgrow manual labor, but colonial elites devised a number of ingenious ways to exploit the productive capacity even of persons presumably free. By the late eighteenth century white southerners would equate black people with slavery, and white people with liberty, but the early colonists in the Chesapeake and Georgia knew that most labor was "naturally" unfree. In these three colonies, the only labor system foreordained was the "hard usage" of men, women, and children, whether red, white, or black. Indeed, almost all workers in early Virginia, Maryland, and Georgia found themselves bound to some form of exploitative relationship—children governed by their elders, servants by their masters, sharecroppers and tenants by their landlords, hirelings by their employers, women by their fathers and husbands, Indians and Africans by white men, criminals and sexual renegades by the state and church. In turn, each of these groups devised means of resistance to the people who sought to work them hard, raising the specter of internal subversion within settlements highly vulnerable to external attack.[6]

Despite differences in their respective political histories, planters in pre-slavery Virginia, Maryland, and Georgia demonstrated a willingness to take advantage of all kinds of labor, no matter what its age, color, sex, or nationality. At the same time, these white men remained profoundly suspicious of "strangers"—men, women, and children who were not English, Christian, or white, or persons who lacked one or some combination of these characteristics. The rush to profit taking pitted English ethnocentrism against a more open, and openly rapacious, attitude toward the labor potential inherent in all groups that peopled the southeastern coastal region. In determining who would work at what jobs, colonial officials and landowners were forced to remain ever vigilant, watchful of enemies in the forests and on the high seas, and watchful of members of their own households.

"IT'S HARD LIVING HERE WITHOUT A SERVANT"

The earliest Chesapeake planters had few colonial precedents to draw upon in their effort to wring a living from a lush but unknown land; the Spanish conquest of South America, and earlier English efforts in Ireland and the West Indies, offered little in the way of a guide for Virginia and Maryland settlers. Confronted by a large, resourceful, and eventually well-armed indigenous population, colonists on the North American mainland failed to subordinate a Native workforce for their own purposes. Nevertheless, the European demand for tobacco quickly convinced seventeenth-century Chesapeake planters that success in the commercial-colonial sweepstakes—with a well-ordered society based on a profitable export economy as the prize—would depend on their ability to control a large number of agricultural workers. In Georgia, too, field labor constituted the heart of the colonial enterprise, but in this colony work fulfilled a moral purpose as well; in the 1740s, the Georgia Trustees determined that the province should serve as a source of earthly and spiritual redemption—through work—for lowly English folk. Before these three colonies turned to black slavery, they all embraced a labor-management system that relied on field work performed primarily by white men, women, and children. In the New World, where critical factors in the production process—from the weather to the price of crops and attacks by animal predators—remained outside the control of individual planters, the exploitation of labor quickly assumed the level of political imperative. And given the fragility of these colonial outposts, modes of supervision of all kinds of workers assumed a particularly brutal form.

By the late sixteenth century, the English could only curse the bad luck and ill-timing that had deprived them of the fabulous gold and silver mines scattered throughout the Aztec and Inca empires of Mexico and South America. The Spanish *conquistadors* proved that New World riches could be harvested quickly and efficiently by maintaining a large army of occupation to oversee indigenous populations put to hard labor; but first, empire builders had to land in the right place at the right time. Relegated to regions devoid of precious minerals and gems—parts of the West Indies and the North American seaboard—English colonists had to content themselves with the more mundane mission of extracting crops and timber, instead of silver and gold plate. The men who founded Jamestown in 1607 had a difficult time reconciling themselves to the idea that a land blessed with such natural abundance would offer up a bare subsistence only with the most strenuous effort.[7]

With their reliance primarily on the labor of colonists of their own nationality, and with their crop-based economies, Virginia, Maryland, and Georgia conformed to neither the Spanish Empire model of Indian slaves nor the English "kingdom" model of Irish serfs. The first planters in these three North American mainland colonies therefore found themselves embarked on a painful process of self-education about the limits of what a single worker, or a single household, might accomplish in the course of a season. In Virginia and Maryland, a shortage of women ruled out the conventional pattern of English husbandry, with a farmer presiding over a houseful of workers—his wife and children in addition to servants, hired hands, or a combination of these groups, depending on his status. In general, early southern colonial elites were not oblivious to the advantages of a family-based labor system, but they gradually dismissed the idea as impractical, for women and children represented a drain on precious resources—especially children, who were consumers for years before they became producers. Thus landholders came to believe that each productive unit must consist of several able-bodied men, and the more the better.[8]

The tribulations of initial permanent settlements boded ill for whites determined to strive for self-sufficiency. The Virginia Company quickly set their "tenants" to work defending the colony and filling company stores with food. Yet during the first few years of Jamestown's history, the men, women, and children there were reduced to eating acorns, dogs, cats, roots, rats, and human flesh. The plentiful fish in the waterways and fowls of the air remained elusive to people who had little experience hunting or foraging—people fearful of venturing too far outside the stockade in any case. Ships from the mother country brought new hands to till the soil, but also new mouths to feed. Sailors and soldiers shared a disdain for field work: they wanted to get on with the business of hunting for gold rather than waste their time scratching the earth for a meager subsistence. These predilections obviously complicated the politics of food distribution. After 1620 or so, company officials faced persistent difficulties in managing settlers who were not only expected to build their own shelter and guard against Indians but also grow their own crops and produce something of value (tobacco) for the Crown besides. High mortality rates blessedly reduced the number of hungry people, but also intensified the demand for men who would spend their time working, "watching and warding," an imperative that did not abate until the end of the century.[9]

The early history of the Chesapeake was marked by the successive seating and abandonment of plantations, for tobacco cultivation demanded, and then within a few years exhausted, fertile soil, and fertile soil remained located (unfortunately) under large trees. Very few English workers arrived in the colonies as skilled axmen, or experienced in felling trees or clearing brush for that matter, yet along with the hoe, the ax was a basic tool of colonial agriculture, and "improvement of the forest"—the planting of "gardens" in the wilderness—was the defining colonial enterprise. The early English colonists hailed from a country plagued by chronic local wood shortages; in England, fuel was scarce and expensive, and so most rural folk had to scrounge for "lops" (branches and twigs) to cook their food and keep themselves warm. Within the specialized English workforce, sawyers and woodwards (wood clearers) were in short supply. The horrible sense of shock expressed openly by the earliest colonists over the tremendous exertions necessary to clear the forest caused one proponent of settlement in the Chesapeake to declare defensively in 1650, "The objection, that the Countrey is overgrowne with woods, and consequently not in many Yeares to be penetrable for the Plough, carries a great feeblenesse with it."[10]

Writing from Georgia soon after his arrival, Thomas Causton observed rather tentatively, "It is impossible to give a true Description of the Place because we are in a Wood, but I can't forbear Saying it is a very pleasant one." Indeed, the deep dense forest of the eastern seaboard seemed to be its distinctive physical characteristic, symbolic of both the untamed nature of the place and its fertile potential. As late as the 1690s, one observer noted of Virginia, "the infinite Number of Trees . . . make that Country more to resemble a Forrest, than one of the Countries of *Europe*." Views of the woods and their meaning ranged from the idyllic to the hellish—from an appreciation of the lushness of the landscape, with its myriad forms of flora and fauna, both edible and aesthetically pleasing, to a terror of what dangers might lurk within it. Among the most prominent of these dangers of course was the Indian; for example, Virginia plantations were situated in "thick woods, swamps, and other covert, by the help of which the enemy might at their Pleassure make their approaches undiscover'd on the most secure of habitations . . . their sculking nature being apt to use these advantages." Even the forests of Virginia—which, cleared of their underbrush by native horticulturalists, resembled the graceful deer parks of England, playground of the gentry— were home to murderous wolves, of which many whites had an almost pathological fear. Somewhere between the association of forests with sweet songbirds and succulent fruits on the one hand, and with skulking Indians and lurking runaways on the other, lay the hard reality that the removal of trees constituted "truely the great labour" of early southern colonial life.[11]

From the Indians, whites learned how to prepare their ground for planting by stripping the bark off trees and then setting fire to the underbrush; in this way the colonists relieved themselves and successive generations of the task of the lowly woodsman to the extent that they did not have to cut huge stands of trees and then rip out the roots. Nevertheless, the building of dwellings and fences necessitated continuous tree chopping throughout the early years of settlement; and the custom of rotating tobacco fields every four or five years or so (rather than draining swamps or using fertilizers) meant that each new cohort of servants throughout the seventeenth century had to struggle with these same tasks anew. Where farmers on the English countryside relied on hedges, the southern planters used fences that had to be picked up and moved whenever new ground was cleared. The production of fence rails involved "disbranching" the timber, dragging the logs to a central workplace, and then assembling the fences on site. During the winter servants customarily cut firewood. In addition, some workers learned how to manufacture naval stores (pitch, tar, and turpentine) and others to raft logs to downstream sawmills.[12]

By the time Georgia was founded, white men realized that the seemingly simple task of clearing the wood was no job for novices with uncallused hands and puny arms. Uncertain how to open up a future homesite, land that was "choked up with old Trees," the Salzburger colonists at Ebenezer obtained permission to import from South Carolina fourteen black slave sawyers, who were then forced to build a road from there to another settlement eight miles away. Four of the fourteen ran away and one of the slaves killed another one.[13]

As early as 1619, then, the tobacco syllogism had become abundantly clear: If "all our riches for the present doe consiste in Tobacco. . . ," then it followed that "our principall wealth . . . consisteth in servants. . . ." In Georgia, the hard work of householders supposedly served as the linchpin holding together the colony's twin purposes of philanthropy and mercantilism. Yet no matter how resourceful a settler and how compliant his wife and children, the demands of a new plantation required the labor of more than one man. Wrote one settler home to a friend in England in 1738, "but I must tell you yt it's hard living here without a Servant, one man being incapable to Move Trees, & fence, with ye other necessary labours that one must go thro; before he can plant." His advice: "I must beg of you to get all ye Servants you can, and be carefull of 'em at Sea, for they'll bring you money, or enable You to live handsomely on Your plantation." About this time, even a seventeen-year-old freeman could write home from Georgia to complain, "I wish I had a servant, which would be extremely usefull to such one as I," assuring his father that the heavy demand for bound labor was "quite different here from what it was in England."[14]

Reluctantly, even representatives of the Georgia Trustees had to admit that each planting season brought fresh humiliations to the most worthy and industrious of farmers. For example, in the spring of 1741, in the vicinity of Savannah, the "infinite Quantity of Worms which infested our Lands" destroyed corn and salad greens alike, causing many a "poor Planter in the Field" to think his "former Labour ill bestowed in Agriculture." Disillusionment among the majority of Georgia settlers proved to be a fertile breeding ground for the pro-slavery sentiments that began to sprout just a few years after the colony was founded, sentiments that bore fruit when the trustees reversed their anti-slavery policy in 1751.[15]

In the colonial South, then, land was worth very little without the requisite labor to improve it. Chesapeake legislators recognized this fact when they established a system of headrights granting land according to the number of dependents imported by a settler, when they levied taxes on landowners according to the "tithables" (that is, white, black, and Indian men, and black and Indian women workers) in a household; and when they instituted the use of a crop—tobacco—as a form of common currency. Among the elite in all of the southern colonies, neither huge landholdings nor an English pedigree could compensate for the lack of a tractable workforce. The immense amounts of time and energy expended in pursuing runaway servants in Virginia, Maryland, and Georgia (by public officials as well as private citizens) indicated that planters literally could not afford to relinquish a single hand if they hoped to maintain their status and sense of well-being, no matter how modest.[16]

The defining characteristic of the southern colonial labor system—the organization of adult male hands into household units—produced a peculiar work ethic among those landowners fortunate enough to control many workers. Initially at least, the physical labor needed to clear the land at times claimed the energies of even the most well-born settler. Captain John Smith watched with satisfaction as two "proper Gentlemen" learned to swing an ax in the woods five miles outside of Jamestown; "within a weeke they became masters: making it their delight to heare the trees thunder as they fell." He noted that "voluntary gentlemen" who worked of their own free will were a far superior labor source compared to many more "presst to it by compulsion." However, the novelty of this type of work soon wore off for most highborn wielders of axes, and they began to see themselves primarily as managers and overseers, cultivating the fine art of making other people industrious. The founders of Georgia too put a premium on the cheerful performance of labor, but they were not so foolish as to believe that the most prominent planters had to perform that labor themselves. Successful planting depended upon the landowner's ability to cajole, or force, other people to work on his behalf. One work ethic enthusiast noted in 1739 that the colony would do well to rid itself of certain gentlemen, not only because "they would not work themselves" but also because they would not "employ their servants on their lands," preferring to hire them out for cash, and then using the income to live "idly" in Savannah instead of in the hinterland. In contrast, the conscientious master devoted considerable effort to making his servants perform his bidding in his own fields.[17]

Throughout the seventeenth century in the Chesapeake, and during Georgia's first generation, English planters needed workers who would prove to be steadfast allies in the battle against the elements, and in the wider war against groups who threatened the social and physical integrity of homogeneous English settlements. Consequently they looked to their own people as the major source of agricultural and military labor. The ideal colonist was a hard worker and a loyal soldier, like John Milledge of Georgia, who won the favor of the trustees (and a grant of four hundred acres) after years of commanding troops stationed along the Ogeechee River. Milledge was particularly adept at "cutting Lumber &c . . . and appear[ing] peculiarly Active to serve the Colony, whenever required, especially in all Disturbances with the Indians, being a good Horseman and well acquainted with the Woods." Nevertheless, planters and colonial officials maintained an open mind about the possible benefits that a limited number of "strangers" might offer to their enterprise. And so different groups of workers became valued—and exploited—to the degree they could be tightly controlled within a New World that was otherwise beyond the control of any one Englishman.[18]

"STRANGERS" AS WORKERS

During the course of the seventeenth century in the Chesapeake, and between 1733 and 1750 in Georgia, English colonists gradually turned to black slave labor, at least partially in response to failed experiments with a variety of other workforces. Population statistics for the Chesapeake during the seventeenth century and for Georgia between 1733 and 1750 reveal the contours of society in these southern colonies. Indentured servants—primarily white men ages eighteen to twenty-five—provided the bulk of labor until slavery began to predominate. From 70 to 85 percent of the immigrants to the Chesapeake before 1700 arrived as servants (a total of 130,000 to 150,000 people for the entire century). Depending on the decade in question, three to five males landed in Virginia for each female, and for Maryland the figure was two to seven men for each woman; at the end of the century the figures were 3.5 to 1 (male-female ratio) for Virginia and 2.5 to 1 for Maryland. Importations of black slaves did not begin to any great degree until 1685 (soon after the chartering of England's Royal African Company, a competitor in the international slave trade), and by 1700, the Chesapeake as a whole had no more than 8,000–9,000 blacks (about half of them tithables), including a few who were servants and landowners. Throughout the seventeenth century, in the area now encompassed by all of the southern states, Indians outnumbered whites and blacks, by four to one as late as 1685. However, by that time white colonists had pushed indigenous groups to the interior, so that whites had become numerically superior (45,200 to 23,000) on the thin strip of eastern coastline stretching from Virginia to South Carolina. Georgia had almost no black inhabitants until the lifting of the ban on slavery; thereafter both the black and white population grew rapidly, from 1,700 whites and 400 blacks (all slaves) in 1751, to 33,000 whites and 15,000 blacks by the time of the Revolution.[19]

Soon after the massacre of March 1622, some Virginia Company officials began to wax enthusiastic about the potential use of Indian labor for English profit. For example, in December 1622, John Martin composed an essay on "The Manner Howe to Bringe the Indians Into Subjection," suggesting that extermination of the enemy might seem to be the logical response to the massacre, but "holy writt" discouraged it, and besides, "other necessarie uses" might flow from a fresh supply of bound laborers. Once harnessed to English purposes, Indians might continue to reduce the numbers of natural predators like "wolves, bears, and other beasts (wch are in greate numbr)." They might also be made to deliver hostages (that is, members of enemy tribes) ripe for religious conversion, and adults and children compliant in growing silk, hemp, and flax. Indian men could serve as guides into hostile territory, as oarsmen "in Gallies & friggetts and many other pregnant uses too tedious to sett downe." Martin advised his countrymen not to "trinke or trade" with nearby Indians, for that kind of interchange might imply reciprocal obligations between the two groups; and he also hoped eventually to render them dependent on English food supplies (under the circumstances, a rather unlikely prospect).[20]

Martin's overly optimistic predictions soon gave way to a more realistic assessment of the relation between Indians and the English demand for labor, an assessment that stressed the uses of friendly groups as diplomatic allies, traders, and hunters, rather than as field workers. At least initially, such a relation was based less on exploitation and more on the accommodation of interests between Natives and interlopers. Indeed, viewed from the perspective of the pre-contact period, Indians managed to incorporate the English into their own political system—based on the exchange of material objects for spiritual and social reasons—more easily than the English were able to take advantage of Indians as bound laborers for their own acquisitive purposes.[21]

From Indians, whites learned a variety of skills related to foraging, fishing, and growing crops like tobacco and corn. Only by observing Indians did the English come to understand how to hunt pigeons, produce cooking oil from acorns, extract syrups and dyes from trees, make canoes, tan the hides of wild animals, and use weirs and poisons to fish. Nevertheless, rather than apprenticing themselves to these "heathens," some English folk persisted in trying to hire, or coerce, them to perform certain types of work. This inclination carried with it obvious dangers. In the Chesapeake, Indians were compensated for killing wolves, retrieving runaway cattle and hogs, fishing, and gathering oysters and muscles. In Georgia, in 1739, a colonial official seeking a thieving runaway Irish servant noted that "some neighbouring Indians whom we sent for, came to assist us by Tracing (which they are very skilful at). . . ." Accounts of Indian hunters abound in the early records of Virginia, Maryland, and Georgia. For example, as "the Archbishop's obedient subjects," the German Protestants called Salzburgers, who settled near Savannah, had never learned to hunt game in their native country; in Georgia they relied on Indians for their fresh meat. Similarly, in England only poachers were skilled with guns, and in America few colonists besides uniformed soldiers knew how to use them at first. The difficulties attendant upon white men venturing too far into the forest in search of a tasty turkey gave these men an added incentive to delegate hunting to members of friendly, or tributary, tribes, and to supply them with guns. On the other hand, of course, the emerging Indian marksman did more than put fresh venison on the table; he also, at times, trained his fowling piece on English men, women, and children. Throughout the seventeenth century, then, the Virginia legislature struggled with the deadly consequences of "the disorderly employing of Indians with gunns." In 1658, lawmakers encouraged county court commissioners to pay bounties on wolves' heads "by imploying Indians or otherwise, *Provided* they arme not the Indians with English armes and gunns contrary to act of Assembly."[22]

Most Indians acquired guns through trade, and intercultural relations in general ultimately rested on a shaky foundation of diplomatic negotiation. (Integral to this process were natives who served as guides, interpreters, and mediators; at least a few of them were women, like Elizabeth Savage of

Accomack County, Virginia, and Mary Musgrove of Georgia.) John Smith expressed well-founded apprehension over the indiscretions of "Gluttonous Loyterers" in Jamestown eager to sell everything from hoes to guns to the Indians in return for a ration of corn. Yet restraint in this regard could prove counterproductive in other areas. For example, the reluctance among mid-century Virginians to trade guns with the Indians caused them to lose out to other colonies in the lucrative beaver trade.[23]

Both Indian and English leaders aggressively promoted trade, but only if they could control it for their own purposes. Werowances (chiefs) sought out steel hoes, alcohol, and copper in order to consolidate their own power and maintain their own status. However, after 1650 or so, control over trade eluded the grasp of leaders on both sides, and aggrieved parties felt justified in seeking redress on their own terms. In Virginia, the bloody upheaval called Bacon's Rebellion was set in motion with a raid conducted by "certain Doegs and Susquahanok Indians" on the farm of an Englishman who "had before abused and cheated them, in not paying them for such Indian trucke as he had formerly bought of them, and . . . they took his hogs for Satisfaction." A party of white men pursued the hog stealers and either beat or killed them all, and then an Indian war chief retaliated with more bloodshed. Soon the entire colony was consumed in a conflict that pitted not only Indians against whites but also groups of whites against each other. Georgia experienced no such conflagration, but it too recognized the hazards of unregulated trade with the Indians of the Creek Nation, and so stipulated that all white traders be licensed. Nevertheless, independent operators continued to pursue their own interests through violence and intimidation of colonial officials.[24]

Outnumbered by Indians by as many as fourteen to one during the early part of the seventeenth century, white men in the vicinity of Jamestown were understandably hesitant to try to put Indians to work in the ground; and indeed, the relatively limited exploitation of Indians as field hands and domestic servants more often reflected trade and diplomatic imperatives rather than labor demand. Indian bondsmen and women did exist throughout the southern colonies in the seventeenth century; some debtors and disturbers of the peace found themselves reduced to servitude by colonial courts, and some prisoners of war were enslaved. However, as a group, Natives proved to be particularly troublesome, if not downright dangerous, workers. Unlike their Latin American counterparts, they remained scattered in small villages, and hence difficult to capture in large numbers; and, too, they tended either to die or to run off before they had produced much of value for their masters. Moreover, most whites understood that they placed themselves in harm's way by holding Indians against their will. South Carolina dealt with the problem by exporting as many as twelve thousand Natives captured in war to New England and the West Indies between 1670 and 1710. Virginia followed suit in 1722, decreeing that any Indian who transgressed colonial statutes "shall suffer death, or be transported to the West-Indies, there to be sold as slaves." Thus from the English perspective, an Indian sold into bondage was better than either a dead or a "domesticated" Indian.[25]

Compared to the uncertainty posed by thousands of Natives who knew their way around the forests of the eastern seaboard, the non-English tradesmen and servants imported into the colonies would seem to offer a safe and reliable source of labor. Yet here again planters and government officials had to balance their demand for workers, and for specialized knowledge, with their queasiness over incorporating foes, and potential foes, into their tiny settlements. In this regard, English ethnocentrism and real security concerns clashed with profit seeking. Within a larger international political climate made volatile by the colonization efforts of rivals like the Spanish, Dutch, and French; by the depredations of pirates and privateers on the high seas; and by coalition building between various European powers and certain Indian tribes, non-Englishmen and women resistant to work discipline could be quickly cast in the roles of spies and traitors.

From their founding, the southern colonies hosted a large number of non-English cultural and religious groups. Enclaves of Dutch and Swedes dotted Maryland's Eastern Shore. French Huguenots settled along South Carolina's Santee River and in the city of Charles Town. Georgia in particular proved an attractive destination for Protestants as diverse as Lowland and Highland Scots, Swiss, Dutch, and German Moravians, Salzburgers, and other dissenters. As long as these groups remained off to themselves they posed few problems for the English, and might even enrich the British Crown through their industry.[26]

More disruptive to the security of colonial settlements were ethnic bound workers of questionable loyalty to English officials and policies. Early Chesapeake planters utilized Irish, Dutch, Scotch, French, and Turkish servants; their Georgia counterparts employed laborers from Germany, Wales, Scotland, and Holland. When French servants ran away from Virginia, and when Dutch and German servants launched collective, "insolent" protests against their condition in Georgia, ordinary forms of worker resistance took on the appearance of treason. According to the findings of a Georgia official in 1748, the unreasonable demands of Dutch servants stemmed from "their Country Men residing in this Colony, who are generally speaking a very troublesome and discontented Sett of People, and many of these last are still worse, no less than five able bodied Men having deserted their Service and the Colony soon after their Arrival. . . ." Scottish prisoners of war, and the Irish, by virtue of their Roman Catholicism and their subjugated status in their own homeland, required close supervision, and amounted to persistent sources of real and potential subversion within individual English colonial households.[27]

The English felt most betrayed by ethnic artisans with special skills. The warm climate of the southern colonies encouraged the first settlers to try to emulate a Mediterranean type of agriculture, and the seemingly endless tracts of standing forests held out the hope of a thriving naval stores and lumber industry similar to that in the Baltic States. The earliest settlers of Jamestown included Polish workers brought over to make pitch and tar, Germans to construct sawmills, Italians to set up a glassmaking house, Languédoc natives to tend grapevines, and an Armenian to grow silk. Georgia conducted experiments growing oranges, and also, within the first twenty years of its founding, imported a French baker and a French hatter-turned-vintner, a Dutch butcher, a French potter, and an Italian family steeped in the mysteries of silk cultivation.[28]

Whatever promise these workers offered to fledgling colonies, most of them soon squandered the welcome they initially enjoyed. The Jamestown Pole had the dubious distinction of being one of the first whites to defect to the Indians (in 1619), and by his "treachery"—"in a manner turned heathen"—caused the colony's leaders to fear that "the salvages would surprize us." In 1630, the Virginia House of Burgesses felt compelled to complain in a formal manner about the deceit practiced by those Frenchmen who were, ten years earlier, "transported into this country for the plantinge and dressinge of vynes, and to instruct others in the same . . ." In their rush to reap the tobacco bonanza, these men and their families had apparently "concealed the skill, and not only neglected to plant any vynes themselves, but have also spoyled and ruinated that vyniard." They were henceforth forbidden to grow tobacco. Georgia officials expressed similar frustration with the Camus family, whose silk-growing exploits were generously subsidized by the colony's trustees beginning in 1733. Appreciative of Mrs. Camus's talents but angered by her arrogance and her fondness for the "Rum-Bottle," William Stephens, the resident secretary, soon tired of humoring the querulous matriarch of the family, and throwing money her way. At one point she declared to Stephens that "we must not think her such a Fool as to bring up any in her Art of winding Silk." Andrew Duchee, the French potter, turned out to be another disappointment; he too relied on the trustees' largesse, promising to become the first man to produce porcelain outside of China, using Georgia clay. The trustees "saw no Fruits of his Works," with the exception of a miserable product that could not "merit the Name of China-Ware." Moreover, the ungrateful Duchee early joined the ranks of the Malcontents, the pro-slavery group at odds with the trustees' policy on slavery, and boldly informed his superiors "that he would not rest till he saw the Use of Negroes granted. . . ."[29]

Although some white ethnic workers confirmed the deepest fears of their suspicious hosts, others forced English men and women to reconsider their own religious and national loyalties. For example, at least one Georgia official cringed when he saw Jewish masters holding Christian servants: "I could not but be somewhat shocked at it, to think of Christians becoming bondmen to those infidels, and . . . it would be ill looked on by everybody in the Communion of our Church." A Jewish physician born in Spain was targeted as a spy soon after his arrival in the colony via Virginia and North Carolina. Yet when colonial officials scrutinized their countrymen, whom they considered to be foul-mouthed, besotted, whoremongering servants, and their idle, ever-complaining English (albeit Christian) masters, these officials could judge hardworking Jewish planters and tradesmen to be honest men and upstanding citizens. In the New World, groups of workers were valued to the extent that they would work hard, and if not actively contribute to the defense of the colony, at least not undermine it.[30]

Workers of African heritage also occupied an ambiguous position in the seventeenth-century Chesapeake. Their skin color set them apart from whites (and Indians) regardless of status. Yet perceived according to a mix of racial, religious, linguistic, and ethnic characteristics, blacks were not always irredeemable aliens in English eyes. Many of the first blacks in Virginia and Maryland had lived in the West Indies, or somewhere in the Spanish Empire, and some were English-speaking and Christian. At least thirty-two blacks, almost evenly divided between men and women, were living with whites in colonial Virginia in March 1619—that is, several months before a Dutch ship deposited "20. and odd Negroes," the event traditionally marking the arrival of the first people of African descent on the North American mainland. The small number of blacks in the region up through the 1680s or so were represented in a range of statuses, from slave to servant to overseer to landowner. Free blacks Anthony Johnson and his wife Mary owned 250 acres and raised livestock in early Northampton County, Virginia. In the 1640s, after a disastrous fire swept through the Johnson plantation, the local court reduced their taxes and exempted three women family members from tithes (a routine exemption for white but not black women). A network of free

blacks—men and women who had managed to buy their way out of slavery—appeared in Northampton; in their struggles to maintain family homesteads, in their dealings with the court, and in their day-to-day labor in the
tobacco fields, they resembled other small landowners.[31]

The institution of slavery developed on a piecemeal basis in the Chesapeake. Most black men and women worked in the fields, black women to a
greater degree than white women of any status. By the late seventeenth century, on scattered quarters in the Chesapeake, black women were performing domestic work (for black slaves as well as white servants). The 1666 list
of tithables for Northampton County, for example, includes "Nan, a negro
woman" in a household of four white men. (In this list blacks are identified
by their race and non-English whites—French, Irish, and Dutch—by their
ethnicity.)[32]

However, certain factors signaled black people's uniquely vulnerable status. In the course of the seventeenth century, Chesapeake legislators passed
a series of discriminatory laws that placed progressively tighter restrictions
on blacks as servants, slaves, and even free people, limiting their choices of
marriage partners and dashing whatever expectations they might have had
about eventually securing their freedom. In contrast, for white men, bound
labor was a condition that most of them realistically expected to outgrow, if
they survived it, allowing them to go on and embrace the new roles of master and father. In the southern colonies, there existed old black servants but
no old white servants. In the mid-1640s, for example, Philip Chapman's
Accomack County, Virginia, estate consisted of an eight-year-old black girl
and "Caine the negro, very anncient," both valued at prices considerably
higher than Chapman's white male and female servants ranging in age from
twelve years to their early twenties. "Caine the Negro, very anncient" had
no counterpart among white servants, all of whom were very young. Moreover, white planters granted a few black men supervisory responsibilities
over white women and children (at least), but whites in positions of political
power felt uneasy about this arrangement. In Virginia, black men were
barred by law from serving as the masters of white servants, though they
might own black or Indian slaves. In 1669 in that colony, the fact that a white
servant named Hannah Warwick labored under a black overseer was considered an extenuating circumstance surrounding an unknown crime that she
had committed. In Georgia in 1741, colonial officials were outraged to learn
that, in the vicinity of Augusta, two Dutch children, servants, "were tasked
at the Discretion of . . . [two] Negroes, who were authorized to punish
them, if they did not fulfil their Task."[33]

Over time in the southern colonies, white ethnics (or their descendants) might become "English." Since they already possessed white skins, they merely had to adopt the English language, worship in Anglican churches, and profess loyalty to the British monarch. In contrast, no matter how gracefully individual blacks managed to acculturate themselves to English ways, their skin color marked them as permanent "strangers." In the seventeenth century, the ethnocentric English planters of the Chesapeake interpreted a dark skin not necessarily as a badge of "racial" inferiority, but rather as a sign that this particular group of people bore close watching; to the extent that blacks could never become English, they would remain a potential threat to the security of the colonies.

WOMEN AND CHILDREN LAST: THE CHALLENGE OF EMPLOYING "USELESS HANDS"

Englishwomen lacked a clearly established place in the hierarchy of seventeenth-century southern workers. The question raised by Virginia settlers in 1619—"In a newe plantation it is not knowen whether man or woman be more necessary"—was a real, not just a rhetorical, one. The answer to the question came slowly, in the form of immigration statistics over the next few decades. In 1621, the planters of Virginia welcomed a shipload of fifty-seven Englishwomen, described by their sponsors as "young, handsome, and honestly educated Maides," whose purpose was "to tye and roote the Planters myndes to Virginia by the bonds of wives and children." Despite this promising start, the twin tasks of defending the colony and planting tobacco shaped the demographic profile of the colony for the next three or four generations. The Chesapeake region was characterized by a sex ratio dramatically skewed in favor of men, and almost all immigrant women arrived as unmarried indentured servants, the majority of whom died before they reached the age of fifty. Very few of the respectable young women who arrived between 1619 and 1621 survived to fulfill their original purpose: to establish stable nuclear families in the English New World. Moreover, since most early settlements more nearly resembled frontier outposts than traditional English villages, women possessed virtually no necessary skills that men themselves could not supply, and they might even prove to be a distinct liability if they could not help to defend the colony with a sword or a gun. In 1626, women and children together constituted a group of "unserviceable people" as the colony once again prepared to meet an Indian attack. Women's one unquestionably unique contribution to a fledgling community—the natural reproduction of the labor force—no doubt promised long-term advantages, but also added to the numbers of hungry and unproductive workers destined to die early, a demographic luxury that these armed garrisons could ill afford.[34]

Certainly early southern history includes examples of women who, like their menfolk, rose to the demands imposed upon them in a new and particularly dangerous time and place. John Procter's wife, left at home with the servants during the Virginia massacre of 1622, "bravely defended their house against the Indians." Women learned to navigate their way through the treacherous coastal waterways in skiffs and canoes; they assisted their menfolk (and fellow male servants) in rounding up wild cattle from the swamps and forests; and they grew all manner of crops in the fields. In colonies plagued by labor shortages, some wealthy wives and widows served as creditors and estate executors, thereby wielding a great deal of influence at the highest levels of colonial government. Still, women's value to the colonization enterprise was ultimately judged in relation to the two great tasks that all colonizers faced: work in the fields and defense of the colony.[35]

Women as loving wives and mothers might "anchor disconnected bachelors" to a new and hostile land, but women as whores, shrews, thieves, arsonists, gossips, slanderers, runaways, and bearers of bastards—in the variegated references of the day—tended to destabilize these fragile communities as much as secure them. A Charles County, Maryland, court heard testimony in 1661 that revealed a woman servant's "good qualities and her bad faults." In an attempt to sell the woman's time to another man, her master reported that "shee was a very good Cooke and that she Coold make very good butter but further [that she] was a whore and a thiefe. . . ." He predicted that "in Case hee [her new master] Coold breake her of thos faults she woold bee an excellent good sarvant. . . ." Until that day, her value as a worker—and as a colonist—would remain in doubt.[36]

The Chesapeake colonies and Georgia attempted to sustain the outlines of a familiar (English) gender division of household labor. It was not unusual for the first ships of English colonists to anchor offshore and send initial parties to the mainland, the men to cut wood and the women to wash the dirty laundry after the long voyage; in the case of the Maryland settlers, these first laundresses set out in a small boat that overturned before they even reached land, and all of their linen was lost. Once settled, most colonists considered clothes laundering an expendable task. In contrast, colonial records reveal abundant evidence of men who baked their own bread, milked cows, looked after children, and performed other types of domestic service—"masculine housewifery" of all kinds.[37]

A large proportion of traditional housewifely duties—such as dairying, ale brewing, poultry tending, spinning, and sewing—depended upon the availability of appropriate resources, which were, by all accounts, scarce. In early Virginia, Maryland, and Georgia, households composed mostly of young men were the norm, and most of those households lacked expensive and cumbersome pieces of equipment for brewing ale, spinning, and making cheese, butter, and cloth. Furthermore, not all masters (or husbands or fathers) were in a position to insist that the workers in their households should milk the cows or tend the chickens after a long day working at other tasks, especially since "beating at the mortar" (grinding corn for bread) was already a duty universally reserved for both men and women during evening hours. John Hammond, an early publicist of the Chesapeake, wrote that women in that region "occupie such domestique imployments and houswifery as in England," but he still condemned them for their failure to make beer or ale: When members of their households had nothing to drink "but Water or Milk and Water or Beverige" (that is, fruit juice or cider), then the womenfolk were by definition "negligent and idle . . . sloathfull and carelesse. . . ." Hammond failed to consider the general lack of material resources available to housewives and women servants, and he also failed to consider that their time might be consumed by backbreaking labor in the field, leaving few of them inclined to devote much energy to household industry.[38]

Men in the southern colonies readily utilized white women as field workers. Contemporary rural Englishwomen weeded, pulled hemp, and used hoes to cultivate corn and sickles to harvest wheat and rye. In the Chesapeake, planters soon adopted the Indian practice of leaving trees standing and planting tobacco in hills around them, and so few whites used plows; almost all field workers relied exclusively on hoes. A white woman with a hoe thus appeared as a familiar figure in the eyes of Englishmen. Planters routinely put their female indentured servants to work in the fields, although in all probability the Virginia statutes that exempted white women from the list of mandated tithables implied that, ideally, planters were not supposed to use these women in this way. Clearly, some planters took advantage of the exemption by using women field workers and then avoiding the payment of taxes on them. For example, in 1662, Virginia lawmakers noted that "diverse persons purchase women servants to work in the ground that thereby they may avoyed the payment of levies. . . ," and so reminded planters that "all women servants whose common imployment is working in the crop shalbe reputed tythable, and levies payd for them accordingly." The Virginia planter who listed "Rich'd Richardson" and "Mary Richardson, his wife," as tithables for the year 1666 avoided the fines levied on employers guilty of this type of "concealment."[39]

In the South, field labor occupied much of the annual calendar, rather than representing a seasonal, and hence limited, activity as in England. Transplanting tobacco seedlings, and worming, weeding, harvesting, and curing the plants constituted tasks that in themselves required less in the way of muscular strength and more in the way of endurance and stamina from any worker. The smaller a plantation, the less its task specialization among men and women, regardless of status. A planter who had to rely on only four servants could not afford to employ an able-bodied adult in tasks unrelated to tobacco production; all four, women and men, were "to make a Cropp." Masters who complained that they lost a considerable part of their year's tobacco when a single female servant ran off indicated that, on the smallest holdings especially, women were primarily field workers and suffered accordingly: In the words of a fictional "Trappanned Maiden," "The Axe and the Hoe/Have wrought my overthrow." Some white women worked in the fields while they were pregnant. Dorcas Howard, a servant of George Unwin near Jamestown, "at worke in the grounde" on a Monday in 1629, suffered from labor pains, and miscarried the next day. (Unwin later testified that he had not realized she was pregnant.) Not until the late seventeenth century could wealthy planters in the Chesapeake (owners of large numbers of black slaves and white servants) institute a system of task assignment on the basis of both sex and race; in those cases, according to Robert Beverley, "Sufficient Distinction is also made between the Female-Servants, and Slaves; for a White Woman is rarely or never put to work in the Ground, if she be good for anything else."[40]

If they were in a position to do so, whites might resist masters who put their female kinfolk to work digging in the ground for persons other than immediate family members. In 1661, John Nicholls petitioned the provincial court of Maryland on behalf of his daughter Easter. John Nicholls had agreed to apprentice his daughter to Captain Thomas Cornewallis on the understanding that the young girl "might come and live with him to wayte on his wife," Cornewallis promising her father "she should doe nothing else but wayte on his wife. . . ." But when Cornewallis sold his estate, along with the hapless Easter, to John Nuttall, John Nicholls feared that his daugher would "be made a slave" (that is, presumably, that she would be made to work in the ground), and he sought her release. The court agreed that Easter should not have to work under conditions radically different from those her father had initially agreed to, and nullified her indentures with Nuttall. Some female orphans and servants benefited from their fathers' foresight in this matter, as evidenced by the wills and contracts that stipulated they were not to be put to work "at the Hoe."[41]

Upon the completion of their indentures, many married women continued to work in the fields, but now as wives—that is, within a new social context. In 1698, the wife of an overseer in Prince Georges was granted use of a plot of her own "to make a Hogshead of Tobacco upon the said Plantation." On small holdings, wives and daughters would likely join their husbands and fathers in the fields, alongside a couple of servants if they were lucky, to plant, weed, and pick. Since only a relatively poor household relied on the field work of its womenfolk, a wife who hoed tobacco probably had a lower standard of living (in terms of shelter, clothing, and diet) than her indentured counterparts on more prosperous plantations. In the latter part of the seventeenth century, a visitor to Maryland's Eastern Shore commented upon the strenuous labors of servants and slaves each forced to produce up to three thousand pounds of tobacco a year, "and some of the masters and their wives who pass their lives here in wretchedness, do the same." The labor performed by white Salzburger women at Ebenezer, Georgia, was emblematic of the settlement's struggling condition in 1748; there wives and daughters worked at rice cultivation, a job reserved exclusively for slaves in South Carolina at that time, and in Georgia after the introduction of slavery. The Salzburgers "consider[ed] the swamps and the work done in them to be unhealthy. The women can hardly start with rice planting and the weeding of grass and weeds before quite soon they feel their health impaired in manifold ways. Laborers are hard to come by, and thus our farmers are in a bad position."[42]

During this period, few women in rural England worked exclusively in either the house or the field; many alternated casual daywork like weeding and raking with specialized cottage crafts like spinning wool and flax; or making buttons, lace, or gloves at home. The more modest households, which were the ones most likely to send young daughters and sons out to service, and off to the colonies, pieced together a living through foraging, wage work, and a variety of seasonal pursuits, only some of which were strictly agricultural. In contrast, English women in the early southern colonies had only limited possibilities to diversify their labor and potential sources of income. Most of these jobs derived from women's roles as caretakers. Local courts might pay a woman to examine a corpse in an effort to ascertain the cause of death; to serve as a wetnurse for an orphaned child; to nurse an ill man or woman back to health; to interrogate an unwed mother about the identity of the father of her baby; or to operate a public poorhouse. A few women and girls, both black and white, worked as weavers in the colonies, and gradually more households became self-sufficient in this regard, though, as in England, men continued to dominate the business of weaving "professionally."[43]

Initially, in both Virginia and Georgia, silk cultivation held some promise as a by-employment for women and children of all races. In 1621, Captain Thomas Nuce of Jamestown pointed to the example of Italy, Spain, and France, "wher are thousands of women and children and such ydle people to be hyred. . . ." As late as 1697, Virginia planters were still calling for the employment of whatever "useless hands" existed in the colony—especially the few slave children—to be instructed in the feeding of silkworms and the winding of silk. In Georgia in 1737, Martha Causton, the wife of a colonial official, took it upon herself to encourage the training of girls in tending silkworms. She invited "the Gentlewomen" of Savannah to view the worms currently under the care of the imperious Mrs. Camus, and noted hopefully in a letter to the trustees that "One of the Indians I mentioned above has promised to bring down his wife and Children in the Summer to live with me & learn the Art of keeping the Worms." But in Georgia, as elsewhere, the "Art of keeping the Worms" proved elusive to women as diverse as upstanding English-born widows and resentful German servant girls.[44]

In the labor-hungry southern colonies, the legal and practical definition of the productive worker expanded to include ever younger persons. An oversupply of workers in England had afforded children under fourteen or fifteen years of age some freedom from formal, contractural labor. In contrast, southern landowners deployed child workers throughout the seventeenth century. It was not uncommon for single parents—both fathers and mothers—to apprentice, or bind out, their children if they lacked the resources to support them; these children in effect became servants, some at tender ages. And, too, at work throughout the fields and households of the southern pre-slave colonies were orphans who had been snatched off the streets of Bristol or London. In 1619 and 1620 at least two hundred children arrived in Virginia, the boys to serve for seven years or until their twenty-first birthday, the girls until they were married (in all likelihood very early, if they survived). In 1661, one Maryland woman, commenting on four "Irish boyes" imported by her husband, wondered aloud why he had not "brought some Cradles to have Rocked them in," they were "soe little." The eldest of these children was judged to be "not above tenn yeares of age," the others "not neere so much." Court records for Virginia as well as Maryland routinely include cases of indentured servants as young as eleven years; they would have to serve until they were twenty-one.[45]

Orphans remanded to the custody of a guardian (high mortality rates in all of the colonies produced large numbers of these children), and offspring bound out by their destitute parents or unwed mothers, could be quite young, of course, and in the absence of written instructions from one or both parents, adults had full discretion in the employment of wards. A well-to-do guardian usually meant a guardian with much land to cultivate and tobacco to grow. Only a few lucky children benefited from a father's will or contractural arrangement that stipulated they were to learn a skilled trade or refrain from field work until a certain age. More common was the collective fate of Charles, William, and Edward Watts, orphans eight, six, and four years old respectively, in St. Mary's County, Maryland, in 1678. In the care of a guardian who forced them to work, the brothers "have noe manner of Cloathes but such Raggs and old Clouts that scarce would cover their nakedness and those given them by the charity of others. . . ." Their daily food rations consisted only of salt and hominy. The elaborate efforts of the Maryland Orphans' Court to protect children suggests that their exploitation throughout the Chesapeake was widespread.[46]

In Georgia, the voracious use of child labor was (characteristically for that colony) cloaked in the rhetoric of humanitarianism. George Whitefield, the Methodist evangelist, traveled up and down the eastern seaboard in the 1730s, exhorting believers to contribute money for his orphanage in Bethesda, which opened with much fanfare, and with "all the children he could get" in 1739. Initially, the Georgia Trustees applauded the idea: Whitefield would take orphans off their hands, and transform them into devout and productive citizens. The routine for the approximately sixty children sent to the institution in the early 1740s included a 5:00 A.M. wake-up call and then a day in which cutting wood, sewing, knitting, carding, spinning, and other "useful employment" took priority over the limited amount of time devoted to school and prayers. Even a most principled proponent of the work ethic, Lord Egmont (president of the Georgia Trustees), complained that the children had "Not a moment of innocent recreation . . . the whole discipline appears to be too strict." Colonial officials reported that Whitefield had a lamentable tendency to break up legitimate families in his pursuit of souls ripe for salvation, and hands ready to labor; though his "Design is for the Good of the People, and the Glory of God," the preacher seemed to forget (according to one critic) "that the Orphans are human creatures, and neither Cattle, nor any other Kind of Chattels. . . ."[47]

In 1643 in Accomack County, Virginia, a planter named James Bruce sent both a neighbor's servant "Girle" and his own son "for hogg weedes and bidd them geather them." Tasks for children throughout the region included not only the preparation of fibers in textile production but also odd jobs like fetching water, gathering melons, tending livestock, pounding corn, ridding the house of vermin, and in the case of girls, helping with dairying. In 1656, one Maryland observer confidently predicted, "Children increase and thrive so well there, that they themselves will sufficiently supply the defect of Servants." However, white children as unpaid family workers became a significant part of the workforce only in the early eighteenth century, when mortality rates declined and family structure stabilized, and then primarily within poor families.[48]

The common plight of sons, daughters, bastards, orphans, young servants, and apprentices indicates that a variety of young workers, regardless of legal status, were subsumed within a universal work experience, namely, field labor. In the case of female servants and the wives of yeoman farmers, women of these two groups often performed the same type of labor, but their work carried with it divergent social meanings, based on their divergent social standings. However, in the end, work in the pre-slave South was notable for its preponderance of young white men, as befitted settlements originally conceived to advance the territorial interests of the British Crown.

ONE KIND OF WORK, MANY KINDS OF WORKERS

Rising to the challenge posed by an infinite supply of land and a chronic shortage of labor, English colonists showed a great deal of flexibility and ingenuity in devising new forms of legal status (and, in some cases, contractural relationships) that bound together parties of different ages, sexes, races, and social standings. Yet these pairings—based on distinctions between young-old, female-male, black-white, landless-landowner, and even bound-free—were no guarantee that the more privileged half of each dyad would gain exemption from agricultural labor. More specifically, the categories of household dependent and servant proved inadequate to meet the Chesapeake and Georgia's insatiable demand for "hands" in the absence of the institution of slavery. The labor provided for any one plantation or master by either family members or indentured servants was by definition of only limited duration (if we assume that children who survived eventually formed households of their own). Consequently, in their capacity as private planters or public officials, the colonial elite freely extended the indentures of their servants; employed hirelings and tenants; and took on purloined laborers, criminals, and social outcasts (some of the last two groups impressed in the service of the state). These arrangements worked to reduce even formally free men and women to a condition of bound, or at

least some gradation of unfree, labor. The land, and efforts to extract surplus wealth from it, exerted a gravitational pull on everyone except those
already in possession of a great deal of human or financial resources.

The system of indentured servitude held out only a tenuous promise that
white men and women of modest backgrounds could someday profit from
New World abundance; servants gained their formal freedom, but economic
independence was rarely a component of it. In Virginia, Maryland, and
Georgia, servitude afforded a means to get young people out of the Old
World and into the colonies, and also to check the "giddy and wild-headed
youth from his profuse and uneven course of life, by a limited constrain-
ment. . . ." Yet relatively long periods of service in the South, combined with
meager freedom dues accorded men and women at the end of their tenure,
meant that most would be unable to afford to purchase land on their own,
and would need to seek out a landowner who would provide them with
shelter and financial support. For former male servants, opportunities for
upward mobility into the landholding class seemed most favorable in Maryland, from the 1640s through the 1660s, to a large extent because freedom
dues in the colony included land grants until 1663. Yet even there, the sur-
veyors' fees and court costs incurred in claiming land proved prohibitive for
cashless young men recently released from servitude. In Georgia, prospects
for former servants remained uncertain, for only those who had sufficiently
impressed colonial officials with their industry and moral character received
land grants. The three young men who, recently freed from their indentures, "debauched themselves" with an "Excess of Rum-drinking" at a house
in Savannah one Sunday night in 1739, had little hope of impressing William
Stephens and others of their fitness to become full and independent citizens
of the colony.[49]

For many whites, like the 40 percent of freemen in Surry County, Virginia, who were landless in 1694, freedom brought with it insurmountable
barriers to economic independence. Chesapeake planters struggled against
declining tobacco prices for much of the seventeenth century; and since
freed servants lacked the resources to buy land, purchase slaves and servants, or employ hirelings, they could not seat a plantation on their own. By
the 1660s the lack of unclaimed, workable land had pushed many young
men out of the tobacco colonies and northward to Delaware and Pennsylvania or southward to North Carolina. As nuclear families stabilized, some
young sons went to work for their fathers, not a master; in one county in
Virginia, the proportion of planters' workers who were their own sons
increased from 10 percent to 33 percent from the 1670s to the 1690s. Landless sons became artisans, overseers, or hirelings, although the possibilities

for an overseer of a great planter probably far exceeded those of a hired hand for a small one.[50]

Women who had served out their time and managed to stay out of trouble (or refrain from pledging their troth to a fellow servant) could probably count on marrying well. One Virginia planter testified in 1649 that "Maid servants of good honest stock may choose their husbands out of the better sort of people." Nevertheless, for a variety of reasons a fair proportion of servants of both sexes never lived to see their indentures terminated at all. Unnamed fevers carried men, women, and children off with frightening regularity. Moreover, throughout the southern colonies, labor contracts were the source of much informal conflict, and formal litigation, with the servant usually the loser either way. A Maryland servant named Jone Nicculgutt became caught in the middle of a dispute centering on an estate appraisal, and served a full thirteen years after she arrived in the colony; her indentures apparently disappeared in the shuffle. In the same colony, Anne Thompson was bound to her master John Floyd for six years, but Floyd subsequently sold her to another man and then he (Floyd) died shortly thereafter; Anne Thompson had served three years over her legal period of service by the time her brother petitioned for her release in 1661. Likewise, the proclivity among planters to trade, barter, or gamble with their servants meant that even a relatively favorable original contract could not necessarily protect a worker from future (contractural) misfortune.[51]

It was not unusual for planters to make at least an effort to hold servants past their contract time in ways that were legal, and colonial lawmakers facilitated this effort by imposing additional demands upon workers who had committed a variety of transgressions, large and small. Indentured men and women had to serve as much as double their original period of service to atone for crimes such as stealing, running away, killing hogs, marrying without a master's permission, and exhibiting any form of "audacious unruliness" toward their superiors. The longest additional periods of service were reserved for those men and women—and especially women—who were implicated in diluting the "purity" of white stock, a sexual misdeed with wide-ranging consequences in southern societies desperate to retain their "English" character and bloodlines. During the seventeenth century, Virginia and Maryland passed laws that decreed the mulatto child of a white mother must remain bound in some capacity—to the church vestry, to a master—until the age of thirty. In Virginia, both free and servant women guilty of such a crime were forced to labor for the colony for five years; Ann Wall, the mother of two children by a black father in Elizabeth City, Virginia, was warned not to return to Elizabeth City after she served her five years of enforced service, under penalty of being "banishd to Island of Barbadoes." It was an unusual young person indeed who could complete several years of labor for a master or mistress and not commit some sort of infraction punishable by extra time.[52]

Maryland, grappling with the legal implications of a biracial society, actually decreed in 1664 that free white women who bore children by slave men must labor as bound workers for the same period of time as the father (that is, presumably for life), and that their children should take their father's status as slaves. This law remained on the books for seventeen years, but its disconcerting implications soon became apparent. At least some Maryland planters lost no time in forcing their white women servants to cohabit with slave men in order to exploit the fruits of these unions—additional slave children to work in the fields. Moreover, the law produced the small but legally distinct category of white women slaves, a development that made colonial officials decidedly uncomfortable. Finally, the measure's intention—to discourage sex between white women and black men—was clear, but its long-range consequences perhaps less so. For one, if paternity uniformly determined legal status, planters who henceforth sexually abused black slave women would have to free any children that resulted from the act. For any number of reasons, then, the Maryland legislature repealed the law in 1681, and eleven years later imposed a seven-year period of service on a white women guilty of sexual relations with a black man (an indentured servant had to complete her time and work an additional seven years). The law further decreed that a free black man who married a white woman must forfeit his freedom and that their children would become slaves. These legislative actions made clear the social significance of white women as conduits of family legacies; but they also added more workers—white women, black men as the husbands of white women, and mulatto children—to the list of bound workers.[53]

In myriad other ways planters, creditors, and purveyors of specialized services used their superior resources to control the energies of people who possessed nothing but the ability to labor. Servants routinely extended their indentures, and free men and women routinely bound themselves to a master, in return for loans and a wide variety of goods and services. In Virginia's Lancaster County in 1666, John Jones received permission from his master to marry a fellow servant in return for serving "foure Complete yeres from the date hereof," though Jones had only two more years on his contract. Morgan Rossier, "a Lame and disseased person," agreed to work for an Accomack County surgeon in return for a cure (which apparently never materialized). The process of self-dispossession on the part of a Georgia settler named Gardener reveals the downward pull exerted on even free men in the earliest years of the colony. Originally a landholder, Gardener "cleared a small Piece of two or three Acres" at Skeedoway; but he "grew weary and deserted it, more than two Years since, as divers others have done; and lived of late by letting himself out to Hire," reported William Stephens in 1739. Unlike indentured servitude, which represented a form of repayment of transportation costs, these self-hire contracts were unregulated by law, and open-ended in their terms.[54]

Hirelings included carpenters as well as women willing to cook and clean for bachelor households; but most were former servants who sought to earn money in a short amount of time—few planters could pay cash wages for more than a few days in a row. Within this fluid labor situation, artisans and overseers occupied relatively privileged positions. However, all contract workers remained vulnerable to employers who reneged on agreements. In response to an offer from the governor of Maryland, William Hewes "imployed his whol labor in setting up the Wind-Mill att St. Maries, & tending & looking to, & grinding in it after it was soe sett up by him," but failed to receive his agreed-upon payment. "Having or possessing little but what hee gets by his hard labor & industry," Hewes sued for the payment of back wages in 1658, but lost. Most aggrieved workers probably had neither the time nor money to press their claim in court. In any case, hirelings who were paid in liquor, corn, shoes, and stockings were unlikely to gain their independence through landowning in the near future.[55]

Planters' frustrations over the unavailability of family laborers, servants, or hirelings of any kind set the stage for illicit arrangements, some of which workers themselves eagerly embraced. The "entertainment" (illegal employment) of Indians and runaway servants produced a great deal of underground trafficking in human labor. In 1676, Ellis Humphrey of Kent County, Maryland, was charged with entertaining William Jackman, "knowing him to be a servant" of another man. For his part, the twenty-four-year-old Jackman testified that he had responded to an offer by Humphrey that he "migt goe to his house & worke for him & he would honnestly pay him for his worke, & sett him home againe. . . ." In a case like this, it is unclear whether or not the arrangement proved of mutual benefit to both parties. Virginia, too, early confronted a crisis of "divers loytering runaways in the collony who very often absent themselves from their masters service."[56]

In the early 1640s, lawmakers instituted a system of freedom certificates for former servants so that new masters could not claim that they had unknowingly taken in someone with time left to serve someone else; but these certificates were routinely forged, or ignored by both parties. A similar policy governing Indian hirelings was designed to curb the security risk posed by employers who exploited members of both friendly and hostile tribes through "their illegall comeing in" (this during a time when "the Tuscarores and other remote nations [were] lying skulking about the English plantations for private sinister commerce"). In addition, mutinous sailors fleeing abusive captains and suffering from starvation inquired surreptiously after employment throughout the southern colonies. In the late seventeenth century, Virginia contended with "Severall stragling Seamen about the Country"—men "haboured and entertained by the Inhabitants" to the detriment of His Majesty's royal service. At the same time, Maryland set penalties for all persons who lodged or conveyed out of the province "Deserting Sailers and other runnewayes. . . ." The business of facilitating the flight of runaway servants developed into a cottage industry of sorts, with men and women selling compasses, boats, food, and maps that pointed the way northward to desperate men and women on the run.[57]

Indentured servants and other workers under contract looked to the state for protection against egregious instances of maltreatment; at times, however, colonial officials themselves took the lead in labor exploitation, when they punished criminals of various kinds by hiring them out, and when they appropriated for themselves labor designated for use by the state. As early as 1624, Virginia lawmakers codified attempts to discourage the already common practice among the colony's elite to commandeer workers reserved for public employment: in that year the governor was instructed not to "withdraw the inhabitants from their private labors to any service of his own." In Georgia, one colonial official, William Bradley, showed great energy and resourcefulness in making improvements on "a five-acre lot of his Sons." The plot boasted "a neat garden, well laid out," "upwards of an hundred Vines" planted, drainage ditches that had been "cast up with great Labour," and a kiln for making bricks. To accomplish all of this, one observer noted, Bradley had indulged in the "flagrant and open perverting [of] the Trust's Servants Labour, to his own and unwarrantable uses." All of the labor in question had been supplied by twenty of the trustees' own German servants, men and women family members who had never "done a Stroke of Work towards clearing or cultivating the Trust's Land." Predictably, then, throughout the pre-slave southern colonies, the temptation among local sheriffs to put their charges to work in their own fields turned out to be just too great to resist. In 1659 a Maryland mistress complained that one of her servants, currently the object of litigation, was being held by the sheriff in the case, "doeing him Labour amongst the rest of the sd Sheriffs servants, & being sett on worke by him."[58]

More generally, seventeenth-century governmental entities—church parishes, counties, and colonies—seized upon any possible pretext to extract unpaid labor from men, women, and children, bound or free, regardless of race. In Virginia, a male fornicator was ordered by a local court to build a ferry (Accomack-Northampton County, 1638), and a Sabbath day fisherman to construct a bridge (Henrico County, 1648). The state claimed the labor of freemen who neglected guard duty or criticized the governor, and servants who insulted their master or ran away. Church wardens literally took advantage of young people abused by their master or mistress, and of mulattoes and the unwed white women who bore them. Colonial officials might exult in the moral efficacy of such punishments, but the fact of the matter was that labor so appropriated served a useful purpose in the realm of public works and public defense. In 1738, one Georgia master noted with grim satisfaction that he had sent an incorrigible servant to the local jail, "where proper employment will be found for him in digging and wheeling, at the public Works carrying on at that Fort, and where I am promised his labour shall not be spared; so yt ye may learn not to be idle or drunken." In the Chesapeake and in Georgia, householders and servants alike were impressed for military service and to work on public works projects of various kinds— clearing underbrush, felling trees, constructing forts, repairing sea beacons.[59]

For white men and women, freedom was fragile, easily crushed under the weight of official mandates related to personal deportment, crop production, and colonial defense. Restrictions on workers affected virtually all persons of any age who fell outside a tight inner circle of planter-lawmakers. Consequently, the defining characteristic of seventeenth-century southern society was the distinction between, on the one hand, the white father and householder who owned property, controlled black or white workers, influenced local parish policy, and helped to write the colony's laws, and, on the other hand, almost everyone else.

THE CHALLENGE FOR pre-slavery southern planters was to employ as many able-bodied hands as possible, and to cultivate the greatest quantity of staple crops possible, without placing the colonial enterprise at risk in the process. In practical terms, this challenge posed a dilemma, for the more expansive and opportunistic the planters' attempts to deploy bound laborers in the fields, the more likely they would find themselves cohabiting with resentful and recalcitrant individuals—youthful, multi-ethnic, multi-racial, and mostly male. Though they might shoulder guns, these workers were not necessarily reliable soldiers.

In the seventeenth-century South, the legal and extralegal force necessary to control unruly workers of all kinds produced whole groups of "slaves" of various colors. Although southern whites used the term with a great deal of imprecision, they believed they knew a slave when they saw one. Englishmen charged that the Spaniards forced indigenous peoples "to doe all manner of drudgery worke and slavery for them," and also believed that the Indians enslaved white women captives. As we have seen, in 1664 Maryland lawmakers created a new (if short-lived) class of "slaves," white women who bore children by (black) slave men. Convicted criminals, transported to the colonies and held against their will, complained bitterly that they "were like old Horses forced to drudge and slave"; and white servants, like Rickett Mecane (also "taken by force out of his native Country"), could claim that extended periods of time stipulated in their indentures (in this case fifteen years) should be nullified, for it "is contrary to the lawes of God and man that a Christian subject should be made a Slave." In Accomack County, Virginia, in 1638, a master's son and male servant were working together in the fields when the servant suggested that, rather than "stay here and bee slaves," they should both run away to "another place and live like gentlemen"—that is, among the Indians. In this case, labor in the fields forged a common bond between the two young men, where kinship or legal status did not.[60]

However, when seventeenth-century English colonists described themselves or unfortunate compatriots as "slaves," they were in fact using the term metaphorically. It is true that some white adults toiled under conditions of extreme duress or dependency—as criminals, servants defrauded of their freedom, children unable to escape a highhanded father and strike out on their own. Still, these workers could claim membership in a historic English community, a community that failed to protect the well-being of its members in all cases, but nonetheless a community of people bound together by certain expectations of what was due them under law and custom. After years of hard work, white ethnics and their offspring might also lay claim to "Englishness," a status increasingly associated with a white skin and a European lineage. In contrast, persons of African descent retained their "strangeness" long after ethnic servants outgrew it.

In 1661 in York County, Virginia, William Clutton, a former servant, incited a revolt among a group of indentured servants. Resentful of the "hard usage" accorded them by their masters, they seemed particularly indignant about their steady diet of corn pone and water, and Clutton, clearly cognizant of the challenges to feudalism that had recently wracked his homeland, suggested that they petition the king of England in favor of a ration of meat three times a week. One co-conspirator testified later, after the plot was foiled, that Clutton and his followers planned to attract at least forty servants, arm them, and then roam the countryside, crying out to all "who would be for Liberty, and free from bondage,"[61] and killing those who stood in their way. This was an exceptionally dramatic incident in the annals of seventeenth-century southern servitude; though many other white servants felt similarly aggrieved, they had neither the resources nor the inclination to launch violent rebellions, or to cloak their resistance in the language of (seventeenth-century English) revolutions. Still, masters and mistresses throughout early Virginia, Maryland, and Georgia had to contend with the demands that their hands made upon them for decent treatment, English style, and for this reason, among others, the days of the white "slave" were numbered.

CHAPTER TWO

MEMORY AND MISERY: WHITE SERVANTS AND THE ORIGINS OF SLAVERY IN THE SOUTH

A s a pioneer planter in the colony of Georgia, William Stephens waged an uphill battle against his own hands and the forces of nature. A former member of Parliament, Stephens had arrived in Savannah in November 1737 to serve as resident secretary on behalf of the London-based trustees. Within two years he had placed two lots of land under cultivation—a five-acre, in-town parcel used as an experimental nursery for mulberry vines, cotton, grain, and vegetables; and a forty-five-acre plantation, Bewlie, located three miles outside Savannah and given over to foodstuff production. The sixty-seven-year-old secretary, a man devoted to upholding the principles of righteous living in himself and in all Georgia settlers, served as a bulwark against the pro-slavery sentiment that developed in the colony soon after its founding. Yet Stephens's detailed accounts of work in the nursery and at Bewlie amount to a lengthy lament about the conditions under which he as a master of servants was forced to labor. Stephens's best-laid plantation plans quickly went awry, literally washed out by heavy rains, burned up by the scorching sun, consumed by worms and insects, blown away by hurricanes, engulfed by other "Extreams in the Weather." Most maddening of all, however, were his dozen or so hands, white men and women who thwarted his demands and desires at every turn, workers who would not or could not work.[1]

Stephens early acknowledged that felling timber, disposing of undergrowth, and constructing fences amounted to "a work that none of them were expert at": "Upon my coming here I found I had not one Servant

among my few, who knew any thing about the work to be taken in hand."
Apparently all of the servants spoke English, but none of them, regardless
of regional identification or ethnic background, had experience in clearing
land of trees and brush. One man balked at working in the ground at all,
claiming that he "was never used to work, but on the Water," while another,
ordered to begin chopping trees, promptly "wounded [himself] by the
Stroke of an Ax in the leg." After a few months' worth of frustration,
Stephens reported that his adult son Thomas was working in the fields as an
example to the servants. This strategy backfired in the long run, for Thomas
Stephens eventually became a leading proponent of slavery, to his father's
everlasting dismay and disgrace.[2]

The servants, afflicted with "an habitual Laziness and Aversion to
Labour," had the added disadvantage of working with tools wholly unsuited
to removing coastal hardwoods, "for some of the felling Axes fly like Glass,
and break out in peices as thick as a Half Crown; and the Cross-cut Saw is fit
for Children only, & of so small a Size, yt they can hardly cut a large grown
Tree thro' with it. . . ." The first year, Stephens planted the wrong kind of
corn seed in the Savannah nursery, and as a result, "it produced scarce any
Thing worth naming, but pined away in Spite of all the Labour I could
bestow upon it, and came to nought. . . ."[3]

With the right resources, Stephens might have instructed honest men and
women in the virtues of hard labor, but by his own admission he dealt with
a "slothful and mutinous Crew, always complaining of too much work, and
too little Victuals . . . daily growing more and more troublesome." Two
women servants—he called them "errant whores"—became pregnant early
on, one of them on board ship en route to the colonies. Since Stephens considered females in general as a "dead Charge" (except to the extent that they
could perform domestic duties for their male counterparts), he was happy
enough to sell the time of these two to someone else. The men servants
indulged in a weekly "Saturday Night's Debauchery," grogshop-hopping
from one Savannah rum house to another. Younger servants were particularly incorrigible—one, "a very idle Boy, and exceedingly addicted to lying,"
took his first chance to run away, and another, "naturally . . . wicked, lying,
and thieving," soon "proved so egregious a Rogue, that now I despaired of
ever seeing any good of him; running away and skulking about in Holes,
was his frequent Practice, without any Provocation. . . ."[4]

Even favored workers disappointed their master. The overseer, a hireling,
"proved such a Rascal in filling [other servants'] Heads with bad Notions of
the Place, and other Discouragements" that Stephens fired him. One privileged and pampered servant, exempted from field work so that he could

attend to matters in Stephens's household, used his spare time to squirrel away stolen provisions for a much anticipated escape. After seeing that the man was sent to jail, Stephens described him as "an egregious sot, and then (no wonder) a downright villain." Though "truly an intolerable Burden," the Bewlie servants were armed with muskets and bayonets in defense against Indians, fugitive slaves, and Spanish soldiers; and Stephens could not help wondering, "but who can safely put Arms into peoples hands, that dont think they have any thing worth defending?"[5]

William Stephens had a genuine love of the fertile Georgia soil, and he delighted in making things grow. Nevertheless, his "weak and wretched Hands" had turned plantation management into "a melancholy Employment" for him. He believed that indulgent masters bred vice-ridden servants, but he was at a loss about the proper route to effective discipline. Offenders whipped in public "have often been observed to grow more hardened," he noted, though workers chastised privately also might grow bitter and resentful. Those incarcerated for suitably long periods of time simply depleted the master's workforce.[6]

In any case, Stephens encountered limits to the amount of work he could expect to extract from his hands no matter what the method. During his first four years in the colony, only half of the men could work at any one time, the rest laid low by fevers and other ailments; one, of a "rotten Constitution," died after only a few months in Georgia. Physicians' fees, plus the construction and support of a hut used to house the ill, threatened to bankrupt Stephens's shaky operation. Moreover, all of the servants insisted on observing traditional English holidays by staying out of the fields; for instance, Christmas, 1738, was "kept as a Holiday (or rather as an idle Day) according to the Custom of our Mother Country," though Stephens noted with grim satisfaction that, in the absence of sufficient provisions, the slackers were forced to forego the usual Yuletide feasting. In early 1741, Stephens expressed "Great mortification" at the impending freedom of his original servants (when their indentures would expire), and panicked at the thought of the fate of his untended corn, peas, potatoes, gourds, and melons.[7]

Stephens's account of his trials provides an indirect testimony to the servants' own tribulations. Cut off from family and friends back in England, isolated in an all-male household (and for the Bewlie servants, at considerable distance from town), these young men found themselves housed under primitive conditions, and forced to perform jobs that were both new and backbreaking. Ill and weak, their arms raw from insect bites, their faces blistered by the sun, they had to contend with a tyrannical, sanctimonious master and with the fear of enemy attacks. The sight of a co-worker whipped, or a co-worker buried, made the dream of a quick escape all the more appealing—for a couple of days, to a rum house, or forever, to South Carolina, where slaves (presumably) did all the dirty work and white men reaped all the benefits.

As an agent of the Georgia Trustees, Stephens was bound to maintain a public stance in opposition to slavery, but he also agreed wholeheartedly with the warning issued by William Byrd II, the Virginia planter, to John Perceval, earl of Egmont and head of the trustees, in 1736. From personal experience Byrd understood that black slaves posed a great threat to the well-being of any community: "They blow up the pride, & ruin the industry of our white people, who seeing a rank of poor creatures below them, detest work for fear it should make them look like slaves." According to Byrd, slaves were by nature thieves, and they necessitated severe discipline; but, he continued, "these private mischiefs are nothing compared to the publick danger" they pose. At the present, he reported, ten thousand black men in South Carolina were "fit to bear arms," and their numbers were increasing every day. A "man of desperate courage" could easily "kindle a servile war . . . before any opposition could be formed against him, and tinge our rivers as wide as they are with blood." This apocalyptic vision framed the question implicitly posed by the Georgia Trustees: Wherein lay the virtues of prosperity, if its price was moral degradation and civil strife?[8]

William Stephens was determined to heed Byrd's warning, but in the process he seemed intent on reinventing the servant-management wheel; for Virginia masters, one hundred years earlier, had confronted exactly the same sorts of servants who demonstrated the same sorts of recalcitrance in the fields as Stephens's own hands, men he described as base and vile, drunken and insolent. The story of the Georgia hands thus represents, on a modest scale, a great drama played out in the seventeenth-century Chesapeake, the first act dominated by white men and women servants before the subsequent, and relatively late, appearance by enslaved Africans. White servants set the initial standard for field workers in the Chesapeake and in Georgia, and it was not a very high one.

THE SERVANTS' NEW WORLD

In early southern society, indentured servants constituted a large group of workers with specific interests in common, interests antagonistic to those of their masters and mistresses. These young people had left England because of a lack of work, and a lack of opportunity to prosper from work, only to arrive in the New World and find themselves worked too hard and denied the commensurate rewards. At the same time, unlike autonomous or free-floating workers, white servants in the Chesapeake and in early Georgia lived within households, and they often shared with their superiors the food on the table and the work in the field. Ultimately, neither class, contractural, nor family relationships fully account for the social status of servants. They were young people keenly aware of the fact that their colonial living and working conditions amounted to a dramatic break with past experience; and they contemplated an uncertain future with bitterness and apprehension. This disjuncture, between past and present, between former experience and future expectations, exacerbated tensions characteristic of the traditional master-servant relationship.

In the seventeenth-century Chesapeake, labor in general and servants in particular constituted by far the most expensive factor in the production of tobacco. (In Surry County, Virginia, in 1687, for example, servants represented fully 96 percent of tobacco planters' total investment, with relatively small amounts tied up in capital and land.) Year by year, and decade by decade, ebbs and flows in the number of immigrant servants transported to the colonies depended upon the labor needs of tobacco planters, and the ability of those planters to pay the costs incurred. The timing of servants' arrival reflected the rhythm of the tobacco growing and marketing seasons; ships with human cargoes reached port in the fall, and filled their empty holds with dried tobacco leaves for the return voyage. Indentured servitude in the seventeenth-century Chesapeake was thus a creature of the tobacco trade.[9]

Though not tied to a staple crop, the Georgia economy of the 1730s and 1740s nonetheless relied heavily on the labor of young men and women indentured to struggling freeholders, and Georgia servants shared with their earlier Virginia and Maryland counterparts the tasks of clearing land, hoeing and harvesting crops, and herding cattle. At first, the trustees turned their benevolent gaze upon the "miserable wretches" exported out of England's largest towns and cities; but the colony's founders soon discovered that such miscreants, while no doubt in desperate need of charity, would prove to be poor pioneers. During Georgia's second decade, its leaders therefore felt "oblidged to employ strangers," and showed a decided preference for the hardy peasants from the British Isles, and for Dutch, Scottish, and German youth who were inured to hard labor outdoors and (ideally) reluctant to complain about it.[10]

At least some servants arrived in the New World involuntarily, and others put their mark on contracts under pretenses that were clearly false. During the seventeenth century, a great number of people were sent off to the colonies in an effort to settle the New World and empty packed English prisons in the process—Newgate "jailbirds" (men and women convicted of any number of crimes from theft to murder), political dissidents, religious dissenters, prisoners of war captured by Cromwellians during the tumultuous Interregnum (1649–60), Scotsmen and the "Monmouth Rebels" (1685) resistant to British rule, and orphans and beggars from large urban centers. In addition, an indeterminate proportion of passengers consisted of men, women, and children lured aboard with fantastic promises, or plied with drink the night before, or, in at least a few cases, literally kidnapped, "spirited away" by force and deposited in the belly of a ship bound for Barbados or Maryland. One sensational, documented episode called attention to an imposter who went by the title of "Owen Evans of the Court of England." In 1618, he roamed the English countryside, trying to pay constables to "press him . . . maidens with all speed," the women "to be sent to the Bermudas and Virginia." Apparently at least one father responded to Evans's call and accepted twelve pence in exchange for his own daughter. This case was unusual because it was so clear-cut; in general, legal means of recruitment often blurred with violent means of abduction, with elements of "persuasion" in between.[11]

As one observer noted in the mid-seventeenth century, it was "only hab nab [haphazard] whether ye go to a good service or a bad," and indeed, a servant's ultimate situation—the daily round of chores, the temperament of a master or mistress—remained a matter of luck, or, more often, the lack of it. Barbados both before and after slavery, and South Carolina from its founding, became known as places without much in the way of possibility for upward mobility among servants, and the Chesapeake always benefited in comparison to other staple-producing, and slaveholding, colonies. Nevertheless, only the most privileged servant—one with a specific skill to offer eager planters—had much say in choosing Jamestown over Bridgetown (in Barbados) as a destination.[12]

The institution of indentured servitude that developed in the southern colonies represented a variation on the servant-in-husbandry system common throughout rural England at the time. That system, which institutionalized high rates of annual turnover among young workers, allowed rural households to deploy laborers according to their needs, and not just the availablity of children in a nuclear family, and it served as a means of socializing young people away from their own parents. By the early seventeenth century, an indentures contract offered a viable alternative to servants-in-husbandry, and it is not difficult to account for the exodus of young English

people out of the rural villages, the alleyways of London, and the base-
ments of Bristol, and into the southern colonies. The England of the late
sixteenth and seventeenth centuries was racked by political upheaval, as the
medieval hierarchal class structure began to crack under the pressures of
commercialization. Civil war was only the most visible and bloody manifes-
tation of long-term transformations in the nation's political economy. Dramatic population growth, combined with a depression in the cloth industry
and periodic poor harvests, deprived farmers and laborers of all kinds of
employment. Estate consolidations and enclosures uprooted the most vulnerable of rural folk, forcing them to take to the road or move to a city in an
effort to find work.[13]

Indeed, migration across the Atlantic represented an extension, a logical
outcome, of more incremental forms of labor mobility in England during
the Tudor-Stuart era. A few migrants to the southern colonies might have
been motivated by ideological or religious principles—one man who wound
up in Maryland had originally indentured himself in 1649 because, he said,
he would "rather serve in Chains, and draw the Plough with Animals, till
death shall stop and say, It is enough," than remain in the country that had
beheaded its own and his beloved king. Nevertheless, economic necessity,
together with a certain youthful adventurousness, remained the predomi-
nant impulse shaping migration patterns to the southern colonies. All over
England, more and more people were severing their connections to a particular plot of land, to their families, and to their kin and community; viewed
from this perspective, sturdy young migrants of both sexes were able to take
advantage of the colonies' chronic shortage of labor.[14]

A constant infusion of new servants into the colonies kept memories of
the mother country alive throughout the seventeenth century in many colonial households. Most English folk of the seventeenth century lived in small
villages, and about 10 percent of the population resided in the great cities,
while in the Chesapeake, and in Georgia, the isolated plantation was the
norm, and towns large by English standards were virtually nonexistent. English servants routinely performed agricultural work, and in all probability
followed some form of by-employment; in the southeastern part of England, home to most of the emigrants to the Chesapeake, people living in the
pastoral woodlands engaged in farming as well as textile production and
dairying. In contrast, in Virginia and Maryland, a monotonous staple-crop
agriculture consumed the energies of men and women workers for most of
the day, and for most of the year.[15]

English servitude was a stage of life for a large proportion of rural young
people; only about one-tenth of the total population occupied this status at

any particular point in the seventeenth century. The proportion of young, bound workers was much higher in both the Chesapeake and Georgia—perhaps as high as 50 percent of all people in Maryland and Virginia during this period. Servants-in-husbandry could count on leaving this status behind them by the time they reached their early twenties, at least, and, while they were servants, they could also count on leaving an individual master within a twelve-month period. The autumn harvest brought with it the payment of wages, in cash or in kind, and a huge, annual turnover of servants—men and women who sought out a similar position nearby within a different household. English rural marriage patterns too reflected the rhythm of servants-in-husbandry contracts, with the number of weddings peaking in August. Although masters and mistresses varied in their treatment of their workers, servants-in-husbandry were well integrated into their new households, and the annual contract system helped alleviate some of the worst abuses. Of course in the colonies, by contrast, servants were bound to serve a particular master for as long as their indentures stipulated—an eleven-year-old boy for a ten-year period, for example—and the chance to work under a new master depended on the fortunes, or death, of the original one. The practice of selling servants, common in the colonies, had no place in the lives of servants-in-husbandry.[16]

By all accounts, servants were a gregarious lot, a fact ironically highlighted by the isolation of plantation life in the seventeenth-century South. The one social institution common to both sides of the Atlantic—the ubiquitous rural gin house, rum house, or alehouse—took servants and family members alike out of the home and offered them a kind of conviviality that household life could not. Southern white men and women workers insisted on congregating during their time off (Saturday afternoon or Sunday), and they saw church services and court appearances as occasions to socialize with each other. The absence of stable nuclear families, and the conflation of household and contractural relationships, profoundly affected the ways young people sought to create or maintain affective ties. Some servants made strenuous efforts to retain contact with their siblings and with shipmates. Michael Hocher, a female servant at St. Inigos, Maryland, found herself in trouble with the law when she responded to the smooth entreaties of a man who promised to take her by canoe to see her brother in Virginia. Colonial court records contain cases of men and women servants who colluded with others whom they had first met in transit from England, and with whom they managed to maintain contact even after they were dispersed to different masters.[17]

Not surprisingly, then, servants often developed quasi-kinship ties with one another, and two or more servants might turn to each other in times of need. Yet they might also suffer from the manipulation of masters and mistresses who sought to drive a wedge between them in order to assert their own power. John Proctor, a Virginia planter and a particularly cruel master (one of his servants died from injuries sustained as a result of a series of beatings), regularly delegated the punishment of servants to their co-workers; one young woman "receved Corectione" from two "boys," the "one named Will the other John Skinner each of them havinge a whip of smale corde and caused her body to bleed downe to her waste. . . ." A Maryland mistress explicitly forbade her servants from coming to the aid of one of her hands, whom witnesses later said was a victim of "very bad usage which was nott fitt for a Christian in his weake Condicon." The other servants in the household were warned against "carrying the said [servant] either Victualls or drinke," and consequently he was reduced to drinking his own urine. Accused of murder, his mistress was tried and acquitted.[18]

Seventeenth-century living arrangements were characterized by makeshift households composed of some combination of masters, mistresses, servants, children, stepchildren, "inmates" (boarders), and adopted orphans; and those households were embedded in networks of nearby plantations. Neighbors, quick to the rescue of an ill friend, might "either voluntarily or upon a request joyn together, and work in it [his crop] by spels . . . so that no man by sicknesse loose any part of his years worke." They might remain ever vigilant in monitoring the behavior of an orphan's guardian, and report instances of "bad usage" of a child to the proper authorities. Planters could also respond to the legal difficulties faced by one of their own, and help to cover up the transgressions of their neighbors in court. In the Proctor case cited above, neighbors assured the jury that the aggrieved woman servant had received only her due—"she never hadd above 20 or 30 lashes atyme and yt wth smale, lyne o[f] whip corde"—and that she was in any case "a very lewd wench & such a one as noe good perswations nor moderate corection could reclame her. . . ."[19]

The factors that shaped a servant's view of his or her immediate world and its possibilities were as infinite in variation as the human psyche itself. Some female servants fell in love with, and eventually married, their master or a fellow servant. Some young men dared to trust their co-workers to carry out a bold plan of retaliation against, or flight away from, a hated master. Relations among servants reflected on the one hand a larger imperative for cooperation among English folk in the New World borderlands, and on the other the sometimes deadly conflicts that wracked individual plantations as well as whole neighborhoods. Servants might bind each other's wounds in a loft by night, and they might testify by day, in public, against the mistress who brutalized them. Yet a servant might just as well simmer with resentment against another worker accorded preferential treatment or boastful of his impending freedom, or determined to lay all the blame for careless work on someone else or to ingratiate himself with the master at all costs. In England, servants looked forward to the hiring fairs each September to save them from an intolerable work situation; but in the southern colonies, extended periods of service could seem like an eternity. Only the uncertainty of being sold, and the finality of death, promised much in the way of change before the day of freedom dues.

THE TROUBLE WITH TREES, AND OTHER TASKS

Young white workers used a variety of means to express contempt for the work they did and for the men and women they served; but mostly they ran away. In August 1664, an unrepentant Charles County, Maryland, servant named Richard Lamb found out the hard way that he had reached the limits of his master's patience. The long-suffering master, Humphrey Warren, complained in court that "Richard Lamb hath Severall times absented himselfe out of his Service," and then offered a familiar litany of other crimes of insubordination committed by the young man. According to Warren, Lamb had sold his clothes for money, and he had "ptended himselfe lame," and then taken the opportunity to abscond. As a matter of habit the servant "did sweare soe extreamely" that he had been sold by his former master, a fact that Humphrey Warren learned too late, to his regret, for "there Can hardlier be A greiueosour swearer in the Country." At his wit's end, Warren hauled Lamb into court and heard him sentenced "to Receive Twenty lashes Uppon his bare back In the publick View of the people att the Whiping Post." As a member of Humphrey Warren's household, Richard Lamb was as morally offensive as he was useless.[20]

Open-ended tenure arrangements galled all servants; but sheer physical discomfort—and pain—compounded their resentment and inspired them to spend a great deal of time and energy contemplating ways to avoid work. English colonists took a century to adapt their dress, diet, and work habits to the ecology and topography of the southeastern seaboard, and servants suffered the brunt of this transition. Most lived under conditions in the colonies that would have been considered primitive at home; seventeenth-century southern plantations in particular were remarkable for their lack of furniture (especially beds) and other creature comforts. The enervating heat preyed upon the minds and bodies of Europeans who worked hatless, in long-sleeved wool clothing, throughout the year. Mosquitoes tormented "both man and Beast" in winter as well as summer. Bug bites and sunburns, minor ailments by themselves, could fester into major preoccupations among young workers. Not only were accidental deaths frequent among servants shouldering axes and firearms for the first time; the southern colonial record is also replete with cases of white people drowning, the fatal consequence of nonswimmers negotiating creeks, branches, and bays in fragile canoes and flimsy pinnances. Former plowmen and dairymaids were now "cutting down Cypress Trees and making Canoes of the Same"; engaging in "very toilsome and laborious and sometimes dangerous" hunting of bears and panthers; and pulling bulls out of boats and chasing wild steers through the swamps. And judging by the quantity and variety of liquid spirits that flowed throughout the colonies—from the records of one neighborhood alone, the wines (canary, mallagoe, port-o-pot, sherry, passadoe), the brandies (Nants, Inglish), and the beer, malt, quince drink, cider, flip, claret, and rum punch—it is apparent that hot and sweaty workers drifted through many a day in a drunken haze. In 1691, Virginia lawmakers admitted that the "loathsom and odious sin of drunkenness is of too common use within this dominion, being the root and foundation of many other enormous sins," one of which was the "disableing of divers workmen." The potentially lethal combination of heat, humidity, and alcohol goes some distance to account for workmen who were both lethargic and accident-prone.[21]

Servants not yet acclimated to a new environment also suffered from the lassitude of "weake and unskilfull bodies." Many planters, like Maurice Smith of Maryland in 1657, assumed that a new hand "would be sick" soon after he or she arrived in the colonies. In addition to the hazards of the seasoning process, servants (and other colonists) endured the consequences of living in a new epidemiological region; they contracted malaria (pregnant women were particularly susceptible), respiratory infections, typhoid, influenza, and dysentery. Specific places were sites of specific health hazards. For example, the earliest settlers in Jamestown contracted debilitating forms of salt poisoning as well as maladies associated with the summertime consumption of shellfish. Even the proud leader of the resourceful and industrious Salzburgers at Ebenezer, in Georgia, had to admit that some of his followers were "so weak in their Bodies, that they are hardly able to cut down a Tree or build a Hutt," and so could not accept the trustees' offer of more land (in 1750).[22]

Sickly, exhausted workers quickly grew resentful of daily routines characterized by heavy, tedious labor. Not only did the seasonal rhythm of the staple-crop economy differ from the more varied agricultural tasks characteristic of rural English life, but many of the essential jobs in the New World required a novel combination of both strength and skill. English workers had had little experience "beating a spell of hominy" for their bread, building fences, hoeing tobacco plants, and dragging cattle out of thickets of thorns. Emblematic of the work was the task of rolling hogsheads of tobacco, great barrels weighing four hundred pounds each, over roads from barn or warehouse to landing; servants, sailors, and other hirelings propelled the casks forward with sheer muscle power, but a misstep could result in crushed limbs and broken bones. Only workers who could boast bargaining power, like Robert Clark, a servant belonging to the great landowner Robert Beverley and possessing some unspecified skill, could manage to avoid the common lot of southern colonial laborers, a lot defined by Clark in his contract as freedom "from working in the ground, carryeing, or fetching of railes or loggs or the like things and beateing at the mortar"—in other words, "useless and and heavy work," the routine forms of drudgery that were "almost perpetuall."[23]

Among the most despised of "perpetuall" forms of labor was the "beating at the mortar," or "beating bread" ("which made my heart to ake"). Virtually every early southern plantation required that this "hard servile labour of beating corn" be performed on a daily basis, and in the absence of wives and children the chore fell to servants of both sexes. A typical household consisting of four or five adults and a couple of children required several hours' worth of this kind of work every single day. Whether a servant pounded soaked corn in a mortar with the use of a large pestle, or used a handmill to grind the corn, the task involved a great deal of upper-body strength and endurance. Most maddening of all, it was work associated with the evening hours, after servants "have worn themselves down the whole day, and come home to rest":

> Sometimes when that a hard day's work we've done
> Away unto the mill we must be gone;
> Till twelve or one o'clock a grinding corn,
> And must be up by daylight in the morn.

In Accomack-Northampton County in 1640, one servant would not beat at the mortar unless beaten himself, and reportedly proclaimed that "hee could not Morter But rather he would goe into the woodes and Dye"; a few days later he was found dead, but it was unclear whether the cause of death was illness, a recent bleeding by a surgeon, or injuries sustained from many whippings. In the same county in 1642, Jarvis Thomas, when asked "why hee runn away," answered that "hee could not beate att the Morter and that was all the excuse hee had. . . ." For men and women accustomed to eating bread made with grain and flour bought at market, the grueling night work was too much to bear.[24]

Beating at the mortar was a prerequisite for keeping body and soul together, but most seventeenth-century white servants defined their status as laborers in relation to the work they did out-of-doors, in or near a forest. Indentured servants were known to spend time "Sitting upon a Tree" and gossiping when they were supposed to be splitting rails or burning brush, their insolence an indirect acknowledgment that work in the woods was endless—and dangerous. Indeed, the novelty of working with trees cost some servants their lives. In the process of felling trees with his master in Maryland in January 1637, John Bryan suffered fatal injuries, though he had been warned right before, "John have a care of your selfe, for the tree is falling. . . ." This was a hazard discovered and rediscovered by each wave of servants newly imported into the southern colonies. Dependent on young sons—children, really—to help clear their land, some families paid dearly when a youth found himself "in great Danger of his Life by the falling of a Tree. . . ." In addition, servants wounded themselves, sometimes mortally, while using the strange and sharp tools necessary to tame the forest—felling, broad, and pickaxes; handsaws and crosscut saws; log chains and handspikes. And finally, servants like those near Savannah, who set fire to piles of wood and brush on a windy day in May 1738, might burn up a part of their master's plantation and injure themselves in the process, if they were not careful. Faced with these life-threatening, never-ending tasks, many planters simply abandoned their land, leaving it "alltogether voyd and uncleered or meddled with. . . ."[25]

A plot readied for planting represented only the beginning of a servant's woes. Dubbed a bitter weed by its contemptuous critics, the tobacco plant actually required a great deal of care and cajoling before it would grow. Fueled by the profit motive, the seventeenth-century Chesapeake economy remained hostage to an export crop that was relatively easy to market at home and abroad, but one that did not always agree with the hands responsible for making it. It is possible that a few of the first servants in the southern colonies had had experience growing tobacco in England; in the 1590s, Sir Walter Raleigh had introduced the crop into his native country, where its cultivation remained geographically concentrated in the areas of Wiltshire, Gloucestershire, and Herefordshire (home regions to at least some of the emigrants bound for the Chesapeake). Small amounts were still being cultivated as late as the 1620s, but with the development of the southern colonial economy, the Crown called for the cessation of domestic production in 1632. In any case, differences in climate and in fertilizing techniques suggest that, in the words of one historian of early Virginia, the plant was "foreign to any agricultural training which [the colonists] had previously received in England."[26]

Tobacco was a labor-intensive staple crop requiring a number of intricate and time-consuming steps. Work with the hoe, or more accurately a variety of them (grubbing hoes and hilling hoes, for example), was a preoccupation for several months of the year. (Proponents of a diversified Chesapeake economy noted that, for at least nine consecutive months, tobacco required "much care and labour, both within and without dores," a requirement that effectively precluded any other crops or products with the exception of livestock and corn.) The busiest summer months at times brought masters into the fields to wield the hoe, and husbands and wives might join their servants during the fall rush to harvest and cure the crop. Yet shared tasks rarely produced fellow feeling between landowners and their workers because the race to produce a good crop was so fraught with uncertainty; the counterpoint to a master's miscalculation was the servant's carelessness in performing assigned tasks. For every drought or torrential downpour that ruined a year's work there was a field worker who let the worms take over the crop, or loaded too many leaves on barn lines that proceeded to collapse under their own weight. The declining price of tobacco after an initial boom in the 1620s produced anxious planters contending with resistant hands.[27]

Compared to the human sweat and the year-round vigilance demanded by each tobacco plant, the pastoral employment of livestock herding would seem to offer colonists a welcome combination of profit and respite. It is true that, in contrast to England, where poor folk could not aspire to own much in the way of farm animals, even very modest southern colonial planters routinely boasted a collection of pigs and cows. Left to roam in the swamps and the woods, or on a nearby island, the animals could multiply quickly and eventually form a significant proportion of a household's wealth. For example, in the Virginia Tidewater county of Surry, herds of livestock made up from 50 to 68 percent of individual planters' holdings during the seventeenth century. Nevertheless, colonists soon discovered that the sublime Old World task of livestock tending must of necessity give way to a more chaotic, New World endeavor. Hogs and cattle at home on the southern range were transformed into wild animals within a matter of months. Consequently, white men delegated the task of rounding them up to Indians whenever they could—and for good reason. Hogs and cows fattened on wild berries and roots, and pursued by a variety of predators, soon developed aggressive tendencies, and violently resisted the efforts of men and women

sent out to bring them in and clip their ears (the seventeenth-century equivalent of branding). In the process of crashing around in the underbrush and
beating bushes for these menacing beasts, servants took their lives into their
hands. Livestock served as a magnet for wildcats, wolves, and dogs. On a
more mundane level, snake and insect bites, scratches, and bruises were a
routine part of a job that took workers into remote and overgrown areas.[28]

Moreover, servants sent out to extricate pigs from brambles, or rescue
cows from drowning in flood-soaked forests, were bound to run into any
number of human predators. Indians routinely preyed upon white men's
cattle. Other poachers included not only runaway slaves and servants but
also planters and "their Servants by Order," groups of men forced to carry
out the elaborate machinations necessary to steal livestock—shooting it,
cutting it up, carrying the meat home, and "bur[ying] the Skin privately."
Knowing that the penalties for poaching were high and meted out swiftly,
men bent on obtaining fresh meat at any cost were not inclined to deal gen-
tly with anyone who suddenly stumbled across them while they were bend-
ing over a bloody carcass or "Carrying a hog out of the woods with out
Ears." Because of the physical demands and social disorder associated with
keeping wild herds, the planters of Ebenezer (in Georgia) went so far as to
give up on livestock altogether; the wild cattle ate and trampled the crops of
the area, and "no Men or Horses that ever have been employed or could be
hired here were found capable of driving that Swamp and Places adjacent."
As a result, "it was conceived no Method could be taken to conquer or master the said wild Cattle otherwise than by shooting them in the Swamps and
Thicketts where they harbour," a solution feared by local officials to open
the way "for Persons of ill character to plunder the Woods. . . ."[29]

Whether they were tracking down lost cattle or hoeing in the tobacco
fields, cutting trees or building fences, most servants saw outdoor worksites
as places of fear, and at times, terror. A near-continuous military alert blan-
keted the Chesapeake through much of the seventeenth century, and Georgia during its entire history as a pre-slave society. As late as the early 1660s,
all hands on Virginia's "frontier" plantations had to possess firearms. It was
during this time that Indians made sporadic raids upon individual plantations for the purpose of retaliating against whites (by killing any or all who
happened to be outdoors or vulnerable), or kidnapping men, women, and
children—especially black people, who could be sold elsewhere as slaves.
During the first two decades of its existence, Georgia remained in a constant state of panic over various "Spanish allarms," exacerbated by periodic
appearances of groups ranging from sailors and soldiers who had deserted
His Majesty's service to fugitive servants and slave runaways from South

Carolina and bands of Spanish marauders from St. Augustine. Thus it was not unusual for early southern workers to associate work, especially work in fields and forests, with physical danger, in contrast to their English counterparts, who rarely worried about surviving yet another day in the fields.[30]

Masters and mistresses did not always have the time or resources to supervise their servants directly, but they did hold those servants accountable for the work they did or did not do. Some landowning men and women understood that brutality was not the most effective means of extracting hard work—let alone cheerful cooperation—from young workers of both sexes; but others, frustrated by the endless expanse of land and the lack of hands to till it, made a calculated attempt to drive their servants mercilessly. To the modern sensibility, the nature and extent of corporal punishment unleashed on children and older servants of both sexes is truly shocking. However, on both sides of the Atlantic could be found communities where witches, pickpockets, and hog stealers were hanged, and other persons considered threatening to civil society were whipped, branded, confined in irons, or deprived of their ears. And certainly, many a southern colonial master was wont to utter the same indictment as his English contemporaries: "There is not a more insolent and proud, a more untractable, perfidious and a more churlish sort of people breathing, than the generality of our servants." It was hard to find good help anywhere, especially when the available hands were all so young and uncooperative.[31]

Still, the exotic social and physical configuration of New World life gave rise to a violent form of labor relations that had no direct counterpart within England at the time (though in the near future the horrific treatment of English convicts as slave laborers in Australia would make the fate of their peers in the western hemisphere seem positively benign in comparison).[32] The most severe cases of servant abuse, at least some of which found their way into the courts, involved various forms of torture, including whippings over a long period of time and instances of starvation and other kinds of deprivation. Some masters discouraged careless work in a swift and violent way; but others engaged in a more enduring pattern of cruelty. A knock on the head with a rake, ax, or hoe was certain to deliver the appropriate message to the recalcitrant field worker on the spot; but more telling were servant homicides or suicides. In the process of sorting out the two causes of death, colonial courts amassed a great deal of evidence of the "barbarous usage" that many servants came to expect. In their rush to exonerate a master with a long history of violent behavior, juries condemned the allegedly self-destructive behavior of a servant who "tooke a Grindstone and a Roape, and tyed it about his middle and crosse his thighes, and most barbarously went and drowned himself. . . ," or of another worker who "hunge himself w'th an irone dogg Chaine . . . in a loft in the house. . . ." In at least some of these cases the corpses showed bruises and other signs of previous mistreatment.[33]

The age and gender of servants to some degree shaped the nature and extent of abuse. Masters might manhandle children of ten or eleven with impunity and without fear of retaliation. (In contrast, when Wiliam Hopkins tried to correct an older servant, Owen Morgan, a chronic runaway, Morgan "struck him his Master wth a Club, threatening him wth many uncivill & opprobious words, wth Cursing, swearing blasphemy &c.") In July 1657, Harry Gouge, a lame boy indented to John Dandy, was found "naked and Dead in the Creeke," his body bearing the marks of his master's attacks on him with an ax and with "Some Small Switch or rod, and that not newly done," as well as ear lacerations resembling rat bites. Dandy claimed that the boy had drowned himself. In an unusual display of collective courage, several witnesses testified to Dandy's persistently cruel behavior, no doubt because the case against him was so clear-cut. These witnesses included servants of neighbors, two inmates in the Dandy household, two of Dandy's own servants, ages fourteen and twenty-one years, and Dandy's wife. In another case, Alice Travellor, the mistress of a little girl named Elizabeth Bibby, showed no remorse after hoisting the girl "upp by a Tackle which they use to hang deare with," whipping her, holding her "over the fyre threatening that she would burne her," and beating her bloody. Elizabeth had enraged her mistress by soiling her bed.[34]

Older girls and young women were the victims of assault and sexual abuse. In 1640, Elinor Rowe of Accomack-Northampton County was "most unconscyonably and dangerousely Beate" by her mistress, leaving the servant convinced that it was only a matter of time before "shee [would] doubtles be murthered." In Lower Norfolk County, Virginia, in 1649, "Deborah Fernehaugh, the Mistress . . . did beate her mayd Sarvant . . . more Liken a dogge then a Christian," and her head "was beaten as soft as a sponge, in one place." According to one of Fernehaugh's male servants, as the maid was weeding one day, "shee complayned and sayd, her backe bone as shee thought was broken with beating. . . ." Considering the near total power of masters over servants, it is not surprising that at least some young women workers were sexually assaulted by the men for whom they worked. In certain counties in seventeenth century England, from a quarter to nearly two-thirds of the mothers of bastards were servants, and at least some of the fathers were either masters or masters' sons. However, the matter assumed somewhat greater dimensions in the colonies, where even established members of the community, like the Virginia lawmakers in 1662, felt compelled to note that "late experiente shew that some dissolute masters have gotten their maides with child, and yet claime the benefitt of their service." In other words, these masters victimized their women servants in two ways: by sexually abusing them, and then extending their indentures as punishment for becoming pregnant as well. Women suffered a whole range of threatening behavior directed at them; one master was brought to trial "for committing a Rape on the body of his Servant Maid," while another routinely taunted his servant by calling her a "whore. . . . Common as the milking payle."[35]

These sketchy details raise more questions than they answer about the pervasiveness of the havoc that masters wrought on the minds and bodies of their servants. In general, cases eventually brought to public attention were particularly dramatic, and monitored over a long period of time by inmates, neighbors, and fellow servants. It is apparent that, in the absence of witnesses willing to testify in the presence of a tyrannical master or mistress, many instances of cruelty went unnoticed and unchecked. Though a servant might endure a beating with a "great ropes end" for spoiling a batch of bread, or assault with a "thre futted stole [stool]" for "takeing a booke in hure hand," a fair number of masters and mistresses apparently considered the matter of worker discipline to be outside the realm of the law: "what hath any man to doe with my Servants?" Called to account for his "severe Usage" of a servant boy, whose "whole Back, Shoulders, Loins, Flank and Belly, were in a dreadful Condition," one Georgia master coolly informed his questioners that "he thought himself the proper Judge, without Controul, in what manner to govern the Boys that he had the care of. . . ." It is likely that mistresses jealous of their husband's attention to a female servant engaged in arbitrary and spontaneous attacks on the young women in their households, the way slave mistresses targeted young black women under similar circumstances. Perhaps there existed a relation between a servant's length of time remaining on his or her contract and the willingness of superiors to indulge themselves in fits of rage. The limited evidence precludes any overarching generalizations, but one verbally abusive mistress "told some of her servaunts saying you Rogues I will hang you all if you had seaven yeares to serve," implying that she was willing to sacrifice a considerable amount of their labor if she could only avenge herself for their "roguishness."[36]

Servant resistance ran the gamut from the verbal sassiness of a dairymaid to open revolt among groups of young men armed with guns and knives, and foul deeds seemed to go hand-in-hand with foul words. Servants made "unlawfull speeches" to their masters and mistresses, vowing to knock them in the head or stab them in the heart. These instances of rhetorical bravado could not always be classified as idle threats. Virginia legislators condemned "the audacious unruliness of many stubborn and incorrigible servants," singling out those who "lay violent hands on his or her master or mistresse." In one notorious case, a young Virginia servant, raised in a middling English family and trained as a bookseller, murdered his master and mistress while they slept in their beds. A man who "abhored the Ax and the Haw [hoe]," the servant had been lured to a Charles City, Virginia, plantation (appropriately called Hard Labour) under the pretense that he would serve as tutor for the owner's children. Instead, he found himself toiling as a field hand. He developed a low level of tolerance for the fulminations of his mistress, a woman who "would not only rail, swear, and curse at him" indoors but also "like a live ghost would impertinently haunt him" while he was outside, plying a labor he found "most irksome" to begin with. Planters guilty of far greater assaults on the dignity of their workers might well have taken notice of this example.[37]

Through deliberate carelessness and overt sabotage, servants burned down their masters' houses, mistreated livestock (by beating a herd of goats "with the bars of the cowpen," for example), and neglected the tobacco crop. One young servant placed in charge of his mistress's cattle alternately played ninepins and fell asleep, and persisted in "lazing all the day," leaving the cows to eat a neighbor's corn, and vulnerable to the attacks of vicious dogs. In defiance of law and their masters, male servants impregnated their masters' daughters, and young workers of both sexes married secretely in violation of their contracts. It hardly comes as a surprise that theft among white servants reached epidemic proportions, beginning in the first years of settlement and continuing thereafter; perpetrators included not only the solo operator who slaughtered a pig for his own secret enjoyment but also men and women who systematically pilfered from the household in order to trade their "truck" with freemen and Indians. The black market in stolen goods was so lucrative that many servants were "thereby induced and invited to purloine and imbezill the goods of their said masters," prompting numerous legal statutes to prevent trade that involved servants in any way.[38]

Servants in the Chesapeake and in Georgia assumed as their prerogative the late-night Saturday and all-day Sunday get-togethers where they could meet to drink, carouse, and indulge in plots of various degrees of dastardliness against their tormenters. To the consternation of more established folk, midnight brawls disturbed the peace and left servants incapacitated from drink or fisticuffs, raw and bleeding, and hence unfit for work the next day. William Stephens believed that the town of Savannah should rid itself of its taverns, or face "utter Ruin," for, he wrote, "these are the Nurserys of all

Villany, where Servants are debauchd, and defraud their Masters of any thing they can lay their hands on, to purchase . . . such Spirits. . . ." Indeed, taverns and servant meeting places of all sorts were emblematic of a whole complex of vices—theft, desertion, drinking, gambling, fornication, and political subversion.[39]

The German servants of Georgia who ventured far into the woods, during late hours, to sit around a fire, "with guns lying by them," prompted fears among planters who assumed with good reason that the dead of night "was not a Time to look for game, whether Venison or Fowls." Some servants began to plan their collective getaway as soon as they arrived on board ship in England, while others hatched plots in the fields, instead of working. Servants who intended to withhold their labor, or to run away, kept colonial officials in a constant state of alert. As early as 1619, the Virginia Burgesses advised against seating a large number of tenants together, on the assumption that they would "overthrowe themselves" by "ill example of Idlenes." William Clutton launched his aborted plot in 1661, and two years later, in Gloucester County, a "desperate conspiracy" of former Cromwellian soldiers in servitude alarmed planters throughout the colony. In 1739, Georgia officials contended with an apparent strike among German servants "(who in general were every Day growing more and more insolent, and lazy) having combined together, and under pretense of not having Justice done them, declared they would not work until their Demands were satisfied." The shock of these well-publicized incidents was compounded by the constant rumors of more modest uprisings on individual plantations, rumors that punctuated the pre-slavery period in Virginia, Maryland, and Georgia.[40]

If white servants in the early southern colonies were soldiers on the front lines of the British Empire, then it is safe to say that many of them were AWOL at least part of the time. The problem of runaways was so pervasive as to cripple the whole system of indentured servitude. Sensing what was in store for them in the New World, or just plagued by second thoughts, some passengers jumped ship before they left port in England, while others waited until the West Indies to flee. Chronic runaways might shrewdly try to exploit their irresponsible behavior by offering to lead a more sedentary existence in return for contract concessions, but most servants apparently just wanted relief from their daily routine of drudgery. One Virginia servant racked up an escape record of sorts: she absconded forty times in the course of a decade (the 1680s). At times, masters launched concerted efforts to locate fugitives—through a colonywide "hue and cry" from house to house—but many more expressed the attitude, "hang him rogue lett him goe, he will Come againe at night or morning, when he is hungry and I shall find him. . . ." Yet the scenario of the famished servant returning home and begging forgiveness proved accurate only in cases where a runaway had not found shelter with nearby Indians, succumbed to the flattering offer of a neighboring planter, or chosen suicide over the prospect of a humiliating return and ceaseless toil.[41]

Servants ran away even though they had certain rights under the law— the right to sue, to enforce contracts, to own property, to testify in courts, and for men (in certain times and places) the duty to serve in the militia— and even though masters were enjoined from mistreating them. However, to save themselves from an abusive master, most young white workers expressed an implicit preference for running away rather than pressing their grievances in court. And no wonder: Servants bold enough to betake themselves to court and denounce their master or mistress were often rewarded for their trouble with countersuits, and, in the case of complaints decided in favor of the defendant, continued (if not additional) service in the household of their nemesis. In Accomack County in 1681, two servants who accused their master of "occasioning the death of a Servant woman" (one of his own) provoked this response: "It appears to the Court a most false and most malitious accusation by the said servants combination. . . ." In fact, the justices found the "information so brought by the said Servants . . . to be notoriously false and Scandalous," and ordered the period of service for each man extended, in order to compensate their master for "their Said Causless information and complaint" and for any court charges he might have incurred. We can only speculate about the fate that awaited the two men upon their return home, as well as the fate of Margarett Roberts, who in 1658 testified that her master "wth all very often striketh her," only to have the case continued and herself returned to her master, who was admonished to "use her well & not strike her."[42]

Whenever vigilant neighbors reported their suspicions concerning adulterous activities on a nearby plantation, servants were compelled to tell what they had seen or heard; and in the cases of mistresses copulating with lovers, and masters raping servant girls, the evidence presented could be quite graphic. For this reason, some masters and mistresses went to extreme lengths to prevent their servants from testifying at all. One married woman killed a servant who had discovered a letter "from one John Hatton to her Dame"; the older woman was afraid that the servant would divulge the note's contents. Under the circumstances, then, we might question the value of a servant's testimony marshaled to exonerate a master of wrongdoing, and we might marvel at the number of servants who risked bodily harm to speak their mind in public. For young white workers, even modest legal protections carried with them definite liabilities.[43]

"BROILING COUNTRYMEN" AND "FAINTING TOWNSMEN"

Toiling together in the woods of Charles County, Maryland, during the winter of 1664, three male laborers—two whites who worked for Francis Pope (Thomas Abbot and Thomas Greenhill) and one black (a "Neger of Mr Popes")—were felling trees. While Abbot and the black man were not looking, Thomas Greenhill was hit by a falling tree ("accdentallie and for want of Care the tree fell on him and killed him," a jury found later). Seeing Greenhill unconscious on the ground, the black man cried out "Lord bless us what ayleth the boy so," which prompted Abbot to run over and implore, "for Christ sake Thomas Greenhill speake but hee could not." These men had gone about their tasks far from the watchful eye of Mr. Pope or an overseer. Yet the equality of condition they shared in the woods was belied by the fact that in public, court officials failed to refer to Mr. Pope's Negro by his name, although he evidently spoke English, and his use of the exclamation "Lord bless us" might even suggest that he was a Christian.[44]

In the course of the seventeenth century, Chesapeake elites undertook the task of creating the legal institution of black slavery; and yet, no "racial" division of labor had yet emerged: in the words of a particularly grim piece of contemporary poetry, "We and the Negroes both alike did fare/Of work and food we had an equal share." On the vast majority of holdings through the 1680s or so, black people of any status were in a minority compared to white indentured servants and few masters had the resources or inclination to enforce color-based segregation in the quarters or in the fields. Lists of tithables and headrights, as well as wills and inventories, show that young white servants predominated on most plantations (with men outnumbering women), with a few Indians or blacks (of either sex, and widely varying ages) rounding out individual holdings. In 1640, for example, Accomack County's Nathaniel Littleton's estate included fourteen Negroes, male and female, plus thirty white men and six white women.[45]

Men and women of all three races mingled outside of workplaces in ways that signaled trouble for their masters. Bound workers' drinking parties were notoriously biracial affairs. Certainly, sexual relations among blacks, whites, and Indians of equal status were not uncommon, despite the efforts of lawmakers (in Virginia, in 1691, for example) to discourage the "abmominable mixture and spurious issue" resulting from intimate contact. More generally, blacks and whites ran away together, and there is some evidence to suggest that non-English white servants felt a particular affinity for colluding with blacks; in Virginia in 1640, three workers belonging to Hugh Gwyn—two whites, "Victor, a dutchman, the other a Scotchman called James Gregory" and the third "being a negro named John Punch"—all absconded together. In their non-Englishness, if not in their race or language, the three may have found a common bond. For their crime, the two whites received lashes, while John Punch was ordered to "serve his said master or his assigns for the time of his natural life here or elsewhere." In 1660, the Virginia legislature decreed that any "English . . . running away in company" with blacks must compensate their own masters for the time lost, and the masters of the blacks for the time they lost as well. If any black died during one of these escapades, the white worker was obligated either to pay "fower thousand five hundred pounds of tobacco and caske or fower yeares service for every negroe soe lost or dead." In this way the planter elite discouraged collective resistance among workers at the lowest echelons of society, even as it acknowledged joint runaway ventures to be a political issue worthy of its attention.[46]

By the last decades of the seventeenth century, an expanded African slave trade increased the supply of black workers available to the colonists; at the same time, improved economic and political conditions in England staunched the outmigration of white servants. Yet these supply and demand factors are insufficient to account for the origins of slavery in the South. In the process of writing letters, recording account-book entries, and writing laws, Chesapeake and Georgia planters created a balance sheet comparing white servitude to black slavery; and the advantages of black labor were always defined in relation to the disadvantages of white labor. Indeed, the choice between the two labor systems appeared less clear-cut at the time than it does for historians three centuries later.[47] In choosing slavery, whites chose not only to force black people to work but also to live with black people, and many planters understood that cohabitation with outsiders carried with it certain risks to English sensibilities, and certain risks to colonial social stability.

Within a few decades of settlement, the shortcomings of white indentured servants were well known. By law, at least, servants labored for a limited number of years only, and though they might grow more skilled as they grew older, they also gradually lost value should a master need to sell their remaining time for cash. Pregnant and nursing servants remained relatively unproductive for weeks on end, scandalized the community, and eventually burdened their masters with extra mouths to feed without any payoff in terms of future labor, since the women's contracts would expire long before the children were big enough to work.

New World workplaces introduced Europeans to what they considered a new and degrading kind of toil, and English men and women in particular wondered aloud about the nature and amount of work that could reasonably be expected of a (white, English-speaking) Christian. Pro-slavery petitioners in Georgia expressed their horror over the degradation of white men and women: "How shocking must it be even to a person of the least humanity to See his own Countrymen, perhaps his own Townsmen, Labouring in the Corn or rice field, Broiling in the Sun, Pale and Fainting under the Excessive heat." Thus, their campaign for black bondsmen and women assumed the character of a humanitarian (or rather, nationalistic) movement on behalf of English workers.[48]

In fact, though, few southern masters or mistresses conceived of indentured servants as potential objects of moral uplift. Living out their days with persons they considered the dregs of English society, planters loftily disdained vice-ridden servants—enduring the mortification that came with boarding a "shameless hussy" or an incorrigible thief in one's own household. And yet no matter how vicious, all white servants expected and even demanded a certain standard of health, diet, and clothing, and they did not hesitate to invoke the "rights of Englishmen" when denied days off from work to mark traditional holidays.[49]

Colonial courts were choked with civil suits, countersuits, and criminal cases revolving around the rights and responsibilities of servants and masters—whenever an indentures contract was in question, or a servant's age in doubt, communities expended precious resources to hear the evidence and in some cases impanel a jury. The fact that a servant might eventually gain his or her freedom served as an attractive recruitment device, but it also meant that insolent young people might someday become the equals of the former mistresses and masters whose personal behavior they had monitored so closely a few years before. And of course, surly, landless bachelors proved to be a disruptive force in pre-slavery society; with fingers on the trigger, these former hands (at least in Virginia) had the capacity to terrorize their former masters, men who monopolized power and property. The planter elite might have overlooked these difficulties inherent in the use of white servants, and their potential for incendiary activities, if young white men and women had worked cheerfully in the fields and demonstrated a proper deference for their betters; but as a general rule they had not.[50]

Given this list of the liabilities of white labor, the arguments in favor of black slavery would seem to be not only self-evident, but also compelling. Masters decided that black people as slaves needed less in terms of shelter, food, and clothing compared to white people as servants, leading eventually to the idea that black people could "naturally" get by with less, compared to white people. Whites had no scruples about putting black women of all ages into the fields, and these women remained vulnerable to sexual abuse that carried no legal penalties. In addition, the offspring of an illicit master-slave relationship became a slave for life. Given the tremendous amounts of psychological intimidation and physical brutality required to force all kinds of workers to toil in the tobacco fields, planters preferred to contend with enslaved workers of African descent—men and women who were no less resistant to their masters compared to white servants, but who were deprived of the ability to pursue their grievances in a court of law or the court of colonial public opinion.

Last but not least, the financial and political payoffs of slavery were undeniable—once "seasoned," a slave represented a lifetime investment; and the existence of a large, readily identifiable group of black manual laborers elevated the position of all southern whites, no matter how grueling their own work or how mean their own standard of living. In the Chesapeake—homeland to the future founding fathers of the United States of America—slavery carried with it its own logic, but it was a logic that was a long time in the making, and not readily apparent to colonists for several generations.

Historians have outlined in great detail the southern colonies' unmistakable (but not necessarily inexorable) move toward slavery. As the seventeenth century wore on, Virginia prevented black men from bearing arms (1640), condemned black children and women to field work, as tithables, (1642), decreed that the offspring of slavewomen were slaves (1662), and that conversion to Christianity did not bring freedom (1667). The colony's official slave code was passed in 1705. To be sure, these measures constituted but a subset of English ethnocentricism; at the same time they served to draw distinctions between people of African descent on the one hand and people of European descent on the other, distinctions that would eventually be stated in exclusively "racial," and not just ethnic or religious, terms.[51]

WHILE THE FACT of blacks' enslavement gave license to whites to treat slaves as they wished, it also posed a serious threat to the security of the colonies, and to principled forms of English social exclusivity. The image of black people that emerges from seventeenth-century southern records conjures up visions of a cunning, bloodthirsty people. Supposedly in a position to know about such life-and-death matters, Barbadian and South Carolina lawmakers proclaimed that Negroes were naturally "of barbarous, wild and savage nature," a group of people "naturally prone and inclined" to "disorders, rapines, and inhumanities. . . ." In Maryland in 1658, Symon Oversee's slave Antonio suffered from severe abuse and neglect, one of his hands and arms eventually "extreme[ly] sore" and rotting from gangrene. Antonio finally died after his master had beaten him with sticks, poured melted lard on his body, and suspended him outside "exposed to the injuries of the weather"—a round of torture no doubt related to the description of the non-English-speaking Antonio (in the words of Oversee's brother) as "a dangerous rogue," "ugly yelling Brute beast like."[52]

Like white servants, black slaves stole, and they bludgeoned unsuspecting masters and mistresses. But even the simple act of running away assumed sinister overtones: they "lie hid and lurk in obscure places." By 1691 in Virginia, ordinary citizens as well as sheriffs were authorized to "kill and distroy such negroes, mulattoes, and other slave or slaves by gunn or any otherwaise whatsover." Within southern colonial settlements, the specter of a slave revolt was inextricably linked to fears of Indians, the Dutch, and Spaniards. As early as 1644, Virginia lawmakers expressed their concern over "the riotous and rebellious conduct" of groups of slaves. In 1680, a "Negro Plot" in the Northern Neck of Virginia was apparently the outcome of the slaves' "Walking on broad on Saterdays and Sundays . . . permitting them to meete in great Numbers in makeing and holding of Funeralls for Dead Negroes"; such clandestine gatherings allowed blacks "to Consult and advise for the carrying on of their Evill and Wichked purposes and Contrivances . . . ." In Georgia, even the rabidly pro-slavery Thomas Stephens, confronted with news about the Stono uprising in South Carolina in 1739, admitted that "perhaps they [slaves] might here and there kill a white, but the hazard must be run, for without Negroes the Colony must drop," an argument that at that point the trustees found less than convincing.[53]

Later, as they set about debating the best way to introduce slavery into the colony, Georgia planters became preoccupied with numbers, wondering how many slaves could be tolerated in one place before they were in "danger of rising, and cutting their Masters throats." Though they might deny the depth of their own fears, these white men, and successive generations of southern slaveholders, never lost sight of the image first suggested by William Byrd II: the slave insurrection that would "tinge our rivers as wide as they are with blood."[54] By 1750, slavery as a system of labor relations and political power was so entrenched in the South that its creation took on the appearance of a foregone conclusion. Nevertheless, the institution of bondage came at a high price, and during an era of revolutionary upheaval, southern planters would all too soon learn the liabilities of forcefully extracting labor from "strangers" who were also domestic insurrectionists.

CHAPTER THREE

THE WORK OF INSURRECTION:
BLACK AND WHITE LABOR IN
THE EIGHTEENTH-CENTURY SOUTH

A few weeks before the signing of the Declaration of Independence, along the shore of Virginia's Rappahannock River, a group of white "minute men" pursued and fired upon a heavily armed band of several "stout men" in a boat on the river. In response to the shots, the "stout men"—described by a Patriot planter as "accursed villains"— beached the boat and then fled on foot, arousing "100 King and Queen minutemen [i.e., Loyalists] in the process." For the residents of Middlesex County, the American Revolution had begun in this brief skirmish, which amounted to an attempt by a group of Patriots to apprehend Joe, Bill, Postillion John, Mulatto Peter, Tom, Panitcove, Manual, and Lancaster Sam— slave runaways belonging to Colonel Landon Carter of Sabine Hall. (These black men thus joined an estimated eighty to one-hundred thousand slaves, most of them men, who would flee to the British in the course of the Revolution.) To make good their escape, and presumably their start on a new life, the fugitives had absconded with guns, powder, ammunition, silver buckles, and assorted pieces of clothing taken from Carter and members of his family. Later in the summer, as he pondered this affront to his authority, Carter speculated about the role of Moses, "my son's man," a free black, in inciting the others to leave; perhaps Moses was determined "to glut his genius for liberty which he was not born to." Carter took grim satisfaction in the fate of these particular slaves and others who followed them from his plantation during the war into the cold embrace of the Redcoats; most of the refugees found only death and disease behind British lines, and the ones returned forcibly to Sabine Hall were put in irons, "secured and confined" until they could be sold.[1]

The return of yet another group of runaways in the summer of 1777—this time Old Will, Ben, and Molly—prompted Carter to spend some time contemplating all the care he had lavished on his slaves, acts of kindness that "should have taught them gratitude if there ever was a virtue of the sort in such creatures." Carter had personally nursed several of these presumed ingrates back to health, and endeavored to "use" all of them "with the greatest respect." From the slaves' perspective, Carter's wounded feelings represented one more assault upon their dignity. As tobacco hands, they were expected to "hill" as many as three thousand plants a day during the spring, to work in the rain if necessary, and to perform myriad other tasks on the large plantation. In response, they feigned illness, snatched naps in the field, and got drunk. Carter allowed his slaves to raise chickens to sell for a little cash, but he withheld adequate clothing so that they would have an incentive to purchase shirts, shifts, and breeches with their modest earnings. And he congratulated himself on his "humanity" for "refreshing such poor creatures," noting the spirit of self-sacrifice that motivated him to spare something "out of my own sumptuous fare" for the benefit of his "Poor Slaves."[2]

During the course of the eighteenth century, the organization of southern workers underwent a number of dramatic transformations. In contrast to the earlier Chesapeake householders, who oversaw a preponderance of young white male indentured servants supplemented by small numbers of white female and Indian and black bound laborers, planters in 1800 were relying on few bound white servants as field workers, and on virtually no Indians as servants or slaves. After 1700, landowners and household heads gradually sorted out workers by "race" (i.e., by West European or West African descent), gender, and specialized skills, and differentiated them from each other according to the terms of their work in the course of the year.

By the time of the Revolution, white elites—and especially the great planters of Virginia—had developed a theory of black inferiority that sought to justify the relegation of Africans and their descendants to lifelong menial toil. In large measure this theory grew out of the fact that slaves were forced to perform amounts and kinds of labor from which white men and women were increasingly exempt. Because slaves were forced to work at a grueling pace, often under dangerous conditions, whites concluded that, in the words of one Virginia planter, black people in general "are by nature cut out for hard labour and fatigue. . . ."[3] In the parlance of Patriots, white men were enlightened and rational beings, governed by a fixed, predictable set of laws (by 1787, the Constitution), and ever hopeful of the material gain that hard work and ambition would earn for them. In the parlance of slaveowners, black men and women resembled animals ("poor creatures"); they were devoid of "reason," vulnerable to the arbitrary whims and wishes of their masters, and condemned (along with their children) to perpetual bondage. White men came to the body politic as individuals, each one guaranteed certain fixed liberties; black people stood indicted en masse, identified as a "race" apart from all whites, no matter how mean or brutish.[4]

Southern slaveowners developed the strategy of "paternalism" to smother, or at least smooth over, these glaring contradictions in the emerging American republic. The challenge of maintaining control over large numbers of blacks engaged in arduous labor prompted planters to liken themselves to ancient patriarchs, protective of whole households of dependents of all ages and both sexes, black and white. Still, paternalism had its practical limits. The institution of slavery was most secure and safe for whites when large numbers of slaves were kept hard at work in the fields and forests; but masters knew all too well that it was not always possible or profitable to confine their hands to these tasks exclusively. In areas where skilled whites were in short supply, slaves dominated any number of trades, and thereby eluded the tight control of their owners.[5] Likewise, slaves as soldiers, traders, herdsmen, boatmen, or producers of wares to be hawked on city streets were less tractable than slaves as producers of staple crops. In the end, the self-congratulatory rhetoric of the planters contrasted mightily with the nature of the particular tasks they pressed upon their slaves, and with the violence necessary to uphold this system of labor control.

Indeed, paternalism reflected less the white men's solicitude for the welfare of their slaves than their attempt to adapt to demographic realities. Unlike masters of servants, slaveowners were forced to clothe and feed a great number of potential workers (children), as well as workers past their prime. Consequently, these white men attempted to break the plantation routine into discrete parts, on the theory that work must be found for all, and not just for able-bodied hands. The householder who employed servants might let the health of a worker deteriorate, especially near the end of his or her "time," while the slaveowner had a vested interest in attending to the physical needs of workers and to make some accommodations for pregnant women (in order to preserve the integrity of his financial investment) at all times. Though also faced with the wearisome task of forcing other people to work, the masters of servants were freed of a major burden borne by the masters of slaves—dealing with workers' simmering resentment over the separation of slave family members through bequest or sale. When planters expressed an interest in the mates their slaves chose, or tried to choose those mates for them, these white men acted in ways that their pre-decessors, as masters of servants, had not. And perhaps most significantly, slaveowners had to contend with workforces desperate to become free, but with little or no hope of outliving their status as bound men and women.

As early as 1700, the division of labor on William Fitzhugh's sprawling Tidewater Virginia plantation provided a model for future large estates: fifty-one black and mulatto slaves, parceled out to several smaller planta-tions, or "quarters"; six English servants, including a glazier and a carpenter; and Fitzhugh and his wife and their children. Toward the end of his life, Fitzhugh sought to bring over from England "a good Housewife," and to pay her a decent yearly wage; he wanted a "good one or none," having little respect for the "generality of [white] wenches." (It would take a couple of generations before slave men and women as a group would be entrusted with the duties of preparing and serving tea, combing a gentleman's wig or grooming his horse.) In his will, Fitzhugh stipulated that one of the woman slaves should be "exempted from working in the ground," a sign, he noted, of his wife's favor toward her. Fitzhugh also anticipated by several decades the appreciation planters in general would have for the self-reproducing nature of the slave labor force: "the negroes increase being all young & a considerable parcel of breeders will keep that stock good for ever."[6]

Complementing the dramatic rise in the number of slaves, several other emerging social groups testified to the maturation of colonial settlements—modest landowners and tenants who relied solely on the labor of their chil-dren in the fields; women and children (in all but the wealthiest households) who devoted considerable time to various household industries, especially textile production; and a class of white artisans, men who had to compete with their black, plantation-bound counterparts. Toward the end of the eighteenth century, black and white men might still find themselves at work together (when they dug the Potomac Canal in 1786, for example), but they were likely to be set apart from one another by their status—the white men either as hirelings or indentured servants, the black men as slaves.[7]

By excluding black people from the body politic of the new nation, and by defining black people exclusively as enslaved workers, theorists of the American Revolution grounded an emergent liberal, democratic state upon the principles of a traditional, feudalistic tyranny. As the first southerner to advance (however tentatively) a theory of scientific racism, Thomas Jeffer-son sought to prove that the rights of landowning white men were precious precisely because children, indentured servants, Indians, black people, and white women were deprived of those rights. (Ironically, Jefferson extolled the simple virtues of tilling the soil while reserving that task on his own estate to the slaves.) The Revolution marked the end of an era when all sub-ordinate workers—red, white, and black, servant and slave—were considered equally dangerous to propertied whites, and ushered in a new period when black people were accorded a distinct, and distinctly threatening, status in American society. To whites, the uniqueness of blacks as a group was compounded by the development of a black collective identity; and that collective identity, juxtaposed to the slaveowners' nationalism, immeasurably complicated the management of southern workforces.[8]

WORK, CULTURE, AND THE BLACK "RACE" IN THE SOUTH

Like Step and Lucy, two "new" Negroes (recently imported from Africa) who ran away from their owner in Petersburg, Virginia, in 1771, "being persuaded that they could find their Way back to their own Country,"[9] enslaved men and women suffered the shock of separation from loved ones, and yearned to return to their homeland. But whites remained ignorant of the slaves' memories and indifferent to their misery. Freed from the political anxieties that went along with exploiting fellow whites, slaveholders now faced a new set of dilemmas. First, the blacks' "strangeness," and more specifically, their retention of certain African cultural forms, made them resistant to work discipline; yet as long as they remained relatively isolated from whites, those cultural forms would continue to shape their emerging families and communities. Second, slave men became more valuable to their owners to the extent that they became skilled in traditional English as well as New World crafts; yet as they became acculturated to English ways and began to take pride in their skills, black artisans grew ever more resentful of their own bondage, more prone to running away and more prone to colluding among themselves to wreak revenge on their tormentors. For these reasons the efficient use of slave labor posed substantial security risks to whites throughout the eighteenth century.

The story of the southern colonies is the story of a series of receding borderlands—those areas where shifting, triracial communities co-existed uneasily and defined their relations with one another through trade—and the emergence of staple-crop economies that relied primarily on slave labor. By the early eighteenth century, in the eyes of European settlers, black men and women had become crucial to the colonization process by virtue of their supposedly unique ability to withstand arduous physical labor—especially the clearing of land—and their (African-based) experience as navigators of rivers, herders of cattle, and producers and traders of a variety of goods.

During the seventeenth century, the physical threat posed by a rapidly growing black population preoccupied white southerners. On the eve of the American Revolution, imports of African slaves combined with native births had pushed the southern black population to 346,000 (up from 13,000 just seventy years earlier). South Carolina changed from an Indian country in 1685 (with red, white, and black populations of 10,000, 1,400, and 500, respectively) to a "Negro Countrey" (of nearly 107,300 blacks, 71,600 whites, and only 500 Indians) ninety years later. The growth of the black labor force thus existed as a demographic fact. But the relation of this noticeable and largely non-English-speaking population to other groups of workers, and to the sworn enemies of the colonists (eventually British Redcoats among them), invested its growth with military and political significance as well.[10]

During the first three-quarters of the eighteenth century, the commercial development of the southern colonies proceeded apace, spurred by massive population movements from abroad and within the British colonies, and by the emergence of specialized and diversified regional economies. South Carolina discovered the profitablity of rice and indigo crops early in the century; Georgia too began to rely on those two staples, and, together with North Carolina, the production of naval stores. As the Chesapeake population dispersed to the Piedmont, to recapitulate the Tidewater's devotion to tobacco, the great seaboard planters of Virginia and Maryland began to produce less of the leaf and more grain, iron, and salt, along with all the craft products and transportation networks necessary to sustain a relatively varied economy. In the 1750s and 1760s, the South was less a unified commercial region and more a collection of places with their own distinctive economic characteristics—the Shenandoah Valley and Appalachian frontier, linked to Pennsylvania and New York through patterns of southward migration; the Eastern Shore of Maryland, dotted by small landholdings, gristmills, and craftshops; the stable, anglicized Virginia Tidewater, with its aristocracy dependent on large landholdings and political influence; the rice districts of South Carolina and eastern North Carolina, modeled upon West Indian monoculture; and the knots of households and commercial outposts scattered throughout Georgia and the Carolinas backcountry.

Each colony used the official machinery of fledgling local governments to shape the nature and deployment of various labor forces; thus private decisions to depend less on European indentured servants, and more on African slaves, as field workers, received public support in the form of tax-supported mechanisms of enforcement. Colonial officials passed regulations governing the licensing of craftsmen, inspection of staples for export, incentives for growing various products, and access to riverways. More specifically, these officials oversaw the operation of various forms of labor organization—indentured servitude, apprenticeship, slavery, and family labor; they bound out orphans to masters and mistresses; decreed that black women, but not white women, must be taxed as field workers; provided for the retrieval of runaway servants and slaves; and put criminals to work on the public roads. To strengthen and sustain the institution of slavery, royal appointees together with native-born elected representatives guaranteed white servants certain rights and left the fate of slaves to their individual owners; stipulated ever more stringent rules governing the manumission of slaves; prohibited the schooling and nighttime assembling of slaves; and in the course of the eighteenth century, began to limit the movements and opportunities of free blacks.[11]

The southern colonial labor force was fashioned not just by planters' needs bolstered by legislative mandates but also by the sword and the musket. Tassel, an Indian leader in the western part of North Carolina, bitterly noted that the whites "rangeing through our country" ("when one goes off two comes in his place") had drastically altered his people's traditional patterns of work; now, he noted, "Our young men are afraid to go out a hunting." In the early eighteenth century, southeastern indigenous peoples confronted a radical "new world," their old one ravaged by disease and war, the new one based on trade and reconfigured tribal and kinship groups. Pushed back from the coast, Indians reacted to their loss of hunting fields and fishing streams in various ways. The Catawbas, an amalgam of fragmented and dispossessed groups, became pivotal in the Carolinas' local and regional networks of exchange—networks fueled by the socially destructive demand for firearms and alcohol, and manipulated by the imperial designs of the European powers. Others, like the Cherokees in the Appalachian Mountains, managed to maintain a precarious subsistence to the extent that they relied on traditionally defined (Indian) "women's work"—tilling the soil—and not "men's work"—hunting, fighting, and trading. Some groups fled further into the interior, while others disappeared altogether. In 1775, the Indian population spanning the territory from the eastern seaboard to East Texas and the Shawnee Interior had decreased to 55,000 (down from 200,000 in 1685); and only 800 Indians made their home within the colonies of Virginia and South Carolina east of the mountains.[12]

"Settlement Indians" resigned themselves to living in proximity to whites and earning meager sums of cash, the men by serving as slavecatchers, scouts, and sellers of venison, the women as spinners and weavers, and both groups as peddlers and basketmakers. Whites still eschewed enslaving Indians in great numbers; in 1724, only two thousand Indians were held in bondage in South Carolina, including fourteen hundred women and children. Indian labor was valuable to the English colonists, but only if prisoners captured in war could be sold to New England for cash, or exchanged in the West Indies for black slaves. Toward the end of the eighteenth century, the new United States government implemented Indian management policies that were intended to "domesticate" remaining populations (the Cherokees, for example) by insisting that they adhere to an English-style gender division of labor—the men and boys put to cattle herding and farming on small parcels of land, the women and girls to spinning and weaving.[13]

Years later, one chronicler of early North Carolina history would write of the Indian man, "With the gun or the net, he was far more useful than he could ever be made with the axe." On the other hand, after 1700, southern pioneers and planters came to see blacks, wielding "their gleaming axes . . . in the deep forests" as crucial to the task of settlement, and crucial also to virtually every commercial enterprise, from processing salt and growing rice to milling corn and cultivating indigo. Despite their respective variations on the themes of land acquisition, commercial gain, and ethnic diversity, the southern colonies moved simultaneously, although along different paths, toward reliance on workers from Africa. Opined a landowner in 1757, " . . . to live in Virginia without slaves is morally impossible." During the first half of the eighteenth century, a conventional wisdom began to spread throughout the South: black people were particularly "well suited" for certain tasks, and the "violent heat" of midsummer provided them with a climate "wherein they delight." This stereotype focused on blacks' supposed physical prowess and resilience, and left largely unstated any generalizations related to their intellectual capacities.[14]

In the process, "great number of negroes . . . to clear the land" came to be listed among "the things which are necessary for the establishment" of a colony, "and which are absolutely indispensable. . . ." The curses of the Jamestown settlers, their hands blistered and bloodied by heavy axes, rolled down and echoed through the decades, as a new generation of English pioneers contemplated draining swamps for rice fields and carving corn fields out of forests. In a tract published in England in 1773, a promoter of emigration to North Carolina tried to allay the fears of would-be colonists with the patently absurd claim that "the land in Carolina is easily cleared, as there is little or no under wood"; a few pages later came the promise, "Five [young healthy Negroes] will clear and labour a plantation the first year, so as you shall have every thing in abundance for your family, with little trouble to yourself. . . ." Some whites felt it was sufficient to note that "a Negro can split 130 to 150 rails a day," on the assumption that only the railsplitter's skin color, and not age, sex, or size, was relevant to the task. It was no wonder that, in mid-eighteenth-century South Carolina, Toney and Jacob, both sawyers, were listed among the most valuable slaves of Hugh Cartwright's estate, in comparison with bricklayers, corkers, tanners, boatmen, black-smiths, butchers, and brickmakers.[15]

Although blacks rapidly became associated with the work of chopping trees and clearing brush from the colonial "interior," whites soon under-stood that the sheer difficulty of staying alive in remote settlements must mandate an expansive definition of labor appropriate for slaves. In the west-ern part of Virginia, "the bears, Panthers, Buffaloes and Elks and wild cats are only to be found . . . where there are as yet but few [white] inhabitants, and the hunting there is very toilsome and labourious and sometimes dan-gerous." Under such conditions, black men were entrusted with firearms and encouraged to hunt, trap, and trade (a development that confounded Englishmen who had always considered the pursuit of game a genteel sport of gentlemen). In coastal South Carolina and the Lower Mississippi Valley during the early 1700s, slaves formed an integral part of the triumvirate of red, white, and black herders, hunters, fishermen, rivermen, and cultivators who cleared the way for staple-crop agriculture. And throughout the eigh-teenth century the English colonists, like other European interlopers, uti-lized slaves and free people of color as soldiers in battles against Indians—in North Carolina's war against the Tuscaroras (1711–12), in South Carolina's campaign against the Yamasees (1715–20), and in Virginia's expeditions against the Kanawha Valley tribes that continued to menace its western frontier. In addition to supplementing their manpower, the whites fervently hoped that the sight of a black man with a musket aimed at Indian men, women, and children would discourage black and red alliances against the whites, and that Indians might be discouraged from harboring the many slave runaways who sought refuge deep in the backcountry.[16]

Gradually, borderland exchange economies yielded to commercial agri-culture and, up and down the southeastern coast, its seasonal complement, naval stores production. Since neither native-born whites nor recently arrived English men and women possessed a historical memory related to many of the tasks associated with eighteenth-century southern (nonto-bacco) commercial development, they quickly constructed a social ideology based on the notion that certain kinds of jobs should be performed by African slaves and their descendants. Tapping pine trees for pitch and tar; engineering the irrigation of vast rice fields for cultivation; and planting and harvesting rice, cotton, and indigo were tasks that the colonists all too readily considered too "troublesome" and too dangerous to do themselves. The epidemiological fact that West Africans were resistant to malaria (in a way that Western Europeans were not) only served to reinforce this evolving "racial" division of labor. In low-country South Carolina, slaveowners soon realized that the cultivation of rice was extremely hazardous to the health of anyone who did it, black or white; strikingly high mortality rates associated with that crop challenged—or should have challenged—the view that black people were hardy enough to survive a regimen that demanded they work in pools of standing water regardless of the weather.[17]

With the importation of large numbers of slaves directly from Africa, especially after 1740, and the subsequent decline of multi-racial workforces, planters were forced to reassess their earlier view of bondage—one based on small numbers of largely assimilated, English-speaking blacks scattered on isolated holdings. The concentration of Africans in the South Carolina low country (in 1740, two-thirds of the colony's population had been born in Africa) caused considerable concern among whites, who made tentative efforts to rank particular West African ethnic groups according to their suit-ability for certain kinds of work—hence claims that the allegedly suicide-prone Ibo made poor rice workers, and that the Angolans as a group were chronic runaways, drawn irresistibly as it were to Spanish Florida. In any case, whites perceived "outlandish," "saltwater," or "New Negroes" (in con-trast to Creole slaves) to be a particularly dangerous group of workers. For these reasons, the acculturation process assumed an air of urgency. Planters made a point of assigning their chattels new names, stripping them of their old ones as soon as possible, and they also sought younger Africans, who tended to learn English more quickly than their elders.[18]

Africans captured and later enslaved in the American colonies had worked at a variety of tasks, depending on the political economy of their homelands. Some men had cultivated tobacco or rice, and many had hoed corn and potatoes and herded cattle. Women, too, often worked in the fields, made pottery, spun thread, and wove cloth. However, like most Eng-lish men and women, new Negroes had had little experience felling trees, tapping trees for turpentine, hunting bears, or working at a forced pace in the fields. More significant than the particular tasks they endured as slaves were the alien and brutal contexts, and worksites, in which they labored; and in their efforts to escape those worksites, or recreate them on their own terms, they forced white people to confront the political implications of African cultures transplanted to American soil.

To the consternation of whites all over the South, African work and social traditions became inextricably intertwined with African-American means of resistance to slavery. Slaves who had recently endured the horrific Middle Passage often proved unpredictable and particularly difficult to control. From the planter's perspective, a "new Negro . . . must be broke," but many refused to conform to their masters' demands, in the words of one sympathetic white man, "either from Obstinacy, or . . . from Greatness of Soul . . . ." In 1731, the actions of Ayuba Suleiman Diallo (known to whites as Job ben Solomon), a highborn African from Bondu, illustrated a logical progression. Put to work in the fields of Kent Island, Maryland, this black man soon fell ill from "work in making tobacco," for he "had never been used to such labour." His master then forced him to tend cattle instead, but "Job would often leave the cattle, and withdraw into the woods to pray." Unable to speak English, and despairing of the treatment accorded him, he used one of these occasions to escape through the woods to safety, and to life as a free man. The act of praying had served as both the incentive and means to escape. Some Africans made good their escape in the company of others. From Henry Hill, North Carolina, absconded Jenning, "an Eboe negro [who] yells and speaks seldom"; John, born in France, presumably a Francophone; and Boston, "an Angola negro" ("scarrified by whipping"). Somehow they managed, perhaps through a pidgin language, to coordinate their plans and flee together. Other Africans took more extreme measures to deprive their masters of their labor. In July 1752, in Williamsburg, Virginia, "a fine Negroe Man Slave, imported in one of the late Ships from Africa, belonging to a Wheelwright, near this City [Williamsburg], taking Notice of his Master's giving another Correction for a Misdemeanor, went to a Grindstone and making a Knife sharp cut his own Throat, and died on the Spot."[19]

In general, the collective impulse among slaves always seemed to bode ill, according to whites. Planters felt no need to grant to blacks the traditional English holidays that their white servants insisted upon, but African-based rituals and communal gatherings brought slaves together in unauthorized gatherings, at night or on Sunday. Virginia lawmakers banned the congregation of blacks wherever they "played on their Negroe drums." Planters throughout the South saw no real distinction between groups of slaves who came together to celebrate feast days or attend funerals on the one hand, and groups of slaves who came together to plot uprisings on the other. An English visitor to a "Negro Ball" in Maryland in the 1770s described the "Dancing to the Banjo" that took place, and observed, "In their songs they generally relate the usage they have received from their Masters or Mistresses in a very satirical stile and manner." His description of the celebration hinted at the explicit danger it seemed to pose to whites: the slaves' "poetry is like the Music—Rude and uncultivated. Their dancing is a most violent exercise, but so irregular and grotesque. I am not able to describe it." These "intriguing meetings" undermined plantation work discipline when they rendered the participants unfit or unwilling to return to the fields early the next day, and when they provided further evidence of the fact that it was impossible for owners to retain complete control over their workers at all times. Like one observer in South Carolina in 1772, most whites concluded, then, that whatever their purposes, such "nocturnal rendezvouses . . . are never intended for the advantage of white people."[20]

Of course in certain instances enslaved Africans' cultural traditions and inheritance of specialized knowledge proved useful to whites. For example, North Carolina whites might marvel at Africans' understanding of "the various uses that the wild vegetables may be put to" and the way they made "vegetable pins . . . from the prickly pear, also molds for buttons made from the calabash, which likewise serves to hold their victuals." South Carolina rice planters were the beneficiaries of the slaves' resourcefulness in ridding the fields of bobolinks with special kinds of noisemakers; in weaving baskets; making pottery and pipes from clay, and pails and churns from wood; and fashioning mortars and pestles for polishing rice. However, Africans' knowledge of herbs and their uses could be implemented in any number of ways; the technique of poisoning fish (for example) had as its sinister counterpoint the poisoning of masters and mistresses. In mid-eighteenth-century Virginia, whites accused slaves of the crime of poisoning more often than any other illegal activity with the exception of theft, and punishments for the offense revealed its seriousness. In pre-revolutionary Williamsburg, the slave Eve, accused of poisoning her owner, was "drawn upon a hurdle to the place of execution and there burned at the stake."[21]

Moreover, the facility with which slaves plied their wares in frontier economies assumed a more threatening cast under the newly instituted staple-crop regimes. Increasingly, whites associated slaves who traded with slaves who stole, and with "sly & artful" behavior in general. In 1772, the *South Carolina Gazette* complained that Charleston's Lower Market was dominated by "loose, idle, disorderly negro women," who made it their business to cheat white customers and ingratiate themselves with the "country negroes" who came to town to buy and sell. Thus were traditional West African (and West Indian) marketing activities transformed from routine economic practices into major sources of black "disorder" and white anxiety. One night in 1780, a group of Moravians traveling through the Maryland interior camped near a "Negro Quarter, whose inhabitants speedily visited us wishing to furnish us apples, blades, and milk"; but the visitors refrained from buying on the assumption that the milk "had been thickened with flour, and the blades might have been stolen. . . ."[22]

Whether or not large numbers of Africans and their descendants lived together reflected the economic interests of slaveowners. More specifically, patterns of slave labor deployment shaped slave family and community life. It was not until the mid-eighteenth century, when the preponderance of black men gave way to a more balanced sex ratio, that white landowners began to expound upon the value of slave women as both workers and reproducers. By this time, rough sexual divisions of labor had been imposed upon the slave population, based on the demands of local economies; as a result, the quality of slave family life varied accordingly. In the more settled areas of Virginia, for example, slave hiring took hold as a highly profitable practice, and the consequent separation of parents from their children (the men hired out as skilled workers, the women as domestic servants) under-mined the stability of black households. The organization of large estates into small, remote quarters, each including perhaps only one woman as cook and laundress for the others, meant many slaves might not be able to find mates at all. Robert "King" Carter settled his four hundred workers on forty-eight different quarters, and some were so small that only six people lived there. In the Virginia Piedmont, pioneer planters of the eighteenth century prized black women and children for their skills in the delicate culti-vation of tobacco; by the last two decades of the century, the region's sex ratios were even, and the black population grew quickly. It was in pre-revo-lutionary South Carolina, however, where large plantations of concentrated Africans were the norm, that families stabilized and African traditions sur-vived in their most dramatic form.[23]

Gradually, the entrenchment and expansion of the institution of slavery served to blur the lines between Africans and Creoles, and between slaves and free Negroes. Indeed, southern free blacks had good reason to identify with enslaved peoples, rather than with whites of any class, so rigid were the legal boundaries between "black" and "white," regardless of status. From the 1660s through the Revolution, for example, free blacks lost rights that they had enjoyed in previous decades: no longer could they hire white indentured servants; testify in court cases; vote; or, armed, join local mili-tias. The fact that free black women were finally able to win exemption from the head tax placed on all black people (but not on white women) amounted to a small victory for otherwise beleaguered communities. The tribulations of the Drighouse family on the Eastern Shore of Virginia revealed the ways legal vulnerabilities contributed to the impoverishment and fragmentation of individual families. Their land preyed upon by their

poor white neighbors, their children forcibly bound out as apprentices by
local authorities, and their job options narrowed through competition from
alternative forms of labor—slaves and white tenants and artisans—free
Negroes like the Drighouses saw their kin scattered and the economic basis
of their households destroyed.[24]

Though constituting no more than 1 or 2 percent of the free population
in any colony, free people of color, most of whom were the descendants of
biracial unions, appeared more threatening to the racial caste system than
their numbers would seem to warrant, for their status as quasi-free people
mocked the emerging racial caste system that relied on a series of stark
dichotomies. White elites scorned the logic of pleas for freedom made by
Christian slaves of mixed white-black parentage—"Releese us out of this
Cruell Bondegg and this wee beg for Jesus Christs his Sake"—and yet feared
the potentially violent implications of this logic. By this time it was becoming abundantly clear that an African heritage—not skin color, legal status, or
religious beliefs—would define an emerging "race."[25]

By resisting the total assimilation of black people into their own culture,
and by singling them out for enslavement, white people in effect invented
the black "race"—that is, the idea that blacks were a group irredeemably set
apart. For their part, blacks understandably identified themselves as separate
from all whites in terms of the work they did and the conditions under
which they did it, but they refused to accept the idea of their "racial" distinctiveness. In the southern colonies, African cultural traditions became highly
politicized, serving to link for black people the memories of the land they
were forced to leave behind and the misery they encountered in the new
land. As a result, then, whites remained highly suspicious of any evidence of
African strangeness, of any behavior that was so foreign to them they could
not even begin to describe it.

THE EVOLUTION OF EIGHTEENTH-CENTURY SOUTHERN
LABOR SYSTEMS

In the eighteenth-century South, a rising native-born white elite struggled to
keep the upper hand over a region persistently and dangerously splintered
into a variety of competing social groups in addition to people of African
descent. The demographic and physical imperatives of empire building—
population growth, political stability, and an opportunistic use of laborers—
were persistently thwarted by the ethnic and religious diversity of southern
colonists. White settlements might attain social stability through institutions

like the church and local government, through networks of mutually supportive kin and neighbors, and through patterns of wealth accumulation; but the Anglo South as a whole remained under siege, plagued by enemies from within and without, up until the Revolution. Consequently, landowners and employers grappled with the task of sorting out various groups by ethnicity and legal status, and then assigning those groups certain tasks. The result was not one labor system—although slavery dominated the scene— but rather a multitude of local, interlocking systems characterized by myriad combinations of workers' tasks, tenure, and divergent backgrounds.

Eighteenth-century planters, like their counterparts a century before, alternately welcomed and rejected much-needed workers who were perceived as subversive to the designs of the British Crown. Though increasingly less significant as field workers compared to African slaves, British prisoners of war together with convicts and members of other European ethnic groups continued to represent real and potential enemies to the British, embedded as all groups were within a transatlantic world of conquest and domination. Thus South Carolina, though bounded by menacing groups of Indians and Spaniards and desperate for more white bodies, could not bring itself to embrace the one thousand or so Roman Catholic Acadian refugees who reached its shores in the mid-1750s. Perceived less as worthy pioneers and more as spies in the service of the pope, the Acadians were dispersed throughout the colony; a few years later, identifiable members of the group were sent off to the West Indies.[26]

Within a volatile empire, the resentful Scottish and Irish rebels and refugees shipped to the New World hardly seemed worth the price of transportation, considering the havoc they might wreak upon fragile settlements. Nevertheless, Chesapeake officials reluctantly accepted shiploads of English pickpockets and highwaymen (between 1700 and 1775, forty thousand arrived in that region of the South alone), suggesting that they might serve as shock troops in skirmishes with the Indians; but most were placed as servants and subsequently lived up to their reputation as purveyors of vicious robberies and other villainies directed toward the masters and mistresses with whom they lived. (Until the Revolution, Maryland planters in particular made relatively extensive use of convicts, most of them men obliged to serve for seven years, and available at a price one-third less than that of slaves; these planters were glad to take advantage of cheap, bound labor, regardless of its color.) In fact, the jailbirds from Newgate apparently differed little from ordinary indentured servants, for southern newspapers continued to brim with advertisements for runaway servants who engaged in murder, arson, and theft at home before striking out for greener pastures.[27]

In 1717, South Carolina legislators acknowledged that the white servants in the colony had "proved of bad consequence to their masters, owners, and overseers," and so passed "An Act for the Better Governing and Regulating" of that group. Provisions of the act addressed instances of covert trucking and trading among servants and apprentices; servants striking their masters and mistresses and "unlawfully absenting" themselves from their duties; tavern keepers trafficking in liquor with servants; and women servants bearing the children of black men, slave or free. The legislators noted that at least some of this illicit activity stemmed from "the barbarous usage of servants by cruel masters."[28]

Nevertheless, two developments in particular sustained a demand for white indentured servants during the eighteenth century. First, in the large rice districts of South Carolina they were heralded as much-needed overseers for the numbers of blacks growing at such an alarming rate. And second, the Chesapeake area continued to import more servants than slaves throughout the period because these servants tended to be more skilled in traditional English trades than their seventeenth-century counterparts, and hence valuable within an increasingly diversified economy that relied on a variety of workers and not just field laborers and wood choppers. For example, in the 1770s the Northampton estate of the Ridgely family, located in Baltimore County, Maryland, included eighty-five white servants (from Ireland, Wales, and England), among them assorted numbers of stoneblowers, nailers, bakers, butchers, wagoners, breeches makers, gardeners, sawyers, pipemakers, collar and harness makers, shoemakers, braziers, tinmen, brickmakers. It is unclear whether or not the soldier, papermaker, and keeper of racehorses found opportunities to follow their listed trades once they arrived at the estate.[29]

Juxtaposed to the restlessness of bound white laborers, the means of resistance employed by slaves at first glance seem to offer but variations on a theme. Yet the spectacular population growth among blacks, combined with an increasing sense of group consciousness among Africans and Creoles, made black slaves appear uniquely threatening to white masters. White servants might combine to run away or steal horses, but those forms of collective action were relatively benign compared to the bloody Stono Rebellion in South Carolina in 1739 during which thirty whites and twenty blacks were killed. All of the southern colonies periodically endured panics and scares about rumored slave uprisings. During the half century before the Revolution, the South Carolina low country and the Virginia Piedmont in particular experienced a rapid "Africanization" of their populations. Under such conditions a single act of aggression on the part of a slave might trigger a wave of hysteria within households of whites regardless of status. In the mid-1750s, the readers of the *Virginia Gazette* might well have asked themselves whether they could be certain that the "Negro Fellow belonging to Mr. Tunstall Hacke, of Northumberland County," who struck his master with a "broad Ax" with "an Intent to murder him"; or the "Negroe Fellow" of Kittery, York County, who, in the dead of night took his master's child "about 6 or 7 years old out of its Bed, and threw it into the well, where it perished," had acted alone, or whether these frightening acts signaled the onset of a more general uprising among the black population.[30]

Still, to a certain extent, in the minds of white masters and mistresses, various groups of bound labor continued to represent generalized sources of subversion and danger. By the third decade of the eighteenth century, the Virginia militia stood armed and ready to fight against insurrections instigated by Indians, blacks, or members of both groups. To the south of Georgia and South Carolina, St. Augustine beckoned to a variegated assortment of Indians and servants and slave runaways, all (presumably) armed and ready to launch assaults against their former tormentors, now fighting under the flag of the Spaniards. Triracial maroon colonies, tucked away in remote mountainous and swampy areas, and used as staging areas for raids upon herds of cattle, confirmed whites' suspicions that domestic and foreign enemies, and black, red, and white enemies, were not always readily differentiated. The commingling of African-American and Native American groups in particular caused considerable confusion, as whites cast a wary eye upon communities of "Indian Negroes," like the Gingaskins settlement on the Eastern Shore of Virginia, which was, it was said, "an asylum for free Negroes and other disorderly persons, who build huts thereon and pillage and destroy the timber without restraint. . . . [T]he honest inhabitants . . . have ever considered it a den of thieves and a nuisance to the neighborhood."[31]

Complicating the social landscape at this time was the emergence of a new kind of worker: the white man who was free and married, but landless. In all likelihood a former servant, he sought work as a tenant, hired hand, or overseer for a planter; or, more ominously, he might choose not to work at all (according to the rhythms established by planters), but instead squat on a piece of land and cultivate it, feeding his family with game and fish, and moving on at the first sight of the tax collector or surveyor. His children might be taken from him and bound out as apprentices to a nearby planter, his wife hired out to work in the fields with slaves during the harvest. These families tended to be highly mobile ("white Indians," they were called), their material standard of living similar to that of slaves. As the eighteenth century progressed and this group became an ever larger proportion of the white population (for example, up to one-third of all whites in the Chesapeake were tenants at the time of the Revolution), the poorest and least stable became categorized as men and women apart from civil society. In the mountains of North Carolina, they were stigmatized as "rusticks" who spent their time "sauntering thro' the woods with a gun," or imbibing New England grog, "the most shocking liquor you can imagine." In Virginia, they were denounced as "divers idle and disorderly persons having no visible estates and who are able to work, [but] frequently stroll from one county to another, neglecting to labour and either failing altogether to list themselves as tithables or by their idle and disorderly life render themselves incapable of paying their levies when listed."[32]

Thus the relatively undifferentiated settlements of the seventeenth century, in which the vast majority of people were bound laborers working in the ground, made way for a more complex society. In the process, gender differences, as well as those based on race and land tenure, became more significant. Early eighteenth-century demographic developments—the equalizing of sex ratios between white males and females, and declining mortality rates for them and their children—affected patterns of domestic work in the southern colonies. Depending upon their access to bulky looms and spinning wheels, white women and children, together with slavewomen and children, began to make substantial contributions to the wealth of white households and surrounding neighborhoods. The extent of domestic manufacturing was contingent upon the size and composition of households; thus in Virginia by the end of the eighteenth century, home manufacturing (including the production of textiles, soap, and candles) "is carried on only by white females in poor families, and, in wealthy families, under the Eye of the Mistress, by female slaves drawn out of the Estates for that purpose, aided by the superfluous time of a superabundance of house-servants." In the earliest stages of colonization, planters had had to rely on the importation of experienced male weavers and female spinners from Great Britain; but a couple of generations later, African-born slaves and their children assumed this kind of work. Still, the specialization of tasks depended upon the size of the establishment. For example, by the 1780s Robert Carter set teenaged male slaves to work as weavers, and used teenaged slave girls, and elderly slave women, as spinners and winders.[33]

Rounding out the social organization of labor within southern neighborhoods and plantations were skilled tradesmen. The whites might work as indentured servants, or as tenants or landowners who combined craftwork with farming; or as full-time master craftsmen, self-employed or beholden to merchants or planters for their livelihood. Slaves became an increasingly visible proportion of the skilled population; ads for runaways described clever, English-speaking, literate black men who could forge passes (certifying either that they were free or on an errand for their master) and in some cases find a ready market for their talents as carpenters and blacksmiths. Peter Deadfoot, a fugitive slave in Stafford County, Virginia, was described in 1768 by his bereft owner as "an indifferent shoemaker, a good butcher, ploughman, and carter; an excellent sawyer, and waterman, understands breaking oxen well, and is one of the best sythemen, eeither with or without a cradle, in *America*: in short, he so ingenious a fellow, that he can turn his hand to any thing. . . ," and as a result, not surprisingly, Deadfoot "has a great share of pride. . . ." A few skilled workers were free blacks, though members of this latter group could rarely accumulate the capital required to purchase equipment necessary for high-status trades. Evidence from Maryland suggests that it was in those trades that fathers (most of them white) were likely to pass their skills and their businesses on to their sons.[34]

Only the largest plantations could aspire to true self-sufficiency, and thus in most areas the fortunes of white and black tradesmen ebbed and flowed in relation to each other. For example, the number of white craftsmen in the rural Chesapeake declined in the course of the eighteenth century, as these men found themselves squeezed by an insufficient local demand for the food-processing and luxury trades; by competition from goods imported by Baltimore merchants; and by the small but steady increase in planters who could afford to devote at least one or two of their slaves to nonfield work (mostly as carpenters, sawyers, or blacksmiths), and hire those men out to neighbors as well. For these reasons, most whites had an incentive to ply their crafts as an adjunct to farming. Skilled workers and tradesmen who lived in or near large towns might find more stable employment if they could attach themselves on a regular basis to merchants and planters in need of specialized services. Yet regional variations remained; while the production of wheat in the Upper South spurred diversified trade and hence an increase in the number and variety of skilled white craftsmen, the Lower South had less need of (and indeed failed to attract) such workers, because of its reliance on slaves for all kinds of labor. Though indentured servants might claim to shun Charleston because of their reluctance to live among "very wild and roguish blacks," in fact the large number of slave "Handycraft Tradesmen" in that city placed constraints on the growth of a class of skilled white men.[35]

One hundred and seventy years after the founding of Jamestown, the Virginia Tidewater had fostered interlocking systems of black and white labor

controlled by the great planters who were also the founding fathers of the
new nation. As the oldest settled area of the British North American mainland, Virginia had developed a number of different socioeconomic groups,
with the labor of slaves supporting a self-consciously gracious way of life
among planter-aristocrats, and free blacks and poor whites of varying statuses trying to make a living for themselves, somehow, in between.[36]

Soon after meeting with one of those planters (General George Washington) during his trip to the United States in 1788, the French visitor J. P. Brissot de Warville commented rather scornfully, "Virginians live in a kind of
tawdry luxury." Regardless of their pretenses, great landlords of the Tidewater could hardly live up to Parisian standards of material comfort and social
decorum: noted de Warville, "Virginians do not use napkins, but they wear
silk cravats, and instead of carrying white handkerchiefs they blow their
noses with their fingers [" . . . I have seen the best bred Americans do this
. . ."] or with a silk handkerchief, which also serves as a cravat, napkin, etc."
Washington might or might not have agreed with his guest about the etiquette of nose-blowing, but the planter-patriot did aspire to live a life of
"republican simplicity" made more comfortable with a wealth of European
luxury goods. Even as a young man, he had implored a London merchant to
send him the best-quality wares; "and you may believe me when I tell you
that instead of getting things good and fashionable in their several kinds we
often have articles sent us that could have been used by our Forefathers in
days of yore."[37]

Washington's huge plantation, Mount Vernon, maintained direct links
with London financiers and tobacco merchants, but its day-to-day operations depended on a variety of workers, white and black, free and slave,
male and female, young and old, within a local labor system. For example,
during the decade or so before the Revolution, Washington owned more
than one hundred slaves, scattered on several quarters and organized on the
basis of their gender, age, and skills, responsible for cultivating wheat, corn,
oats, and rye; milling grains; and producing cloth. During the slack seasons,
Washington hired his slaves out to friends and neighbors nearby; for the services of his blacksmith he received in return at various times butter, eggs,
and chickens. Wealthier customers paid in port wine, cash, and cattle.[38]

Yet the general also secured the employment and services of whites in a
variety of capacities. In order to increase his cash flow and provide for the
clearing of his vast landholdings, he leased property to tenants in Frederick,
Berkeley, Fauquier, and Loudoun counties. At Mount Vernon, he personally
supervised the labor of white overseers and a seemingly endless parade of
white craftsmen—plasterers, chimneymakers, bricklayers, millwrights, and

construction workers of various descriptions. A white master carpenter resided on the estate in a rent-free house. At harvest in the summertime, Mount Vernon's grain fields appeared to be relatively integrated worksites; several kinds of wheat ripened at the same time, rendering it impossible to make do with slaves only, and so male slave wheat cradlers worked alongside local white men who had been hired to perform the same work. Of the white hands engaged in general field labor on a daily basis, Washington found that they "workd but indifferently," though his only recourse was to refuse to hire them the next season; wages were "exorbitantly high," and he hoped someday that "hirelings of all kinds may be dispensed with." In May 1770 Washington decided to give up on his hired white ditchers altogether, because they worked carelessly, or not at all; he replaced them with his slaves.[39]

Nevertheless, these complementary workforces were continually disrupted by slaves who ran away. Like Tom ("both a rogue and a runaway," sold to the West Indies in 1766), George Washington's slaves as a group refuted their master's contention that plantation society functioned like a healthy organic whole. As a private citizen, Washington was forced to rely on the vigilance of his neighbors and local government officials for the retrieval of his fugitives. But later, after the Revolution, as the commander-in-chief of the Continental army, he was forced to bargain with British officials over the return of thousands of blacks (including some of his own) who had either absconded with, or were taken off by, departing Tories in the course of the war. Thus did the southern elite confront a war at home, within their own homes, a war that showed no signs of subsiding after the last gun was stilled at the Battle of Yorktown.[40]

THE CONTAGION OF "INGRATITUDE": SLAVES IN THE REVOLUTIONARY SOUTH

If the glory of the American Revolution was the unity of purpose that bound thirteen colonies together in battle, then the terror of the slaves' counterrevolution lay in the apparent singlemindedness with which black men and women resisted forced labor on plantations all over the South. As a result, the founding fathers cast themselves in the same role as their British rulers, protesting that their own subjects (the slaves) had turned vicious in response to the benevolence bestowed upon them. In the ensuing conflict between master and slave, forests, fields, and kitchens became transformed into domestic battlefields. For black men and women, labor for whites was the emblem of their bondage, even as labor on their own behalf was the basis of free families and communities after the war.

In June 1776, about the same time that Landon Carter's slaves were making a break for freedom, white pioneers in the Mississippi Delta north of New Orleans got wind of a conspiracy among their own slaves. Most were engaged in cultivating corn, rice, indigo, and peas; in clearing new lands and felling trees; and in producing barrel staves out of red and white oak. One of the planters, William Dunbar, a Scottish immigrant, kept a record of his estate's daily routine, and his account is dotted with references to women sawing logs to make a boardwalk through the forest, workers pressed to produce a record number of staves each day, and men cutting their feet and nearly severing their fingers as a result of accidents with axes. Dunbar and his neighbors had planned a competition to determine whose slaves could make the most staves in the shortest amount of time, a neighborhood get-together that was canceled when rumors of the conspiracy surfaced. Dunbar was disappointed—he had planned to win the competition by "regulating the work among my People in such a manner that I had not the slightest doubt/from former experiments/of making at least four thousand staves. . . ." Like Landon Carter, he could not comprehend the rage that motivated slaves "kept under due subordination & obliged to do their duty in respect to plantation work"; two of the three alleged plotters had never even suffered a whipping: "Of what avail is kindness & good usage when rewarded by such ingratitude [?]" he asked rhetorically. Dunbar considered the whole matter so distressing, "occasion[ing] such fatigues of [his own] body & mind," he suspended stavemaking in order to recover his bearings. Nevertheless, the suicide of one of the slaves, and the hanging of two others, failed to deter two women, Ketty and Bessy, from running away two weeks later. Bessy was captured, brought home, and put "in Irons"; and Ketty came home on her own, "finding it uncomfortable lodging in the woods."[41]

As slave plots and rumors of plots surfaced throughout the South during the two years leading up to war, planters and military leaders contemplated the various uses to which blacks and their labor might be put in service of their respective causes. On plantations, the slaves were subjected to speedups as their owners attempted to increase the production of both food and textiles in response to the exigencies of war. Ever vigilant to opportunities to escape or otherwise avoid new and brutal work regimens, some slaves gradually withdrew their labor from their owners, scorning the importations of overseers and mistresses alike; the "impudent" Sarah on one estate in North Carolina in 1781 deigned to "come and Iron a few clothes" only after she "was repeatedly ordered to do so. . . ." Sarah's mistress faced the same dilemma as the Baltimore slaveholder who counseled his overseer to indulge the slave Ruth, or "she will run off, for she is an arch bitch." Deprived of overseers who had gone off to fight, their estates gradually or suddenly depleted of food, work implements, and livestock, most planters nevertheless knew that brutality toward resentful slaves would probably be counterproductive in any case.[42]

In the colonists' eyes, King George III committed the unpardonable crime of instigating "domestic insurrections" within the colonies; but in fact the monarch merely tried to manipulate an ever present rebelliousness among enslaved men and women. The planters who for decades had contended with slave runaways and individual acts of resistance now confronted the specter of massive retaliation on the part of the "enemies in their bowells"—slaves, indentured servants, Indians, or some combination thereof.[43]

In November 1775, Virginia's governor Lord Dunmore encouraged a wholesale exodus of slaves from their Patriot owners with his promise of freedom for all who would take up arms and fight for His Majesty. Yet, as British military policy, the proclamation amounted more to little more than a cynical ploy, a matter of military necessity rather than any putative anti-slavery principle. In fact, the British used black volunteers primarily in non-combatant roles—as foragers for the advancing armies, as guides, and as diggers of trenches and builders of fortifications. (Patriots scoffed at the idea of black freedom fighters, suggesting that "lord Dunmore's *Royal Regiment of Black Fusileers*" were recruited to do "the drudgery of the day . . . acting as scullions, &c. on board the fleet.") In British-occupied Charleston, for example, 134 fugitives and slaves impressed from their Tory owners were put to work clearing the Cooper River of sunken boats. Still, all over the South, the British offensive triggered massive slave runaways (perhaps a quarter of all South Carolina slaves deserted their masters during the war), most of whom absconded in families. The fugitives then had to scavenge to keep themselves alive—appropriating boats and guns wherever they could find them, stealing food from farms regardless of the political allegiance of their owners. Yet for the most part the black men and women who sought refuge and the promise of a new life behind British lines found during the war only hunger, disease, and the degradation of forced labor at the end of a bayonet. During the American seige of Yorktown, in 1781, British troops expelled from their lines all of the black volunteer soldiers who had contributed to the Crown's cause, most of them by now famished and exhausted. Remarked one Redcoat officer, "We had used them to good advantage, and set them free, and now, with fear and trembling, they had to face the reward of their cruel masters."[44]

Early in the war, George Washington drew upon his own experiences as a slaveholder to suggest that the Continental Congress use black men as teamsters and other laborers in the army; but the issue here was legal status as much as skin color. He noted: "They ought however to be freemen, for slaves could not be sufficiently depended on. It is to be apprehended that they would too frequently desert to the enemy to obtain their liberty. . . ." As for the use of blacks as soldiers, Washington felt compelled to follow the lead of the Redcoats, assuming that the slaves would no doubt make invidious comparisons between the British eager to arm slaves and the Patriots reluctant to do so. About five thousand blacks eventually fought on the side of the colonists during the war, on land and on sea, most of them from New England and most in the Continental army (which mandated three years' service, or the duration of the conflict), in contrast to the local militias. Georgia and the Carolinas accepted no slaves, and only a few free blacks, into their ranks of fightingmen. Joseph Ranger, a free man of color from Elizabeth City County, Virginia, who served in the Navy of Virginia, received cash wages for his service, a grant of land after the war, and later in life a pension from the U.S. government. In contrast, David Baker, a slave on the Isle of Wight, joined the American navy as a substitute for his master Lawrence Baker, who then re-enslaved him after the war.[45]

Of the perhaps as many as one hundred thousand slave fugitives during the war, fifteen thousand left aboard British ships for Nova Scotia, and many more fled rural areas for southern towns, in search of safety and paid labor. In Upper South cities, in particular, added to the large numbers of slave runaways were blacks freed by masters imbued with Quaker or evangelical (Methodist or Baptist) religious principles of equality, and troubled by the narrow—i.e., racially exclusive—application of the Whigs' "natural rights" theory. The liberal Virginia manumission law of 1782 inspired owners (George Washington among them) to liberate at least ten thousand slaves within the first decade of its existence, and many freedpeople migrated to nearby towns, a few finding employment as preachers and shopkeepers— work qualitatively different from the kind they had performed as slaves. Between 1790 and 1810, Baltimore witnessed a dramatic increase in its free black population (from 323 to 5,671 persons) and Alexandria saw a comparable rate of growth (from 52 to 836 free Negroes).[46]

To sustain these small communities, free Negroes found that traditional kinds of labor had been imbued with new significance. Many of the black women who continued to toil over washboards and in hot kitchens, and the men who sought wages as day laborers and carpenters, now worked in the hope of using their meager pay to release loved ones from bondage, and in the hope of sustaining benevolent societies that nourished the well-being of their neighbors and kinfolk. For example, by dint of hard labor, between 1792 and 1805, Graham Bell of Petersburg purchased and then freed nine slaves, a collection of his relatives and other blacks. Yet relatively substantial free Negro populations—the small tenant class of rural Maryland and the artisans of Richmond, for example—remained an Upper-South phenomenon. In 1810, 10 percent of southern blacks were free in the area to the north of South Carolina (a threefold increase since 1790), but less than 4 percent in the Lower South (Georgia, Mississippi, Louisiana, and South Carolina).[47]

The American War for Independence transformed the scope and meanings of the tasks performed by African Americans in the South without altering the region's social division of labor in any significant way. The crosscurrents of the Revolution flowed in one direction, toward freedom for thousands of runaways and for thousands more freed by masters inspired by egalitarian ideology; but simultaneously in another direction, toward a harsher, more stridently "racialized" slavery for the vast majority of slaves exploited within geographically expanding commercial and agricultural economies. (After the Revolution, William Dunbar moved to Natchez, Mississippi, to continue his experiments in scientific plantation management—now with cotton—and become a correspondent of Thomas Jefferson.) Although an emerging class of free Negroes embraced the new task of institution building within their own communities, most black people continued to toil as slaves on plantations, and to struggle to carve out time for their own work over and above the demands imposed upon them by their masters and mistresses.

Changes and continuities in the labor of black women foreshadowed the devastation wrought upon the well-being of slaves in the nation the Whigs made. The Constitution of 1787 provided for the closing of the foreign slave trade by 1808, spurring planters to intensify their reliance on slave women as reproducers of the labor force as well as producers of staple crops. Noted one British traveler in the early 1780s, "The female slaves fare, labour, and repose, just in the same manner [as the men]; even when they breed, which is generally every two or three years, they seldom lose more than a week's work thereby, either in the delivery or suckling the child." The widespread practice of giving young slave women to the betrothed daughters of the planter elite further fragmented enslaved families in the interests of the physical comfort of young white households.[48]

As slaves and free women, black women performed menial labor for whites within the relatively narrow realm of agriculture, burning stubble and heaping dung and thrashing oats in the Chesapeake, and domestic service, working as cooks and laundresses in southern cities. The particularly harsh field-work regimes associated with Virginia Piedmont tobacco, low-country rice, and southwestern cotton lowered black women's fertility rates, increased their incidence of miscarriage, and contributed to high rates of infant mortality. These tasks contrasted mightily with the niche prepared for elite women, under the banner of Republican motherhood. (Of the socially useful roles of poor white southern women, the founding fathers said virtually nothing at all.) Wealthy women were charged with rearing virtuous citizens for the new nation. But when black women (slave or free) were not attending to the intimate and immediate needs of whites, or loading their barns with rice and tobacco, they were supposed to be rearing the children who would soon take their "self-evident" places as members of a subordinate labor force.[49]

Regardless of the relative financial well-being they enjoyed, the revolutionary generation of planters paid a steep price for the institution of slavery. Not only did masters and mistresses have to contend with black workers who carried on in the time-honored tradition of indentured servants and refused to accept passively the grueling work assignments meted out to them; whites also had to contend with a group of workers who understood that the revolutionary rhetoric of resistance to tyranny applied to them, too. In this way the slaves posed a fundamental political challenge to the foundations of the new nation, a challenge underscored with bloodshed, or at least the perpetual threat of it.

The life of Olaudah Equiano illustrates the ironies of American slavery in the age of the American Revolution. An Ibo captured from the area that is now eastern Nigeria, Equiano (who became known as Gustavus Vassa) mourned his whole lifetime for the sister who was kidnapped along with him in 1756, when he was eleven years old. He hoped someday to find her during his extensive travels throughout the Atlantic world, but he never saw her again: "Though you were early forced from my arms, your image has been always riveted in my heart, from which neither *time nor fortune* have been able to remove it." As an enslaved seaman, he became "almost an Englishman"; he spoke, read, and wrote the language; made an effort to "imbibe . . . [the English] spirit and imitate their manners"; and accepted baptism as a Christian. In 1766, at the age of twenty-one, he gained his freedom, and yet he soon found that in Georgia, at least, his "Englishness" afforded him little protection from the worst abuses of slavery—random beatings and the threat of kidnapping. Of Savannah in 1766 he wrote, "I knew there was little or no law for a free negro here." Later, he became active in the transatlantic abolitionist movement, noting at one point, "I hope to have the satisfaction of seeing the renovation of liberty and justice resting on the British government, to vindicate the honour of our common nature." Deprived of honor because of their skin color as well as their legal status, Africans like Olaudah Equiano and their descendants would both appropriate the ideals of the Revolution and struggle against the constricted world the Revolution had wrought.[50]

BY ELIMINATING THE French and British presence in the transmontane regions of the eastern United States, the Revolution opened the way for the final assault on the Indians remaining east of the Mississippi, and then cleared the path for massive migrations of American citizens westward and southwestward. The forced migration of blacks to the Lower South in the early nineteenth century broke up as many as 20 percent of all slave families in the Upper South; three-quarters of those "sold down the river" left Virginia without their kin. Many white settlers took their slaves with them (75,000 to Kentucky and Tennessee alone), or imported large numbers from Africa (63,000 into South Carolina between 1800 and 1808) or from the Upper South. The invention of the cotton gin in 1791 served as the catalyst for the spread of cotton culture into the southern backcountry and the Old Southwest.[51]

Patterns of settlement in these lands recapitulated the social structure characteristic of the eastern seaboard. White men with commercial interests (agricultural or otherwise) relied heavily on slave labor because free labor was unavailable in sufficient quantities. By the late eighteenth century, Kentucky slaves numbered forty thousand—more than 18 percent of the state's total population. The plantation frontier perpetuated traditional forms of subservience, and at the same time subjected African-American laborers to new forms of danger and isolation. In 1793, near Newport, Kentucky, the slaves Moses and Humphrey informed their master James Taylor that the arduousness of their tasks—clearing the land and planting corn—was exacerbated by the lack of a black community in the vicinity. Declared Moses, "there are no colored people here, we have no women to wash for us, on Sundays we stalk about without being able to talk to any one."[52]

Where white planters saw unlimited land and opportunity in the new territories to the west, their slaves saw backbreaking toil unrelieved by companionship or family ties. Yet at the same time, on the eastern seaboard, Africans and Creoles, free Negroes and slaves together forged an African-American culture built upon extensive kinship networks and shared grievances. The war confirmed and accelerated impulses toward acquisitive individualism among whites, but it also confirmed and accelerated impulses toward a collective consciousness among African Americans. As slave families formed extended kin networks in locales all over the South, planters faced a new kind of foe with a black face—not the "outlandish," dangerous Africans who took off at the first opportunity, but rather devoted family members, determined to provide for their kin, and in the process costing their owners much in the way of time and stolen property.

The era of Revolution and nation building highlighted the South's distinctiveness: a substantial amount of the region's capital was tied up in its principal labor source, chattel slavery. Yet the era also highlighted the South's political bonds with the North. Though blacks were, and would remain, a much more substantial portion of the population in the South, both sections shared a vested interest in maintaining civil order throughout the colonial period, and beyond. In the North, too, English ethnocentricism gradually emerged as American nationalism; but not before bound red, white, and black workers had demonstrated their potential to wreak havoc within individual households, to the mortification of English settlers who valued social harmony and political consensus as much as they valued a compliant labor force.

CHAPTER FOUR

"DOMESTICK ENEMIES": BOUND LABORERS IN NEW ENGLAND AND THE MIDDLE COLONIES, 1620–1776

I n the 1630s, the English fishing outpost on Richmond Island, Maine, had much in common with English tobacco plantations in the Chesapeake region far to the south. Sponsored by London merchants, the Richmond Island enterprise was a virtually all-male affair. In the absence of wives and daughters, the merchants' agent, John Winter, hired a man "to brew our beare and to bake our bread. . . ." The fishermen, contract workers from England, broke up the monotony by bouts of drinking "sacke and aquavite." John Winter hinted darkly of the discipline problems that would continue to plague the business, when, in July 1634, he noted that recruits should be warned about the strenuous nature of winter fishing, "otherwise when they Com heare they will forgett their promyse and slacke their business." He added, "This is no contry for loyterers. . . ."[1]

Richmond Island fishermen were not indentured servants: they agreed to serve for a year or two for a stipulated wage, and they worked at a variety of tasks in addition to fishing. For example, during the warmer months they made clapboards and pipe staves, and during the summer they were expected to grow Indian corn in the rocky soil of Maine. Yet like tobacco workers in Virginia, they had a nasty habit of running—or more usually, stealing a boat and sailing—away. Admitted Winter, "I haue a bad Company to deall with all, beinge heare in a lawles Contry. I have a hard taske to vder go, beinge I hardly know my friend from foe." The root of the problem seemed to be that the workers quickly abandoned the contractual obligations stipulated in their "covenants" in favor of the idea that "they Cann do them selues more benyfitt to be [masters] of them selues for fishinge or any thinge els which is heare to be donn in the Country, & for selling their fish at a greater prize." Those who remained on the island proved to be even more troublesome than those who ran away. The carpenter was "a stubborne lasy fellow," and by August 1637 the brewer had been sent back home; he was "very vnwilling to do vs any servize," and besides, Winter feared that he would "poyson sum of [the] men" if he stayed. Unlike tobacco workers, Richmond Island fishermen were in close proximity to settlements where they could make much higher wages than their employer was willing to offer. Winter noted that artisans and farmers alike received "great wages heare in this Country," even if they were not inclined to do much work. His own men demanded that he double their pay, or they would leave. Winter concluded that, if matters continued, "the servants wilbe [sic] masters & the masters servants."[2]

The early history of Richmond Island suggests that the direct relationship between family life and the social stability of a community transcended regional differences. Confronted with the prospect of more bitter winters of fishing, and far from wives and other family members, contract workers on the island were inclined to leave at the first opportunity. Nevertheless, these Englishmen had distinct advantages over their laboring counterparts to the south; they were working for wages, for less time, and they were conscious of the opportunities that awaited them—no questions asked—in the fledgling seaport communities along the northeastern coast. Thus relatively small grievances— the sour beer and the moldy bread, the sound of howling wolves by night and the stench of fish by day—provided more than enough reason to leave.[3]

The Richmond Island fishermen were not "free"; technically, they were bound by contractural obligations to their employer for a stipulated number of years. Nevertheless, the relative openness of early New England society provided these men with the incentive and the wherewithal to strike out on their own, and that openness also spawned various forms of tenure status tailored to meet the needs of specific local economies. In contrast to the slave-servant-planter schema of the seventeenth-century South, patterns of northern labor relations included not only slaves and indentured servants but also redemptioners, contract laborers, agricultural tenants and share-croppers, wage workers and laborers hired by the task, neighbors who "swapped" work, apprentices, and wives and children. The poor, and criminals of all stripes—felons convicted in the colonies or transported from England, and prisoners of various wars of empire—also supplied labor within specific, limited contexts, and under specific constraints.

Clustered in seaport towns, farming villages, and frontier outposts, northern colonists built for themselves a highly militarized society, one that depended on the mobilization of young men as soldiers; on aggressive population growth achieved through immigration and large farm families; and on the deployment of ever scarce labor within the sectors of commerce, industry, and agriculture. Given the Puritans' premium on socioreligious homogenity, and the pervasive threat from the French and Indians to the north and west, white Englishmen would seem to have offered the most efficient source of labor. Young men and their fathers could simultaneously serve as pillars of religious communities, defend those communities from outside attacks, produce food and goods for the marketplace, and propagate future workers. Yet it was apparent from the beginning of settlement that, despite a balanced sex ratio and rapid rates of natural increase, English whites were not plentiful enough to fulfill all of these functions at once.

Northerners in both the New England and Middle Colonies eschewed dependence on a single staple crop, and created interdependent local economies; and the enterprises of commercial farming, extractive industry, and regional and international trade contributed to a dynamic form of economic growth.[4] Nevertheless, northern and southern elites agreed on certain key principles related to labor deployment. Historians have focused on the much-vaunted northern work ethic, but in fact most propertied whites at the time, regardless of region or religion, realized that even "men that are of weak constitutions" made suitable colonists as long as they had money and as long as "their estates can . . . maintain servants."[5]

Throughout the colonial period, northern slavery represented not a unique labor system based on a distinctive "racial" ideology, but rather one labor system among many, and one characterized by myriad trade-offs depending upon which groups were enslaved—Indians or blacks, men or women, field hands or skilled artisans, children or the elderly. The earliest white settlers, including the Puritans of Massachusetts and the Quakers of Pennsylvania, used an explicit economic-cost, social-benefit analysis (specifically, financial and security considerations) when contemplating the use of black slaves in relation to other forms of bound labor. In 1638, in the aftermath of the Pequot War, New Englanders enslaved captive Indian women and children, sold captive Indian men to the West Indies, and brought black slaves back to Massachusetts on the return voyage. Thus they fervently (if mistakenly) hoped to rid themselves of their enemies and gain presumably compliant hands in their place. On this early balance sheet, then, African slaves seemed to have much to recommend them: they were supposedly cheaper than white servants and safer than Indians. In the course of the eighteenth century, however, northern whites increasingly perceived slaves to be too dangerous and the system of slavery too inflexible for the needs of a vibrant, growing economy.

In the South, the ideology of white superiority flowed from the grueling, dangerous, and forced pace of the labor performed by blacks; in the North, that ideology flowed primarily from black people's persistent "strangeness" within a society based upon corporate values. These values were expressed through nuclear families and through religious and village life. Early on, northern landowners came to rely upon the members of their own families for labor, and when they did hire servants, the lack of staple-crop agriculture throughout the region favored a more diverse workforce than in the South, where large numbers of people were required to perform the same function at the same time and place. Like southern planters, northern colonists initially failed to distinguish among Indian hirelings, English indentured servants, and African slaves in their desire to exploit labor and in their fear of internal subversion. Still, northern whites believed that slaves were too different (in terms of their skin color and African heritage) to be easily incorporated into the dominant society, and too few in number to enrich their masters sufficiently in order to make the risk of incorporation—economic no less than social—worthwhile.

AN "ORDENARY TIME OF DAINGER"[6]:
WORKING AND SOLDIERING

By virtue of its elevated location, John Winthrop's "City Upon a Hill" served as a beacon to Christians all over the world, and also doubled as a fortress, an armed camp, for the people who lived in it and remained under siege throughout the colonial period. Like the colonists to the South, northerners soon discovered that military conflict defined citizenship and shaped patterns of work—who would work where and under what conditions. And security demands understandably produced ambivalent views toward the real and potential contributions of Indians, blacks, and young servants as workers. However, unlike southern white men, northern white men faced an ongoing struggle with French and Indian forces that lasted well into the eighteenth century, and in that respect military service emerged as the single most important kind of "work" that bound white men of property together with each other, and with their sons. Widespread gun ownership among white landowners cemented the bond; of this group (with the exception of the pacifist Quakers), it could truly be said, "there is no man there that bears a head but that bears military arms."[7]

For the early New England colonists, planting a settlement, fighting Indians, and praising God were all of a piece, all of the same "worthy" and "intricate" "worke." Writing in 1653, Captain Edward Johnson of Woburn, Massachusetts, exhorted his compatriots to pursue a religiosity forged in blood, "to behave themselves in War-like Discipline," and to "incourage every Souldier-like Spirit among you." He pleaded, "spare not to lay out your coyne for Powder, Bullets, Match, Armes of all sorts, and all kinde of Instruments for War," suggesting the massive infusion of money needed to sustain violent conflicts. One-fifth of all Massachusetts's original settlers had formerly served as soldiers in England; and in the New World, temporary military service made up a normal part of the life cycle for white men. Consequently, the early colonists apparently made a remarkably swift transition from toiling as peaceful English farmers, clergymen, artisans, and merchants to serving as "the severall Regiments of these Souldiers of Christ."[8]

The colonists' hunger for land provoked bloody battles on several fronts. From the 1620s until (and during) the Revolution, virtually all settlers from Fort Christina on the Delaware to the upper reaches of what is now Maine found themselves in a state of war at some point. The settlements positioned on or near a three hundred–mile-long frontier that followed an arc from Albany to York (Maine) remained particularly susceptible to attack throughout the period. In the 1630s and 1640, the beleaguered New Swedish colonists (in what is now Delaware) fended off raiding parties composed of Dutch, English, and Indian men, and various combinations of all three groups. New England fought the Pequot War in 1637 and King Philip's War in 1675 (when fully one-half of all Massachusetts towns were the targets of Indian raids) and King William's War from 1689 to 1697. Maine bore the brunt of skirmishes with Dutch warships as late as the 1660s, and labored to repel the French and Indians until the second third of the eighteenth century. During Queen Anne's War (1702–13), colonists in the Provincial army were sent on expeditions to Canada against the French. The period 1739 to 1763 saw battles at home and abroad—an English-sponsored incursion to Cuba, King George's War (against Canada), French and Indian attacks on the Pennsylvania backcountry, and an all-out war between the English and an Indian-French alliance (1754–63), a war that required colonywide mobilization. During this last conflict, which ended the French presence in North America, fully one-third of Massachusetts men served as soldiers at one time or another, and much of the colony's population contributed to the war indirectly, by producing or distributing supplies to the army.[9]

These colonial wars were punctuated by intracolonial conflicts in regions most vulnerable to enemy attacks. Throughout the mid- and late eighteenth century, backcountry farmers, fearful for their lives and their futures, rose in violent protest against landowning elites. Yeomen in New Jersey (in the 1740s and 1750s), tenants in New York's Hudson River Valley (beginning in the 1750s), and squatters in Maine, Vermont, and western Pennsylvania (from the 1760s until after the Revolution) gave expression to a militant "defensive localism"—collective anxiety over impending poverty and land-lessness brought on by wartime taxes, devastating Indian raids, and chronic indebtedness.[10]

Population growth produced military conflict throughout the northern colonies. New England mushroomed out of a single settlement of a handful of souls clinging to the Atlantic coastline in 1620 to more than 580,000 people scattered throughout Massachusetts, Connecticut, Vermont, New Hampshire, and Rhode Island by the time of the Revolution. The Middle Colonies grew from the 400 people clustered in New Amsterdam in 1630 to about 556,000 in 1770 (in Delaware, New Jersey, New York, and Pennsylvania). As the seaboard region became more crowded and older sons had considerably fewer acres to till compared to their fathers, new towns sprang up all along the northern and western frontier of New England; for example, between 1660 and 1710, 209 settlements were founded, and during the fifteen-year period following 1760, 264 new towns were formed, an average of 16 a year. Sporadic "Blooddy & Expensive" warfare with the Indians threatened all of those living in "open and wide Country" until well into the eighteenth century; moreover, even whites in relatively safe areas remained conscious of persistent Indian threats. In 1750, Indians were still "annoying and disturbing the Frontier towns [throughout New England] . . . and the Inhabitants put in Great Fear and Terror." Around this same time outposts in the colony of New York were forced to remain ever vigilant, "to watch the Motions of their Neighbours the *French*, and the frenchified *Indians*."[11]

In contrast to Pennsylvania's more dispersed settlements (the result of relatively peaceful relations between settlers and Indians, at least until the early 1760s), New England towns fortified themselves as military garrisons, the first line of defense against Indians and French and Dutch intruders. The ever present threat of Indian raids had immediate and far-reaching effects on patterns of work in these outposts. In 1764, the beleaguered inhabitants of Pownalborough, Maine, were busy building shelters for their families "in this uncultivated frontier country," and found themselves unable to meet their fiscal obligations to the colony of Massachusetts; they pleaded that they be exempted from taxation "till our Ground Shall be Subdued that we shall be able to Maintain our Selves & Families from it by our Labour." To "subdue the ground," many small towns first had to subdue the surrounding Native populations. Bands of Indians killed and maimed the cattle and pigs that wandered into their corn fields. Huddled in garrisons, farmers and their families refrained from venturing outside to till their lands or harvest their crops. A New England town might employ a "Small pty of men whereby our people may be inabled to prserve their feilds & Cattle & the sd Souldiers ready upon any assault here or elsewhere. . . ." In some places, Indians, those "Sundery Skulking rogues," emerged from the forest to attack English men, women, and children engaged in raking hay, fetching water, catching fish, or retrieving livestock. The Maine naval stores industry suffered during periods of Indian unrest, when work in the woods was hazardous: "the Tarr burners are forc't to straggle in ye Woods, & are often in Danger of the Enemy where they work, as well as that they are necessarily taken off from their Labour into the Service of the War, to guard the Frontiers. . . ."[12]

The tensions produced by frontier life spilled over into internecine warfare. Thus at times it is difficult to distinguish settlers' fear of Indians from their resentment toward their social betters—men who in their roles as creditors, land speculators, colonial legislators, employers, and landlords represented a threat to a householder hanging on to a small piece of land whether he owned it or not. In western Massachusetts in the town of Springfield, inhabitants armed themselves to repel the Natives who prevented them from working: "we Cannot with safety follow out ourselves in the Fields." Then, just a few years later, the same militiamen, many of them tenants, banded together and turned their wrath against John Pynchon, the town's patron and great landlord; they demanded to be free of his interference in choosing their own officers. In other colonies, backwoods antiauthoritarianism took the form of bloody and protracted warfare. For example, civil disorder in Maine lasted from 1760 through the Early National period, as "liberty men" battled the "great proprietors" of landed wealth. Thus the militiamen who protected the community from outside attacks might also instigate a form of class warfare directed against the Crown, and the most prosperous beneficiaries of its land-granting, and land-grabbing, policies.[13]

Throughout the northern colonies, soldiering away from home assumed the form of productive labor that might occupy young men who otherwise would have remained dependent upon their fathers until they could inherit land of their own. In small towns, sons might leap at the chance to join the Provincial army for a summer expedition to the North, an expedition that might earn them cash wages, or even some plunder or an Indian slave. In New York in 1760, the Provincial army recruited among the city's laboring classes by offering pay that was roughly equivalent to the amount ordinary workingmen could make at their regular jobs. In some cases, men with special skills were able to put those skills to use in the army, as when a soldier-millwright from Massachusetts earned wages over and above his regular pay by constructing a sawmill near the battlefront. And finally, army life entailed discipline and a variety of tasks, like driving wagons and felling trees—in other words, work experience that might prove useful to a young man later in his life.[14]

The relationship between colonial governments and the men who composed their armies had revolutionary repercussions. Volunteers understood that they were entering into an implicit contract with their "employer," the province, a notion that would pave the way for a political theory based on the mutual rights and responsibilities of political leaders and their constituents. On the other hand, impressment into the service could be deemed onerous—like fealty to a distant monarch, or involuntary servitude. As a form of wage earning, military service had to compete with alternative opportunities, and good times on the home front spelled disaster for the recruitment of volunteers. Governor Hamilton of East Jersey wrote to his counterpart in New York in 1696 to complain of his difficulties in procuring men who would agree "that in case of an invasion they should march to the fronteers and be at liberty to return when the acc'on was over or the enemy retreated. . . ." Noted Hamilton, "they live so plentifully at home and have so great wages besides severall of our youth gone to the Southern Colonies to be free from detachments, and several as I am told gone aboard Captain Kidd [the pirate], that there is not a possibility to prevail them to continue in garrison, and indeed very difficult to effect any thing." For some men, then, resisting military service proved to be their first experience resisting the demands of the state, or the demands of a potential employer.[15]

Ill-clad, famished, and diseased, many soldiers made less than reliable "workers." Regardless of how they came to find themselves in the army, some rebelled against the barbaric physical conditions and against all forms of military discipline. In 1689, the troops advancing from the south toward Indian settlements near Casco, Maine, were "Sick & some lame . . . in much want of Cloathing & Tobacco," and without fresh food. If they survived, these men could look forward to sharing memories of such hardship with their compatriots in the future; but few men at the time were in any shape to romanticize battles in the forest, or the arduous preparations necessary to fight them. Instead, ungovernable volunteers and impressed men alike deserted, pillaged from the civilians on the neighboring countryside, impregnated local young women, and generally exhibited "dangerous & mutenous Carages."[16]

The northern colonies defined themselves according to the number of inhabitants who qualified for military service; the rule of thumb was "Five to one for Old Men Women and Children Against the Mustered Souldiers." Predictably, then, mobilization policies directly affected the dynamics of labor supply and demand characteristic of any particular time and place. The young men mustered into provincial service could leave their home-towns depleted of hands during the summer season, or even worse, depleted of defenders in case of attack. The residents of Westborough, Massachusetts, in 1740 watched as "Several companys of Volunteers [read-ied themselves] for the Expedition against Cuba," and worried about the fate of the harvest and the fate of their own families' safety. Too, the recruit-ment of one group of workers for the battlefield at times mandated the increased use of another group for civilian service. For example, during the mid-eighteenth century, Pennsylvania householders became alarmed at the large number of their servants pressed into military service by the Crown; consequently, they became more receptive to owning slaves, and the black population in the colony increased accordingly.[17]

Military service yielded specific codes of citizenship. Isolated examples to the contrary notwithstanding, warfare was a distinctly masculine enterprise, and concurrently, the use of lethal weapons was a prerequisite of civic responsibility. Menaced by marauding Dutch, thieving Indians, and even traitorous Englishmen, Rhode Islanders in the mid-seventeenth century were required to own muskets. Worried that Massachusetts might not sup-ply the requisite amount of powder and shot, the Rhode Island legislature decreed that all men and boys should become skilled in the practice of "archerie"—that is, they should learn from the Indians how to use bows and arrows in place of guns. Though a champion of freedom of conscience, the governor of the colony, Roger Williams, nevertheless drew the line when it came to defense, insisting on universal manhood service. White women in New England were urged to "war their warfare," but they were not expected to take up arms. The most famous (and bloodthirsty) latter-day Jaels, or women warriors, used muscle power and primitive weaponry, not guns, as instruments of attack. In Marblehead in 1677, Indians taken captive by local fishermen met a gruesome fate at the hands of the town's women. Furious that the prisoners had been taken alive, the women fell on them: "with stones, billets of wood, and what else they might, they made an end of these Indians." Recalled one observer, " . . . we could not see them till they were dead, and then we found them with their heads off and gone, and their flesh in a manner pulled from their bones." In 1697, the fearless captive Han-nah Duston of Haverhill, Massachusetts, scalped ten of her Indian tormentors with a hatchet. Noted Cotton Mather, "she thought she was not forbidden by any law to take away the life of the murderers by whom her child had been butchered." Duston rose to meet the dangerous demands of her circumstances; but she and her sisters were not mobilized in any systematic way against the various enemies of the English.[18]

Landowner-farmers were the prototypical northern citizen-soldiers: not only were they the most numerous of householders, they also used firearms routinely in the course of their workdays, to hunt for food, or kill wolves and other wild animals that might threaten their livestock. Marblehead fishermen attacked by Indian raiding parties at sea were described by a contemporary as "a dull and heavy-moulded sort of People, that had not either Skill or Courage to kill any thing but Fish . . . [and so] they were easily taken. . . ." These views conformed to the widely held contemporary (and Old World) view that tilling the earth was a noble enterprise, while catching batches of stinking fish was not.[19]

Many white men followed the familiar and preferred trajectory that led from youthful army volunteers to heads of farming families as active militiamen, and finally older men as respected officeholders.[20] Yet once citizenship became associated with soldiering, this congruence of roles relegated Indians, blacks, and white women to the margins of civic responsibilty, and later to the margins of republican rhetoric during the era of the American Revolution. And so the problem remained: What was the proper place of men and women workers who played only an incidental part in military struggle?

The "Miserable Drove of Adams Degenerate seede, and Our Brethren by Nature":[21] Indian Workers

In the North, European colonists' views of indigenous populations revealed the settlers' own philosophy of life and labor: a transitional philosophy between feudalism and modernity, one that combined a devotion to industry with a suspicion of the material blessings that industry could yield. In the eyes of whites, the Indian way of life (generally defined) remained rootless and hence "idle," tied to the natural rhythms of the seasons and scornful of the accumulation of food or material goods. In 1634, one observer noted critically that, for the Indians, "time is not so precious," and others chastised them for their failure to need or want things of any kind; "they have little Houshold stuffe." Yet these contemptuous renderings of Indian labor and community life found a counterpoint in some whites' suggestion that whatever Indians lacked in creature comforts, they made up for in simplicity of spirit and purity of heart; though unfamiliar with bills of lading and fine clothing, Native populations possessed "heathen virtues." In the words of one Pennsylvania cleric, Indians rightly rejected the ways of "nominal Christians," white men and women who spent their days "seek[ing] their pleasure in eating, drinking, gambling, and debauchery, in usury, fraud, envy, cursing and quarreling."[22]

When the Pilgrims landed at Provincetown, they entered a region inhabited by a variety of indigenous groups already reeling and regrouping in response to their first encounters with fishermen and traders who plied the coastal waters from Newfoundland to Massachusetts Bay. Their ranks decimated by epidemics in the early seventeenth century, in 1620 only 70,000–125,000 Indians were located within the Northeast culture area, extending from the Maritimes of Canada past the Great Lakes to the west and south to the Delmarva Peninsula. Europeans had learned all too quickly that individual groups differed in their military might and their inclination to trade with whites.[23]

Like settlers in the southern colonies, whites in New England and the Mid-Atlantic region devoted little effort to absorbing or assimilating the Natives, whom they considered too dangerous, and too different, to be welcomed as cohabitors, even as slaves. However, the colonists remained open to the notion of a "usable Indian," Native men, women, and children employed in productive labor for the benefit of whites. In contrast, only a handful of missionaries entertained the idea that whites could prove "useful" to Indians—as preachers of the Gospel. In fact, Indians in general were in no position to launch systematic efforts to harness the productive energies of whites. Some Indian bands managed to drag a few white captives back to their settlements, but the work performed by these white women, men, and children only served to keep them alive, and not to enrich their captors (although Mary Rowlandson found favor with the Wamponoags by sewing shirts and knitting stockings for them). Captives frequently referred to individual Indians as "masters" or "mistresses." A prisoner of the Mohawks in western New York, Father Isaac Jogues, cut and fetched wood, and called himself a "slave of savages," the term calculated to highlight his humiliation. Likewise, William Bradford offered a definition of degenerate behavior in the New World by describing a group of Plymouth colonists who, in their hunger, sold all their worldly possessions, "fell to plain stealing," and, most shocking of all, "(so base were they) became servants to the Indians, and would cut them wood and fetch them water for a capful of corn. . . ."[24]

In assigning Natives a place in the emerging northern economy, white people, like their southern counterparts, faced the daunting task of sorting out Indian friends from Indian foes. Since northern and western frontiers remained unsettled throughout much of the colonial period, whites cautiously experimented with Natives as traders, hunters, interpreters, and military allies, even as those whites continued to perceive Indians as a group as menacing. The rapid decline of Native populations, especially after King Philip's War (1675–76), and the enclosure of the few who were left within colonial boundaries, reduced most Indians who lived among whites to the status of wage workers, slaves, or servants. In contrast to southern Natives— pushed westward and so by 1700 largely out of sight of most whites—some northern Indians became "settled" (that is, converted to Christianity). These people were permitted to live either within white households or in officially mandated, segregated communities; but they represented only a tiny percentage of the region's total laboring population. In 1765, Narragansett missionary Joseph Fish noted with approval that the Indians in that area were "Industrious—Dwell in comfortable Houses and have Things about them." Nevertheless, that ideal—of Indians who worked for whites and had "things about them"—never materialized on a large scale, for the northern colonists wanted the Indians' land more than their labor.[25]

Predictably, "usable Indians" in the North as well as the South were more likely to work for whites as wartime allies and as warriors than as domestic servants or field hands. For their part, Native groups sought to turn alliances with the English to their own advantage in larger struggles for captives and political influence. To compensate for the lack of white bodies to defend the colonies' northern frontier, "our friend Indians," men and women, served as spies and guides, and alongside whites suffered from a lack of food, clothing, and blankets in expeditions against the French in Canada. In 1746, the colony of New Jersey sought to enlist "Five Hundred Freemen, or well-affected native Indians into his Majesty's Service, in the present Expedition against Canada," paying them a cash bounty return. In 1755, the Battle of Lake George called forth 3,500 provincial soldiers and 400 of their Indian allies. Narragansett Indians were allowed to keep small parcels of land in Rhode Island in return for the aid they rendered His Majesty's service in the Seven Years War.[26]

Nevertheless, the military and political consequences of relying on Indians as soldier-workers could be disastrous. In 1676, some settled Indians from Massachusetts fought on the side of the colonists against King Philip and his supporters; but the Nipmucks, from other "praying towns," defected to their Indian brothers. Whites continued to learn the hard way that a "good Indian" was hard to find. In some cases they proved unreliable foot soldiers; if they became weary of a march, or "weary of the War," they would disappear back into the woods. In 1712, a Boston official, reporting on the most recent campaign against the "French and their Dependant Indians," complained that the provincials' own Indian allies "are weary of Warr, having Lost some Hundreds of their Number . . . but we Can never be assured of their fidelity. . . ." In their campaigns against the French in the late 1750s, American and British generals acknowledged that their foes stood in awe of native warriors, but that these same warriors proved to be poor soldiers away from the battlefield. General Thomas Gage complained that "neither orders nor entreaties can prevail on them to do service, always lying drunk in their hutts, or firing round the camp." Lord Jeffrey Amherst concurred, declaring, "I have as vile opinion of those lazy rum-drinking scoundrels as one can have."[27]

In the northern colonies, the English sacrificed peaceful trade relations with indigenous groups upon the altar of violent conquest of territory. Yet from the beginning, trade represented a major security issue, for men on both sides had little incentive to confine themselves to the buying and selling of beaver skins, baskets, and brooms. Liquor and guns, axes and knives, powder and shot soon became the currency of choice among Native hunters and their new European customers, an explosive mix in the powder keg of colonial conflicts. And gradually, trade undermined the viability of Indian populations that engaged in it. In turning from hunting for subsistence to hunting for commercial gain, for example, northern woodland groups became more nomadic, and in the process men and women devoted more of their energies to procuring and processing skins, and less to producing their own food.[28]

In the early seventeenth century, their normal seasonal migrations shattered in response to epidemics, war, and the loss of traditional hunting grounds, Indians—and especially Indian men—were decried by English settlers as lazy, and as lacking in the personal responsibility that only hard, sedentary labor could produce. A European visitor echoed the prejudices of his American hosts when he claimed that New York Indians possessed "an aversion to labour, and an itch from roving from place to place . . . they are not likely soon, if ever, to make good farmers." By "labor," most whites had in mind agricultural work; one observer could watch a group of Indians gathering oysters and conclude, "They are a lazy, indolent generation and would rather starve than work att any time. . . ." A strict gender division of labor within most groups meant that men spent more time away from villages—as warriors, diplomats, and hunters—compared to women, who stayed near their settlements to care for children and tend fields of squash,

beans, and corn; to process food and make clothes and baskets; and gather
shellfish and trap small animals. These gender roles prompted whites to
conclude that Indian men "be right infidels, neither caring for the morrow
or providing for their own families," enjoying their meals while their wives
waited upon them with "a spaniel like-attendance," eating the scraps the
men cast aside.[29]

White and Indian men alike filtered their views of the other group's
women through their own preconceptions of women's worth as workers.
While Indian men apparently had nothing new to offer the English in terms
of agricultural technology or animal husbandry, Indian women had developed a constitution of "hardnesse" that conformed to the whites' notions of
industry. Roger Williams referred to "their extraordinary great labour (even
above the labour of men) as in the Field . . . [their] carrying of mighty Bur-
thens, in digging clammes and getting other Shelfish from the Sea, in beating
all their Corne in Morters: etc." For their part, Indian men considered English women "lazie squaes," mistaken in their impression that white women,
confined in or near the house, did nothing but languish about all day.[30]

Colonists early sought to take advantage of Indian men's physical
strength and prowess without confining them to routinized day labor. The
early Swedes hired them to "do the lugging" of supplies from New York to
Fort Christina. From Pennsylvania to New Hampshire, colonists paid Indians to kill wolves; to carry messages long distances; to retrieve slave runaways and fetch wild horses; and to hunt, fish, and fowl. In the latter part of
the seventeenth century, Massachusetts tried to walk a fine line between
maintaining security and procuring food when the legislature decreed that
Indians had to obtain an official certificate in order to carry firearms for the
purposes of hunting. In 1726, a New Jersey official could sound the alarm
about the persistent threat posed by the Indians to the peace of the colony,
and then in the next breath acknowledge that "many familyes now have
Indians to hunt for them for a Trifle. . . ."[31]

It is probable that most Indians perceived new ways of working under the
English to be part of a larger package of demands that whites sought to
impose upon them. In this view, for men, working with a hoe in a corn field,
and for women, learning to spin and weave, were part and parcel of convert-
ing to Christianity and receiving an English education. As a group, for example, Indian men resented attempts to "domesticate" them. In the words of
one white man in Pennsylvania,

If one of these savages allows himself to be persuaded by a Christian to
work, he does it with complaining, shame, and fear, as an unaccustomed

act; he looks about him all the while on all sides, lest any of his people may find him working, just as if work were a disgrace, and idleness were an inborn privilege of the nobility, which should not be soiled by the sweat of toil.

Some colonists employed Indian men to tend their cattle, on the assumption that such tasks would keep them outside, away from whites, and yet usefully employed. Highly supervised labor proved to be another matter. Missionaries complained bitterly about the time and trouble it took to oversee groups of Indians set to work building schoolhouses and bridges. While constructing stone fences in Massachusetts, Indian laborers were "summarily flagallated" if they shirked their responsibilities. One Indian in Dartmouth seized upon a British raid on that town during the Revolutionary War to flee from his employer, writing on a barn door before he left, "I make no more stone wall for Joseph Russell."[32]

Whites gradually realized that Indian male wage workers, slaves, and servants as a group were more trouble than they were worth. After the Pequot War, Indian prisoners from Rhode Island were exported to Long Island to work as slaves and indentured servants; but these men turned out to be resentful and resistant laborers, eventually dying out and forming no part of the region's bound labor supply. In Connecticut, the importation of Indians defeated in the Carolinas Tuscarora War spurred a ban on such importations in 1716, because of "divers conspiracies, outrages, barbarities, murders, burglaries, thefts, and other notorous crimes at sundry times and, especially of late . . . perpetrated by Indians and other slaves . . .being of a malicious and vengeful sprit, rude and insolent in their behaviour, and very ungovernable. . . ." As a result, the northern colonies (like the southern ones) tended to deal with recalcitrant Indians, whether prisoners of war or thieves, by selling them as slaves outside their boundaries, rather than overseeing their labor at home.[33]

Indian men in general made less than satisfactory workers, but the children (like their mothers) seemed a bit more promising. In 1637, Governor John Winthrop of Massachusetts received "48 or 50 women and Children," booty from the Pequot War. In the process of parceling them out, he considered requests like the one for "a little Squa that Steward Calacot desirth," and "Lifetenant Damport allso desireth one, to witt a tall one that hath 3 stroaks [scars] vpon her stummach. . . ." Around this time Winthrop's counterpart in Rhode Island, Roger Williams, suggested reducing Indian women and children to servitude as a military strategy: "I doubt not but the Enemie may be lawfully weakened and despoiled of all comfort of wife and children etc. . . ." Not until the end of King Philip's War (in 1676) did the colonists believe they could harness Indian female and child labor productively on a scale hitherto deemed unmanageable. In Cambridge, Massachusetts, in 1676, thirty-two Indian children were "put to service" until they were twenty-four years of age. Included were

> 1 Boy. To old Goodman Myls of Dedham, a boy of fower years old, son to Annaweeken Deceased, who was late of Hassanameset, his mother p'sent. . . .
> 1 Mayd. To mr John Flint of Concord a mayd age about feeten years; her parents dead, late of Narraganset.
> 1 Boy. To mr. Jonathan Wade of mistick, a boy named Tom Aged about 11 years sonne to William Wunukhow of Magunkog deceased.

The fate of these children represented no doubt a wide spectrum of outcomes; some probably found themselves assimilated into English society, while others endured a lifetime of bitterness in response to the loss of their own culture and people.[34]

Over the course of the colonial period, from the Delmarva Peninsula to the upper reaches of Vermont and New Hampshire, and from the Narragansett region of Rhode Island to Albany, New York, Indians became ever more dependent on whites as masters and employers. Despite variations in local political economies throughout the northern colonies, whites in the region used similar tactics to deprive Indians of their claims to the land, and their claims to their own labor. Beginning in the 1720s, the landowning "praying Indians" of Natick, Massachusetts, in order to make improvements on their land, sold pieces of their small holdings to raise cash; gradually, as their collective indebtedness increased, the women turned to weaving, and peddling baskets and brooms, and the men to wage labor or servitude. A variety of groups served as "venison merchants" in towns up and down the eastern seaboard. During the early eighteenth century, the whaling industry of Nantucket recruited seamen from the Indian communities of that island. These groups had lost their livelihood in the wake of English intensive cultivation practices, and had simultaneously become dependent on English technology. Caught up in a vicious cycle of a liquor trade financed by credit, they were reduced, by violence or the threat of it, to debt peonage, and exploited for their knowledge of (Native) whaling practices. By 1720, the island's traditional Native economy had all but disappeared. Thus throughout the North, "domesticated" Indians gradually lost their exotic quality and became associated in the minds of whites with various groups of poor people in the past and in the present. Meanwhile, enemy Indians would continue to resemble the "wild Irish," roving and resistant to subordination.[35]

During the early eighteenth century, Governor Joseph Dudley of Massachusetts gained a reputation for extracting from Indians the kinds of labor that benefited whites. In 1709, an English visitor to Boston recounted a story that Dudley told him in order to illustrate the true nature of the Natives. One day the governor happened upon a "lusty *Indian* almost naked, [and] took occasion to ask him, why he did not work to purchase something to keep him from the cold?" The Indian asked Dudley why he himself did not work, and the governor replied "that he worked with his head, and had no occasion to work with his hands as he [the Indian] must." The Indian agreed to slaughter one of Dudley's calves for pay, but then refused to skin the animal until paid an additional sum. He proceeded to squander what little he had made in a local alehouse, and then went back to the governor and, presenting him with some brass coins, managed to convince him that the alehouse keeper would not accept the money. After falling for this trick twice, Governor Dudley decided that it was time to punish the fellow, and gave him a letter addressed to the Boston jailkeeper, ordering that the bearer of it be "well lashed." The Indian, "apprehending the consequence, and seeing another *Indian* on the road," gave him the letter, and as a result, the second one "was whipped very severely. . . ." Confronting his former employee later, Governor Dudley asked if he delivered the letter, to which the Indian replied that he had not, and then by way of explanation said, "Headwork, pointing to his head."[36]

This story captured the white view of Natives as sly and crafty people who would use their considerable wiles to avoid work, and to avoid punishment for shirking work. Yet it is significant that some of the contemporary newspapers that carried accounts of this (no doubt apocryphal) story substituted two blacks for the two Indians in the retelling. Although the black population was growing while the number of Indians was shrinking, both groups were poor, and perceived by whites as conniving and averse to hard work monitored by whites. Therein lay the challenge for northern Anglo colonists who sought to profit from the labor of Africans and the children of Africans within the confines of their own households.[37]

THE LIMITS AND LIABILITIES OF NORTHERN
BLACK SLAVERY

In 1700, eight years after he passed judgment on the witches of Salem, Judge Samuel Sewall turned his attention to the fate of black slaves. In his anti-slavery tract, *The Selling of Joseph*, Sewall noted the practical difficulties of maintaining enslaved Africans in colonial New England. He wrote that "their continual aspiring after their forbidden Liberty, renders them Unwilling Servants," a reference to the harsh discipline necessary to keep black men, women, and children hard at work. Because of slaves' distinctive physical appearance and alien origins, according to Sewall, "they can never embody with us, and grow up into orderly Families, to the Peopling of the Land"; therefore, even free blacks would "remain in our Body Politick as a kind of extravasat [superfluous] Blood." Sewall considered the five hundred Bay Colony blacks, actually a tiny percentage of the colony's total number, too "numerous" for comfort; like the Salem witches, their very existence (in Sewall's eyes) threatened the stability of well-ordered Massachusetts communities. Black men, slave and free, took up places in the population that would be better filled by young white men, citizen-soldiers who could serve in town militias to defend the colony, men "that might make Husbands for our Daughters."[38]

On constant military alert, the New England and Mid-Atlantic colonies calculated the relative merits of various forms of bound labor, but this reckoning was not static; propertied whites figured the pros and cons of black slavery on the basis of their local economies and the state of their local defense network, and those factors changed over time. It was not surprising that Sewall's ideal of harmonious and homogeneous New England villages tended to discourage the importation of large numbers of bound laborers from Africa. For the most part banned from defending the colony, they were less useful in the overall scheme of things compared to musket-wielding whites who were also either sons or indentured servants. The close quarters characteristic of northern slavery in both towns and rural areas rendered cohabitation between the races necessary, a fact noxious to ethnocentric Western Europeans of various nationalities. The harsh measures used to discipline slaves easily spilled over into violence, offending the religious scruples of some household heads and their dependents.

Nevertheless, whatever distinctiveness northern colonists could claim in terms of their devotion to godly, upright communities, they resembled other white settlers throughout the western hemisphere in their willingness to extract labor from Africans and their descendants as slaves. (The Quaker William Penn, for example, saw slavery as a purely economic issue, noting that with slaves, in contrast to indentured servants, a master "has them while they live.") Black bondage took hold earlier in the North than in the Chesapeake. The first settlers on Long Island eagerly embraced enslaved Africans as workers because labor was always in short supply, and because the absence of threats from either foreign invaders or Indians lessened security considerations. As part of a small-scale commercial economy, Long Island farmers engaged in a lively slave trade within their own region, leasing and hiring out slaves as their needs dictated; in 1700, slaves constituted 13 percent of Long Island's population, and almost three-fifths of all King's County households contained at least one slave, though the average sizes of individual holdings was small (only a little more than half had more than one slave).[39]

Other parts of the North as well developed into local "slave societies"— that is, areas where slavery was *the* determinative institution." Beginning in the seventeenth century, Quaker dairy farmers in Narragansett, Rhode Island, relied on the Newport slave trade for their workers. In 1730, that region included 965 whites, 333 blacks, and 223 Indians. By the mid-eighteenth century, blacks constituted 40 percent of the population of the largest city in the region, Charlestown, 17 percent of Newport County, and 15 percent of Kings County. The Quakers of Bergen, New Jersey, also maintained slaves in relatively large numbers up until the Revolution; for example, in the first half of the eighteenth century, blacks accounted for almost 20 percent of that county's population. In the vicinity of Fairfield, Connecticut, in the 1770s, 60 percent of all the household inventories included slaves (though black people made up only 6.6 percent of the colony's population).[40]

The price and availablity of various groups of laborers, rather than any ideology of "racial" inferiority, determined the extent of slavery in specific cities and regions. Routinely, the adjustment of duties levied by individual colonies on the importation of Africans served also to regulate the supply of white servants, on the assumption that masters preferred whichever form of labor was cheaper. In 1714, for example, the governor of New Jersey noted: "The Act Laying a Duty on Slaves is Calculated to Encourage the Importation of white Servants for the better Peopeling that Country, a law something like that in Pensilvania haveing evidently had that effect." In Philadelphia, the importation of slaves slowed when German and Scottish immigrants (redemptioners and indentured servants) arrived in the middle of the eighteenth century, and then rose again when white servants went off to fight in the Seven Years War. Between 1731 and 1750, fully one-half of all Philadelphia artisans owned at least one slave, a trend linked directly to the relatively cheap cost of imported Africans. A decade before the Revolution, about 20 percent of Philadelphia families were slaveowners, and slaves represented three-quarters of all the bound laborers in the City of Brotherly Love. By that time, the flow of indentured servants to the colony had virtually ceased, and the available white servants were destined either to gain their freedom or go off to war eventually in any case.[41]

Similarly, in New York City, blacks (most of them slaves) represented nearly one-fifth of the city's total residents by the early eighteenth century, constituting a labor pool that might or might not be augmented by white servants. As early as 1626, the Dutch West India Company had used slaves procured through its own trade to bolster the general labor supply in the fledgling colony of New Netherland, and in its largest settlement, New Amsterdam (seized by the British and renamed New York in 1664). Throughout the colonial period, New York City remained a slave city, and in the late eighteenth century its black population was surpassed in absolute numbers only by that of Charleston, South Carolina, a result of large number of Africans imported directly from their homeland, beginning in the early 1730s.[42]

Observers like J. Hector St. John Crèvecoeur (writing in his *Letters from an American Farmer* in 1782) claimed that,unlike those in the Chesapeake, slaves in the "northern provinces" enjoyed "as much liberty as their masters, they are as well clad, and as well fed; in health and sickness they are tenderly taken care of; they live under the same roof, and are, truly speaking, part of our families." Though appealing in its simplicity, this benign (and inaccurate) view of northern slavery reveals little about its basic similarity to southern slavery; nor does it reveal the unique hardship faced by northern slaves as workers and family members. The institution of bondage was characterized by a bottom line that transcended regional differences. In 1745, a farm for sale in Piscataway, New Jersey, included three hundred acres situated along the Raritan River, a "good Dwelling-House and Out-Houses, a Barn, a Grist-Mill, and Bolting-House with two Bolting Mills, and Things necessary for the carrying on grinding, bolting, and baking," as well as "two good Orchards." Noted the advertisement: "There is also to be Sold or Let with the said Plantation, three Negro Men, one of them a good Miller, and the other two understand Baking, Bolting, and Country Work; also one Negro Wench, and sundry Horses, Cattle, Hoggs and Sheep, and divers Utensils necessary for Farming." This farm presented a distilled picture of northern slavery, characterized by small slaveholdings (relative to southern plantations), a workforce engaged in proto-industrial as well as agricultural tasks, and an unbalanced sex ratio in favor of men. Regardless, these three slavemen and one woman remained at the mercy of a master who could sell them at will; in New Jersey, as in Virginia, they might share the fate of livestock and farm tools.[43]

A small farm located within a diversified regional economy proved to be no haven from the greatest hardship of slave life—the fragility of family ties. Northern masters showed no greater interest than their southern counterparts in keeping black family members together whenever their separation (through sales or bequests) was deemed necessary. Indeed, the absence of large-scale staple-crop plantations hindered the development of the black family as a viable institution in colonies north of Maryland. In towns where living space remained at a premium, masters and mistresses discouraged marriages, whether "abroad" or not, and they might sell their domestic slaves "for no other Fault than being too fruitful." The ideal black woman worker was one who, in the words of a New York advertisement for her sale, "drinks no Strong Drink, and gets no Children; a very good Drudge. . . ." Under such circumstances, masters considered slave children useful only to the extent that they could be sold or bound out as apprentices. As a result, the northern black population failed to reproduce itself naturally (relative to the burgeoning white population) during the colonial period. In 1780, Africans and their descendants made up barely 2 percent of New England's population, and about 6 percent of the total in the Middle Colonies.[44]

According to the historian Lorenzo Johnston Greene, "There was no color line in colonial industry." More accurately, we might note that that during the initial phases of settlement, slaves were forced to do the kinds of heavy work that Europeans avoided if at all possible. For example, in 1639, the Dutch installed an overseer over a workforce of black men belonging to the West India Company; these slaves proved their usefulness by "cutting building timber and firewood for the Large House as well as the guardhouse, splitting palisades, clearing land, burning lime and helping to bring in the grain at harvest time, together with many other labors. . . ." As time passed and the black population in the North (very gradually) increased, the deployment of slave labor conformed closely to the use of bound and waged labor in general. Slave women predominated as domestic servants, especially in the cities, and they filled the English gender-specific role of dairymaid in the Narragansett region. Slave men rapidly learned skilled trades if their masters so demanded. In New Jersey and Pennsylvania, slaves labored in iron furnaces and produced ironware. Throughout the northern colonies they worked in the shops of printers, sailmakers, shipbuilders, and coopers. Yet in most rural areas, the lines of a gender division of labor blurred as both men and women worked in the vicinity of the house and in the fields. In mid-seventeenth-century Flushing, Long Island, Black Mary (the slave of a Quaker master) hoed and harvested Indian corn, tilled a garden and tended an orchard, carded wool, and made hay.[45]

The history of slavery in the North reveals a variation on a central paradox in colonial history: the fact that a system of genteel "status ownership" of slaves among the wealthiest of urban residents could co-exist with forms of social control so brutal that they rivaled the efforts to contain and subordinate the much more numerous slave populations in the South. Northern lawmakers followed southern planters in early enacting statutes intended to curb runaways (whether Indian or black, servant or slave) and to restrict bound laborers of all kinds from engaging in the illicit trade of liquor and stolen goods. Yet because whites remained numerically superior to blacks in all areas of New England and the Mid-Atlantic, they permitted slaves some rights and privileges not granted to their southern counterparts. At the same time, a relatively liberal legal code for slaves in general was counterbalanced by barbaric punishments for individual slaves who posed a violent threat to the white population. In Massachusetts, though slaves could be bought and sold and taxed as chattel, they were allowed to testify in court cases (even against whites) and to own property, seek counsel in case of arrest, and petition for their freedom. However, such apparent laxity vanished at the first sign of smoke from a suspicious fire. In 1681, a slave woman named Maria was convicted of arson and burned alive in Boston, her fate no doubt the result of whites' fears about a number of other fires in the city preceding this one. New Englanders associated arson with slaves, and punished black perpetrators more harshly than white servants for the same crime.[46]

Throughout the northern colonies, and especially in the largest towns, mechanisms of social control were designed to respond quickly to criminal acts committed by slaves, and to slave uprisings or the rumor of them. The most stringent slave codes in the region characterized areas where the concentration of blacks was the greatest—in localities like Boston and South Kingstown, Rhode Island, and throughout the colony of New York, with its large slave populations on Long Island and in New York City. For example, in 1712, a slave uprising was quashed in New York, with condemned slaves burned alive slowly, broken on the wheel, and suspended in chains to die a slow death. A statute enacted in that colony shortly thereafter stipulated that slaves could be put to death for crimes that included not only rape and murder but also arson and other forms of property damage.[47]

Because black resistance to bondage at times assumed the form of collusion between two or more slaves, most town and colony officials refrained from mobilizing black men for the purposes of military defense. In 1708, citizens of the town of Haverhill, New Hampshire, were fending off Indian raids with the help of soldiers enlisted from other parts of New England; the following year, reports circulated that Colonel Saltonstall's house in that town had been "blown up by negroes." Regardless of the accuracy of the report, the juxtaposition of Indian attacks and slave attacks—combined with the fact that, on the frontier at least, runaway slaves were often assumed to take refuge with the French—no doubt confirmed in the minds of many whites the folly of calling upon black men to take up arms, no matter how scarce the supply of local militiamen and provincial soldiers. Some colonies codified their restrictive military recruitment policies in response to specific instances of slave rebellion; for example, a 1741 slave conspiracy in New York prompted Delaware to bar black men from militia service in all cases because foreign threats were compounded by the threat of slave insurrection. Some locales mandated that slaves and other black men perform public service in lieu of military service. Still, by the time of the Revolution it had become clear to white elites that the cities that served as the cradles of liberty for Patriots could also serve as nurseries of crime and rebellion for slaves.[48]

Though all white men regardless of economic status could aspire to the legal status of freemanship (the nexus of political and economic independence), the vast majority of black men could not. Even those black men allowed to serve as soldiers in defense of the northern colonies did not receive commensurate rewards—in particular, the rights of citizenship—because their service was contingent on military necessity (as perceived by whites) and not upon principles of social equity. In general, the provincial armies were more welcoming of armed blacks than were local militias, no doubt on the assumption that, if gun-bearing slaves were to be useful, they should be as far away from home as possible. Some black sailors fought on the high seas in His Majesty's service, and there are isolated instances of black men serving in the colonial wars of the mid-eighteenth century. When solicited for troop enlistments during the French and Indian War, the hard-pressed citizens of Massachusetts and Connecticut towns willingly acquiesced, and met their quotas of white men by sending blacks and Indians in their place. Like their white counterparts, free Negroes volunteered to fight out of a sense of adventure or patriotism, or in hope of making some money; but like slaves, most of these free black men would never own the parcel of land that signified the independence of the sturdy citizen-soldier.

The most striking differences between northern and southern systems of slavery were the number of black people residing in these two regions of the colonies, and the kinds of work they were forced to perform. Only gradually did slave craftsmen become integrated into local southern economies; in contrast, northern slaves performed a variety of tasks, skilled and unskilled, agricultural and proto-industrial, from the earliest period of settlement onward. Economy and demography, rather than some transcendent notion of "racial" difference, shaped these two divergent labor systems. At the same time, slave resistance to forced labor prompted similar responses among whites in both regions—raw fear that resulted in legal liabilities for all black people, slave or free. For their part, few northern slaves would have calculated their individual or collective well-being in terms of the skills they acquired or the grueling plantation work they managed to avoid. Instead, they understood all too well that the work they did was equal to the work done by any number of northern white men or women, while the promise of northern life—its openness and political vitality—remained closed to them. In this sense, even the shivering, begrimed fishermen of Richmond Island could contemplate life possibilities infinitely more expansive than those of well-dressed slaves in Philadelphia town houses.

"WE DOE DECLARE . . . IT A KIND OF REBELLION":[49]
NORTHERN SERVANTS

From the earliest days of settlement, northern colonial landowners and householders embarked (in the words of Massachusetts Governor John Winthrop) on a search for "boys and young maids of good towardness"— that is, for servants who would work hard and in the process contribute to the peace and well-being of God-fearing families. The English system of servants-in-husbandry would at first glance seem particularly well suited to a region of the New World characterized by family farms and a developing commercial economy. Nevertheless, for several reasons white indentured servitude failed to flourish north of Maryland to the extent that it did in the southern colonies. From the 1620s onward, northern household heads could count on the labor of their own family members in the kitchen and in the fields, an advantage accentuated by dramatic population growth. Moreover, in the North, laborers occupied a wide variety of tenure statuses, many of which were more flexible than indentured servitude, in contrast to the South, where the hierarchy of workers was more truncated and more rigid. Northern servants represented a broad social spectrum, from the near slaves who were Indian and black children, to the native-born neighbors set to work in the fields, and the foreign-born, highly skilled craftsmen who emigrated voluntarily and managed to negotiate favorable terms of service and pay. And finally, community life in the North, and the collective priority placed on order and stability, rendered the presence of "multitudes of idle and profane young men" unwelcome to say the least; good, Godly help was hard to find, and expensive.[50]

As early as 1627, Governor Bradford of Plymouth Colony was already decrying the presence of "the meanest servants," who soon after arriving in the colony "fell to great licentiousness and led a dissolute life, pouring out themselves into all profaneness." Later, Bradford cited the presence of servants as partial explanation for the fact that "so many wicked persons and profane people [had] quickly come over into this land and mix[ed] themselves amongst" the righteous:

> Men being to come over into a wilderness, in which much labour and service was to be done about building and planting, etc., such as wanted help in that respect, when they could not have such as they would, were glad to take such as they could; and so, many untoward servants, sundry of them proved, that were thus brought over, both men and womenkind who, when their times were expired, became families of themselves, which gave increase hereunto.

Servants not only fomented contention in the households of their social betters; they also eventually gained their freedom and in too many cases (according to troubled elites) spawned more troublemakers.[51]

The history of indentured servitude in the North varied by time and place. New England imported few young men and women as servants after 1640, and in general servants in that region represented a far smaller proportion of the total workforce (one-third in the first half of the seventeenth century, and less thereafter) than in the South, primarily because the children of large families supplied a great proportion of all agricultural labor. During the first four decades of Pennsylvania's history, householders employed young English servants under a relatively benign system (many were kin to their masters and mistresses). As the supply of these workers dwindled, the use of unskilled German redemptioners and Scots-Irish servants increased, and so too did servant resistance to what was becoming an increasingly harsh institution. In general, northern servants represented a greater age range, and brought with them a greater variety of skills, than their southern counterparts. Throughout the colonial period, northern servants bound for more than three or four years remained something of an anomaly; in a society characterized by geographical expansion, rapid population increase, and a growing and dynamic economy, the servant who could not move on quickly to bigger and better things was considered a sorry excuse for a worker.[52]

The northern colonies refrained from embracing servants who came to the colonies under duress—convicts and prisoners of war in particular.

Struggling to sustain his fragile community of New Sweden on the banks of the Delaware River, fighting off alternate raids from the "savages" and the English, Governor Johann Printz delicately inquired of his superiors in 1644 "to be informed what difference there was between the free people and those who had been sent over here on account of crimes." The out-post desperately needed tobacco workers, carpenters, tenders of livestock, and soldiers, but it remained susceptible to internal subversion from peo-ple "who in no wise wish to remain here." Over the next century the northern colonies as a whole (like their neighbors to the south) would col-lectively resist English transports, as well as men captured in various impe-rial conflicts in the Atlantic world, and foreign-born workers of various kinds. Nevertheless, the Middle Colonies contended with Acadian (French-speaking) prisoners of war from Nova Scotia, Irish "papists," and Germans who stubbornly clung to their own language in a sea of English speakers. Carefully, Massachusetts took advantage of a few Scottish prisoners of war and French and Irish Catholics. Yet in 1654 the Massachusetts General Court attempted to ban Irish immigration altogether, "considering the cruel and malignant spirit that has from time to time been manifest in the Irish nation against the English nation." Attempts to isolate convicts by sending them to outposts like Sagadahoc, Maine, no doubt only added to the turmoil of the frontier; from the point of view of English masters, runaways rivaled those who stayed as threats to the security of their own well-being. Though relatively few compared to the total of northern work-ers, foreign-born servants and imported English criminals were ever on the brink of causing a disproportionate number of headaches for their masters and mistresses. In 1745, a local newspaper in Boston pointedly characterized an alleged servant uprising in that city as a conspiracy insti-gated by Irish servants.[53]

More generally, even "untoward" behavior taken for granted on Chesa-peake plantations assumed a more menacing cast in the northern colonies, where the socialization of youths was deemed just as worthy an enterprise as the efficient appropriation of their labor. Yet if northern servitude was a school for youths, then it was one filled with sullen and unruly pupils. In 1647 the founding fathers of Rhode Island noted that "we doe declare that we counte it a kind of Rebellion for a servant to threat, assault, or strike his master." However, most servants apparently perfected the art of passive resistance rather than active physical aggression. Servants throughout the colonies on occasion flaunted conventional moral standards by going to bed with each other or with the children of their master, by taking to the bottle, and by spewing out profanity with wanton disregard for the sensibilities of those within earshot. They daily slacked off, embracing "the devil's pillow" of idleness.[54]

Typical perhaps was Priscilla, a young Englishwoman sent to the John Winter household on the bleak fishing outpost of Richmond Island in 1636. Two years later, Winter found himself writing to his merchant-sponsors in London defending his wife's decision to beat the "idle" maid. Bitterly resentful of her new life on the desolate, windswept island, Priscilla insisted on sleeping later in the morning than her mistress, and she had a habit of rambling in the woods and losing her way home. Noted Winter, "we cann hardly keep her within doores after we ar gonn to beed, except we Carry the kay of the doore to beed with us." She was a bad cook, and a worse dairymaid; and "She Cannot be trusted to serve a few piggs. . . ." She wore her clothes to bed at night, and in general, "She is so fatt & soggy she Cann hardly do any worke." Winter felt fully justified in overseeing "2 or 3 blowes" upon her; because of this young woman, an otherwise tranquil household was the site of sloth and violence.[55]

Indeed, just as troubling as the intractability of servants was the discipline necessary to subdue them. Reacting to the same types of youthful disobedience as their southern counterparts, northern colonists placed prohibitions on trafficking with servants, "entertaining" them, and selling liquor to them. Like southern planters, northern householders hard pressed for labor might beat or whip their servants, strike them with any handy object, force them to work on the Sabbath, and even engage in sadistic kinds of torture. Puritan communities were forced to police their members who abused the young people in their charge, and forced to worry about the disgrace that might contaminate entire communities.

Northern servants, though relatively well off compared to southern ones, ran away in great numbers and with great frequency, and masters and mistresses at times bade good riddance to particularly dangerous or foulmouthed young men and women. (That so many of the fugitives carried off with them the family's pewterware, clothing, and jewelry was cause for real anguish.) In 1734, John McDowel, "a Servant Man" in New Jersey, was thirty-five years old and a "Taylor by Trade"; he was thus much older, and presumably more skilled, than his tobacco-field working counterparts in Maryland and Virginia. Yet he, and countless others like him in the North, ran away, causing their masters considerable aggravation and expense. Southern field hands ran away from hard usage in the tobacco fields and the forests; and it is true that some northern fugitives felt similarly aggrieved, like George Owens of Chester County, Pennsylvania, who "despaired because his work consisted entirely of chopping wood." Nevertheless, northern servants were probably more often running toward a better future, either certain or uncertain, that seemed to beckon to them from the wharves of Boston, Philadelphia, and New York. Labor was scarce in all of these places, and the fewer questions asked by a potential employer, the better off both parties would be.[56]

In a similar vein, runaway servants might head straight for the nearest encampment of the Provincial army, on the (frequently accurate) assumption that even volunteers of questionable background, men with Irish brogues and "leering down looks," would be welcomed unconditionally into His Majesty's service. During the colonial wars of the mid-eighteenth century, servants could win their freedom by enlisting in the army; in Pennsylvania, for example, as many as 10 percent of all servants took advantage of this opportunity, most of them from rural areas. For these young men, as for others who went before and came after them, military service offered the promise of cash wages and the chance to see a wider world (even if it consisted mainly of the Saratoga wilderness). Despite these putative advantages to military service, it is questionable that enlistees found much that was appealing in the experience itself, if they survived it. The army offered good work only in that it served as a way station to freedom.[57]

Though few northern runaways viewed themselves as political actors on the raucous stage of colonial life, their bravado carried considerable political meaning within this fluid, well-armed society. In certain respects, these men and women served as the link between feudalistic patterns of labor deployment, based on ascribed status at birth and a persistent dependency on one's father, husband, or master, on the one hand, and the free labor system that would emerge in the new nation in the early nineteenth century, on the other. If only for a short time, runaways got a taste of individual freedom, going as far as their wits and skill and luck would take them. They severed ties of obligation to their masters, and sought to contract with an employer on their own, to haggle, lie, or bluster their way into a wage-earning position.

Within the ranks of bound laborers, barriers based on skin color, language, and culture collapsed under the weight of shared grievances. Blacks and Indians as servants, slaves, and day laborers, and as marginal members of northern society in general, often worked in proximity to each other, lived together, and intermarried. Throughout New England and the Middle Colonies were scattered small communities of Indians and free blacks—in the Narragansett region of Rhode Island, within Massachusetts praying towns, on Martha's Vineyard, among the Moors of Kent County, Delaware, and the Nanticokes of Sussex County in the same colony. Together, Indians, blacks, and poor whites might find themselves in the same place as objects of charity or as the targets of proseltyzing efforts. The Philadelphia Bettering House included "both Negro men and women . . . mixed here with the whites and sleep in the same wards." Transients might be confined to shelters like the one in Marshpee, on Cape Cod, that included blacks and Indians. On Staten Island and in Rhode Island, prayer meetings and other forms of religious instruction sponsored by the Society for the Propagation of the Gospel in Foreign Parts attracted black and white audiences, adults and children, and sometimes Indians as well. The Reverend Joseph Fish of Narragansett preached to Indians, blacks, mustees (the offspring of those groups), as well as to whites.[58]

Thus propertied colonists routinely threw Indians, blacks, and white servants and criminals in the company of each other. In New Amsterdam, Dutch officials punished white settlers for minor infractions by forcing them to work with blacks on the streets. Throughout New England and the Middle Colonies, white servants and black slaves together mowed hay in the fields and beat and cleaned flax by day, and then rubbed elbows while drinking surreptitiously at night. Members of the two groups colluded to steal from their social betters. In early eighteenth-century Connecticut, "A negro Slave belonging to a man in ye town, stole a hogs head from his master, and gave or sold it to an Indian, native of the place. The Indian sold it in the neighbourhood, and so the theft was found out." Some farmers in that colony allowed their black and white workers to sit down and eat together, an arrangement defended, "as they say to save time." Around the mid-eighteenth century, a Pennsylvania ironworks employed black slaves and indentured servants from Germany and Ireland. Alongside white men, black sailors—slave and free—hoisted sails and scrubbed decks on ships that crossed the Atlantic and plied up and down the East Coast. A large farm in southeastern Pennsylvania might include a free black man along with day workers and tenants (with the immigrants described as "slow, indolent, and dirty"). Servants and slaves of both races apparently possessed the same proclivities to avoid work and aggravate their masters and mistresses. In 1734, Judith Vincent of Monmouth County, New Jersey, advertised for three runaways: "an Indian Man, named Stoffels, speaks good English, about Forty years of age, he is a House Carpenter, a Cooper, Wheel Wright, and is a good Butcher also." Accompanying this jack-of-all trades were two men, "one being half Indian and half Negro, the other a Mulatto about 30 years old, & plays upon the Violin, and has it with him."[59]

Black and Indian workers were potentially more threatening to the well-being of a household if they stayed home and plotted together than if they ran away. In 1708, in Newton, Long Island, a black slave woman and an Indian slave man conspired to murder the entire family of their master—the husband, wife, and five children. The Indian was executed by hanging in chains, and his co-conspirator was burned alive. Rightly or wrongly, white officials believed that the Hallet Affair was part of a wider plot among Indian and black bound workers. The murders inspired a new law in 1708, providing that "all and every Negro, Indian or other Slave or Slaves within this Colony" who attempted to murder their master, mistress, or any other white person should "suffer the Pains of Death in such manner and with such circumstances as the Aggravation and Enormity of their Crime in Judgment of the Justices shall merit and require."[60]

An episode somewhat misleadingly called the "Great Negro Plot" of 1741 served to confirm the deepest fears of New York City's masters of servants and owners of slaves. In the spring of that year, an assortment of workers, including black and Indian slaves and Irish servants, plotted together and torched the city's "symbols of Royal Majesty and civil authority," including Fort George, the Governor's Mansion, and the imperial armory. These workers had met to concoct their strategy in a tavern that was known as a place for late-night interracial encounters, sexual and otherwise, and as a place where servants and slaves might fence goods stolen from their masters. White officials responded swiftly to the fires and the inevitable rumors that sprang from the flames—rumors that the arsonists were the agents of Spanish or French forces, Catholics all, bent on conquering the city, rumors that there was some connection between their own troubles and the bloody Stono Rebellion in South Carolina of 1739. Eventually thirteen black men, most of them slaves, were burned at the stake, and seventeen others were hanged; two white men and two white women were also executed by hanging, and an additional seventy-seven persons were transported out of the colony. In the fall of 1741, after the executions, George Clarke, lieutenant governor of New York, warned that the colony remained in mortal danger as long as blacks consorted with whites of questionable loyalty to the Crown. He described the "Great Negro Plot" as "the late most execrable conspiracy and the hellish and barbarous designs of a perverse and bloodthirsty people for the ruin and destruction of the whole province. . . ." Thus colonial elites reaped what they had sown—a multi-racial workforce aggrieved.[61]

HISTORY HAS LONG since redeemed the reputation of a certain conniving fugitive: a youth who broke the bonds of obligation between master and apprentice, and between older brother and younger brother, a youth who abandoned the Puritan stronghold of Boston in 1723 in favor of the City of Brotherly Love. Later in his life, poised on the brink of a new world that he had a large part in forming, Benjamin Franklin paused a number of times to reflect upon the presence of black slaves in the colonies. He noted in 1751 that he lived in a land "where no man continues long a labourer for others, but gets a plantation of his own, no man continues long a journeyman to a trade, but goes among those new settlers, and sets up for himself, etc." A slaveowner himself for many years, Franklin acknowledged that the appeal of black bondage lay in the fact that "slaves may be kept as long as a *man* pleases, or has occasion for their labor; while hired men are continually leaving their masters (often in the midst of his business,) and setting up for themselves. . . ." Despite the financial justifications for slavery, however, Franklin suggested that other factors militated against it: he considered "almost every Slave . . . *by Nature* a Thief." At the outset of the French and Indian War, Franklin issued an alarm against drafting indentured servants into the army, arguing that such a move would heighten the demand for slaves, and thereby weaken the province "(as every Slave may be reckoned a domestick Enemy). . . ."[62]

Yet as late as 1770 Franklin continued to defend the institution of slavery, and he insisted that slaves in general were treated "with great Humanity," considering that "the Majority are of a plotting Disposition, dark, sullen, malicious, revengeful and cruel in the highest Degree." He further suggested that American slavery, when viewed in a worldwide context, was not the worst of all labor systems. American slaves, he wrote, lived lives similar to those of "poor labouring people in England," men and women condemned to toil in workhouses and coal mines. Convicts toiling as indentured servants in the colonies, sailors serving on the high seas, and soldiers fighting in the king's army all faced varying degrees of coercion, and a loss of individual freedom, as workers. By acknowledging the ties that bound together nonfree workers of both sexes and various races and nationalities throughout the English-speaking world, Franklin implicitly recognized the collective challenge posed by these workers to a political economy that, while based on a rhetorical foundation of egalitarianism, would persist in excluding them.[63]

The northerners' eventual peaceful abandonment of bound labor regardless of its color should not conceal the fact that they remained suspicious of slaves in particular and descendants of Africans in general. Although he favored emancipation, Samuel Sewall probably agreed with his pro-slavery critics about the nature of blacks: "He that exasperates them, soon espies/Mischief and Murder in their very eyes./Libidinous, Deceitful, False and Rude,/The Spume Issue of Ingratitude."[64] In fact, in the North, anti-slavery principles flowed from two directions: from revolutionary "natural rights" principles imbued with Quakerism and evangelical Protestantism, but also from propertied whites' suspicion of blacks and reluctance to cohabit with them. This latter view—that blacks constituted an ever present threat to civil order—meant that northern pro-slavery and anti-slavery ideologues could eventually join in common (anti-black) cause; that Massachusetts Puritans shared the prejudices of Pennsylvania deists; and that New England Yankees and southern cavaliers would demonstrate an enduring commitment to keeping blacks in positions of menial labor. Noted Samuel Sewall, "Few can endure to hear of a Negro's being made free; and indeed they [black people] can seldom use their freedom well. . . ."[65] Unlike southern planters, northerners sought to defuse the radical potential of slave laborers by freeing them, and in the process, freeing white households of their "domestick enemies." These political calculations proved a shaky foundation for black freedom. Well into the nineteenth century the fate of free black wage earners in the North would reflect, albeit in altered form, the fate of their brothers and sisters in chains to the South.

CHAPTER FIVE

....

THE EMERGENCE OF FREE LABOR, FETTERED, IN THE NORTH

O ne day around 1750, on the western coast of Africa, a father sent his two sons—one about ten, the other six years younger—into his rice field to keep the birds away from freshly planted seeds. While engaged in this task, the two boys were set upon by a group of white men. The elder brother picked up the smaller one and ran, until, exhausted, "he was obliged to give him up and escape for his own life." The little boy left behind was then seized by the men, gagged, and taken to a waiting ship. "It was twilight when they brought him on board. He saw . . . a large number of men, women, and children who had been also thus stolen, [but] he did not recognize them. He was, therefore, lonely and distressed." The youth survived the Middle Passage, and eventually found himself slave to a ship carpenter in East Guilford, Connecticut. The carpenter gave him a new name, Gad Asher.

When the Revolution broke out, the slaveowner was drafted, but he either allowed, forced, or persuaded Gad Asher to serve in the army in his place, promising in return to allow the black man to buy his freedom. Gad Asher fought at the Battle of Bunker Hill, next to white men, and lost his eyesight as a result of his time in the army; but when he returned home, his master refused to accept the $200 in Continental money he had received as a soldier. Eventually Asher managed to earn that amount on his own, again, and finally secured his freedom.[1]

In 1785, Gad Asher and his wife had a son Ruel, and in 1812 Ruel had a son Jeremiah, who later in life became pastor of the Shiloh Baptist Church in

141

Philadelphia. When he was growing up in East Guilford, Jeremiah would listen to his grandfather Gad and two other black veterans of the Revolution discuss "the motives which had prompted them to 'endure hardness'" during the war. Recalled Jeremiah around the time of the Civil War,

> I was so accustomed to hear these men talk, until I almost fancied to myself that I had more rights than any white man in the town. Such were the lessons taught me by the old black soldiers of the American Revolution. Thus, my first ideas of the right of the colored man to life, liberty, and the pursuit of happiness, were received from those old veterans and champions for liberty.

Though surrounded by whites in a small New England town, Gad Asher managed to begin a family, and seek out the company of other veterans. Most blacks in the North, scattered in farm households throughout the region, were not so fortunate, and spent their lives "lonely and distressed." Yet in any area, the presence of just one or two black men or women could keep alive memories of Africa, and younger generations would take from those stories the conviction that freedom was their birthright.[2]

For slaves of African birth and African descent, the commercial development of the northern colonies provided little in the way of tangible rewards, material or otherwise. The towns and rural villages that gave rise to a diversified economy elevated work to a collective effort, as interdependent households pooled their tools, skills, and labor. Within this context of (white) sociability, black people retained a separate identity; though they might toil in the company of whites, and perform the same tasks as whites, their enforced subordination in America produced among them a distinctive political sensibility. At the same time, the fluid labor relations that served as the underpinning of commercialism weakened the institution of bound labor, for slaves and indentured servants failed to offer to their masters the flexibility necessary for a variety of artisanal and other pursuits. By the late eighteenth century, the former slaves found themselves emancipated, but lacking in the resources that would have made freedom a real, and not just rhetorical, condition.

Because in the North (as in the South) even free Negroes remained stigmatized by virtue of their skin color and their association with slavery, and limited in their opportunities to make a decent living, blacks as a group remained very poor during the colonial period and into the nineteenth century. In an era when "independence"—from the mother country, masters, landlords, and physical want—assumed heightened political significance, black people's impoverishment seemed to represent an enduring condition of dependency. In Rhode Island, a black woman named Elleanor Eldridge grew up hearing stories told by her father, who was, like Gad Asher, forcibly taken from his African homeland when he was a child. Eldridge's father too served in the Revolution, and he too felt the bitter disappointment of an unredeemed promise: "At the close of the war they were pronounced FREE; but their services were paid in the old Continental money, the depreciation, and final ruin of which, left them no wealth but the one priceless gem, LIB-ERTY.—They were free [but] having no funds they could not take posses-sion" of the lands (in New York State) to which their service had entitled them. "Freedom without funds" could impose its own kind of slavery.[3]

By the late eighteenth century, artist-craftsmen such as silversmiths and fine furnituremakers were plying their trades among the well-born, and with the loosening of the English grip on the American economy, domestic man-ufactures of all kinds grew up in response to the insatiable demands of a restless people. Not unexpectedly, the asceticism that characterized both the early Puritans and Quakers—their commitment to plain dressing and right-eous living—eventually fell victim to the lure of commerce and consump-tion; by 1724, in Philadelphia, in the words of one observer, "According to appearances, plainness is vanishing pretty much." Meanwhile, the large-scale production and widespread distribution of necessities and luxuries alike created hierarchical job structures on ships and in shops, in mines and mills, making manifest emerging, dramatic class and gender distinctions; the men, women, and children who produced certain kinds of goods were not necessarily those who could afford to buy them.[4]

The political dimensions of acquisition were liberal in nature, and the northern colonies increasingly came to glorify individual preferences—whether in choosing a place to live, an employer (over a father, master, or landlord), a marriage partner, or a style of dress or personal adornment. The Constitution harnessed the national state as an agent of white men of prop-erty, men with an interest in the regulation of commerce and trade through public improvements and banks. Nevertheless, outside of this new civic order were the estimated 80 percent of all Americans who remained legal dependents at the end of the colonial period; in the North this included all women, children, servants, and slaves, as well as landless white men.[5] The emergence of a liberal labor market, then—one ultimately shaped by volun-tary contractural relations and the demise of indentured servitude and slav-ery—must be juxtaposed to the persistence of the patriarchal household, on the one hand, and the emergence of a new class of dependents on the other: the laboring folk of both sexes, all races, and all ages for whom the notion of choice in any realm of personal experience was severely circumscribed. During the first years of the new nation, these contradictions were illustrated most poignantly by the plight of the white women and children textile workers who were shifted from home production into factories, and that of the black people who emerged from slavery only to confront persistent discrimination and hardship. Though legally free, these laborers remained fettered by poverty, and subject to the vagaries of a seasonal and casual labor market.

SPHERES OF LABOR IN THE NORTH

During the mid-eighteenth century, the labor performed in the household of the Reverend Ebenezer Parkman (1703-1782) in Westborough, Massachusetts, partook of a community enterprise. The Parkman farm yielded fruits, grains, and vegetables; and with the aid of specialized equipment, an assortment of family members, neighbors, neighbors' sons and daughters, extended kin, slaves, servants, and hired hands brewed beer and produced cloth, butter, and cheese. As the town's Congregational minister, Parkman made special claims on the energies of his congregants, and adults and children of both sexes provided the elbow grease necessary to till his fields and harvest his crops. Still, compared to other substantial New England and Mid-Atlantic farms, the Parkman household was fairly typical in terms of its extensive use of the labor of family members; its willingness to experiment with a variety of types of workers outside the family circle; and its agricultural production combined with the processing of natural materials into food, drink, and clothing.

At times exasperated by the endless details of maintaining such an elaborate establishment, Parkman regretted that the energy he devoted to earthly matters came at the expense of exertions more spiritual. If the nonspecialized nature of his household provided a key to the economic vitality of northern life, it also meant that, as a father, husband, and farmer, he would feel restless "under Confinement to so narrow a Sphere of motion." Parkman's lament suggested that his life resembled less that of a simple farmer than that of a weary patriarch orchestrating the labor of a large group of people ever changing in its size and social composition.[6]

Parkman's woes dealing with his "Tedious . . . Hirelings," with an irreligious maid servant, "saucy" and "Rude and Vile" male servants, calculating wage-earning lads, and a slave who died within eighteen months of his purchase seemed to confirm the prophecy of William Wood in 1634: "He that hath many dronish servants shall soon be poor, and he that hath an industrious family shall soon be rich." The Parkman children engaged in a variety of tasks appropriate to their gender and ages. Molly received a flax spinning wheel at age five and accompanied her sisters on huckleberrying expeditions. A niece might come for the day to help the girls pull flax. The sons labored in the fields in the summer, and repaired fences and took apples to the cider mill in the late fall. The two (successive) Mrs. Parkmans, we may assume, oversaw all of the dairying, gardening, and spinning operations, though not unsurprisingly Ebenezer failed to document their labors in his diary. He sometimes grumbled about the ingratitude of his congregants; nevertheless, over the decades, a long procession of friends, neighbors, and church members helped Parkman to mow hay, weed crops, stack wood, gather corn, and build his house and fences. When, in the middle of one summer, the Reverend Benjamin Pomeroy, a Yale-educated minister from Connecticut, together with his wife, visited the Parkmans, Mrs. Pomeroy took to the field and helped her host rake and pole hay. In some cases older neighbors lent their sons or daughters to Parkman for a few days, as a favor to the clergyman; the young men might be put to work reaping rye or digging a cellar, the young women boiling the soap or helping Parkman's wife when she was ill. Economic relationships between members of the Parkman household and the surrounding community were not static. The family's life cycle dictated the tasks demanded of any one person at any particular time, and the availability of neighbors and their children varied according to the seasons and their own family needs.[7]

Unlike the servants and slaves used extensively in the South, northern family members and neighbors remained bound to a farmer or a farm wife not by force, or by formal contractural agreements, but by ties of mutual obligation based on kin relationships (children who worked for their parents, wives whose work complemented that of their husbands), on age (younger sons who worked for a nearby older farmer), and on wealth (the sons and daughters of poorer farmers who worked for a more prosperous neighbor). These myriad sources of labor were flexible—that is, responsive to seasonal demands—and dynamic, reflecting the changing economic and demographic composition of a family, town, or region. Yet they still formed a hierarchy of dependency. Poor families lacking in land and equipment depended on their social betters for credit and for employment for their children. Parents had a relatively free hand in parceling out tasks to their children, and wives remained economically dependent upon, though not necessarily servile to, their husbands.

The difficulties faced by persons who wished to sever either parental or marital ties during the colonial period and long after suggest the constraints placed upon children and wives who resisted their dependent status for whatever reason. Throughout the northern colonies, intermingled with newspaper advertisements for runaway Irish and Indian servants and black slaves of both sexes were sporadic notices for fugitive wives, like Rachel Pricket, who absconded from her husband John Pricket in Burlington County, New Jersey, in 1734, and who (in his words) "by her extravagant Conduct and Behaviour, is like to ruin her said Husband and Family, she being eloped."[8]

Between 1620 and 1790, several simultaneous (and uneven) processes transformed the rural communities north of Maryland from small agricultural outposts of early modern England to regional networks of free laborers poised on the brink of the Industrial Revolution. Over time, some of the women's household tasks, especially the production of soap, clothing, and candles, were transferred outside the home. The Revolutionary War briefly halted this process, as women were exhorted to patriotic spinning and weaving; nonetheless, by the early nineteenth century, the flexibility and fluidity inherent in the early colonial roles of women had disappeared, hardening into more class-specific and narrow kinds of work. At the same time, the by-employments so characteristic of northern farms (and so distinctive compared to the South's staple-producing plantations) served as a foundation for the factory system that appeared soon after. The increasing efficiency of agricultural production in New England and the Middle Colonies in turn freed a greater portion of the population for mechanical pursuits, and yielded the cash surpluses that would enable farm families to consume, and not just produce, goods. Despite these gradual transformations in the organization of work and the gender division of labor, the majority of the population continued to live as members of farm families, the women and children subject to the direction of their husbands and fathers.[9]

After the first couple of generations of settlement, northern households accumulated the tools and resources that allowed them to engage in profitable handicraft production as well as agriculture. In the northeastern colonies, along the coast, farmers combined fishing and lumbering with the tilling of their fields, and even specialized craftsmen such as weavers ran farms and tended livestock. On large estates worked by tenants, like the extensive Pynchon family holdings in Springfield, Massachusetts, the concentration of workers and centralization of management gave rise to proto-industrial communities. Men, women, and children divided their time between the fields (during the growing season) and a whole host of other enterprises facilitated by gristmills, sawmills, tanneries, and naval stores manufactures. In the late seventeenth century, fully two-thirds of the men in Springfield were skilled craftsmen of some kind—blacksmiths, tanners, or cobblers, for example. The Pynchon estate was exceptional by virtue of the fact that its owners actively recruited men with diverse skills. Still, the principle of supplementing agriculture with diverse forms of production and processing pertained throughout the North.[10]

Women and girls tended to work in the house or its immediate environs, though well into the nineteenth century their "place" did not necessarily imply a specific number of tasks, or a limited "sphere" in general. Wives kept chickens, and tended gardens that produced herbs and vegetables; dairy workers might be mothers, daughters, hired girls, or servants, but they were inevitably female—"dairymaids." Mothers supervised the labor of their own children and any younger women in the household. Anglo wives and daughters were expected to help with the harvest, and they wielded sickles, raked clover and mowed hay, and pulled flax. German women labored in the fields on a more regular basis, throughout the spring, summer, and fall, as did women whose menfolk spent long stretches of time away from home, fishing or whaling. In the community at large, women might be called upon to provide particularly "womanly" services—to minister to the ill child of a neighbor, to offer spiritual advice (either solicited or unsolicited) to anyone who appeared to be in need of it, "to cure simple diseases by means of simple medicines," this last service at times performed by a "skilful grandmother, who formerly learned of the Indians of her neighbourhood," and now "ransacked . . . the swamps and woods . . . to find the plants, the bark, the roots prescribed." Indeed, the general term "housewifery" fails to convey the social dimensions of colonial rural women's work.[11]

By the mid-eighteenth century, in the most crowded areas of the eastern seaboard north of the Chesapeake Bay, the lack of affordable farmland, combined with a robust commercial economy, precipitated a decline in women's household-industrial pursuits, as readymade goods appeared on the shelves of town and village stores. At the same time, an increasing array of imports from the mother country provided women of means with a new role: that of consumer. Whether or not consumption entailed personal effort akin to productive labor is debatable, though shopping was certainly a service provided for the household. In any case, in the period immediately preceding the Revolutionary War, some women, and not just those in the largest towns, began to consider themselves discriminating buyers when it came to choosing from a variety of porcelain tea sets, silver buckles, and pretty pieces of silk and lace that might adorn the drabbest linen or woolen garments. Around this time, then, the basic characteristics of a consumer culture began to emerge in the northern colonies: the fickleness of fashion; the wide price range of specific items; the infinite variety of goods associated with personal raiment, and household decoration and maintenance. These features of women's domestic consumerism contrasted with the buying patterns of their menfolk, who faced more limited choices associated with the tools of their trades, from plows to axes, oxen yokes to sickles and scythes.

Age rivaled gender as an organizing principle of the social division of labor in the northern colonies. The work of the young and old, like the work of men and women, complemented each other; noted a New England divine, "One is sometimes ready to wish that the aged who have the most wisdom and experience, had most strength; but while we have old heads to contrive and advise, and young hands to work, it comes to much the same." Age established patterns of authority in households and in communities, the result of patterns of landownership and inheritance that (through at least the mid-eighteenth century or so) kept most sons dependent on their fathers until they could inherit property and establish households of their own. In some areas of the northern colonies, like Long Island, a dearth of immigrants and servants placed pressure on individual households to rely on children as an especially significant source of labor; and the enduring premium placed on sons over daughters testified to the needs of a persistent agricultural economy.[12]

Around 1700, in the John Abbot family of Andover, Massachusetts, six sons worked for—that is, remained dependent upon—their parents, from ten to twenty-nine years each. John Abbot benefited from a total of ninety-two years' worth of his sons' labor—a sum that could hardly be matched by employing a succession of indentured servants or hired hands. (Together, two daughters added another twenty-four years' labor to the household.) For young sons, work within the family was not always a labor of love, as evidenced by the Connecticut youth who remained miserable, toiling in the fields under the direction of both an "unfealing father" and a "tirant brother." (Of the latter, he remarked later, "I have not seen him for upward of twenty years [and] I would not go to my nighest neighbour to see him unless he was in distress.") Of course, the children of "strangers," especially blacks and Indians, were vulnerable to a system of "apprenticeship" that served as a thinly veiled rationalization for appropriating the labor of children of powerless parents. Thus child labor existed on a continuum from one extreme of a loving family to another, a workplace marked by misery and woe.[13]

For poor and middling folk, in contrast to the very wealthy, old age often brought a return to dependency. The relatively healthful population of the northern colonies created a whole group of elderly men and women at risk of poverty, a demographic category that did not exist in the disease-ridden South. Like the New Hampshire farmers who, in 1683, "being sundry of us about and above seventy years of age, some of us above eighty, others near ninety, being past our labor and work," some aged colonists were forced to throw themselves on the mercy of town officials—if not for direct aid, then for exemption from per capita taxes: "we humbly crave our heads may be spared, since our hands can do so little for them." The age division of labor within regional economies revealed the inevitable decline in physical strength and productivity on the part of men who had earned their living through muscle power. On Martha's Vineyard, in the vicinity of Edgartown, young and middle-aged men plied the Atlantic, and beyond, as whalers and fishermen; but "the elderly men [were] employed in cultivating the land," their confinement to agricultural pursuits a sign of their infirmity. Fishermen in general, who retired as early as age forty from a life of arduous labor on the sea, prized large numbers of sons, who were needed to support them early in their old age.[14]

The diary of Thomas Hazard ("Nailer Tom") suggests the ways in which a mature community—in this case Kingston, Rhode Island, during the Revolution—organized the productive energies of its inhabitants. Tom led an exceedingly social life that revolved around the services he provided for the community. Still single in the late 1770s (he would marry in 1780), he supplied the surrounding neighborhood not only with nails but horseshoes, bridles, hoe handles, buckles, knitting needles, and clasps for boat masts (among other products) made in his forge. He kept a garden; herded his own cattle; and made regular fishing, hunting, and berrying forays (he had a special fondness for spearing eels at night by firelight). Part of an extended Hazard clan in the Kingston area, Tom routinely helped relatives to construct stone walls, plant corn, hoe potatoes, mow hay, make cider, and fetch wood.[15]

During the war years, he hired a black man to work in his fields, two white men to work in his shop, and a washerwoman to do his laundry. The wife of one of his white workmen made him a pair of trousers, in return for Tom's hatchelling some wool for her. The wife of a cousin cut his hair periodically, and he routinely conveyed people and products around the neighborhood on his horse. He ingratiated himself with his future mother-in-law by mending a pair of her candlesticks. Later, as a married man, he would operate an oil mill for flax seed, rely more heavily on a tailor who came twice a year to outfit his growing family, and continue to barter for a variety of other services with a variety of commodities, from applesauce to fish and shoe tacks. Thus, Tom's household was not self-sufficient, but rather embedded in neighborhood networks based on barter and trade.[16]

Within these overlapping spheres of labor—household, neighborhood, and region—black workers represented a position that was at once representative and unique. As servants, slaves, and eventually free men and women, they worked closely with whites in virtually every aspect of northern agricultural, craft, and commercial production. At the same time, age played much less of a role in determining a black worker's dependence on a property owner; mature slaves, and mature black day laborers, occupied positions of subservience that white servants and white day laborers tended to leave behind once they passed their twenties or so. Moreover, the extensive use of black women in northern agriculture suggests that a gender division of labor did not affect their assigned tasks to the extent it did white women in rural areas. Enslaved workers developed a rich oral tradition that helped them to meet the distinctive demands imposed upon them by a life of relative isolation from other black people. Of a small group of blacks working in a Connecticut field soon after the Revolution, an English visitor noted, "they love to associate with one another."[17]

A native of Guinea, on the western coast of Africa, and the daughter of a king there, Jin Cole was abducted by slavecatchers when she was twelve years old (in 1713) and, as she remembered later, she and her shipmates "nebber see our mudders any more." Jin spent seventy years of her life working for the family of a clergyman in Deerfield, Massachusetts. She performed many of her chores in the company of the minister's wife, but as she went about those chores, she remained tormented by the loss she had suffered as a child, and

> she fully expected at death, or before, to be transported back to Guinea; and all her long life she was gathering, as treasures to take back to her mother land, all kinds of odds and ends, colored rags, bits of finery, worn out candlesticks, fragments of crockery or glassware, peculiar shaped stones, shells, buttons, beads, cones,—*anything* she could *string*. Nothing came amiss to her store.

Thus did ordinary, everyday objects take on a talismanic quality for this New England slave, and Jin Cole's son Cato "shared with his mother in this expectation and preparation."[18]

For some slaves of African birth, the work they performed as cooks, cattleherders, weavers of cloth, or field laborers in the northern colonies did not mark a radical break with a work world of the past; on the other hand, certain tasks, like polishing silver in a Philadelphia town house, or shoeing a horse in a Boston stable, did. More significant than the objective nature of the jobs themselves was the fact that enforced loneliness often cast a pall over the workplace. The youth who was sent out by the town fathers of Groton, Massachusettts, to spend the spring and summer watching over their cattle pastured in the nearby hills assumed a task not uncommon in the villages of Africa, but one now transformed by sheer lack of human companionship since he labored not as a family or community member but as a slave among whites. In urban areas, too, the few slaves within individual households—usually no more than one or two—served as an incentive for black people as a group to seek out other blacks from other workplaces. Exceptional indeed was the Newport, Rhode Island, slave merchant, Abraham Redwood, who owned 238 slaves, and put equally large numbers of men and women—180 altogether—at work together in the fields.[19]

For blacks in the northern colonies, affective relationships forged in the larger community transcended the routine of work. In three arenas in particular did blacks affirm their place within a wider web of social relationships: in church congregations; in formal annual celebrations; and in weekly neighborhood gatherings (contemptuously labeled "tumults" by anxious whites). For some servants and slaves, a church afforded an egalitarian meeting place, where spirituality counted for more than skin color, and where the congregants called each other "brother" and "sister." In rural New Jersey, Baptist Church members periodically listened attentively to black preachers, and blacks participated actively as members in German Lutheran, Dutch Reformed, and Quaker congregations. The Great Awakening of the 1740s acted as a leveler of sorts, and black folk in out-of-the-way places eagerly sought the spiritual nourishment, and the weekly rituals, that a community of converted souls could provide. More often than not, however, segregated seating arrangements and a double standard in church discipline for "moral turpitude" intruded into even these relatively color-blind settings.[20]

In contrast, the black-sponsored festivals observed each year in certain areas of the North—Pinkster in New York, Negro Election Day or Coronation Day in New England—provided opportunities for black people to come together, apart from the supervision of whites, and proclaim the integrity of their own communities and African heritage. White and Indian servants and hirelings often attended these celebrations, which, though representing a blend of ethnic rituals and traditions, were notable for African foods, forms of dance and music, and parade-style "strutting." For several years, Noah Brown, a slave freed by his Narragansett Indian wife, worked in the household of Moses Brown, a prominent Providence family. Noah Brown worked with white field hands, but he was ostracized by the mistress of the house, and made to retire to his sleeping quarters at eight o'clock every night, alone. No wonder then that he delighted in Providence's annual Election Day celebration, consisting of a dinner, parade, and dancing; he was "anxious," as his son later recalled, "to have a good time." And finally, throughout the northern colonies, black people established Sunday evening as a time for late-night conviviality in the streets, occasions that whites came to associate with disorderly behavior of all kinds. All of these venues served as social connectors for a group of people considered alien (by whites) because of their skin color and status as slaves or as the children of slaves, a group that naturally developed an intense self-consciousness because of their shared African heritage and their shared oppression.[21]

In the New England and Mid-Atlantic Colonies, then, patterns of labor reflected the needs and life cycles of individual families and households. The demographic realities that affected the black population—the low fertility rate, the difficulties in establishing independent residences even after emancipation—meant that slaves and their descendants could not partake of these generational rhythms. The political realities that affected the black population—the efforts of whites to mark all people of color with a badge of inferiority and subservience—meant that slaves and their descendants would conceive of their work in unique terms, compared to white family members, church members, and community members. In Jin Cole's "store" lay a lifetime of hopes and bitter disappointments; but these objects also represented a legacy that her son and the handful of other black people of Deerfield would not soon forget.

WORKERS SEEKING TO BE "MASTERS OF THEM SELVES"

Throughout the New England and Middle Colonies, masters and employers showed great resourcefulness in linking a particular social group to a particular tenure status and at times to a particular job. Most Africans and men and women of African descent were slaves, and therefore enjoyed little or no choice in following a certain kind of work or setting the conditions of that work. Likewise, prisoners of war and transports remained at the mercy of their New World employers, who used these laborers any way they saw fit. For example, in 1651, 272 Scottish prisoners of war were supplied to the Saugus (Hammersmith) Iron Works outside of Boston, there to do the bidding of John Gifford, who made some extra money for

himself by hiring the men out when they were not needed in the furnaces.[22]

In 1710, the Lords of Trade initiated a New York naval stores project
designed simultaneously to provide for the Crown's shipbuilding needs, to
settle the English-French frontier, and gainfully employ twenty-four hundred "poor Palatine refugees" who otherwise threatened to present a drain
on the domestic English economy. The Germans, though, proved less than
satisfactory laborers; they considered the work itself to be arduous and
demeaning, and they complained bitterly that their children were apprenticed to families outside their group (only men could make tar), "by which
means they were deprived of the comfort of their children's company and
education, as well as the assistance and support they might in a small time
reasonably have expected of them." This particular naval stores experiment
was soon abandoned as a result. In the 1760s, another project, this one utilizing German labor in iron forges along the Mohawk River in New York,
foundered when the immigrants, most of them contract workers,
demanded higher pay from their Prussian-born employer. The young men
employed at the ironworks were more likely to run away than to fulfill their
three-year, four-month contracts.[23]

In other areas of the colonies as well certain ethnic groups predominated
in certain kinds of tenure statuses. Pennsylvania received four hundred Acadian prisoners of war as bound laborers, and Philadelphia alone greeted
thirty-seven thousand German and Scots redemptioners (bound family
members obliged to work off the costs of their transportation to the
colonies) in a single five-year period (1749–54). The tenants of the sprawling
Dutch estates in New York's Hudson River Valley were primarily Scottish
and Irish immigrants. Though originally characterized by feudalistic social
relations, this particular system of tenancy gradually developed so that it
held out the promise of landownership, or at least cash accumulation. Tenants on Livingston, Rensselaerswyck, and Cortlandt manors (for example)
were allowed to use their landlords' farming equipment and to keep the
improvements they made on a piece of land, thus providing some with the
ability to purchase their own land, and others with the determination to
challenge their landlords in a series of civil uprisings beginning in the mid-
eighteenth century and continuing through the Revolution.[24]

Extractive industrial establishments, with their hierarchy of job categories, were especially varied in the diversity of the contractual status of
their laborers. Over time the Rocky Hill copper mine in Somerset County,
New Jersey, pieced together a workforce of imported professional miners,
farm laborers from the surrounding countryside (available only in the slack

season), and black slaves and white indentured servants. Ironworks were highly sophisticated enterprises, utilizing machinery brought over from Europe and a range of workers, including colliers, hammermen, and forgemen, and a whole host of unskilled workers who labored as woodcutters and teamsters. In his string of ironworks in Burlington and Gloucester counties, New Jersey, Charles Read employed immigrants bound to him as indentured servants, black men bound to him as slaves, artisans employed as wage earners, and a motley assortment of nearby fishermen and lumberworkers who eagerly sought out part-time employment depending upon the time of year. Workers regardless of skill level or status sought solace from the heat and noise of the forges in drinking and fighting, in cursing their employers, and, of course, by quitting. Ironworks runaways found ready employment in nearby competing furnaces, though few managers were prepared to admit to encouraging these defections: "We have always made it an invariable rule at our Works never to be assistant in robing a Person of his Property by Secreating his Servant[;] the Contrary Conduct is base and unjust as well as ruinous to the Interest of Iron Masters." Local economies like these forced men to alternate among different kinds of work that were either seasonal or unpredictable in nature. At times, then, the "fluidity" inherent in a local labor pool revealed the marginal economic status of fathers, husbands, and sons, rather than any putative upward mobility they might have enjoyed.[25]

The ingenuity employers exhibited in their quest for an efficient workforce was matched, if not exceeded, by that of the men and women who sought to cut themselves loose from formal employment relations of all kinds, and in the process create their own opportunities, legal or illegal, to make a living. Once again, Benjamin Franklin emerges as a representative figure of larger trends in the mid-eighteenth century, for his own success made him a particularly juicy target for professional thieves. In 1750, Franklin's residence in Philadelphia "was broken open," and the following things

> feloniously taken away, viz., a double necklace of gold beads, a womans long scarlet cloak almost new, with a double cape, a womans gown, of printed cotton of the sort called brocade print, very remarkable, the ground dark, with large red roses, and other large and yellow flowers, with blue in some of the flowers, with many green leaves; a pair of womens stays covered with white tabby before, and dove colour'd tabby behind, with two large steel hooks and sundry other goods, etc.

Throughout the colonies, "very remarkable" clothing and household wares proved irresistible to a wide range of ambitious entrepreneurs. Franklin was the quintessential self-made man, but in the process he became the likely victim of another kind of "self-made" men and women.[26]

During the colonial period, stealing became a calling for an increasing number of persons who organized themselves in a variety of ways, in order to carry out their "work" more safely and efficiently. At times family members worked as a unit to acquire and dispose of goods in an illegal way. In 1675, Sarah Spurwell and her mother Julian Cloyce of Cascoe, Maine, were punished for operating a fencing ring. Sarah made forays south to Boston and returned with stolen goods that her mother was charged with "Concealeing & disposeing." Other thieves preferred to labor on their own, to be their own masters or mistresses. The life histories of unrepentant criminals like Isaac Frasier of Fairfield, Connecticut, for instance, reveal the thief as solo operator. Born in Kingston, Rhode Island, in 1740, Frasier was the son of a father killed in the military expedition to Louisbourg in 1745. His poor but honest mother apprenticed Isaac at age eight to a shoemaker; the lad had already shown a disposition toward stealing (he pilfered corn from a neighbor at the tender age of eight). As an apprentice, Isaac fell under the baneful influence of a mistress who encouraged him to steal not only snuff but also "sundry other articles I pilfer'd, which she seem'd to countenance."[27]

At sixteen, Isaac Frasier enlisted in the Provincial army, but over the next few years he alternated among stealing, fleeing from town in order to escape capture, and then reenlisting, and, in at least one instance, working as a farm laborer. He roamed the colony of Connecticut, indulging in what he later described as his "covetous disposition, being extremely desirous to be rich." Jailed in Fairfield, he escaped, and recalled, "Now being at liberty to pursue my thievish calling, I was not long out of employ for I repair'd to Woodbury," where he continued to pursue his livelihood of choice. No number of arrests, and no form of punishment (teeth extractions and brandings), could deter him from what he called his "career." At the age of twenty-eight, he was apprehended for the last time, and hanged in the town of Fairfield. Isaac Frasier was reviled as a common thief, but the description of his exploits— provided by himself with the help of his pious biographer—emphasized the dark side of an acquisitive impulse, an impulse that was, under more favorable circumstances, glorified by many persons in the colonies. Frasier sought a life of "liberty," free from the constraints of masters or military officers or employers, and followed a "calling," though it was a "thievish" one.[28]

Some professional thieves lived lives of derring-do, but people more modest in their aspirations—poor people in general—struggled to piece together
a threadbare existence, one that signified their precarious economic and
legal status. Both groups were "free" laborers, although perhaps not for
long. The servant who ran away intended to escape dependence, but, like
members of other vulnerable groups, she probably found her newfound
freedom slip away all too soon. In some towns, suspicious-looking vagrants,
especially black people and young white men and women, were promptly
arrested, and then, lacking the requisite identification (or convincing story),
bound out to the highest bidder at a public auction. Men like the "English
Servant Man, Named Isaac Tailer," spent years in a cycle that revolved
around working for a master, running away, languishing in jail, working for
a court-appointed master, and then starting the cycle all over again. Other
men, like "one John Wilson Marriner," found themselves picked up by pirate
ships, or British warships, and impressed into service. Too often, then, a
worker's "freedom" from an owner or master placed him or her at the
mercy of other labor-hungry men and women. Such workers were "free" to
be exploited by any number of individuals or state-sponsored institutions.[29]

By 1700, the Chesapeake had turned decisively toward slavery, and by
1800, the North had embraced at least the rhetoric, if not the fact, of free
labor. Until the Civil War, northerners would boast that they were the true
political heirs of the Revolution, that the emergence of a system of free
labor was a natural and necessary triumph for a society based on principles
of republicanism and liberalism. Yet the "free labor" standard carried so
proudly by revolutionary-era artisans might better have been hoisted, however weakly, by transients and casual workers during the latter part of the
eighteenth century, for these men and women (outside the prisons and the
almshouses) were truly "independent" of long-term legal constraints. In the
late eighteenth century, at least, it is to their trials and tribulations that we
must look if we are to understand not just the differences but also the similarities between northern and southern work patterns.

OVERSEEING THOSE "WHO WOULD OTHERWISE
BE IDLE" IN NORTHERN SEAPORTS

The Revolution's immediate and long-range effects on the labor of white
men and women of the "middling clases" are well known. To compensate
for the lack of imported British textiles, mothers and daughters intensified
their spinning, knitting, and sewing efforts, and reveled in patriotic—

"Nationaly"—pride. During the war, wives attended to their husbands' businesses, agricultural or otherwise, and afterwards assumed the role of "republican mothers," now charged with preparing their children for virtuous and enlightened citizenship in the world's first modern republic. On the countryside, tenants sought to throw off the remnants of feudalism in a bid for household independence achieved through landownership; and in the seaport towns, craftsmen and mechanics proclaimed the dignity of labor and ensured for themselves a potent political voice in the new nation.[30]

Yet, as a gauge of the larger meaning of the Revolution for the history of work, the fates of several other overlapping groups are also revealing. Throughout the country, poor white women and their children served as the first hands to labor in the emerging industrial system, as textile production began to move out of the home and into factories. These workers were not necessarily employees, at least initially, for factory work took on the cast of a charitable enterprise under the direction of elites who sought to redeem the poor from a life of "idleness," and by extension, a life of crime. In towns and cities, the dislocation of war added to a growing class of laborers who scrounged for daywork, released from the ties of patriarchal authority within the household-shops of master craftsmen. Finally, the plight of the emancipated slaves demonstrates that the Patriots of 1776 drew too sharp a distinction between freedom and slavery; though gradually released from their bonds in New England and the Middle Atlantic states, black men, women, and children remained in a legal limbo, constrained by the dynamics of labor competition among free workers.

Beginning in the early seventeenth century, the problem of clothmaking assumed a central place in the political economy of the British colonies, and a central place in the moral order fashioned by colonial elites. In 1642, the Massachusetts General Court proclaimed that bound-out children should learn the skills of spinning and weaving, a move that reflected both the shortage of adult textile workers and the hope that idle folk of tender age might find suitable employment. In 1656 the court went further, mandating that "all hands not necessaryly imployed on other occasions, as weomen, girles & boyes" must work at spinning, and that towns should enforce spinning quotas for households. In the early eighteenth century, textile production remained confined to households, which supplied unpaid workers; and yet during the Revolution, just as women's roles as consumers (in this case, boycotters of tea) assumed new political signficance, so too did their traditional roles as textile producers, now that "our republican and laborious hands spun the flax [and] prepared the linen for the use of our soldiers. . . ."[31]

Nevertheless, spinning carried quite different social meanings when carried out by women outside their own households. In the mid-1700s, town fathers in the largest northern cities moved to compel poor women and children in workhouses to spin for their livelihood, not only for their own good but also for the public good, thereby seeking to encourage personal responsibility and self-discipline, and to discourage widows from draining a town's charitable resources. In the minds of the well-to-do, poverty and criminality among the dependent had become conflated. In New England, public officials had always exercised their prerogative to appropriate the labor not just of convicts and prisoners of war but also of ordinary citizens—men and women alike—whose behavior contributed to civil disorder, variously defined. In 1680, a New Hampshire town council responded to "sundry indictments against John Waldron, for drunkenness and neglect of his calling, and disorderly living. . . ." For these crimes, and other instances of "vicious living," Waldron was remanded to jail, and there provided with "materials to work at his trade," while "one of his legs be constantly chained to a post"; and "if he refuse to labor he shall be kept with prisoners' fare, and to be whipt, with ten stripes at a time, at the discretion of those gentlemen of the council." The proceeds of Waldron's labor went "for his own and his children's maintenance and livelihood." Criminals of various kinds were routinely bound out to employers, and afforded no more rights than slaves, forced to atone for their flagrant laziness.[32]

The establishment of workhouses in several colonial cities before the Revolution made explicit the perceived link between poverty and immorality. By the late seventeenth century, the tradition of "warning out" indigent persons (that is, expelling them, forcibly if necessary, from a town) had become inadequate to deal with the growing number of war refugees and other persons who could not find full-time work. War widows and women whose husbands went off to sea for long periods or simply disappeared remained overrepresented among the colonial poor. To cope with the increase in poverty, the largest cities experimented with "outdoor relief," almshouses, and workhouses. Gradually, the efficient operation of workhouses, where labor was regimented to an extreme degree, encouraged merchants, lawyers, and their political allies to see the business of ministering to the poor as a potentially profitable enterprise.

In the eighteenth century, workhouses cum textile manufactories utilized simple forms of machinery characteristic of home production, including the housewife's spinning wheel and the itinerant weaver's loom. At the same time, these workplaces were new and notable for the way they were organized: in large establishments, employing a number of people closely supervised (in contrast to the informal routine of the small, household-based artisan's shop). With financial support from concerned citizens, the city of Boston established the Workhouse on the Common in 1735, its purpose to put to work the poor, mostly widows of soldiers, and their children, at picking oakum (a jute fiber used for caulking the seams of ships), carding wool, and spinning wool and flax. Yet these women resisted attempts to incarcerate them in a factory; they resented the daily punishments inflicted upon them for poor work, the restrictions imposed upon their movements, and the paltry pay accorded them for their labors. In 1748, the United Society for Manufactures and Importation revitalized these efforts, and with a name change initiated two years later, established itself as the Society for Encouraging Industry and the Employment of the Poor. The society opened a linen manufactory, with women and children as its principal employees. An infusion of Boston taxpayers' money in 1753 put the public stamp of approval on the venture, but even this gesture of support was insufficient to keep the factory afloat. Once again, poor women preferred to toil at home rather than at long hours within the walls of the factory, at wages that would not support themselves and their children.[33]

The other two major northern seaports followed a similar path. Philadelphia established a workhouse—called a bettering house—in 1766, where poor people and vagrants and criminals could be punished and rehabilitated, all in one place and all at one time. Like the Boston Linen Manufactory, the Philadelphia Bettering House represented a link between domestic (home) manufacturing based on unpaid labor, and manufacturing work based on poorly paid labor. A minority of the inmates worked at manufacturing (spinning), though here again the enforced work regimen made all the more glaring the similarity between a prison and a factory. The Philadelphia Bettering House failed to earn its subscribers a profit, and after the Revolution it closed its doors. In 1775, the United Company of Philadelphia for Promoting American Manufacture organized hundreds of poor women as spinners in their own homes as part of a putting-out system, an effort based on the notion that uplift and moneymaking could go hand in hand with enterprises that relied on the labor of the indigent. The New York Poorhouse, founded in 1737, also relied on inmates to produce goods that could be sold in the marketplace. In 1776, the New-York Society for employing the Industrious Poor, and Promoting Manufactory, was initiated, with the intention of "exciting a general and laudable spirit of industry among the poor, and putting the means of supporting themselves into the hands of many who at present are a publick expense." However, this effort fell victim to the British occupation of the city that same year.[34]

Towns and regions varied in the ways they parceled out work to the poor, relying on a system of home handicrafts, outwork, and "machineless factories." White women and children constituted a sizable proportion of early manufactory labor. This was particularly true in Boston, which lacked Philadelphia's near-continuous infusion of skilled clothmakers from the British Isles before and after the Revolution. A 1794 survey of Boston revealed that a sailcloth manufacturer employed a number of women spinners, out of a total of four hundred hands; and a cotton card manufacturer provided work for twelve hundred persons, mostly women and children.[35]

In contrast, the New York and Philadelphia entrepreneurs who invested a great deal of money in elaborate textile mills soon discovered that their reliance on skilled (that is, in modern terminology, "overqualified") immigrant workmen was hardly the boon to business they hoped it would be. For example, Henry Wansey, an English visitor to the Hell's Gate area of New York City in 1794, observed the opening of a cotton manufactory that was "training up women and children to the business, of whom I saw twenty or thirty at work; they give the women two dollars a week, and find them in board and lodging; the children are bound apprentices till twenty-one years of age, with an engagement to board, clothe, and educate them." In the same breath, though, Wansey sounded a warning note that foreshadowed both the increased use of time-saving machinery and the increased reliance on women and children over skilled workmen imported from Europe: "The English workmen are dissatisfied, and ready to leave the factory as soon as they have saved up a few pounds, in order to become landholders up the country, and arrive at independence." New England would in effect bypass this particular stage of industrial development by tapping into its large labor pool of women and children, and by pioneering the use of textile machinery that proved more reliable than men who sought to "arrive at independence" through landownership.[36]

In 1791, Secretary of the Treasury Alexander Hamilton offered an optimistic *Report on Manufactures*, suggesting ways to render labor more efficient as well as more responsive to the moral life of the new nation. First, Hamilton lauded machinery, "an artificial force brought in aid of the natural force of man; and, to all the purposes of labour, [it] is an increase of hands; an accession of strength, *unemcumbered too by the expense of maintaining the laborer*." Second, he predicted that woman power could now be freed from its domestic moorings, and contribute to the nation's wage-labor force. As a result, "The husbandman himself experiences a new source of profit and support from the increased industry of his wife and daughters; invited and stimulated by the demands of the neighboring manufactories." In clarifying these remarks, Hamilton noted the connection between poverty and "idleness" that made certain groups of people suitable for manufacturing pursuits:

> Besides this advantage of occasional employment to classes having different occupations, there is another, of a nature allied to it, and of a similar tendency. This is—the employment of persons who would otherwise be idle (and in many cases a burthen on the community) either from the bias of temper, habit, infirmity of body, or some other cause, indisposing or disqualifying them for the toils of the Country. It is worthy of particular remark, that, in general, women and Children are rendered more useful, and the latter more early useful by manufacturing establishments, than they would otherwise be.

Hamilton added that American businessmen had much to learn from the British lords of the loom, factory owners whose workforce consisted of a majority of women and child workers.[37]

Hamilton's observations represented less a ringing endorsement of a new direction for the new nation than a confirmation of public and private priorities established during the colonial period. Specifically, he was calling upon women and children to continue their labors, but now within a changed venue—the manufactory rather than the household. At the same time he maintained that wage work was also the proper remedy for the "idle" and for other kinds of miscreants, thus providing a class dimension to a type of production that traditionally depended exclusively upon women workers regardless of class and age. Finally, by implication the treasury secretary acknowledged three forces driving the new nation's commercial economy: the encouragement of technological innovations as labor-saving devices; the denigration of women's unpaid domestic labor in favor of the wage labor of women and children; and the increasing social inequality fostered by commercial development in general.

A series of depressions and epidemics, coupled with the economic dislocations caused by the Revolutionary War, the embargo of 1807-09, and the War of 1812, created a new, readily identifiable group of poor people—the able-bodied poor who scratched out a meager living through seasonal and casual work. As the hubs of colonial and new-nation commerce, the seaport cities beckoned to widows and children left homeless by military conflict, to sons lacking an inheritance of land, and to the "wandering poor" warned out of towns because of rising welfare costs. The cities served as entrepots for soldiers and sailors; offered employment to the unskilled, as teamsters and dockworkers; and provided ample customers to goldsmiths and carpenters. In 1775, a visitor to New York noted the fierce rivalry among tradesmen, the city's "overstocked" labor market swollen by "the arrival of so many adventurers from Britain and Ireland." Successive waves of in-migration from the countryside, and immigration from Europe, would exacerbate this job competition among the "lower orders."[38]

At the same time, master craftsmen and their journeymen employees developed a sense of "craft consciousness"; their politicization stemmed from pride of work and their status as small producers, rather than class consciousness per se. Residing within the households of their masters, yet not part of their masters' socioeconomic group, were journeymen-employees who owned their own tools, and bound apprentices who did not. In contrast, the laboring poor lacked both craft and class consciousness; this group consisted of persons whom elites dubbed "the meaner sort"—a hodgepodge of vagabonds, unskilled free Negroes and freed servants, "the strolling poor," and the chronically underemployed. As many as one-fifth of all residents of Boston (beginning in the 1740s) and New York and Philadelphia (beginning in the 1760s) could be classified as the poor; by the time of the Revolution, this highly transient group was a permanent fixture on the urban landscape, in the vanguard of "free" laborers.[39]

Swelling the ranks of free laborers were former servants like Philadelphia's Polly Nugent, married to a blacksmith fallen on hard times; and Grace Biddle, newly widowed. Both of these women were compelled by hardship to return to their former mistress, Elizabeth Drinker, and beg for assistance between 1796 and 1797. Women outworkers of New York City toiled by day, and by firelight at night, just a batch of spinning or a bundle of shirt collars away from the almshouse. War veterans sought work in the warehouses and along the docks of Boston Harbor; child scavengers were forced to fend for themselves on the streets of the largest towns; and as a matter of life course, elderly folk inevitably lost out in a lopsided race with younger workers. Both male and female, varying in ages and in the sources of their misery, these workers were united only in their lack of resources, whether tools or land; in their mobility, from neighborhood to neighborhood, and city to city; and in the precariousness of their everyday existence. Discharged from indentured servitude, William Moraley "roam'd about [the Middle Colonies] like a Roving *Tartar*," finding "no Abiding Place" for weeks on end, and later rendered his tribulations as an itinerant in picaresque terms; "Sometimes I have acted the Blacksmith; at other times, I have work'd in the Water, stark naked, among Water Snakes. Sometimes I was a Cow Hunter in the Woods, and sometimes I got Drunk for Joy that my Work was ended." But for "a Woman, with two Children, walking the same Road," to Philadelphia, the life of the wanderer held little promise and many dangers. Such was the fate of labor—especially women's labor—"independent" of the constraints imposed by fathers, husbands, and masters.[40]

By the late eighteenth century, in the North, any sharp economic distinctions that might have existed between the white laboring poor and former black slaves had begun to erode. Most New England and Middle Atlantic slaves underwent an incremental process of emancipation, and possessing very little, if anything, in the way of property, the majority of freed blacks also found themselves beholden to a labor market that afforded only casual work. Yet they suffered the added liability of a skin color that marked them as persistently vulnerable to exploitative labor relations and to attacks from their resentful white counterparts, for they lacked the legal protection and political influence that would have enabled them to resist such assaults.

With the exception of Vermont, which abolished slavery in one stroke with its constitution of 1777, the northern states gradually (and in the cases of the Mid-Atlantic region, grudgingly) approved emancipation plans, and then only in response to political pressure from free blacks and organized abolition societies. As a movement, abolition of course derived its inspiration and its moral fervor from the revolutionary "rights of man" ideology. Interpreting Whig rhetoric in favor of freedom and opposed to slavery more consistently than the founding fathers, groups of free blacks, evangelical white women, Indian clergymen, and Quakers offered a view of bondage that carried much moral force, but little political or economic appeal. Nevertheless, slaves played a relatively small part in the economies of New England and the Mid-Atlantic states as a whole, and gradual manumission plans ensured that slaveowners would lose their investments only over an extended period of time.[41]

Ultimately, the collective white ambivalence toward emancipation revealed not only dismay over the confiscation (as it were) of their property, but also a deep-seated fear of a new group of black people whose movements and labor were no longer closely regulated by the institution of bondage. This fear reached the point of near hysteria in 1791, when the slaves of St. Domingue initiated the bloody, systematic destruction of the French planter class on that island, all in the name of the same "liberty" and "freedom" invoked by the American Patriots of 1776. It was during this period that white elites transformed their traditional suspicion of all poor people into a more specific anxiety about the nature of black people in particular. Whites' fears, most evident in the largest seaport towns, found institutionalized expression in the gradual emancipation legislation passed by Pennsylvania, Rhode Island, Connecticut, New York, and New Jersey between 1780 and 1804. These plans mandated that the children of slaves should labor for their mother's master as indentured servants for extended periods of time after the passage of abolition statutes—from eighteen to twenty-eight years for females, and from twenty-one to twenty-eight years for males, depending on the state. Consequently a whole generation of "free" blacks would remain under the tight control of white masters and mistresses. The last vestiges of slavery were not abolished in New York until 1827, in Rhode Island until 1842, and in New Jersey until 1846.[42]

Whites, then, approached the politics of emancipation in terms of their own property rights and the need to ensure worker discipline. In contrast, black people attempted to carve out for themselves lives as free men and women, as free family members, and as builders of free communities. By 1800, over ten thousand free blacks (and three thousand slaves) were living in Boston, Philadelphia, and New York. During the Revolution, colonial patterns of black resistance to white authority led directly to wartime patterns of black migration among runaways as well as recently manumitted blacks and free Negroes. Like their southern counterparts, some black men and women opted to join the Tories in their flight; in 1783 alone, approximately three thousand former American slaves joined British sympathizers when they were evacuated from New York to Nova Scotia. Others, apparently mostly single young men—in other words, those free of physical infirmities and family responsibilites—stole themselves away from their masters, regardless of political affiliation. During the period immediately after the Revolution, this process of black withdrawal continued, as free people of color began to move out of the households of their owners and form nuclear families. For example, in Boston, one-third of all black people lived in white households in 1790, but by 1820 more than eight out of ten blacks lived apart from whites. Blacks in northern towns created their own churches, schools, newspapers, and voluntary associations, apart from whites of all classes.[43]

Black men and women remained persistently vulnerable to white people who perceived a black skin as license for kidnapping and various dramatic forms of labor exploitation. In the eighteenth and early nineteenth centuries, free blacks in the North found little security in their legal status. As a routine part of imperial conquest and commercial trade, privateers and naval warships had always seized black seamen and passengers with impunity, just because, in the words of one victim captured in 1709, "he differ[s] in Colour & Nation," and no matter that "he is a Christian & was Born Ffree." These incidents illustrated a larger principle: That blacks in general "by reason of their colour which is swarthy . . . were said to be slaves and as such were sold, among others of the same colour and country." Revolutionary rhetoric glorifying natural rights failed to stem this practice. In 1788, a group of Boston blacks petitioned the state's General Court on behalf of "Three of our Brethren free citizens of the Town of Boston." The master of a ship in the harbor "got them on bord put them in irons and carred them of, from their Wives & children to be sold for slaves." Demanded the petitioners, "What then are our lives and Lebeties worth if they may be taken away in shuch a cruel & unjust manner as these...?"[44]

For these reasons, some free blacks chose to bind themselves to their former master or mistresses so that they might receive some protection from the depredation of whites. Such slaves-turned-servants attempted to avoid the uncertain fate that awaited, for example, an elderly black woman in Newport, Rhode Island, manumitted by a master who remarked of this "one old Negro woman, I have offered her Freedom, I do not value her at anything." In Philadelphia, some former women slaves bound themselves to white households for as much as sixteen years of "housewifery" in order to provide for themselves and their families. Throughout the northern states, large numbers of black men, women, and children abandoned by their masters and mistresses swelled the ranks of the wandering poor.[45]

In the latter part of the eighteenth century, northern blacks left slavery and entered a commercial economy marked by fluidity in the relations between rich and poor, men and women, artisans and journeymen, whites and blacks. For black workers, the Revolution possessed a meaning profoundly different from that experienced by whites, especially white property owners. In the seaport cities, white tradesmen and mechanics forged a link between republican citizenship and the dignity of labor; groups like the Sons of Liberty and worker-based local militias celebrated their political independence and a collective tradition that made their interests inimical to those of merchants, financiers, and elites in general. In contrast, black artisans recently released from slavery might have demonstrated a pride in their specialized skills, in their mastery of the mysteries of woodworking, blacksmithing, or cordwaining; but they could hardly associate their labor with a glorious past, or even with the bright promise of the new nation. As former slaves, they considered the terms of their work, and not just the physical labor itself, to be their defining experience as members of the labor force.

As the first days of the new nation dawned, white widows spinning in workhouse-manufactories shared an unseen bond with former slaves toiling in the kitchens and stables of white households, a bond that lacked formal political expression. Together, these workers, though free, remained vulnerable to the whims of their "charitable" sponsors, and to the vicissitudes of the local economy. Yet, together, they hardly constituted a class, for they remained disenfranchised and isolated from each other. Separating the two groups were poor white men, similarly lacking in skills and material and financial assets, moving from dockwork to petty thievery, from picking rags to hauling lumber, the insecurity of their livelihood a price they paid for their status as free laborers. The uncertain fate of these workers illustrated the mixed blessings that flowed from the dissolution of various forms of political authority during the late eighteenth century—the decline of slavery, the disappearance of indentured servitude and apprenticeship (by the 1820s), and the assault upon, if not the demise, of the patriarchal household, especially among poor city folk. Thus the northern seaport cities of 1800 saw the birth of a producing and consuming society in which recognizable groups of people had virtually no opportunities to consume goods above the level of barest subsistence.

THE STORY OF Venture Smith is the story of revolutionary struggle carried out in the fields, barns, and waterways of New England. The well-born native of Africa was captured as a prisoner of war at the age of eight, and sold as a slave in Rhode Island (in 1737), where he was put to work carding wool and working in the fields by day, and pounding corn by night. Twelve years later he married Meg, another slave, and tried to spirit her away with him in a thwarted attempt at escape; subsequently Smith was sold to another master and separated from his wife and baby daughter. Smith's new master reunited the young family, but more than once Smith had to intervene to protect his wife from her mistress's horsewhip. Over the next few years, he managed to earn some money for himself by performing tasks over and above his stipulated assignments, by cutting cordwood and threshing grain, "cleaning gentlemen's shoes and drawing boots, by catching muskrats and minks, raising potatoes and carrots &c., and by fishing in the night, and at odd spells."[46] At age thirty-six Venture Smith paid his master £71 and secured his own freedom, but his efforts to free his family continued. He moved to Long Island, grew watermelons, fished, and served on a whaling ship, thereby raising enough money to buy his enslaved wife, daughter, and two sons, as well as (eventually) three other black men. Yet his life continued to be marked by hardship. The owner of his own "fishing and trafficking business," Smith was sued in court by a well-to-do white captain, and forced to pay a substantial sum of money for a misdeed he maintained he did not commit. Noted the black man in his autobiography, "but Captain Hart was a *white gentleman*, and I a *poor African*, and therefore it was *all right.* . . ." To compound his sorrow, one of his sons, "induced to join the crew of a whaling ship" for the promise of "a pair of silver buckles, besides his wages," had died at sea of scurvy. Still, at the age of sixty-nine, Venture Smith could declare, "my freedom is a privilege which nothing else can equal."[47]

Smith's story, and the fate of his son, suggest the ambiguous nature of sailing as an occupation for black men. Since the beginning of the colonial period, blacks had served on a variety of vessels as slaves, as hired-out slaves, as servants, and as free men. It is revealing that work on the high seas proved so appealing to so many black men throughout the eighteenth century, and later. Some considered their relative autonomy and the variety of their routines aboard ship to be preferable to field work, labor in a master's shop, or domestic service. An Atlantic community of seamen afforded black men a cosmopolitan view of the world, a view that, together with a transient way of life, they might share with Irish hands and English apprentices on deck, or in the taverns and brothels of port cities. A few well-known black men in Boston, Providence, and southeastern Connecticut developed sailing careers and businesses that provided their extended families with a sense of collective identity and the financial resources necessary to establish a stake on the mainland and a claim to leadership within the larger black community. Paul Cuffe of Westport, Connecticut, became one of late eighteenth-century America's richest black men. As a merchant-captain with a fleet of ships under his command, he was in a position to employ all-black crews (and take on a white apprentice now and then), to build schools for black children, and to pursue his pan-African ideal of black solidarity.[48]

Yet the life of a seaman required that fathers and husbands spend long periods of time (in some cases, even years) away from their families. Black sailors tended to be older, and more often married, compared to their white counterparts, suggesting that the relative freedom of life at sea (and relative paucity of alternatives) made them willing to endure such hard and dangerous work longer than white men. In turn, black women as wives and community members were forced to labor within communities deprived of (in some cases, substantial numbers of) husbands and fathers.

The organization of shipboard labor mirrored both the employment patterns characteristic of a commercial economy and the prejudices of the larger society. Operating within a vertical hierarchy of assignments, black crew members found it difficult to achieve much in the way of occupational mobility, and most remained clustered at the lower end of the wage scale. Workers who performed unsatisfactorily faced certain and bloody discipline. Some blacks joined with their white co-workers in defiant mutiny, while others seized the opportunity to desert at a port that offered a safe haven from a brutal master or merely a respite from life before the mast. With a few exceptions (Nantucket's Absalom Boston, in addition to Paul Cuffe), most free black seamen had to contend with sporadic employment, for they could never aspire to owning their own ships and hiring their own crews. Black sailors worked on British and American ships during the Revolution, yet they rarely received either the compensation they deserved or the gratitude of the nations they served.[49]

Well into the nineteenth century, black whalemen, fishermen, merchant seamen, and sailors faced the persistent threat of impressment by British naval authorities, or kidnapping by pirates and merchant vessels; and as Venture Smith understood all too well, young men were susceptible to the blandishments of ship captains who held out promises of good pay. For these reasons the seafaring life remained emblematic of the trade-offs faced by black men and their families, even within one of the most racially integrated worksites of the early republic.

For the most part, northern Whig ideologues took for granted that indentured servants and apprentices should continue to obey their master; that wives should remain dependent upon their husbands; that people of African and Native descent should remain content with a legal status somewhere between slavery and freedom; and that Indians should be deprived of their ancestral lands, and of life itself. The Revolution did little to challenge these traditional forms of inequality. Now, in ever-increasing numbers, black, white, and Indian men, women, and children would escape familiar kinds of dependence only to find themselves bound to the uncertainties of rural capitalism in the countryside and merchant capitalism in the cities. Among the poor, black people demonstrated a unique sense of self-consciousness borne of their collective memories of Africa and their collective experience as enslaved Americans. And so, in rejecting their ascribed places as field hands and domestics, blacks not only kept alive the spirit of the American Revolution; they also sought to fuse political rights to economic rights, and thus to advance the agenda of freedom in a truly revolutionary way.

American Work:
A Photo Essay

The English colonial enterprise mandated the use of large numbers of agricultural workers, but the colonists perceived indigenous groups primarily as traders and warriors. Although whites at times put Indian women and children to work as field hands or domestic servants, Indian men were considered too dangerous—and as a group too heavily armed—to subordinate to the demands of an agricultural economy (1, 2). For southern colonists in particular, the novelty and arduousness of certain types of work, like moving large tobacco casks (3) and cutting down stands of trees, intensified the need for a bound labor force— primarily English indentured servants and African slaves.

The founding fathers of the United States sanctioned the institution of human bondage (4), and slaves were employed in a variety of tasks, not only as field hands and domestic servants (5), but also as textile machine operatives and turpentine camp laborers (6). In the North, the social nature of work in villages and small towns (7) highlighted the relative isolation of black men and women, who were nevertheless well integrated into the northern craft economy (8).

During the Civil War, black men embraced the opportunity to fight for their own freedom and for the freedom of their families. They served proudly in regiments like the 54th Massachusetts (9). However, the Union army, like private employers, tended to relegate black soldiers to manual labor (10); and indeed, the work relationships between blacks and whites in Union military encampments mirrored those in the civilian sector (11).

In the late nineteenth century, the vast majority of black workers were using the same tools, and engaged in the same tasks, as their slave forbears (12, 13, 14). They remained barred from machine work in general until northern factories opened their doors to them (temporarily) during World War I (15).

Work patterns over the next half century yielded striking contrasts in the opportunities afforded black and white workers. For example, like white men, white women found jobs operating sophisticated kinds of machinery (16). Black women remained concentrated in the domestic service sector; the advent of the railroad sleeping car perpetuated their roles as cleaners and maids (17).

Companies conscious of their public image highlighted white workers in promotional literature, even though blacks performed similar tasks within different workplaces—for example, food preparation in private homes instead of food-processing plants (18, 19). As more and more whites entered the burgeoning white-collar sector of the economy, blacks continued to perform seasonal and backbreaking labor, outside (20, 21). The myth that blacks were incapable of working machines persisted through the early 1940s, when whites entered defense-industry plants (22, 23), and black men either remained in their old jobs (24) or found ill-paid war-related jobs (25). Distinguished for their bravery in combat, black service-men like the Tuskegee airmen (26) were subjected to discrimination within the armed services as well as in civilian life.

Beginning in the 1930s, the federal government responded to persistent pressure from black activists, and to the growing political power of black voters in northern cities, by opening up new kinds of jobs to black workers. Public works projects allowed blacks to bypass racist labor unions, such as those that dominated the con-struction industry (27), and provided training in the use of heavy equipment (28) and office machines (29) to substantial numbers of African Americans for the first time. By the 1960s, the United States military was the most racially integrated institution in the country (30).

The final assault on the legalized Jim Crow workplace came at a time when the heavy manufacturing sector was eroding and the service sector was expanding. Lead-ership in the country's growing service-sector labor unions passed from white men to people of color, such as members of the Service Employees International Union (31). By this time, a host of other groups of workers throughout the United States were reeling from the effects of a transformed global economy. In their everyday struggles, they served as a reminder that a high-tech economy would continue to depend upon traditional forms of labor exploitation (32, 33). By the late twentieth century, African Americans as professionals (34), politicians, artists, athletes, and entertainers had attained an unprecedented degree of public visibility and influence.

Nevertheless, as a group African Americans remained disproportionately poor, confined to communities where a lack of good schools and good jobs would continue to hinder the life possibilities of future generations.

1. Sa Ga Yeath Qua Pieth Ton, King of the Magua (Mohawk sachem of one of the five Iroquois Confederacy Nations), c. 1710 *Massachusetts Historical Society*

2. Indian family groups, from Sir Richard Phillips, *A View of the Characters, Manners, and Customs of the North Americans . . . Northern Indians* (1810) *Courtesy, American Antiquarian Society*

3. Tobacco wharf along the shores of the Chesapeake, c. 1750 *Schomburg Center for Research in Black Culture/ New York Public Library*

4. Slaves en route south, near the U.S. Capitol after it was burned by the British during the War of 1812. From Jesse Torrey, *Portraiture of Domestic Slavery* (1817) *Courtesy, American Antiquarian Society*

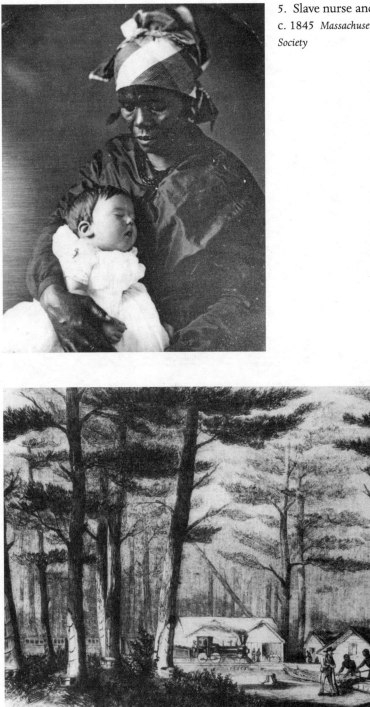

5. Slave nurse and white baby, c. 1845 *Massachusetts Historical Society*

6. South Carolina turpentine camp *Schomburg Center for Research in Black Culture/New York Public Library*

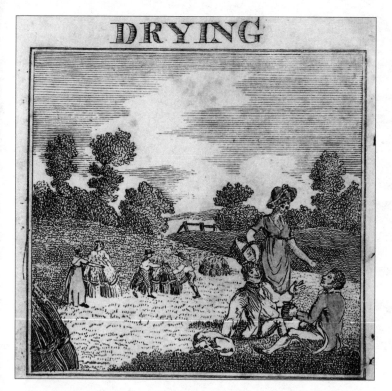

7. Drying the wheat, from *Harvest Home, Representing the Progress of Wheat* (1809) *Courtesy, American Antiquarian Society*

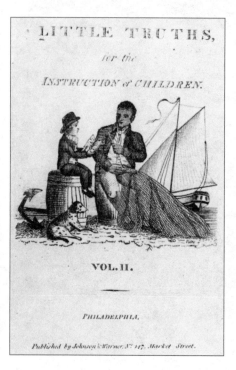

8. Black sailmaker, from William Darton, *Little Truths*, Vol. II (1812) *Courtesy, American Antiquarian Society*

9. Sergeant. Henry Steward, 54th Massachusetts Regiment, United States Army, c. 1865 *Massachusetts Historical Society*

IN THE TRENCHES.

10. Black worker for the Union army (drawing by Winslow Homer) *Courtesy, American Antiquarian Society*

11. Civil War *carte de visite* showing a black serving woman with white military officers *Massachusetts Historical Society*

12. Farmhand in Alabama cotton field, c. 1895 (photo by C. E. Battey) *Courtesy, American Antiquarian Society*

13. Mattress maker at Tuskegee Normal and Industrial Institute, c. 1895 (photo by C. E. Battey) *Courtesy, American Antiquarian Society*

14. South Carolina laborer on oxcart (photo by Doris Ulmann) *Schomburg Center for Research in Black Culture/New York Public Library*

15. Workers making webbing for bed springs, 1919 *National Archives*

16. General Electric employee winding relay coil, 1927 *National Archives*

17. Car cleaner for Southern Pacific Railroad Company, n.d. *National Archives*

18. Workers posed for General Foods Corporation promotional photograph, c. 1945 *National Archives*

19. Domestic cook, c. 1940s *National Archives*

20. Clerical workers, Aetna Life Insurance Co., 1931 *National Archives*

21. Construction workers, c. 1930s (photo by Bill Cummings) *National Archives*

22. Machine shop workers, Glen. L. Martin Aviation Co., Baltimore, c. 1941 *National Archives*

23. Portion of second shift, B-19 workmen in front of aircraft wing, c. 1942 *National Archives*

24. Fireman, c. 1930s *National Archives*

25. Workers constructing emergency wartime office space, Washington, D.C., 1941
National Archives

26. Charles A. Burns, Tuskegee airman, c. 1946 *National Archives*

27. Construction workers in Washington, D.C., c. 1942 (photo by Charles W. Collier) *National Archives*

28. Civilian Conservation Corps worker operating road-surfacing roller, Beltsville, Maryland, c. 1940 *National Archives*

29. Works Project Administration workers, c. 1943 *National Archives*

30. Marines from First Platoon, Company C, Third Reconnaissance Battalion, cross-
ing the Nong River in Vietnam during an operation to sweep clear the area, 1965
National Archives

31. Harlem service workers on strike, 1980 (photo by Coreen Simpson) *Coreen Simpson/Schomburg Center for Research in Black Culture/New York Public Library*

32. Mexican immigrants waiting for work, Alpine, San Diego County, California (photo by Richard Steven Street) *Richard Steven Street/Street Shots*

33. Mexican girls cutting grapevines for wreaths, Mecca Slope, California (photo by Richard Steven Street) *Richard Steven Street/Street Shots*

34. Ibrahim Sundiata, Victor and Gwendolyn Binfield Professor of African and Afro-American Studies, Brandeis University, c. 1996 (photo by Julian Brown) *Julian Brown/Brandeis University*

WORKERS AND OVERWORKERS

Black and White Labor in the Era of Slavery

CHAPTER SIX

BLACK AND WHITE HANDS IN A
SLAVEHOLDERS' REPUBLIC,
1790–1860

Seventy-three years after she was freed from slavery, Sarah Wilson could still remember with razor-sharp clarity the work she was forced to do as a young girl on the large plantation where she was born in Indian Territory, north of Arkansas: "Work from daylight to dark!" By the time she was fifteen, Sarah Wilson had already hoed and chopped and picked cotton in the fields, sheared sheep, fetched water, cut firewood, sewed clothes, and tended a garden; "all we done was work," she said. The elderly woman laced her recollections with reminders that the essence of slavery was forced labor of one group of people for the profit and well-being of another: "Lord, I never earned a dime of money in slave days for myself but plenty for the old Master." Other masters used incentives to extract more work from their slaves, but "Old Ben Johnson," the slave girl's owner as well as her paternal grandfather, used mainly fear and physical force. Sarah Wilson saw her sister Lottie sold "because she wouldn't have a baby," and when her aunt physically attacked Johnson, the older woman was sold, too. Sarah Wilson noted that her white mistress, Ben Johnson's wife, was afraid of the adult slaves, "but she beat us children all the time." Yet not all of the labor on this plantation took place at the behest of white people. Because the rations issued each Monday morning were inadequate to see them through the week, Ben Johnson's slaves scoured the surrounding woods for wild greens and sweet potatoes, and if they got the chance, Sarah's Cherokee grandmother and her uncle Nick would steal a cow and butcher it: "Old Master had so many cows he never did count the difference."[1]

A powerful institution of political domination, slavery nevertheless did not paint the southern social landscape in grand swaths of black and white exclusively. Sarah Wilson's mixed parentage—she was part Indian, part Caucasian, and part African-American—underscored the disingenuousness of the claim that slavery was based on "racial" differences between the master class and their slaves. Sarah Johnson and her kinfolk remained resistant to the demands imposed upon them by Ben Johnson, but they did not necessarily shirk work; clandestinely, they worked to provide for their own families through "overwork," productive labor over and beyond the tasks forced upon them by whites. Moreover, within the South's staple-crop economy, slave labor remained a relative concept—one contingent upon the alleged defects of other kinds of labor. Indeed, from the early eighteenth century through the Civil War, the status of landless whites as potential agricultural and industrial laborers remained a subject of political debate among elites. Though they rarely articulated their principles, Old Ben Johnson and thousands of other southern planters operated under the assumption that slave labor was superior—presumably for its cheapness, tractability, and self-reproducing quality—to free labor of any color.

Traveling through the slave states in the 1850s, the northern journalist Frederick Law Olmsted maintained a keen interest in this very issue, "the labor question" as it affected black and white men and women. For example, he spoke with white men who claimed that the workers they assigned to menial jobs "will not do such work if they can very well help it, and they will do no more of it than they are obliged to . . . they work reluctantly, and will not bear driving. . . ." Such complaints, expressed in the late antebellum period, anticipated the comments of staple-crop planters in the early postbellum period; after 1865, the freedpeople resisted gang labor in the fields, and preferred to cultivate small parcels of land on their own, much to the disgust of their landlord-employers. However, this particular lament quoted by Olmsted referred not to the shortcomings of slaves but to the shortcomings of free laborers—specifically, poor white men.[2] Most southern taskmasters understood that black people were more "efficient" not necessarily because they were black, but because they were slaves.

On assignment in the South on and off between 1852 and 1854, Olmsted observed a number of local economies that suggested the organic relationship between enslaved and free workers. In Virginia, planters hired their slaves out to work in mills, on canals and railroads, and in gristmills and tobacco factories. Poor whites along the coastal areas of that state "generally followed boating"—they worked by the day, for fifty cents to a dollar, and they helped farmers in their fields during the harvest, for a dollar a day.

In the turpentine forests near Fayetteville, North Carolina, Olmsted found slaves and poor whites working together; the whites ("vagabonds"), who were squatters making a living by cultivating a little corn, hunting, and foraging, were considered by their employers to be inferior workers "because they cannot be relied upon to finish what they undertake, or to work according to directions. . . ." New Orleans afforded the sight of German and Irishmen journeymen working side by side with slave artisans; although white immigrants "were rapidly displacing the slaves in all sorts of work," on Canal Street it was still possible to glimpse an "Irishman waiting on negro masons."[3]

On a backcountry cotton plantation visited by Olmsted, the twenty slaves not only worked in the fields but the women spent their evenings spinning thread "with the old-fashioned great wheel" and weaving cloth on an "ancient rude hand-loom," while men worked at a variety of other skilled tasks. By selling the baskets and cloth they made, the slaves were able to purchase religious tracts from itinerant peddlers. Even the largest staple-crop plantations boasted complex local labor systems. A sugar estate in Louisiana included a dozen white tenant families, some of whom were skilled workmen. The slaves themselves appropriated food and equipment from their master's sugarworks, and then sold their ill-gotten gain to white men who plied the Mississippi River in boats called "chicken-thieves." And on an expansive rice plantation in coastal South Carolina, Olmsted documented the task system, which allowed slaves to finish their work early in the day, and devote the rest of their time to producing handicraft goods and marketing those goods, together with poultry and garden crops, on the plantation and within a wider regional economy. Like their Louisiana counterparts, these slaves too persisted in illegal trafficking with white traders.[4]

The slave South consisted of local communities that produced and exchanged goods and services and deployed labor to accomplish those tasks. Free and slave, black and white, agricultural, industrial, and artisanal, young and old, and male and female workers stood in symbiotic relation to one another throughout the region, much as they had since the seventeenth century; yet these communities were not static, and from 1790 to 1860 the mix of labor shifted over time. It is true that in some parts of the Appalachian Mountains, demographic realities meant "that whites alone were used for every description of labour,"[5] and that, in contrast, the largest slave plantations existed as relatively self-contained entities, dependent entirely upon black workers. Yet most subregions of the South included complementary white and black and free and slave labor forces.

Members of the master class spoke eloquently about the "organic" nature of slave society—the ties of "family" that bound together the residents of a plantation or a neighborhood. Nevertheless, local patterns of hiring, selling, and volunteering labor, and of producing and exchanging goods, revealed a tangible "organic" southern community at odds with the planters' mythical one. Slavery was a political system, defined by the words and the physical power wielded by white elites; but slavery was also an economic system, defined by the work that blacks were forced to do, and the work that "common whites" either did also or refused to do.

LABOR MARKETS AND ILLICIT TRADE NETWORKS
IN THE RURAL SOUTH

The plantation served as the political and economic center of the rural antebellum South, and the plantation, variously defined, claimed a considerable proportion of the labor of the enslaved men, women, and children who resided on it. Yet black people managed to carve out separate spheres of labor for themselves as family members and community members. To a great extent, the plantation also determined the labor—the kinds of jobs, and the terms and conditions under which they were performed—of nonelite white people who lived nearby. At times the work lives of slaves and "common whites" intersected, and these encounters served as a reminder that, even within this most rigid of caste societies, the social division of labor was not static. Some cotton and tobacco fields were racially integrated worksites. Morever, outside the sight of slaveowners and overseers, blacks and whites surreptitiously attempted to redistribute some of the bounty of the plantation away from elites and into their own hands. Like the planters themselves, poor folk did not let abstract notions of racial caste stand in the way of their immediate self-interest.

The local economy, size of plantation, and labor-management proclivities of the master and mistress exerted a profound effect upon the structure of slave family life and work. The system of task labor, characteristic of the rice economy, offered slaves relatively more autonomy in terms of providing for themselves and marketing small surpluses compared to the gang system that found favor with cotton planters. For example, with as many as five hundred slaves each, the huge South Carolina low-country rice plantations boasted an impressive degree of job specialization among the enslaved men, women, and children whose labor sustained them. These plantations resembled proto-industrial, self-contained villages, with blacksmith and carpentry shops; tanneries; water-driven rice-pounding mills;

salt-boiling operations; and pottery, basket, and textile production. Slaves were assigned a variety of tasks, and at least some of them performed these jobs on a full-time, year-round basis. This list of slaves' jobs was compiled from a variety of plantation records:

> animal raisers, baby keepers, barbers, blacksmiths, boatmen, bricklayers, butchers, butlers, carpenters, coachmen, cobblers, cooks, coopers, engineers, gardeners, gunkeepers, laundresses, lumbermen, maids, nurses, pantry minders, saltworkers, seamstresses, shoemakers, stock tenders, tailors, tanners, tinsmiths, trunk minders, valets, waiters and weavers.

Years later elderly black men and women would remember with remarkable precision the tasks assigned to themselves and their parents, and distinguish boatmen from oarsmen, the steerman from "an extra man." In many cases children served as apprentices to their mothers, fathers, and grandparents: "My father run the blacksmith shop for the master on the place. I worked around the place." Young girls picked up the shuttle for their grandmothers and learned to weave in the process. Young boys helped their parents make "fish baskets, feed baskets, wood baskets, sewing baskets and all kinds of baskets for de Missus." In the early nineteenth century, as many as 25 percent of all slave men in the South Carolina low country worked outside the fields at more specialized tasks; the comparable figure for slave women was 8.5 percent.[6]

Nevertheless, these rice estates remained exceptional, and throughout the South, the overall percentage of slaves engaged in skilled labor declined during the period 1790 to 1860, a development that reflected the expansion of cotton cultivation rather than any rigid notions about the proper work for slaves. The fresh lands of Alabama, Mississippi, and Louisiana drew slaves out of the Upper South, where skill levels were high, and put them all—male and female, adult and children alike—into the fields, in a frantic drive to produce as much of the staple within as short amount of time as possible. In the Cotton Belt in 1860, the vast majority of slave men and women worked as field hands. Men predominated among the skilled crafts, mainly carpentry and blacksmithing, but only 2 to 5 percent were so employed. In that region, slave women represented more than three-quarters of all house servants, with from one-fifth to one-third of all enslaved girls and women assigned to these jobs. In the Upper South, a different dynamic obtained. A study of skilled blacks in St. Mary's County, Maryland (in the southern part of the state), suggests that increased competition from goods produced in nearby Baltimore meant that older skilled men (most of whom were carpenters, blacksmiths, and boatmen) were not replaced by younger ones. Over the generations, then, skill levels among black men deteriorated.[7]

The historic trend toward nonspecialization was in fact most striking in the case of slave women (though tobacco and cotton cultivation relied less on a gender division of labor than did sugar and rice). Women and children received specialized training in the areas of cooking and textile production, they cared for black and white babies, kept chickens and tended gardens, while men dominated the whole host of other crafts that a plantation or neighborhood might depend upon. However, where cotton was king, slave women were first and foremost field workers, and domestic servants and textile producers only if the size of the plantation warranted their diversion to work outside of agriculture. For example, in Alabama, Bill and Mary Slaughter of Opelika put their slave Sarah Colquitt to work "in de fields every day from 'fore daylight to almost plumb dark," but then sent her to the spinning house to continue to labor at night. At other times Sarah Colquitt would "hope wid de cooking up at de Big House when de real cook was sick or us had a passel of company." More often than not, the few slave men working at skilled or specialized tasks were married to women field hands. Growing up on a plantation near Mobile, Charles Hayes remembered that "My mammy was a fiel' han' an' my pappy was a mechanic . . . makin' eve'thing f'um churns an' buckets to wagon wheels."[8]

Formal work assignments depended upon a wide array of factors, and enslaved men and women exercised little direct control over them. At times a man, woman, or child might perform a task slowly or carelessly in the hope of leaving one worksite for another, but this effort entailed considerable risk of punishment or even permanent separation from loved ones, and met with success only in specific situations—the resentful young cook who wished to work in the fields, closer to members of her family, for example. In contrast, field hands could count on little in the way of job mobility, either upward or lateral. In the end, the heaviest, dirtiest work of a plantation was least likely to be gender-specific.

The tasks assumed by slaveholding women increased in proportion to the number of their bondswomen deployed exclusively in the fields. A Mississippi plantation mistress, together with her two daughters, performed the bulk of domestic work on their Marion County place because her husband (in the words of a former slave) "wouldn' waste no Nigger to help 'em out. His family was as scared o' him as we was." Later, some planters, now Confederate die-hards, would declare their determination to preserve slavery in order to preserve the privileges of their mothers, wives, and daughters, supposedly ladies of leisure. One Colonel McNairy, for example, vowed that "before he'd let his mother bake bread and his sister wash and iron, he would wade in blood up to his stirrups." Instances of planter bravado like this one concealed the fact that most slaveholding white women, like virtually every other group in antebellum southern society—with the notable exception of elite men—regularly engaged in manual labor. It was a rare mistress indeed who could avoid all of the domestic chores necessary to the smooth operation of any plantation (though even work performed together by a white woman and her slave carried with it radically divergent meanings for the two of them).[9]

Between the work that slaves were forced to perform in the fields, and the work they chose to do for themselves in the quarters, lay a realm of labor for which at least some slaves received specific kinds of payment. These incentives were highly contingent upon the whims of a master; while slaves in the Cotton Belt of Georgia came to expect cash wages for the cotton they picked on Sunday, their customary day off, at least some of the slaves on Morris Island, South Carolina, could not: "Master paid us no money for work," recalled Joe Rutherford many years later, adding however that his master did allow the slaves to "hunt and fish, and [get] lots of game round there." In the wintertime, plantation ditchers on James Henry Hammond's Silver Bluff, South Carolina, plantation received a dram of whiskey every night (liquor mixed with water), a form of compensation for cold, wet work. In some instances slave women could count on rewards for having children, and drivers and craftsmen might get cash bonuses at the end of the year; in other instances they did not.[10]

Slave family members also toiled on their own behalf when they provided directly for their own needs. Women cooked, and they mended and laundered clothes, but only after they had met the demands of their master and mistress. They remained at the spinning wheel and the loom, their assigned nightly tasks completed, to make clothes for their husbands and children. Men fished, went hunting, and fashioned household utensils and furniture from wood, but only at night, or on Saturday afternoon or Sunday, and in fact the nature and extent of this kind of work depended on the organization of the plantation. As a matter of principle, the less time devoted to forced labor, the more time devoted not to "leisure" but to labor performed within the context of an internal slave economy.

In the antebellum South, the slaves' bartering and selling practices were not nearly as extensive as those characteristic of their West Indian counterparts, who dominated the internal economies of their respective islands. Nevertheless, presented with the opportunity, American bondsmen and women engaged in a lively form of trade that afforded them a modest amount of control over their material lives, and in some cases allowed them, either openly or clandestinely, to recoup a small amount of the fruits of their own labor. As we have seen, barter relations among Anglos, blacks, and Indians were integral to borderland economies, and those traditions persisted, in constricted form, within subsequent plantation societies. For example, when the United States acquired Florida in 1821, Anglo settlers could not help but comment on the presence of slaves who operated as "free dealers" in soliciting work for themselves, venturing forth to "trade as . . . free person[s]."[11]

The southern internal slave economy was part of larger, local informal economies that claimed the energies of several groups—the slaves themselves, masters and mistresses, poor whites and free blacks in the vicinity of plantations, and even in some cases interregional traders. When slaves appropriated supplies from their masters' corncribs and smokehouses, and traded their booty with poor whites, they tried to carve out a sphere of autonomous behavior for themselves, not unlike their efforts to name their own children, conduct their own worship services, and choose their own mates. This form of activity—which slaves considered taking their due and masters considered stealing—was of a piece with breaking farm equipment and mistreating livestock, for it represented a direct assault on the private property of slaveowners (a problematic concept on the plantation, where people too were considered private property). On the other hand, in some cases planters encouraged slaves to provide for themselves, over and above the allowances allotted them, when they deliberately withheld adequate supplies of food and clothing. The whites intended that black men and women would either grow some of their own food or use whatever money they had earned from overwork to purchase necessities of life. Viewed from this perspective, efforts by slaves to market small surpluses of eggs (for example) reflected a central principle of the slave regime—the determination of white men and women to wring every bit of energy from their slaves, and to hold out modest material gains as "incentives" for black men and women to work even harder.[12]

Petty commodity production reached its most dramatic form in the coastal regions of South Carolina, those areas where West African marketing traditions survived to the greatest extent. By the time of the Civil War, Mary Jess, a slave "dairy woman" on one of James Potter's rice plantations, had accumulated cows, "full-grown hogs—fat," turkeys, chickens, household utensils, blankets, bedding, thirty beehives, syrup, stone jars filled with lard, a sack of coffee, two sacks of flour, sugar, chewing tobacco, and port wine, among other things. "This property all belonged to Mrs. Jess [because] she was allowed privileges that other servants didn't enjoy," recalled a neighbor in admiration. "She was allowed to raise poultry & stock & cattle. She sold them when she pleased—& she worked a garden. She worked and earned money outside her regular task work—." In other areas of the South the same impulses obtained, though with less dramatic results. In the late 1840s, a northern visitor to Mississippi marveled that some slaves made money "so as to be able . . . to supply [their] own little wants" by "raising poultry, making baskets and brooms, gathering moss, doing overwork Saturdays and evenings, for which they are paid, and by cultivating a crop for themselves. . . ." On the Gay family estate in the sugar district of Louisiana, slaves received payment from their masters for certain services like fixing kettles and cutting wood, and for gathering moss and cutting hay. With the money they earned they purchased coffee, food, cloth, saddles, boots, shawls, and eating utensils, among other items.[13]

Yet it was slaves in this same general area of Louisiana who earned a bad reputation for succumbing to the blandishments of Mississippi riverboat traders, stripping their masters' estates of expensive pieces of machinery and bits of pipe and brass—in effect handing over hundreds of dollars' worth of material, often in return "for a drink." Thus the slaves' spirit of enterprise could spill out of the confines of the plantation and into an immediate neighborhood, where whites of various stations waited eagerly to receive the goods purloined from "swell-head" (arrogant) aristocrats, and to offer commensurate payment, usually liquor. (In return for one and a half bushels of corn, James W. Wilson gave to a slave in Jasper County, Georgia, in 1846, "cider whiskey rum gin and other intoxicating liquours for his own use.") Indeed, the beverages flowing from countless stills helped to lubricate relations between slaves and poor whites all over the South. Slaves furnished to whites a variety of stolen supplies and foodstuffs, but usually received clothes, liquor, or money in return.[14]

This trade relied primarily on the resourcefulness of slave men and poor white men within a specific neighborhood, but other groups participated as well. In Georgia, Patsy Elliot (it is unclear whether she was a free Negro or a white woman) was sentenced to five days in the county jail for buying seven pounds of bacon and a "handkerchief of flower" from "a certain negro Man slave named Joe the property of Henry Walker. . . ." Respectable whites regarded transients of both races, as well as itinerant peddlers, with justifiable suspicion. In 1858, a planter near Vicksburg alerted readers of the city's newspaper to the fact that officials had recently apprehended a "certain white man of your city, by the name of Landfair, and a negro by the name of

Peterson." Together the pair made forays into the surrounding countryside with their peddling wagons, "hiding in the woods in order to traffic and trade with our negroes, buying all the stolen property and other things they can get, paying them in whiskey." The black man, a slave, reported that he had hired "his own time," though he had no pass to prove it. Yet not all of these illicit traffickers were outcasts and reprobates; even respectable factory owners, tavern keepers, and grocery-store owners proved ready and willing customers of slaves who were traders.[15]

Out of these impulses, slaves and their white customers forged a material economy that had moral and political implications. On one level, planters fully comprehended the forces that impelled the landless of both races to create trading networks, no matter how fleeting or flimsy. In the words of one South Carolina bard:

> Barnwell district, Aiken town
> O Lord in Mercy do look down!
> The land is poor, the people too;
> If they don't steal what will they do?

Nevertheless, most slaveowners agreed that "The crime of trading with slaves, is not such an offense against the person or property of the citizen, as can be privately settled by the mere act of the parties"; in other words, it warranted state intervention, or at least formal community action. When slaves claimed some of their masters' food, they filled their own bellies and that was pretty much the end of it. But when slaves marketed their illicit gain among themselves, and among whites, they participated in a wider network of exchange that threatened the master's authority over all poor people in the immediate area. Near Augusta, Georgia, planters formed the Savannah River Anti-Slave Traffick Association in 1846, an effort to limit the depredations of both the trading slave, described as a "serpent knawing at [society's] vitals or a demon ready with knife and torch to demolish its foundations," and the poor white man, whose actions were "more potent than [those of] the abolitionist" in undermining the institution of bondage. Still, some prominent white men could do little but watch uneasily as defense lawyers urged juries to nullify statutes that outlawed the practice of slaves trafficking in stolen goods. In 1854, a Bryan County, Georgia, attorney aggressively defended a white man accused of trading with a slave. The plaintiff, the son of a local slaveholder, had suspected the defendant of purchasing goods illegally from one of his father's slaves, and so had furnished the slave with cotton and sent him off to the defendant's house "while [the slaveowner's son] went to watch their pro-ceedings." Presumably the lawyer hoped to convince the jurors that this type of entrapment represented an affront to community standards of jus-tice and fair play. Nevertheless, the defendant in this case was found guilty.[16]

Historians disagree about the extent to which the ties that bound together the community of whites—ties based on shared bloodlines, reli-gious practices, and reciprocal obligations of debtor and creditor—tran-scended their divergent economic statuses. The very poorest southern whites in all probability were too transient to be bound by such relations in any case. Still, nonelite whites, slaves, and free Negroes might perceive their immediate, day-to-day (or night-to-night) material interests to be somehow interrelated, without expressing those interests in any formal political way. Because liquor ranked high on the slaves' list of desired black-market com-modities, many no doubt saw their white partners in trade merely as vehicles for obtaining a brief psychological release, rather than as co-conspirators against the planter elite.[17]

The illegal trading practices of blacks and poor whites represented a rem-nant of colonial days, when slaves formed an integral part of local barter economies. In the South during the era of the American Revolution, the planter elite helped to justify and codify dramatic distinctions between the black poor and the white poor. These developments gave new meaning to interracial illicit trade, for the poor of both races sought to advance their immediate material self-interest in ways that were inimical to the planters' ideology of race. Even elaborate slave codes could not deter black men and women from seeking to provide for themselves and their families, relying on neighboring poor whites if need be. Under the cover of darkness, then, the trafficking carried on between free whites at the lowest echelons of the labor force and enslaved blacks gave new meaning to the planters' ideal of an "organic" society in which black people's labor complemented white people's labor—or the lack thereof, as the case might be.

EXPENSIVE SLAVES, "WORTHLESS" WHITES, AND FREE NEGROES IN BETWEEN: COSTS AND BENEFITS OF FREE AND BOUND WORKERS

Faced with the arduous and disagreeable task of clearing his swampy fields for cultivation, one of the few remaining Virginia Tidewater planters who grew large quantities of tobacco in the 1850s decided to contract with "an Irish gang" of workers to do the job for him. The planter eventually expressed disgust with what he considered their slovenly work pace, and with the "sprees and quarrels" that seriously impaired their efficiency. Although a slaveowner, he preferred to use white men in this case because draining swamps was so injurious to health: "It's dangerous work, and a negro's life is too valuable to be risked at it. If a negro dies, it's a considerable loss, you know." With slaves as hired workers commanding high prices from urban and industrial employers throughout the region, and with slaves as property commanding high prices from domestic slave traders, the planter calculated that bondsmen and women served him better as investments, and free white men served him better as laborers.[18]

This particular plantation, with its slave capital and free labor, was a product of a specific time and place—late antebellum Virginia. Outside the cities and the Upper South, few southern landowners enjoyed the option of hiring relatively cheap Irish immigrants in lieu of risking the physical well-being of expensive slaves. Nevertheless, many (but not all) planters throughout the southern states were forced to sort out a tangle of economic and political factors in deciding whether to buy slaves or hire them, whether to hire free labor—and if so, white or black, as tenants or hirelings—for any part of the year, or all of the year. Within this slave society, free Negroes, together with landless whites, represented potential sources of alternative and supplementary labor even as their very existence mocked the rhetorical premises of the slaveholder's republic: that all black people were slaves, and that all white people, rich and poor, prospered in relation to black people.

The fluidity in land-tenure relations among whites, and in material well-being among blacks, suggested that class and "racial" lines remained somewhat ill-defined in the antebellum South. April Ellison, a South Carolina free Negro cotton gin maker who was also a slaveowner, together with the poor white woman who worked as a domestic servant for a free black artisan in the North Carolina Piedmont, offered striking examples of "racial" role reversals; but their numbers were too small to have much social significance in the South as a whole. During the late antebellum period, elites began to debate the merits of reenslaving the free black population, and controlling white "vagabonds" and "idlers" lacking any "visible means of support." By that time the war for southern independence was at hand.[19]

The early nineteenth century witnessed the receding of the late eighteenth-century egalitarian impulse among elites that had freed so many slaves. Thereafter, new manumissions centered in the cities, where skilled artisans and relatively privileged house servants were much more likely either to buy their own freedom or receive it from a master or mistress. As a result, free blacks became ever more concentrated in the cities; in 1860, about a third of free Negroes in the Upper South, and more than half in the Lower South, lived in urban areas (compared to 15 percent of all southern whites and 5 percent of all southern slaves). Further, many free Negroes lived along the coast, in Delaware, Maryland, Virginia, and North Carolina, where fully one-half of the total group was located.[20]

As a political issue, free people of color were far more visible than their relatively small numbers would suggest. Although less than 2 percent of all Lower South blacks were free in 1860, most of the states in that region took pains to detain or sequester the free seamen who sailed into their ports from other parts of the country, or the world, out of fear that these outsiders would provoke domestic black populations to rebel against their masters. In the Upper South, where 13 percent of all blacks were free by the late ante-bellum period, the needs of a revitalized industrial economy—that is, a heightened demand for labor—clashed with efforts to regulate free blacks and their movements. Virginia's revised manumission law of 1806 provided that all freed slaves must leave the Commonwealth within twelve months or face reenslavement. Twenty-five years later, determined to rein in the small but potentially dangerous free Negro population after Nat Turner's revolt, the Virginia legislature provided that free blacks might not learn to read or write, assemble for religious purposes apart from whites, immigrate into the state, bear arms, or sell goods without written proof of their ownership. Some towns went so far as to prohibit blacks from holding jobs as preachers and shopkeepers.[21]

As efforts to limit the growth of the free black population, these legislative initiatives were largely successful, and they forced black parents and children to confront the painful choice between remaining in an area with loved ones as slaves, or leaving their ancestral homes altogether, without family members, as nominally free people. But at times these laws also worked against the economic priorities of local white communities. Some free Negroes solicited and received the support of white patrons in gaining an exemption from the law; and black men and women who performed traditionally "black" work had an advantage in these cases. For example, in 1850, the ninety-three white men (including judges, lawyers, and members of the county executive council) who supported the successful petition of Harriet Cook, a black washerwoman in Loudoun County, argued, "It would be a serious inconvenience to a number of the citizens of Leesburg to be deprived of her services as a washerwoman and in other capacities in which in consequence of her gentility, trustworthiness and skill she is exceedingly useful." The petitioners added that as long as Harriet Cook devoted herself only to laundering for whites, "no possible injury" could come from her residence in the county.[22]

Although some free Negroes were members of large, extended networks of proud, landholding kin, most remained desperately poor. Those without even a small piece of land, and without a white patron or guardian, patched together a living through fishing, foraging, and odd jobs, avoiding long-term commitments to landowners who would just as soon reduce them to a state of near peonage as pay them at the end of the year. Skilled craftsmen, their ability to move in search of better work opportunities restricted by law, and faced with increased competition from whites, turned to day labor to make a living for their families. As field hands paid in food or clothing, not cash, they were dependent on the whims of white landowners who might or might not prefer to hire white men and women during the busy harvest season. Compared to poor white women, black women were disproportionately the economic mainstays of their households, and found limited employment as domestic servants, laundresses, weavers, and spinners. Yet these wage-earning activities could not insulate them from a persistently precarious legal status; they remained subject to imprisonment or an indeterminate sentence of forced labor for minor criminal offenses. Convicted of the crime of bearing a mulatto child, or bearing any child out of wedlock, poor black women could do little but watch helplessly while their children were bound out as "apprentices" to local white landowners.[23]

The poverty and vulnerability of free Negroes of both sexes and all ages had a mixed impact upon their status as workers. Within local labor markets, white employers practiced a great deal of selectivity in hiring. The free black man, woman, or child who resided on a slave plantation under "contract" for years at a time lived a life not that different from a slave; on the other hand, groups of free black kin who sought to negotiate with a landowner eager for harvest hands more nearly approximated the ideal of free laborers, with some leverage over their wages.

Between these two extremes lay a host of trade-offs for the employers. Chronically underemployed, most free blacks tended to work for less pay than poor whites. In some cases they possessed a sufficient amount of experience (as watermen or sawyers, for example), or demonstrated a sufficient amount of deference (as cooks and domestics) to make them appealing to white employers. Tavern patrons in general had no patience for white workers like the one encountered by a traveler in North Carolina, a woman servant "so drunk that she would not cook me any Dinner." Indeed, whites universally perceived black people (compared to poor whites) as relatively if not absolutely obsequious, a condition attendant upon their legal status. Yet some white employers were sensitive to the warnings of their (white) neighbors, who claimed that for every free Negro hired, one white man suffered the loss of a job, and perhaps even left the county for good. In areas where tensions between free Negroes and poor whites ran high, employers might reckon the political costs of hiring even very cheap black labor as unacceptably high.[24]

Depending on the structure of their regional economies, nonslaveowning whites all over the South participated in local labor markets either as hirelings or as the hirers of slave or free labor. White tenants and small landowners in the Upper South lived in an area where gristmills and tobacco factories offered wage-earning possibilities; their Cotton Belt counterparts on the other hand found themselves moving to the rhythms of the staple-crop economy, and dependent upon their wealthy neighbors for loans of slaves and money. In the Piedmont of the Lower South, yeomen farmers and poor whites attempted to insulate themselves from the larger national and international market economy, relying on barter and exchange in a bid for regional self-sufficiency, free of cotton merchants and bankers. In the South as a whole, about three-quarters of all white families owned no slaves, and they ranged in status from yeomen farmers, who together with their wives and children worked with a hired slave or two during the busiest seasons of the year; to tenants who attempted to make do with family labor employed either on their own holdings or hired out to neighbors for part of the year; to squatters and transients, men and women who resisted sedentary labor (if they could avoid it) in favor of herding cattle, fishing, hunting, and foraging.[25]

Within this variegated class system, elites argued that the sight of white men, women, and children stooped over picking cotton with blacks (bound or free) was not particularly threatening to the South's peculiar division of labor as long as those "labourers in the lower strata above the slaves" aspired to a better life—that is, as long as they hoped to own slaves of their own. Thus the southern editor James B. DeBow and other ideologues could argue that manual labor was personally degrading only when performed by slaves, not by men and women who worked with future gain in mind. The sweat of a young tenant nourished his dreams of landownership; the exertions of the apprentice paved the way for a shop of his own someday; the artisan's skills served as a ticket to the accumulation of capital and slaves; and the destitute father's load was lightened by the relative success of his son, a young man "who had nothing to do but drive a team; he did n't [sic] have to load, and he had a nigger to take care of the horses when his day's teaming was done."

Nevertheless, some older men who had little to show for a lifetime of labor, or a lifetime of avoiding it, earned little more than the scorn of their social betters, along with a dollar a day, for venison delivered or cotton rows hoed. At times, too, the slaves expressed their contempt for that group of whites who seemed bent on squandering their (purely relative) advantages. Charlie Hudson, born a slave on an Elbert County, Georgia, plantation, leveled the ultimate indictment against a poor white man, the head of the Sims family, who lived just down the road. Though he had "a big drove of chillun," Sims "never wukked a lick in his life—He jus' lived on other folkses' labors." Slaveowners did not work either—they lived off the labor of other people— but few lived in squalor like the Sims, separated from their livestock by a partition in their dirt-floor cabin.[26]

Many nonslaveholding whites, landed and landless alike, pieced together a livelihood that required the energies of all family members, but provided only sporadic and unpredictable income. James Bennitt in Chatham County, North Carolina, managed to parlay loans and a small inheritance into a farm of 325 acres by the time he was forty years old. After that he farmed and made money by selling liquor to neighbors and hauling their crops to the market in town. His wife Nancy performed most of the labor necessary to run a small boardinghouse business, and she also sewed clothes that she later sold. All of the family members, together with a hired slave, made shoes for their own use and also for extra income. A family economy like the Bennitts' ensured that local planters could count on extra hired hands during the harvest season, but it also raised the specter of able-bodied whites subsisting on their own for part of the year, without engaging in "productive" (i.e., waged) labor of any kind.[27]

Slaveowners periodically hired landless whites, but with the exception of skilled craftsmen who rendered highly specialized services, these workers were considered stubbornly resistant to any kind of task that required much in the way of either deference or discipline. Overseers were notorious for their high rates of turnover; on the job they were either too lax or too eager to wield the whip. (Noted one exasperated South Carolina rice planter, "I have not an overseer that is intrinsically worth the hominy he eats.") Some planters hired rent collectors to make monthly or annual rounds among tenants, and some took in poor white children as "apprentices," to be used whatever way they deemed appropriate. Some white women found places as governesses and seamstresses within the households of wealthy whites; they occupied an awkward place within the household, insisting upon being called "Mrs." or eating at the same table with the family, though their employers saw them primarily as employees. Whites of all classes abided by racially exclusive labor codes and customs of their own devising. Thus, in certain areas of Virginia, it was common knowledge that white men would not herd cattle or fetch wood or water for household use, and that white women and girls would sew for wages but not perform menial labor in the home of another white person.[28]

White men, women, and children worked in their own fields, and yet some also worked alongside slaves in the fields of planters. Though primarily responsible for their own parcels, white tenants might be called upon to supplement black labor when the cotton bolls appeared and the peas grew high. Some whites hired for a day or week at a time expressed bitterness that they were driven to such lengths. In Randolph County, North Carolina, Brantly York and his brother had to work for neighbors after their father's business failed. Brantly recalled, "We had shoes, but not socks or coats. Soon after we reached the place of our destination, the weather turned quite cold and very heavy frosts fell at night. We with the negroes were sent out before sunrise to pull corn. . . . We suffered extremely from the cold. This was our lot every morning." Children often resented the highhandedness of fathers who forced them to work under such conditions, but parents might place family need over personal pride. The wife of John Brown, a hunter with a large family in northern Alabama, requested a neighbor to allow her to go into his fields "with the niggers and pick" some cotton, taking "her pay in corn" for the benefit of her hungry children.[29]

On the fringes of rural southern society, whites and blacks continued to be thrown together as paupers and as workers, as they had been for generations. During the first four decades of the nineteenth century, the Beckford Parish Poor House in Shenandoah, Virginia, was a racially integrated worksite reminiscent of colonial institutions that lumped social outcasts and the infirm together with the elderly and children on the assumption that poverty, disease, and criminality were all interrelated. The white inmates included elderly farmers and "spinsters," men and women no longer able to care for themselves and lacking supportive networks of kin and friends. Some were listed as blind or "insane." Another group of whites consisted of unmarried mothers with their children. The black inmates were primarily free women with children, with at least one older slave woman ("Mary [negro]") apparently committed to the institution because her owner no longer wished to be burdened by feeding her. The poorhouse was a working farm, and the inmates were expected to labor in the fields (at times with a hired white man), the crops they produced sold to maintain the operation. Some of the women of both races saw their children bound out to white landowners in the area—Nancy Beech's one-month-old was taken by

Samuel Summers in October 1837, and Frances Henry's four children, ages one to thirteen, were divided between two different white men. Some of the inmates left "by consent," and others in time-honored fashion "deserted" or "absconded" from their poorhouse guardians.[30]

Southern planters, then, did not limit field work to black people exclusively. At the same time, certain kinds of field work became associated with blacks—or rather, with slaves—because whites managed to steer clear of such tasks. For example, in antebellum Kentucky, hemp became known as a "nigger crop" not because poor whites eschewed all kinds of agricultural labor but because growing hemp (and also breaking the tough stalks in particular) was "very dirty, and so laborious that scarcely any white man will work at it." Apparently whites in the area could take care of themselves and their families by finding other work. The view that "none but our strong able negro men can handle [hemp] to advantage" gave rise to the widespread belief after the Civil War that black men were somehow naturally suited to this type of work, "superior" in their abilities to grow hemp compared to white men. Other crops like cotton and tobacco were seen not necessarily as "nigger crops," but rather as crops that whites as well as blacks might grow, with the crucial difference that the white men, women, and children had the freedom to imagine a point in their lives when they might escape that kind of work altogether.[31]

In the antebellum southern countryside, interracial workforces anticipated the expansion of the proto-industrial and extractive sectors after the Civil War. Blacks both slave and free worked with whites in ore mines, on roadbeds, and on railroad construction projects in the southern Appalachian Mountains. In 1856, the account book of D. B. Hawkins & Co, contractors for the Raleigh and Gaston Railroad, included hired slaves, and white hands hired by the day or month, several of whom, like Preston Lyle, were illiterate. These whites included draymen and laborers as well as blacksmiths and stonecutters. Men of both races toiled together in backcountry forests, as miners and timber and turpentine workers, and on the canals of the Upper South as ditchdiggers.[32]

Planters might have few options other than to tolerate the collective shortcomings of blacks, slave and free, and poor whites—their laziness, promiscuity, and supposedly congenital disposition to lie and steal. However, elites were prepared to take stern measures at the first hint of overt political collusion between blacks and nonslaveholding whites. Rumors of slave conspiracies invariably implicated alleged white conspirators—northerners, shopkeepers—men happy to provide slaves with moral support, even if that "support" came only in the form of sharing a bottle of whiskey down a road deep in the countryside in the middle of the night. At times, confessed black rebels confirmed such rumors. These were men who claimed, perhaps out of hopefulness as much as conviction, "I have joined with both black and white which is the common men or poor white people, mulattoes will join with me to help free the country, although they are free already." (This from Arthur, a slave admitting to his involvement in a plot in Goochland County, Virginia, in 1802.)[33]

Yet by many accounts of slave plots where white men and women figured prominently, the liberal use of alcohol considerably clouded the issue. The slaveholding elite worried that slaves and free Negroes and poor whites would make common cause against that group of whites that variously owned, employed, or otherwise lorded over them. But so powerful were the mechanisms of social control over all blacks, and so entrenched the political and economic power of the master class, that neither biracial groups of cotton pickers, nor biracial groups of late-night revelers could muster the requisite number of firearms, or the requisite amount of moral authority or even desire, to challenge the existing political order. Instead, together, they resisted working the way overseers and employers wanted them to work.[34]

Together with other planters, James Henry Hammond, the South Carolina politician and theoretician of slavery, well understood that all labor systems were relative; pressed to state whether or not he was "an advocate of Slavery in the abstract," he would "probably answer, that I am not. . . ." Still, compared to the heartless wage slavery of the North, southern slavery had much to recommend it, in Hammond's view. Ordained by God as a means of harnessing the energies of, and providing moral and physical sustenance for, the ignorant and degraded, slavery stood as testimony to the glory and honor of the slaveholding elite. Within Hammond's private writings, however, another story unfolded, one considerably less tidy than his black-and-white defense of slavery would allow. For his public audience, Hammond wrote as if the black population constituted the South's sole laboring "mudsill" population; but he himself rarely tired of denouncing the "worthlessness & obstinacy" of the white hirelings he encountered in the Augusta hinterland.[35]

In 1850, Hammond advocated the employment of poor whites in southern textile mills on the assumption that steady wage work would give them more settled occupations compared to scavenging, hunting, and fishing, and also keep them from "a precarious subsistence by occasional jobs, by what is in its effects, far worse—trading with slaves, and seducing them to plunder for their benefit." As the owner of hundreds of slaves, Hammond relied less on white labor than did some of the smaller slaveholders in his area. Still, even he had to contend with overseers who indulged too freely in drink and who resisted the terms of employment outlined in their contracts; they must always inform him of their whereabouts "on any day" and never absent themselves from the plantation "for a single night or whole day" without receiving permission from their employer." Hammond also listed "running away" and "getting drunk or having liquor" as the two most serious offenses of slaves on his plantation.[36]

This is not of course to suggest that there existed a rough symmetry of black and white landless folk on either side of the planters' ledgerbook. Black men slaves might serve as "drivers" over other slaves, but they never served as overseers. Likewise, planters made extensive use of white field hands if such hands were available and willing to work, but no matter how arduous their labors, whites were never reduced to slavery. The demands of plantation work necessitated a certain fungibility between bound and free labor. However, in the end, the social and political limitations imposed upon free Negroes revealed that status in the slave South grew out of "racial" considerations based not on color or legal condition but on a family heritage that whites identified as either African or non-African. Presumably that fact was sufficient to allow even the poorest whites to accommodate themselves, no matter how grudgingly, to the slaveholders' republic.

"WHENEVER WE SEE A NEGRO WE PRE-SUPPOSE A MASTER": URBAN SLAVERY

Urban slavery too was part of a larger labor system that claimed the energies of whites as well as blacks; but the city scene was complicated by the sheer diversity of available jobs and by the ethnic diversity of the whites who stood ready to do those jobs. Though boasting less in the way of industrial development compared to northern urban centers, early nineteenth-century southern cities included busy ports (Charleston, Savannah, St. Louis, and New Orleans), cotton entrepots (Louisville, Mobile, and Memphis), and centers of manufacturing (Richmond). Slaves, free people of color, southern-born whites, Western European immigrants, men and women, adults and children: The urban labor force brought together a number of overlapping groups competing for work, legal and illegal. The intensity of this competition is suggested by the fact that although slaves or free Negroes might dominate certain jobs, there were no "racially" exclusive jobs at the lower echelons of the labor force in any southern city. At the same time, among all of these groups the skilled slave and skilled free man of color stood out as symbols of a larger dilemma: in asserting their competence they made money for their owners and employers, but mocked slavery as a system of social control, and riled their white rivals in the process. By the late antebellum period, a substantial proportion of slaves had been siphoned off from southern towns and relocated to the spreading cotton fields in the southwestern part of the region. Vulnerable to attack from poor whites, free Negroes remaining in urban areas faced a bleak future that foreshadowed life in the postwar South.[37]

In the cities, many employers favored slave labor over free labor, claiming that enslaved blacks were more easily controlled than free whites (or free blacks), prompting white workers (native-born and foreign-born) to call for the election of "faithful members to the Legislature, who will make it penal to prefer negro mechanic labor to white men's." These disagreements stemmed from the ultimately ambiguous nature of the institution of bondage itself. Slavery was simultaneously a legal status assigned to an individual at birth, a system of labor force management, and a system of regionwide political control. At times these multiple facets of slavery came into conflict with one another, with elites as urban masters allowing their slaves considerable latitude in seeking work on their own, but elites as city councilors and state legislators passing measures to limit the freedom of city slaves. Within the antebellum South, the value of white workers was gauged by a complicated formula, one that took into account the relative financial advantages and the relative military and internal-security disadvantages that flowed from the use of slave labor.[38]

Between 1815 and 1860, the social division of labor in the urban South shifted to reflect population movements and changes in demographic patterns. In 1860, about 10 percent of southern urban workingmen had been born in the North (suggesting a modest but noticeable north-south migration flow in the antebellum period), and workers born in other countries (primarily Germany and Ireland) constituted a large proportion of free men employed in all of the major southern cities. For example, 44 percent of all the skilled free workingmen in Baton Rouge were immigrants, 54 percent in Mobile, and 36 percent in Richmond; the comparable figures for immigrant unskilled free workingmen in those cities were 57 percent, 69 percent, and 46 percent, respectively. In the largest cities, free blacks numbered no more than one out of ten of all workers, but the proportion of slaves ranged as high as more than one-half (in Charleston).[39]

Much like their northern counterparts, the southern white working classes advanced the idea that no urban job at all was the appropriate province of black people exclusively, and challenged slaves and free people of color in manual and skilled work alike. Nevertheless, slavery and black labor in general continued to reach deep into nonagricultural pursuits. In Charleston, blacks predominated in the construction trades as carpenters, plasterers, bricklayers, and coopers. In Richmond, free men of color constituted more than half of all barbers and plasterers, and slaves were used extensively in iron forges and tobacco factories. In Savannah, free black women were prominent among the city's pastry cooks, seamstresses, and hawkers, as well as among washerwomen and domestic servants. During the half century before the Civil War, immigrants displaced free black workers in certain cities, eliminating free black cartmen in St. Louis and Baltimore, for example, and free black tailors in Richmond. The "slave-holding bosses" of the New Orleans construction trades worked immigrants and slaves together, but in other occupations in that city a combination of ethnic groups and migrants from New England were pushing slaves out of their jobs as "cartmen, hackney-coach men, porters, railroad hands, public waiters, and common labourers, as well as of skilled mechanics."[40]

In contrast, the skilled free black men of Charleston held their own despite an influx of unskilled Irish laborers, beginning in the mid-1840s, highlighting the uniqueness of local economies in establishing particular social divisions of labor. In the primitive law enforcement system of that city, Irish laborers found jobs as policemen at night, an occupation that was ill-paid but remained for obvious reasons all-white; on the other hand, free men of color served in the slave patrols of antebellum New Orleans, and Savannah residents relied on slave firefighters exclusively. Depending on the time period, in Columbus, Georgia, the textile mill workers were all white; in Athens, they were mixed, black and white; and in Saluda Factory near Columbia, South Carolina, they were all black. Even black women found it increasingly difficult to maintain an occupational niche which, for free blacks, served as the only means to support their families; for example, in Charleston in 1860, the number of Irish domestics (280) was almost equal to that of free blacks in that job category (287). In sum, within the realm of manual and skilled work, there was no single southern notion of "black man's work" or "black woman's work," but rather a fluid definition of the appropriate work for certain groups, depending on the relative supply of black and white, slave and free, skilled and unskilled workers in any particular time and place.[41]

A restless mix of sailors from distant lands, quasi-free slaves and quasi-slave free Negroes, and poor white laborers (many of them packing knives, pikes, or pistols), all made southern cities cauldrons of social disorder and sources of fear for the slaveholding elite. Nevertheless, in their quest for schools for their children, customers for their businesses, and safety for their families, some free people of color aimed for a settled and respectable life pointedly at odds with the riotous urban scene that engulfed the poor of both races. For example, a group of relatively well-to-do (and propertied) free black women in Savannah helped to found the First African Baptist Church in that city (in 1788) and served as "church mothers," the backbone of the Sunday School and benevolent and temperance societies. Yet over the course of the antebellum period, a gradual constriction of job opportunities boded ill for the future of relatively well-to-do free blacks and their children. Thus, from the 1830s through the 1850s in Savannah and throughout the urban South, the American Colonization Society found a receptive audience for its emigration plans among some well-educated free people of color. In 1848, H. B. Stewart requested more information about Liberia on behalf of other free people in Savannah, seeking "delivernce fr the present Bondege an degredation they ear labering ounder." He listed machinists, tailors, engineers, masons, blacksmiths, farmers, and ministers among those considering the move. Increased competition from white tradesmen, combined with the growing suspicion with which all whites regarded free men and women of color, struck at the heart of otherwise relatively stable families and communities.[42]

The efficient exploitation of slave and free black labor mandated that whites recognize and utilize talent wherever they could find it. However, the drive for efficiency provoked unintended social consequences, especially in the case of the urban slave artisanal class. Skilled black men derived pride from a kind of work that provided them with cash incentives and a modest control over their productive energies, a kind of work that blended artistry and usefulness, at times under physically hazardous conditions. These men (too proud, in the eyes of whites) served as leaders of their communities and as inspirations for their children. Drawing upon his own skills as a ship caulker, Frederick Douglass developed a political consciousness that eventually threatened the authority of his master; Douglass transformed himself from a slave at the beck and call of whites to a slave biding his time until he could make good his escape. Still, pride of craft came at a high price—for some men who were hired out, separation from loved ones, and for all of them, the fate of all slaves in the form of year-in, year-out work without commensurate compensation. The contrast between their sense of competence and their degraded legal status could have explosive ramifications. The plot associated with Denmark Vesey, a former slave and a carpenter in Charleston in 1822, provided more than enough proof to nervous whites of the revolutionary potential of skilled blacks in cities.[43]

Whites had no trouble identifying those tasks that they considered dangerous to the public order when performed by black people. Boatmen and teamsters had access to other people's goods, and the lively black-market trade included everything from building construction materials to food and liquor and clothing. Carriage drivers, waiters, and domestic servants had access to information provided by unself-conscious whites bantering with each other about subjects of great political sensitivity—the evils of abolitionist literature, the need to quell the loud, "rude" behavior of the black population on Sundays. Jobs like domestic service necessitated intimate contact with whites; though a fixture in southern households, black cooks were also prominent in the pantheon of notorious slaves who had poisoned masters, mistresses, and their dinner guests. Rivermen and seamen of all descriptions had access to water, which provided escape, and the means to other ports where racial restrictions played less of a part of public life. It was unclear who was more threatening to southern slavery, the fugitive slave boatman hired by an obliging captain and making his way north, or the free Negro sailor recently returned home with news about the latest speech of abolitionists in Boston.[44]

Besides singling out certain kinds of tasks that seemed to lend themselves to danger, whites also quite rightly pinpointed the conditions of any number of jobs that allowed black people the time and opportunity to engage in suspect activities. Enslaved men and women who learned to read, and then seized the chance to read in the course of the workday, were considered potential troublemakers. Jobs that involved group labor, or provided time for carousing at night in a waterfront tavern, encouraged breaches of the peace, and might also serve as a cover for the plotting of slave "risings." Thus crews of black street construction workers were equally implicated with slave blacksmiths who hired themselves out, the first group by virtue of their collective labor in close proximity to each other day after day, the second by virtue of their relative freedom to spend their time away from work as they wished. Clearly, if white elites had been consistent in limiting slaves and free people of color only to "safe" jobs that afforded the requisite amount of supervision, they would have had to forego much of their dependence on black labor altogether.

Throughout the South, lawmakers grappled with ways to control the apparently subversive consequences of the employment of free blacks and self-hired slaves. The city of Richmond took steps to ban blacks from the drayage (cart transportation) trades (1810), and to curb the "tumultuous assemblies of negroes in the streets of our City on Sundays" (1815); but these measures found little support among the city's slaveowners and merchants, white men who enjoyed high profits when their slaves were allowed a modicum of freedom in hiring their own time, and even in establishing independent residences apart from whites. Nevertheless, state legislatures throughout the South persisted in their attempts to limit the mobility of this group of blacks. It soon became clear that the ensuing regulations flew in the face of riverboat owners who relied on slave pilots, and indeed all businessmen with commercial and industrial interests dependent upon tractable labor. Thus, conflicts emerged between the maintainance of public order on the one hand, and the prerogatives of slaveowners to use their property the way they wished on the other.[45]

In 1860, an editorialist for the Atlanta *Daily Intelligencer* wrote of the "unnaturalness" of "finding negroes anywhere in white communities not under the control of whites." Expressing his support for a proposal in Augusta "to sell into slavery free negroes convicted of a violation of the city laws," the writer declared, "Whenever we see a negro, we pre-suppose a master"—and presumably the closer the master to the Negro, the better. However, some slaveowners failed to share their neighbors' sense of urgency when it came to the public monitoring of slave activities. A whole host of antebellum regulations governing the behavior of slaves—the outlawing of "loafing every evening in crowds at the doors of . . . places of dissipation," gambling, dancing, playing loud instruments, indulging in "spiritous liquors and refreshments of every kind," and dressing up in fancy clothes, were enforced only sporadically, if at all. For many urban masters, a little commotion from slaves at night was well worth the price if the profits earned for them by slaves each day met their expectations.[46]

In the cities, blacks and whites intermingled promiscuously, not only after work, in back-alley grogshops, but also on the job. On the docks of New Orleans, as late as 1855, Irish and black workers strained shoulder to shoulder to unload "the legions of steamers from the upper country," and then, just as swiftly, labored to "build another mountainous pile on board" before the boat was sent on its way. Yet more often than not, these integrated worksites bespoke not a fellow feeling between members of the two groups but rather its opposite: an intense struggle on the part of whites to stake out that place as their own territory. White employees assaulted black co-workers on the Baltimore and Washington Railroad in 1834, in the Baltimore shipyards in 1838, and on the Hazel River Works in Culpeper County, Virginia, in 1851. Free black workers were particularly vulnerable to attacks. For their part, slave masters were forced to choose between holding their ground, possibly resulting in the injury or death of expensive chattels, or withdrawing blacks altogether from tense workplaces.[47]

White mechanics in the South cast aspersions on the character of their black competitors, and appealed to various governmental bodies to remove those competitors from the labor force altogether. Their arguments echoed those of the sturdy (white) sons of toil north of the Mason Dixon line—that is, the idea that black men were simultaneously lazy and determined to deprive whites of their jobs at all costs. For example, in 1850, Rowan County, North Carolina, white mechanics complained that

> free negroes are with us a degraded class of men living in a condition but little better than the brute creation and, having no regard for an honest name, and fair reputation, can procure such a living by pilfering and theft. As a general rule, they idle away their time and only labour when more dishonest means fail them, and hunger oppresses them, and then at prices regulated by such temporary necessity. . . .

The Mechanics Association in Portsmouth, Virginia, declared that the mere presence of black mechanics was offensive to them; and a white carpenter in Georgia expressed the same idea when he wrote that the use of slave labor in his trade was "unjust, oppressive, and degrading." In 1858, two hundred white workers of Atlanta excoriated the absentee slaveowners "whose negro mechanics can afford to underbid the regular resident mechanics of your city to their great injury"; these owners were white men, "who pay nothing toward the support of the city government," and at the same time deprived honest white citizens of the chance to make a living. Charleston's native-born and immigrant leaders of the white laboring classes regularly spoke out against the ability of free blacks and hired slaves to follow their trades unmolested, yet these measures met with as little success in city hall chambers as in state legislatures. In fact, white elites at times even raised the alarm that, in advocating curbs on slavery, the petitioners were giving aid and comfort to northern free-labor advocates, and to heretical abolitionists in particular.[48]

Beleaguered on every side, by scornful slaveowners and free men of color, by large numbers of slaves with skills and politicians all too eager to preserve the advantages of capital, some groups of workingmen organized to assert their "rights" as whites. In their fight against the "Rich man's Negro," these workers conflated their class and "racial" interests. Often, however, they found that their only "right" an employer was bound to respect, in the words of Joseph Reid Anderson, manager of the Tredegar Iron Works, was "the right of any individual to leave my employment at any time." Responding to a strike on the part of his employees who refused to work for him until he dispensed with his highly skilled slave puddlers alto-gether (in 1847), and to these workers' demands for higher wages, the Rich-mond employer informed his "late workmen . . . you have *discharged yourselves*," and promptly installed an all-black workforce. To drive home his point, Anderson later sued his former employees, charging that they had conspired to deprive him of his slave labor: "It must be evident that such combinations are a direct attack on slave property, and, if they do not origi-nate in abolition, they are pregnant with its evils."[49]

The failure of such "race-based" calls to action among white workmen served to inflame prejudice against blacks, and to remind all white workmen that their labor was more often valued according to its price than the color of its skin. However, in antebellum southern cities, racial solidarity among whites was only one of many factors that shaped the local labor force. The southern slave trade, an influx of northerners and foreigners, and the effi-ciency of slave labor all contributed to permutations of a system that pro-vided for the political power of whites over blacks, but left the economic arena a site of contention among whites with conflicting self-interests. In urban areas, then, white employers faced a challenge that would similarly bedevil the planter class in general during the Civil War: How to sort out their priorities as southern citizens and as southern businessmen.

UNDERNEATH A BLAND veneer of pro-slavery pronouncements, the South remained a volatile region up until and through the Civil War. The colonial society forced to cope with a diverse set of resentful workers and European and Indian foes gradually gave way to a more stable antebellum society forced to cope with increasing numbers of resentful black workers. The Patriots of 1776 had attempted to create a new body politic by juxtaposing powerless blacks to whites possessed of varying degrees of power, but the everyday reality of southern life and work confounded their fondest hopes. By the time of the Civil War, plantation overseers were driving some slaves who were light-skinned and blue-eyed. Some plain white folk picked cotton in the fields with slaves, while some blacks managed through the dint of industry to accumulate more cash, chickens, and furniture than the desti-tute poor white family down the road.

After 1830 or so, in response to growing consumer demand within the United States and growing competition from the world market, assorted business enterprises in the South began to expand and reorganize their oper-ations, increasing their reliance on slave labor. Louisiana sugar farms installed new forms of technology to render their processing operations more efficient, eliminating smaller farms in the process. Virginia tobacco processors and iron manufacturers enjoyed a surge in profits within an industrializing Upper-South economy. A variety of groups of black and white workers registered these changes in different ways. The variable price of cotton impelled upcountry planters to regiment their slave labor forces, and the flood of imported goods from the North and Europe threatened the livelihood of specialized craftsmen in the vicinity of port cities. In the years leading up to the Civil War, yeomen in the Piedmont region devoted fewer acres to corn, and more to cotton; and even in the most remote of regions, crews of black and white men laid railroad tracks that would link upland crossroads to the low-country hubs of cotton distribution.

On the plantation, slaves and free people of color worked primarily as field hands, domestic servants, or artisans. In the cities and in various industrial enterprises, the scope of jobs performed by blacks was much broader. Yet a compelling question remained: Might not the slaves profitably employed as literate urban tradesmen, textile machine operatives, and independent-minded rivermen also serve as sources of subversion, and work to undermine the very institution that dictated the terms of their labor? If so, where did the needs of employers end and the needs of the white community as a whole begin? For their part, slaves pushed hard against the forces that circumscribed their labor. By making themselves indispensable to the southern urban and industrial economies, but also by flaunting their desire for freedom in seemingly unpredictable ways, they made these questions both more urgent and more difficult for whites to resolve.

As the nation plunged deeper into the sectional crisis of the late antebellum period, the planter elite began to consider seriously the civic responsibilities that an incipient southern nationalism would demand of it. In the process it confronted the novel idea that certain forms of labor assigned to poor whites might prove both beneficial to that benighted group, and necessary to the future of southern white people in general. Planters already understood that they might turn the productive energies of poor whites to their own advantage and make a profit; now they contemplated sacrificing a measure of that profit for the sake of founding a new nation and ensuring the political loyalty of nonslaveholding whites whose work was less satisfactory than that of slaves.

CHAPTER SEVEN

THE RACIAL POLITICS OF SOUTHERN LABOR IN PEACETIME AND WAR, 1820–1870

I n late 1863, a group of South Carolina gentlemen suggested to Confederate commander P. G. T. Beauregard that he begin to rely less on slaves as manual laborers, and more on the white "troops recruited from the upper Districts" of the state. The petitioners expressed certainty that this class of poor whites (with whom the planters claimed to be "familiar") would "cheerfully volunteer to do the work now conducted almost entirely by slave labor, if they were paid for, such work the extra per-diem now paid for the service of the negro." This suggestion would seem to address several problems at once. Slaveholders would not have to send their slave property off to an uncertain future at the hands of military officials. The unruly, unpredictable slaves conscripted as trenchdiggers and hewers of wood would be replaced by white men already enrolled in the Confederate army. Working overtime, as it were, these whites could make a little extra cash, thus presumably helping to relieve the destitution suffered by their kinfolk at home, and all the while proving their patriotism.[1]

Nevertheless, Beauregard was unmoved by the petitioners' professed concern for the welfare of their poor white neighbors, and he dismissed the scheme as "impractible in every military point of view." He explained to a South Carolina state legislator that "too many soldiers are already diverted from their legitimate duties, whose places should be filled by negroes—that is, teamsters, company-cooks and hospital nurses." The real obstacles to the successful prosecution of the war, he implied, were the masters who were "holding back," refusing to place their slaves "freely in every possible position by means of which a soldier may be restored to the ranks." In Beauregard's view, in order to preserve the new Confederate nation, gentlemen must relinquish their slave property for a higher cause, poor whites must accept their appointed station as soldiers, and black people must remain slaves, performing the ignoble work that supported the glorious fight for southern independence.[2]

Between 1861 and 1865, military officials and planters throughout the Confederacy waged a contest over the control of slave labor, a contest that pitted the future of the would-be new nation against the private interests of the men who founded it. Southern whites spoke with one voice when they called for the continued subservience of all black people; yet within the ranks of white men who stood to gain directly from the labor of slaves emerged bitter disagreements about the proper work, and terms of work, for southern blacks in service of the Confederate cause. At the outset of the war, faced with a revolt from a subordinate who refused to use his soldiers as dockworkers on the assumption that "there are Negros & hirelings enough to do the menial labor," one commander asserted that "Under the circumstances, the wants of the service ought not to be embarrassed by points of etiquette." During the war, "racial etiquette" faced its severest test.[3]

This debate over the relative uses of black and white labor off the plantation was not entirely new, of course; in fact, it had surfaced in a particularly revealing way during the founding of the antebellum southern cotton textile industry. A few outspoken textile mill owners sought to balance their need for dependable labor with a sense of civic duty toward chronically underemployed poor whites in the countryside. In opposition to this view stood the white men convinced that the cheapness and tractability of slaves suited them for all kinds of work under all kinds of conditions, and that profitmaking must remain the employer-landowner's chief priority. In 1850, a writer in *DeBow's Review* hailed slave labor as "the best and cheapest factory labor in the world," and many industrialists apparently agreed.[4] However, what would have otherwise been a straightforward decision to hire all-slave labor forces was considerably complicated by the rise in slave prices during the late antebellum period, and by the conviction among some mill owners that the political advantages involved in favoring white employees over black slaves or hires should outweigh financial considerations. In this debate were conjoined, on the one hand, employers' recognition of the flexibility in the institution of slavery—the fact that groups of slaves could be set to work in a variety of settings, for short or long periods—and, on the other, a growing uneasiness among some white men about the problem of "idle" whites in the rural South, and about the problem of utilizing slaves in any capacity off the plantation.

The histories of individual worksites brought these political and economic conflicts into focus. William Weaver, a Pennsylvania-born ironmaster in Rockbridge County (east of the Blue Ridge Mountains), Virginia, initially experimented with a workforce of free whites and enslaved blacks. In the early 1840s, after twenty-five years of contending with white men who insisted on remaining idle (when they were not drunk), who used afternoon frolics as excuses for week-long absences, and who demanded cash advances and then took off with the money, Weaver installed slave men at all levels throughout his ironworks at Buffalo Forge. The ironmaster conceived of himself not as a philanthropist obliged to take on white workers, no matter how unreliable, but as a businessman determined to make money from the production of iron. So he bought men like Sam Williams, a highly skilled forgeman, who together with his wife Nancy, a cook, alternated between work at the forge and in Weaver's fields, and also made time for "overwork," including raising crops and tending chickens to sustain their own family. In 1844, Sam Williams's extra work at the refinery earned him $31, which he spent on presents of food and clothing for his wife, his children, and his extended kinfolk. Weaver supplemented his own slave force with hired slaves, for whom he had to negotiate each January in the open market; and owners were loathe to send a slave back to a place where the jobs were particularly hazardous or the white man in charge neglectful of his workers' physical well-being. These realities inspired William Weaver to favor cash incentives over the lash in extracting compliance from his workers.[5]

The coming of the Civil War shocked Weaver into a recognition that his iron forges were not just places of business but also places vulnerable to the intrusion of state authority; in the process, the ironmaker began to lose control of his own operation. In 1859, one of his slaves, Henry Towles, was brutally beaten by a local slave patrol, white men ever vigilant to perceived lapses in slave decorum, especially in the weeks and months after John Brown's raid on Harper's Ferry. And during the war, Confederate officials impressed some of Weaver's slaves for fatigue duty, while other blacks left on their own to find family members, and thus start a life of freedom before freedom came formally in the spring of 1865. In choosing to use slave labor in his forges, William Weaver had reckoned his short-term gains, but failed to calculate the long-term costs of a workforce that had become a source of political controversy.

With the end of the Civil War and the emancipation of the slaves, white southerners, like their northern counterparts three-quarters of a century earlier, began a systematic campaign to repudiate a history of black artisanal skill. Without the constraints of bondage, freedpeople must be eliminated as competitors of white artisans and factory operatives alike, and limited to agricultural and domestic work. Hence the emergence of a new ideology— a new mythology—that blacks as a group were "unsuited" for more skilled jobs. Sam Williams's talents, and William Weaver's keen appreciation of those talents, gradually became relics of the period of slavery.

ANTEBELLUM SOUTHERN INDUSTRIALIZATION: THE BUSINESS OF HIRING SLAVES, THE CHARITY OF RESCUING WHITES FROM "THE VEGETABLE LIFE"

During the antebellum period the vast majority of slaves labored on plantations; yet southern elites had always remained receptive to commercial ventures that provided agriculturalists with useful goods and provided investors with at least the possibility of profits. Early colonial enterprises included lumber and naval stores (in North Carolina); salt and iron mining and production (Virginia); and flour, grist, and sawmilling (throughout the South). By the antebellum period, tobacco manufacturing, leather tanning, and textile production had been added to the list. Moreover, canals, railroad lines, and turnpikes claimed the energies of black and white workers off the plantation. Proto-industrial activities took place on the plantation—cotton ginning, rice milling, sugar refining, spinning and weaving of cloth—and in some cases provided the basis for more extensive and sophisticated commercial enterprises. Because so many of these activities complemented staple-crop production (allowing workers to alternate between one type of employment and another in the course of a year), it is difficult to pinpoint the number of free Negroes, slaves, and whites at work at any particular time in the nonagricultural sector of the economy. Still, estimates that no more than 6 percent of slaves were at work in manufacturing in 1860 understate the significance of industrialization as it shaped the labor relations among whites and blacks in the antebellum South.[6]

Like all southern slaveowners and employers, those who operated factories, forges, and mills wanted an ample supply of workers who were cheap, tractable, and, if necessary, skilled and experienced; with the exception of some textile mill owners, most employers of wage labor and hirers of slaves downplayed "racial" (that is, political) considerations in fashioning a labor force out of myriad groups of southerners. Because antebellum whites were not bound by work-related racial stereotypes to such a degree as their grandsons later in the century, they considered black men to be suitable workers for virtually every kind of nonagricultural job that existed in the South, and at virtually every level of operations except (in most cases) that of supervisor. Black women too worked as textile operatives, distillery hands, and tobacco processors; in mining and railroad camps; and in the rural villages that grew up around sawmills and iron forges, they worked primarily as cooks and laundresses, their children serving as apprentices in gender-specific tasks.[7]

Industrialists faced labor-management issues that planters routinely did not. For example, in the coal-mining and salt-processing industries, where a substantial proportion of the labor force was leased slaves, managers had to factor into their annual calculations additional costs incurred as a result of occupational hazards—the loss of their lease payment, and funds expended on lawsuits brought by disgruntled owners. (The danger inherent in these occupations, combined with relatively low wage levels, made them unappealing to most free laborers.) In the salt mines and processing plants of western Virginia, slaves suffered bodily injury, and in some cases death, when they were caught under collapsed roofs, when they fell into pans of boiling water, and when they found themselves in the path of exploding steam engines. In the Upper South, masters not only commanded high prices for the slaves they hired out, they also demanded that their chattels arrive home each Christmastime healthy and preferably willing to return to the same worksite (for a high price) the following year. In addition, the prevalence of epidemics like cholera and smallpox in relatively isolated rural sites forced a preoccupation with the physical well-being of slaves; the untimely demise of a free worker signaled "merely" the hiring of another man, but the death of a slave constituted a considerable and immediate cash loss.[8]

Employers pieced together their workforces from whatever labor supply was available locally. Thus at certain times and in certain places ironworks, gold and coal mines, brickworks, hemp factories, salt-processing plants, and lumber, railroad, and canal camps included slaves and free workers, most of them men. Of all the antebellum southern worksites, textile mills tended to be the most mixed in terms of the gender, race, and age of workers. The Vaucluse Mill in Horse Creek Valley in the South Carolina Piedmont had twenty slaves and thirty white wage earners at work in 1836. The looms in one of the first steam-powered cotton mills in North Carolina, the Mount Hecla Mill, in Greensboro, relied on the labor of young white women and young slave women, who tended machinery built in Paterson, New Jersey, and learned their tasks from two supervisors who had come with the machines from New Jersey (in 1838). About a decade later, the DeKalb factory at Camden, South Carolina, had "1,680 spindles and 40 looms, 93 hands; two-thirds white and one-third black."[9]

Regardless of the composition of their workforces, most antebellum southern cotton mills had failed by the time of the Civil War because of labor problems—the high cost of slaves, and the high turnover (and thus ultimately high cost) of whites. It was significant that the first successful textile mill in Mississippi was located in a state prison and manned by convicts; this mill not only utilized a cheap, captive labor force, it also dumped its products on nearby markets without worrying about the prices they would bring. Nevertheless, the regionwide debate over the use of slave versus free white labor in the mills offered a telling commentary on the larger challenges of deploying efficient workforces in a society where various groups of unskilled workers carried with them their own liabilities.[10]

In the early 1840s, an English visitor stopped at a cluster of three textile mills on the banks of the Oconee River, near Athens, Georgia, and noted that each mill employed equal numbers of blacks and whites among its one hundred or so workers. The blacks were slaves, some of them the property of the mill owner and others hired from local planters. When he stepped inside one of the buildings, the visitor saw adults and children of both races quietly going about their work: "There is no difficulty among them on account of colour, the white girls working in the same room and at the same loom with the black girls; and boys of each colour, as well as men and women, working together without apparent repugnance or objection. . . ." He therefore felt justified in concluding, that, based on his extensive travels throughout the United States, "colour prejudice" was not as strong in the South as in the North.[11]

Blacks were systematically denied employment in all northern textile mills, and almost all northern manufacturing establishments, while southern whites seemed much more receptive to exploiting black labor in every facet of the commercial economy. Yet, clearly, the widespread use of black labor did not necessarily signal the relative absence of "colour prejudice" in the South, and neither did the existence of a few integrated worksites. The white men, women, and children who toiled next to slaves in the Oconee River factories had made a decision, consciously or unconsciously, that working next to black people for wages, modest though those wages might be, was preferable to the alternative—in this case, probably days and nights foraging for food over the countryside. Still, that decision was not a permanent or irrevocable one; job turnover among white textile operatives was high, in contrast to the immobility of slaves.

Some mill owners advanced the proposition that their proper role was that of public-spirited citizens first, and businessmen second, and that their primary duty was not to their stockholders but to the poor whites who were (they feared) languishing in wretchedness in the southern hinterland. In 1849, Solon Robinson, a pro-slavery northerner, contrasted the energetic, industrious, and schooled factory workers of the North with the rural poor in the South, "as inert as indolence and total want of education for ages can make a people," and noted with approval the efforts of William Gregg, the crusading South Carolina textile manufacturer and founder of a company town called Graniteville. Gregg decided to lift local whites out of their "indolence" by employing them in his mills, and Robinson was impressed with the results:

the change wrought upon such a population, by transposing them from their miserable log-cabins in the pine woods, and equally miserable food and raiment, to the state of civilization that they meet with in such a beautiful manufacturing village as Graniteville, must be seen to be appreciated. It is no wonder that Mr. Gregg estimates the benefits to the body politic so highly. The whole tract around Graniteville, three years ago, was a wild barren waste, and the greater part of the operatives as wild as the aborigines—living a sort of vegetable life, of little profit to themselves or others.

Daniel Pratt, founder of the Prattville Manufacturing Company in Alabama, in 1846, shared Gregg's vision that southern businessmen must approach textile manufacturing as a political investment as well as an economic investment. The goal was to provide poor whites with a stake in a slave society that seemed to offer them so little in the way of either moral "uplift" or material blessings. Some observers might have dismissed such rhetoric as a cynical ploy on the part of cash-starved manufacturers who hoped to wrest subsidies, tax rebates, and other favors from state legislators; but the fact of the matter was that this argument on behalf of an all-white textile force carried the day, after the Civil War, in a stunning victory of politics over the raw profit motive.[12]

Both Gregg and Pratt were swimming against a tide of industry opinion that held that slaves were superior textile operatives compared to free labor of either color. As a rule, slaves could not leave work for a day, or quit their jobs altogether; they thus offered a stable labor force for employers who needed to know how many hands they could count on from one week to the next. Slaves might engage in slow or careless work, they might play sick and sabotage machinery; but white workers had the same faults, with the additional liabilities of "turning out" or striking for higher wages and better working conditions. Slaves owned by the manufacturer were especially valuable because they cut down on the time and expense necessary to train new workers; managers who hired slaves by the year, or employed white wage earners, could not rely on continuity among their most highly trained workers.

Moreover, according to some observers, textile manufacturing helped to strengthen and render more profitable the slave system as a whole by siphoning off those women, elderly people, and children who were less than full field hands, and providing them with productive labor. For example, in 1828, David R. Williams, owner of a mill at Society Hill, South Carolina, specified that he could use ten children not yet ready for field work, and five young women spinners and winders.[13] (The fact that so many slave women had had experience in plantation textile production made their employment in the mills all the more compelling.) Deprived of compensation, and their expectations of decent treatment low in any case, slaves tended to react favorably to incentives that extracted even more labor from them: the lure of cash bonuses, increased control over their own work, extra holidays, mobility up the occupational ladder within the mill. Since employers had no need to attract slave laborers to their worksites (just buy them or negotiate for them in January), they saved considerable money by foregoing the building and maintaining of cottages, schools, and churches that so appealed to rural whites moving into mill villages.

And, last but not least, mill owners well understood that black people proved just as adept as white people in learning every aspect of mechanized textile production, including the repairing of equipment. As a factor affecting the performance of mill hands, "racial" characteristics could be affirmed or denied, depending on the immediate interests of specific groups of white people. The superintendent of the Saluda Factory in South Carolina offered to the company's stockholders this rather defensive testimonial of his black workers in 1849: He had "never seen an equal number of entirely new hands become efficient operatives in less time," and their ability to pick up new skills meant that "whatever they see done they are very quick in learning to do." The slave carders and spinners "perform their duties as promptly and as well as any hands I have ever seen."[14] Other managers echoed these sentiments, and northerners who came south to work in the mill either as supervisors or operatives, only to be quickly replaced by slaves trained to do their (that is, the white men's) jobs, had little choice but to arrive at the same conclusion.

Proponents of white workers countered that the economic advantages of slaves were illusory, especially during periods of high demand for cotton. A mill owner might in the long run profit from buying his own slaves, rather than replenishing his force with leased hands annually; but then he would ultimately face the additional expense of caring for slaves who were too infirm or ill to earn their keep in the mill. Leased slaves tended to be young and robust, but they had the disadvantage of appealing to their owners and refusing to return if they suffered in any way at the hands of the mill manager. Moreover, since southern factories were rather small and precarious affairs, they were subject to even more seasonal and mechanical interruptions in their operations compared to larger establishments in the North; spring floods swamped riverbank villages, and August droughts brought waterwheels to a grinding halt. Thus a long-term black labor force necessarily spent at least part of the year outside a shutdown mill, seriously impairing their "efficiency." Broken machinery could take days or weeks to repair, and given the primitive state of the southern transportation system, years to replace (from northern machine shops). White workers could be fired, or laid off, with no notice, while resident black workers represented a substantial financial investment and so had to be fed and clothed whether or not they were tending machines at any particular moment. Further, some southern whites warned that, like other slaves released from the confines of the plantation, black operatives, especially those with skills and responsibility, might become "spoiled" and "corrupt," the vanguard of a restless southern proletariat.

Despite these considerations, employers of whites felt they were on firmest ground in defending their choice when they avoided making explicit comparisons between black and white labor, and instead focused on the absolute (rather than relative) advantages of whites. In 1850, one observer in *The Merchants' Magazine and Commercial Review* added his voice to those urging white men, women, and children into the mills by proclaiming, "A great good to society must result from the employment of thousands of idle and immoral persons, who are now consumers and not producers." Certainly the appeal of this call was a dubious one for the intended recipients, who were often compared to Indians and Gypsies, and denounced as "not only unproductive, but actually a burthen to us," by their would-be benefactors. Portrayed as vagrants and mischiefmakers on the countryside, where the landed gentry had only limited use for them, poor whites supposedly served no useful purpose and faced a future of continued degradation. This appeal to their usefulness as mill employees conveniently ignored their shortcomings on the job.[15]

Deep South antebellum southern textile mills existed in relation to the cotton plantation economy, their sites chosen for the most part on the basis of demographic and geographical factors. Upper South and border state mills drew upon the labor of whites who already combined farming with wage work in a variety of industrial settings. Too, in the Piedmont, where rushing creeks and rivers provided ideal sites for water-powered machines, poor whites tended to be more numerous than blacks, and hence more prevalent in the mills. In contrast, factories established in the Black Belt naturally drew upon the workers nearby—in this case slaves, bought and leased.

The first southern mill was established in 1789 near Statesboro, South Carolina, but it was a drop in cotton prices in the 1820s that provided a stimulus for the industry, as the cost of both raw materials and slave labor declined accordingly. Throughout the period before the war, the price of slave labor varied directly with the price of local staple crops; and the relatively low rate of investment in the mills reflected conventional wisdom among southern elites that they could best invest their money buying more land and slaves to produce more rice, cotton, or sugar. Compared to northern factories, southern mills tended to be less well capitalized and smaller (some employed only a dozen or so workers), and in 1850 all of the establishments in the region were producing less cotton cloth than the state of New Hampshire alone. (Overall, in that year southern mills accounted for about 10 percent of the nation's output, a figure that grew to between 20 and 25 percent a decade later, with Georgia's fifty mills leading the region.) Southern mill owners spent much money trying to build up the resources and experienced workforce already in place in New England and the Middle Atlantic. Spindles imported from Lowell and managers brought in from Pawtucket, and even, in one instance, white hands coaxed away from Georgia to work in Mississippi (in 1848), all amounted to start-up costs that made individual ventures particularly costly and risky. For all of these reasons, New England textile workers in 1860 numbered 74,260; the comparable figure for the whole South was only 9,111.[16]

As a vehicle for social regeneration, the textile mill village itself had unique advantages, at least according to its boosters. Most mills were located on riverbanks, in the Piedmont, and the rural setting was deemed particularly appropriate for the task of "civilizing" and "domesticating" poor whites. Entrepreneurs constructed whole towns around textile production, and added gristmills, blacksmith shops, and tanneries. Many of these owners took pains to provide their workers with schoolhouses and with preachers determined to link industry with salvation, and they also aimed to eliminate all the evil influences to which city folk necessarily fell prey—the taverns and brothels, the gaming parlors and music halls. Villages free from the contamination of town life thus represented a presumably irresistible package for rural folk, offering backwoods "crackers" a whole new way of life as well as a source of livelihood. As whites poured into the textile mills, they would find they had a "place" in slave society after all, their own place, apart from blacks, and would consequently feel none of the rush to migrate west in search of homesteads of their own, depleting the southeastern seaboard states of white voters. Whites of all classes who might otherwise cast a suspicious eye upon so many black machine operatives clustered in one settlement could gaze proudly upon the all-white mill village with its message of mercy and uplift. Nevertheless, this vision of the future of rural southern society depended upon a sufficient number of common whites accepting at least part, if not all, of it its promise.

The bulk of southern white textile mill operatives were young white women from poor rural families. Women were logical employees since many had had some experience spinning and weaving at home, they could easily master the machinery in the mills, and they could be paid one-third to one-half less than white men. During the 1840s, the Salem Manufacturing Company in Salem, North Carolina, employed about three-hundred seventy hands, of whom 85 percent were female, and this proportion was not unusual. (Men were hired to supervise, repair machines, tend the boilers, and serve as "hands of all work.") Reaching out to the "piney woods people" in the vicinity of Graniteville, William Gregg began his operation in the late 1840s by modeling it on the Lowell system, with matrons presiding over boardinghouses composed exclusively of young women. This arrangement failed, however, because, in the words of one observer, "Girls were unwilling to leave the home of their birth for strange places." In some cases the girls' mothers, or fathers, or both parents, followed them to Graniteville, there to camp out patiently nearby while their daughters worked in the mill. This situation was hardly conducive to the elevation of family life among the poor, and Gregg promptly switched from boardinghouses to tenant houses in order to formalize the residence of parents and other family members. At first, the change did not bring parents into the mill; for "while the sons and daughters worked in the mill, the father would engage in cultivating his land, hauling wood, &c., and the mother would attend to the housekeeping department." In the 1850s the complex at Graniteville consisted of between eight and nine hundred people, but probably no more than one-third of that number were actually employed in the mills.[17]

Thus parents saw the village as a place to live more than as a place where they themselves might earn a living, a perception that would eventually have disastrous consequences for the long-term stablity of the mill workforce. Elizabeth Carrigan accompanied her two daughters to a textile mill village in the North Carolina Piedmont in 1855. She liked the preacher she heard every third week, despite his Methodism, and she considered their small brick house "a pleasant place to live"; but deprived of any means of making money on her own, Carrigan found the cost of living there too high. Prices were so dear at the company store that the girls' wages were quickly consumed by the necessities of life.[18]

Most white workers considered the charms of mill village life to be only temporary, or seasonal; as families and as individuals, they resisted committing themselves to factory work and to their paternalistic employers. Reasons for the high rates of turnover among operatives are not difficult to understand. Landless southerners were a highly transient group even under the best of circumstances, but mill work provided plenty of disincentives to stay at any one workplace very long. Coming from the farm, some operatives resented the fact that work took place in the dark for at least part of the day, and some parents had little inclination to turn over their offspring so completely to foremen and managers. Twelve-year-old children employed in the Graniteville mills worked up to fourteen hours a day (with eighty minutes for two meal breaks) in the summer, and twelve to thirteen hours in the winter. The pay was neither as regular nor as high as ideologues implied it would be; children earned a dollar or two a week and skilled weavers as much as six dollars per week, but average wages were about three dollars. Annual totals were always disappointingly small, reflecting the periodic layoffs that were standard in the industry. Like rural folk everywhere, southern whites conveyed their contempt for factory discipline in a multitude of ways. They broke machinery; sauntered into work late, after the whistle, and then left early in the day to go fishing; stretched their breaks from forty minutes to an hour; alternated loom tending with whiskey drinking; and answered the foreman's demands with curses and walkouts.

Moreover, the villages quickly and justifiably earned a bad reputation as particularly unhealthful places to live. Graniteville had to contend with a high infant mortality rate, and many other sites periodically suffered epidemics of tuberculosis and pneumonia. Mill work was not for the fainthearted; workers lost their digits, limbs, and even heads in the machinery, and the hot air saturated with fiber particles caused headaches and respiratory diseases. Some employees, like Prattville's J. H. and Sarah Lilly in 1857, became indebted to the company store and had their wages garnished by their employer; they could choose either to continue to subsist as debt peons, or move on to another job.[19]

This litany of workers' grievances places into context the employers' complaints about the "unreliability" of white workers. Few mill owners paused to consider that the work itself was "unreliable" for those who wanted a steady source of income; that the employee who felt little "loyalty" to the company and went fishing for the afternoon, or left for weeks on end, mirrored a company that routinely laid off workers and suspended operations in the mills. Employers rightly claimed that high turnover rates not only detracted from mill discipline but also ensured a lack of "aging" within the workforce, necessitating an endless cycle of retraining younger operatives. The moralistic underpinnings of village mill life grated on workers (and nonworking family members), who resented the mandatory religious indoctrination; they preferred to choose their own preachers on their own terms, or perhaps none. And finally, employers recognized that, as a group, rural whites were unlikely to think of mill work as a long-term option. Fathers, given the opportunity to save a few of their daughters' hard-earned dollars, would buy a cow and a piece of land; young women, derided as "Cracker girls"[20] no better than slaves in terms of the work they did, looked forward to the day when they could marry and rid themselves of the grueling mill routine and the social stigma that came with it.

Factory owners expressed their exasperation with workers who refused to stay on the job, and with workers who persisted in getting drunk on and off the job, though they could not and did not attribute those personal failings to their workers' "racial" characteristics (the way they would characterize blacks' work habits after the Civil War). The large number of adults living in the villages but not working in the mills—primarily fathers and older brothers of the operatives—showed little inclination to abide by the temperance strictures the owners tried to enforce. Graniteville demanded that its workers and the lessees of its company houses promise to refrain from drinking at all times. But even William Gregg himself could not control local liquor traffickers, like the one who (in 1860) "puts himself at defiance & has the most boisterous nuisance that has ever been within 5 miles of Graniteville. . . . Most of our reformed drunkards have returned to the bottle and lay about this nuisance day & night." The sporadic work stoppages that plagued many of the mills stemmed from predictable causes—low wages and speed-ups, demeaning working conditions (for example, laboring in a building where the window had been painted over to lessen distractions for the operatives), and complaints about hard-driving supervisors.[21]

Despite these obstacles to efficient production, and despite the extra costs incurred with the use of such a mobile and undisciplined workforce (clearly whites were in the long run more "expensive" than their low wages would suggest), the trend in the 1850s was toward all-white factories. The cotton boom meant that slaves were becoming increasingly unavailable for nonagricultural labor, and employers realized that their only hope of attracting a sufficient number of whites to mill work was to "render it a genteel employment" by excluding all blacks from it. The factories in Columbus and Augusta hired only whites in order to avoid the contempt heaped upon operations with biracial workforces: "*Negroes*, slaves and White men, and *White Women*, co-operating in a cotton factory! What an association! Disgusting!" In Alabama, Daniel Pratt took a different tack in the 1850s, when he increased the contingent of slave workers in his racially integrated mills in an effort to inhibit collective resistance among the whites. More generally throughout the South, poor whites took "a Negro's place" with little hesitation. The Rocky Mount Mill in North Carolina, which quickly made the changeover from slave to white operatives in the 1850s, installed a few black men as draymen and other menial laborers, a pattern that foreshadowed the postbellum model for the social organization of labor in textile factories.[22]

Together with the great planters, antebellum southern industrialists valued poor whites equally as an ever available, cheap complement to their slave workforces, and as political (and ultimately military) allies in the emergent conflict with the Yankees. For their part, most landless white men and women refused to embrace either function gracefully or gratefully. During the Civil War, landlords and employers continued to wrestle with a form of "racial" solidarity at odds with profitmaking. But these questions soon assumed life-and-death consequences, now that black workers, as much as white soldiers, held the fate of the Confederacy in their hands.

PUBLIC AND PRIVATE ADVANTAGES: USES OF BLACK LABOR DURING THE CIVIL WAR, AND ITS AFTERMATH

During the Civil War, conflicts among the Confederates over military and industrial manpower mobilization represented the culmination of labor-management debates that had originated in the antebellum period. As workers, free people of color and slaves could provide valuable service to the Confederate cause, and as potential soldiers, they might even hold the key to an independent Confederate nation. At the same time, as freedom fighters in their own right, black men and women were dangerous to the cause, "traitorous" in their cunning. The hysteria over slave insurrections that swept white communities in the years and months before the war simply brought to the surface fears that had remained suppressed earlier, concealed under the rhetoric of slave contentment and docility. As early as May 1861, an Alabama lawyer warned Jefferson Davis, the would-be new nation's recently elected president, of the "horrors of [slave] insurrection, which may be an incident of the war." Yet whites in the Piedmont and the Black Belt, in the cities and in the countryside, slaveowners and nonslaveowners alike, failed to muster the political will to offer a united front against this enemy within.[23]

The politics of mobilizing black labor during the war confounded ideologues of slavery and Confederate nationalism. Elites were loathe to yield up their bonded workers to impressment officers and owners of railroads; observed Major John A. Campbell in 1863, with considerable understatement, "the sacrosanctity of slave property in this war has operated most injuriously to the Confederacy." It was no wonder, then, that poor whites resented bearing the brunt of wartime sacrifices while they believed that large numbers of slaves remained safely ensconced on the plantation. At the same time, black people seized freedom when and where they could find it, breaking from the confines of the slave quarters to seek out long-lost family members and to take advantage of wartime ways to make a living. In January 1865, when Georgia general Howell Cobb observed, "If slaves will make good soldiers our whole theory of slavery is wrong," he highlighted the self-delusional nature of the planters' paternalism. Slavery was a viable (though brutal) labor system in the South, justified by a theory of black people's inherent inferiority, and white people's solicitude for them, a theory that was a sham.[24]

Confederates agreed that blacks must be put to work as part of the effort to secure southern independence, but they disagreed among themselves about the best uses of specific groups of blacks during the war. Those disagreements centered upon contested military priorities: Would slaves further the successful prosecution of the war if they continued to toil in the fields, or if they went to work in factories and on fortifications? Some planters found it difficult to forego their own role as cotton producers and so kept their slaves hard at work chopping and picking for as long as possible. However, outside the Black Belt, white communities considered slave labor to be their lifeblood in terms of producing food, not staple crops, and they expressed strong feelings on the subject. In August 1861, the requisition of slaves in the Richmond area had "engendered some little feeling of discontent" among farmers who relied on them to thresh the wheat crop, prompting both a Confederate congressman and a colonel to appeal to military authorities on behalf of a group of aggrieved citizens. By 1863, the yeoman farmers of Randolph, Alabama, objected to Confederate impressment agents depriving them of the only able-bodied labor they had left. With white women and children scrounging for food—"seeking & feeding upon the bran from the mills" and instigating bread riots as well—white residents of the county insisted that Confederate officials would be better off looking to the cities, where "large numbers of negroes . . . used for the pleasure of their owners [were] idling about; a curse to the community—*consumers not producers.*" The former governor of Virginia, John M. Gregory, offered strategic reasons for confining slaves to agricultural areas for the duration of the war; in army camps, he suggested, slaves became "mere consumers," using precious food and supplies better reserved for the soldiers, and they also deserted in wholesale numbers. On the plantations, slaves would continue to serve as producers, and help to ward off starvation for soldiers and civilians alike.[25]

Nevertheless, thousands of slaves and free blacks were deployed in army camps throughout the South, as Confederates maintained that "Soldiers cannot be expected to work night and day [building fortifications and breastworks], and fight besides." A significant number of politicians and military planners took steps to ensure that the Confederacy mobilize "Negros & hirelings enough to do the menial labor" upon which every regiment depended—loading and unloading ships and railroad cars, chopping wood, constructing roads, driving wagons, digging trenches, nursing the sick, washing clothes, and cooking. These kinds of jobs drained the energies of white men away from the honorable task of fighting; it was better that slaves and free blacks die a wretched death laboring during the "sickly season [when] . . . the Army could no longer work," rather than commit the lives of white men to such drudgery. A. P. Hayne, a South Carolina planter, made the point emphatically in August 1861: he recommended that each regiment attach to itself "*One Hundred Blacks* to be used for various kinds of menial labor, noting, "The *hardest,* and *most painful duty* of the *young Volunteers,* is to *learn how* to *Cook,* and wash—." He could not abide the notion that "*our Brave Volunteers*" might have to consume "*Food . . . hastily* and *badly prepared. . . .*" In his conviction that male slaves should be assigned the work routinely performed by women in the civilian sector, Hayne stated an early version of the principle that would shape the African-American military experience from the Civil War through World War II.[26]

No doubt individual soldiers brought to the service their own expectations about the proper social division of labor on the battlefront. At least some of the men who by their own admission "had never labored a day in their lives" might have disdained manual toil—these were the ones who could afford to hire slave runaways as personal cooks and valets. Meanwhile, others went about new and physically arduous tasks with the zeal of converts, knowing their work with pickaxes and shovels (if not bedpans and frying pans) to be just as crucial to the cause as their courage under fire. On the other hand, poor white men might resent the fact that military service brought them no respite from heavy labor, especially if the bulk of that labor fell to them while the sons of wealthy slaveholders escaped it.[27]

Confederate officials managed to gain control over slaves in a variety of ways: They requested that masters voluntarily relinquish their bondsmen (or bondswomen) for a specific period of time; they forcibly impressed blacks from their owners; and they seized runaways and put them to work before bothering to locate their owners. At first, the use of slave labor in Confederate ordnance factories, on railway lines, and the front lines would seem to conform to the traditional practice of using slave labor in any way that would enhance the safety and well-being of white people. But the fact that slave labor had traditionally been placed in the service of profitmaking considerably complicated the Confederacy's plans to make efficient use of blacks in its fight against the Yankees. More than one commander was disappointed when his urgent and eminently reasonable plea went unheeded: "I am sure that no patriotic citizen, with the issue truly at heart, would hesitate to respond, most cheerfully, to the call which I now make (viz) 'One negro man with his axe, or spade, to be furnished at once, by each propietor'"— this near Lee's Mill, Virginia, in April 1862.[28]

All over the Confederacy, slaveholders showed apparent more willingness to relinquish their sons to the army than to relinquish their slaves. Avoiding formal debate over the matter altogether, they simply did their best to thwart the quotas and requisition orders that would have deprived them of control over their own property. They "refugeed" their slaves away from the coast and into the Southwest or the upcountry, out of the way of the Federals and Confederates alike; they fended off impressment officials with guns and curses; they pleaded for local politicians to intercede on their behalf with labor-hungry generals. Sensitive to the wishes of the slaveholders in his own area, the chief of police of Nashville advised Confederate military officials in March 1863 that they should make an effort to find sufficient numbers of "Col'd Laborers . . . in and about the City & from the Work Houses & Jails," and not "effect the Interest of Persons engaged in Planting—."[29]

Those officials who managed to pry slave labor from the grasp of their owners must have wondered at times if the effort was worth it, for they were constantly bombarded with queries about the physical well-being of the blacks under their control. In April 1862, General J. B. Magruder had to take time away from meeting with his staff and planning his next move against the Yankees in order to answer a letter from the Confederate secretary of war, who passed along several masters' complaints about the treatment of their slaves by the army. Wrote Magruder, "Every precaution has been adopted to secure their health and Safety as far as circumstances would allow," pointedly adding that the slaves in his jurisdiction, in Virginia, slept under covers and next to fires, while the soldiers, "more exposed," did not. The chief surgeon of the Confederate hospital for black laborers in Richmond found it necessary in December 1864 to dispute the claim of a slave (who had returned to his owner after working on nearby fortifications) that the patients there "are very much neglected & almost starved." An owner had forwarded the complaint to his congressman in Richmond, prompting the surgeon to offer an elaborate defense of himself and his staff, from the medicines they prescribed to the food they provided: "Fresh beef, & beef soup chickens & chicken soup, eggs, milk, Rice, stewed fruit, apples & peaches, Potatoes, molasses Tea & Sugar. . . ." If this list represented an accurate rendering of the care afforded the slaves in the Richmond hospital, the patients in all likelihood were eating better than almost anyone else in the Confederacy in December 1864. If, on the other hand, the surgeon felt compelled to exaggerate the quality of their care (and this is more likely the case), it is an indication of the lengths to which Confederate officers were forced to go to answer to the angry charges of nervous slaveowners.[30]

Considerable numbers of white men and women complained to authorities about the drafting of their sons, urging their release from the service for a variety of reasons; but few communicated in such detail their preferences for specific tasks assigned to their sons, compared to those who demanded specific tasks be assigned to (or, more often, withheld from) their slaves at the front. Virginia owners insisted that their (hired) slaves recently put to work in a Confederate hospital be released immediately when they learned that the place had "been appropriated for the reception of cases of smallpox." In Alabama, owners protested when their impressed slaves were forced to construct a railroad "for the benefit of a *private* corporation." Planters' formal complaints and lawsuits over the "hard usage & starvation" of their property, and over the death of slaves from illness or from a firing squad, flooded the Confederate bureaucracy and ate into the precious time of harried politicians and distracted generals. To the commander of the

Confederate army in Florida, the enraged owner of a runaway slave "destroyed" (that is, executed) by Confederates represented but one more "citizen unwilling to make a sacrifice of his personal interests to the public welfare," a selfish troublemaker who had the audacity to interfere with the official duties of an army offficer.[31]

Under these conditions, military strategists would seem to have been justified in targeting free people of color for service; these black people were not encumbered by owners consumed with worry about the fate of their personal investments. In the summer of 1861, a number of generals called on the free men of color within their districts to report immediately for Confederate service, declaring that they would be "impressed if they refuse to come and a force will be sent to bring them in." And there were plenty of white workingmen in southern cities who saw the war as the perfect opportunity to rid themselves of their free-Negro tormentors. In July 1861, John Lenahan of Lynchburg, Virginia, made this plea to Confederate president Jefferson Davis:

> There is a large number of Free Negroes in this City a great portion of which are Mechanicks af various trades viz: Carpenters Bricklayers Stone masons, & Blacksmiths a large portion of which are now liveing on the honest industry of our Volunteers already in service by stealing and robing their families out of the provisions stored to them before their enlistment in the Confederate army. I want to know if that degraded and worse than useless race could not do something in the way of defending the south such as throwing up Brea[s]t works Building tents or any thing els that wuld be of advantage to us.

General Roger A. Pryor, a proponent of the reenslavement of free blacks before the war, predictably endorsed their widespread use after April 1861, so that "the community [would be relieved] . . . of a thriftless and vicious class and compel them to labor for the public advantage." Yet the list of trades represented by the Lynchburg free Negroes revealed they were hardly "worse than useless."[32]

The fact that a general impressment order covering all free black men between the ages of eighteen and fifty was not issued until the fall of 1864 suggests that employers refused to yield control over even this obvious source of labor. While some whites registered their outrage over able-bodied free men of color lounging about the countryside and inciting the slaves to rebel, other civic-minded citizens (like those in the coastal region of Virginia in October 1863) made it clear that they were "*decidedly* and *strongly* opposed to any attempt" to impress free Negroes, workers who "furnish the only means in our reach of getting our wood cut, rails mawled, or any other labor whatever, performed—." In February 1864, a North Carolina farmer appealed to his congressman, stating that the whites in the vicinity of Pitch Landing were "now wholly dependent on free negro labor"; the legislator then forwarded the request to the secretary of war in an effort to gain an exemption for all of the "free negroes who are industriously engaged in culti-vating the soil and raising crops" in Hertford County.[33]

In the midst of this cacophony of voices emerged a crystallized restate-ment of the antebellum view that black people as skilled artisans and trades-men were necessary to local economies even as they posed a potential threat to the black-white caste system. Faced with the prospect of losing prized workers to the Confederate war machine, southern masters and employers sang the praises of the resourcefulness and skills of black men. For example, Lynchburg millers, in the business of filling government contracts for flour, resisted the impressment of their coopers, free men of color essential to their business. Likewise, a Richmond manufacturer made a personal request to the Confederate secretary of war to exempt from service James Robin-son, a free black man who "has four Waggon Teams working on the Street," arguing that "we are dependant on them for pursuing our business." Con-federate commanders wrote similar testimonials to their own superiors, lauding the abilities of the "excellent artificers" (in this case two slave black-smiths) upon whom they now relied for ordnance work. Insisting that he be permitted the leeway to maintain a competitive edge over other employers, one superintendent of a government harness shop defended the extraordi-narily high wages paid to free black carpenters and blacksmiths "selected as the best of that class of mechanics to be found in the neighbourhood, some of them in fact superior workmen to many white men." He further justified the $182 per month paid to the master of "a slave . . . the best blacksmith in the shops; on piece work at harness; this boy excells in industry any of the workmen; [if payments are reduced] in this case, we most certainly will loose one of our *best hands.* . . ."[34]

Slaves hired and impressed by the army faced unprecedented kinds of hardship, the assurances of their wartime caretakers to the contrary notwithstanding, but they also sought to turn work off the plantation to their advantage whenever possible. Even as they came to rely on all sorts of black workers, Confederate officials understood that they were losing their grip on the traditional social order. A few months after the black pilot Robert Smalls, a slave, commandeered the rebel armed steamtug *Planter* in May 1862 for the Union cause, one Charleston engineer understandably expressed concern about whether the government should "allow negroes to Run Steam Boats as Engineers in the Confederate States." When the slaves at work in a hospital near Jackson, Mississippi, protested that they would not be sent to nearby saltworks at the behest of their owners, a planter named Robert Shotwell recognized their intransigence was "fostering & encouraging this spirit of insubordination now so dangerous & general in our country." Shotwell also desired to move a select group of his slaves out of the way of the advancing Union army, men and women who "would not be controuled should Vicksburg fall . . . as they would no doubt shoulder the musket willingly & be dangerous negroes in that capacity." Among the most insubordinate of all his slaves was a blacksmith; "a valuable workman. . . . He is a dangerous negro if he should rebel & I understand swears he will not be taken off."[35]

The threat posed by fearless slave runaways necessitated reserving certain forms of labor for white men. Plantation owners managed to win draft exemptions for their overseers (the notorious "twenty slave" law, passed in 1862), but coal mine owners and other managers had to make their individual cases that "intelligent and experienced white men should constantly supervise and control" specific workforces. In March 1864, a group of twenty-two slaveholders from Darlington District, South Carolina, petitioned the secretary of war to release from active duty one John B. Rhodes; black people in the area were "stealing everything the [sic] can lay their hands on knowing we are not able to help ourselves," and they needed Rhodes, a man "acquainted with Creeks bays & swamps in this part of the Country where the negroes hide themselves, he has likewise a excellent trained pack of dogs for that purpose which no person with any success manage but himself. . . ." The South Carolina dog owner and slavecatcher should continue to serve his country at home instead of on the battlefront.[36]

In their desperate attempts to withhold their slaves from public service, a core of influential slaveholders made clear their conviction that private interests should take precedence over civic duty. In response, Confederate officials in a variety of capacities cited the risks inherent in assigning white men to jobs crucial to the war effort, especially if those men did not share with their superiors an unwavering commitment to the cause. (The high rate of desertion within the army's ranks was emblematic of a historic "unreliability" of white workers for any tasks that demanded discipline and loyalty to higher-ups.) For example, in February 1864, J. W. Lapsley, a Confederate railroad director stationed in Selma, Alabama, complained that the men at work in his iron forges, "nearly all foreigners from Europe, or natives of the Northern states, the majority being foreigners," were an unstable source of labor. Most of them were single men, without families, and they had no longstanding ties to the South and no short-term loyalty to the Confederacy. The workers were susceptible to two kinds of insidious rumors: first, that they could make higher wages working for the Union; and second, that they might at any day be "summarily taken from their work to a conscript camp" or "some day be suddenly summoned into the [battle] field." Around this same time, Confederate managers at the Wilmington, North Carolina, saltworks drew a connection between the forced labor of a group of white Unionist sympathizers and the desertion of their slave co-workers soon after. Regardless of whether or not they in fact collaborated with the Yankees or offered tangible aid and support to black people, southern white men of uncertain loyalties, in the eyes of die-hard Confederates, served as practical allies of both groups.[37]

Beginning in late 1864, the debate over soliciting black volunteers into the Confederate army (in return for the promise of freedom for themselves and their families) reflected, on the one hand, Confederate leaders' appreciation of black men's potential as soldiers, and, on the other, their recognition that blacks of both sexes were already aiding the Union army in overt and covert ways. Military officials in the vicinity of Pensacola, Florida, had initiated court-martial proceedings against five runaway slaves in 1862, charging that "the said slaves are intelligent beings possesing the faculties of Conveying information which would prove useful to the enemy and detrimental to the Confederate states." Georgia slaveholders also elevated their slaves from the childlike cotton-hoeing machines extolled in antebellum paternalist rhetoric to the position of "Traitors, since they go over to the enemy & afford him aid & comfort, by revealing the condition of the districts and the cities from which they come, & aiding him in erecting fortifications & raising provisions for his support. . . ." By early 1865, the heroism demonstrated by black northerners and by southern slave runaways who joined the Union army had inspired Robert E. Lee to suggest that the Confederacy arm its slaves, a proposal that was simultaneously radical and reasonable: "we must decide whether slavery shall be extinguished by our enemies and the slave be used against us, or use them ourselves at the risk of the effects which may be produced upon our social institutions." The war showed that paternalism was ultimately a fragile ideological construct, crumbling in the face of military conflict and political necessity.[38]

In the fields and factories, in iron forges and army camps, black men, women, and children as workers bore the burdens of a war fought to keep them in chains. Yet, given the opportunity, some enterprising souls managed to turn the conflict to their economic advantage. For almost two decades before the war began, Alonzo Jackson, a slave, hired his own time, paying his master $140 each year, and "working only for whom I chose." At the start of the conflict, the fifty-one-year-old man worked as a hostler in a livery stable; but in February 1864 he hired a flatboat and began a freighting business on the riverways along the South Carolina coast. After Federal troops arrived in the area, Jackson returned to the stables, where he kept two horses that he owned, and hired them out for the duration of the war. Other slave men and women ran away at the first opportunity and earned their first wages as valets to Confederate soldiers, teamsters for the Union army, or laborers for Confederate employers under the cloak of anonymity in towns and large cities. For men like Henry Ellis, a slave near Fredericksburg, Virginia, working for wages was his first step as a free man, and enlisting in the Union army was his second, suggesting the intimate connection between gaining control over one's own labor and fighting for freedom.[39]

During the Civil War, politics, profits, and military imperatives all collided with each other in the Confederate debate over the use of black labor. Many slaveholders persisted in their apparent self-destructive determination to withhold slave labor from the Confederates at all costs if they could manage to; though they watched plantation discipline disintegrate all around them, they could not bear to relinquish the capital that even homebound enemies represented. When Appomattox settled the question of secession once and for all, most white southerners remained prepared to do battle all over again—this time within a context of a regional civil war of aggression that pitted all classes of whites against all blacks.

As southern soldiers retreated to nurse their wounds in the spring of 1865, the conflict shifted from the battleground to the halls of state legislatures and the halls of Congress; but underlying the clash between northern Republicans and southern Democrats was the assumption on both sides that black people would continue to till the soil. To white landowners in the postbellum South, the sight of the vast majority of freedpeople stooped over in the cotton fields evoked a not-so-distant past when blacks were "efficient" agricultural workers because they were slaves. To southern white tradesmen and small farmers, blacks now became even more threatening as potential economic competitors, but also more vulnerable because they lived without the patronage and protection of the planter class. To northern free labor advocates, the sight of black field hands hard at work held out the promise of a black peasantry (of independent landholders) in the not-so-distant future. The Republican Party, through Bureau of Refugees, Freedmen, and Abandoned Lands agents, held that annual rural labor contracts would offer incentives for employers to provide decent treatment for their workers, and allow them over time to accumulate enough cash to buy their own land. But to the planters, the contracts were little more than a nuisance, easily flaunted in splendid, rural isolation far from meddlesome bureau and military officials alike.

In 1867, the plan of Radical Reconstruction guaranteed southern freedmen the right to vote, and black communities throughout the region hastened to transform what had amounted to a twoway debate between groups of whites into a more expansive and significant struggle over the great political issues of the day—the rights of blacks as citizens and as workers.[40] Lacking land, capital, or credit, freed men and women nonetheless sought to seize control over the conditions and terms of their labor. Thus, during the first five years or so after the war, blacks loosened the power of whites who attempted to reorganize slavelike gangs; and then, gradually, kin-based "squads" of workers gave way to household units of production. Thereafter, in a bid for economic self-sufficiency, blacks aspired to grow corn for themselves rather than cotton for whites. But in the coming years they would find themselves constrained through a variety of laws that limited their geographical and social mobility. As renters, tenants, share-wage earners, sharecroppers, day workers, peons, and convict laborers, most African-American men and women remained confined to extractive industries and staple-crop agriculture in the "New South" economy.

The diversity of black occupations under slavery contrasted with the largely menial agricultural pursuits to which the freedpeople and their children and grandchildren were confined. As the manufacturing, clerical, and retail sectors of the U.S. economy expanded, whites rushed to fill these jobs. Urban skilled blacks (descended from antebellum free men of color) gradually disappeared from southern cities, their craftwork now taken over by a new generation of whites and new kinds of machines. With their disappearance went the possibilities for the emergence of a vital African-American entrepreneurial class. In the countryside, sharecroppers' contracts placed severe limitations on families' abilities to tend a garden or raise some chickens when they were not working in the fields, although the trade developed under slavery could not be suppressed entirely. During the last decade of the nineteenth century, in the Cotton South fewer than fifteen out of every hundred black persons worked at something other than farming (most of them were sharecroppers), unskilled labor, or domestic service.[41]

ENSLAVED AMERICANS SHOWED remarkable unity of purpose in struggling to divert their energies from work that would enrich their owners to work that would sustain their own families and communities. After emancipation, this impulse toward individual and collective autonomy became manifest in regions throughout the South; regardless of the type of crop under cultivation, or the social configuration of a particular urban landscape, freedmen and women attempted, with varying degrees of success, to reclaim their labor as their own. Though still bound by the demands of whites, now in the role of employers and landlords, blacks expanded the realm of "over-work"—tasks performed over and above stipulated assignments, tasks that in some cases could yield a little cash or otherwise enhance the well-being of family members and extended kin. Freed communities all over the South embarked on a concerted campaign of institution building, an effort that earned them little in the way of financial gain, but contributed to the overall quality of African-American life. The black churches, schools, political associations, and benevolent societies that emerged immediately after the war thus represented a culmination of the slaves' determination to withdraw from "work" (for whites), in favor of "overwork" (for themselves) whenever possible.[42]

After the war, a few black men parlayed the skills they had learned as slaves into the basis of a free life: "My father was a blacksmith on master's place, and after the war, he was a blacksmith for himself," recalled Eugenia Fair of Greenwood, South Carolina, many years after the war. Phoebe Banks's father "got to be a good horse trainer" as a slave, and then for "a long time after slavery he helped to train horses for the Free Fairs around the country." His daughter noted, "I suppose the first money he ever earned was made that way." Yet even those black people who escaped farm labor found few opportunities to advance up the occupational ladder. Born a slave near Hodgenville, Kentucky, Billy Slaughter "worked on a steamboat in his earlier days" as a free man. He started out cleaning the decks of the boat, and later progressed to work "cleaning up inside the boat," mopping up the floors and making up berths. Then, "the next job he held was ladies' cabin man," and he was subsequently assigned to take "care of the quarters where the officials of the boat slept." Finally, as "a second pantry man," Slaughter waited on passengers in the dining room. For this job he had to wear "spotless" clothes and sometimes "change his shirt three times a day." Billy Slaughter's moves to different jobs—from outside to inside, from cleaner to waiter—represented the constricted world of black occupational mobility after the Civil War.[43]

In the early 1870s came indications that the freedpeople would find few job opportunities in the factories of the New South because whites now claimed the former slaves were incapable of operating "delicate machines."

It was about this time that the manager of the Eagle and Phenix Mill, in Columbus, Georgia, explained the composition of his workforce, eight hundred white operatives and ten black "yardmen": "We do not think the negroes adapted to the labor of cotton-mills. Their lack of quickness, sensitiveness of touch, and general sleepy characteristics disqualify them for work which needs the requisites they lack. Being far better fitted for outdoor labor, they will no doubt always be kept so employed."[44] Though the mill had never actually used black labor before the war or since, the manager's words had a ring of finality about them, and they gave no hint of the difference of opinion—and practice—among his predecessors all over the South just a generation before. Quickly, the new idea that black people could not work textile machines—and the implication that they had been tried and failed—assumed the exalted form of "racial" ideology among white businessmen, opinionmakers, and ordinary folk alike.

About this time, elites began in earnest a concerted campaign to link the moral "uplift" of poor whites to a nascent industrial revival. However, as a group, textile mill owners soon learned that their reliance on white operatives was doomed to produce less than satisfactory results as rendered by annual business statements and stockholders' standards. Released from bondage, black people were no longer deemed "reliable" workers, either. Instead, they were more like whites, because they were free—"shiftless" and "intractable"—and so employers had few incentives to seek them out and simultaneously alienate poor whites. The near-total exclusion of black men, women, and children as machine operatives from southern textile mills until the mid-1960s testified to the owners' cynical manipulation of white workers' prejudice and desperation to provide a decent life for themselves and their families. Ultimately, the late nineteenth-century southern road to white "racial" solidarity, paved with a social contract between mill owners and their white employees, was fraught with obstacles; for the mills simply could not fulfill their promise of a work life that afforded rural whites not only cash wages, but dignity as well.

Traveling through the South in the summer and early fall of 1865, Carl Schurz, a Republican Party stalwart and brigadier general in the Union army, described the wave of terrorism that was sweeping over the vanquished Confederacy. White landowners were attempting to keep black men and women hard at work on the plantations "either by ruse or violence," and at the same time these whites were driving off the young and infirm who would not be able to earn their keep as "free" workers. Schurz foresaw for African Americans a future of legal ambiguity: no longer the property of slaveowners, neither could they become their "own master."

Instead, they remained hostage to whites who were motivated by "profit, caprice, or passion." Politicians in the southern states lost no time in passing legislation that imposed harsh penalties against black workers who left the plantation without permission from white overseers and owners, making "liberty of locomotion" among the former slaves a crime.[45]

Already, white vigilante groups were forming all over the region, in an effort to block freedpeople physically from seeking to participate in the political process, send their children to school, and find a better job down the road. Schurz accounted for the violence directed at black men, women, and children by citing a "most singular notion [that] still holds a potent sway over the minds of the [white] masses—it is, that the elevation of the blacks will be the degradation of the whites." By embracing this idea—that the welfare of black people must necessarily come at the expense of the welfare of white people—southern white yeoman farmers and urban tradesmen adopted a view that had held "potent sway over the minds of the [white] masses" in the North since the Revolution, one that laid the basis for national, and not just regional, systems of black labor exploitation in the future.[46]

WHITE MEN "IN A TIGHT PLACE": BLACK POVERTY AND BLACK PROTEST IN THE ANTEBELLUM NORTH

O n the night of October 18, 1824, a group of young white men, armed with clubs and axes, entered a black section of Providence, Rhode Island, attacked its inhabitants, and left the neighborhood itself "almost entirely in ruins." Later, the men who had virtually razed Hardscrabble (for that was its name) defended their actions by claiming that it was the site of "debaucheries and riots," where crowds collected for "revels and midnight orgies," and where servants came to pawn the "plunder" they had stolen from their masters. The town's bad reputation was further tainted by the fact that it apparently attracted seamen and other highly transient black people. One white observer held that, while a few were "honest and industrious," the mass of residents of Hardscrabble "can hardly be considered a valuable acquisition to any community, and their return to the respective places from whence they came, probably would not be considered a public calamity."[1]

The catalyst for the 1824 attack was an incident that had occurred the day before, when black men and women in the city had tried to "maintain the inside walk in their peringinations through the town"—that is, when they had refused to yield to white pedestrians who had historically claimed for themselves the inside of the sidewalk, a cleaner, more "respectable" place to walk compared to the outside. The attorney general prosecuting the case against the four white men indicted in the Hardscrabble riot acknowledged "the insults which the whites have suffered from the numerous black population in this town"; nevertheless, he added, black residents "have a right to be protected by the law in their persons and property." The jury decided otherwise, and found the defendants not guilty.[2]

Hardscrabble was home to poor working families as well as carousers. The house of one black man, Christopher Hill, was dismantled and his possessions seized, leaving the woodcutter and his three children to live in their cellar for the rest of the winter. The following year he emigrated with his family to Liberia. Hill's precarious existence was emblematic of Providence's impoverished black community. In 1824, Rhode Island's blacks had been free only a generation or so (since the new state's constitution of 1794 banned slavery). Former slaves who were artisans found it difficult to retain (their masters') old customers or attract new ones, and they lacked the resources to invest in or replace tools necessary to their trades. Most of the black workers in the state were concentrated in domestic service and day labor; though a number of machine-powered textile mills were appearing in the region around Providence and Pawtucket, the jobs in those mills were reserved for white men, women, and children. Hardscrabble no doubt had more than its share of places where people fenced stolen goods, and places of dancing and late-night conviviality. Like other poor neighborhoods, the town became associated with vice and crime, and thus vulnerable to the incursions of moralists of all classes; the Hardscrabble attackers were described in their indictment as "gentlemen, alias labourers, alias traders. . . ."[3]

The refusal of black pedestrians to defer to whites on the sidewalks of Providence appeared to be a defiant and provocative act. In Providence (and other cities at this time), groups of white men lounging on street corners considered it fine sport to harass blacks on their way to work, or on the sidewalks for any reason; they would knock the hats off the heads of black men, and pull the shawls off black women, all in an effort to humiliate people who considered public thoroughfares to be their rightful domain.[4] In Providence (again, as in other urban areas in the North), encounters between black and white workers often took place out-of-doors; the most integrated worksites were outside, on wharves and construction projects. As greater numbers of whites moved out of the fields and into shops and factories, most black laborers remained exposed to the elements, and to the taunts of pedestrians and potential rivals. They performed their jobs, or certain tasks associated with their jobs, in full view of city crowds—the washerwomen lugging their bundles through the streets, the men driving carts and carriages or just waiting expectantly on the docks or on a street corner for a day's work. For these reasons, relations between black and white members of the "laboring classes" often assumed the character of street performances. However aggressively or inadvertently, the refusal of Hardscrabble blacks to yield to whites on the street was part of a larger challenge to white power in the courthouse, in city hall, in the statehouse, and in the workplace.

On the eve of the Civil War, blacks constituted only 2 percent of the total nonsouthern population, and only 6 percent of that relatively small number could vote. During this period, northern whites continued to associate the free blacks in their midst with slavery—white mobs in Philadelphia and New York even drove blacks away from Fourth of July celebrations in those cities—and the generally impoverished condition of the black population perpetuated this association. Yet African Americans as a group expressed themselves in a political voice that resonated throughout the nation, a voice disproportionate to their numbers in the New England, Mid-Atlantic, and midwestern states. Beginning in 1790, and especially after the 1820s, free people of color intruded upon the white public consciousness with their newspapers, temperance associations, literary societies, suffrage conventions, schools, mutual aid societies, and religious meetings. Complementing these institutions were frequent and dramatic public displays of distinctive styles of music and dance, styles that insistently proclaimed an African heritage. In 1801, and several times thereafter, crowds of New York blacks massed to liberate by force slaves who had been brought into the city by their owners. Philadelphia blacks paraded to celebrate the First of August (British Emancipation Day) each year after 1838. Beginning in 1854, Cincinnati black men donned their "Attuck Blues" militia uniforms for drills in public places.[5]

And throughout this period black communities all over the North assembled to hear an illustrious array of abolitionist orators, male and female, black and white, decry the evils of slavery. The fact that black women played a prominent role in these meetings, as listeners and as speakers, did little to allay the fears of white men that black people in general were fomenting a multifaceted revolution that would inevitably alter the existing balance of power in the North. Sojourner Truth, author, itinerant preacher, and abolitionist, mocked the pretensions of white men in a speech she delivered to a crowd of women's rights advocates assembled in Akron, Ohio, in 1851: " . . . man is in a tight place, the poor slave is on him, woman is coming on him, and he is surely between a hawk and a buzzard."[6]

During the last three decades of the antebellum period, when so many social conflicts among northerners—between immigrants and the native-born, between white men and white women, Catholics and Protestants, bosses and workers—assumed a raucous form, blacks appeared menacing to whites in a variety of workplaces. The lowly immigrant canal digger determined to hold on to his sense of superiority while toiling alongside a black co-worker; the failing artisan, who saw in the black hod carrier's poverty his

own future degradation; and the haughty Philadelphia merchant, dependent
on his southern slaveholding customers—all of these whites believed that
they had much to lose in any situation where blacks had anything to gain.
From these tensions arose an image of African Americans as doubly dangerous: as poor people, and yet also as politically aggressive people.

Apparently, whites saw no contradiction in charging that black men and
women were "naturally" lazy and indolent, and at the same time "naturally"
predatory in pressing for rights and jobs that would inevitably diminish the
relatively privileged but increasingly tenuous standing of white people. For
these reasons, patterns of black residential and labor mobility loomed large
in the minds of whites in general, and white voters in particular. The sight of
even a relatively small number of black migrants into a region—men and
women seeking jobs to provide for their families—personified, for whites,
social disorder and social distress. Illinois frontiersman were convinced that
every free black in-migrant would inevitably languish, jobless, and prove a
drain on every white taxpayer's resources. Irish workers in Civil War Boston
believed that every former slave who came north during the war would be
one more source of impoverishment of the Irish community. In sum,
according to a British visitor to the United States in the early 1830s, whites
saw blacks as both a "burthen to the rich by their idleness, and a nuisance to
the poor by their industry."[7]

In the minstrel hall, white men of the laboring classes might have fashioned for themselves a seductive image of African Americans as sly, sensual
beings, resistant to the dictates of a disciplined, industrial society; and in
their writings and speeches, white abolitionists of the emerging middle
classes might have developed the idea that blacks, and especially slaves, were
inherently childlike and passive—a "feminine" race of people.[8] Yet in everyday life these creations of the white imagination mattered less than the
drama of black action and white reaction, especially as that drama affected
work and politics. In some instances, blacks and whites competed fiercely
for jobs at the same worksite; but more generally, whites deeply resented the
assertive and at times boisterous way that black men and women pressed
their claims as American citizens.

"THEY LIKE US VERY WELL IN OUR PLACES, AND THEY HAVE SELECTED OUR PLACES FOR US"

In 1834, a group of New Haven white men petitioned the Connecticut legislature on a matter related, they claimed, to their "self-preservation."

Alarmed at a recent in-migration of blacks, the petitioners charged that the newcomers had launched both a collective assault upon public morality and a rapacious attack upon the economic well-being of white residents. Not long before, a public spectacle in New Haven had proved particularly alarming: "a band of negroes paraded the streets . . . armed with clubs, pistols, and dirks, with the avowed purpose of preventing the law of the land from being enforced against one of the species." Apparently, some of the New Haven petitioners encountered black men as co-workers also, declaring indignantly that if a white man "is employed in the same work with a colored man, he is subjected to constant insult and abuse, if he refuses to descend to familiarity. . . ." The petitioners' main grievance centered on the notion that the blacks, "who have just emerged from barbarism or slavery, have few artificial wants" (in other words, they were accustomed to poverty and failed to purchase their share of consumer goods), and could thus afford to work for lower wages than more "civilized" white men. When he was not depriving the white man of gainful employment, the black man was helping himself "from the public-storehouse, as a legal pauper." The result was the immiseration of Connecticut's white residents:

> Whenever they come into competition, therefore, the white man is deprived of employment, or is forced to labor for less than he requires. He is compelled to yield the market to the African, and, with his family, alternately becomes the tenant of an almshouse, or is driven from the state to seek a better lot in Western wilds . . . banished from home and kindred for the accommodation of the most debased race that the civilized world has ever seen. . . .

Following this line of reasoning, the petitioners concluded that the abolition of southern slavery would hasten the process by which the noble white sons of Connecticut would be driven from their native state by "black laborers of every description." Indeed, "black porters, black truckmen, black sawyers, and black mechanics" stood ready to strike a mortal blow against the young republic. Therefore, the campaign to impose legal restraints upon black immigration into the state amounted to nothing less than a moral crusade. Only the ridding of blacks from the workplace, from the state, would "render labor respectable, by making the [white] laborer respected." A Democratic Party toast expressed these same backward-looking sentiments succinctly: "To the light of other days when liberty wore a white face and America wasn't a Negro."[9]

The petitioners' statement would seem to suggest that New Haven black men were poised to overrun the city's workplaces and muscle whites out of their jobs. In fact, in 1830, blacks accounted for only 5 percent of the city's total population (564 out of 10,180), and only 3 percent of the total population of New Haven County.[10] Given their small numbers, black workers could not have in any significant way offered much economic competition to whites. What animated the protesters was not the current "racial" balance of power, but rather the possibility that in the near future that balance might shift (if ever so slightly) toward African Americans. As political activists (who remained disenfranchised), New Haven black people made it abundantly clear that they would demand their rights as American citizens; and those rights included not only freedom from slavery and the freedom to vote but also the freedom to pursue jobs that afforded economic stability and upward mobility—this at a time when increasing numbers of whites feared they were losing their grip on the same kinds of jobs.

The white men in New Haven in 1834 were reacting to two specific educational initiatives sponsored by the city's African Americans and their abolitionist allies. In 1831, delegates to the First Annual Convention of the People of Color (held in Philadelphia) declared their support for a proposed black college that would combine instruction in the skilled trades with a classical curriculum of instruction, to be located in New Haven. Supporters of the college were outspoken in their desire to attract the children of well-to-do West Indians of African descent, a move that would presumably further ties between merchants in New Haven and in the Caribbean. In 1833, the founding of a school for black girls (taught by a white woman, Prudence Crandall), in nearby Canterbury, also prompted fears of massive black in-migration: "Once open this door, and New-England will become the Liberia of America." That year, a white opponent of the school characteristically combined the notions of blacks as economic dependents and blacks as economic predators when he declared in one breath, "The colored people can never rise from their menial condition in our country," and then in the next, "they ought not to be permitted to rise here." The townspeople of Canterbury proceeded to jail Crandall and attempted to set fire to her school. The state legislature acknowledged the anxieties of its white constituents by approving a statute that outlawed any black educational institution enrolling out-of-state residents. The college never materialized, and Prudence Crandall was forced to flee the state, but the petitioners of 1834 were still smarting from the two-pronged insult. They wrote: "Not satisfied with depriving us of our labor, they are determined to become our Lawyers, Physicians, Divines, and Statesmen."[11]

The social turmoil in Connecticut during the first half of the 1830s indicates that it is not possible to extract regional political issues from their national context, or to distinguish the "public" anxieties of white men from their "private" lives as husbands and fathers. In the minds of white New Englanders, Nat Turner's revolt in Virginia in 1831 raised the specter of a massive migration of freed slaves out of the South and into the northern states. Connecticut residents as workers and voters took their cause to the state legislature, and in their physical attacks on abolitionists, to the streets. Mobility—not just ascent up the job ladder, but movement from place to place—formed the crux of antebellum northern free labor ideology; but mobile black men supposedly hindered white men who wanted to make use of their relative advantages. As white Americans embraced "universal manhood suffrage," free public schools, western homesteads, and the rhetoric of Jacksonian individualism, and as white "ladies" inspired a new social ideal of consumerism and idleness, black Americans retained only a precarious hold on their life and liberty. But they also demanded the right to vote, started their own schools, and moved in search of better jobs so that husbands might relieve their wives of the drudgery demanded of them by whites. Blacks lobbied, agitated, and spoke out for an inclusive definition of American citizenship; repression followed; and then racial prejudice intensified. In the words of a New York City abolitionist, "We dislike them because we are unjust to them."[12]

Between 1803 and 1867, the United States consolidated its territorial boundaries from Florida to California and from Texas to Oregon. The politics of expansion—more specifically, the question of the spread of slavery into the new territories—encapsulated a number of issues that went to the heart of the new nation's experiment with democracy: whether a country devoted to freedom should countenance the growth and nourishment of the institution of bondage; whether men of modest means must compete with wealthy slaveowners for land and labor; whether the two major parties could withstand seismic shifts in the congressional balance of power. Yet lurking beneath the surface of these grand debates was another practical concern of the people who had settled in the territories: whether free black people should be permitted to migrate into them. This concern reflected the fears of white workingmen in the eastern states (like the Connecticut petitioners), fears that former slaves, or people descended from slaves, would seize whatever jobs were available and in the process reduce white families to poverty.

By the 1850s, these sentiments, and the bloody attacks they inspired against black communities all over the North, had taken a devastating toll on African-American workingmen and women and their families. As the nation was witnessing the birth of the first major anti-slavery political party, and as voters all over the country fixed their gaze on the future of the South's "peculiar institution," the black abolitionist Frederick Douglass called upon northern whites to acknowledge the economic crisis that afflicted their African-American neighbors right at home. Douglass painted a picture far different from the one offered by the New Haven petitioners of 1834. The black man spoke not of blacks competing successfully with whites for jobs, but rather of the massive displacement of blacks from their jobs by whites: "It is evident, painfully evident to every reflecting mind, that the means of living, for colored men, are becoming more and more precarious and limited," he noted. "White men are becoming house-servants, cooks and stewards on vessels—at hotels.—They are becoming porters, stevedores, wood-sawyers, hod-carriers, brickmakers, white-washers and barbers, so that blacks can scarcely find the means of subsistence." In the United States, where men were valued not "for what they are," but rather "for what they can *do*," the rapid loss of even menial job possibilities for African Americans signaled the group's larger liabilities within the body politic.[13]

Douglass maintained close personal friendships with many white abolitionists (and indeed, in 1884, after the death of his first wife, he married a white women whose parents had been active in the cause). However, he refused to exonerate even relatively enlightened northern whites of their responsibility for a labor system that kept free people of color in a state akin to bondage. As Douglass put it, bitterly, "here at the North, our white friends—not our friends but our fellow citizens—have a regard for us—like us very well in our places,—and they have selected our places for us, and they have marked out the boundary lines for us,—and while we remain in the narrow circumference that they describe for us, we are 'good fellows,' and they pat us on the head and say we are good boys." Even the most ardent white abolitionist—the merchant, the manufacturer, the steamboat owner—showed his true colors (or rather, his true color) when he failed to offer employment to any blacks at all, Douglass charged. It was no wonder, then, that members of the northern black community in general believed that their fates were inextricably entwined with those of southern slaves.[14]

Together, Frederick Douglass, his wife Anna, and their children had encountered firsthand the forces of racial discrimination that restricted the productive capacity of African Americans in the North during the first three-quarters of the nineteenth century. As a slave in a Baltimore shipyard in 1836, attempting to go about his job as a caulker, Douglass had provoked a hate strike among white shipbuilders; in 1838, as a fugitive slave in New

Bedford, Massachusetts, he found that "such was the strength of prejudice against color, among the white calkers, that they refused to work with me, and of course I could get no employment." The young man proceeded to scavenge for odd jobs in the town of New Bedford until a year later, when he entered the ranks of foremost New England abolitionist agitators. Yet the acclaim that he won for himself on the national and international political stage was not transferrable to other members of his family.[15]

His son Lewis, a veteran of the Civil War, had learned the printer's trade in Douglass's own newspaper office in Rochester, New York, during the 1850s, yet white editors refused the young man work in that city; in 1869, Lewis accepted a job as a compositor with the Government Printing Office in Washington, D.C., but the local typographical union denied him membership, charging that he had once worked as a nonunion printer for less than union-scale wages. Presiding over the first meeting of the Colored National Labor Union in 1869, Frederick Douglass declared that his son Lewis was made "a transgressor for working at a low rate of wages by the very men who prevented his getting a higher rate." Closer to home, Anna Murray Douglass continued to toil in traditional ways despite her husband's increasingly cosmopolitan life. In New Bedford, as newlyweds working according to a gender-based symmetry, her husband made a living "with saw, buck, and axe," while she labored bent over the washboard. However, when he traveled to Europe in 1845, she stayed at home, now in Lynn, Massachusetts, and "sustained her little family by binding shoes." As Frederick Douglass gained in public stature, Anna retreated to the kitchen as cook, laundress, and servant, regarding her husband as her "honored guest," in the words of their daughter Rosetta.[16]

Frederick Douglass was keenly aware of larger economic changes that were dramatically transforming the labor of many white antebellum northerners. The welding of regional economies into a national marketplace through new networks of transportation and new methods of business organization and financing spurred a nascent industrial revolution in the northern countryside and in seaport cities. The artisan's shop—the shoemaker's ten-footer or the blacksmith's shed—gradually gave way to larger workplaces where employees toiled at machines of various degrees of technical sophistication. The face-to-face relations between a master and his servants, slaves, apprentices, and journeymen now yielded, haltingly, to the more formal, time-based discipline imposed by employer upon employee. Both parties had to adjust to the new realities of the workplace: workers, no longer bound by indentures and apprenticeship agreements, were free to come and go; but employers were also free to fire them at will. Meanwhile, the majority of American workers—women and children who engaged in some combination of waged and unwaged labor, in and out of the home—simultaneously labored at new kinds of tasks while remaining under traditional patriarchal arrangements, legally and economically dependent on fathers and husbands.

Historians have described in detail the wrenching effects of deskilling on early nineteenth-century artisans and mechanics, and it is true that master craftsmen in the textile and shoe industries in particular feared and loathed the factory. Wrote one woolen weaver from England, soon after his arrival in central Massachusetts in 1828, as he contemplated his son's job as a "Condenced Spiner": "This is a new meserable business for making money . . . the Factory Sistem which Sistem I hate with a perfect hatered as being only calculated to create bad feelings bad principles and bad practices." Workers throughout the Mid-Atlantic and the Northeast responded to the loss of craft pride and work-based community with resignation in some cases, and militant resistance in others. Yet the fact that the antebellum economy produced so many kinds of new jobs, and absorbed so many hundreds of thousands of immigrants, rivaled the long-range political and economic significance of the deskilling process. In contrast to their grandfathers, who worked primarily on farms—in colonial America or pre-famine Ireland—early nineteenth-century men found jobs digging canals and laying railroad ties, stoking the engines of steamboats, and manufacturing sewing machines and threshing machines. Their women and children engaged in a variety of manufacturing enterprises organized around outwork, and served as the vanguard of machine operatives during the earliest stages of the Industrial Revolution. The expansion of the construction and metalworking trades in the largest cities opened up not only new jobs but also possibilities for upward mobility among native-born whites and immigrants alike.[17]

Many Americans, then, faced dramatic changes in their work lives, or in work lives that had historically shaped the intergenerational well-being of their families. They labored in new kinds of places and under new conditions, forced to wield, or master, new kinds of tools. In contrast, as a group, African Americans stayed clustered in jobs that remained strikingly static, in terms of both organization and technology, during this period. A few skilled men and entrepreneurs continued to ply their trades; black barbers shaved white customers in New York and Boston, and black caterers served a Philadelphia elite. But for most black workers, intergenerational continuity in their work revealed their persistent poverty within a world otherwise notable for its expansiveness. Black teamsters and stevedores continued to load and unload ships on the docks of Cincinnati, and black laundresses continued to wash the clothes of white people throughout the Northeast, Mid-Atlantic, and Midwest. These men and women toiled not under one roof with many co-workers, but out in the streets, on the wharves, in small work-places, or at home. And they worked with relatively primitive forms of technology, or in the absence of technology altogether: The drayman callused his hands by dragging his cart through congested alleyways, and the washer-woman rubbed her knuckles raw on the fluted washboard. Together with waiters and carriage drivers, these workers remained at the mercy of white men and women who expected deference from them. Their jobs tended to be irregular and ill-paid, and offered little in the way of opportunities for advancement, cash accumulation, or home ownership.

For black northerners, work patterns differed from town to countryside, but within narrow parameters. In rural areas, black people labored as land-less, lifetime domestic servants and farmhands; unlike many of their white counterparts, they did not secure economic independence as they grew older. In 1860, six out of ten of all northern blacks lived in cities; indeed, as a group they were more urbanized than any other at the time. Some cities offered a slightly wider range of (lowly) jobs for black men and women. New York's rush to commercial predominance, Philadelphia's emergence as a manufacturing center, and Cincinnati's status as a western entrepot all affected to some degree the kinds of jobs available to African Americans in those respective places. With their more traditional economies, antebel-lum Boston, Providence, Pittsburgh, and Washington, D.C., earned well-deserved reputations for their particularly narrow job structures for blacks. Still, the range of openings in even the most hospitable of cities was only relative. In New York, black men and women peddled oysters, but they did not work in the metal trades; in Philadelphia, black men found work as sea-men in relatively large numbers, but they did not operate power looms in textile factories; and in Cincinnati, blacks worked as waiters and dockhands, but they found no jobs as shipping clerks.[18]

In 1860, the sheer numbers of (white-dominated) occupational categories grew apace, reflecting the growing need for specialized tenders of technology and the splintering of production processes into incremental steps. In contrast, about seven or eight out of every ten black men in the North found work only as laborers, mariners, cartmen, porters, waiters, and ser-vants; individual towns included small numbers of shoemakers, barbers, cooks, blacksmiths, tailors, and shopkeepers. The paltry range of options for men was limited, but greater than that for women, who toiled almost exclu-sively as farm laborers and domestic servants in the northern countryside, and as laundresses and seamstresses in urban areas. A few women hawked their wares on city sidewalks, or pieced together a living sewing or baking for white customers. In 1859, one investigator for the New York Anti-Slavery Society estimated that blacks in that state were concentrated in only ten or twelve occupations out of the more than three hundred jobs enumerated in the census. Because of the prejudice of white employers, blacks were relatively numerous among the ranks of the so-called self-employed—as woodchoppers, hucksters, bootblacks, and chimneysweeps as well as laundresses and seamstresses—but those jobs reflected their extreme poverty, and not any putative self-sufficiency.[19]

Shades of skin color were significant social indicators among the free black population of the North, for mulattoes retained some advantages over their darker-skinned brothers and sisters: they more likely had opportunities to become skilled, and they found it easier to attract and retain white customers. Yet in general the black social structure remained truncated to an extraordinary degree compared to its white counterpart. During the antebellum period, the northern white elite consisted of wealthy merchants and land speculators, men who made their living from traditional means, as well as an emerging class of urban professionals, chiefly physicians and lawyers, and owners of large businesses in manufacturing and construction. In contrast, the black men who served as pillars of their respective communities came disproportionately from the ranks of barbers, preachers, skilled tradesmen, petty proprietors, teachers, and waiters; women leaders included teachers, charismatic preachers, and entrepreneurs of modest means. Frederick Douglass and Sojourner Truth had both escaped from slavery, and whatever financial security they enjoyed derived primarily from their efforts as public speakers and writers (of their respective autobiographies). Robert Gordon, a Cincinnati coal dealer; John Jones, owner of a Chicago tailoring business; William Brown, Worcester upholsterer, carpetmaker, and inventor; and James Forten, the Philadelphia sailmaker, were typical of African Americans who acquired standing and influence not because their businesses were particularly large by early nineteenth-century standards, but because those businesses were relatively stable and employed a small payroll of workers. The success of these men depended less on dramatic forms of upward social mobility, and more on the dependability of their clientele, black or white.[20]

Between on the one hand the prominent artisans and preachers, and, on the other, the largely anonymous hod carriers, sawyers, and ragpickers who just managed to scrape by, were a host of ordinary black men and women notable for their enterprise and their nonspecialized labor. Born a free person in Rhode Island in 1785, Elleanor Eldridge entered the world of paid work ten years later, soon after her mother died. For the next six years, she washed and performed "all the varieties of house-work" for a white family in Warwick, and learned to spin and weave as well. Later she worked for other employers as a spinner and dairymaid. In 1812, together with her sister, she "entered into a miscellaneous business of weaving, spinning, going out as nurse, washer, &c, [and she also] entered considerably into the soap boiling business." With the proceeds of this business she moved to Providence and embarked on "white-washing, papering, and painting," supplementing her pay with the wages she made as a domestic in hotels and boardinghouses, or as a servant or nurse for private families. In Boston, one of Elleanor Eldridge's contemporaries, the African-born Chloe Spear, "worked early and late," taking in boarders, scrubbing and ironing clothes, and finding other jobs so that she could eventually buy her own home. Up and down the eastern seaboard, the male counterparts of Elleanor Eldridge and Chloe Spear combined work as mariners and boatmen with farming, woodcutting, selling produce at market, and seeking out odd jobs for whites.[21]

With the decline of indentured servitude, more and more white workers began to acquire skills on the job—not as bound servants or as apprentices, but as employees who had already secured wage-earning positions. Limited to jobs in the service and manual labor sectors, black men, women, and children were excluded from the most extensive system of vocational education that the antebellum North had to offer; without the requisite jobs or job-training opportunities, blacks as a group suffered from a kind of poverty that was not episodic in nature, but rather intergenerational and self-perpetuating. In sum, African Americans performed the menial labor that served as the legs of a ladder of upward occupational mobility that so many whites, and their children and grandchildren, had realistic aspirations to climb.

WHY NO BLACKS WORKED AS MACHINE OPERATIVES
IN THE ANTEBELLUM NORTH

Because blacks for all intents and purposes occupied a separate labor market from white men, and to an extent, white women and children, it was unusual for white employers to encounter a black and a white applicant for the same job. (As the exception that proves the rule, whites in some cities "preferred" blacks as hired carriage drivers, in the hope that passersby would mistakenly view the drivers as their own personal servants, and not as hirelings.) In the antebellum period, when most positions required no for-

mal education, employers often hired people according to their demographic characteristics—some combination of a worker's gender, age, ethnicity, physical strength, and skin color. Homogeneous groups alternately
suffered or benefited from this type of hiring strategy for a variety of reasons: because one group or another constituted an underutilized, local labor
pool; because one or another had predominated in a certain industry during
its preindustrial stages; or because social norms, or worker "preferences,"
dictated that in specific worksites men not work with women, or Irish immigrants with the native-born. Most devastating for the long-run prospects of
African-American workers was the universal exclusion of northern blacks
from the position of factory machine operative (though not factory
sweeper).[22]

Throughout this period, public officials, popularly elected and otherwise,
implemented policies that either directly or indirectly favored white workers
over black workers. Though weak by modern standards, the early nineteenth-century federal government helped to shape the northern labor force
in several ways. Black men and women were routinely rejected for federal
employment until 1861, when Boston's William Cooper Nell received an
appointment as a clerk with the United States Postal Service. Cabinet officials and military officers felt free to devise overtly discriminatory hiring
policies; for example, though routinely ignored on the high seas, regulations
barring blacks from naval service were promulgated by the secretary of the
navy in 1798. More generally, Congress voted subsidies to railroad companies, and protected a variety of enterprises—including iron, glass, and textile
manufacturing—all of which provided a wealth of job opportunities for
employees of these racially exclusive industries. The Dred Scott decision
handed down by the Supreme Court in 1857 reiterated the widely shared
belief among whites in all areas of the country that blacks had no rights that
white people were bound to respect, and thereby put its (retroactive) stamp
of approval on a whole host of "black laws" enacted by states in the Midwest and North to limit the rights of black taxpayers to vote, serve on juries,
testify in court, join the state militia, receive poor relief, attend public
schools, move from state to state, make contracts with whites, hold office,
and receive passports. Taken together, these measures affected the composition of labor market and the mobility of workers within it.[23]

Historically in the North, black artisans had been tolerated to the degree
that they remained under the control of whites through the institutions of
bondage, indentured servitude, or apprenticeship. As slavery receded,
whites as public officials, union members, employers, and co-workers felt
compelled to devise a number of constraints on black ambitions, constraints

that had the short-term effect of impoverishing black workers, and the long-term effect of restricting their upward mobility and poisoning the welfare of their households and communities. Artisans in particular began to register some of the unanticipated effects of emancipation in the late eighteenth and early nineteenth centuries. In 1798, a runaway slave, "Black Abraham" Johnson, voluntarily returned to his master in Berks County, Pennsylvania, because he soon found that "chances for my kind of employment" (as a blacksmith) were virtually nonexistent for a free man of color. Because they more often than not engaged in nonspecialized labor, slaves in the colonial North were mostly unskilled. However, the case of New York City, where artisans often depended on slave labor, reveals how quickly and irrevocably even the small group of skilled black workers and tradesmen could be displaced after emancipation. In that city, as the number of free blacks increased more than twofold between 1790 and 1810 (from 3,332 to 7,470), and the number of slaves decreased, the proportion of black men who worked as artisans fell from 38 percent to 29 percent.[24]

Throughout the northern states, black men began to lose whatever tenuous connection to the skilled trades that they had claimed as slaves, eroding the possibilities for their households to achieve a "competence"—that is, a level of material well-being commensurate with their status as free citizens as opposed to slaves and other kinds of dependent workers. By 1860, about one out of ten New York City black men labored at a skilled trade; the comparable figures for Richmond and Charleston were 32 percent and 76 percent, respectively (largely due to the fact that blacks constituted such a large proportion—one-third—of the entire southern population). Although some northern black men passed their trades on to their sons, these younger men found it more and more difficult to eke a living from skilled work that attracted white customers. In 1856, nearly 40 percent of the black artisans in Philadelphia reported that they had been "compelled to abandon their trades on account of the unrelenting prejudice against their color."[25]

The "racial" sensibilities of white employers and customers were not the lone culprit here. In certain instances, black men fell victim to the same process of forcible deskilling that affected their white counterparts; the introduction of a patented machine sweep in the 1820s meant that master chimney sweeps (almost all of them black) were bound to become increasingly superfluous. Moreover, recently emancipated free blacks, no matter how proficient at their craft, often lacked the resources that would propel them into the ranks of self-employed tradesmen and entrepreneurs; they remained dependent, now on employers instead of masters, for their livelihood. The unevenness of technological development meant that in some

industries certain groups of skilled craftsmen (like glassblowers) would continue to find a demand for their services within a factory setting; without a
niche in those crafts during the late colonial period, black men and women
(like whites without the requisite skills) could gain no entry into them.[26]

At the local level, municipal licensing practices and public works hiring
practices had an immediate and dramatic impact on the chances of black
men to find gainful employment. Responding to the demands of whites as
voters and as purveyors of "mob rule," public officials protected the interests of various groups of white workers. In the early 1820s, the mayor of
New York City refused to license a black cartman who, he acknowledged,
possessed the requisite qualifications; he added "that he would grant no
license to any but a white." The mayor explained his decision by "expressing
his fears that a compliance would endanger not only the man's safety but his
own. He said the populace would likely pelt him as he walked along the
streets, when it became known that he had licensed a black carman." By
1835, a foreign visitor could report, "the black carman in that city was as
rare as a black swan." In a similar manner, Philadelphia officials bowed to
the economic interests of their white constituents when they hired only
whites to shovel snow and clean gutters during winter snowstorms; among
all of these emergency municipal employees in 1831, for example, "there
was not one man of color to be seen, when hundreds of them were going
about the streets with shovels in their hands, looking for work and finding
none."[27]

Because industrial development was uneven during this period—few
crafts followed the New England "textile model" and mechanized completely and quickly, within the space of a couple of decades—it is difficult to
generalize about the forces that shaped the social organization of labor in
different job categories. At one extreme was the early appearance of the
automated flour mill that needed very few employees to keep it running. In
contrast, paper factories and textile machinery shops continued to rely on
skilled workers even after their operations had been consolidated and their
technology rendered more efficient. In some instances, white women were
tapped as factory workers because of their role in the colonial antecedents
of various industries—papermaking, shoe binding, and textiles, for example.
(On the other hand, despite their, or rather their grandmothers', experience
in household industry, women were excluded from Philadelphia's new soap
and candlemaking factories during this period.)[28]

A number of factors account for black people's absence from the emerging industrial workplace in the North. The prevalence of outwork in New
England—from nail to shoe and straw hat production—and the availablity

of land in the West made it difficult for early manufacturers to recruit sufficient laborers. The late eighteenth-century Connecticut mill owners forced to rely on an initial workforce of English army deserters and prisoners of war had an incentive to mechanize their operations and simplify them so that nearby farmers and their family members could learn them quickly. Pawtucket, Rhode Island, cotton mills began their operations by hiring native-born children; Lowell recruited Yankee farm girls; and rural Massachusetts mill towns made do for several decades with a relatively heterogeneous force of old and young, male and female, skilled and unskilled, native-born and immigrant workers. Despite their differences in ethnicity, age, and gender, these laborers were uniformly white, primarily because as young unmarried women, or as Irish immigrants regardless of gender, or as children (for example), they received "preference" for mill jobs, and not necessarily because mill owners made a conscious decision to exclude blacks because of their skin color. Nonetheless, such employer choices could adversely affect the job opportunities of blacks who existed in sizable numbers in any particular area. For example, although blacks constituted 7 percent of the area's population, Berkshire paper mills in Massachusetts employed thousands of white men and women between 1850 and 1880, but only two black people, and those two worked as outside menials. In Providence, and all other northern cities, blacks were conspicuously absent from factory payrolls, though their patterns of irregular employment in the service sector would have made them a likely labor source as machine operatives.[29]

Textile mill owners who relied on the boardinghouse system for single women might have been reluctant to integrate employees' residences, out of a desperate need to coax Yankee women out of their fathers' households and into the factories. The relatively small black labor pool—the tiny numbers of African-American men, women, and children scattered throughout the northern states—might have worked against their finding jobs within all-white, ethnically homogeneous workplaces. On the other hand, as a group, blacks were just as mobile as other (mainly propertyless) members of the laboring classes, and no doubt they would have migrated to those worksites where the presence of even a few machine workers of their own race would have signaled relatively egalitarian hiring practices.

Towns in general remained particularly contentious places. There the employment of any black manufacturing workers had the potential to incite white men and women eager to retain whatever meager advantages they could muster within a dynamic and unpredictable industrializing economy. In Westchester County, New York, in 1860, the African-American community known as "the Hills" constituted 15 percent of the total population of the town of Harrison. Black men could find work only as laborers, teamsters, sailors, carmen, gardeners, and waiters, while in the surrounding area Irish, French-Canadian, German, and English immigrants labored in such establishments as the Waring Hat Manufacturing Company of Yonkers; in silkworks, foundries, and brickworks; and in shoemaking as outworkers. Black men with families more often had to combine several kinds of employment to make ends meet; in the words of one wife, her husband worked at "Anything in fact that he could earn an honest penny." In sum, throughout the northern states, fledgling manufacturing enterprises followed different paths toward consolidation and technology efficiency; but all of these enterprises restricted machine work to whites.[30]

It is possible that a severe labor shortage in the North during the late antebellum period might have impelled employers to hire black factory workers. However, between 1840 and 1860, 4.3 million immigrants, 70 percent of whom were either German or Irish, entered the United States, and the latter group especially began to supplant black men and women, not only in the skilled trades but in service jobs as well, as hod carriers and stevedores, barbers and cartmen. Immigrants in general—the Irish in particular, but by the 1860s in northern New England the French Canadians too—provided a foundation upon which native-born white workers might escape manual, irregular employment. In the process, these same groups of newcomers effectively pushed many black workers down to the very lowest echelons of the workforce. In Philadelphia, the presence of a large Irish population by midcentury meant that

> when respectable women of color answer an advertisement for a dressmaker, either in families or with a dressmaker, they are invariably refused, or offered a place to cook and scrub, or to do housework; and when application is made at manufacturies immediately after having seen an advertisement for operators or finishers, they meet with the same reply, sometimes modified by bidding you "call again," "just suited," "will want more hands in the course of a few weeks," etc. There are many respectable workmen of color competent to fill any of the above named positions and who eke out a scanty livelihood at home, who would gladly take permanent situations, to sew, operate or finish; and some have advertised to that effect, making their color known, and received no answers.

In the city's dynamic manufacturing sector, the Irish newcomers constituted 23 percent of the workforce and blacks only 1 percent. Although blacks made up only 5 percent of the city's total population, their near-total exclusion from factory and machine work testified to an oversupply of unskilled labor in the region.[31]

Patterns of labor deployment established early in the Industrial Revolution could become elevated to the realm of family tradition for willing groups of workers and their offspring. Once a group gained a place in the industrial economy through factory work, it either left voluntarily (in the case of native-born women, who abandoned the textile mills in the 1840s and 1850s) or held on to its position by bequeathing it to the next generation. Kin networks, combined with ethnic affiliation, could serve to preserve the status of building, construction, metal, and machinery production workers through the generations; these jobs remained reserved for certain groups of whites and thus closed to all black people.

Unlike their postbellum southern counterparts, northern antebellum factory owners never developed a full-blown rationale, or an ideology based on "racial" difference, for excluding blacks from machine work. (The idea that black people were unable to perform effectively in worksites characterized by technological complexity would emerge in the North in the late nineteenth century; but it was the enforced absence of blacks from those worksites that created that situation.) Presumably, blacks as a group aspired to factory work. They probably resembled less the disaffected "republican" craftsmen descended from the Sons of Liberty, and more the Irish canallers and ditchdiggers who considered shoemaking among other factory jobs to be an improvement over outside work, and believed that such jobs, performed with appropriate attention to punctuality and discipline, might serve as stepping stones to better positions. Relying to such an extent on native-born widows, young girls, and on children as young as eight years old (especially in the largest establishments), and on the Irish, employers would have been hardpressed to argue that blacks were "ill suited" to work as machine operatives. To the contrary, their labor in a variety of colonial crafts would seem to make them logical workers in any number of jobs, including shoes and textiles. In any case, so rigid was the color bar in northern factories on the eve of the Civil War that Frederick Douglass urged his people to seek out employment with wheelwrights, blacksmiths, joiners, cabinetmakers, milliners, and seamstresses. And an Ohio convention of black leaders resolved "that they, the colored people, should not settle in large numbers in cities, but go to the country, cut down trees, split rails and be farmers."[32]

The sporadic violence directed at black workers and their communities in the 1830s and 1840s coincided with a newfound preoccupation with personal and public morality on the part of native-born white skilled and fac-

tory workers. In attempting to distance themselves from "disreputable" elements in the population—the poor in general, and African Americans and
Irish Catholics in particular—anxious Protestant tradesmen seized upon the
imperative of public order to regulate the behavior of increasingly presump-
tuous and rowdy workers. This concern was not entirely new. White northerners had always expressed their apprehension over emancipation in
moralistic terms, and as early as the eighteenth century they claimed that
free black laborers had shown a lack of restraint in public, allegedly "racial"
behavior that white city dwellers in particular found galling. By the early
1800s, various groups of black workers came under attack for advertising
their services in an unseemly way. In 1817, residents of New York City's first
ward charged that black nightmen (workers who emptied the privies in private homes) routinely breached the peace:

> A number of vagabond negroes who have taken upon themselves the
> business of nightmen excercise their functions in such a manner as is
> excessively offensive and outrages all propriety. These persons scream
> through the streets at all hours of the night with such a vociferation as to
> disturb everyone within reach of their destestable cries. . . . They transact
> their business often at a very early hour of the evening when the streets
> are full of passengers. . . . It is not only their savage yells that are offensive
> but they are in the habit of bawling out such expressions as are most
> shockingly indecent—They commonly go in pairs and perform a duet of
> this description, but a person in the neighborhood of Franklin Square
> may often hear a dozen or twenty of them at once vieing with each other
> in such noise & indecency as no stranger would believe could be tolerated
> anywhere but in an encampment of Savages.

The petitioners acknowledged that the nightmen were "people employed in
a work that cannot be dispenced with"; but as the self-proclaimed "industrious part of the community," these whites preferred that the lowliest job in
the entire city be carried out more quietly, more discreetly.[33]

Through various forms of labor organization white workers began to
assert their claims to workplace control, better wages, and shorter work
days, and those in a number of different industries initiated formal labor
unions, some more durable than others, during the antebellum period. But
in seeking to shape the social composition of their respective workforces,
employees engaged in spontaneous demonstrations of solidarity—through
turnouts, and also through mob action on the streets—that sent a clear message to their employers, and to black men and women: African-American
assertiveness, whether in the form of political activism or public job seeking,

would not be tolerated by white people who believed that they had every-thing to lose if blacks had anything at all to gain.[34]

Despite some notable exceptions in the shoe and textile industries, for the most part the white working classes of northern cities showed little sympa-thy for abolitionism as a movement based on justice or moral principle. They fixed their attention upon their own uncertain situation, and they had little inclination to initiate political alliances with the anti-slavery clergymen, merchants, and evangelical reformers who went out of their way to express their contempt for white wage earners of all descriptions. Moreover, some white workers who broke with their fellow Democrats and supported the anti-slavery cause consistently advocated keeping blacks "in their place"—that is, in the South—so fearful were these whites of the specter of black migrants eventually overrunning northern shops and factories. In the North, then, manual labor was considered honorable because it was there that *free laboring white men* do the working." In Pittsburgh in 1856, a group of several hundred white workers who met to oppose the spread of slavery argued that, wherever slavery reigned, there "Labor is servitude." In the end, to northern whites, the possibility that they might have to work alongside blacks in the North or in the new states to the west constituted a real crisis, for such physical proximity would supposedly herald the descent of free white men to the status of slaves or neo-slaves.[35]

These fears found confirmation whenever black workers asserted their presence and their competence in the public marketplace. It would be diffi-cult to tell which group more offended whites within sight and earshot—the "bawling," vociferous New York City garbagemen or the subservient wait-ers of the same city, who by their very industry challenged whites. Accord-ing to one foreign observer in 1833, "the better portion [of blacks] are spoken of with a degree of bitterness, that indicates a disposition to be more angry with their virtues than their vices." In northern seaport towns, when black hucksters hawked their wares and tradesmen advertised their services in boisterous songs with loud cadences, they assaulted the senses of white folks who came to resent the sound of these voices in the workplace as well as in the court of public opinion. Strolling down a narrow street in New York City one day in the 1840s, a white observer from the "respectable classes" might be struck by encounters with several forms of black "expres-sion"—a blind beggar "with horny hand and tattered garments"; a water-melon peddler chanting his unique work cry; and a black woman "preaching to a full audience" in a Methodist church, and "gradually rising in her tones, until she arrived at the shouting pitch," her "rude eloquence" spilling out of the pulpit and into the street. Indeed, many whites came to consider these sounds to be a kind of "war-song" calculated to mock their own moral and political sensibilities.[36]

When Cincinnati black wharfmen and boatmen sang slave songs as they worked, when oyster vendors in Philadelphia and streetwise chimney sweeps and peddlers in New York insistently and plaintively called out to potential customers, they trumpeted their role as economic actors, as free men and women of color who were also workers. Whites at times regarded these black intrusions into the cityscape to be sufficiently abhorrent, and sufficently provocative, to warrant a violent response. On the day before the outbreak of the Philadelphia anti-black riot of 1834, the *Commercial Herald* published a letter from a white citizen who referred to "the conduct of the black porters who infest our markets," meaning the intermingling of white women customers and black porters hired by hotels to transport foodstuffs to their restaurants. He wrote, "Is there no way in which the rudeness and violence of these ruffians can be prevented? If not, is it high time for the ladies at least to retire, and give up the privilege of marketing to those with whom might is right?"[37]

The public presence of black workers blended with other kinds of infor-mal "performance" staged by African Americans in a variety of settings, prompting charges that in their efforts to seek out each other's company, urban blacks were "particularly exposed to the contagion of bad example." The angry black crowds that congregated to liberate fugitive slaves from the clutches of policemen represented a peculiar, "race-based" kind of lawless-ness, in the eyes of disapproving whites. These mob actions partook of a dramatic, theatrical quality. Boston blacks who forcibly freed the runaway slave Frederick Wilkins, a black waiter seized at work, "rushed in [to the courthouse], and to the consternation and alarm of the authorities, yet without inflicting wounds or shedding blood, disarmed and overpowered the slave-catching officers. . . ." One sympathetic observer noted that "the blacks divest[ed] the marshall himself of his sword, and with a dexterity worthy of the Roman gladiators, snatched the trembling prey of the slave-hunters, and conveyed him in triumph through the streets of Boston. . . ." Thus did political protest, performance, and parades meld into one another in a fashion peculiar to antebellum America.[38]

In 1841, black Cincinnatians staged a celebration commemorating British Emancipation Day (on August 1) with a public meeting at one of the large black churches, followed by an outdoor dinner that featured orators who "admonished all oppressors in every nation that the day is at hand when the hand of Almighty God will sunder the chains of the oppressed in every land." Just a few days later, and as prelude to the attack a white mob launched on the city's black population, a white workingman expressed his outrage: "White men . . . are naturally indignant when they see a set of idle blacks dressed up like ladies and gentlemen, strutting about our streets and flinging the 'rights of petition' and 'discussion' in our faces." In other cities as well, whites saw in lively black street festivals, notable for the musicians playing African-style percussion instruments and marchers dancing down the street, not the African-American counterpart to their own exclusively white celebrations, but a threat to civility and the racial caste system. In 1842, just such a demonstration in Philadelphia precipitated a devastating race riot against the black community. In both of these instances the attacks led to black out-migration from both cities, as black workers and leaders came to understand that white authorities would afford them little if any protection, in the present or in the future. Indeed, more often than not, white officials provided the rioters with moral, if not actual physical, support. A commission established to investigate the 1834 riot against blacks in the Moyamensing area of Philadelphia confirmed popular racial prejudices when it concluded that "many whites, who are able and willing to work, are left without employment, while colored people are provided with work, and enabled comfortably to maintain their families; and thus many white laborers, anxious for employment, are kept idle and indigent."[39]

For free people of color, voting was also a public, and ultimately courageous, act, and wherever the law allowed it, black people went to the polls and exercised their rights as citizens, to the outrage of white politicians who found themselves among the losers on election night. In some cases, the support of blacks was pivotal in contests between two major parties. For example, in early nineteenth-century New York City, African-American men consistently allied themselves with the Federalist Party. In the 1840s, Rhode Island blacks sided with the conservative, nativistic Whig Party, in opposition to the state's white workingmen and their party, the Rhode Island Suffrage Association (which in fact opposed black suffrage). Blacks took their civic responsibilities seriously, prompting several northern state conventions to disenfranchise black men who had had the right to vote since their release from slavery. New Jersey (1807), Connecticut (1818), New York (1821), and Pennsylvania (1838) all revoked in absolute terms, or for all practical purposes, the legislation that had enabled black men to vote in previous years. In Bucks County, Pennsylvania, in 1837, a group of Democrats who resented the part played by black voters in swinging a recent election petitioned delegates to the state's Constitutional Convention with the admonition that "Negroes, whether slaves or free, from the first settlement of our country, have always been considered and treated by our laws, as an inferior race, and never until quite recently, thought or even dared to take any part in the management of our government." The petitioners concluded with a now familiar theme, that they believed their "rights as white citizens and freemen have thus been violated and trampled upon by negroes." Once again, whites charged that the assertion of black rights—in the workplace or in the streets, in the voting booth or at the courthouse—served to degrade and humiliate all white people.[40]

With the implicit support of merchant elites who depended on slave-grown products for their fortunes, and of politicians who sought popularity by condoning attacks upon disfranchised black men, mobs exercised a form of political power over the structure of the northern labor force. At a work-site in an industry that showed no growth, one position granted to a black job seeker equaled one less position available to a white man; that equation was straightforward enough. But the viciousness of attacks on individual blacks during mob actions—their pogromlike horror—suggested deeper psychological tensions among whites, and not just economic competition. Black people served as a collective scapegoat for whites seeking to make sense of the dramatic structural changes that were affecting their own liveli-hoods. Consequently white mobs reacted violently to demonstrations of black solidarity and assertiveness by storming neighborhoods and maiming, mutilating, and killing African-American men, women, and children, and destroying their homes, churches, and shops.[41]

On the job, whites drove hundreds of blacks from their workplaces and out of the city (for example, in Cincinnati in 1829), directed their rage against employers of black men (New York, 1834), and refused to work at a site in the presence of blacks (Philadelphia coal heavers in 1842, New York dockworkers in the mid-1850s). In cases that anticipated the targets of late nineteenth-century southern lynch mobs, whites vented their fury not against blacks of modest means but against the relatively more prosperous and stable class of black workers—the steamboat stewards and servants of Cincinnati, a black restaurant owner named Beverly Snow in Washington, D.C., James Forten's son in Philadelphia. Many of the perpetrators of vio-lence were young men insecure in their trades, declining artisans and jour-neymen; but in fact, while "hunting the nigs" called out masculine bravado and homoerotic thrill seeking, young white men in the streets put into prac-tice the prejudices so glibly uttered by their elders and their social betters.[42]

In the 1850s, the struggling white workingmen's labor movement that had fallen prey to the depression of 1837 reemerged, and a handful of unions with the requisite bargaining power sought to wield some influence over who entered the workplaces of their respective industries. Without the patronage and protection afforded them by slaveholders, black mechanics in particular became vulnerable to white workers' quest for trade monopolies. Founders of a national union in 1850, the bookbinders and printers not only restricted memberships in their respective organizations to whites; they also influenced the hiring practices of their employers. Journeymen bookbinders justified their racially exclusionary policies by arguing that "although the employer is the part who selects the boy and the work that he is to do, [we] are the parties to instruct him, and we do think that we have as good a right to place a limit upon the number we instruct, as the employer has to compel us to instruct any." Throughout the second half of the nineteenth century, as white workers' organizations gained in numerical strength and political power, they became more effective in achieving lily-white memberships and in relegating black workers to the margins of an expanding, dynamic economy.[43]

It was no wonder, then, that the multilayered divisions between African Americans and whites in the antebellum North seemed so stark to virtually all observers. Foreign visitors (and native-born ones as well) commented on the apparently more virulent form of racial prejudice that flourished in the "free" North, compared to the slave South. Wrote Alexis de Tocqueville in the early 1830s, "Race prejudice seems stronger in those states that have abolished slavery than in those states where it still exists, and nowhere is it more intolerant than in those states where slavery was never known." In fact, of course, the white North was wrestling with the problem of controlling the labor of black nonslaves, a problem that the South would face after 1865. In the North (as in the South, later), "Memories of slavery disgrace the race, and race perpetuates memories of slavery." It was in the various worksites of the North that white people's collective "memories" took tangible form, to the detriment of black people as workers and citizens.[44]

IN THE EARLY nineteenth-century North, black political protest melded with black labor and cultural "performances," and white people reacted accordingly. The early New England colonists feared slaves (and especially groups of slaves who acted in concert with indentured servants and Indian hirelings) for the potential danger they might wreak on white households; the grandchildren of those colonists resented the fact that black people assumed such a dramatic public presence as laborers, agitators, and streetwise pedestrians. That presence served as a constant reminder to whites that black people would continue to ply their wares from house to house, continue to denounce the institution of bondage, and continue to assert their rights as free men and women no matter how constricted their job opportunities.

By the time of the Civil War, white northern employers, consumers, workers, and public officials had constructed a social division of labor that kept blacks out of factory work and other expanding sectors of the economy. Denying certain kinds of employment opportunities to black northerners assumed the level of moral imperative, for whites believed that any advances made by black workers—any gains that would take them out of kitchens and off street construction crews—would necessarily come at the expense of white workers and their families. Thus emerged a racialized "zero-sum game" principle of labor relations that would pollute the American workplace for the next century, and beyond.

Despite their striking economic and demographic differences, the free North and the slave South showed some marked similarities in labor relations during the early nineteenth century. In the cities in particular, whites of the laboring classes regardless of region perceived the economic interests of black men to be inimical to their own, and city councilmen and municipal licensing boards, heeding the calls of their supporters, favored white artisans and tradesmen in open and unapologetic ways. In the South as well as the North, the relative fluidity of labor relations in urban areas contradicted the rigid hierarchies of caste, and signaled a larger threat to political and moral order. The fact that the vast majority of black people in the rural North toiled as landless field workers mirrored, if only obliquely, the concentration of southern slaves within the plantation system.

Despite these parallels between the two regions, there arose at this time no unified ideology of black inferiority that assigned the former slaves and their descendants to certain jobs; black people remained limited to lowly kinds of employment because they were politically vulnerable in relation to whites regardless of class or ethnicity. As particularly poor people, blacks presumably would have shown a willingness to work in factories next to other people similarly determined to earn steady cash wages. Nevertheless, different groups of white people acted with their own interests in mind, and justified those interests with a hodgepodge of different ideologies. Although only a few white workers felt directly threatened by the small numbers of blacks in the North, the cry of "unfair competition" resonated with white politicians eager to sustain the support of their constituencies. Moralists tended to conflate black people with the poor in general, and thereby impugned their ability to serve as trustworthy or reliable workers. Employers remained ever sensitive to the sensibilities of their customers and their own employees, on the assumption that even a few blacks dealing with patrons or working alongside whites could cause more trouble than they were worth. Whites in general believed not that black people were incapable of doing jobs which so many other poor workers obviously managed to master, but rather that they should not be allowed to do those jobs.

In another time and place, the poor but industrious African-American washerwoman might have represented the struggles of an oppressed population to overcome through productive labor the burdens that history had placed upon them. But to whites in the antebellum North, the woman of color who lugged her bundles through city streets, and at times perhaps even cursed the whites who obstructed her path, appeared to whites to be both a reminder of a slave past and a harbinger of an uncertain future. As the population of the antebellum North grew in number and ethnic diversity, the black washerwoman would continue to serve as a symbolic counterpoint for whites of all classes, not just because of the work she did and the poverty she endured, but because the color of her skin and the texture of her hair had acquired a new meaning of profound political significance.

························

CHAPTER NINE

WHITE CITIZENS AND
BLACK DENIZENS: WORKERS
IN THE NORTH DURING THE ERA
OF THE CIVIL WAR

F or two families in the rural Midwest, the end of the Civil War brought joyous relief intermingled with uncertainty about what the future might hold. In September 1865, John Roberts was mustered out of the Union army, and returned home to Bureau County, Illinois, to his wife Sarah and his six-year-old son Alexander. For the next twenty-four years John and Sarah Roberts would move at least fourteen different times, but always within three contiguous counties in northwestern Illinois. John Roberts sought out work as a woodchopper, a coal miner, and a farm hand; meanwhile, he and his wife retained ties to kinfolk and friends who remained in the same general area, about one hundred miles west of Chicago. The family's restlessness brought them little in the way of material blessings; when John died in 1892, Sarah was left with no personal property except her clothing.[1]

Soon after Eliza Brown welcomed home her husband William from the war in 1865, the couple moved north from Greene County, Indiana (just west of Bloomington), right over the Michigan state line to a town called Dowagiac. The Browns' journey was part of a group migration of extended family members and longtime neighbors who had lived together in Indiana. In Dowagiac, William Brown took a job working for a cooper, cutting hoop poles, and he settled his family in the vicinity of close relatives and a number of former co-workers from Indiana. By the time they made the move, Eliza and William had three daughters, Ann (nine years), Sarah E. (six), and a baby whom they named Harriet Beecher Stowe Brown. Yet William's health was poor (he had contracted measles in the service and never fully recovered) and he died in 1869. Three years later Eliza Brown remarried, but her new husband absconded after just a few months with all her savings, and she died penniless in 1874.[2]

Taken together, the Brown and Roberts family histories constitute two distinct yet tightly intertwined stories. The first of these stories tells of the hardships of rural folk in the last half of the nineteenth century. Both John Roberts and William Brown lived, worked, and went to war in the company of kin and friends; those ties helped to determine patterns of their own migration and employment. Yet both men faced an uphill battle providing for their families. The landless and peripatetic Roberts joined the ranks of a rural proletariat, while the more settled Brown cast his (brief) lot after the war working for a cooper, a skilled trade that was gradually disappearing with the advent of labor-saving machinery. This story was not unique to the Midwest. Rural tenants in Chester County, Pennsylvania, and farm laborers in the Massachusetts countryside all faced the same struggle to make ends meet without the resources of land, money, and new kinds of technology that an increasingly commercialized agricultural economy demanded. So they moved often, scrambling to piece together a livelihood in a seasonal, unpredictable economy.[3]

The second story revealed by the Browns and the Robertses constitutes a chapter in African-American history. Born slaves, John and Sarah Roberts had married "slave fashion" on a Tennessee plantation in 1856, and in 1862 they ran away together, finding their way to Illinois sometime in the fall of that year. Their many moves after the war resembled the "shifting" of southern black sharecoppers, men and women unable to accumulate cash or buy land despite years of hard work, and always on the lookout for a better contract, or a better employer, down the road.[4] In an era of industrial job creation, black people in the North and South, in the cities or on southern cotton plantations or midwestern wheat farms, remained confined to menial labor, far from mill village clocks and foremen's whistles.

The Brown chain migration out of Indiana after the war (between 1865 and 1866) included a number of black people—R. S. Russell, a farmer who had known William Brown since boyhood; Jonathan Brown, who had "worked around by the month" with his brother William after their parents died; Warren Mitchell, William's brother-in-law; and William's employer, Daniel Purcell the cooper. Born in Green County in the mid- to late 1830s, William Brown and his circle of kin and friends no doubt understood full well the legal restrictions imposed upon the state's blacks mandated by a new state constitution in 1851 and codified the following year. Black migrants were prohibited from entering the state; all contracts between blacks and whites were null and void; employers of black men, women, and children could be fined. Indiana blacks could not vote, and they could not serve as witnesses in trials that involved whites. Though taxpayers, black parents had to contend with the whims of local school boards, whites who might or might not allow black children to attend the public schools. The end of the war impelled the Browns to begin a new life in Michigan.[5]

Nevertheless, in order to understand the historical significance of the Brown and Roberts families, we would do well to avoid segregating them from their white neighbors in the Midwest, or from white workers in the North in general. The men of the Brown and Roberts families, like other farm laborers at the time, would soon have to reckon with the incursion of sophisticated agricultural technology into the wheat and corn fields, and wives and daughters of the two families would continue to share with other groups of women a whole realm of unwaged domestic labor. Moreover, by the time of the Civil War, groups of northern whites who sought to win advantages in the labor market over black people could no longer argue that the descendants of Africans were distinctive by virtue of their poverty and the lowly jobs they performed. The industrial-commercial revolutions of the Northeast and Midwest created whole new categories of workers displaced and dispossessed by regional economic forces, and a white skin did not necessarily insulate men, women, or children from the effects of these forces. To stake their claim to superiority over blacks, then, whites would have to rely on forms of self-definition other than their relative economic "independence"—for instance, ideologies of "whiteness" as opposed to "blackness." These ideologies were calculated to forge white unity and overcome rivalries that pitted Protestants against Catholics and the native-born against immigrants. In practical terms, "whiteness" proved to be an effective organizing strategy for the Democratic Party, as well as a boon to Irish immigrant laborers, who, because of their destitution and their history of serfdom in their native land, otherwise had precious few claims to superiority over black people in the urban North.[6]

The emancipation of 3 million southern slaves intensified the economic fears of northern workers, even as black people all over the country sought to win the rights that white men already enjoyed. In the North, black people were free, but until 1867 they did not possess (formally) the full rights of citizenship accorded whites regardless of wealth, ethnicity, or social standing. They were "denizens"—native-born residents of the United States, but without the requisite legal protection—as opposed to white "citizens." That black people only belatedly and grudgingly were afforded the opportunity to fight in the war to save the Union testified to a larger system of prejudice that relegated them to the meanest labor, and more often than not to positions of service to white people. Black soldiers suffered indignities, and worse, at the hands of their officers and comrades-in-arms on the battlefield, and in this respect Union encampments mirrored the civilian workplace. After the war, "whiteness" served as the underpinning of national reconciliation, its usefulness revealed in the similarity of work patterns among black people in the industrial North and agricultural South. And the forces preventing black denizens from achieving the status of citizens would survive until well into the next century.

BLACKS AND OTHER ANTEBELLUM WORKING CLASSES

Just as "race" is a concept based on relatives—there can be no "black" without a "white"—so the status of African-American workers in the antebellum period was a relative one, at the same time revealing of and dependent upon the fates and fortunes of other kinds of laborers. By 1870, blacks represented 2 percent of all northerners, a drop of a percentage point since the turn of the century (despite some northward black migration and due to large-scale white immigration), and most formed a tiny subset of the two-thirds of all American workers who were not self-employed. Juxtaposed to the southern system of slavery, the northern labor system seemed to offer whites absolute, and not just relative, advantages. Yet, as more and more northerners lost their ties to the land and to trades practiced by their fathers, they began to understand the limits and liabilities of "free labor." Meanwhile, rhetorical glorifications of "free labor" gave the impression of a similar well-being among a variety of workers, a condition that did not exist.[7]

In the early republic, traditional forms of bound labor—indentured servitude, redemption, and apprenticeship among them—were replaced not by a single free labor system, but rather by various combinations of the old and the new systems. More than half of the population (women and children under patriarchal control) continued to have only limited potential to enter the ranks of "independent" wage earners. New England and Mid-Atlantic small towns persisted in "selling" their paupers to the highest bidder well into the nineteenth century; the elderly, widows, and children were the groups most likely to be dragged to the auction block, where they joined criminals and moral reprobates as part of a bound labor force. In 1825, the town fathers of Manchester, New Hampshire, distributed Marjory Boyes and her four children among five different bidders who expected to get their money's worth from these workers for the foreseeable future. In some cases at public auction, buyers paid a lump sum to purchase an entire workforce for years at a time. This practice hearkened back to a colonial past. As we have seen, the poor in general were unlikely candidates as positive exemplars of free labor as opposed to slave labor; the starving needlewomen of the largest northeastern cities, closeted in tiny garret apartments and toiling for pitiful wages earned during sixteen-hour days, suffered from a kind of poverty and dependence that represented the wave of the urban-industrial future.[8]

Blacks were disproportionately represented among other groups of bound, or otherwise unfree, laborers during this period. Although all of the northern states had passed gradual emancipation laws by 1804, those laws provided for the continued enslavement of the children of slaves (usually until daughters were eighteen years of age and sons twenty-one); as a result, at the start of the third decade of the nineteenth century, twenty thousand slaves lived in the North, and many of their children were condemned to work as indentured servants for years after. (Even in Indiana, always a "free" state, black youths could be indentured for periods up to ninety years.) These children thus made up a transitional class of bound servants, persons legally dependent upon a master or mistress under the terms of emancipation legislation. Born in 1790 in Canaan, Connecticut, James Mars was sold eight years later by his owner for the sum of $100. The clergyman who bought the boy counted on using his labor for seventeen years, until he was legally free. Although a gradual emancipation plan was enacted in New Jersey in the early nineteenth century, the white residents of Hunterdon County were still advertising for "runaway slaves" in 1825, though any one of the blacks in question might have been, in the words of one historian, "a slave for life, a slave till the age of majority by the law of 1804, or an "apprentice," bound out by the overseers of the poor. . . . It is doubtful that in actual practice there was much distinction."[9]

Black seamen as well as black people accused of crimes were among those groups that found freedom to be a tenuous category in the nineteenth-century North. When shipmasters contracted the recruiting of their crews to independent "crimps," they opened the way for the widespread practice of "shanghaiing" blacks and whites alike—the kidnapping of men for the purposes of forced labor aboard ship. Furthermore, along urban waterfronts as well as rural byways, black men and women remained vulnerable to arrest and incarceration to a degree greater than their white partners in crime, and in the process they came under the jurisdiction of public officials who sought to appropriate their labor. In 1841, upon his conviction for "cuting [a] sapling," Moses McColly was "disposed as a servant" by Delaware authorities to the highest bidder for a term of seven years. From the seaport cities came reports that blacks filled state prisons and municipal jails in proportions far larger than their numbers would suggest. In 1846, blacks constituted 16 percent of Sing Sing and Auburn prisoners, though the black population in the state of New York was only 2 percent; 16 percent of New York City's Blackwell Island inmates were black, though African Americans as a group represented only 5 percent of the city's residents. Often forcibly prevented from attending the public schools, blacks nonetheless found state and local officials more than willing to remand them to public almshouses and workhouses, until those tax-supported institutions gave way to private, racially exclusive charitable efforts in the 1830s.[10]

At the same time that they remained uniquely vulnerable to exploitation from public authorities and private employers, blacks demonstrated forms of worker resistance not unlike those utilized by a variety of white workers. Indeed, the apparent differences in workplace experience represented by the white employee of a shoe factory in Lynn and the black cook in Philadelphia reveal little about the relative status of the two workers, and indeed, they shared more than meets the eye. For example, high rates of job turnover were characteristic of many laborers along the time-oriented and task-oriented continuum. Antebellum northern workers of virtually every description demonstrated a lack of commitment to a particular job at a particular worksite, and for certain urban groups, this turnover was complemented by high rates of residential mobility. Such disparate groups as canal diggers, rural New England and Delaware Valley textile mill operatives, Massachusetts and southeastern Pennsylvania agricultural laborers, and urban dockworkers up and down the eastern seaboard followed the custom of their colonial forbears and "ran away" from (that is, quit) one workplace in favor of another every few months or so. Some skilled workers, like cigar, tool, and diemakers, and metal and machine tradesmen, institutionalized the practice of moving from one employer to another in the course of their careers. These voluntary leavings, or "quits," stood in symbiotic relation to "fires," for virtually all enterprises—whether based on manufacturing, construction, or agriculture—responded to periodic upturns and downturns in demand, seasonal rhythms of production, or the vicissitudes of the weather. Thus farmers might combine wage work on a local railroad with labor in their own fields; young girls might teach school during part of the year and stay at home to manufacture straw hats or buttons for the rest of the time; and tenants and their families might alternate between the harvest and labor in a local gristmill.[11]

By the 1830s, northern employers in the canal construction business, in cotton and woolen textile mills, and even on farms had dropped all pretense of paternalism in favor of a more formal relationship with their employees, a relationship that depended on strict discipline to control and shape the workplace. However, few antebellum workers of any race showed much enthusiasm for conforming day in and day out on any particular job to the dictates of employers who engaged in both moral suasion (promoting the conscience as self-regulator of individual behavior) and workplace sanctions (threatening employees with fines and lost pay in order to encourage compliance on the job). A funeral, a circus in town, a communal bottle of whiskey, or even just a balmy spring day could promote wholesale defections from the weaving room, the wharves, or the wheat fields. More dramatic were the turnouts and other spontaneous forms of collective action that put employers on notice that they slashed wages, instituted speed-ups, or extended hours at their peril.

And too, black-white, factory-service dichotomies conceal the times and places where members of the two races labored together during this period. A few black businessmen hired both black and white workers; for example, Henry Boyd, who established a business manufacturing bedsteads in Cincinnati, reportedly employed several men of both races. Once in a while a black man took on a white boy as an apprentice, though these instances too were rare. The rough work of digging canals claimed the energies of black men who shoveled dirt next to white men, until Irish immigrants came to dominate the labor force in the 1830s. In rural areas throughout the North, black hired men worked with whites; on a farm in Setauket on early nineteenth-century Long Island, men of the two races planted crops, threshed, carted posts and rails, made cider barrels, and cut wood together. Buffalo, New York, sailors forged a biracial group consciousness, a pride of craft that transcended skin color, and in the New York City dock areas black and white tavern owners, prostitutes, con artists, cobblers, and cigar sellers intermingled "all on an equality." Black and white stevedores were still co-existing, if uneasily, on the wharves of Boston and Cincinnati during the time of the Civil War. In Philadelphia, the city's poorest residents, black and white, native-born and immigrant, huddled together in shanties, venturing out to scavenge for food, rags, bones, and other things that would bring them "hard earned (or ill gotten) pennies."[12]

Despite their common lot, northern workers throughout the antebellum period identified themselves not just by the tasks they performed on the job but also on an almost "tribalistic" basis. Conflicts between employees and their employers were at times rivaled by the hostility that certain groups of workers felt for each other—hostility based on Old World loyalties (Catholics vs. Protestants among the Irish), between and within ethnic and religious groups (Catholic immigrants vs. Protestant natives; French-Canadian Catholics vs. Irish Catholics), between workers within a craft (shoe factory employees vs. rural outworkers; male cordwainers vs. female stitchers). Moreover, groups of workers developed critiques of their own distinctive place in the economy. In the Manayunk textile mills outside Philadelphia, immigrant English spinners and weavers drew upon English radical theory and the Luddite tradition to denounce the evils of the factory system, while native-born workingmen in Boston and New York called for solidarity among the proud sons of the American Revolution, upholders of a republican tradition of independence. Native-born women factory workers resisted their male co-workers' notion that they should aspire to a ladylike domesticity and leave organizing and public speaking to their brothers and fathers. Declared the striking women shoemakers of Lynn, Massachusetts, in 1860, "American ladies will not be slaves"—and neither, apparently, would they acquiesce in a patriarchal ideology that relegated them to roles as guardians of morality and the home hearth exclusively.[13]

The vast majority of women of both races, native-born and immigrant, were engaged in some type of domestic labor, either as paid laborers or as wives, mothers, and daughters; but different groups viewed their status through different lenses of historical precedents and future possibilities. In the cities, Irish women soon began to predominate in white households as cooks and maids—in New York in 1852, as one observer noted, "all servant girls here are named Bridget"—but as soon as other opportunities presented themselves, they began "to assert the supremacy of [their] white blood," on the assumption that "black men and women are the only proper servants," and that they should limit their own domestic exertions to "their own households and in behalf of their own husbands and children." Yankee domestic servants, seamstresses, and governesses resented their declining status, their fall from helpers of friends of the family to mere employees. Louisa May Alcott, famous for her fiction but also experienced in a variety of low-paid antebellum "women's jobs," spoke through her fictional heroine in a novel appropriately entitled Work (published in 1873): "I like to work for people whom I can respect." These were women "willing to work, yet unable to bear the contact with harsher natures which makes labor seem degrading, or to endure the hard struggle for the bare necessities of life when life has lost all that makes it beautiful." Even some of the housewives they worked for lamented the sacrifices entailed in their own transformation from household industrialists to the supervisors of resentful cooks and maids, and in the process these white women embraced an ideology of loss and regret.[14]

By the 1850s, these cross-currents of intra- and interclass conflicts had by no means been resolved. What, then, made black workers unique in relation to the emerging white proletariat, in the countryside and in cities, and in relation to white women and children, who bore the brunt of industrialization as family dependents and as machine operatives? First, most black workers remained atomized, unable to wield the collective power, formal or informal, that accrued to large numbers of white employees who labored together inside. Black canal diggers and railroad and dockworkers toiled in settings where a tough, brawling work life, combined with high rates of turnover, discouraged the unity necessary for labor organization. Black people tended no machines, and they were singled out for legalized forms of segregation and discrimination. Unlike the white poor, they remained prey to mercenary bounty hunters like the New York City "Blackbirders," men ever on the lookout for fugitive slaves, or any particularly vulnerable black people, for that matter. Beginning in the 1830s, the abolitionist press routinely carried accounts of black families like the Butlers, esteemed "for their industry, sobriety, and [a] general good family . . . an unoffending and meritorious family," kidnapped near the Maryland line in Cumberland County, Pennsylvania, by a slavecatcher who "doesn't hesitate to say that he follows the business of hunting up runaways. . . ."[15]

In the North, as one foreign visitor observed with amazement in 1835, the formal institutions of public life mandated that blacks and whites remain apart from one another

> in infancy and in manhood—in sickness and in old age—in the manufactory and the poorhouse—in the school and the hospital—in the house of prayer and in the house of mourning—in the public festival and in the private assembly—in the day of battle and in the hour of death—in the funeral procession, and in the grave itself.

No other group of workers, native-born or immigrant, was targeted for deportation en masse, or restricted in its movements from one part of the country to another, within and between the free and slave states. In 1851, the few black men eligible to vote in New York decried the fact that they had helped to elect Whig candidates, white men who then turned around and debated the merits of removing all blacks to Africa, "as if we were wild Indians, or tares growing among the wheat." Patterns of interstate and urban inmigration among blacks, combined with escapes from the South to the

North, and then on to Canada, were not merely a variation on white population movements, but rather evidence of a distinctive political imperative
borne of unrelenting oppression.[16]

The peculiar liabilities of black workers become obvious when their history is compared with that of the Irish in antebellum America. As refugees
from poverty and the tyranny of their English landlords, and clustered at the
bottom of the job hierarchy, in seaport cities, too poor to move west with
the Germans and Scandinavians, the sons and daughters of Ireland would
seem to be potential political allies of African Americans, or at least imbued
with fellow feeling for them. The victims of street-brawling, native-born
gangs and their Know Nothing political mentors, the Irish—the "white niggers" of America—endured a kind of opprobrium that resembled prejudice
against blacks. Significantly, many Americans of Western European descent
initially identified the Irish not just as a group of desperately poor people
but as a separate "race," identifiable by their distinctive physical features as
well as their ragged appearance.

Throughout the Northeast, nativist mobs attacked the homes of Irish
immigrants and the churches and convents of Irish Catholics. Philadelphia
was the site of a full-scale riot of native-born white workers against Irish
men, women, and children in 1844. White elites charged that the Irish as a
group were the dupes of various sinister interests; a prominent Protestant
clergyman referred to the group collectively as "a dead mass of ignorance
and superstition . . . priestdriven human machines"; and a prominent
Republican in Illinois denounced the "thousands of roving—robbing—
bloated pock-marked Cathoic Irish" who cast their votes for Democratic
candidates in his state. However, rather than repudiating the "American-
ism" that humiliated them, the Irish wrapped themselves in the flag, and
embraced Negrophobia and the partisan-political apparatus that sustained
it, the Democratic Party. Ultimately, anti-black sentiments proved irresistible to people who possessed white skins, the advantage of numbers,
and the franchise.[17]

Like their native-born counterparts, Irish laborers came to believe that
the presence of blacks contaminated workplaces and cheapened the status
of free white men. This conviction had severe repercussions for black workers. In New York City, the Irish competed with blacks aggressively and successfully for jobs as domestic servants, common laborers, waiters, coach-
men, boatmen, and carters. Anti-black violence was so endemic to the
workplaces that claimed the energies of both groups that black workers
termed the missiles heaved at them "Irish confetti." It would be difficult to
label these encounters forms of "job competition," a term that fails to con-

vey the raw physical force used by Irish workers to maintain their hold over even the most arduous and low-paying of jobs.[18]

The decision among Irish workers to embrace the privileges of "whiteness" would have come to naught had they lacked tangible sources of leverage over employers and influence over political leaders. After the Irish Potato Famine of 1845, emigration from the Emerald Isle accelerated; between 1845 and 1855, almost 2 million Irish arrived in America. These immigrants were more likely to be Catholic, and more likely to be very poor, compared to their compatriots who had arrived in the United States a decade or two earlier. Still, despite such obvious liabilities, the post-1845 newcomers soon found that the weight of their numbers positioned them well in northern labor markets. For example, five years before the Civil War, Irish laborers made up nearly 90 percent of the New York City unskilled workforce, while black people constituted only three out of every hundred workers in that category. Therefore, when Irish dockworkers, waiters, teamsters, and ditchdiggers declared that they would refuse to work with blacks, employers realized that they could indulge these demands with very little cost to themselves; sufficient replacements were not difficult to find, and a major source of job disruption was eliminated in the process. Referring to trends apparent in many northern cities, a writer for the New York *African Repository* noted in 1851, "You no longer see [the black man] work upon buildings, and rarely is he allowed to drive a cart of public conveyance. White men will not work with him."[19]

Moreover, the Irish were adept at turning demography to political advantage, an effort that provided them not only with a loud, partisan-political voice, but also with new sources of jobs and new sources of upward mobility. In 1850, all fifty thousand naturalized Irish immigrant men in New York were eligible to vote, and those who did vote cast their ballots overwhelmingly for the candidates of the Democratic Party. Gradually, in that city, as in Boston and Philadelphia, Irish immigrants, and especially their children, began a collective ascent out of unskilled labor and up into patronage jobs, as teachers, policemen, and political appointees; and as beneficiaries of a city spoils system that awarded lucrative municipal construction jobs to loyal Democratic contractors, and lucrative licenses to liquor dealers and tavern owners. Thus the route to Americanization via racial prejudice made good business sense to the much-maligned newcomers, and the advantages they derived from racially exclusive political clubs and worksites helped to sustain their families, churches, and neighborhoods for generations to come.[20]

In contrast, the discriminatory social organization of labor, combined with blacks' inability to vote in an increasing number of northern states, served to impoverish black communities; but these handicaps also intensified their politicization. Free black northerners shared with black slave southerners the conviction that their collective futures were linked through the abolitionist movement, and together they also felt keenly their inability to rise as a people from menial subservience to whites. Even from white political allies, northern blacks could expect little sympathy or support on this score. Some anti-colonizationist activists suggested that black people should remain in the United States, not as a matter of justice or rights-based principle but because they could free all whites from the burden of dirty work if they stayed: "When they are gone, white men must hew our wood, draw our water, and perform our menial offices. . . . Why then should we drive so many humble and serviceable Helots from our soil?"[21]

As black people contemplated their past, present, and in all likelihood future status as "humble and serviceable" workers, they pressed their protests against a racially defined job structure. Indeed, the plight of black women workers in particular seemed to symbolize the plight of the group as a whole. Even within the category of domestic service, black women fared more poorly than their white counterparts. In the cities, the work of washerwomen was more physically arduous, and more ill-paid, compared to the work of live-in servants. In the countryside, black women domestics suffered from desperate isolation in the absence of a larger community. In her autobiographical novel *Our Nig: Or, Sketches from the Life of a Free Black, In a Two-Story White House, North* (1859), Harriet E. Wilson described her ordeal as an indentured servant in a New Hampshire household in terms that evoked southern slavery. A friend of Wilson's noted, "She was indeed a slave, in every sense of the word, and a lonely one, too." Physically abused by a white mistress, the main character in the novel endured the contempt reserved for "little *niggers*," even in the heart of the "Granite state."[22]

From the entire spectrum of northern black leadership came condemnations of a division of labor that was calculated to demean the African-American community by the collective humiliation of its women. The preacher Maria Stewart linked the prevalence of service to a thwarting of spiritual contemplation and aspirations: "How long shall the fair daughters of Africa be compelled to bury their minds and talents beneath a load of iron pots and kettles? . . . The Americans have practised nothing but head-work these 200 years, and we have done their drudgery. And is it not high time for us to imitate their examples, and practise head-work too, and keep what we have got, and get what we can?" An advocate of removal to Africa, the black physician and journalist Martin Delany, suggested that the "position of a people" was revealed in "the *condition* of their *females*," and asked, "Then what is our condition? Our *best ladies* being washerwomen, chamber-maids, children's traveling nurses, and common house servants, and menials, we are all a degraded, miserable people, inferior to any other people as a whole, on the face of the globe."[23]

Black leaders also issued critiques of the more general social and psychological demoralization that accompanied a lifetime of menial labor. In his fiery *Appeal*, published in 1829, David Walker ridiculed the notion that blacks should be content with more boots to black and forego the ambition that motivated whites of all stations. In the largest cities, some successful barbers who served a white clientele came in for a measure of criticism for their willingness to defer to the racial prejudices of their white customers; for example, a barber in New York said that "he dare not shave one of his own race, for fear of losing the custom of the whites." The black neighbors of these barbers envied them their jobs but resented the sacrifice of moral conviction that those jobs seemed to entail. Charged a group of well-to-do Ohio blacks in 1852, "a colored man who refuses to shave a colored man because he is colored, is much worse than a white man who refuses to eat, drink, ride, walk, or be educated with a colored man because he is colored, for the former is a party *de facto* to riveting chains around his own neck and the necks of his much injured race."[24]

The black barbers forced to choose between making a living and maintaining their own self-respect were representative of the many black workers who had to seek out work anywhere they could find it. In turn, the irregular, ill-paid labor of the vast majority of northern blacks adversely affected the social fabric of their communities, all too often severing families and destabilizing neighborhoods. High residential turnover rates, common among workers of both races and all classes during this period, hindered the ability of blacks to form viable political communities over time. In several cities, an unbalanced sex ratio in favor of women reflected the relatively plentiful jobs that awaited washerwomen and cooks, in contrast to the more unpredictable opportunities for men who labored outdoors. Without the income of a husband or father, black wives and children had to demonstrate extraordinary resourcefulness to make ends meet. For example, around the time of the War of 1812, the family economy of the Princes in Newburyport, Massachusetts, mandated that all of the children work to help their mother support the household. Their seaman-father a victim of British impressment, the Prince children picked and sold strawberries, raspberries, blackberries, and whortleberries, caught and sold fish, ran errands, hired out as domestics, and "scattered all about" in search of work. Scrambling to piece together a livelihood, some black men and women turned to illicit activity on a part-time basis. These were the tavern keepers who fenced stolen goods, the hucksters who shoplifted, and the barmaids who turned to prostitution to pay the week's rent; many of them relied upon victims and customers of their own race. Without representation on the bench, in the jury box, or at the police station, black lawbreakers were fined and sent to prison in greater proportion than white offenders, further weakening mutually supportive networks of kin and friends.[25]

On the other hand, all sorts of workers might labor to strengthen a community's bonds. Black women who accepted boarders into their homes helped country folk and southerners to adjust to northern city life; shopkeepers kept the hard-earned dollars of their customers within the neighborhood and used the money to support churches, lodges, and other institutions that benefited large numbers of people; the more modest barbers, those who had no white clientele, offered their tiny shops up for informal community centers, where the issues of slavery and justice could be debated freely every day; and seamen transported news and incendiary material from port to port, their communications the lifeblood of a politically engaged community.[26]

Given this tradition of political activism on their own behalf, it was no wonder that, during the Civil War, northern free blacks, together with southern slaves, readily joined the ranks of the Union army when the barriers to their service began to crumble. As black people, they saw the conflict clearly as a fight for freedom; as brothers, husbands, and sons, they vowed to reclaim a manhood denied to them within the highly charged politics of white political fraternity during the antebellum period; and as workers, they sought to distinguish themselves on a battlefield where—in theory if not in practice—strength and courage counted for everything, where bullets cut down men and boys, Catholic and Protestant, black and white alike, and where rewards flowed freely to those who did a job well . . . and survived. Yet in the end, for most black soldiers the daily work of war itself remained an old kind of work, and the glory that followed from victory on the battlefield failed to penetrate the postbellum workplace.

"LABORING FOR THE GOOD OF THE UNION"

In March 1863, Second Lieutenant R. H. Isabelle of Company H, Second Regiment of the Louisiana Volunteers, Native Guards, wrote to his superior at the headquarters of the Department of the Gulf to tender his resignation as a Union army officer. The target of a purge of black officers by General Nathaniel P. Banks, Isabelle explained his decision to leave the service in these terms:

> When I Joined the united States army I did so with the sole object of laboring for the good of the union supposing that all past prejudice would be suspended for the good of our Country and that all native born americans would unite together to sacrefice their blood for the cause as our fathers did in 1812 & 15.

But instead, Isabelle's experience in the army had convinced him that "the same prejudice still exist[s]." Isabelle's disillusionment was not limited to the higher ranks of black soldiers, or to southerners in contrast to northerners, or free people of color in contrast to newly freed slaves. All of these men endured indignities that served as reminders that their status as slaves, or as the descendants of slaves, would continue to mark their place in the postbellum North as much as in the antebellum South. Echoing Isabelle's sentiments was Nimrod Rowley, a private from the state of New York. Rowley wrote to President Lincoln in the summer of 1864 charging that black soldiers were consigned to fatigue duty day after day, and were forced to labor like beasts of burden, rather than proud fightingmen: "Instead of the musket It is the spad[e] and the Whelbarrow and the Axe cuting in one of the most horable swamps in Louisiana stinking and misery."[27]

The process by which black men were recruited into the Union army derived more from military and political necessity than from principles of justice. Blacks had proved to be a conspicuous military presence during the War of 1812; observed one white naval officer in 1813, "I have yet to learn that the color of a man's skin, or the cut and trimmings of the coat, can affect a man's qualifications and usefulness." Andrew Jackson's force of six thousand men included five hundred blacks when he defended the city of New Orleans in 1814, and that same year free people of color were prominent among New York City's defenders against the British. Nevertheless, black men had been excluded from the nation's militia from the time it was formed in 1792. In the decade before the Civil War, black leaders in northern cities formed their own militias in response to the passage of the Fugitive Slave Act in 1850, but the functions of these companies—the Massasoit Guard in Boston, the Attucks Guard in New York City, as well as the Attucks Blues in Cincinnati, and others—were more ceremonial than military.[28]

During the war, the debate among northern white politicians and military officers over manpower mobilization reflected both "free labor" employment practices and southern slaveholding traditions. For example, black soldiers remained segregated from white workers, and assigned lowly positions of manual labor. They had few if any opportunities to advance the ranks to the position of officer, and until the middle of 1864, they received paychecks smaller than those of their white comrades-in-arms, regardless of the work they performed. Moreover, military discipline for blacks at times resembled the sadistic punishments inflicted by slave overseers, and protests against these outrages were crushed with great brutality. Like northern employers and southern slaveholders, Union army officers demanded obedience from the men under their command, and they remained convinced that black men could—or should—endure heavy and dirty labor better than white men. As workers, southern and northern black men alike perceived the demoralizing continuity between the war and the period before the war; "compelled to remain at home" early in the conflict, they felt "themselves humbled and disgraced and treated with more contempt and disgrace than by the Southern Slave drivers and rebels." On the battlefield, subject to fresh humiliations, "Wee are said to be U S Soldiers and behold wee are U S Slaves."[29]

Northern public opinion militated against the recruitment of black soldiers until the war dragged into its third, bloody year and the rising death toll depleted the Yankee ranks. Republican and Democratic politicians began to realize that drawing blacks into the service might help to subdue the angry whites, male and female, resentful over the suffering of an all-white army. In August 1862, Samuel J. Kirkwood, the governor of Iowa, gave a succinct expression of the dual impulse that would eventually liberalize Union recruitment policies: Blacks would relieve whites of fatigue work—"I have now *sixty men on extra duty* as teamsters &c. whose places could just as well be filled with *niggers*"—and blacks would take bullets otherwise aimed at white men—"When this war is over & we have summed up the entire loss of life it has imposed on the country I shall not have any regrets if it is found that a part of the dead are *niggers* and that *all* are not white men—." The images of black men as trench diggers and as cannon fodder contrasted mightily with their own sublime rhetoric about the magnificent task that awaited them as freedom fighters.[30]

Once released of their inhibitions, northern military recruiters drew blacks into the conflict with unparalleled ruthlessness. From 1863 on, not only did white officials rely on the large numbers of black men, slave and free, who volunteered to fight to liberate their own people; they also engaged in strong-arm conscription tactics. These tactics went beyond the normal methods utilized to draft white men into the army, and instead evoked the methods of slavecatchers, press gangs, and man-stealers. Wrote one army engineer of the Florida men seized at the point of the bayonet by Union soldiers in April 1863; "My men, Colonl, *have not been drafted. They have been kidnapped in the night.*"[31]

Within northern ranks, the segregation of black and white troops was a foregone conclusion, for just as biracial workforces in the civilian workplace supposedly degraded the status of white labor, so it was deemed "unjust to the brave [white] soldiers and volunteers who are fighting as those who compose this Army do, to place them on a par with" black troops. White officers made the same complaint. Refusing to work with their black counterparts, white surgeons stationed in Maryland in February 1864 declared, "we cannot in *any* cause, willingly compromise what we consider a proper self respect." A white officer who promised a black chaplain an appointment later reneged on the promise, explaining that the action had placed both his honor and his life in peril. Black men who expected to shoulder arms and prove their courage on the battlefield instead found themselves restricted to hauling wood and erecting fortifications, assigned to work up and down the Mississippi Valley "during the sickly season, [so] it will afford much relief to our armies." Mortality statistics told the story in cruel detail: Fewer than two white soldiers died of disease during the war for every one killed or mortally wounded in battle; the figures for black soldiers were ten and one, respectively. From the front came reports of black troops chafing under such constricted work assignments, at times even forbidden to engage in military drills. The injustice was palpable: "No white troops lifted an ax or a spade while out on that trip to work . . . [they] lay in the shade [while] we were hard at work."[32]

Like slaves, black soldiers understood all too well that their fate depended to a large extent on the whims of individual white men free to exercise unlimited power over them. For some whites, command of a black regiment represented a shortcut to higher pay and higher rank; abolitionist-minded commanders like Massachusetts's Thomas Wentworth Higginson and Robert Gould Shaw were in a distinct minority. When a white officer referred to the flag of his Louisiana black regiment as a "dam pettiecoat and A disgrace to the brigade," or called the black men under his command "*Black sons of bitches*" or "d—d Niggers," or robbed them of their rations and forced them to work for nearby white civilians so he could pocket the money himself, or when he tied them up by the thumbs or "Bucked and gagged" them in retaliation for minor infractions, he dramatized the connection between serving as a United States army officer and serving as a southern slaveholder.[33]

In a host of other ways patterns of military service among blacks resembled their labor in the civilian workforce. Like black workers more broadly, black soldiers relied on meager paychecks, laboring under a wage system that limited black officers to the pay of white privates and ensured that ordinary black soldiers would barely have enough money to buy stamps for the letters they sent home. A black volunteer from Worcester, Massachusetts, wrote bitterly of the discriminatory pay rate in April 1864; "such a Government as this dont Suit me," he declared, though he was prepared to lay down his life to preserve it. Soldiers' dependents suffered the way the wives and children of ill-paid civilians suffered, and for this reason money could rival patriotic fervor as a stimulus to action. In Virginia, the federal government competed "against itself" when former slaves chose to work for staff departments for pay greater than they could earn as soldiers. Yet among black soldiers angered over unequal or deferred pay, the consequences for collective action were predictably severe. Sergeant William Walker, who led a strike among the former slaves in the Third South Carolina Volunteers over this issue in November 1863, was executed by a firing squad for his "mutinous" actions three months later.[34]

Even before the war's end, black veterans who returned home to northern cities found whites determined to preserve all-white workplaces. The violent attacks perpetrated by northern white workers upon blacks during the summers of 1862 and 1863 in particular represented a continuation and intensification of antebellum conflicts, and pitched battles fought on the home front rendered even more precarious the hold of black workers on gainful employment. As the second year of the war began, white Chicago meatpackers refused to work "for any person, under any consideration, who will, in any manner, bring Negro labor in competition with our labor." In July 1862, desperate to seize the shrinking supply of Cincinnati dock jobs for themselves, Irish laborers through sheer force and intimidation managed to oust their German competitors from the wharves, and then turned their wrath upon the black stevedores who were going about their work, shouting that "no d——d niggers should work on the levee." Three days later a white mob stormed a black neighborhood, to make their message that much more explicit. Anti-black rioters in Detroit in March 1863 attacked black babies and the elderly indiscriminately, and torched a whole neighborhood—first stripping the homes of black workers of "a large number of musical instruments," symbols of a black public presence, which they then ceremoniously burned in a pile.[35]

In the spring of 1863, one hundred sixty white caulkers walked off their jobs in the Boston Navy Yard to protest the hiring of a black caulker from

Baltimore. The whites were fired as a result, provoking outcries that once again blacks had deprived white men of their right to make a living. About this same time, the Boston *Pilot*, an organ of the conservative Roman Catholic hierarchy in that city, sounded the alarm over the impending doom that awaited white workers should the fondest hopes of abolitionists be realized and "these [black] wretches crowd our cities, and by overstocking the market of labor do incalculable injury to white hands." Taking refuge in the patriotism of his readers, the *Pilot* writer charged: "What has the African done for America? What great or even decent work has his head conceived, or his hands executed? We pity his condition: but it is unjust to put him in the balance with the white laborer. To white toil this nation owes everything; but to *black, nothing*." And then came this warning: "*Let no man employ a black while he can get a white laborer.* He who prefers the black to the white may yet find his own injured by the choice."[36]

William Lloyd Garrison reprinted this *Pilot* editorial in its entirety in his abolitionist paper *The Liberator*, and followed up the piece with a letter to the editor from a writer (Garrison himself perhaps) who made an invidious comparison typical of antebellum abolitionists. Wrote "Justice," "for all the purposes of intelligent citizenship, free black men are more tractable and thoughtful, less inclined to fight among themselves or with others, to brawl, to quarrel about trifles, to drink whiskey and get themselves into the hands of the police authorities, than free Irish men." (By the last comment he no doubt meant to remind the readers of the *Pilot* that they too had been slaves, of the English, in their own land.) This exchange revealed some of the animosities that had simmered within antebellum Boston—the raw contempt of Brahmin for Irish, white for black, rich for poor, Protestant for Catholic, Republican for Democrat. And in July 1863 these conflicts boiled over, as Irish immigrants took to the streets to protest the newly instituted Union military conscription law.[37]

That same month, draft riots directed at Lincoln's Republican administration in general and at black workers and their families in particular swept across the Northeast, from New York to Hartford, Boston to Brooklyn, Troy to Newark. White workers in all of these cities feared that freed slaves would migrate north, and there engage in a vicious bid to undercut whites for the remaining low-paying jobs on the wharves and city streets. The rioters were convinced they faced a formidable array of foes—Republican nation-state builders and haughty merchant-employers, some of whom had enlisted their minions, black men, in an effort to degrade all honest white workingmen. In New York City these fears assumed a particularly virulent form, as mobs proceeded to destroy the Colored Orphan Asylum and subject individual black men to mutilation, castration, and lynching. Irish workers in that city triumphantly managed to uphold the "white-only rule" on dock areas, a "rule" that had been violated recently by black men who found sporadic work there as strikebreakers; now these men were expelled from that workplace altogether.[38]

Apart from these conflagrations inspired by the political imperative of "whiteness," black workers in general felt the devastation of war on several fronts. As unskilled workers within the North's commercial economy, they lost their jobs when the bustling docks of Boston, Philadelphia, Cincinnati, and New York registered the effects of disrupted national and international trade. As a subset of poor northerners, they found it difficult to pay for basic necessities in the midst of runaway wartime inflation. As dependents of black soldiers, black women, children, and the elderly bore the brunt of the army's callous wage policy. In September 1864, Rachel Ann Wicker of Miami, Ohio, wrote to "the Governor of Massachusetts or the President" demanding to know why her husband, who enlisted in the 54th Massachusetts Regiment, had not been paid:

> i think it a Piece of injustice to have these soldiers there 15 months with out a cent of Money. . . . i speak for my self and Mother and i know a great many others as well as ouselve are suffering for the want of money to live on when provision and Cltheing wer Cheap we might have got a long But Every thing now is thribbl and over what it was some thre year Back.[39]

Just as the blatant injustice embedded in the northern workplace served to politicize northern black communities, so too did the hypocrisy of the Union army as an "employer" of black men serve to spur black soldiers and civilian leaders to action. Military men aggressively sought redress of their grievances from higher authorities, an opportunity for protest rarely available to them as workers at home. And, too, black men attempted to draw out of their experience as soldiers any advantages they could garner: some learned to read and write during the long hours of relative inactivity in camp, while others grasped at the chance to discuss the great issues of slavery and freedom with their comrades-in-arms. Black veterans, and especially the few men who served as officers, went on to leadership positions in their own communities, and to positions of national prominence in the postbellum black conventions of freedpeople in the South. In some cases they were able to parlay their experience as Union army men into jobs with the Freedmen's Bureau, the northern freedmen's aid societies, or the postwar army that moved on to the Indian wars in the West.[40]

Networks of kin and friends that had helped to shape the antebellum workplace carried over into wartime. When disabled veterans applied for federal pensions due them after the war, they could call upon brothers and former co-workers to testify both to their physical well-being before the conflict and to the specific incident that led to their disability. In the vicinity of the town of Eldorado, in Saline, a southeastern county of Illinois, the veteran James H. Patton referred pension officials to nine black farmers and farm laborers, men who had known him "before, during, and after our term of service," to corroborate his account that he had entered the war a healthy man and "came home, a badly diseased, and broken down man."[41]

Many black soldiers returned home suffering from chronic ailments they had contracted while performing heavy labor during the war. These were not the amputees who had escaped with their lives but lost a limb to a sharpshooter's bullet; instead, they were men like Minos Miller, a farm hand before the war, who soon after his discharge "found he could not make half a hand" working on an Iowa prairie farm, fencing and plowing. Simeon Schultz, born in New York City in July 1832, was as a youth taken to New Jersey by a white man for whom he was bound to labor until he reached the age of twenty-one. Schultz married Mary Van Deveer in 1860, and three years later he and two of his wife's cousins took off for New Haven, where they enlisted. Recalled his wife later, "We did not want him to enlist and he was afraid we would not let him leave if he enlisted at Bound Brook [in New Jersey]." While on fatigue duty near Petersburg, Virginia, in November 1864, Schultz was working as part of a detail carrying logs to help build a breastworks fortification; a log slipped from the shoulders of the men in front of him, and struck his foot, leaving him crippled. After the war he worked in a grocery store in New Brunswick, his days as a physically active "laboring man" over. For men whose livelihood depended upon their muscle power, such disabilities could substantially reduce their already meager earning capacity. Though he was "a good spry boy before the war," Henry Ellis's postwar life in the nation's capital was limited to taking jobs as a messenger, teamster, and custodian in the U.S. Marine Hospital. The rheumatism that plagued him after the war prevented him from taking any employment that required much in the way of physical exertion—again, a distinct liability in the case of any black job seeker.[42]

About 180,000 black men (33,000 of them from the northern states) fought in the ranks of the Union army during the Civil War, and black women served the effort as teachers of the former slaves, and as nurses, cooks, and laundresses in Yankee encampments. Yet neither these specific contributions, nor black men's newly won status as enfranchised citizens (with the passage of the Fifteenth Amendment in 1870), had a discernible impact on the northern social division of labor. Black men in the North volunteered for service in large numbers—in some states, in higher proportions than whites—and they distinguished themselves on the battlefield when provided the opportunity to do so. Yet this patriotic commitment counted for little among the white workers and white employers who contended with a volatile postwar labor market. The increasingly militant white trade union movement, which garnered numerical strength and political influence in the course of the war, failed to offer black men a role in their great crusade for labor reform. During the conflict, white women gained a foothold in the expanding federal bureaucracy, and stayed on after 1865, when government agencies processed growing numbers of land claims and veterans' pension claims. In addition, white women nurses and teachers emerged from the war to embark on a new path toward professionalism, yet specialized institutions of higher learning in these fields excluded black women altogether. Four years after the war's end, Frederick Douglass saw the future of black workers "shrouded in doubt and danger," because unresolved was "Whether this newly emancipated race shall be allowed to work in any other than menial occupations." For black men—and women—who after 1865 aspired to positions other than fatigue duty, the war experience held out little hope.[43]

The end of the Civil War opened a new chapter of the white working-class trade union movement, one that depended ultimately on racially exclusive policies to provide white men with the collective "self-respect" to challenge employers. The founding of the National Labor Union (NLU) in 1866 brought together representatives of typographers, mule spinners, stationary engineers, wool hat finishers, morocco dressers, locomotive firemen, tailors, iron molders, and cloth cutters, among other unions. Although women shoe binders (as members of the Daughters of St. Crispin) were a sporadic presence at annual meetings of the NLU until its demise in the early 1870s, and although some of the group's leaders made gestures in the direction of biracial organizing, for the most part this organization reinforced antebellum forms of "racial" self-identification among white tradesmen: they continued to define themselves as not poor, not black, and not female—that is, as white men. William Sylvis, a founder of the Iron Molders International Union in Philadelphia and second president of the NLU, could break with tradition and call for "consolidation" between black and white workers, and at the same time express his contempt for biracial equality, in the courtroom or in the parlor. As long as even the white "friends" of black tradesmen persisted in denigrating them in social and political terms, a cynical opportunism would characterize their calls for biracial "unity."[44]

Isaac Myers, leader of a union of black ship caulkers in Baltimore, attended NLU meetings but found little common ground with the other delegates. As a workingman who had had his livelihood violently stripped from him by white competitors, and as a loyal Republican who remained suspicious of both the Democratic Party and all calls for a third (Labor) party, he soon realized that the interests of the men he represented were not necessarily the same as those of the whites who dominated the NLU. Consequently, in 1869 Myers helped to found the Colored National Labor Union (CNLU), in Washington, D.C., and put white onlookers on notice:

American citizenship is a complete failure if [the black man is] proscribed from the workshops of this country—if any man cannot employ him who chooses, and if he cannot work for any man whom he will. If citizenship means anything at all, it means the freedom of labor, as broad and as universal as freedom of the ballot.

By linking the right to work with the right to vote as standards of citizenship, Myers exposed the intentions of white tradesmen who worried less about the rights of all workers and more about the preservation of their own exclusive domains.[45]

Still, if the odds against black men gaining access to apprenticeships in the skilled trades were daunting, the odds against black women moving out of the "lamentably circumscribed" occupational sphere seemed overwhelming. In 1871, the CNLU established a special women's committee headed by Mary Ann Shadd Cary. (Cary, typical of mid-nineteenth-century black leaders, followed several kinds of work in her role as activist. She served as a teacher, Union army recruiting officer, journalist, and outspoken women's rights advocate, and she was also the first black woman lawyer in the United States.) In the committee's final report, they called upon their sisters to seek out "profitable and health-inspiring employment," jobs in "market-gardening, small fruit and berry culture, shop and storekeeping, upholstering, telegraphing, and insurance and other agencies," a list that pointedly omitted the manufacturing sector, the greatest source of new opportunities for white women.[46]

By the end of the 1860s, it was clear that African-American women and men, white women wage earners, white non-waged housewives, white tradesmen, and the white laboring poor would remain isolated from each other, unable to achieve even a mutually agreed upon definition of American citizenship. White male union members regarded the women who labored under the same roof with them but in a separate room as competitors willing to work for cheap wages, and as the instigators of a demoralized, mechanized workplace. White women who took up the standard of social reform came to think of their moral and legal crusades as distinct from the economic and civil rights issues that united black men and women of all classes. Soon after the Civil War, the coalition between abolitionists and women's rights activists that had emerged in the 1850s splintered, as white women of the "respectable classes" began to narrow their own goals to the vote, and to identify their interests in opposition to black and white working people.

These divergent impulses derived from divergent work experiences, among other factors. It was difficult for the harried mistresses of cooks and servants, the resentful black tradesmen and laundresses, the young white women factory workers, the disgruntled white male farm hands and wage earners to make any connection between their own struggles in the marketplace of labor, waged and unwaged, and the struggles of other groups. Yet all of these working classes entered a new, postwar "gilded" world, in which the measure of men—and women—depended not only on what they did but how much money (if any) they earned while doing it; the healthfulness (or lack thereof) of their work; and the degree of control over their lives they had to, or continued to, yield to someone else, in or outside of their own homes.

DURING THE CIVIL War decade, the Republican Party's commitment to the elimination of race-based restrictions in federal law resulted in significant legislation: the Thirteenth Amendment (1865); the Civil Rights Act of 1866; and the Fourteenth (1868) and Fifteenth amendments (1870). But although these provisions would serve as the basis of a revolution, a Second Reconstruction, one hundred years later, they had no real impact on the social division of labor at the time. It was during this period that northern and southern principles of black labor deployment converged; as free people, blacks would be confined to menial labor, and gradually stripped of their status as tradesmen, craftsmen, and entrepreneurs with white customers. By the 1870s, they could only brace themselves for a fresh new wave of foreign immigration, a wave that would confirm the major theme of antebellum northern labor relations: "Wherever the interests of the white man and the black come into collision in the United States, the black man goes to the wall."[47]

It might be true, as some historians have suggested, that the riotous political rallies and torchlight parades sponsored by antebellum local party lead-

ers (whether Democratic, Whig, Free Soil, or Republican) distracted substantial numbers of native-born white workingmen from the real source of
their troubles—industrial capitalism—and gave them only an illusory power
over their own lives.[48] (After the war, black communities initiated their own
tradition of Emancipation Day celebrations that once again linked public
performance to political protest, and also served as a counterpoint to
whites' partisan gatherings.)[49] However, the ballot box offered whites in general, and the Irish in particular, concrete rewards in the marketplace, though
they might reap those rewards only gradually, over the generations. If
notions of white "racial" superiority represented a "wage" or wage supplement to whites, then at times the material benefits came only in the form of
deferred compensation, if at all. Still, "whiteness" was a prerequisite if not a
guarantee of economic mobility and political power, and too often "blackness" represented a liability that could not be overcome through hard work,
talent, or ambition.[50]

For nineteenth-century African-American workers, the blessings of
American citizenship were contingent upon the time and place in which
they lived. Within five years after the end of the Civil War, it was apparent
that black men would retain the right to vote only to the extent that local
white politicians and their constituents would allow them to vote, and that
aside from the few who were self-employed in modest ways, black men and
women workers would find jobs only to the extent that they did not deprive
whites in the same locale of their advantages in the realm of gainful
employment. For these reasons, the key to the future of the collective well-
being of black workers was their ability to move from place to place—not
within the shifting sharecropper's narrow boundaries, but to regions of the
country where (they could hope) a high demand for labor could render
racial ideologies counterproductive and irrelevant for employers and workers alike. Therefore, the black workers who chose to move in search of political and economic rights reinvigorated a most distinctive American
value—the value of taking a risk by taking a mind to leave, unfettered by the
chains of slavery or by the taunts of a mob.

PART III

THE RISE AND DECLINE OF THE RACIALIZED MACHINE

Technological and Political Change in the Workplace

THE MODERNIZATION OF PREJUDICE: ECONOMIC CHANGE AND THE SOCIAL DIVISION OF LABOR, 1870–1930

One morning in the summer of 1951, soon after reporting for work in an East Chicago, Indiana, steel foundry, seventeen-year-old James Comer caught sight of a black man, "with broad shoulders and taut muscles, sweat pouring off his body, straining to perform an operation at the furnace," and realized that the man was his cousin, Johnny Lee. Comer's father Hugh had helped Johnny Lee to get a "good job" at the steel mill, and within the racial hierarchy of the mill, the dirty, dangerous work in the foundry qualified as a good job. Noted James Comer, "None of the black men had clean jobs." Moreover, black men went to work every day knowing that "no matter how hard they worked they could not move up" to a skilled, more secure, and better-paying position; the brick-layer's helper could never aspire to become a bricklayer, and Johnny Lee could never hope to become a welder or machinist. Some white employees new to the steel industry also started out in the blast furnace, but they did not remain in those jobs very long, and when they moved on, they left behind older, more experienced black men.[1]

Hugh Comer had migrated from Alabama to Indiana in 1916 and labored in a steel foundry until 1949, when he contracted severe emphysema "as a result of the heat, smoke, and dust he had worked in over the years." Nevertheless, he and his wife Maggie had managed to make their way into the middle class through hard work and good luck. Maggie Comer, born in Mississippi, had moved north in 1920, and in the course of her married life with Hugh, she ironed, washed, cooked, operated a small grocery store, took in boarders, worked for a caterer, served as a poll watcher on election days, and performed other "little jobs here and there." Hugh Comer labored for a time as supervisor of the foundry's janitors (all of whom were black), and as a beneficiary of his white boss's patronage, he received a generous cash settlement from the company for his respiratory illness. The five Comer children eventually earned a total of thirteen college degrees. After his summer job as a steelworker in 1951, James Comer went to college, then medical school, and on to a faculty position at Yale University: "The steel mill had given us a small piece of the American dream that the cotton fields could not."[2]

Yet more representative of twentieth-century black laborers than Hugh Comer were the other leaders of the Comers' church—the men who, though attired in "white shirts and ties, robes and roles of dignity" every Sunday morning, remained "covered in soot, grime, and grease from head to toe" every work day of their lives. These black foundry employees were working at jobs that were less "black men's jobs" than jobs that carried no chance of promotion because they were performed by black men. The poet Claude McKay compressed the muted outrage of all black workers: "Your door is shut against my tightened face / And I am sharp as steel with discontent."[3]

Between 1870 and 1930, transformations in the "racial" division of labor resulted primarily from the initiative of black men and women themselves—the sharecroppers who abandoned the neo-slavery of the cotton fields in favor of wage work in sawmills and "public work" in southern towns; the domestic servants who left the kitchens of their employers to work long hours as tobacco stemmers; and the 1.5 million black southerners who migrated from the South into northern cities between 1916 and 1930 to take jobs in steel mills and meatpacking plants, on auto assembly lines and in garment factories. Nevertheless, for virtually all blacks regardless of the region of the country or the economic sector in which they labored, upward mobility within the workplace was restricted by the intransigence of employers and the hostility of white co-workers. Even relatively egalitarian labor unions enforced the ironclad dictum that black people should never rise above their appointed station. William R. Riley, a black organizer of coal miners, noted in 1892 that the installation of a black man as assistant bank boss at a mine in Laurel County, Kentucky, prompted the whites to declare that "they won't work under any negro and the drivers won't pull the coal that is dug under a negro boss." Demanded Riley, "And now I would like to know how under heaven do the white miners expect for the colored people to ever feel free and welcome in the order of Knights of Labor or United Mine Workers of America, when their so-called brothers don't want them to get not one step higher than the pick and shovel."[4]

During these years, industrial expansion followed an uneven and bloody course, characterized not only by technological innovation but also by traditional, and coercive, means of labor deployment. The "good roads" movement of the South was symbolized by the pickax of the convict laborer, and middle-class prosperity heightened the demand for black women domestic servants. Concentrated in "stagnating" industries, black men and women sought out employment opportunities (as strikebreakers if need be), which prompted violent retaliation on the part of whites determined not only to hold on to their own jobs but also to gain more control over their own wages and working conditions. The disenfranchisement of virtually all rural southern blacks between 1890 and 1916; the ritualistic murder of one hundred fifty black men, women, and children each year during the decade of the 1890s; and the deaths of hundreds more as a result of anti-black riots in East St. Louis, Chicago, and other northern cities during World War I, told a grim tale of white backlash.[5]

Wherever they lived, black workers could count on few white allies of any class during these years. In political terms at least, the much-heralded principle of *laissez-faire* proved one-sided, as sheriffs and judges aided and abetted the power of factory owners over workers, and the power of southern whites over southern blacks. For their part, most Progressive reformers, alternately fascinated and appalled by the swelling ranks of white factory workers, ignored the plight of blacks, except for the youthful black oyster shuckers and cotton pickers included in exposés of child labor. During the era of Jim Crow, whole categories of black workers disappeared. Around the turn of the century, Isaac Murphy and other black horse jockeys who had dominated the Kentucky Derby winners' circle since the end of the Civil War found themselves shut out of the major racetracks. Black jockeys then took their place at the back of an employment queue headed by native-born white men: "The only place in the world of labor that the colored man can win . . . is the place that no one else wants."[6]

White employers and employees could always find a "racial" justification for either favoring or opposing blacks in certain kinds of jobs, but those rationales differed according to whose interests were at stake. In addition, variations between North and South, between industries within regions, and even within industries revealed a certain capriciousness about the process of excluding blacks from specific kinds of jobs. The sociologist Charles S. Johnson pointed out in 1925 that the black man "may be a porter in charge of a sleeping car without a conductor, but never a conductor; he may be a policeman but not a fireman; a linotyper but not a motion picture operator; a glass annealer, but not a glass blower; a deck hand, but not a sailor." Chicago meatpackers barred black women from handling finished products like bacon on the assumption that "the public dislikes the idea of Negro women handling food," yet thousands of black cooks prepared meals for the consumption of white people in restaurants and private homes every day. A complex matrix of corporate "public relations" considerations, local factors of labor supply and demand, union members' prerogatives and white bosses' prejudices, and racially exclusive "customs" all tended to harden into the "natural order" of a particular workplace. Yet, regardless of time or place, there were two cardinal tenets of black labor patterns. In an era of industrial growth, southern black men and women would remain concentrated in agriculture, and in northern and southern cities "men-[and women]-of-any-work" would continue to be denied promotions and the opportunity to supervise whites at any level.[7]

These years witnessed the birth of both the modern civil rights and black nationalist movements. There existed no single black ideological assault upon white supremacy, but the issue of jobs—getting and keeping more of them, and better ones—united various insurgent groups. Though they differed in their means, members of the newly formed National Black Business League (founded in 1900), the National Association for the Advancement of Colored People (1909), the National Urban League (1911), and the United Negro Improvement Association (1919) dared to try to liberate black folk from exploitative white landowners and employers. Though they reached out to different constituencies, leaders like Maggie Lena Walker and A. Philip Randolph sought to redress the humiliations endured by blacks in workplaces controlled by whites. And northern black politicians wheeled and dealed in an effort to parlay their constituents' newfound political clout into patronage jobs above the level of street cleaner or bootblack.

In 1895, W. E. B. DuBois drew a distinction between menial toil that served as a stepping stone to a better job, and menial toil that amounted to "a lifework" regardless of a person's skills or ambition. DuBois was referring to the fact that, for black men, "Once a porter, barring the phenomenal, always a porter." During the years that marked the emergence of the United States as a world power, the all-white workplace became a bastion of both white aggression and white defensiveness; and as a group, black men and women remained condemned to various forms of "lifework" that simultaneously harkened back to a preindustrial past and presaged a postindustrial future.[8]

THE POLITICAL DYNAMICS OF WHITE PREDOMINANCE
IN THE WORKPLACE

Throughout the nineteenth century and into the twentieth, the least privileged American workers struggled to follow an upward trajectory out of jobs that were dangerous, ill-paid, and subject to the whim of a landowner, housewife-employer, or factory boss. Blacks complained bitterly that, in the quest for good jobs, "they had not been allowed to compete freely, *as individuals*, for any types of jobs to which they aspired and for which they were qualified." To a certain extent, the status of all demographic and social groups of workers rose or fell collectively; the structure of the workforce relied upon the categorization of people according to their country of origin, skin color or "racial" heritage, gender, and age. However, just as significant as the objective conditions under which African Americans labored were the relative disadvantages that set them apart from white workers. For every generation of blacks deemed unworthy of promotion, there was a generation of whites favored for advancement.[9]

It is difficult to generalize about "racial discrimination" as it affected the employment of black men, women, and children during this period. According to their own interests, different groups of whites invoked different stereotypes of blacks and their abilities in a particular workplace. Such was the case during a Georgia railroad strike in 1909. In an effort to cut labor costs, railroad officials fired ten white assistant hostlers (firemen) and installed in their place black workers who were paid one-third less than the whites. In the South, blacks had traditionally served as firemen, shoveling coal into the engines of locomotives, but by the early twentieth century technological changes had rendered the job more acceptable to white men, who hoped to advance to the position of engineer after they had served as firemen. Members of the Brotherhood of Locomotive Firemen and Enginemen called a strike of their white members in May 1909 to protest management's policy of replacing white workers with blacks. In the course of the strike, employers and white employees drew upon different stereotypes of blacks to bolster their arguments. White unionists charged that blacks lacked the intelligence and judgment to serve as "practically an assistant engineer," while managers countered that black men's brute strength and endurance made them particularly suited for this kind of work. In June, a board of arbitration upheld the railroad's decision to use black firemen, concluding that the attempt to deprive black men of unskilled work in this instance raised the specter of vast numbers of them thrown out of a variety of other jobs. Thus a number of competing interests—the white firemen's job security, the employers' payroll, and the maintenance of civil order in the Jim Crow South—collided to produce divergent perspectives on the proper place of black men workers.[10]

In 1930, black men and women workers were still concentrated in agriculture, mining and extraction, domestic service, and other forms of manual labor, but 60 percent of all black men in Cleveland, Pittsburgh, Detroit, Chicago, Milwaukee, and Birmingham labored in some industrial capacity. Still, it is possible to overestimate the growing significance of nonfarm employment as it affected the structure of black communities and the welfare of individual workers. First, major centers of manufacturing—including New York, New Jersey, Pennsylvania, and New England—opened few if any industrial jobs to black people during this period. Second, within the category of industrial workers, blacks of both sexes remained at the lowest levels of the labor force, effectively barred in many instances from achieving semi-skilled positions. Throughout this period they were "compelled to loiter around the outer edge of industry, and to pick up such menial work or odds-and-ends pursuits as white men do not care to undertake." Thus the industrial sector duplicated the structure of southern agriculture, where blacks worked primarily as wage laborers and sharecroppers, and whites predominated in the categories of renter and landowner.[11]

African Americans lacked employment "niches" of the kind that provided for upward mobility among individual immigrant groups. Black men retained a monopoly over the positions of Pullman porter and "Red Cap" porter throughout the country, and in any particular city they worked in service jobs to a degree disproportionate to their numbers; yet outside the South there existed few if any exclusively "black jobs," or clusters of blacks in vertically organized entrepreneurial activity. For example, in early twentieth-century New York, black people were overrepresented in the categories of servants and waiters, janitors and sextons, and laborers. However, although the percentages of black servants and waiters were tenfold greater than the percentage of black people in the city, those workers still accounted for only one-fifth of the total number of New Yorkers engaged in those kinds of jobs. Black men in Cleveland in 1930 were concentrated in the jobs of porter, drayman, chauffeur, servant, and waiter, and black women found employment disproportionate to their numbers as boardinghouse keepers, laundry operatives, seamstresses, home laundresses, and servants (with the bulk of wage earners in the last two jobs).[12]

In some southern cities like Charleston, South Carolina, black men managed to hold on to skilled positions in the "trowel trades," as masons and bricklayers. Nevertheless, outside a small number of modest businesses such

as beauticians' and undertakers' establishments, and an even smaller number of more substantial endeavors in banking and insurance, blacks as a
group had no specific, broad-based avenues of mobility comparable to the
success achieved by Jews in the garment industry, Italians in grocery stores
and contracting, the Chinese in laundries; or through political patronage
jobs (the Irish), or even organized crime (Italians and Jews). For relatively
privileged immigrant groups, entrepreneurial niches held out the possibility
of economic expansion and the development of a wide range of skills and
jobs, from production through marketing and sales.[13]

Remarked one black Pittsburgh steelworker bitterly in 1925, "Plenty of
hard work here but there is no chance to get anywhere. Colored men work
at the same jobs from year to year while white men and foreigners are promoted in 2 or 3 months after coming here." His lament echoed throughout
the black workforce. Most sharecroppers could hope only to pay off their
debts at the end of the year. The large numbers of blacks who toiled long
hours as cooks, porters, or laundresses understood all too well that these
were "'blind alley' jobs which lead to nothing beyond the merit of long and
faithful service." Within industrial occupations, blacks had no access to
internal ladders of mobility. Although black men as a group had worked in
the iron industry for many generations, by the early twentieth century
three-fourths of all of them employed in that capacity were still classified as
laborers, and only 8 percent were skilled. Nathaniel Leach, a longtime resident of Detroit, recalled that, on the city streetcars, "a motorman could be
black, but the conductor had to be white. That was a standard rule; you just
couldn't get that job." Black men worked as "inside men" in the coal-mining
industry, but they could advance only to the jobs of mule driver and brake-
man, which paid less than the coveted positions of motorman and manager.
In Chicago meatpacking plants, with departments segregated by gender,
race, and even ethnicity, black people could go no further than their own
"rooms": men could become "splitters" within the beef-killing room, for
example, and could serve as informal, or "straw," bosses over workers of
their own color, but they could not work machines in another part of the
factory. In the 1920s an investigator found that many of the oldest workers,
including black men and women, held jobs paying the lowest wages. Some
black workers reached their maximum wage rate after only a few months'
on the job; no matter how long or devoted their service, they could earn no
more in the way of a wage increase or promotion.[14]

Consequently, the black boss was a relatively rare phenomenon throughout the country, and the black boss who supervised whites was virtually
nonexistent. A survey of eighteen cities for the period 1920 to 1940 suggests

that black foremen in manufacturing were far less common (relative to their white counterparts) than black physicians and surgeons. In one Chicago business, for example, a black starch tester was ordered to "teach his duties to a Polish workman" because his boss did not approve of blacks holding jobs superior to whites working in the same department. However, because "the Negro declined to do this . . . it was decided to permit the Negro to retain his position as tester, but he was given no authority over the men" in the department, including whites. These managerial decisions ensured that white workers would retain a substantial advantage over blacks regardless of skill, and that employers would not have to worry about the logistical difficulties of segregating black workers who were promoted to "white" departments.[15]

Under these conditions, the low pay received by black workers was a source of contention, but so too was the lack of opportunity to earn a better wage in the near future. Because most businesses kept black and white workers separated, performing different tasks, the issue of equal pay for equal work rarely arose. (However, in a survey of black women workers in the early 1920s, the Women's Bureau located one workplace that was particularly "tense," because "colored girls were being paid a lower wage than the white workers for similar and equal work, and in their resentment a feeling of hostility had arisen between the two groups.") Black employees in Trenton, New Jersey, were paid very little (an average of $15 a week by manufacturers of floor and wall tiles and brooms), but in response to an investigator's question, "Do you think Trenton industries are fair to Negroes?" workers said, "They are fair in the sense that they pay the same wages to all who do the same thing, but they keep us out of certain jobs where wages are high." Most black laborers had no way of knowing that their white counterparts within the same industry but segregated in "white" departments were receiving, on average, wage "premiums" for performing unpleasant work as their first step on a ladder that would eventually lead to a better job.[16]

As the American economy expanded, the contrasts between different types of workplaces became ever more striking. Insurance agency offices staffed by native-born white men and women were light, clean, quiet, and safe—dramatically so, compared to an automobile foundry or a phosphate mine. Other comparisons highlighted the relative advantages of certain kinds of jobs over others. Black landowners often tilled the poorest southern soil, but in contrast to sharecroppers, they might be able to leave a legacy of economic independence, however modest, to succeeding generations. Manufacturing workers received wages, and not castoff clothing or the "service pan" accepted by domestic servants in lieu of cash. Employees in agriculture and extractive industries faced regular, seasonal shutdowns, while department-store clerks could count on steady employment throughout the year. Professionals like teachers and social workers enjoyed a degree of control over their workplaces unknown by sweatshop and assembly-line workers.

It was no wonder, then, that many black workers felt keenly their exclusion from "modern" kinds of employments, or at least ones that would eventually provide relief from dirty and demeaning labor. Within a new consumer society, domestic service in particular amounted to "a badge of humility and a relic of slavery," and white girls—native-born and foreign-born—hastened to flee a workplace notorious for its drudgery, "awful lonesomeness," irregular hours, and humiliating conditions: "It's hard to give up your whole life to somebody else's order. . . ." Outside of agriculture and service, too, black wage workers regardless of gender remained concentrated in those jobs scorned by whites who could locate anything better; for example, in Richmond during the 1920s, blacks formed at least half of the labor forces of the following industries: fertilizer and guano, canneries, candy and chewing gum, brick and tile, tobacco, and meatpacking.[17]

The jobs performed by black women were representative of the liabilities faced by black workers as a whole, for those jobs were by and large less affected by technology than those of most American workers at the time. In the South, wives and mothers labored in the fields and kitchens, and the industrial centers of Pittsburgh and Birmingham afforded them little employment outside of hand laundry work. While white women worked machines in Virginia tobacco factories, black women stripped the leaves by hand, and suffered from respiratory diseases and canker sores, all for as little as $6.55 for a fifty-five-hour week during World War I, when average wages reached unprecedented highs. In recalling her own work experience as a young woman in Alabama, Sara Brooks made explicit the comparison between her tasks and those performed by whites, first at a barrel factory and next at an orange crate factory:

> I never did mind workin—I liked to work—but you'd have the heaviest and the hardest job all the time—coloreds. 'Cause we was handlin that wood and the white guy would be usin the electric saw that would be cuttin it. It was just a small little place but no white ladies were workin there—
>
> [At the crate factory] White women didn't work like that—they were workin in the office at the shipyard.

Around this time Women's Bureau investigators found that women's meatpacking jobs were "disagreeable in the extreme," and as examples cited the black workers who in one particular department of a Chicago plant were every day "braining heads, taking out hogs' eyes, ripping guts, measuring bladders, shaving ears, plucking lungs, and skinning sheep tongues"—all tasks performed in rooms with floors covered with standing water.[18]

To a degree greater than white women, some black women, such as garment workers in Chicago, preferred to do industrial home work rather than wage work, for they could monitor their own productivity and watch their children at the same time. Blacks in a variety of other settings made a bid to escape the close oversight that many low-paying jobs entailed; for example, as natives to the area, black oyster shuckers on the coast of Georgia managed to avoid the fate of Polish immigrants "imported from Baltimore and living in the factory quarters," men, women, and children who "could be worked for longer hours and more regularly than the Negroes." Black ore miners in the Birmingham district made it clear that they prized their relative autonomy compared to those men working in foundries. And even Annie Tucker, a black woman convicted and sent to prison in Alabama in 1883, understood that all jobs were relative. She told a state board of inspectors in 1888 that she preferred to work at the Pratt prison mines than at the state prison, where women cultivated crops and performed domestic service chores. Tucker said that at the mines she "was not locked up" (though she had once been whipped for trying to run away).[19]

As slaves, black people had been confined primarily—although not exclusively—to agriculture and domestic service, and after emancipation these kinds of jobs constituted a "self-perpetuating color bar." In the words of Gunnar Myrdal, by 1940 or so, "the vicious cycle of job restrictions, poverty, and all that follows with it tends to fix the tradition that Negroes should be kept out of good jobs and held down in unskilled, dirty, hot, or otherwise undesirable work." He added that for whites, "it becomes a matter of social prestige not to work under conditions of equality with them."[20] These arguments, however, tell only part of the story, for they fail to explain why in certain circumstances whites might have made a positive effort to hire blacks, even before (or after) the World War I labor shortage.

With new jobs and job categories expanding quickly enough to encourage the in-migration of millions of foreign workers, some employers considered black people more reliable laborers, given their relative lack of alternatives within even a dynamic economy. As Charles S. Johnson suggested, "employers know that with the normal outlets blocked for superior Negro workers, the chances favor their getting better Negro workers than white for the wages paid." Consequently, although blacks in general were disproportionately represented among manual laborers, their "range of occupations in unskilled work . . . was fairly wide." Foremen in turpentine camps, phosphate pits, and blast furnaces generally agreed that black men were "Quicker, huskier, and can stand more heat than other workmen," an indirect acknowledgment of the difficulty of securing whites for these kinds of jobs. In the rural South, the political powerlessness of black sharecroppers made them particularly attractive to white landowners, who continued to defraud and threaten their workers without fear of judicial reprisal. Similarly, labor barons who established isolated mining and lumber camps presided over near-captive labor forces, men and women in some cases literally held hostage at gunpoint.[21]

Southern whites remained convinced that, when it came to meeting their daily needs, the black person "makes a better servant" compared to the white. During this period, domestic service was one of the few occupations for which prospective employers specified black applicants. Along these same lines, a 1918 study found that certain white southern railroad engineers advocated reserving the position of fireman to blacks because they considered black men to be uniquely vulnerable to highhandedness—"They can treat them differently—make them wait on them."[22]

And finally, the volatility of the labor force encouraged some employers, depending on the time and place, to embrace black workers as a source of wage discipline for their white ones. During World War I, the manager of a Pittsburgh plant spoke for many of his colleagues when he pointed out that "one of the chief advantages of the Negro migration lay in the fact that it gives him a chance to 'mix up' his labor force and so secure 'a balance of power.'" His strategy represented the continuation of a tradition among northern employers who saw in "colored workers the effective means of staving off or preventing the movement toward organization . . . which is now spreading among the foreign workers." Black people were not the only group so manipulated by their employers; meatpackers pitted Polish strikebreakers against German workers, cigar manufacturers sought to replace skilled Bohemian cigar makers with semi-skilled women machine operatives, and textile mill owners drew freely upon a pool of child laborers to depress wages for workers throughout the industry. Nevertheless, out of all of these groups, it was black people alone who came to symbolize the scab.[23]

Unlike South Africa, the United States passed no federal laws barring blacks from specific jobs, though localities at times imposed such restrictions if they could get away with it. (In 1915, the South Carolina state legislature banned the use of black people in textile mills in all but the most menial jobs.) However, after 1865, black people were accorded at least formal citizenship, a status that discouraged broad-based legal assaults on their right to earn a living. Perhaps more tellingly, politicians wished to reserve for employers a flexibility in creating their own workforces. In certain well-defined situations, black workers could serve a political purpose as part of a larger labor relations strategy, and in certain areas, demographic realities meant that ample numbers of whites were not always available to fill the current labor demand. And so, when northern employers swung open the factory gates to southern migrants for the first time, they acted not out of (in the words of one labor economist) "altruistic motives," but out of the "sheer economic interests" that embraced an increased labor supply.[24]

The boundaries between skilled and unskilled work represented a gray area where firms might or might not employ black people. In 1923, in Baltimore, "There were plants employing Negroes for certain grades of work and others refusing to employ them on the similar processes. . . . Some of the plants have what they call 'labor policies' which summarily exclude all Negroes as below the standard for workers; others with identical processes regard them as best fitted for the work." Through the 1930s, southern whites in particular persisted in claiming that black people's "lack of mechanical sense" disqualified them from working textile machines or driving tractors, the presence of black delivery truck drivers notwithstanding. These apparent inconsistencies derived from the history and the contemporary needs of individual workplaces. In 1899, a visitor to Jonesboro, Georgia, commented on the fact that "not far from the 'heading' factory, which employed chiefly negroes, was a stave-factory which had never employed anything but white labor." The manager of the latter establishment declared, "People don't think it right to employ negro labor when there is white to be had." Other stave manufacturers in the area had experimented with black employees, but had failed because of the unwillingness of local farmers to sell them lumber, a novel kind of "boycott where men of Anglo-Saxon instincts refused to sell." These employers had learned the hard way that the use of cheap black labor could have unanticipated consequences.[25]

Indeed, any lessons that employers might have learned about the efficiency or competence of recently hired black workers were often overshadowed by other, overtly politicial lessons about the depth of resistance that whites as employees, customers, and foremen could mount against new workplace configurations. Tentative attempts among southern textile owners to save money by introducing black workers into spinning and weaving rooms provoked walkouts and hate strikes on the part of white workers. In Macon, Georgia, in 1919, white rioters killed two blacks in response to a rumor that black workers would be hired at a local mill. Unions that operated employment bureaus, thus controlling hiring at a particular site, could retaliate against an employer who dared to bypass these traditional channels of hiring workers.[26]

Employers at times anticipated these difficulties and managed to resist the temptation to reduce their payrolls by taking advantage of blacks who would work for less money than whites. (On the other hand, when union pay scales determined wages, employers had little incentive to recruit blacks. Noted a Chicago landlord dependent for workers on the Flat Janitors' Union, "If I have to pay these wages I'm going to get a good white man.") Some critics accused northern foremen and bosses in particular of shifting the responsibility of all-white workplaces onto their employees, when in fact those workplaces simply reflected their own prejudices. In glass factories—where white women decorated and then inspected and packed the finished products while black women worked in hot oven rooms "where at times bits of broken glass were flying in all directions"—neither white supervisors nor white employees had an incentive to challenge a discriminatory division of labor.[27]

The effort to segregate workplaces on the basis of "race" could entail considerable time and expense. Not surprisingly, some employers considered the rearrangement of floor spaces, and the need to provide separate dressing rooms and restrooms for black and white employees, to be prohibitively expensive and hence an insurmountable barrier to employing blacks. In company towns, where employers provided churches, schools, and other social services to the residents, the employment of black men and women signaled a host of managerial headaches, since not just workplaces but also whole communities would supposedly have to be redesigned to accommodate the Jim Crow imperative. In 1927, a West Virginia coal-mining superintendent cited the company's pride in its schools and churches as a rationale for excluding black people from employment: "We do not want to bring in colored men and undesirable people and decrease the standing of the community, particularly the schools." Nevertheless, union activity on the part of white miners, and the need for black strikebreakers, could cause the immediate revocation of this principle.[28]

Pressed by questioners about the absence of blacks on their payrolls, employers responded with a variety of answers that blended traditional complaints of all kinds about poor, unskilled workers (they demanded close supervision, they never stayed in one job very long) with stereotypical pronouncements about black people in particular (they were particularly "suitable" for agricultural and domestic work). In the early 1920s, Baltimore employers offered a fairly representative (if redundant) list of reasons for all-white workplaces:

1. Traditional policy of the plant not to employ Negroes.
2. Fear of racial difficulties if whites and Negroes are introduced into the same plant.
3. Fear of the objection of white workers and resultant labor difficulties.
4. Traditional beliefs about the Negro which concern their mentality and character, and general inability to perform the work required.
5. Fear of bringing Negroes into contact with white women workers.
6. Lack of training of Negroes for certain jobs.
7. Unsatisfactory experience with Negro workers in the past.
8. Advocacy of certain jobs as belonging exclusively to the white race.
9. Expense that would be involved in making alterations in the building to accommodate white and Negro workers separately.
10. Objection of labor unions.

Ultimately, the first reason—variously termed "custom" or "precedent"—was the most difficult to overcome, for employers needed less a reason to continue to exclude black workers than a reason to break with the past and begin to hire them.[29]

Moreover, the way workers went about finding a job tended to exclude blacks as a matter of course. Some firms hired on the basis of kin connections or ethnic loyalties among workers, or between workers and bosses; others relied on union-sponsored apprenticeship programs more akin to fraternal organizations than employment bureaus. Compared to their white counterparts, blacks were more often forced to depend upon placement agencies (that charged a fee) or the goodwill of individual whites—a housewife's letter of reference for a domestic servant, the patronage of a white man for a town's first black policeman, the recommendation of a black clergyman for an automobile worker. Black men in cities all over the country tended to congregate on street corners in the hope of finding day work through a labor contractor (prompting passing whites to conclude, wrongly, that they were always idle). What counted for very little in this process was formal education, for the vast majority of positions, unskilled, semi-skilled, and skilled, entailed on-the-job training (and internal promotion ladders) rather than a specific level or kind of schooling.[30]

Nevertheless, the divergent policies of southern tobacco and textile owners indicate that "race-based" exclusion was not a foreordained or unyielding principle of workplace management. As we have seen, black people had worked in textile mills as slaves before the Civil War, but they would not work in the mills again for another one hundred years; the mill village became home to a socially constructed "mill family" that by definition did not include black men, women, or children. In contrast, the use of black women as tobacco stemmers and rehandlers continued through the early twentieth century; but in the 1930s, the introduction of machinery opened up whole new kinds of "clean" jobs that were then assigned to white women. Indeed, as the social division of labor continued to evolve, it became clear that the march of industrial "progress" would reinforce, in new and ever-changing ways, centuries-old traditions of labor exploitation.[31]

MAKING "A LARGER PLACE FOR COLOR PREJUDICE" IN A NEW ECONOMY

Around the turn of the century, when W. E. B. DuBois surveyed the condition of black workers in a variety of settings—from blacksmiths in the southern countryside and in small towns, to undertakers and lawyers in large cities—he sounded an alarm about the seeming inexorable loss of a whole class of tradesmen and skilled artisans. DuBois recognized that not only were white workers jealous of their prerogatives in the workplace, but trends in business consolidation and mechanical innovation necessarily threatened to eliminate persons who lacked the resources—and especially the capital—to expand, innovate, and adapt their small enterprises. In the South, vocational schools provided black men and women with training for a world of horsedrawn buggies, wooden barrels, and hand-sewn clothing, a world rapidly disappearing. In the largest northern cities, black grocers and barbers faced ruinous competition from immigrant entrepreneurs. The plight of black caterers offered a case in point. According to DuBois, the "application of large capital to the business" of catering in general meant that this kind of business was now in a better position to respond to cues "as to propriety and fashion from New York, London, and Paris." Under these conditions, a business that originally depended on the "talent and tact" of its owners now relied increasingly on economies of scale; and "with this new and large clientele that personal relationship between the caterer and those served was broken up, and a larger place for color prejudice was made."[32]

Black people did find work in certain expanding sectors of the economy, although the nature of the work itself offered them no guarantee of upward mobility, and in fact served to relegate them further to the margins of the new consumer economy—on truck farms, in coal mines and canneries, on passenger trains, and in warehouses. Yet the correlation between jobs and social status was not always a simple one. A black carpenter who migrated from Mississippi to Milwaukee and lost his craft and his trade in the process might have considered his work as a common laborer for the International Harvester Company as much a blessed avenue of escape from southern Jim Crow as a way to make a living. Ultimately, though, the search for "efficiency" in American business had a decidedly negative impact upon the status of black workers as a whole.

Although the percentage of all Americans gainfully employed in agriculture dropped from 55 percent to 20 percent between 1870 to 1930, black people became a significant proportion of workers employed in new capacities in the rural South. Throughout this period, the vast majority of blacks lived in the South, and more than eight out of every ten of those lived in rural areas, forming a large and constantly increasing part of the laboring population. Black landownership reached its heyday in 1915, when 15 to 20 percent of all black farmers held title to their property; after that, most owners saw their land "taxed, taken, stolen and frittered away." For most rural black southerners, the line between freedom and neo-slavery was an exceedingly narrow and fragile one, as employers resorted to ever more blatant attempts to restrict the regional mobility of their workforces. Among sharecroppers, "many colored people look upon every great plantation as a peon camp," for planters readily encouraged chronic indebtedness as a strategy for forcing some workers to stay, while not hesitating to evict the troublesome ones.[33]

Cotton prices showed an overall marked decline between the 1870s and the 1930s, but other agricultural and extractive products found new sources of marketing and demand. The invention of the refrigerated railroad car in the 1880s spurred the growth of truck farms up and down the East Coast and up and down the Mississippi Valley; by the 1890s, black sharecroppers were taking their place in the annual migrations of families who worked "on the season" and put their children in the fields. During the off-season, the men in these families might seek out wage work in local sawmills or lumber camps, while the women and children might take jobs in local canneries or fish-processing plants.

In addition, the rapid development of southern extractive industries after the Civil War gave rise to state-supported forms of coercion and labor "recruitment"; work in mines, on railroad beds, and in the naval stores industry was just too dangerous and dirty to rely wholly upon wage workers. For the three decades or so after the war, local law enforcement officials and state legislators formed an unholy alliance with commercial developers to channel able-bodied young black men through the judicial system and into convict lease programs. Large state penal institutions began to work gangs of prisoners on the public roads, in brickyards and mines. Thus did black convicts, the victims of "fearful brutalities" and "disproportionately long sentences," help to construct the "New South," illustrating in a particularly grim way the compatibility between economic expansion on the one hand and the use of bound labor on the other.[34]

Observers could hail the presence of blacks in rural southern industry as "providential," and employers of agricultural migrant workers agreed with the southern landowner who declared that the black laborer was a "God-given instrument," tractable and in seemingly endless supply. Nevertheless, rural worksites were far from homogeneous. In the post-Reconstruction South, Chinese worked as field laborers in Louisiana, and in the 1890s, young, naive Italian immigrant men found themselves lured by labor agents from Ellis Island to the turpentine swamps of Florida. By the early twentieth century, Mexican extended families were spending their summers in the company of African Americans, stooped over picking cotton in Texas and beans in Georgia. The introduction of the tractor during the 1920s hastened the displacement of all landless southern farmers, sending native-born whites into orchards and canneries from Florida to Virginia, where they worked alongside blacks and Mexican immigrants. On the West Coast, Filipinos, Japanese, and Mexicans formed the bulk of the agricultural workforce, suggesting that international patterns of migration, rather than a fixed "racial" division of labor, determined the social composition of "factories in the field."[35]

From the 1880s to 1910, the percentage of the American workforce engaged in common labor grew from 40 to 60 percent; within the category of working-class people in general, this group outnumbered both skilled workers and machine operatives. In the pre-World War I North, black men hauled trash and stoked fires in steel mills, wielded pickaxes on construction projects, hauled fresh produce from supply depots to restaurants, and worked as longshoremen on city docks. Though census takers might list these men under the occupational categories of manufacturing, construction, or trade and transportation, almost all of them were engaged in similar kinds of menial labor. In Milwaukee in 1900, nearly 70 percent of black men were working in domestic service; thirty years later that figure was 13 percent, while the percentage of black men performing unskilled work rose from 8.5 percent to 55.6 percent (with the greatest numbers working in iron and steel plants and tanneries). Again, the signficance of these developments lay less in the switch from domestic to industrial work per se, than in the persistence of certain patterns of black marginalization.[36]

In the late nineteenth century, black people began to find jobs in the expanding sector of commercial entertainment within the nation's largest cities. By the first decade of the twentieth century, cabarets and vaudeville shows supported African-American musicians, actors, dancers, and comedians in numbers two to three times their proportion of the population in cities like New York and Cleveland. New York had five black orchestras and twenty-four black acting troupes around the turn of the century, even before the Great Migration. Among the actors was the team of Bert Williams and George Walker, who performed in vaudeville shows around the country, billing themselves as "The Real Coons." By the teens and twenties, black musicians were introducing white Americans to blues, ragtime, and jazz on Chicago's South Side and in Harlem, and artists like Duke Ellington and Billie Holiday were performing for white audiences. But the roles assumed by Williams and Walker spoke to the kind of entertainment that white people often demanded of black performers. Black journalists decried the sight and sound of a young black woman, a graduate of the Chicago Conservatory of Music, playing in "a low concert hall in one of the worst sections of the city"; talented black piano players finding work only in brothels and gambling dens; and serious actors grinning and shuffling in front of jeering, drunken white audiences. By the late twenties, the fledgling film industry centered in Los Angeles also had established a stereotypical screen presence for black actresses and actors, one that remained intact for at least the next three or four decades. Black people found roles to the extent that they conformed to white notions of what a (servile) black person should look and act like. Even formally trained actresses like Teresa Harris and Evelyn Preer had little choice but to embrace regular work in spite of their demeaning assignments; and outside of the movie studio they could rarely find jobs much better than the ones they performed on screen.[37]

In the largest northern cities, the world of professional entertainment was intertwined with the provision of various illicit services. Singers and dancers performed in nightclubs that served as sites for prostitution, gambling, the selling of drugs, and (after 1919) bootlegged alcohol. Public zoning policies insulated middle-class white residential areas from organized criminal activities, but ensured that black workers in dance halls, gambling dens, speakeasies, and brothels would stay within easy commuting distance of their jobs. The monopoly of various ethnic groups over organized crime in any one urban area meant that black communities helped to subsidize the rise of white criminals who would bequeath to their sons and daughters a good education and a life in the suburbs. If the big business of prostitution and bootlegging syndicates offered a "queer ladder of mobility" for the Jews, Irish, and Italians, it offered to black people more dead-end jobs as domestic servants, sweepers, and messengers. In contrast, the policy business (a form of lottery) was controlled primarily by black men, though they too could hardly escape dependence on whites—in this case, the politicians and policemen and judges who received kickbacks for looking the other way. Just as northern black communities grew after World War I, so too did the policy business. By the 1930s, five hundred policies stations scattered throughout Chicago's South Side provided jobs for two thousand people, including numbers runners, "walking writers" (who collected bets), porters, and other kinds of employees, and accounted for a weekly payroll of more than $15,000. One young black man in Chicago, a former coalheaver, remained "a warm defender of the game" as a source of employment for men like himself and for women who would otherwise be working in a kitchen; as a policy runner, he said, "You can make a living without slaving for it." Nevertheless, with the exception of a few wealthy black "policy kings," most organized crime employers were white, and blacks who engaged in illegal activities themselves—prostitutes, drug dealers, and liquor runners—remained disproportionately vulnerable to arrest and physical abuse.[38]

World War I of course represented a watershed, providing an entree for half a million rural black southerners into northern industries and jobs in "white" workplaces for the first time. Though they found little more than "the type of work, generally speaking, that requires considerable physical strength but not so very much head work," black men and women seized this opportunity to take their place behind the "white men [and women] who have been called to more difficult and better paying positions since the cessation of immigration" in 1916. As a destination, the North held out the hope of a life of labor with dignity, a fair wage for an honest day's work, and the opportunity to cast a ballot, send one's children to a decent school, ride unmolested next to a white person on a streetcar, and go to a moving picture show for the very first time. Yet the jobs that the war offered to blacks were by and large those that white people could afford to shun.[39]

In general, black men and some white women took the unskilled industrial and other blue-collar jobs left by immigrant men who entered the army; white women replaced native-born white men who had served as clerks and other kinds of white-collar workers; and black women took the positions abandoned by white women and boys. All over the country, as groups of white workers moved up the ladder by a single rung, private employers and government officials did their best to maintain segregated workplaces despite rapid labor force turnover. Thus a poor white woman in the rural South might agree to drive a team of horses in a lumber camp, but she "was not called upon to load" the wagon, for that was "a negro's job." White women worked "as timekeepers, as talleymen, or checkers" inside lumber yards, while black women worked on "clean-up gangs and in repiling lumber." A relatively small number of black women did make inroads into the garment industry, and into processing jobs in leather, paper, and textiles; and as employees of the government, they worked as cleaning women in arsenals and on railroads. Most striking of all, some five thousand black women found at least temporary employment in federal offices as typists and stenographers. Still, these new kinds of work remained contingent upon local economies; cities dominated by a single heavy industry, such as Pittsburgh, offered little to prospective black women wage earners.[40]

Black men served in the armed forces in numbers proportionate to their place in the general population—380,000 blacks out of a total force of about 4 million soldiers. Nevertheless, the numbers alone reveal little about the increasingly bitter public debate over, and the increasingly violent civilian response to, the role of blacks in the military. Between 1906 and 1917, Texas congressmen introduced so-called elimination bills that would have denied blacks the opportunity to serve in the army—or in any military capacity at all. A chronic lack of volunteers, and a large number of western outposts to defend, had opened a place for black soldiers during the Indian War period (1865–90), but a swelling of the ranks fed by the national war mobilization efforts in 1898 and 1917 made possible new forms of discrimination and humiliation for black servicemen. Black troops deployed during the Spanish American War were considered particularly suited for combat in Cuba and the Philippines because of their alleged tolerance for heat. During World War I, black men volunteered in great numbers to serve in eight all-black regiments; but at every step of the way, from the induction ceremony to the barracks, from the journey across the Atlantic to foxholes in France, they remained strictly segregated from their white counterparts. At mealtimes, black officers took their place at the table only after white infantrymen had finished eating. Black soldiers in the Great War at times found themselves issued discarded Civil War uniforms, or forced to sing spirituals for the amusement of Allied audiences: Declared one serviceman, "The spirit of Saint-Nazaire [where he was stationed in France] is the spirit of the South."[41]

Throughout this period, black servicemen continued to contend with the kind of hostility from government officials and white officers that had enraged their grandfathers who had fought for the Union. Noted Ethelbert P. Moore, a Kentucky volunteer who endured hours of fatigue work at a camp in Georgia in 1898: "Any [railroad] section hand has a better time than we do. We are nothing but slaves, and treated accordingly. . . . We do more work than the rest of the companies put together." During World War I, only 11 percent of black troops saw combat; the rest worked in now familiar capacities as stevedores and other kinds of menial laborers. Again, then, the rigid internal segregation of the army mirrored the larger civilian workforce: black men were blocked from receiving commissions commensurate with their expertise and length of service, and specialized corps, like the Marines, barred them altogether.[42]

Yet the wave of physical attacks on black soldiers stationed within the United States, especially in the South—attacks that went unpunished by either civilian or military judicial officials—marked a new stage in the history of military service. Between 1906 and 1917, in Brownsville and Houston, Texas, and in Manhattan, Kansas, and Spartanburg, South Carolina, whites assaulted and harassed black soldiers, who then paid dearly for their efforts to protect themselves or retaliate against their tormentors. The so-called Brownsville Raid in 1906 (initiated when two black privates were beaten by whites for taking the inside of a city sidewalk) led to the dishonorable discharge of 167 black soldiers. In Houston in 1917, thirteen black soldiers were secretly hanged for their role in challenging Jim Crow streetcars, and for wreaking revenge on white police officers who routinely beat black men and women without provocation. The acquiescence of whites in authority in violence against black servicemen suggests a more actively racist U.S. military establishment than the Grand Army of the Republic of the 1860s.[43]

Black servicemen returning home from the war chafed under the strictures of Jim Crow, but at the same time they found that economic changes did not bode well for job seekers of their race. The rise of large corporations, the emergence of a consumer culture, increased foreign immigration, and the introduction of new mechanical processes displaced a whole host of black entrepreneurs and other workers. These included the Chicago tailor who lacked the resources either to locate his shop in an attractive location or to offer customers the range of services provided by the new, large department stores; and the Detroit drayman, a man who "didn't know how to drive," employed by a coal company "in the process of changing over to trucks . . . [that eliminated] the back-breaking job of shoveling and wheeling."[44]

At the same time, throughout the country, black nonagricultural workers were being overwhelmed by the sheer number of whites who sought jobs. In Athens, Georgia, native-born rural whites were gradually eliminating black plumbers and carpenters, and "Greeks have superseded negroes as waiters in some restaurants." In the largest cities, black waiters, chambermaids, and valets lost out to immigrants who were increasingly preferred by owners of grand hotels and fancy restaurants. In New England, black waterfront workers could not hold their own against their immigrant rivals. At times this form of job competition transcended demographic imbalances and entered the realm of overt political conflict, when trade unions simultaneously monopolized employment and barred black people from membership, and when white workers found new and creative ways to drive blacks from the labor force. In 1912, white chauffeurs in New York City, resentful of the black men who would work for lower wages, "would put mothballs in our gasoline tanks, short-circuit our ignition system and throw the carburetor out of adjustment." Ironically, southern cities remained a last bastion of black trades and craftmanship. For example, three-quarters of all masons in Atlanta in 1900 were black, but only 1 percent of the masons in New York City. On the other hand, even small, out-of-the-way southern towns gradually decreased their demand for wheelwrights, coopers, blacksmiths, shoemakers, and whitewashers, regardless of color.[45]

As new machine jobs appeared, they quickly became classified as "white men's jobs." (An exception to this rule was the case of the Little Rock, Arkansas, white women laundry workers who lost their jobs to cheaper black women when management installed new presses deemed "too strenuous" for white girls. At the same time, commercial laundries in general displaced black washerwomen.) The use of electricity in the cities and sophisticated forms of agricultural techonology like tractors on the countryside, the introduction of the mechanical coal cutter in mining camps and steam power in phosphate pits, all eliminated the need for raw muscle power and certain kinds of hand tools. In the iron and steel industries, black puddlers (highly skilled workers) became virtually obsolete between 1890 and 1910, replaced by semi-skilled machine operatives; and the number of unskilled black workers decreased as well, as new production processes rendered a proportionately smaller workforce ever more efficient. As long as sufficient numbers of whites were available to fill these new positions (and the ranks of displaced unskilled men stood ready and eager to do so), new kinds of workplaces would automatically exclude black people.[46]

The use of labor-saving machines was part of a larger "scientific management" movement designed to streamline operations, especially in the largest plants, producing textiles, autos, iron and steel, and machines. Often among the least skilled employees, blacks were vulnerable to these efforts to trim workforces, particularly during a period of unprecedented labor unrest

compounded by high rates of foreign immigration. Nevertheless, it is difficult to generalize about the effects of scientific management on black workers as a group. In the late nineteenth century, the mechanization of the
meatpacking industry in Chicago displaced skilled German and Irish butchers, creating openings for unskilled blacks and Italians. Frederick Winslow
Taylor, the person credited with initiating the movement, helped Bethlehem
Steel eliminate 460 of its 600 shovelers; but he also oversaw personnel policies at Midvale Steel (near Philadelphia), which in the late 1890s hired large
numbers of blacks to work alongside whites at all stages of the production
process. Taylor's avowed goal was to eliminate fraternization, and hence the
threat of collective action, among unskilled white immigrant workers. Presumably the disconcerting presence of blacks would force the other employees to fear for their jobs and thus concentrate on the business at hand. This
particular experiment in shop-floor racial mixing proved only temporary,
and in the early twentieth century, Midvale reverted to a policy of racial segregation.[47]

A devotee of Taylor in general and the assembly line in particular, Henry
Ford was unique among automobile manufacturers in his willingness to hire
large numbers of black workers, but he limited them primarily to foundry
work. For example, between 1918 and 1927, about three-quarters of all
black men hired by Ford were assigned to the River Rouge Foundry (three
times the percentage of whites so assigned). In contrast, General Motors,
Chrysler, Packard, Murray, and Hudson maintained racially exclusionary
policies through the 1930s. Henry Ford was able to turn this to his advantage: he hailed black workers as particularly loyal employees because they
could find no work in the plants of his competitors. Ford also relied on a formal screening process by which black clergymen in the Detroit area had to
offer their personal recommendation of a job applicant before he could be
hired. In the self-consciously "racial" construction of his labor force, then,
Ford exemplified scientific management principles designed to secure a
workforce with a high degree of loyalty and a low rate of turnover.[48]

In general, though, most black people worked in settings far removed
from personnel managers of any kind. Southern lumber barons persisted in
their conviction that the best way to handle a black worker was to "keep
him broke." Observed a tobacco factory boss in Richmond of his black
women employees, "Rough treatment is the only thing that will reach
them." The majority of southern blacks worked for white housewives and
landowners, employers who learned their labor-management techniques
from the textbook of slavery, rather than from twentieth-century scientific
management seminars.[49]

White employers assumed that black people were destined to remain producers, but not consumers—or indeed, participants of any kind in the modern world of business or retail sales: "In work requiring contact with the public in the capacity of salesman or representative, Negroes are infrequently employed (if they are known to be Negroes) except in Negro businesses." Within the new department stores of the early twentieth century, native-born white women—preferably young, soft-spoken, and stylish—embodied the glamour of the products they sold, while native-born black women served as maids, warehouse workers, and late-night floorsweepers. During the 1920s, four out of every ten new white women workers went into "clean work" as sales clerks or secretaries (some of them immigrants' daughters who had completed commercial courses of study in public high schools), but only 5 percent of all new black women workers found similar jobs, and those were hired primarily in black businesses or in mail-order operations, out of sight of white customers.[50]

The premium placed on white notions of female attractiveness pervaded advertisements in mass-circulation magazines, and extended into the reception offices and stenographic pools of large businesses. Even telephone operators, presumably rarely seen by their customers, were chosen on the basis of age and physical type, and applicants who were older, Jewish, or black were rejected out of hand. This last example suggests the relation between a firm's effort to project a particular image of itself and its need to employ attractive white females. The Bell Telephone Company routinely ran photos of its operators in advertisements, just as meatpackers promoted their products with public tours through the bacon department, staffed exclusively with white women. In contrast, black employees found their way into company brochures as workers in fertilizer production and tanning cellars. After World War I, the sales and clerical sectors of the economy continued to expand, and, combined with the highly stylized images of female beauty that flickered across the silver screen, shaped a white public consumer consciousness that actively denigrated the role of black people in the annals of "progress."[51]

During the 1920s, as young white men and women continued to find increased job opportunities in the fields of advertising, journalism, sales, and business management, first the process of war demobilization and then a slackening of demand for unskilled labor plunged northern black communities into depression. Acknowledged an employer of black women during the war: "They were employed solely on account of the shortage of labor, and it was not the intention of the management from the beginning to retain them when white girls were available." Black men like Charles Malone, an employee of the Pennsylvania Railroad, were told "that the war was over, and they [employers] could get plenty of [white] men now." The Brotherhood of Locomotive Engineers seniority rules did not apply to Malone, for the union had decreed that "men of any Nationality could belong to the Brotherhood excepting the colored man." The postwar recession of 1919 to 1921 hit black workers particularly hard, and even those who had been active union members during the great wartime organizing drives found themselves victims of a seniority system that led to automatic layoffs. In Detroit between 1920 and 1930 (that is, within a maturing industrial economy), the proportion of blacks employed as domestic servants actually increased slightly, from 14 to 17 percent of all black men, and from 74.6 to 77.1 percent of all black women. When Detroit factories started laying off blacks after the war, James Jennings (age ten) and his younger brother started selling newspapers, and the money they made was their family's sole source of income. The coming of the radio in the 1920s caused the household some trepidation, as they worried that more and more people would rely on the airwaves for their news.[52]

Throughout the period 1870 to 1930, labor unions exercised little control over the ongoing process of industrial efficiency, but they did make strenuous efforts to retain control over the social compositions of their own workplaces by retaining control over their own members. In southern cities like Richmond, the Knights of Labor aggressively organized workers of both genders and both races in all kinds of jobs, but its successes were relatively short-lived (during the decade of the 1880s). Similarly, the Industrial Workers of the World (founded in 1905) made its greatest inroads into the ranks of black workers toiling with their white co-workers in the dense forests of Louisiana, but only before employers and government officials violently suppressed the union during World War I. The mainstream American labor movement, represented by the American Federation of Labor (AFL—founded in 1881 by Samuel Gompers, a cigar maker), concentrated on organizing only skilled workers; this bias accounted in part for the fact that, by the mid-1920s, only 82,000 blacks (out of a total black workforce of 2.5 million) were union members. Anti-black membership policies afforded a potent means of limiting the labor supply within an industry, and domestic servants, unskilled laborers, and farm workers remained outside the purview of the AFL. Gompers himself took an opportunistic view of the problem of black craftworkers, urging they be brought into local organizations if necessary to eliminate their use as strikebreakers. In general, however, white workers acted aggressively to reserve skilled and better-paying jobs for themselves: noted an astute writer for the *Atlantic Monthly*, "wherever the union develops effective strength the black workmen must put down the trowel and take up the tray."[53]

Nevertheless, the story of black workers in unions is richer and more complex than these generalizations would suggest. Within any particular work setting, the region's history of biracial cooperation (or lack thereof), the social organization of labor, the effects of technology, as well as local demographic and political considerations, all played a part in shaping union membership policies. Some locals, like those of the Molders' International Union, the Ironworkers Union, Sons of Vulcan iron and steelworkers, the railroad brotherhoods, Iron Shipbuilders, and Boilermakers, refused as a matter of principle to admit black members; but other groups followed more circuitous paths. In 1911, editors of the NAACP's paper, *The Crisis*, brought to their readers' attention the case of the New York City Pavers' Union, which managed to rid itself of a black local that had fallen behind in its dues. In Memphis, black and white workers belonged to the masons and plasterers union, but only white members were admitted to the city's Builders Exchange, which enforced the stipulation that "no contractor could sublet his work to a contractor who did not belong to the exchange," thereby shutting black contractors and their employees out of work altogether. In Chicago, Polish and Irish meatpackers insisted that blacks join the union, but they also harassed black workers on the job, and instituted differential benefits for members on the basis of race; as one black meatpacker observed, "you pay money [dues] and get nothing." In Atlanta, black brickmasons could join the "white unions 'if they knew their business,' although the initiation fee was larger for colored men and the sick and death benefits much smaller for them than for whites." These strategies at times had the desired effect of discouraging black union participation, and at other times the unanticipated effect of encouraging black strikebreaking.[54]

Biracial unionism enjoyed its greatest successes in industries where black workers were numerous and already established (for example, the United Mine Workers [UMW] in the Birmingham mineral district and the International Longshoremen's Association [ILA] in New Orleans), and where workers labored together under life-threatening conditions in isolated camps (the Brotherhood of Timber Workers in Louisiana and the smelters in the phosphate pits of Florida). In some areas, a history of political cooperation between the races—in the form of support for the Greenback Labor Party in the 1870s, the Knights of Labor in the 1880s, and the Populist Party in the 1890s—might spur inclusive organizing efforts. In other

areas, the militant activity of unions during the World War I organizing drives, combined with the growing numbers of black migrants seeking jobs in
defense industries, opened the ranks of individual locals to people of color
for the first time.[55]

In almost all cases, those international unions that did admit black members relegated them to separate locals. Nevertheless, historians have documented impressive cases of black and white union members meeting
together, eating together, and sharing positions of union leadership during
the darkest days of Jim Crow in Birmingham, New Orleans, and the former
capital of the Confederacy, Richmond. In these instances, black and white
workers found common ground within communities that were otherwise
rigidly segregated. Not surprisingly, such efforts were for the most part fleeting, in many instances crushed by race-baiting employers and their hired
guns, private security forces. Moreover, biracial unions, no matter how out-
wardly egalitarian and savvy in their strategies of dealing with employers,
included within their ranks white men who felt free to vent their own prejudices on the shop floor or in the mine. And significantly, most "integrated"
unions like those affiliated with the UMW and the ILA failed to challenge
internal, racially discriminatory divisions of labor. In this specific respect,
otherwise progressive unions did not differ so much from overtly racist
ones, like the AFL Metal Trades Department, which decreed that no black
man could be employed as an apprentice, and that no black man could be
promoted until he received authorization from his local auxiliary board, his
supervisory (white) local, and the international union president.[56]

The consequence was that black workers were disproportionately
affected by the technological innovations that characterized all major U.S.
industries, especially after 1900. In West Virginia during the 1920s, staunch
(white) members of the UMW, "white men in strongly organized territory,"
refused to "permit the employment of Negroes as motormen, brakemen on
motors, head-house operators, machine runners, track layers . . . and other
higher waged . . . jobs even though the Negroes are members of the union
also. . . ." In New Orleans around the turn of the century, black longshoremen waged a major battle within their own union, the ILA, to gain equal
access to the position of cotton screwman, a job long dominated by the
waterfront's elite white workers. Thereafter, black men constituted half of
all cotton screwmen, but the ILA made no move to open up supervisory
jobs to black men, or to address an internal division of labor that kept the
majority of black workers in poorly paid jobs like those of teamster and
freight handler. In Birmingham in the 1920s, the modernization of mills
owned by the United States Steel Corporation led to the elimination of

unskilled labor jobs (performed by blacks) and, between 1910 and 1930, the fourfold increase in semi-skilled jobs (performed by whites).[57]

Not surpisingly, then, most black workers tended to approach all-white unions with either skepticism or outright hostility. And in fact, strikebreaking provided substantial numbers of blacks with their first chance to crack certain previously all-white jobs. In 1906, black graduates of an industrial school in New York City took advantage of a strike on the part of Typographical Union No. 6 ("it was generally known that Negroes could not get into this union") to secure jobs in the city's printing shops for the first time. Black teamsters in Boston, black steelworkers in Pittsburgh, black women garment workers in Chicago and Philadelphia, and black construction workers in Chicago were some of the many groups that owed their livelihoods to the troubles, or in some cases the demise, of a white union. In Birmingham in 1908, black workers won some of the coveted skilled jobs they had long been denied by reporting for work at the Hardie-Tynes Machine Company while white men were out on strike. And New York City waiters previously displaced by immigrant competitors regained a modest place in the industry with the strike of the International Hotel Waiters' Union in 1912.[58]

White union leaders often labeled blacks incorrigible scabs, echoing their grandfathers' view that the elevation (or promotion) of a black person necessarily resulted in the degradation (or lack of promotion) of a white. Yet the proliferation of all-black labor unions around the country revealed that blacks as a group were less averse to unionization than to second-class status within organizations that purported to represent the interests of all their members. At particular times and in particular places, black charwomen and laundresses, porters, hod carriers, and hotel waiters, all formed trade-specific organizations to advance their interests in the workplace. Most of these black unions were too small to prosper, or even survive, for very long; but at least their members could concentrate their energies on battling employers alone, and not fellow white unionists.[59]

In the end, the history of the Pullman porters, who launched the first successful all-black labor union (in 1925), encapsulates all the ironies and contradictions inherent in the ongoing relations between black workers and trade unions. Though they owed their livelihood to a peculiarly modern form of transportation—the luxurious Pullman sleeping car—the porters performed traditional kinds of services for wealthy white people. Before the formation of the Brotherhood of Sleeping Car Porters (BSCP), these men received only a quarter to a third of the pay of the white conductors who worked on the trains with them. No matter how many years of experience they accumulated, they could never look forward to wage increases or promotions that reflected their seniority; they endured the so-called P.M. rule, which required an "extra" porter (one without a regular run) to work without any compensation at all between noon and midnight; and their jobs took them away from their families for days, even weeks, at a time.[60]

However, with tips the pay was—or could be—good, depending on the whims of individual white passengers, and Pullman porters took pride in doing their work well. Thus the position was an appealing one relative to other "black jobs." As Ernest Ford, Jr., put it, "I used to wave at the white-suited porters when the train ran through, and I left South Carolina to get one of those jobs. Neckties were mandatory, and you have to understand, blacks were *elated* to get out of denims." The nature of the work meant that porters were threatened neither by white competitors nor by mechanization; the passengers came to expect the personal attention that black men were paid to deliver. Out of this peculiar and socially homogeneous workplace, black men forged a union that was officially recognized in 1937. As the key to the Pullman mystique, the porters held a relatively strong bargaining position, one that few other black workers enjoyed. Porters developed a strong political consciousness, and in the 1940s and 1950s played a prominent role in challenges to a Jim Crow job structure all over the country. In 1941, A. Philip Randolph, the union's founder, initiated the March on Washington movement, and in 1955, E. D. Nixon (another leader of the BSCP) helped to arrange the legal defense of Rosa Parks in Montgomery.[61]

In sum, the logic of industrial capitalism moved companies inexorably down one of two paths: either toward greater profits, usually achieved through lower labor costs and greater technical efficiency, or toward failure. No piece of machinery was predestined to favor the workers of any particular skin color, but blueprints for shop-floor organization took into account all workers' potential animosities and loyalties, as employers attempted to discourage collective action and encourage higher rates of productivity. Throughout this period, black people, by virtue of their already vulnerable position in the American economy, found themselves forcibly pushed to the end of the employment line in all jobs except those that demanded servility and strong backs. By the 1920s, the creators of this new economy had decreed that black people would not participate in it as sellers, as consumers, as managers, as operators of sophisticated machinery, or as advertising icons touting new apparel or appliances. In the United States, modernization wore a white face.

CHALLENGING THE MYTHOS OF BLACK SERVICE
AND SERVILITY

Between 1890 and 1930, the first complete generation of African Americans born as free persons came of age, and enriched the nation's civic, intellectual, and cultural life. The flowering of black literature and of black musical styles like the blues, jazz, and ragtime; the published studies of progressive black scholars; and the defiant vitality of religious and political organizations all testified to the diverse effects of an African heritage transformed by the legacy of slavery, and to the sense of urgency produced by persistent prejudice and discrimination. These years witnessed a range of not only individual but also collective creative expression, from mutual aid and "race uplift" societies, the Baptist Church and all-black colleges, to the nationalistic Universal Negro Improvement Association. During World War I, the glaring contradiction between the nation's professed ideals to "make the world safe for democracy" and the reality of black second-class citizenship spurred grass-roots organizing—even in the rural South—to challenge lynching, disfranchisement, and Jim Crow jobs.[62] Meanwhile, the structure of the paid labor force consistently thwarted black talent and ambition. In this context, the efforts of black people to provide employment opportunities to members of their own group—especially jobs commensurate with their training and abilities—took on a special historical significance.

Most black workers struggled to resist the daily demands made upon them by exploitative employers. For example, over the generations, women domestic servants had perfected a whole range of strategies designed to insulate themselves from the worst abuses of a system that evoked the days of bondage. More and more, they insisted on "living out," thus maintaining both a residence and an identity apart from their employers. They retained the prerogative of taking unauthorized holidays: "When revivals and baptizings are the order of the day the cook must be handled tenderly." They formed their own mutual aid associations to compensate for the pitifully low pay, and they refused to work for an employer who had been particularly nasty to one of their own. Long-term economic considerations mandated that a servant must keep her tongue while hard at work, but the chronic shortage of "good help" enabled her to find a new position relatively easily, and leave with a rhetorical flourish if she wished. Indeed, the "impudence" of their servants proved to be the bane of many a white housewife's existence. Inquiring of a group of black women where she could find a cook, she might be told to "go home and look in the mirrow [sic]."[63]

As the mainstays of their communities, black women domestics came to represent the archetypical black worker when black scholars, politicians, and activists debated the problem of employment writ large. Some argued that menial labor was the black worker's destiny, while others, less resigned to the idea, agreed that though employees must remain ever vigilant to better-paying alternatives, individuals must invest every task, no matter how lowly, with dignity and honor. Black nationalists were adamant in their conviction that performing domestic service for whites was inherently demeaning, and some black businessmen and women were in a position to offer white-collar positions to members of their own community. Still, only national groups (by the time of the war, the National Urban League and the NAACP) had the clout to press successfully for openings in white-owned factories and department stores; most black women remained in the kitchen full time while their husbands, brothers, and sons tried to make do with irregular and seasonal wage work. Complicating the situation were the strenuous efforts that activists found necessary to keep blacks out of certain kinds of jobs. In the South, Walter White and other officials of the NAACP, with the help of countless black clergymen and concerned relatives, sought to rescue black peons—the men, women, and children held against their will by planters and rural industrialists. In comparison, the domestic servant, free to quit whenever she wanted, represented a step above forced labor.[64]

Founded in New York City in 1906 as the Committee for the Improvement of the Industrial Condition of Negroes, the organization that evolved into the National Urban League (NUL) remained committed to the idea that northern migrants would fail in their quest for freedom if they possessed only the franchise but not the means of making a living. Established in all of the major northern cities by the 1920s, and boasting a formal Department of Industrial Relations by 1925, the league aimed to serve as both an employment bureau that placed workers in traditional kinds of "black" jobs, and as a wedge to prod employers to drop the barriers to "white" positions. In this latter effort, league officials had little leverage, and so relied on personal contacts and moral suasion in dealing with whites. For example, John Dancy, head of the Detroit NUL, claimed that his personal encounter with John Dodge in 1919 turned on the fact that the auto maker was a fan of the black singer Bert Williams; wrote Dancy, rather grandly, "When he found out that I was a friend of Bert's the way was opened for Negroes to create a new frontier on Detroit's industrial scene," an overstatement at best, since only Ford Motor Company had more than a token number of black workers through the 1920s. In Chicago, T. Arnold Hill appealed to employers' self-interest when dealing with oil company executives: he declared that hiring "colored salemen, filling station managers, and demonstrators will increase your sales among Negroes." Overall, the black elevator operators, department-store clerks, and factory workers placed by the league represented a tiny fraction of all black employees, and it had little choice but to continue to respond for requests for more maids, cooks, and chaffeurs.[65]

A smaller, weaker black business community existed parallel to its white counterpart and provided jobs for highly trained and specialized workers, from printers to physicians, nurses, and lawyers. Black businesses, hospitals, and other institutions needed no cajoling to hire black workers at every level of operations, but by and large these sources of employment were few in number, and after 1929, too vulnerable to depression, to affect the overall job structure in any dramatic way. Black entrepreneurs concentrated not on manufacturing but on the provision of personal and financial services—beauty shops and undertaking establishments, insurance and real estate. After 1900, they tended to lose whatever white clientele their predecessors might have claimed.[66]

These businesses ranged in size from the hairdresser's shop located in the kitchen of its owner to the big business in cosmetics and hair products founded by Madame C. J. Walker; from small mutual aid burial groups to the impressive North Carolina Mutual Life Insurance Company based in Durham. By the 1920s, the largest businesses had achieved a high profile and an impressive payroll—for example, Robert Abbott's *Defender* and Jesse Binga's real estate company, both in Chicago—but more typical were the confection shops, taverns, liquor stores, groceries, drugstores, and shoe-shining and repair shops characteristic of communities in the South as well as the North. As we have seen, in contrast to more lucrative organized crime activities like bootlegging, prostitution, and racketeering, the policy business was controlled by blacks, from the powerful "policy kings" at the top to the custodians at the bottom. However, policy too spawned a plethora of smaller businesses, primarily individuals who appealed to the fervent desire among gamblers (especially recent southern migrants) to find their lucky number through the intercession of fortunetellers, dream interpreters, root doctors, "Professor Edward Lowe, Astro-Numberologist," and peddlers of books offering "approved, verified, sympathetic and natural Egyptian secrets."[67]

Regional factors affected the growth and development of black businesses throughout the country. In the Far West, black communities were too small to support shopkeepers of any size for any great length of time. In the South, black businesses that were conspicuous by virtue of their success were vulnerable to attacks from whites. In 1892, the three black owners of the People's Grocery in Memphis, which diverted trade from a rival white store, were lynched by a white mob. As journalist Ida B. Wells noted at the time, "lynching was merely an excuse to get rid of Negroes who were acquiring wealth and property and thus keep the race terrorized and 'keep the nigger down.'" In contrast, in the North, the assaults on black businesses were mainly economic. Queried about his persistent patronage of white stores, one black man in Chicago replied, "My real friend is a dollar," alluding to the superior services (including charge accounts) and lower prices that the largest (white-owned) stores could offer their customers. The "Double Duty Dollar Campaign" to encourage blacks to shop in stores owned by other blacks thus pitted economic self-interest against "racial" pride, a tough call for many community members living on the thin edge of economic distress. When depression slowly invaded black communities in the 1920s, businesses of all sizes folded in response to their customers' low pay and irregular employment. As a consumer base, then, the ghetto could sustain, but also undermine, black business enterprise.[68]

Although they inhabited opposite ends of the ideological spectrum, black Republicans ensconced in the two-party system on the one hand and black nationalists on the other proved to be particularly assertive in broadening job possibilities for black people. Between 1890 and 1934, Charles W. Anderson served as a leader of New York black Republicans and found jobs for his constituents in a truly impressive array of workplaces—as draftsmen and tax collectors, customhouse inspectors, post office employees, stenographers, and assistant district attorneys. In the South, Maggie Lena Walker, founder of the St. Luke Penny Savings Bank in Richmond and the country's first woman bank president, was a moving force in the Independent Order of Saint Luke (IOSL), a mutual aid society that evolved into an engine of local black economic development. Walker described herself as "not born with a silver spoon in my mouth; but instead, with a clothes basket upon my head," and she remained committed to opening up a wider range of job options for black women. "How many occupations have Negro women?" she asked. "Let us count them: Negro women are domestic menials, teachers, and church builders." White women were pushing black women out of tobacco work and even, in some cases, domestic service. Consequently, the IOSL sponsored a department store that employed fifteen black women as sales clerks. The Universal Negro Improvement Association (UNIA), founded by Marcus Garvey, a Jamaican, was an international organization with grand designs. Its Black Star Shipping Line provided jobs for black seamen, lawyers, and clerks; and local branches, like the one in New York City, sponsored cooperative economic efforts that produced a variety of businesses, including grocery stores, restaurants, laundries, and publishing houses. Both the IOSL and the UNIA lived on as symbols and examples of black self-determination, and their political significance transcended their (relatively brief) economic role as employers.[69]

More enduring were the all-black towns formed after Reconstruction, small communities concentrated in Oklahoma and scattered throughout the South and Far West. Places like Boley, Oklahoma, founded in 1904, employed its own teachers, controlled its own utilities, and elected its own mayor and councilmen: "Oh, 'tis a pretty country / And the Negroes own it, too / With not a single white man here / To tell us what to do—in Boley." Velma Dolphin Ashley was a little girl when her family moved to Boley from Alabama in 1907; her father was motivated by the conviction that "You were supposed to be independent. You weren't supposed to bow to anybody." His daughter became a teacher in the local school, and thereby avoided a life "in which white people would expect her to clean and cook but not, for example, to teach Shakespeare." These towns were not always able to offer gainful employment for all their residents, some of whom were forced to commute long distances between their homes and their jobs. Nevertheless, they represented places of "thrift and self-government" where the accommodationist views of Booker T. Washington and the nationalist views of Garvey and Walker converged in a dramatic way.[70]

The struggles of these small black towns to survive served as a reminder that jobs were the fulcrum of family and community life everywhere. Throughout the country, compared to whites, a larger percentage of black people worked for wages (because of the large number of black women and children forced to find jobs), and blacks worked for longer years over the course of their lifetimes compared to their white counterparts. Constricted employment opportunities in the mainstream labor force impoverished the black community, and forced prospective wage earners to seek out jobs in the underground economy of gambling, prostitution, and petty crime. Because the possibilities for promotion were so limited, individual aspirations of necessity remained low—painfully so. Asked by a high school principal what he wanted to do for a living, a black youth in New York City answered, "I am going to be a doorboy, sir." Pressed, he replied, "I should like to be an office boy." His questioner continued:

"Well, what next?" A moment's silence, and "I should try to get a position as bell boy." "What next?" A rather contemplative mood, and then, "I should like to climb to the position of head bell boy."

The principal concluded, "He has now arrived at the top; farther than this he sees no hope. He must face the bald fact that he must enter business as a boy and wind up as a boy." This youngster and black teenagers all over the country took their cues from the sight of black women trained as secretaries forced to scrub floors for a living and black bricklayers forced to become day laborers.[71]

What white employers universally condemned as "irresponsible" behavior—high turnover within most "black" jobs—was actually a highly conscious strategy among workers who remained alert to the possibility of finding not necessarily a better job in an absolute sense, but a position that offered fewer relative disadvantages—occupational hazards, low pay, a "Ku Klux" boss, a long commute and long hours on the job, little or no control over the workplace. In 1916, railroad owners expressed dismay over the refusal of large numbers of southern migrants to stay at work on the lines for very long, their labor forces "fluxing . . . from the start." In fact, these were black men housed in filthy, congested railroad boxcars, men who eagerly left after hearing rumors of better wages and living conditions in steel mills and auto factories in other parts of the North. The checkered work histories of individuals, and the population movements from southern countryside to nearby small town, from small town to southern city, and from the South to the North, betrayed a restlessness among all black workers, and their refusal to accept for any considerable length of time the conditions of work that an employer sought to impose upon them.[72]

AS A FORCE assigning African Americans certain kinds of work between 1870 and 1930, the political process of mechanization had a threefold impact. First, technological innovation placed at risk those workers at the lowest echelons of the industrial workforce; it was the engine stokers and the shovelers, the hand laundrywomen and tobacco stemmers, who were easily replaced by labor-saving devices. Second, as whole sectors of the economy expanded, new kinds of machine jobs came to be defined exclusively as "white." Thus, symbols of a new economy—the typewriter, the telephone switchboard, the mechanical coal cutter, the tractor, and (with the exception of Ford) the assembly line—served to perpetuate the second-class status of black men and women as workers. And finally, the increasing technological sophistication of American life was accompanied by the rise of a consumer culture that depended upon a racialized "style" not only to sell but also to produce certain products. That style was invariably young, white, and wealthy—and so deemed glamorous. No matter that the vast

majority of white workers could neither conform nor aspire to such glamour; it was black people as a group who, by virtue of their labor, seemed to
represent its antithesis in the eyes of white advertisers, employers, and consumers.

During this period, "racial" ideologies of black inferiority remained
remarkably malleable, as different groups of whites sought to advance their
own interests (variously defined). However, white people in general
invented new rationales to justify certain traditional patterns of black labor.
More often than not, critiques of black workers and their abilities followed
from the specific jobs they already performed; hence black men were considered "particularly suitable" for hot, dirty work because they had done
that kind of work for so long, and they were considered "ill-qualified" to
work with machines, because they had been barred from that kind of work
since the end of slavery.

As workers, activists, and national political leaders, blacks continued to
demand workplace opportunity. However, it was not until the 1930s that
African Americans could count on even a modest amount of support from
whites in their roles as government officials, politicians, and policymakers.
For black workers clustered on the very lowest rungs of the job ladder, the
coming of the Great Depression in 1929 proved devastating. Not only were
these employees the first to lose their jobs when businesses closed their
doors and housewives could no longer afford domestic help; they also had to
contend with an onslaught of white competitors, now forced to take any
jobs they could find, regardless of the "racial" label attached to them. Out of
the despair of white workers emerged a new national commitment to protect citizens from the cyclical unemployment that was a byproduct of industrial capitalism. Yet ironies abounded: the federal government, through the
New Deal, attempted to counter the conditions that produced a workforce
constantly vulnerable to downturns in the economy, but the majority of
black workers remained unaffected. To gain the benefits of the modern welfare state, workers must first partake of modern industrial employment.
Thus did congressmen make yet another place for color prejudice in the
twentieth-century political economy.

CHAPTER ELEVEN

....

CAN YOU SEE A TOMORROW THERE? INDUSTRIAL TRANSFORMATION AND FEDERAL CIVIL RIGHTS LEGISLATION, 1929–1978

In his memoir *Colored People*, Henry Louis Gates, Jr., recalls that during the 1940s and 1950s, almost all of the black men in Piedmont, West Virginia, "made the same money" because they all worked at the town paper mill as "platform loaders," forklifting giant crates of paper onto tractor-trailer trucks. Until 1968, when the craft unions at the mill began to admit black members, the platform loaders labored apart from whites, and served as a "Colored Genealogical Society. . . . The loaders were the Senate, the House, and the Supreme Court of Public Opinion. . . ." In Piedmont, black people as a group lived in their own world, and "The soul of that world was colored," writes Gates. "Its inhabitants went to colored schools, they went to colored churches, they lived in colored neighborhoods, they ate colored food, they listened to colored music, and when all that fat and grease finally closed down their arteries or made their hearts explode, they slept in colored cemeteries, escorted there by colored preachers. . . ." The familiarity of this world meant that some of the older people in particular experienced racial integration in the 1960s as, in Gates's words, "a loss." Now that young people could aspire to skilled jobs in the paper mill, or even to illustrious academic careers at Yale and Harvard, the platform loaders began to recede in significance as the keystone of African-American community life. Henceforth, successive waves of black "pioneers," men and women who entered previously all-white jobs, would turn their backs on the paper mill platform in favor of a more expansive, if less predictable, world.[1]

In fact, by the middle of the twentieth century a significant proportion of African Americans all over the country were more than ready to bid farewell forever to Jim Crow jobs. By migrating north, litigating in the courts, picketing, and protesting, black people succeeded in dismantling the formal legal apparatus that had helped to sustain "race-based" divisions of labor in both North and South for more than a century. The gradual disappearance of jobs on cotton plantations and in private households, and the gradual folding of the South into the national economy, made all the more urgent blacks' demands that they finally take their rightful place as workers within a modern industrial state.[2]

Nevertheless, the legal and political gains won by the civil rights movement—represented by integrated schools, access to better jobs, and the right to vote—came at precisely the same time that larger economic trends arrested, and eventually eroded, new employment opportunities for many blacks. As early as the 1940s, the supply of well-paying, low-skilled jobs began to dwindle, and fully one-half of all black workers were employed only part of the year, as day or seasonal laborers. During the next half century, blacks as a group would continue to be disproportionately harmed by the forces of economic displacement and dispossession. Referring both to the devastating effects of the continuous coal-cutting machine on the jobs of black pickax miners, and to the acquiescence of the United Mine Workers in this process, a West Virginia miner named Oliver Gholston would indict "automation and the race thing." Southern textile mills, which hired black operatives in large numbers for the first time in the 1960s, would begin to suffer from foreign competition soon after; this industry alone accounted for 40 percent of all the manufacturing jobs that disappeared in the early 1990s. In essence, black people fought their way into jobs in transition, jobs that were fast disappearing from auto plants and steel mills, rubber plants and paper mills.[3]

The degradation of labor, byproduct of the genius of American enterprise, continued to assume ancient as well as new forms. By the 1960s, black men like Jim Grayson, an auto factory spot-welder, had escaped the plant foundry, but not the heat, smoke, carbon monoxide, and heart-pounding pace of the assembly line. As technology forced speed-ups on the shop floor, black workers were hired in ever greater numbers.[4] The three generations of Americans who lived during the last two-thirds of the twentieth century witnessed not only the rise and fall of a blue-collar dream (rooted in the good jobs and benefits offered by major industrial employers) but also the rise and fall of a tentative federal commitment to facilitating the integration of black people into previously all-white workplaces. The New Deal welfare

state anointed industrial workers the beneficiaries of a variety of entitlement programs; but it left the majority of all black men and women workers, who remained locked outside the gates of the largest corporations,
bereft of health insurance and unemployment compensation.[5]

In 1942, personnel officials at a newly (and grudgingly) integrated West
Coast aviation plant countered criticism of the plant's racist shop-floor culture with the argument that to root out such a culture "would not be in
accord with racial traditions in the United States, that it would prove futile,
and that the plant was a commercial enterprise interested in production, not
in social reform."[6] These officials recognized that the social configuration of
the workplace merely mirrored life away from the job. Ultimately, the hiring
policies of American corporations constituted a weak foundation on which
to build an egalitarian society, for those policies flowed from calculations
related to profits and stock prices, and not from the ideal of a society purged
of past injustices. Thus, the nation chose to yield the well-being of its workforce to the operation of the free enterprise system, and so tolerated a growing division between rich and poor (regardless of color) as a matter of
economic and political principle.

RACIAL POLITICS IN WORKPLACES SHAPED BY DEPRESSION AND WAR, 1929–50

The crises that beset the United States in the 1930s and 1940s spurred the
process of technological innovation, and this process remained racialized.
During the Great Depression, federal policies to regulate wages and working conditions provided industrial employers with an incentive to mechanize
their operations. The entry of the United States into World War II produced
thousands of new jobs, and new job descriptions, in the defense industry,
but employers and union officials alike aggressively reserved sophisticated
machine work for whites. When blacks did find defense work during the
early months of the war, it was only because government and personnel
officials believed that "the available supply of Negro labor . . . could be
absorbed as janitors." Given white workers' determination to preserve their
prerogatives on the shop floor, combined with such institutional structures
as discriminatory seniority policies, work rules, and job classifications, only
the most strenuous political pressure on the part of civil rights activists
could open new jobs to black workers, or secure for them a more equitable
share of the old ones.[7]

In the 1930s, the forces of economic contraction compressed the job assignments of the poorest workers of both races, and then squeezed out the most vulnerable. While the notion of "white people's good work" remained hard and fast, the notion of "black people's dirty work" was only tenuous, subject to redefinition by poor whites made desperate in those hard times. A few whites retained the best positions, while other whites either integrated formerly all-black workplaces or displaced black workers from their jobs altogether. The social customs that reserved managerial and skilled positions for white men, and clerical and sales positions for white women, persisted, though older and less educated white workers lost out to their younger counterparts. Southern white men, by this time stereotyped as excellent "all-round mechanics," continued to retain favor over blacks in the auto industry and other kinds of heavy manufacturing. Indeed, by making competition for blue-collar jobs even more intense than in past decades, the depression exacerbated historic forms of exclusion in any number of worksites. For example, through the 1930s, Philadelphia plants producing ships, railroad locomotives, cans, machinery, lace, streetcars, and textiles remained off-limits to black workers altogether.[8]

Yet soon after the stock market crash, the vast middle ground that separated poor blacks from poor whites began to soften, and then dissolve. At times all it took was a name change; for example, some railroads fired white "stewards" and replaced them with black "waiters in charge," men who did the same work as the whites, but for less than half the pay. It was not uncommon for whites to descend the ladder of occupational mobility, step by step. Arthur Barnes, a black employee in a North Carolina tobacco warehouse, observed in the late 1930s, "We've been getting right smart white hands in late years." White women joined black women in southern canneries, and white men broke a color barrier in the public service sector when they deigned to accept "Negro jobs" as custodians, messengers, and elevator operators in the nation's capital. In Chicago, white men working as porters clashed with blacks over control of the Red Cap union, and in areas outside the South particularly, white female commercial high school graduates now vied with black women for domestic day jobs. (In 1940, 18 percent of all white women workers were domestics, up from 12 percent ten years earlier.) More revealing of the plight of whites, and the utter hopelessness of many blacks, was the downward trajectory of perhaps as many as one-quarter of all white men from relatively secure jobs into casual labor and transiency, and then unemployment. Technological advances in textile production, glassblowing, the printing business, and cigar making (to cite just a few examples) caused white men to lose steady paychecks, and then to look for "occasional odd jobs," before finally abandoning their homes and in some cases their families to embark on a fruit-less quest for employment.[9]

Shifting patterns of employment and poverty had political repercussions during the 1930s. The growing concentration of African-American voters in northern cities, combined with their transferral of party loyalties from the party of Lincoln to the party of FDR in 1932, helped to raise the racial-polit-ical consciousness of Democratic leaders during the decade. African Ameri-cans did benefit from general New Deal policies and specific New Deal programs. The first government-sponsored program of affirmative action hiring, in the Public Works Administration (PWA) Housing Division, helped to distribute construction work between blacks and whites on a more equi-table basis; over the opposition of local white unions, the PWA mandated that minimum percentages of certain kinds of black craft workers be hired on its public construction projects. More broadly, President Roosevelt's pro-union stance spurred the organization of auto and steelworkers, as well as New York City's commercial laundry employees, women "standing ten hours and sticking their hands into almost-boiling starch," a substantial number of whom were black. Intervention on the part of the National Labor Relations Board was crucial to the successful organization of the Mine, Mill, and Smelter workers with their large proportion of black mem-bers. Monthly allowances distributed via the Aid to Dependent Children provisions of the Social Security Act of 1935 benefited some black female-headed households, especially in areas outside the South.[10]

For the first time in American history, a chief executive (and a Democra-tic one at that) openly solicited the counsel of a "black cabinet" consisting of Mary McLeod Bethune, Robert Weaver, and others. A handful of black writ-ers like Zora Neal Hurston, Ralph Ellison, Margaret Walker, Arna Bon-temps, and Richard Wright found work with the Federal Writers Project. About a quarter of a million young black men worked for the Civilian Con-servation Corps (CCC); although it instituted racial quotas and established strictly segregated camps in the South, the program offered a few blacks the opportunity to use the machines that the private sector denied to them. Laurinburg, North Carolina's Elias Covington remembered that it was as a staff sergeant in a CCC camp that "I saw a typewriter for the first time in my life, and every time I got a chance, I used it." Ralph S. Plummer was assigned to the National Arboretum in Washington, D.C., where he had a chance to drive a truck, "and I learned how to operate a bulldozer, which brought me some good money in my lifetime."[11]

Certain individual blacks, and groups of blacks, gained from specific pieces of New Deal legislation. Nevertheless, federal programs during this decade did little to crack open all-white workplaces. The New Deal exhibited a profound bias in favor of wage earners employed full time by large industrial corporations, and against workers in the agricultural, personal service, and casual labor sectors. Federal legislative initiatives in the 1930s linked medical insurance, paid vacations, school tuition benefits, and relatively generous pension plans to employment in the country's largest companies, and in this way actually worsened the relative economic and social position of black workers. These provisions placed white women at risk also—only three out of ten benefited from the maximum hours and minimum wage provisions of the Fair Labor Standards Act of 1938, for example; but only one in ten black women gained protection under the act.[12]

Deprived of minimal benefits like unemployment compensation, Social Security, and medical insurance, or legal safeguards against hazardous working conditions, the vast majority of African-American domestics struggled with the same assaults to their dignity that their great grandmothers had contended with generations before. Paid only with "sometimes nothin but somptin to eat," servants were vulnerable to speed-ups within private homes—in Jacksonville, Sarah Rice "had to babysit, do laundry, scrub the woodwork, and get down and scrub and wax the floor with my hands." Even more critical to a woman's sense of self-worth was the fact that she remained outside the federal system of entitlement, not because she failed to work hard enough but because she worked at the wrong kind of job. An elderly black woman in Milwaukee remembered her long years of domestic service this way: "I never received social security, not till I quit doing domestic work altogether. For all those years I'd worked, I didn't have anything for my future." Moreover, the relatively high rate of occupational accidents associated with unregulated industries, and the weak health of poor workers in general, meant that the exclusion of black workers from employee-sponsored health plans would have devastating consequences for the well-being of households and entire communities in the years to come, as in years past.[13]

In the South, New Deal officials doled out government jobs and cash relief in such a way as to preserve the social division of labor. Thousands of southern black sharecroppers lost their jobs under New Deal crop-reduction programs, and the tractors that replaced hands were driven exclusively by whites. The newly defined educational role—and implicit political objectives—of farm extension agents and all-white public vocational schools preserved inequalities in job training by depriving black southerners of the opportunity to learn "to operate and repair tractors, cotton pickers, mechanical milkers, and other machines" that were appearing on "the emerging mechanized and livestock farms." Public works supervisors withheld jobs from blacks as long as there was local cotton to pick or laundry to be washed, and placed black women on "trash crews" while white women worked on sewing projects indoors.[14]

During the 1930s, other policies approved by various government agencies had far-reaching consequences in terms of reinforcing the privileges of white workers at the expense of blacks. Even the legendary hallmark of pro-worker legislation, the Wagner Act of 1935, left intact the racist membership policies of AFL affiliates, most of which were concentrated in the transport, trade, construction, and services areas of the economy—the areas where most black men and women found employment outside the cotton fields. Consequently, in the process of encouraging collective bargaining between Jim Crow unions and their employers, the National Labor Relations Board implicitly backed the white members who denied blacks a voice in contract negotiations. Minimum wage legislation spurred mechanization in certain key industries such as coal mining and tobacco stemming, and thereby deprived black men and women of traditional sources of livelihood without facilitating their entry into other kinds of jobs.

In Memphis, blacks referred to the National Recovery Act (NRA) as the "Negro Removal Act," and charged that NRA wage codes accounted for rising rates of black unemployment. Katie Hurston, a black woman in the city, wrote to President Roosevelt that "here in the South they think that shorter hour and more money is for white only and therefore they are dismissing the negroes from their jobs and taking white ones their places." Most New Deal–era public housing remained segregated by race, and the new Home Owners Loan Corporation gave its blessing to the practice of "redlining" by local banks, a policy that deprived would-be black homeowners of the federal assistance that whites came to take for granted.[15]

To counter forces of reaction, blacks around the country launched a multi-pronged assault on institutionalized prejudice. Neighborhood groups such as Housewives Leagues pressed local merchants to hire black men and women in supermarkets of the Roxbury section of Boston, in Baltimore shoe stores, and in Manhattan department stores, winning an estimated seventy-five thousand new jobs—and new kinds of jobs—for their communities in the depths of the depression. Launched in 1936, the National Negro Congress (with backing from the Communist Party) sponsored direct action against lynching, job discrimination, and police brutality. Meanwhile, the NAACP and the National Urban League continued their attempts to pierce the color barrier in hiring, and placed private and public employment issues at the center of their larger civil rights agenda.[16]

Yet what distinguished the 1930s from previous decades was the (at least tentative) welcome that industrial unions offered to black workers as members, if not as rivals for specific "white jobs." In the words of Hosea Hudson, a CIO organizer of steel workers in Birmingham, "They done seen that strength of the union, white and black together. That was something unusual, to see white and black together." During these years, substantial numbers of employees of both races made common cause—North Carolina tobacco workers and Florida cannery workers; sharecroppers in Arkansas and Alabama; garment workers in New York City; and blacks and whites engaged in a variety of tasks under a single roof in auto, steel, and rubber plants. (Black and white radicals—especially the men—tended to focus their organizing energies somewhat narrowly on industrial workers, on the assumption that, in the words of Hudson, "if you don't get that basic worker, what can stop the wheels of production, you lacking, you still lacking.") Throughout the country, the politics of resistance melded previously self-consciously distinct groups of people. In the South, the NAACP, the CIO, and the Communist Party all equally attracted the outrage of white elites who derived great benefits from a social structure that depended on the estrangement of blacks from whites, industrial workers from farm hands, the poor from the rich. In New York City, the organizing drive aimed at laundry workers brought together West Indian immigrant workers and their middle-class supporters, members of the Women's Trade Union League. In Detroit, black auto workers marveled at the novelty of socializing with their white co-workers off the job for the first time—a development that received implicit support from the egalitarian membership policies of the CIO. Blacks and whites alike thus opened up the possibility of a day when racial conventions on the job floor would be abandoned.[17]

Nevertheless, in a number of different settings, white activists informed their black comrades-in-arms that "The Negroes will have to forget they are Negroes" and instead concentrate on being Marxists, or Democrats, or members of the United Automobile Workers (UAW). Even those unions that welcomed black members, and the monthly dues they contributed to union coffers, balked at demands that they should serve as advocates for men and women who were the victims of racial discrimination in job assignments. In the South, stubbornly all-white auto factories testified to the acquiescence of the UAW in explicitly racist hiring policies outside the North. (As late as 1957, a General Motors manager noted, "When we moved into the South, we agreed to abide by local custom and not hire Negroes for production work. This is no time for social reforming and we're not about to try it.")[18]

A leader in the combined black union and civil rights struggles of Memphis, Clarence Coe, tempered his praise of the progressive impulses of the CIO by stressing the organization's commitment to maintaining "black jobs": "I tell you when both of us get in a ditch together and stay long enough, we'll find the means to get out together, and the CIO was that. But once they got it set up and got that thing working, the white leadership just wasn't going to support you in job equality or equal pay. We had the dirtiest, the cheapest jobs—there was a certain job the white man didn't do, he just didn't do it." Moreover, the public attention garnered by bold, biracial groups of labor organizers tended to overshadow the fact that the CIO focused its energies on durable goods workers who were overwhelmingly white, while the American Federation of Labor (AFL) unions felt little compunction to alter their exclusive membership policies with the times. Indeed, during the turbulent 1930s and the 1940s, AFL leaders in specific industries successfully played upon the fears of white workers who believed that a CIO victory on the shop floor would mean more jobs for blacks, and fewer jobs for themselves and for their kinfolk and friends.[19]

In March 1941, defense industry officials sounded the alarm over a dwindling supply of skilled labor needed to produce armaments for export to aid the British war against Germany. William S. Knudsen, director of defense production, called for employers to "give every skilled man three helpers to learn his work." That same month, J. H. Kindelberger, president and general manager of North American Aviation, Inc., announced the opening of a ten-million-dollar bomber plant in Kansas City, and indicated that the plant would employ about ten thousand workers. However, Kindelberger specified that "Negroes will be considered only as janitors and in other similar capacities," and that "under no circumstances would Negroes be employed as aircraft workers or mechanics in the plant." To make his intention clearer, Kindelberger declared that even blacks trained as skilled aircraft workers would find no employment in the North American plant. His announcement set off a series of public protests coordinated by local branches of the NAACP.[20]

Soon after the United States entered the war in December 1941, National Urban League official Ann Tanneyhill created a seemingly innocuous slogan that evolved into a direct and bitter challenge to racially exclusive hiring practices: "One tenth of America's citizens are Negroes: Train, hire, work with them." Even in industries organized by relatively egalitarian industrial unions, the hard-won seniority prerogatives of white men meant that black workers would continue to languish at the end of the employment queue when mobilization for war led to the exponential growth in relatively well-paying blue-collar jobs. During the war, manpower shortages, combined with intensified pressure from black advocacy groups, eventually produced breakthroughs (at least in the North) for black men who gained access to semi-skilled industrial jobs and then managed to hold on to them after 1945. Nevertheless, these gains had only a limited impact on the long-term structure of the black labor force. The process by which northern black men eventually rose from the jobs of custodians and foundry workers to machinists and assembly-line workers failed to affect the work opportunities of black southerners, or of black women nationwide who would play an increasingly significant role as the providers for individual families. Moreover, these new jobs remained concentrated in a sector of the economy that would begin to decline in the early 1950s.[21]

In his book *Negro Labor: A National Problem* (published in 1946), Robert C. Weaver, a Harvard-trained economist, detailed the painfully slow process by which some blacks overcame the historic barriers to their entry into light manufacturing and machine work during the war years. A member of Roosevelt's "Black Cabinet," Weaver served on both the National Defense Advisory Committee and the War Manpower Commission during the war, and he witnessed firsthand the combined forces of technological change and old-fashioned racism that denied African Americans any jobs—let alone those commensurate with their talents—until well into the conflict. In 1941 and 1942, on the battlefront and on the home front, not even the immediate national security threat posed by the German *luftwaffen* and Japanese kamikaze fighters could dislodge the color line that barred blacks from so-called white jobs.[22]

Weaver offered a succinct analysis of the policies and prejudices that actively excluded blacks from serving as citizen-workers in the "arsenal for democracy." In 1940, when the United States began to mobilize war production on behalf of its Western European allies, employers like those in Detroit and Charleston, South Carolina, decided to import thousands of rural whites rather than hire the black people already resident in their own cities. The United States Employment Service reinforced these policies, going so far in some cases as to declare that their offices would continue to refuse to place black women in any defense jobs as long as such action "would occasion the wrath of the wives of most influential employers" (white women who relied on black domestics) in any particular area. The United States Office of Education funded white but not black vocational education programs, and workers in a variety of settings launched hate strikes to protest both the hiring and the upgrading of token numbers of black workers.[23]

Black men made their surest gains in industries where they had established a foothold before the war, but racist hiring policies remained in place and much defense work fell under the rubric of "white men's work." Forty percent of all steel mills refused to hire any blacks at all in the course of the war, and the ones that did held them to unskilled, traditionally "black" jobs. As a group, black men were at a competitive disadvantage with whites who had gained previous experience with machines; but even S. Liplin, Jr., a Panama City, Florida, man who had worked previously as an operator of drill presses, lathes, and punch presses, was told by employers at local paper mills and shipyards as late as November 1942 "that all ther had for Negreos was Slabers and Laboers regardes of what you know." Most whites, too, lacked experience as welders, riveters, and steamfitters, but defense work training programs, whether sponsored by private employers or the United States Office of Education, enrolled all-white trainees throughout the country. In Alabama, government defense projects went begging for welders because the supply of white men was exhausted and no local blacks were provided with the requisite training. In his semi-autobiographical novel of his years as a defense worker, *If He Hollers Let Him Go*, Chester Himes describes the dream of his protagonist. The black man, a job applicant, encounters two white men: The whites "looked as if they didn't want to give me the job but didn't want to say so outright. Instead they asked me if I had my tools." The black man replies that he does not have any tools, but insists that "I could do the job. They began laughing at me, scornfully and derisively. One said, 'He ain't got no tools,' and they laughed like hell."[24]

In shipyards, blacks were closed out of hiring and training for skilled positions, including welding, a new technique immediately identified as a "white" job. In converted auto factories, the manufacturing of airplanes provided employment for white machinists and electricians in light manufacturing occupations, jobs that had customarily excluded blacks. While sounding the alarm over a perceived critical shortage of available workers as early as 1940, aviation industry officials such as W. Gerald Tuttle of the Vultee Aircraft Company in Southern California declared bluntly, "I regret to say that it is not the policy of this company to employ people other than of the Caucasian race. . . ." The association between aircraft construction and light manufacturing meant that even blacks in auto foundries would face barriers in their attempts to find employment in plants converted to wartime production. A black journalist in Detroit noted in 1941, "We are in a hell of a spot out here as a result of the curtailment in auto production. Our boys are being laid off and they are not getting transfers to defense work."[25]

The element of timing—the belated entry of blacks into defense work—

told a larger story about the mobilization of the black workforce. In 1942, black men—and in 1943, black women—gained entry to decent defense jobs only as a result of the shortage of white workers, and the combined pressure applied by organizations like the NAACP, the National Urban League, the Communist Party, the Congress of Racial Equality, the national "Double V" for Victory campaign, and local workers' groups like the Portland, Oregon, Negro Shipyard Organization for Victory. In the middle of 1942, black workers were still conspicuous for their presence in southern cotton fields and on Mid-Atlantic truck farms, workplaces that whites had quickly abandoned in favor of highly paid defense work. Not until later that year did black migration rates begin to increase appreciably, in response to critical labor shortages around the country. Between 1942 and 1944, the proportion of blacks engaged in defense work increased from 3 percent to 8.3 percent.[26]

Black women had to wait even longer than black men to gain access to skilled jobs like those paying $85–$95 weekly, which seemed like a fortune to refugees from domestic service. Early on, in June 1941, a group of black women leaders sponsored a conference at Howard University to "discover ways and means through which Negro women should aid in the protection of America from external dangers and set up precedents by means of which true democracy may be maintained within." Public and private officials alike were slow to respond to the first objective, and ultimately unsympathetic to the second. Throughout the war, the United States Office of Education sponsored courses in domestic service for black women, on the theory that black private household workers could make their unique contribution to the war effort by doing the laundry and cooking the meals of white women employed in factories and shipyards. In a 1945 report on "Negro Women War Workers," the Women's Bureau quoted the "president of a large west coast aircraft corporation late in 1943: *We think every worker we can place in a laundry is worth three new workers in our own plants. . . .* Bomber production was being affected because workers in these plants could not get their washing done, nor buy their meals in restaurants." In late 1943, when employment levels in general were reaching all-time highs, some black women were hired as welders and other kinds of skilled workers; but many found themselves employed in particularly dirty kinds of work traditionally reserved for black men—in steel mill sintering plants, for example.[27]

Throughout the war, whites in a number of industries sent clear signals to their employers that they considered the introduction of blacks to be an infringement on their shop-floor rights, and an unwanted form of management encroachment—in other words, a threat to workplace "democracy." Hard hit by stagnating wages and numbing speed-ups, whites saw new black co-workers as one more aggravation in an already nerve-shattering work-day routine. Employers who took the first steps to hire blacks, like the own-ers of the National Smelting Company in Cleveland, were accused of "fascist practices": "were we not compelling him [the white worker], against his wishes, to work with people he didn't like—people who were a menace to his health and well-being, physical as well as moral?" Members of Port-land's Longshoremen's and Warehousemen's Union, Local 8, took this pecu-liarly perverse rhetoric of "freedom" and "self-determination" even further, defending their policy to exclude blacks by declaring, in late 1943, "We are fighting the Negro race!"[28]

From this perspective, the hate strikes that wracked the Detroit defense industry in response to the hiring and upgrading of black workers repre-sented but an extension of white workers' militant determination to protect their jobs against the highhandedness of managers and personnel officials. But such justifications rang hollow in light of incidents like that at a Beau-mont, Texas, shipyard where whites dropped hot rivets on recently hired skilled blacks. With numbers on their side in virtually every workplace con-frontation, whites could rally around the principle of "workers' control" without acknowledging the reality of anti-black prejudice. It was no won-der, then, that black workers failed to partake of a workplace culture that was defined by whites and served as a source of self-definition for white workers.[29]

Faced with an increasingly militant white workforce, employers were reluctant to utilize black workers until absolutely pressed to the wall by wartime necessity. Employment officials in the railroad industry, notorious for its discriminatory hiring practices and tolerance of violent attacks by white workers upon blacks, released this statement in 1943:

The railroads cannot undertake to push the solution of these problems [ie., racial prejudice] beyond that reached by the civilization as a whole. Railroads do not operate in a vacuum, or in a theoretical utopia. They have to operate in and serve the civilization in which they find themselves and must adopt [sic] their operations and employment practices to the social solution of racial questions as worked out by the prevailing mores and legal systems of the states they serve.

A few employers offered more detailed rationales for their exclusionary poli-cies. Echoing the complaints of manufacturers (and military officials) nationwide, southern paper mill officials maintained that black people as a group were "ill-qualified for machine training," and (in the words of an official of the Michigan Manufacturers' Association) lacked the "speed and rhythm" demanded of the modern assembly line.[30]

In some cases, employers deferred to the demands of unions that refused to accept any blacks as members, leading to scenes like the one at Bethlehem Steel's Sparrow Point plant near Baltimore, where "15 Negroes, skilled and unskilled, stood in line for six hours . . . in front of the employment office and watched 150 white men receive certification for employment [from the Steel Workers Organizing Committee], while the Negroes were ignored." In other cases, employers deferred to a region's racial mores. Bell Aircraft hired blacks as production workers in its Buffalo plant in 1942, but refused to institute a similarly open policy at its Atlanta facility. A report issued by a southern Regional Labor Supply Officer for March 1942 noted that the largest shipbuilding and aircraft plants were prepared to reach deep into local reserves of white women, married and unmarried, rather than provide training, and then employment, to blacks of either sex. Years later, a black man would describe the affront this way: Most employers "would rather see a cracker do wrong than give a black man a chance to do right."[31]

Still, some employers integrated their workforces relatively successfully once they put disgruntled whites on notice that they could either accept their new black co-workers, or quit. One measure of the eventual movement of southern black workers into defense jobs by 1945 was the extent to which German prisoners of war had been put to work in Georgia peanut fields; North Carolina fertilizer plants and turpentine orchards; Arkansas cotton fields, gins, and mills; and Louisiana lumber mills. Tellingly, some work camp officials suspected that these specific forms of forced labor violated international standards of conduct prescribed for the humane treatment of prisoners of war.[32]

A study of the racial integration of a large West Coast aviation plant employing twenty-four thousand workers suggested the link between the shop-floor politics of manpower mobilization on the one hand, and patterns of segregated housing and education on the other. A recent white migrant from Missouri made an effort to "tolerate the situation" when forced to work with a black woman, admitting, "I have never lived around colored folks. I have never played with them as a child. About five years ago we visited down South and they had everything separate; I thought that was good." Whites and blacks had few opportunities outside the workplace to deepen or extend on-the-job relationships—at church, at a school meeting, at a dance hall. No matter how accommodating an individual union or employer to black workers, when whites spent their lunch hours at Jim Crow restaurants and their after-work hours at Jim Crow bars, when they played on all-white baseball teams in the evening or attended all-white company picnics, they naturally came to think of all-white workplaces as part of the natural order of things. It was no wonder, then, that a shortage of housing in wartime Detroit contributed to a clash between whites and blacks on a hot summer day in 1943, and a bloody riot ensued. Such civil disturbances were but community manifestations of factory-based hate strikes.[33]

For its part, the federal government took tentative steps toward pressuring private employers to enact egalitarian hiring policies, but the Roosevelt administration acted only in response to overt political pressure. When A. Philip Randolph, leader of the Brotherhood of Sleeping Car Porters, threatened to organize a massive March on Washington to protest racial discrimination in defense hiring in June 1941, Roosevelt created the Fair Employment Practices Commission (FEPC), a weak and temporary agency that nevertheless eventually boasted some local successes in opening selected positions to black workers. The FEPC lacked the power of enforcement, and instead relied on black militants, progressive unions, and local civil rights organizations to attack some of the most egregious cases of racist hiring policies. For example, on the West Coast, blacks launched a court fight against the Boilermakers' segregated ("auxiliary") union system that relegated nonwhites in the trade to second-class citizenship. The resulting decision of a California superior court judge (in 1943) helped to dismantle that system and provided legal backing to FEPC directives. In the South, hearings held by the FEPC encouraged black firemen to come forward to document the efforts of the Brotherhood of Locomotive Firemen and Enginemen to displace them from their jobs. Despite progress in the desegregation of transit systems in Philadelphia and Pittsburgh, among other cities, the chronic shortage of manpower, and not the FEPC, was the factor most responsible for opening up new kinds of jobs for black men and women between 1943 and 1945.[34]

Black FEPC field investigators like the southerners John Hope II and Virgil Williams spent a good deal of their time monitoring a whole host of taxpayer-supported agencies that actively upheld discriminatory hiring practices. The United States Employment Services steadfastly refused to place blacks in supervisory positions, or in "refined settings"—that is, in all-white workplaces. The National Mediation Board and the National Railroad Adjustment Board continued to put their stamp of approval upon the railway unions' exclusionary policies. Blacks made some temporary wartime gains in achieving administrative positions in public employment, no doubt due to Executive Order #8802, which officially outlawed discrimination in the Civil Service; however, on average, whites could count on a promotion for every two man-years of service, while blacks had to wait seven times as long for a similar upgrading. And by the end of the war, the 7 percent of all Postal Office employees who were black were still not allowed to join the National Alliance of Postal Employees, an all-white union of federal workers.[35]

The ultimate test of the federal govenment's commitment to the full and equal utilization of black men and women as war workers of course came in the form of military policies, and here the FDR administration (and the subsequent wartime Truman presidency as well) failed miserably. Some African-American recruits had decidedly low expectations when they joined the armed forces. A Chicago man, Louis Banks, homeless and unemployed "when the war came . . . was so glad when I got in the army. I knew I was safe . . . I'd rather be in the army than outside where I was so raggedy and didn't have no jobs." Banks would soon discover that military manpower deployment practices represented a blend of nineteenth-century customs with twentieth-century sensibilities about the "unfitness" of black soldiers for technologically advanced modes of combat.[36]

At the most basic level, U.S. military policy had not changed much since the Civil War, when black men too often served as fatigue workers and the valets of white officers. In *Colored People*, Gates describes a by now familiar "racial" dynamic that assigned the service work performed by women in civilian life to black men in army life:

Camp Lee was where colored soldiers were sent to learn to be quarter-masters—butlers, chefs, and service people, generally. Because the Army replicates the social structure of the larger society it defends, almost all black draftees were taught to cook and clean. Of course, it was usually women who cooked and cleaned outside the Army, but *someone* had to do the work, so it would be black men.

In the words of one contemporary critic, the army placed southern white officers over black troops on the assumption that "Southern whites 'understood' Negroes best, and also that Negro troops preferred Southern white officers because they knew exactly where they 'stood' with them." These officers continued to assume "that Negroes could not be trained for combat duties and were fit only for unskilled service jobs." Men of the 96th Battalion built docks and causeways in New Guinea, but, armed only with old Springfield rifles and deprived of rigorous military training, played virtually no fighting role in the South Pacific. Secretary of War Henry Stimson attempted to justify the assignment of black troops to fatigue work when he suggested that "a relatively large percentage of the Negroes inducted in the Army have fallen within the lower educational classifications, and many of the Negro units accordingly have been unable to master efficiently the techniques of modern weapons."[37]

In the armed forces, innovations in administration and strategy were accompanied by innovations in the tactics of humiliation of black servicemen and women. As a matter of general policy, the armed forces declared that all blood collected from troops be separated by the race of the donor, a policy in which the American Red Cross readily acquiesced. In 1945, 40 percent of a black postal battalion of the Women's Air Corps (WAC) sent to the European theater assumed unskilled tasks, but only 1 percent of the white WACs. The U.S. Navy, which had gratefully accepted the services of black seamen in the Revolutionary War, had devolved to the point that a male mess steward named Dorie Miller could be awarded a Navy Cross for sharpshooting two Japanese aircraft out of the skies over Pearl Harbor in December 1941, and yet fail to receive a promotion out of the kitchen and onto the deck as a gunner (he died at sea, the victim of a Japanese torpedo, two years later). In 1943, Judge William H. Hastie (a former Howard University Law School dean), in his capacity as civilian aide to the secretary of war, protested that the air force, a new branch of the service, was perfecting new techniques of discrimination, insisting on segregated officer candidate schools (such as the one at Tuskegee, Alabama), and then relegating trained black pilots to "the performance of such odd jobs of common labor as may arise from time to time at air fields." The 99th Pursuit (later Fighter) Squadron consisted of all-black personnel, from janitors and clerks to fighter pilots, as the air force enforced its segregation policies with a vengeance. Warned Hastie in his letter of resignation (dated January 5, 1943), "Men cannot be humiliated over a long period of time without a shattering of morale and a destroying of combat efficiency."[38]

For blacks as a group, the war left a mixed legacy. Between 1941 and 1945, black activist groups refined and expanded their protest strategies, sponsoring court test cases, lunch-counter sit-ins, mass picketing, consumer boycotts, and political lobbying to achieve greater employment opportunities. At the end of the war decade, the number of black men engaged in manufacturing stood at 22.3 percent, just slightly lower than that of similarly employed white men (26.6 percent), and white women (24.6 percent), and up from 15.4 percent ten years earlier. Still, agriculture continued to claim the energies of one-fifth of all black workers (and only 12 percent of whites), and six out of ten gainfully employed black women still toiled as service workers in private households or in commercial establishments and office buildings. Although 38 percent of white women found jobs as secretaries and retail clerks after the war, only 5 percent of black women were similarly employed. In 1946, New York City's Hilda Fortune, like other members of the National Council of Negro Women, expressed alarm at the prospect of black women war workers once again forced to enter white households through the back door; said one reluctant domestic, "I could stand the work if I were just treated respectfully by the family and the children." For many others, no amount of respect could compensate for the pitifully low pay and lack of benefits they earned for unpredictably long hours.[39]

The FEPC was disbanded in 1946, but the logic of political equality highlighted by the war years could not be denied by the process of demobilization. Several states formed their own FEPCs—New York in 1945, and Washington State in 1949, for example—and individual cities, among them Chicago, Minneapolis, New York, and Cincinnati, enacted municipal anti-discrimination ordinances. In 1947, the National Urban League launched a Pilot Placement Project, its goal to open all-white jobs (like those with U.S. Atomic Commission subcontractors) to at least fifty black workers each year. However, these efforts had less impact overall than the growth in black voting strength that gradually yielded public-sector jobs in the nation's largest northern cities. Will Robinson remembered the pride he felt when he was hired as one of Chicago's first bus drivers in 1945. At that time, "The job was predominantly white," and so on Sundays, he and his co-workers would wear their drivers' uniforms instead of suits to church—"it was a prestige thing."[40]

If Will Robinson represented black people's impulse for a respectable job in the paid labor force, a group of young men in the cities in the 1940s elevated their resistance to such work to the level of a distinctive, proto-political, and highly public style; these were the "draped-shape-clad hipsters" known as "zoot suiters," men like Malcolm Little (later Malcolm X) and other "hustlers" who talked tough and walked even tougher. They rejected the jobs of ditchdiggers and cooks in favor of a streetwise identity carved out of illicit forms of moneymaking. Malcolm Little himself understood that white people often measured themselves against the demeaning roles that black wage earners were forced to assume. Referring to his own stints as a sandwich maker on a commuter train and as a shoeshine boy in wartime Boston, he wrote: "We were in that world of Negroes who are both servants and psychologists, aware that white people are so obsessed with their own importance that they will pay liberally, even dearly, for the impression of being catered to and entertained."[41]

During the postwar period, it was clear that there existed no groundswell of public (white) opinion in favor of black civil rights. While the federal government might typically engage in discrete reform, it would refrain from launching a concerted assault on the whole apparatus of inequality. In 1948, President Harry S Truman desegregated the armed forces; but he left intact de jure systems of educational and housing segregation throughout the nation. By this time, few educated Americans in high positions of public service could claim ignorance of the laws, procedures, and behaviors that relegated blacks to second-class citizenship. Indeed, a succinct report issued by the President's Committee on Civil Rights in 1947, *To Secure These Rights*, outlined in stunning detail the means by which qualified black applicants were denied jobs in private industry and government service. In terms of federal complicity in Jim Crow hiring practices, little had changed since the founding of the republic.

INDUSTRIAL DECLINE AND THE DESTRUCTION OF LEGALIZED JIM CROW, 1950–78

The consolidation of black voting strength that resulted from the massive migration of 4 million blacks out of the South in the 1940s and 1950s wrought a genuine revolution in American political life. The passage of the Civil Rights Acts of 1964 and 1965 amounted to the legislative fruits of a civil rights movement initiated by abolitionists and culminating in the protests of thousands of ordinary black men, women, and children in the 1950s and 1960s. In dramatic fashion, Title VII of the 1964 act outlawed racial discrimination in hiring, and created administrative machinery, in the form of the Equal Employment Opportunity Commission (EEOC), to enforce its provisions. The election of several black big-city mayors in the late 1960s and early 1970s—in Cleveland, Atlanta, Chicago, Detroit, Los Angeles, and Newark, for example—represented a seismic shift in the urban political landscape. Yet even these dramatic departures were insufficient to erase the effects of generations-old patterns of black inequality.

Interviewed in the late 1980s, T. C. Johnson of Lexington, Mississippi, a member of the Freedom Democratic Party in the late 1960s, recalled the realm of public jobs in his native state. "Blacks were left out of most positions. Everything you went to—if you went before the judge, ya goin' 'fore a white judge. If you went 'fore the sheriff, you goin' with all white in there and you bein' mistreated in jail. If you went before the polices in town, ya going against all whites."[42] During the 1950s and 1960s, film footage and still photographs showed black protesters of all ages confronting white county sheriffs and white voter registrars; white policemen unleashing dogs and wielding billy clubs; white firemen aiming water hoses at black schoolchildren; white mayors defending lunch-counter segregation; and white governors barricading schoolhouse doors.

The elimination of racial discrimination was easier to invoke in court cases and legal statutes than it was to achieve in reality. Ultimately, the psycho-social dynamics of color-based inequality were impervious to legal action, and neither the ballot nor government legislation proved to be wholly effective weapons against the forces that rendered blacks economically insecure. Yet it was during this period, when the struggle against Jim Crow was waged on the national stage for the first time, that southern businessmen began to worry: Northern companies might readily relocate to a part of the country where unions were weak and production workers cheap, but not to a region where black girls were killed in church bombings and peaceful demonstrators set upon by attack dogs. If the South were to partake of the blessings of a booming postwar economy, then it would have to moderate its image and loosen the vise of black subordination. The public relations imperative acknowledged by southern chambers of commerce thus complemented the moral imperative articulated by black activists and their white allies.[43]

A number of long-term demographic, economic, and political developments ultimately counterbalanced the effectiveness of equal opportunity legislation passed in the mid-1960s. Within well-defined regional labor markets, two groups in particular appealed to the "racial" loyalties of employers and stalled blacks' efforts to partake of postwar prosperity. Through the 1950s, middle-class white women solidified their monopoly over retail and clerical jobs, and successfully competed with black women in their bid to work as waitresses, factory operatives, nurses, and schoolteachers. Occupational statistics confirmed that fewer black women were working as farm hands, but as a group they remained concentrated in declining traditional women's jobs—as household and laundry workers—in contrast to the white women gaining positions as secretaries and telephone operators.[44]

Moreover, white southern migrants to the urban Northeast and Midwest effectively shut out large numbers of blacks from the factory jobs that provided a more secure foothold in the industrial sector compared to traditional "black" jobs. Northern-born blacks and southern black migrants alike found themselves at a distinct disadvantage when competing with rural whites for entry-level factory jobs, whether in Bakersfield, California, or Cincinnati,

Ohio, or Middletown, Connecticut; everywhere, whites were often able to count on the help of friends and kin who had already found jobs as industrial laborers, while blacks usually had to rely on more formal devices like employment agencies to secure work. Because poor whites received priority in hiring, they were more likely to advance to semi-skilled positions, compared to blacks, who remained in menial positions if they were hired at all. By this time, the notion that southern white men were especially adept at operating and fixing machines had hardened into conventional wisdom. Despite similarities in their wage-earning histories (on farms and in coal mines) and their lack of formal schooling, black and white southern migrants followed separate paths once they reached the North; and the residential mobility enjoyed by the whites ensured that they would be able to move as far in search of safer neighborhoods, better jobs, and better schools as their incomes and ambition would take them.[45]

Persistent residential segregation confined black workers to poor, overcrowded inner-city neighborhoods where the schools presented a striking contrast to the new ones attended by white children in the all-white suburbs. Generations of black workers had learned through bitter experience the connection between housing and job patterns, and more specifically, the disadvantages that flowed from living far from factories and other industrial workplaces. Employers looked askance at black job applicants who had to travel long distances to work, on the assumption that tardiness and high turnover rates would be the inevitable result. Long commutes prevented black employees from participating in company and union activities that necessitated a return to the job site in the evening. And finally, the expense of traveling to and from distant workplaces kept blacks from applying for positions that were bound to pay them low wages in any case.

By the mid-1950s, the enforced spatial concentration of blacks in northern ghettoes had reached crisis proportions, as the discriminatory policies of suburban "neighborhood improvement associations," regional zoning boards, city councils, and bank loan officials confined blacks to areas of decaying housing and deteriorating schools. White suburbanites continued to react violently to the prospect of residential integration, out of the conviction that civil rights was at odds with "homeowners' rights." In cities, massive public construction projects, such as the Interstate highway system and urban renewal ("Negro removal") programs, razed entire neighborhoods, replacing them with concrete high-rises in some cases, and nothing at all in others.[46]

The processes of economic restructuring and technological innovation that had already begun to destablize black work patterns in the early 1900s intensified after World War II, pushing African Americans off the southern countryside, but also depriving migrants of blue-collar jobs in the urban North. Machines threw hundreds of thousands of black southerners out of work between 1950 and 1970. In Delta cotton fields, the appearance of the mechanical cotton picker in the late 1940s, and its pervasive use twenty years later, signaled the end of an era, a 150-year period during which rural black southerners were identified almost exclusively with the cultivation of cotton. North Carolina tobacco companies completed a process begun two decades earlier, and virtually eliminated the job of tobacco stemmer through the use of labor-saving machinery, a move intended to crush the Tobacco Workers Organizing Committee (composed of large numbers of black women). In southern Appalachia, dislocations in the coal industry hit black workers the hardest. Continuous coal-mining machines mined half of all underground coal by 1967 (up from 2 percent in 1950), eliminating black hand loaders in the process. (According to coal mine operators in the late 1960s, "you can't trust [blacks] with a machine, even the educated ones.") Strip-mining, which relied on heavy machinery, became more pervasive throughout the region, but failed to provide jobs for unemployed black miners. And the "dog hole mines" dug by unemployed (but landowning) whites remained independent operations owned by kin groups that insisted on racial exclusivity. Throughout this period, the policies of the United Mine Workers revealed that union leaders could garner national reputations as outspoken advocates of black civil rights, and yet by their support of mechanization condemn black workers in their own industry to a life of insecurity, or joblessness.[47]

At the same time that machines were squeezing southern blacks out of jobs, several major northern industries, including autos, appliances, and defense, began to expand their use of skilled workers with technical proficiencies over unskilled and semi-skilled production workers. Black men had enjoyed relatively low rates of unemployment for the first eight years or so after the end of World War II; but black migrants arrived in northeastern and midwestern cities in the 1950s and 1960s only to experience the loss of unskilled industrial jobs throughout those regions. For example, postwar Trenton, New Jersey, offered southern blacks jobs only as custodians and sweepers in factories, and as potato grubbers and chicken pluckers in the surrounding rural areas. In the city, AFL unions, public housing, restaurants, and public schools and colleges operated on Jim Crow principles, providing most whites with an automatic advantage in the job market.[48]

Within a decade and a half of the war's end, in cities like Harrisburg, Pennsylvania, and St. Paul, Minnesota, as well as Trenton, "white-collar bureaucracies" replaced smokestack industries, bringing into center cities by day the well-educated suburbanites who retreated each evening by auto and commuter rail to their all-white neighborhoods. In Chicago, Cincinnati, Cleveland, Detroit, New York, Newark, Philadelphia, and Pittsburgh, 1960 represented the high-water mark of total number of workers employed in manufacturing; between 1960 and 1964, Chicago, Detroit, and Cleveland, major centers of black industrial employment, lost an average of ten thousand black manufacturing jobs each. During that same period, the number of blacks engaged in manufacturing in New York dropped by almost eighty thousand, or 8 percent.[49]

The cumulative effect of these transformations in the shape and demographic composition of the American workforce was the impoverishment of a substantial proportion of the black population. Employers who abandoned the inner city left behind a shrinking tax base, resulting in resource-starved schools in black neighborhoods. Although black youth were close to reaching parity with whites in terms of the number of years of formal education, employers made the connection between inner-city schools on the one hand and overcrowded classrooms, overburdened teachers, and inadequate resources on the other. As a result, a quality (i.e., suburban) high school education replaced the high school diploma as the minimal requirement for a decent job. The trimming of unskilled workers automatically cut off possibilities—however rarely fulfilled—for substantial numbers of black men to climb internal ladders into skilled jobs and supervisory positions. When black men lost their factory jobs and entered the ranks of casual laborers, black women were forced to bear a larger share of the responsibility for family breadwinning.[50]

By the early 1960s, the essential mix of racial discrimination in job hiring—the part played by private and public employment agencies, employers, and union officials—had not changed substantially since the turn of the century. Soon after the end of World War II it became clear that the unions most determined to exclude black members altogether—the Railwaymen, Boilermakers, and Shipbuilders, for example—were concentrated in declining sectors of the economy. At the same time, unions like the United Auto Workers and the United Mine Workers evinced little interest in directly addressing the process by which automation was displacing large proportions of black (or white) workers. The building trade unions still enforced so-called gentlemen's agreements to ensure that black workers remained in auxiliary, or "independent" unions. In 1954, in a letter to NAACP official Herbert Hill, a Miami attorney noted that the AFL craftsmen of the city were not going to integrate their own ranks "until they have to." Paper mill unions devised a convoluted system of seniority progression, so that black jobs, such as those of laborers, brakemen, and car loaders, were left off the tracks that led to promotions. Roll handlers and bundle cutters, all white men, could hope to reach the position of sheet cutter operator, while the black lift-truck operators they worked next to could not. Employers continued to defer to the perceived sensibilities of white workers, who preferred not to work with blacks if at all possible and who insisted that certain dangerous kinds of work—like spray-painting in auto factories—be labeled particularly appropriate for blacks, or reserved exclusively for them.[51]

And whites in a variety of official capacities proved adept at using new ideologies, organizational structures, and bureaucratic procedures to maximize their own opportunities at the expense of black workers. Increasingly conservative white labor leaders tended to conflate all forms of radicalism, automatically branding as Communists black workers like New York City's Florence Rice, a member of the International Ladies Garment Workers Union (ILGWU), who spoke out against racism on the shop floor. Charged Rice in 1962, "Whenever a new type of machine was brought into the shop the white employee was always taught how to operate it first. They were given preference." ILGWU officials strongly disapproved of such complaints, and Rice was blacklisted from union jobs after her public testimony on the issue.[52]

For jobs that required formal application procedures, personnel officials and office administrators devised ingenious strategies to circumvent color-blind employment policies, including machinations that reflected an emerging emphasis on "credentialism"; now applicants were required to provide proof of formal education and previous work experience for a growing number of jobs for which such prerequisites were hardly necessary. The Civil Service used application photos and the "rule of three" (the ability of department heads to choose among three applicants) to advance whites over qualified blacks. In the early 1960s, private employment agencies stamped the application forms of blacks with codes like "NFU" ("not for us") and "POK" ("people of color") to alert prospective employers.[53]

Subjective forms of color-based preference were especially difficult to root out by means of federal legislation. Created as the enforcement machinery of Title VII, the Equal Employment Opportunity Commission, which served as an "updated FEPC," soon ran headlong into the problem of combatting elusive forms of racism in hiring. In 1966, the EEOC sponsored a survey of 26 million workers and 43,000 employers throughout the country, and found that "Negro workers, both male and female, are clustered in those industries which have the fewest jobs to offer in the top-paying occupations," and that only about one-third of the differential in black-white job status was attributable to the superior educational attainment of whites. The principal author of the study, Alfred W. Blumrosen, offered a case study of entrenched discrimination in the construction industry, and provided a "partial catalogue of tactics" that had been used by unions to exclude blacks. These tactics included, among others, a ban on all new black members by a particular union; the failure of a union to notify members of the black community that it was accepting new applicants for the positions of apprentice and journeyman; the decision not to refer black union members for work; and "the establishment of the barriers of delay, of subjectively evaluated tests, of unreasonable test standards not uniformly applied to whites. . . ." Clearly, any union determined to maintain anti-black policies possessed a great deal of latitude in pursuing that objective, and, as equal opportunity advocates would eventually discover, it would be impossible to litigate the finer points of exclusion.[54]

The Civil Rights Acts of 1964 and 1965 were part of a series of social welfare initiatives hailed by President Johnson as "the Great Society," and the consequent growth of the federal bureaucracy, combined with the creation of thousands of (mostly low-paying) jobs in the public sector, brought substantial numbers of African Americans onto the federal payroll for the first time. The expansion of the Aid to Families with Dependent Children (AFDC) program, and the launching of Head Start and other local community action programs, gave employment to as many as fifteen thousand African-American men and women as teachers' aides, social workers, leaders of local youth job corps, Model Cities administrators, and Vista volunteers. Although these positions served as the foundation of a grass-roots leadership base in the cities, and although part-time employment opportunities enabled some black youngsters to remain in school longer than they would have otherwise, for the most part Great Society jobs failed to provide black (or white) people with the skills that would have enabled them to transfer into the private sector; and indeed almost all of the jobs remained contingent on federal funding, which gradually dried up after 1972. In Washington, the vast majority of federal appointees remained at the lowest echelons of the government bureaucracy; and the typical federal worker of the 1960s was not a social services administrator but (in time-honored fashion) a postal worker. By failing to address the structural causes of intergenerational poverty in inner cities, Great Society programs did little to alter the long-term prospects of black job seekers within chronically depressed neighborhoods.[55]

Between 1964 and the late 1970s, federal anti-discrimination initiatives shifted from an emphasis on individual grievances to more aggressive "affirmative action" programs intended to root out institutional bias affecting the job opportunities of specific groups, particularly black men and women and white women. Initially, the EEOC investigated exclusively on a case-by-case basis, thereby leaving intact whole systems of racial preference. However, the chronically understaffed and underfunded commission was soon overwhelmed by a floodtide of complaints (15,000 in its first eighteen months alone; by 1974, the annual figure was 57,000). The weakness in this scattershot approach was acknowledged in 1969, when the Nixon administration approved the Philadelphia Plan, a successor of the PWA quota system targeting racial bias in the construction industry. Under this initiative, industry officials had to submit hiring schedules (based on the percentage of blacks in the Philadelphia workforce) before their applications for government contracts could be reviewed, or accepted. (From a partisan Republican perspective, the plan's great virtue was its potential to alienate from each other two key constituencies of the New Deal coalition: black workers and trade unions.) In the early 1970s, a series of Supreme Court cases outlawed hiring and promotion procedures that disproportionately harmed black workers, regardless of their intent. Thus the federal government had moved beyond the original mandate posed by the 1964 Civil Rights Act, which outlawed discrimination in hiring, to a more energetic role in rectifying the effects of historic patterns of discrimination. Nevertheless, in the famous *Bakke* case of 1978, Allan Bakke (denied admission to the University of California-Davis Medical School) argued that he had lost his place to a less qualified black applicant. Though Bakke lost the case, the Court put schools and employers on notice that strict, numerical racial quotas were unacceptable means to combat historic patterns of racial prejudice in education and employment.[56]

The fourteen years subsequent to the enactment of the Civil Rights Act of 1964 revealed both its strengths and its limitations as a device for opening previously all-white jobs to African Americans. Taken together, Title VII and the Voting Rights Act of 1964 removed longstanding legal barriers to the integration of black men and women into a variety of workplaces, and provided blacks (at least those with the economic wherewithal) with the kind of residential mobility that was key to their search for better jobs and safer neighborhoods. Specific groups of blacks—those with formal schooling, women, and southerners—benefited in dramatic ways. Well-educated black workers gained employment opportunities that their grandparents only dreamed about. By any number of measures—percentage of blacks employed as professionals, household income, number of black college students, increase in home ownership—the mid-1960s represented a watershed for the black middle class, and especially households with two wage earners. Between 1960 and 1980, the percentage of black women in clerical work tripled (from 9 to 29 percent of all black women wage earners), a development that affected younger women in particular, and during that same period the percentage of black women in professional jobs increased from 6 to 15 percent. Nevertheless, many black workers were left behind, in inner-city neighborhoods and in jobs shaped by historic white supremacist ideologies. In 1980, the 15 percent of black women workers who were factory operatives remained concentrated in the least desirable positions within that category—as employees of dry-cleaning establishments, for example. Similarly, black women stayed clustered at the lowest echelons of the service sector, as nursing home aides, office custodians, and cafeteria workers.[57]

Changes in the social structure of local labor forces were most apparent in southern states, where black field hands began to move into semi-skilled manufacturing jobs now that de jure discrimination had been eliminated. Successful attempts to integrate public schools and register black voters provided the necessary political context for economic advancement. In the textile industry, employers eagerly tapped into a hitherto neglected labor pool, for whites were leaving the industry in droves in search of better jobs—the men to higher-paying factory jobs, the women to cleaner, lighter clerical work. Thus, in South Carolina between 1960 and 1980, the percentage of white women employed in manufacturing dropped from 43 percent to 28 percent; the corresponding figures for white men were 40 to 33 percent. At the same time, blacks increased their participation in the manufacturing sector—women from 4 to 32 percent, and men from 24 to 38 percent. As foreign imports flooded the domestic textiles market, black workers served to keep the shaky low-wage industry competitive in the world marketplace. In southern mills, shop-floor integration proceeded relatively smoothly, not only because employers had a financial incentive to facilitate the process but also because a whole generation of black workers had labored in intermediary positions between floor sweepers and machine operatives, and were therefore already familiar with the machinery they would operate full time after 1964. Almost overnight, plant managers found it easy enough to dispense with "the idea that Negroes were not intelligent enough to work with modern technology."[58]

However, employers and labor unions continued to favor white employees and still escaped the scrutiny of equal opportunity commissions and the courts. In 1968, Lucy Sledge and a white co-worker were laid off from their jobs as terry inspectors at the J. P. Stevens textile plant in Roanoke Rapids, North Carolina; but when it came time to rehire one of them, the white woman was called back, reflecting a larger, industrywide trend to favor whites in times of industry downturns. (Sledge also noted that Stevens personnel officials preferred "light and nice-looking" blacks in their hiring.) In the southern service sector, hotels and restaurants could boast of hiring substantial numbers of black workers for the first time, while assigning all of them to menial positions and blocking their promotion to supervisory jobs. Reports issued by the Kentucky Commission on Human Rights documented unstated policies that kept blacks in the kitchens and reserved the positions of bartender, food server, cocktail waitress, hostess, and executive for whites. A 1973 study of building craft unions nationwide revealed that qualified black job seekers faced roadblocks at every step of the application process: They were denied application forms, told that the local's business agent was unavailable, instructed to fill out multiple forms, and excluded from training programs reserved for the male kinfolk of (white) members. Locals continued to thwart the promotion of blacks by redefining jobs and thereby manipulating the seniority system to favor whites.[59]

During these years it became apparent that structural changes in the economy would continue to exert a gravitational pull downward on relatively unskilled and uneducated workers, blacks foremost among them, who were already handicapped in the competition for good jobs. Of the nearly 1 million new jobs created in the New York City region between 1959 and 1967, fully three-fourths were located in the suburbs, creating in the city a mix of jobs and workers that would become typical of late twentieth-century America: white-collar jobs (for suburban white commuters) in the legal and financial services industries, and minimum wage jobs (for inner-city blacks and Hispanics) in food services, health care, and building maintenance. During the recessions of 1974–75 and 1977–78, black unemployment rates reached depression-level highs of 15 percent. The much-vaunted political power of black mayors—and for that matter, grass-roots organizations of tenants, welfare recipients, and the parents of schoolchildren—propelled some black workers into the ranks of municipal political employees, and a few into high positions of leadership as police commissioners and heads of housing and welfare agencies. Nevertheless, these developments would have only minimal impact on the social organization of the African-American labor force, and on the life chances of a poor population (both urban and rural) increasingly wracked by joblessness. Neither black judges nor black policemen nor black voter registrars, landlords, or teachers could restore jobs that had vanished.[60]

The twin impulses behind black job creation half a century earlier—the integrationist efforts of the National Urban League on the one hand, and the black nationalist emphasis on indigenous enterprise on the other—appeared again now, in altered form, to fill the economic vacuum left by tentative government programs and indifferent private employers. "Operation Breadbasket," founded by the Southern Christian Leadership Conference (SCLC) in 1962 to open new jobs for blacks and encourage black businesses, yielded five thousand new jobs in Atlanta in the early 1960s. During the late 1960s, the locus of the campaign shifted to the North, and especially Chicago, where under the leadership of the Reverend Jesse Jackson activists focused on supermarkets, and by picketing and boycotting managed to wrest commitments from employers to hire more black workers and utilize more black businesses as suppliers. From a different point on the ideological spectrum came the calls of Black Muslims to concentrate on building black economic power, block by block, business by business, and lessen dependence on white people as landlords, employers, and leaders of all kinds. Yet no amount of faith, whether inspired by the preaching of Southern Baptists like the Reverend Martin Luther King, Jr., or Black Muslims like Malcolm X, could create economic opportunity out of whole cloth. The loss of jobs over the course of a decade or more shredded the social fabric of poor black neighborhoods all over the country.[61]

Emblematic of the deepening distress of urban communities was a radical turnabout in mainstream white perceptions of black men as soldiers. Beginning in 1950, with the integration of the armed forces and the abandonment of racial quotas, black men began to play an increasingly significant role as fighters, and not just fatigue workers, in the U.S. military. By the late 1960s, black GIs were dying in Southeast Asia in numbers disproportionate to their representation in the general population. It was during this era that some politicians and policymakers came to see the army as a means of moral regeneration among black men, even though American military engagements around the world were becoming less clearcut as moral crusades. In his report *The Negro Family: The Case for National Action*, prepared for the U.S. Department of Labor, Harvard University sociologist Daniel Patrick Moynihan argued that the service afforded poor black men a necessary kind of work, for in the army they would find "an utterly masculine world . . . a world away from women, a world run by strong men of unquestioned authority, where discipline, if harsh, is nonetheless orderly and predictable, and where rewards, if limited, are granted on the basis of performance." Yet few Vietnam veterans who reentered the civilian labor force found that their combat experience overseas, and the drug use and post-traumatic stress that often accompanied it, adequately prepared them to make a living in a transformed civilian economy.[62]

Moynihan's analysis of the black family attracted a firestorm of criticism, but it was his proposal about Uncle Sam as employer that told a larger story about the the gradual breakdown in a division of labor that assigned black people certain kinds of work. By this time it was clear that the economy would serve less to force poorly educated black people into particular forms of productive labor than to consign them to joblessness; under these conditions, the army would supposedly offer to African-American men the kind of discipline and direction that gainful employment had supposedly provided in the past. No longer did poor blacks fill a need as a civilian "reserve army" of workers available to pick up the slack in times of labor shortages and national emergencies; modern industry was just too technologically efficient to rely upon large numbers of unskilled laborers, regardless of economic conditions. This fact of business life suggested that, without the creation of large numbers of new jobs at good wages, federal equal employment legislation would have only limited impact upon the chances of many blacks. Civil rights activists in the streets and church pulpits, on the federal bench and in the Congress, achieved impressive gains in integrating American workplaces, but more and more of those workplaces were disappearing. For the poorest workers in particular, employment opportunity meant integration into a job structure that had little room for them.

IN THE 1970s, noncollege-educated black workers fell into two categories: those who remained relatively untouched by Title VII legislation, self-consciously toiling in, as one sixty-year-old women put it, "the work that my grandmother's mother did"; and those who now labored in integrated workplaces, but at jobs that broke body and spirit, with no commensurate reward in either pay or status. Situating herself in a long line of black workers, one woman observed: "I have never been anywhere where there were not some black people there before I got there. I have been a waitress, laundress, cook, cannery worker, and domestic." A household worker named Maggie Holmes declared to interviewer Studs Terkel, "I don't want my kids to come up and do domestic work. It's degrading. You can't see no tomorrow there." Domestic servants resented "people hanging overtop of me all day long," their every move monitored by a white person impossible to please; "the best work is work that you want to do that you do for yourself." Men and women confined to scrubbing floors or cleaning out hospital bedpans revealed the historic liabilities of black workers in general: "Now, you know our people can't do the kind of work they want to do anyway, so one kind of job is like another." For this reason, heavy, ill-paid labor, no matter how innocuous, carried with it a stigma borne of a slave past.[63]

Few blacks now employed in previously all-white positions had any illusions about the intrinsically liberating aspects of working together with white people. Among the first generation of women coal miners, Patricia Brown did battle with racist bosses and with racist co-workers, men who "would take my bucket, or my jacket, and they would put them in a hangman's noose." After securing a job in the spinning room at the J. P. Stevens plant in Roanoke Rapids, Ernestine Brooks was amazed to encounter poor whites for the first time in her life: "I had no idea those old white ladies had it so bad coming up. They got no education, and they started working twelve hours a day at ten years old. I never heard whites had it like that." Still, Brooks compared the factory itself to a prison, where "they got you shut in with brick. They got you closed in with earplugs." Paid the minimum wage to keep up with the spinning frames ("hopped up as fast as you can hop them up"), she "worked until my feet about fell off"—hers was a "stinking job." The last straw came when her boss said, "Unless you're smart enough to keep all those machines going [while you're gone], you can't go to the bathroom." Ernestine Brooks quit to fry chickens at a nearby restaurant.[64]

From workers in the postal service, transportation, and the auto and steel industries came similar cries of distress about the speed-ups, automation, and mandatory overtime that owners claimed were necessary to meet the challenge of a new era of cutthroat competition. In the auto industry, 550,000 workers produced 3 million cars in 1947, and 750,000 workers turned out 8 million cars annually twenty-five years later. Since World War II, the composition of the labor force had gradually changed, so that by 1970 about one-fifth of all Detroit auto plant employees were black, most of them young and male. What had not changed was that most of them were working under the supervision of white foremen and superintendents, more and more of whom were college educated. In 1968, the Dodge Revolutionary Union Movement was formed to protest speed-ups on the assembly line and racism on the shop floor. Critical of both the UAW and management, a writer in the *drum* (the organization's newsletter) charged:

(1) 95 % of all foremen in the plants are white; (2) 99% of all the general foremen are white; (3) 100% of all plant superintendents are white; (4) 90% of all skilled tradesmen are white; (5) 90% of all apprentices are white . . . systematically all of the easier jobs are held by whites; (7) Whenever whites are on harder jobs they have helpers; (8) When black workers

miss a day from work they are required to bring 3 doctors' excuses as to why they missed work; (9) . . . seniority is also a racist concept, since black workers were systematically denied employment for years at the plant.

In this list of grievances was encapsulated a self-perpetuating cycle of black worker marginality going back to the early nineteenth century, when blacks were barred from the first factories that dotted the hills of New England.[65]

Despite more than a decade of unprecedented federal efforts to eradicate racial discrimination in job hiring, by the late 1970s it was clear that long-term trends held out little promise for many black workers who hoped to make a living unfettered by the vagaries of history. Allan Bakke's challenge to affirmative action policies signaled a thickening of white reaction to equal opportunity legislation. Like generations of white workers and would-be white workers before him, Bakke claimed that the gains of black people (within a certain school or job) necessarily came at the expense of white people. As fewer worksites employed whites exclusively, other grievances came to the fore: racist office and shop-floor work cultures, and the failure of white supervisors to promote black employees in the same way or at the same rate as their white counterparts. And finally, the winds of economic change blew ill for large numbers of black workers, who found little consolation in the fact that more and more white workers had begun to fear for their own livelihoods as well.

CHAPTER TWELVE

....

INDUSTRIAL DEVOLUTION AND THE PERSISTENCE OF THE "RACE WATCH" AT THE END OF THE TWENTIETH CENTURY

By the 1990s, African-American workers in a wide variety of jobs were buffeted by the upheavals that had transformed the political economy of the United States, and the world, since the Great Depression. Moving to the tick-tock rhythm of the stopwatch, "gutpullers" in Mississippi chicken-processing plants struggled to keep pace with high-speed, carcass-laden assembly lines, and found themselves rewarded for their frantic efforts with meager pay and the crippling pain of carpal tunnel syndrome. Employees in outdated auto, textile, and steel plants were gradually yielding their places to robots and to the younger, well-educated people who operated them within new "white-collar factories." Construction workers languished in hiring halls, still beholden for jobs to the whites who stubbornly favored their own kin and kind; a Philadelphia foreman called on white workers exclusively, and explained, "they are the people I know best." Secretaries and banktellers, rendered increasingly superfluous by computer technology, saw their newfound security and status washed away in a flood of pink slips, while social workers and "human resources" officers too lost their jobs to the relentless forces of government downsizing and business restructuring. Meanwhile, in the boardrooms of Fortune 500 corporations, and in the downtown offices of prestigious law firms, black graduates of Ivy League schools remained ever vigilant, on a "race watch": white colleagues might applaud their individual achievements, and yet, "what you do poorly—well, that's when what you do will be dumped on the whole race." Further complicating the social landscape were a few newsworthy and tremendously wealthy artists, entertainers, and professional athletes who enriched the nation's public life, and yet in no meaningful way reflected the structure of the labor force as it affected ordinary African-American workers. Indeed, as many as one-third of all black people had good reason to worry not only about the terms on which they would be admitted to the paid labor force, but whether or not they would enter the mainstream world of work at all.[1]

In their quest for workers who were cheap and tractable, late twentieth-century employers felt little compunction to abide by any rigid racial division of labor, or even indeed to confine their quest within national boundaries. Employers with mobile forms of capital sought local supplies of immobile workers; thus a particular region of the United States might offer a surplus of illegal aliens, or the destitute sons and daughters of isolated rural folk, or inner-city blacks and Hispanics, all potential employees willing to work long hours for low wages. As a result, the African Americans who remained at the lowest echelons of the workforce found that they were not alone there, as multi-ethnic, multi-racial distressed communities proliferated throughout the country. At the same time, by virtue of their resistance to various forms of labor exploitation, black people as a group continued to bear the stigma of "troublemakers," in contrast to allegedly quiescent "Fourth Wave" immigrants from Latin America and Southeast Asia. In every sector of the economy, employers responded warily to the blacks at all levels of the workforce who were declaring, in the words of Thomas Rush, an airline skycap, "I look at everybody at eye level. I neither look down nor up. The day of the shuffle is gone."[2]

By the time federal lawsuits had begun to chip away at overtly discriminatory union membership policies, white industrial workers had begun to contemplate their increasingly beleaguered position. As the standard of militancy passed from industrial workers (mostly male and white) to service workers (mostly female and nonwhite), rising to the forefront of organized labor leaders were African-American women like Hattie Canty, a hotel worker in Las Vegas in 1996. Of her efforts that helped to organize forty thousand employees of Las Vegas's largest casino hotels, Canty said, "It has not been a picnic for me, but I don't think I'd like to go on a picnic every day. I have enjoyed the struggle. I'm not the only Hattie. There's lots of Hatties out there."[3]

Nevertheless, few of even the most determined of labor activists could hope to penetrate late twentieth-century worksites that recalled systems of bound labor. Now reliant for workers upon Latin American and Southeast Asian refugees as well as African Americans, labor-intensive industries spurred the growth of garment sweatshops, prison workshops, and "sweat-shops in the fields" (migrant labor camps). The exploitation of Chinese seamstresses in New York City, black prisoners in Arizona, and Mexican strawberry pickers in California testified to a never-ending quest for laborers who were at once cheap and lacking in political power. In spite of the infusion of large numbers of immigrants of color into the low-wage jobs long associated with black men and women, many black people continued to work as nursing aides and hospital attendants, cleaners and servants, and maids and housemen in numbers disproportionate to their representation in the general population. The poorest black urban residents remained confined to "hypersegregated" inner cities, deprived of quality health care and schooling, virtually precluding intergenerational upward social and residential mobility. Members of the black middle class (now 30 percent of the total black population) escaped from the ghetto, but many found themselves in newly racially segregated suburbs, and in new "racialized" jobs, working as administrators dependent on increasingly insecure sources of public and private funding for their livelihood.[4]

"When the plant lights go out, we all look same in the dark," observed the Reverend Jesse Jackson;[5] but in the labor force, and in workplaces throughout the country, history would continue to matter. In the midst of social dislocation caused by rapid technological change and large-scale immigration, it was no wonder that the race-baiting rhetoric of antebellum New England echoed in late twentieth-century pronouncements about the place of African Americans in the national labor market. Desperate to avoid a forced relocation to the end of the employment queue, whites would assert their claim to a moral and intellectual superiority over blacks, unknowingly imitating the political strategies of anxious tradesmen and mechanics a century and a half before.

African-American Workers within the "Global City" and in the Global Countryside

Located within an ever-shifting kaleidoscope of ethnic and class identities, late twentieth-century Americans came to realize the inadequacy of static "racial" categories as sources of group identification. For centuries, whites of European descent had borne children with blacks of African descent, and their offspring had been classified as "black," a label fraught with no real physiological meaning, but with great political significance. Various groups of African heritage—Jamaican Anglophones, together with Puerto-Rican

Spanish speakers, and Haitian Francophones, together with Brazilian Por-
tuguese speakers—confounded the easy equation of blackness with a distinctive African-American culture. By 1995, Hispanic Americans were on the
verge of overtaking African Americans as the nation's largest "minority"
group. Under pressure from an increasingly diverse workforce, the historic
underpinnings of a black-white racial division of labor gave way; at the
same time, time-honored tactics of prejudice against African Americans
endured.

From a variety of social indicators came proof that the destruction of the
legal basis of job discrimination was unequal to the tasks of erasing or
reversing the effects of generations-old systems of racial oppression. Of all
black female-headed households, more than half qualified as poor (compared to a little more than a quarter of similarly situated white households).
In the 1990s, almost half of all black children lived in households below the
poverty line (compared to 16 percent of white children). Although blacks
represented 12 percent of the total population, they constituted about two-
fifths of all recipients of Aid to Families with Dependent Children. More
than a fifth of all African Americans lacked health insurance. Black unemployment rates were consistently two or two and a half times greater than
the rates for whites, and nationwide, three out of ten of all "discouraged"
workers were black. Among wage-earning household heads with less than a
high school education, almost 40 percent of fully employed black women,
and 24 percent of fully employed black men, lived "beneath economic self-
sufficiency." In their average weekly compensation (among all full-time
wage and salary workers), black women ($336) and black men ($380) lagged
behind white men ($518) and white women ($388). These indicators of
social well-being (or rather, the lack thereof) were key determinants in a
country rapidly taking on all the demographic characteristics of an aristocracy, for the best jobs went to workers who were the children of workers
who lived in the wealthiest communities and attended elite schools.[6]

By this time, some observers were arguing that the U.S. armed forces
now provided an institutional model for civilian society, a dramatic claim
considering the abysmal historic record of the military establishment in
treating black soldiers equally or fairly. It is true that the army of the post-
Vietnam era boasted a high degree of racial integration at all levels, including the officers' corps, and that black men and women volunteers (who
tended to reenlist at a much higher rate than whites) found their talents and
hard work rewarded to a much greater degree than in nonmilitary work settings.[7] Nevertheless, it was unclear whether or not the army provided specific "lessons" that were transferrable to the civilian labor force. Indeed, in

the 1990s, allegations of widespread sexual abuse of female recruits by male drill sergeants suggested that the U.S. military was a less than satisfactory model for social relations of any kind. Moreover, army recruitment impera- tives bore little resemblance to the hiring considerations of government or private employers determined to match certain kinds of people with certain kinds of jobs, to hire or fire at will, and to create novel job arrangements in response to financial incentives. And, too, even the structure of the army continued to reflect the social realities outside. Almost all enlisted personnel had similar levels of education—as high school graduates—but they were assigned to jobs on the basis of entrance test scores. Because blacks came from poor neighborhood schools in disproportionate numbers, they tended not to do as well as whites on these tests, and therefore more often worked as truck drivers, cooks, and other kinds of "support" (rather than technical) workers. Such disparities in job assignments affected the overall status of blacks as a group within the military organization, and served as a predictor of opportunity in the private sector once individuals left the service.

The private sector itself consisted of four distinct battlegrounds of eco- nomic competition, battlegrounds on which black people were handicapped in ways both new and old. The first site covered well-paying professional positions in law, medicine, high technology, business, and finance. Between 1970 and 1990, a rising number of blacks ages twenty-five to forty-four worked as architects (1.8 percent of all persons in the profession in 1970, to 3.0 percent in 1990), lawyers and judges (1.5 percent to 4.0 percent), physi- cians and surgeons (2.9 percent to 4.7 percent), stock and bond salespeople (1.5 percent to 5.0 percent), and aeronautical engineers (2.0 percent to 5.3 percent). However, in every one of these categories, average black income was less than that of whites, and in some cases strikingly so. For example, in 1990, white surgeons earned on average $62,000 annually, and white bond salespeople $36,023; the comparable figures for blacks in those jobs were $40,000 and $24,000, respectively. In many cases, black people's gains in high-status jobs were directly attributable to the opening of the suburbs (and hence quality public education) to black families, the lowering of his- toric formal admissions barriers in colleges and postgraduate institutions, and the implementation of affirmative action programs in education and employment.[8]

A second locus of job rivalry centered on middle-level jobs that required specialized training but not necessarily a graduate degree. In this area, black firefighters, police, construction workers, and teachers benefited from the relatively open hiring policies enforced, or at least encouraged, by Title VII legislation. Black law enforcement officers, banktellers, public officials and

administrators, mail carriers, social welfare workers, and telephone operators all equaled or surpassed their proportionate representation in the population, and their annual incomes tended to approximate that of their white
co-workers; for example, in 1992, black and white public officials and administrators made about $25,000 annually. Nevertheless, this tier of jobs was
particularly vulnerable to government and business downsizing, heighten-
ing the resentment of whites who felt that blacks gained favor, by virtue of
their skin color, during times of both hiring and firing. For the broad white
middle class, then, affirmative action policies represented a federally backed
gambit in the zero-sum game; in the absence of job creation, the entry of
one black person into a previously all-white office place would virtually
guarantee the absence of one more white person. The job aspirations of
white women and Hispanic workers only served further to splinter the
workforce into shards of competing ethnic, racial, and gender groups. In an
exceptional case of interethnic alliance building in the 1980s, the Boston Jobs
Coalition pushed for a residency requirement among workers hired on city-
funded building projects to counter the predominance of suburban white
men in the construction industry. African Americans, white women, and the
Latin, Asian, and Native American communities all joined together to challenge the socially exclusive policies of local contractors.[9]

Positioned at a level between the jobs of lawyers and police officers were
those related to the implementation of "diversity" policies within the personnel offices of businesses, and those related to the administration of social welfare services within local, state, and federal governments. Using a metaphor
based on residential segregation, Vikki L. Pryor, senior vice president of operations at Blue Cross Blue Shield headquarters in Boston, noted in 1995, "Certainly there is ghettoization of jobs in corporate America." These jobs were
often earmarked for black applicants, and therefore, not unexpectedly, carried
with them certain liabilities. In contrast to mainstream jobs, lines in the
"human resources" or "community outreach" departments of corporations,
nonprofit organizations, and public agencies were often the first ones to be
affected by cutbacks. These jobs tended to keep blacks segregated from whites
working for the same organization; they rarely offered opportunities for promotion up and out of the "racialized" realm and into the mainstream (or
white) realm; and they failed to provide workers with the credentials necessary to make the move into more traditional management positions in private
industry. In the process of applying for a nonracialized management position,
the director of a community center, or the affirmative action officer at a large
corporation, would inevitably founder on the query from a prospective
employer: "Have you ever run a profit and loss operation?"[10]

The final tier of jobs—low-status, low-paying, and often highly exploitative positions—constituted the traditional preserve of black workers. In
labor-intensive industries with low profit margins, employers sought out
workers whom they believed were particularly nimble with their fingers,
accommodating in their demeanor, and vulnerable in their legal or political
status. Thus, managers of chicken hatcheries claimed that "only Asians have
the physical dexterity and small hands needed to feel a chick's tiny sexual
organs and determine whether they're male or female." (Manufacturers of
computer components and other kinds of electronics equipment offered
similar rationales for their hiring practices, whether at home or abroad.)
Pockets of immigrants were tapped for specific low-skill jobs: for example,
hotel owners recruited recent Vietnamese and Hmong immigrants for jobs
as chambermaids and buspersons, using videos as training devices, since so
few of the newcomers spoke English. In out-of-the-way places like Storm
Lake, Iowa, employers found Hispanic and Laotian hands willing to do the
dirty work that more settled groups shunned—a hog slaughterhouse offered
"lots of knife work" ("not a pleasant job"), while Somalis found employment in the local turkey-packing plant. In 1996, commenting on the subhu-
man conditions under which Honduran immigrants worked at an egg farm
in rural Maine, labor officials termed their plight the "worst in the nation."[11]

For increasing numbers of desperate men, women, and children, the
concept of "free labor" rang hollow. Amid a growing outcry over illegal
immigration, agribusinesses persisted in hiring a quarter of a million undoc-
umented workers to toil in the fields. An employer-sponsored influx of Mexicans (including Mixtec Indians) into the California strawberry fields
depressed wages, evoking the days of bondage: in the words of one worker,
"They use us all year as slaves." In the early 1990s, as many as 13,000 garment sweatshops employed 300,000 workers laboring up to 90 hours a week
for compensation far below the minimum wage. Reports of Thais virtually
imprisoned in Southern California garment factories, and of Chinese workers smuggled into New York City and then held as debt peons until their
friends and relatives redeemed them for up to $30,000 each, prompted com-
parisons of modern-day working conditions with slavery and indentured
servitude.[12]

In the 1990s, immigrants made up 9 percent of the U.S. workforce;
according to the President's Commission on the Future of Worker-Management Relations (in a report released in 1994), most of these newcomers
were concentrated in "low-wage import-competing industries . . . in several
sectors: apparel manufacturing, leather and footwear; private household
jobs." The commissioners added that "many immigrants, particularly those

who enter the country illegally, work in poor conditions outside the normal rules of the labor market." However, a case could be made that, to the contrary, these men, women, and children worked in poor conditions that exemplified the normal rules of the labor market. Indeed, the full measure of the horrific conditions endured by this group—and the lengths to which hardpressed employers would go to secure a cheap labor force—were revealed not only in persistent reports condemning the cramped quarters of sweatshop seamstresses, but also in the exposés of child labor on truck farms and in fruit orchards.[13]

For a century and a half, immigrant workers from Asia, Latin America, and Eastern Europe had challenged the division of labor that wrongly posited a stark dichotomy between blacks and whites in the labor force. Chinese immigrants found niches in traditional women's work in mid-nineteenth-century California (as servants and the owners of laundries); and by the turn of the century, Japanese, Filipino, and Mexican field workers were deemed indispensable to the state's largest agricultural enterprises. In the post-Reconstruction South, Chinese and Italian immigrants picked cotton in the Mississippi Delta, and Greek men waded in waist-deep water in the turpentine swamps of Florida. In the early twentieth century, Polish migrants from Baltimore were employed as seafood processors along the Gulf Coast; and in the next few decades, Mexicans, Puerto Ricans, and Bahamians would be imported under a federal program to recruit migrant laborers on the East Coast and in the Southwest, while Cape Verdeans found their way to Cape Cod cranberry fields and Jamaicans to Maine potato and Connecticut tobacco farms.

The wave of immigration in the 1990s encapsulated a whole host of fears that plagued native-born whites, who resented the fact that they were now expected to subsidize, through their tax dollars, the cheap labor force that enriched a variety of businesses (but in the process also provided consumers with affordable clothing, fruits and vegetables, and house cleaners). Bilingual education, public systems of schooling and health care for immigrant children, the political ramifications of the growth in the numbers of people of color—these highly charged issues distracted the voters of California, Texas, and Florida in particular from a preoccupation with black-white ideologies. The southern states, once the bastion of black-white dyads, now acknowledged but did not necessarily embrace the reality of multi-ethnicity. Native-born black and white workers alike contended with local labor markets transformed by specific immigrant groups—Chinese grocers, Asian-Indian motel owners, and Lebanese restauranteurs in Mississippi; Vietnamese county administrators in Georgia; Mexican migrant workers in

Alabama; and Guatemalan day workers in Texas. In the early 1980s, the Ku Klux Klan in Cedartown, Georgia, responded to changing times by harassing and ultimately condoning the murder of Mexicans who worked at Zartic Foods, the town's meatpacking plant; the Klan thereby simply expanded its historic mission of keeping vulnerable minority groups "in their place."[14]

The modern equivalent of bound labor found its most dramatic expression in the incarceration of increasing numbers of men—particularly black men—throughout the country. Forced labor under the supervision of white jailers and corrections officers resonated in a unique way within the African-American community, for prisons and chain gangs were enduring symbols of state-sanctioned neo-slavery. Groping for words to describe her arduous work from sunrise to sundown for a succession of white farmers in Georgia in the 1940s and 1950s, Irene Nixon exclaimed. "I don' know what to say, be like the *chain gang* then! . . . I couldn't a worked no harder. I worked *hard*! . . . I worked *so* hard, couldn't do no harder work on a chain gang." In Alabama in 1995, the Commissioner of State Prisons made explicit the connection between past and present forms of labor exploitation when he not only reinstituted chain gangs for roadwork but forced inmates to spend their days breaking rocks—a kind of labor more useful as a means of humiliation than as productivity, since the state had no need for the crushed rocks. The spectacle of African-American men shackled in chains, sweltering in the sun and wielding pickaxes under the direction of armed guards, represented a legacy of state-supported slavery that endured in a particularly stark and brutal form.[15]

Whatever the political purposes served by such public displays of southern chain gangs, the fact of the matter was that state officials all over the country were aggressively tapping into a pool of prison labor for cheap workers, and half of that pool was black. With as many as one-third of all black men under some kind of court supervision (either in jail or on probation or parole), it was clear that the war on drugs, initiated in the 1980s during the Reagan administration, had taken a devastating toll on the demographic integrity of black families and communities. In the early 1990s, almost 2 percent of all potential workers in the United States were in jail, 47.3 percent of them black. By this time, more than half of all states had legalized the practice of prison labor contracting to private employers, covering an impressive array of jobs:

In Arizona . . . prisoners test blood for a medical firm and raise hogs for John's Meats. In New Mexico prisoners take hotel reservations by phone.

In Ohio inmates do data entry; they made Honda parts as well until political pressure from labor unions forced an end to that particular arrangement. Spalding golf balls are packed by imprisoned labor in Hawaii. In
Lockart, Texas, inmates held in a private prison owned by the Wackenhut
Corporation build and fix circuit boards for L.T.I., a subcontractor that
pays $1 a year in rent and supplies companies such as Dell, I.B.M. and
Texas Instruments. In 1994 a Chicago-area Toys R Us used a night shift of
prisoners to restock shelves. The list goes on.

Possessing a "captive labor force," and freed from providing benefits like
health care, employers were able to pay prisoners less than the minimum
wage (up to 80 percent of that went back to the state) and in the process
undercut the "free" labor market.[16]

Prison labor provided a good example of the way certain late twentieth-
century political and economic imperatives assumed a legally nonracialized
form, and yet affected blacks as workers disproportionately. Law enforcement officials rounded up drug abusers of cocaine regardless of race; but
judges sentenced those caught with the less expensive "crack" cocaine to
longer sentences compared to those with the powdered form of the drug.
Theoretically, prison workshops were racially integrated, but the high percentage of black men in them reverberated throughout whole communities,
leaving the women and children in them impoverished.

Indeed, in many poor inner-city neighborhoods, drug trafficking was
revealing of structural—both historic and recent—sources of distress. Without transportation to the suburbs, poor black youth in the inner city found
themselves limited to jobs in fast-food restaurants, jobs that paid very little
and promised little in the way of advancement. Underground economies—
markets in fake Social Security cards and immigration green cards, in drugs
and weapons—offered to poor youth of all races the chance to make money
in a particularly dangerous work setting. For example, by the mid-1990s,
Camden, New Jersey, had lost the Philadelphia Navy Yard, the Campbell
Soup factory (the white-collar headquarters remained in place, however),
and electronics companies. The end of the cold war meant further that
Camden would continue to pay a high "peace dividend" now that blue-collar jobs associated with the space and defense programs had all but disappeared. With a jobless rate of 20 percent, and two-thirds of its residents on
public assistance, Camden was wracked by street violence; in 1995, the city
had the highest murder rate of any urban area in New Jersey. Referring to
the flourishing and bloody business in the illicit drug trade, Lonnie Watkins,
a Camden resident, noted: "Long as there's no jobs, people going to deal

drugs. And if that's how you make your living, then you protect your business any way you can, know what I mean?"[17]

Because law enforcement policies and the decline of heavy manufacturing jobs affected black men disproportionately, the labor of black women continued to assume heightened significance in the African-American community. These demographic developments had far-reaching political consequences. Throughout the United States, black women toiled on the frontier of a transformed world economy, their low-wage jobs testament to stubborn forms of labor exploitation that undergirded the glitter of late-century high finance and high technology. They served as cleaning women in gleaming skyscrapers; as chambermaids in luxury hotels; as nannies for harried, high-powered dual-career couples; as clerks in discount department stores; as the backbone of the catfish- and chicken-processing industries in the rural South; and as health care workers in hospitals and nursing homes. They clung to jobs as typists and textile machine operators, as similar jobs disappeared all arouund them.[18]

In 1990, black women headed one-third of all black households (more than half of them poor), and they figured prominently in organizations of public service workers (for example, the Association of Federated State, County and Municipal Employees); hospital orderlies; southern catfish-processing employees; and hotel, restaurant, and other service workers (for example, the Service Employees International Union). The historic efforts of white male craft and industrial workers to assert control over organized labor (from 1830 to 1980) became but a chapter in workers' ongoing search for power, on the shop floor and in the halls of city council chambers and the U.S. Congress. Now service workers, and black women in particular, would write the next chapter of that story.[19]

Despite the power of "institutional racism" as a force channeling black men and women into certain kinds of jobs, or forcing them out of the paid labor force altogether, blatant instances of "racial" stereotyping also continued to affect the hiring policies of employers who were hoping to install a particular type of wage earner in the postindustrial workplace. The ill-defined quality of employee "attitude" assumed great significance, now that workers had to be closely supervised in order to ensure high levels of productivity, and low levels of grumbling, on the job. Employers might eagerly tap into the pool of previously unemployed minority women, but at least some supervisors claimed that these women had been out of the labor market for too long, and lacked the requisite tractability that efficient workplaces demanded. A study of hiring practices conducted in 1989–90 in Chicago suggested that employers of entry-level workers conflated the categories of race, ethnicity, class, and space (that is, residential neighbor-hood), and as a result dismissed young black job seekers as too poor, uned-ucated, and temperamentally ill-suited for the rigors of modern office work. In the view of these employers, racial integration of the workforce was a recipe for tensions among workers who did not attend the same schools or churches, and did not live in the same neighborhoods. Said one employer: "I wanted a person who was going to fit into this area. . . . You're looking for skills, but you are [also] looking for someone who will fit in. . . ." Poor blacks as a group also suffered under the widespread misperception that they were unwilling to accept low-paying jobs, a charge belied by cases of multiple inner-city job applicants for single fast-food restaurant jobs. In fact, black male workers, with fewer opportunities, continued to show a willingness to accept jobs at lower wages than whites—on average, half the "white rate."[20]

Some observers claimed that black women as a group had secured a rela-tively advantageous position in the workforce (compared to their mothers a generation before, and compared to their sons and husbands now) by mov-ing up into clerical and administrative positions; nevertheless, those gains were hardly absolute, especially in comparison to the newfound opportuni-ties of white women. In 1990, black and white women worked for wages in about the same proportion—60 percent of all women; but black women's unemployment rate was more than twice that of their white counterparts. As a result of Title VII, women of both races achieved access to traditional male-dominated blue-collar jobs, but white women went on to predominate (among women as a group) in the high-skilled construction trades like car-pentry and electrical work. For most black women blue-collar workers, "opportunities" came in fits and starts, at the lowest level of the workforce. Born in 1948, Connie Johnson began earning wages as a young girl, working as a household cleaner, and then moved around to a variety of jobs—as an armhole creaser and presser in a shirt factory, a restaurant cashier and fry cook, janitor in a spa, nurse's aide in a convalescent home, and butcher in a grocery store. By the time she was in her thirties, affirmative action policies in the construction industry had opened up a place as a laborer to her, but this amounted to one more in a series of low-wage, high-turnover positions. For women like Connie Johnson, relatively open employment policies yielded new kinds of jobs, but not careers.[21]

Therefore, few black women wage earners were inclined to measure their success solely on the basis of their freedom from scrubbing floors and ironing clothes for wages. Jewel Jackson, a single mother and a secretary for a university in Boston, shared a sense of frustration with other women trapped in dead-end jobs: "I hate being a secretary. It's boring. It's demeaning. The pay is bad and it's got a royal stigma wrapped around it: single mom. Secretary. Dumb. . . . The lack of money reflects a lack of respect." Jackson was hardly willing to pay homage to the postindustrial labor market merely because it now offered her employment possibilities outside the realm of domestic service. In an interview in 1995, she also took pains to distance herself from her white co-workers: "more and more it's white women getting out of clerical into management . . . I see the clerical staff getting blacker and blacker."[22]

Just as significantly, black women who worked at home as mothers and caretakers endured the opprobrium of policymakers, politicians, and the general public in return. Social scientists denounced them as the agents of "dysgenesis" (the "dumbing down" of America), and exhorted them to betake themselves to the nearest employment office. (Meanwhile, the white middle-class wives who chose to stay home with their children were glorified as the pillars of their respective communities.) Living in dangerous neighborhoods with few material resources at their disposal, negotiating the social welfare bureaucratic maze, poor women understood full well that caring for their children was a form of productive labor, no matter how little it earned them in terms of money or respect. In the words of Denise Turner, a welfare recipient in Wisconsin, "I mean if you got a family, what're you talkin' about lazy?! . . . in today's economy a woman is considered lazy when she's home taking care of her children. And to me that's not laziness. If she's doing a good job at that, she has to use a lot of skills . . . a woman is not lazy when she's taking care of her family."[23]

The passage of so-called welfare reform legislation in 1996 aimed to push recipients of Aid to Families with Dependent Children (38 percent of whom were black) out of the home and into the workforce, thus worsening an already overcrowded market for low-wage labor, without adequately providing child care services for the mothers affected. The state thereby denigrated the responsibilities incumbent upon parents in favor of the interests of employers who sought to prey upon the most desperate of workers, while ideologues simultaneously scapegoated the poor and vulnerable as the root of all of the country's social ills. Public and private employers alike prepared to reduce their unionized labor forces through attrition in order to make way for "workfare" employees. For the most part, an apparently indifferent public, composed of all kinds of workers fearful of losing their own jobs, shrugged off predictions of the impending immiseration of hundreds of thousands of mothers and their children throughout the country.

AS THE TWENTIETH century came to a close, politicians of both parties resisted initiating the bold measures necessary to counter the disastrous impact of global economic forces on vulnerable populations. The sources of poverty transcended national borders and thus remained out of the control of individual neighborhoods. Yet Americans in positions of power abnegated their responsibility to construct an industrial policy that would facilitate cooperation between the public and private sectors in stimulating job creation, providing affordable health care for all citizens, and equalizing educational opportunity among poor and rich youngsters. By this time, the concept of a "living wage"—a rate of compensation that would permit a full-time worker to support a family—seemed hopelessly outdated, naive in the extreme, as contract and part-time laborers continued to swell the ranks of the gainfully employed. Calls for an increased minimum wage produced grudging hikes of only a few cents at a time, amid cries that higher increases would jeopardize the well-being of the nation. Local officials at the state, county, and municipal level began to reel under the financial burdens of newly impoverished communities, where a single plant or army base closing foretold the demise of that community's lifeblood, its jobs. The devolution of federal responsibility for the poor to the states was matched by an expanding power among individual corporations to seek out and hire the most tractable workforces possible, and to extract from those workers the highest rates of productivity at the lowest possible wages.[24]

Although the American political economy of the late twentieth century relied on the low-wage labor of a variety of ethnic groups (both at home and abroad), the idea of race continued to serve as a basis of social organization. Recent immigrants living in ethnic clusters and laboring within larger, diverse metropolitan areas could locate seemingly few reasons to view African Americans other than as rivals apart from themselves. As a group, African Americans retained a heightened political self-consciousness that allowed little room for alliances with newcomers who were in the process of asserting their claim to the American workplace. And native-born whites throughout the workforce—in good jobs as well as bad—persisted in seeing black co-workers as interlopers and as a threat to their own job security and economic well-being. The debate over affirmative action policies in particular revealed just how little had changed in the political rhetoric that originated to justify a "racial" division of labor, even though that division of labor was fast succumbing to a new world economic order.

FAMILIES, FRATERNITIES, AND SITES OF DIVERSITY: AFFIRMATIVE ACTION IN HISTORICAL PERSPECTIVE

Title VII of the 1964 Civil Rights Act, which spurred federal efforts to crack open exclusionary workplaces, represented an achievement of unprecedented proportions. Long the guardians of white privilege, presidents, lawmakers, and judges now devised public policies to counter institutional biases and employers' prejudices in order to enable African Americans to work at a variety of jobs. For blacks, as for all Americans, steady and relatively well-paying employment held out the promise of stronger families and safer neighborhoods within their communities. More broadly, the greater integration of black workers into the late twentieth-century workforce, and the subsequent dramatic increase in the size of the black middle class, appeared to represent the culmination of a centuries-long struggle for black equality, a struggle that had long fused the ideal of economic opportunity with the ideal of American citizenship. By attacking job application procedures and union membership policies intended to bar African Americans from specific worksites, the United States finally renounced state-sanctioned Jim Crow employment.

Yet thirty years after the elimination of race-based statutes governing American life, the federally sponsored drive to ensure black people access to good jobs and quality education had stalled. The debate over affirmative action on behalf of blacks in employment represented a new chapter in the history of politicized workplaces, and drew upon several time-honored truths of American labor deployment. Meanwhile, the definition of "affirmative action" itself remained imprecise, as some critics condemned all

forms of outreach to potential black job candidates, and others voiced objec-
tions to more specific numerical quotas and set-asides (reserving certain
places for black workers) in hiring and contracting. Yet definitions of "discrimination" also lacked rigor. It is not possible to eliminate generalized
forms of "discrimination" in job hiring, for that process is inherently a selec-
tive one that favors certain groups over others. And participants in the affirmative action debate tended to act and write as if larger structures of
inequality in American life—and particularly class-based systems of educational and residential segregation—were irrelevant to the task of opening up
employment opportunities for black people. As long as the economy favors
the highly educated at the expense of the poorly educated, and as long as
poor communities lack the educational resources of middle-class suburbs,
affirmative action policies will yield only superficial results.

Job competition invariably produces political conflict. In an industrial-
capitalist economy, the number of good jobs available at any particular time
is finite (and in some eras decreasing), and these jobs are reserved for certain
classes of people variously defined—for example, by their skills, skin color,
formal education, gender, country-club connections, religion, ethnicity, kinship, or some combination of these factors. As long as workers outnumber
good jobs, all kinds of employers will continue to have the luxury to pick
and choose among applicants, some in seemingly arbitrary ways. The term
"reverse discrimination" (a reference to the practice of favoring certain
minorities over whites, or women over men, in employment or education)
therefore remains redundant. A personnel official might seek to hire among
Ivy League graduates, finding that black people are now included in that
elite labor pool for the first time; but in the process the official "discrimi-
nates" against graduates of less prestigious colleges, regardless of their
"qualifications" or skin color. In some cases, then, black graduates of Harvard University might have an advantage over black or white graduates of a
state university. And, of course, the ability of black people to gain or hold on
to certain types of jobs at times reflects the structure of the economy, more
than forms of "racial bias." The decision among major car makers to auto-
mate their assembly lines in response to foreign competition in the 1970s
threw many black men out of work—a form of employer "discrimination"
that affected great numbers of blacks but one that was not necessarily motivated by racial animus on the part of plant managers and supervisors.

Although some people argue that affirmative action programs trump the
premium placed on formal credentials, the conflict between "merit" and
"racial preference" is not nearly as stark as these observers assume. Black
and white critics alike charge that black people hired under the rubric of

affirmative action raise the specter of "unqualified" blacks getting jobs at the expense of "qualified" whites (as if a pure meritocracy would flourish in the absence of affirmative action). However, these critics are seemingly oblivious to the generations of male workers who benefited from biased hiring practices on behalf of whites but wasted precious little time worrying about whether or not they were deserving of a good job.[1] In the 1990s, many employment opportunities, even in the business and high-technology sector of the economy, still provide a substantial amount of on-the-job training, suggesting that applicants with a variety of credentials, formal or otherwise, possess the potential to succeed in any particular position. Blacks in those jobs are drawn from a (presumably large) applicant pool of "qualified" workers of all races, rather than plucked from a pool of "unqualified" workers of all races. Denied particular jobs of their own choosing, whites focus their wrath on more fortunate black applicants without acknowledging that other qualified whites and blacks inevitably lose out in this process too.

From a historical perspective, the dual charge that blacks as a group are both lazy (as welfare recipients)[2] and predatory job seekers (as beneficiaries of affirmative action policies) recapitulates the defensive and confused rhetoric of early nineteenth-century white workers. Postindustrial America is wracked by a number of social and economic dislocations similar to those that shaped the antebellum North a century and a half earlier. New technologies displace whole categories of workers, and waves of immigration lead to the rearrangement of employment queues. In the 1990s, these dislocations are made manifest when black people take their place in line for skilled and professional "white" jobs, when women vie for blue-collar "men's" jobs, and when immigrants seek access to jobs traditionally reserved for the native-born poor of both races.[3]

Yet new sources of job insecurity among whites of various classes continue to produce political backlash, as academics and political observers help to reify suspect categories such as the "black family" and "black culture." Asserting that social pathologies like out-of-wedlock births and drug addiction constitute the core of an African-American "culture," Dinesh D'Souza, writing in *The End of Racism* (1995), suggests that "For many whites the criminal and irresponsible black underclass represents a revival of barbarism in the midst of Western civilization. . . . If blacks can close the civilization gap, the race problem in this country is likely to become insignificant."[4] This kind of rhetoric, juxtaposing "white civilization" to "black barbarism," amounts to a modern variant of the nineteenth-century white tradesmen's indictment of black workers as immoral and hence unworthy of good jobs. To complement this perspective, ethnographic studies of inner-city neighborhoods provide voyeuristic middle-class whites with a view of people whom they consider exotic "others,"[5] yet at the same time these studies imply, wrongly, that black folks are unique among the poor in general in terms of the afflictions they suffer and the toll those afflictions take upon their health and emotional well-being. Moreover, whites in general persist in believing that affirmative action amounts to a "zero-sum game," positioning all black people to win at the expense of all whites. Given the fact that black people constitute only 11 percent of the U.S. population, it is clear that many whites are at greater risk of losing their jobs to sophisticated technology and to other, better-educated white people than to blacks as a group.

Though often framed in either-or terms, the debate over affirmative action exposes a number of social fault lines. The black community is not unifed in this debate, with critics of "racial preferences" emerging from the ranks of black (mostly male) professionals.[6] Glenn Loury, Shelby Steele, Clarence Thomas, Robert Woodson, and Stephen Carter are among the academics and legal and public policy experts who charge that affirmative action programs stigmatize and promote a "victim mentality" among their beneficiaries. They also suggest that such policies have outlived their usefulness, since the black professional upper middle class is now relatively secure, and the black "underclass" has derived little if any gain from them in any case. (Left out of this analysis are workers like firefighters, carpenters, and banktellers whose futures perhaps rely more heavily on policy interventions in the labor market.) Too, the question of employment opportunity highlights gender divisions within the African-American community. Some critics charge that black women benefit disproportionately from affirmative action programs. It is true that black women tend to find jobs in the expanding service sector while manual labor and heavy manufacturing, traditional sources of black men's employment, are declining. Moreover, black women find favor among personnel officials who can count them twice, as women and as blacks, in their affirmative action progress reports. Nevertheless, as we have seen, the plight of black working women in general makes it difficult to argue that affirmative action policies have benefited black women at the expense of black men.[7]

Liberals who once favored the use of race-neutral written examinations to overcome employers' personal prejudices in job hiring now realize that such examinations perpetuate an emerging aristocracy of whites and blacks who live in the wealthiest suburbs and educate their children at the best schools, public or private. For their part, conservatives who decry the folly of workplace "diversification" must confront the fact that some of its most outspoken supporters come not from the cramped cubicles of government

bureaucrats but from the tastefully appointed offices of international corporate executives.[8] Meanwhile, blacks, white women, new immigrants, and
indigenous groups (ranging from Eskimos to Wampanoags, from Aleuts to
Cherokees) seek access to wider job opportunities, in the process frequently
engaging in bitter recriminations among each other. And in time-honored
fashion, many whites react personally and defensively to issues related to
affirmative action. Said Joseph L. Ruhnke, a thirty-one-year-old Arizona test-
ing technician, "I'm a white single male and they try to make you feel guilty
because they're not getting jobs and that it's our fault. It's not my fault that
somebody can't get a job."[9]

Free market purists decry the interference of the federal government in
hiring practices, but ignore the myriad ways that federal policies have always
shaped, and continue to shape, the composition and size of the domestic
labor market. The Federal Reserve Board sets interest rates and makes
money-supply decisions, policies that directly affect the unemployment rate
as well as the rate of inflation. Government defense contracts, licenses to
casinos located on Indian reservations and in poor rural counties in the Mississippi Delta, free trade and immigration policies, and educational programs for veterans all bestow advantages upon groups of workers and
potential workers who either possess the requisite personal characteristics
or live in the right place at the right time. Some government policies deliver
large numbers of cheap workers directly to the factory gates and hiring
halls. In the mid-1990s, the Clinton welfare "reform" program provided a
boon to low-wage employers who enjoyed a labor supply swollen by mothers now denied AFDC benefits. States, counties, and municipalities lavished
companies with tax breaks in order to attract jobs to their areas, though
employers retained the option to move on if they could cut a better tax-
payer-sponsored deal elsewhere or locate cheaper workers outside the country, leaving stranded communities in their wake. Therefore, calls for the
cessation of "government interference" in hiring practices have a disingenu-
ous ring about them; employers object to such "interference" only when
they perceive it to hinder their own economic interests.

For critics of affirmative action, a mythology of the American past offers
up ideals of harmony and justice, ideals smothered under the weight of a
"rights rhetoric" run rampant. In their best-selling book *The Bell Curve*,
Charles Murray and Richard Herrnstein move backward in time, chapter by
chapter, from the Jim Crow era, when even "unintelligent" (i.e., black) people could live "productive" lives; to slavery, when plantation owners helped
to "civilize" (that is, improve the Intelligence Quotient) of Africans; to the
late eighteenth century, when Thomas Jefferson and the other founding

fathers posited an aristocracy of intelligence as the key component of a virtuous republic.[10] Indeed, *The Bell Curve* is at its core a polemic about the
structure of the American labor force; by ranking in one long queue all
potential workers according to their "IQ," the authors seek to reserve the
best jobs for people who score well on standardized intelligence tests—that
is, people who have had access to the best formal education, the vast majority of whom are white. Observers like Herrnstein and Murray tend to
romanticize the past, when, they suggest, different groups literally "knew
their place" within the structure of American society, and accommodated
themselves to various forms of inequality. Like the anxious native-born
workers of the early nineteenth century, these observers interpret black
demands for employment opportunity and political representation as a
threat to civic order—a loud, insistent, and ultimately impolite assault upon
the sensibilities of the privileged.

Assuming that affirmative action is a form of "punishment" aimed at
whites, some critics believe that they must disprove the notion that white
workers as a group bear any collective responsibility for the oppression of
black people. For example, Supreme Court Justice Antonin Scalia has
claimed that "There are, of course, many white ethnic groups that came to
this country in great numbers relatively late in its history—Italians, Jews,
Irish, Poles—who not only took no part in, and derived no profit from, the
major historic suppression of the currently acknowledged minority groups,
but were, in fact, themselves the object of discrimination by the dominant
Anglo-Saxon majority."[11] Scalia here misses the point: that white workers
regardless of ethnicity profited, no matter how indirectly or modestly, from
a turn-of-the-century segmented labor force that relegated black workers to
the bottom of the job ladder. Because immigrant Italian carpenters found
work in New York City, black carpenters, regardless of their skills, too often
could not.

At the end of the twentieth century, the Supreme Court decisions outlawing numerical quotas of black workers, college scholarships for black students exclusively, minority set-asides in the awarding of local and federal
contracts, and legislative districts redrawn in favor of blacks all signaled a
withdrawal of federal and state governments from the realm of equal
opportunity in employment and public education, and from the development of minority businesses and black voting strength. The 1996 Civil
Rights Initiative (Proposition 209) approved by voters in the state of California aimed to outlaw public policies that took into consideration race or gender in hiring, contracts, or education. Anti-affirmative action politicians,
columnists, and academics insist that the destruction of de jure discrimina-

tion has already yielded an egalitarian society, and that racial preferences are therefore regressive measures destined to plunge the country back into a period of bitter color-consciousness.[12]

Lacking a national consensus as a basis of political support, affirmative action supporters continue to press for packages of more locally configured measures. In Atlanta, Georgia, the private corporation that produced the 1996 Summer Olympics dispensed about one-third of its budget of $387 million to companies owned by minorities and women. Bill Campbell, the black mayor of the city (with a two-thirds black population), remained an enthusiastic proponent of policies that were under attack from voters and judges elsewhere in the country: "The sad truth in this country, the sad truth even in the city of Atlanta, is that without our affirmative action programs, our minority businesses would wither." In order to win contracts for the Olympics, white-owned businesses had to form partnerships with minority companies. Former mayor Andrew J. Young, co-chair of the city's Olympic Committee, noted that these expectations had produced the intended effect. "People soon realized that the team with the greatest minority participation was usually the team that won the contract if all things were equal," he said in June 1996. Unsuccessful white contractors felt aggrieved. "There was some serious injustice here," said one architect, who noted the difficulties he and others in his profession faced in initiating contacts with their minority counterparts. Still, the Atlanta case suggests that the fate of substantial numbers of black workers will remain contingent not necessarily upon their skills or ambition, but whether as voters they have sufficient numbers to affect the hiring policies of local governments.[13]

By this time many of the largest U.S. corporations had reached a consensus that workplace "diversity" was good for business. Some companies instituted "mentoring" and summer internship programs for black employees, provided managers with financial incentives to recruit and retain black workers, and offered "sensitivity-training" workshops for white employees. Cynics argued that these programs exist to promote corporate self-interest; chief executive officers and personnel officials agreed and made no apologies. Extensive in-house affirmative action programs forestall costly lawsuits brought by applicants or workers who consider themselves victims of racial prejudice, improve a large firm's competitive advantages over smaller companies in securing federal contracts, and better enable a company to appeal to minority consumers. Prying open all-white workplaces has evolved, or devolved (depending on one's point of view), from a theoretical question of justice to a practical question of public relations.[14]

Yet such optimism about the redemptive nature of corporate culture is premature. In the mid-1990s, the Texaco Oil Company proclaimed that "a work environment that reflects a diverse workforce, values diversity, and is free of all forms of discrimination, intimidation, and harassment is essential for a productive and efficient workforce." However, statements like this one, combined with colorful, glossy brochures outlining "Texaco's Visions and Values" for public consumption, were not sufficient to assure black employees of job promotions commensurate with their experience and performance. Nor were these public relations ploys sufficient to assure black employees the respect of white managers and co-workers, who harassed blacks by scribbling "KKK" on their cars, and referred to them as "niggers" and "porch monkeys." Shaped by a shallow and ultimately callous attempt to conform to vague public notions of "diversity," Texaco workplaces were little more than creatures of the marketplace, always subject to redefinition dictated by shifts in "customer relations."[15]

Faddish attempts at workplace "diversity" will falter in a society where black and white people continue to live and attend school apart from each other. Black employees of all kinds know from firsthand experience that even an advanced degree and a satisfying paycheck do not necessarily insulate black workers from racial slurs and other forms of routine humiliation.[16] Though white workers can hardly claim ignorance about the social dynamics of their own workplaces, no doubt most are oblivious to the emotional and physical toll that harassment, no matter how subtle, takes on blacks. Even middle-class black workers are more vulnerable to stress-related ailments like hypertension, angina, and gastrointestinal illnesses compared to their white counterparts. Kelly Smith, a black woman with an MBA, "a high-ranking officer in an international corporation," described the emotional turmoil she felt as a black worker in a white business world trying to distinguish ruthless, color-blind corporate politics from ruthless, color-conscious racial politics: "I can't sleep—my mind is racing—because I can't figure out how they are going to come at me next. So I have to work twice as hard to think about this person and what is going on and to try to figure out what they [her co-workers as well as supervisors] are going to do next." The presence of blacks in formerly all-white workplaces often altered the work "environment" while leaving intact the balance of power in favor of whites.[17]

Jill Nelson, who worked for a time as a journalist for *The Washington Post*, titled her account of her experiences there *Volunteer Slavery*, and claimed that the fact she had to work under the supervision of white people—especially arrogant white men—conditioned her view of her job. Of her stint at the *Post* she wrote, "I walk around with a stomachache, my standard physiological alert to mounting disaster. . . . From a distance, it's easy to start thinking that white folks run things because they're especially intelligent and hardworking. This, of course, is the image of themselves they like to project. Up close, most white folks, like most people are mediocre. They've just rigged the system to privilege themselves and disadvantage everyone else." Nelson also charged that white news managers' decisions to hire black journalists or to cover stories related to the black community were little more than "paths to career development": "black folks . . . exist mostly as potential sociological, pathological, or scatological slices of life waiting to be chewed, digested, and excreted into the requisite number of column inches in the paper."[18]

Given the persistent estrangement between blacks and whites, it is no wonder then that public opinion constitutes a slippery slope rather than a firm foundation for corporate-sponsored affirmative action policies. In 1995, a nationwide poll sponsored by *The Washington Post*, the Kaiser Family Foundation, and Harvard University revealed a number of misconceptions among whites about the size and well-being of the black population. The summary of the poll's findings (published in the *Post* under the headline "A Distorted Image of Minorities: Poll Suggests That What Whites Think They See May Affect Beliefs") noted that about 50 percent of all whites believed that blacks as a group now held jobs equal qualitatively to those of whites, and another 12 percent believed that blacks as a group were better off than whites. White people tended to downplay what they considered past discrimination as a cause of problems affecting the black community. And like whites in the antebellum period, whites in 1995 tended to overestimate the economic threat posed by blacks by exaggerating the size of the black population, now making them 24–25 percent of the total instead of 11 percent. In the words of one journalist, whites as a group had "become more hostile to minorities, fearful that more minorities would further erode their diminishing quality of life."[19] These results suggest that it is only a matter of time before corporate sponsors of "diversity" programs decide that their efforts no longer find favor with white voters and white consumers, and abandon all pretense in that direction. Certainly any residual federal affirmative action programs would generate little enthusiasm among white taxpayers who believed that blacks had already achieved parity with whites in terms of the jobs they held and the schools they attended.

In fact, workplace "diversity" as a corporate strategy, 1990s-style, offers a variation on the historic theme of workplaces crafted under political as well as economic pressures. In postbellum textile mill villages, workers and owners alike (albeit for different purposes) embraced the analogy of the family and therefore found it easier to believe that all-white mills were a "natural" and not a social construction of relations among workers. Throughout much of the twentieth century, white construction workers conceived of the job site as an extension of fraternity, a source of fellow feeling in opposition to intruders who happened to be black or female. Because managers and personnel officials continue to shape their workforces in response to perceived political needs, and because private life outside the workplace remains so rigidly segregated by race, the integration of previously all-white worksites will amount to only a tentative first step in the eradication of social distinctions defined as "racial."

The persistence of specific anti-black work cultures reveals the inherent limitations of equal employment strategies within a nation that continues to uphold customs of racial residential segregation, though now these customs are justified as the predictable if unfortunate outcome of inequalities based upon class differences. By isolating employment and public higher education as their targets, many affirmative action proponents and opponents alike distract themselves from the stubborn reality of slavery's broader legacy, and from worldwide political-economic trends that place at risk relatively uneducated and unskilled workers in the global labor market. Large corporations might boast of their progress in "diversifying" their lower- and middle-level workforces. But as long as those corporations aim to compete in an international marketplace, continuing their restless, worldwide quest for cheap workers, affirmative action "schedules" will do little to rectify longstanding injustices toward black people, and especially toward poor black people who do not live in middle-class suburbs. The tenuousness of affirmative action programs indicates not a straightforward march toward a society devoid of racial (or any other kind of) prejudice, but rather a convoluted path pockmarked with persistent, overt conflict among employers, the state, consumers, and different groups of workers.

In sum, the debate over affirmative action pushes to the forefront the issue of "equal employment opportunity" while minimizing the larger tangle of inequality that characterizes American life: inferior public schooling for poor youngsters; a maldistribution of job-related benefits like health care, Social Security, and unemployment compensation; the devastating effects of corporate consolidation on distressed populations; and the exploitation of increasing numbers of workers in fields, food-processing plants, and garment sweatshops. Moreover, a narrow focus on jobs obscures the fact that black people as a group still lag far behind whites in wealth accumulation, and therefore cannot always enjoy the fruits of a middle-class life derived from a middle-class income. The red-lining practice of many big-city banks (the refusal to approve mortgages for any families regardless of income within poor neighborhoods) makes home ownership difficult even for middle-income blacks. Many black families have relatively greater financial responsibility for extended kin, and receive from parents relatively modest legacies in the way of cash and assets, compared to their white counterparts at similar income levels. In 1990, blacks and whites earning $25,000 to $50,000 annually had the same net income, but whites in that bracket had an average net worth three times that of their black counterparts ($44,069 compared to $15,250). Therefore, working at the same jobs with middle-class whites, black people would have difficulty affording the down payment for a house in a middle-class suburb, or foregoing the paycheck of a working wife and mother; and the children of these black parents stood to inherit far less than whites of the same age.[20] The stubborn economic vulnerability of black families regardless of income level will continue to stoke the fires of political conflict for the foreseeable future.

In the late twentieth century, Americans tend to support in principle and law the ideal of equality, but they remain remarkably tolerant of the most dramatic market-based inequalities. Indeed, when the ideal of racial integration runs afoul of the free enterprise system, in practical terms it too often disappears altogether. In several respects, the precarious political fortunes of affirmative action are parallel to those of court-ordered busing to achieve school desegregation. In 1954, the Supreme Court outlawed de jure school segregation based on race; ten years later, Congress outlawed de jure workplace segregation based on race. From the pure ideal of school racial integration flowed the more ambiguous policy of busing, a policy that by the 1990s had lost favor with both the courts and the general public.[21] The result was a solidification of public school systems segregated by class, for integration proceeded apace only within regions where the political climate allowed and facilitated such efforts. Likewise, from the pure ideal of workplace integration flowed the more ambiguous policy of affirmative action, a policy that by the 1990s had also lost favor with both the courts and the general public. The result was the continued immiseration of the black poor, immobilized within neighborhoods that lacked good jobs to sustain the families of relatively uneducated people. Integration of workplaces proceeded apace only within regions, and individual businesses, where the political climate allowed and facilitated such efforts. The American public would not abide invidious distinctions based on race to remain codified in law; but they launched few meaningful or sustained challenges to invidious distinctions based on class.[22]

When "rights" are dependent upon the approval of taxpayers and voters, they are not rights at all, but rather contingencies subject to constant rene-gotiation within the political arena. Neither blacks nor any other group have a constitutional right to a decent job, or to any job at all; therefore work-places will continue to reflect the raw social tensions that characterize the larger society. The history of employment opportunity legislation thus reveals one of the central ironies in American law and politics: that a nation ultimately determined to eradicate legal distinctions among various groups would prove so accommodating to real distinctions between the rich and poor.

A good job is the key that opens the way to quality health care, a home in a good school district, a life free of the fear of poverty in old age. Despite the elimination of legal barriers to certain kinds of workplaces, Americans of African descent are now likely to find their employment opportunities dependent upon whether or not they attend a school rich in computer resources, and whether or not they live in a neighborhood where substantial numbers of adults hold good jobs.[23] Ambition and intelligence most often find their just rewards within exclusive communities that can afford to nur-ture those qualities in ways befitting a credentials-conscious postindustrial labor market. Confined to menial jobs and poor communities for three and a half centuries, most African Americans were at a competitive disadvantage when Jim Crow was formally laid to rest in the mid-1960s. Today, labor exploitation is for the most part color-blind; but the legacy of slavery and other enduring forms of "racialized" labor practices reach their most con-centrated form in poor places, urban and rural, where good jobs have all but disappeared, and where a history of oppression is not a textbook abstraction but a bitter, everyday reality.

NOTES

ABBREVIATIONS FOR PERIODICALS CITED
IN THE NOTES AND BIBLIOGRAPHY

AER	*American Economic Review*
AH	*Agricultural History*
AHQ	*Alabama Historical Quarterly*
AHR	*American Historical Review*
AJES	*American Journal of Economics and Society*
AJS	*American Journal of Sociology*
AL	*American Legacy*
AM	*Atlantic Monthly*
AmH	*American Heritage*
Annals	*Annals of the American Academy of Political and Social Science*
AnnalsCHS	*Annals of the Chinese Historical Society of the Pacific Northwest*
APSR	*American Political Science Review*
AQ	*American Quarterly*
ArHQ	*Arkansas Historical Quarterly*
ASR	*American Sociological Review*
AV	*American Visions*
AW	*Arizona and the West*
AWJ	*Aframerican Woman's Journal*
BCTWLJ	*Boston College Third World Law Journal*
BG	*Boston Globe*
BHR	*Business Historical Review*
BS	*Black Scholar*
CH	*California History*
CHSB	*Connecticut Historical Society Bulletin*
CM	*Century Magazine*

EEH	*Explorations in Economic History*
Eh	*Ethnohistory*
EHR	*Economic History Review*
EIHC	*Essex Institute Historical Collections*
FHQ	*Florida Historical Quarterly*
GHQ	*Georgia Historical Quarterly*
HJM	*Historical Journal of Massachusetts*
HJWM	*Historical Journal of Western Massachusetts*
HN	*Historic Nantucket*
HNMM	*Harper's New Monthly Magazine*
IJPCS	*International Journal of Politics, Culture, and Society*
ILRR	*Industrial and Labor Relations Review*
IR	*Industrial Relations*
IRSH	*International Review of Social History*
ISR	*International Socialist Review*
JAH	*Journal of American History*
JB	*Journal of Business*
JBlS	*Journal of Black Studies*
JBS	*Journal of British Studies*
JEH	*Journal of Economic History*
JEL	*Journal of Economic Literature*
JER	*Journal of the Early Republic*
JES	*Journal of Ethnic Studies*
JF	*Journal of Forestry*
JHG	*Journal of Historical Geography*
JHS	*Journal of Historical Sociology*
JIH	*Journal of Interdisciplinary History*
JIR	*Journal of Intergroup Relations*
JLS	*Journal of Legal Studies*
JMH	*Journal of Mississippi History*
JNH	*Journal of Negro History*
JPE	*Journal of Political Economy*
JSocH	*Journal of Social History*
JSouH	*Journal of Southern History*
JUL	*Journal of Urban History*
KHQ	*Kansas Historical Quarterly*
LH	*Labor History*
LRR	*Labor Research Review*
MdHM	*Maryland Historical Magazine*
MHSP	*Massachusetts Historical Society Proceedings*
MJ	*Mother Jones*
MLR	*Monthly Labor Review*
MP	*Marxist Perspectives*

MQ	Midwest Quarterly
MVHR	Mississippi Valley Historical Review
NCHR	North Carolina Historical Review
NEHGR	New England Historical and Genealogical Register
NEQ	New England Quarterly
NJH	New Jersey History
NLR	New Left Review
NYH	New York History
NYRB	New York Review of Books
NYT	New York Times
OSV	Old Sturbridge Visitor
PAAS	Proceedings of the American Antiquarian Society
PH	Pennsylvania History
PHe	Pennsylvania Heritage
PMHB	Pennsylvania Magazine of History and Biography
PresSQ	Presidential Studies Quarterly
PSA	Plantation Society in the Americas
PSQ	Political Science Quarterly
RHR	Radical History Review
RIH	Rhode Island History
RKHS	Register of the Kentucky Historical Society
ROA	Research on Aging
RRPE	Review of Radical Political Economy
RS	Rural Sociology
SAQ	South Atlantic Quarterly
SAUS	South Atlantic Urban Studies
SCHM	South Carolina Historical Magazine
SCQ	Southern California Quarterly
SE	Southern Exposure
SEJ	Southern Economic Journal
SF	Social Forces
SH	Social History
SI	Sociological Inquiry
SQ	Sociological Quarterly
SSH	Social Science History
SW	Southern Workman
THQ	Tennessee Historical Quarterly
VH	Vermont History
VMHB	Virginia Magazine of History and Biography
UMJLR	University of Michigan Journal of Law Reform
WHQ	Western Historical Quarterly
WMQ	William and Mary Quarterly
WP	Washington Post

WULQ   *Washington University Law Quarterly*
WVH   *West Virginia History*

INTRODUCTION

1. Frederick Douglass, "[Free Blacks Must Learn Trades]," in Michael Meyer, ed., *Frederick Douglass: The Narrative and Selected Writings* (New York: Modern Library, 1984), p. 350.
2. See for example Evelyn Brooks Higginbotham, "African-American Women's History and the Metalanguage of Race," *Signs* 17 (Winter 1992): 251–74.
3. Frederick Douglass, "[Free Blacks Must Learn Trades]," p. 350.
4. Tomás Almaguer, *Racial Fault Lines: The Historical Origins of White Supremacy in California* (Berkeley: University of California Press, 1994); "gap": Mary Roberts Coolidge, "Chinese Labor Competition on the Pacific Coast," *Annals* 34 (1909):120; Lawrence M. Lipin, "'There Will Not Be a Machanic [sic] Left': The Battle Against Unskilled Labor in the San Francisco Harness Trade, 1880–1890," *LH* 35 (Spring 1994):216–36; Alexander Saxton, *The Indispensable Enemy: Labor and the Anti-Chinese Movement in California* (Berkeley: University of California Press, 1971). For examples of rhetoric similar to expressions of racism against blacks, see California Legislature, *Senate Special Committee on Chinese Immigration: Its Social, Moral, and Political Effects; Report to the California State Senate of the Special Committee on Chinese Immigration* (Sacramento, CA: State Printing Office, 1878).
5. See for example "More Blacks in Their 20s Have Trouble with the Law," *New York Times*, Oct. 5, 1995, p. A18; Christian Parenti, "Making Prison Pay: Business Finds the Cheapest Labor of All," *Nation*, Jan. 29, 1996, pp. 11–14.
6. Scott L. Malcolmson, "Having Their Say," *New Yorker*, April 29 and May 6, 1996, p. 139.
7. James Freeman Clarke, *Present Condition of the Free Colored People of the United States* (New York: New York Anti-Slavery Society, 1859), p. 5.

CHAPTER ONE

1 Philip L. Barbour, ed., *The Complete Works of Captain John Smith*, Vol. II ("The Generall Historie of Virginia . . .") (Chapel Hill, NC: University of North Carolina Press, 1986), pp. 285, 185, 225.
2. *Ibid.*, pp. 265, 306, 298, 235.
3. "lusty": T. H. Breen, James H. Lewis and Keith Schlesinger, "Motive for Murder: A Servant's Life in Virginia, 1678," *WMQ*, 3rd series 40 (January 1983):117; "strong": Robert Patterson to Harman Verelst, Dec. 5, 1737, in Allen D. Candler, ed., *Colonial Records of the State of Georgia*, Vol. 22, *Correspondence, Trustees, General Oglethorpe and Others, 1737–1739* (New York: AMS Press, 1970; orig. pub. 1904–16), Pt. 1, p. 23 (hereinafter cited as *Colonial Records of the State of Georgia*, Vol. 22).

On the history of South Carolina, see Peter Wood, *Black Majority: Negroes in Colonial South Carolina from 1670 Through the Stono Rebellion* (New York: Knopf, 1974); on Virginia, Edmund S. Morgan, *American Slavery, American Freedom: The Ordeal of Colonial Virginia* (New York: W. W. Norton, 1975); on Maryland, Gloria L. Main, *Tobacco Colony: Life in Early Maryland, 1650–1720* (Princeton: Princeton University Press, 1982); on Georgia, Sarah B. Gober Temple and Kenneth Coleman, *Georgia Journeys* (Athens, GA: University of Georgia Press, 1961). In the mid-seventeenth century, John Hammond in "Leah and Rachel, or, Two Fruitful Sisters Virginia and Mary-Land," described Virginia and Maryland as marked by "one nature, both for produce and manner of living," in Clayton Colman Hall, ed., *Narratives of Early Maryland* (New York: Barnes and Noble, 1946; orig. pub. 1910), p. 284. David Hackett Fischer discusses the Chesapeake as a regional culture in *Albion's Seed: Four British Folkways in America* (New York: Oxford University Press, 1989).

In significant respects, Virginia, Maryland, and Georgia followed different paths of political development. A joint-stock venture, the Virginia Company of London operated as a paramilitary organization for several years. In 1619 the colonists established a representative assembly, the House of Burgesses, and discovered the profitability of tobacco. Five years later, James I revoked the Virginia Company's charter and Virginia became a royal colony. Maryland began as a proprietary colony under the control of the Calverts, and provided a haven for Roman Catholics; by the last decade of the seventeenth century, Protestants had seized the government and England had assumed control of the colony. In the Chesapeake, reliance on black slaves as field laborers developed gradually, over the course of a century.

In contrast, the first generation of Georgia settlers remained beholden to London-based trustees who believed in the moral efficacy of hard work for a group described at the time as the English "middle poor . . . decayed tradesmen, or supernumerary workmen in towns and cities," men who, as it turned out, "cannot put their hands to country affairs, or are too proud to do it." Under intense pressure from a band of pro-slavery "Malcontents," the trustees relinquished their principled stand against slavery in 1751, and in 1754 King George assumed authority over the colony. For the quotation, see Temple and Coleman, *Georgia Journeys*, p. 38. See also Wesley Frank Craven, *The Southern Colonies in the Seventeenth Century, 1607–1689* (Baton Rouge, LA: Louisiana State University Press, 1949); Trevor Richard Reese, *Colonial Georgia: A Study in British Imperial Policy in the Eighteenth Century* (Athens, GA: University of Georgia Press, 1963).

4. See for example J. Frederick Fausz, "An 'Abundance of Blood Shed on Both Sides': England's First Indian War, 1609–1614," *VMHB* 98 (January 1990):3–56; Helen C. Rountree, *The Powhatan Indians of Virginia: Their Traditional Culture,* Civilization of the American Indian Series, 193 (Norman, OK:University of Oklahoma Press, 1989).

5. "ignominiously": H. R. McIlwaine, ed., *Minutes of the Council and General Court of*

Colonial Virginia, 1622–1632, 1670–1676 (Richmond, VA: Colonial Press, 1924), p. 12; Ralph Gray and Betty Wood, "The Transition from Indentured to Involuntary Servitude in Colonial Georgia," *EEH* 13 (October 1976):355. See also Karen Ordahl Kupperman, *Settling with the Indians: The Meeting of English and Indian Cultures in America, 1580–1640* (Totowa, NJ: Rowman & Littlefield, 1980); James H. Merrell, "Some Thoughts on Colonial Historians and American Indians," *WMQ* 3rd series 46 (January 1989):94–119; Wesley Frank Craven, *White, Red, and Black: The Seventeenth-Century Virginian* (New York: W. W. Norton, 1971), pp. 40–67.

6. Oscar and Mary F. Handlin, "Origins of the Southern Labor System," *WMQ* 3rd series 7 (April 1950):199–22; Robert J. Steinfeld, *The Invention of Free Labor: The Employment Relation in English and American Law and Culture, 1350–1870* (Chapel Hill, NC: University of North Carolina Press, 1991), chap. 2; Winthrop Jordan, *White Over Black: American Attitudes Toward the Negro, 1550–1812* (Chapel Hill, NC: University of North Carolina Press, 1968), chap. 2.

7. See for example Edward P. Cheyney, "Some English Conditions Surrounding the Settlement of Virginia," *AHR* 12 (April 1907):507–28; Richard Beeman, "Labor Forces and Race Relations: A Comparative View of the Colonization of Brazil and Virginia," *PSQ* 86 (December 1981):609–36; Ronald Wright, *Stolen Continents: The Americas Through Indian Eyes Since 1492* (Boston: Houghton Mifflin, 1992). For comparisons of the English colonization efforts in Ireland and Virginia, see Nicholas P. Canny, *Kingdom and Colony: Ireland in the Atlantic World, 1560–1800* (Baltimore: Johns Hopkins University Press, 1988); and "The Marginal Kingdom: Ireland as a Problem in the First British Empire," in Bernard Bailyn and Philip Morgan, eds., *Strangers Within the Realm: Cultural Margins of the First British Empire* (Chapel Hill, NC: University of North Carolina Press, 1971), pp. 35–66. See also Karl S. Bottigheimer, "Kingdom and Colony: Ireland in the Westward Enterprise, 1536–1660," pp. 45–63, in K. R. Andrews, N. P. Canny, and P. E. H. Hair, eds., *The Westward Enterprise: English Activities in Ireland, the Atlantic, and America, 1480–1650* (Detroit: Wayne State University Press, 1979); and David Thomas Honig, "Colonization and the Common Law in Ireland and Virginia, 1569–1634," in James Henretta, Michael Kammen, and Stanley Katz, eds., *The Transformation of Early American History: Society, Authority, and Ideology* (New York: Knopf, 1991).

8. Hilary McD. Beckles, *White Servitude and Black Slavery in Barbados, 1627–1715* (Knoxville, TN: University of Tennessee Press, 1989); Richard S. Dunn, "Masters, Servants, and Slaves in the Colonial Chesapeake and the Caribbean," in David B. Quinn, ed., *Early Maryland in a Wider World* (Detroit: Wayne State University Press, 1982), pp. 242–66; Lois Green Carr and Lorena S. Walsh, "The Planter's Wife: The Experience of White Women in Seventeenth-Century Maryland," *WMQ* 3rd series 34 (October 1977):542–71; Terry L. Anderson and Robert Paul Thomas, "The Growth of Population and Labor Force in the 17th-Century Chesapeake," *EEH* 15 (July 1978):290–312; Ruth S. Green, transcriber,

"The South Carolina Archives Copy of the Fundamental Constitutions" (July 21, 1669), *SCHM* 71 (April 1970):86–100. South Carolina did utilize white indentured servants; but the bulk of the field work after the introduction of rice cultivation was performed by slaves. See John Donald Duncan, "Servitude and Slavery in Colonial South Carolina, 1670–1776," Ph.D. thesis, Emory University, 1972.

9. "watching": Barbour, ed., *Complete Works of Captain John Smith*, Vol. II, p. 306; Virginia Bernhard, "'Men, Women and Children' at Jamestown: Population and Gender in Early Virginia, 1607–1610," *JSouH* 58 (November 1992):599–618; Morgan, *American Slavery, American Freedom*, pp. 44–91; Sigmund Diamond, "From Organization to Society: Virginia in the Seventeenth Century," *AJS* 63 (1958): 457–75; Karen Ordahl Kupperman, "Apathy and Death in Early Jamestown," *JAH* 46 (June 1979):24–40.

10. Abbot Emerson Smith, *Colonists in Bondage: White Servitude and Convict Labor in America, 1607–1776* (Chapel Hill, NC: University of North Carolina Press, 1947), p. 256; "The Advantages of Enclosure. 1697," in Joan Thirsk and J. P. Cooper, eds., *Seventeenth-Century Economic Documents* (Oxford: Clarendon Press, 1972), p. 186; "The Objection": E. W. Gent, "Virginia . . . More Especially the South part thereof. . . . (1650)," in Peter Force, ed., *Tracts and Other Papers, Relating Principally to the Origin, Settlement, and Progress of the Colonies in North America . . . ,* Vol. 3 (New York: Peter Smith, 1947; orig. pub. 1836), no. 11, p. 13.

11. "It is impossible": Causton quoted in Temple and Coleman, *Georgia Journeys*, p. 10; "the infinite": Henry Hartwell, James Blair, and Edward Chilton, *The Present State of Virginia, and the College* (Williamsburg, VA: Colonial Williamsburg, Inc., 1940; orig. pub. 1697), p. 6; Michael Zuckerman, "Identity in British America: Unease in Eden," in Nicholas P. Canny and Anthony Pagden, eds., *Colonial Identity in the Atlantic World, 1500–1800* (Princeton: Princeton University Press, 1987), p. 120; "thick": "A True Narrative of the Late Rebellion in Virginia, by the Royal Commissioners, 1677," in Charles M. Andrews, ed., *Narratives of the Insurrections, 1675–1690* (New York: Barnes and Noble, 1952), p. 108; Timothy Silver, *A New Face on the Countryside: Indians, Colonists, and Slaves in South Atlantic Forests, 1500–1800* (Cambridge, UK: Cambridge University Press, 1990); "truely": "A Perfect Description of Virginia" (1649), in Force, ed., *Tracts and Other Papers*, Vol. 2, no. 8, p. 10.

12. "disbranching": Allen D. Candler, comp., *Colonial Records of the State of Georgia*, Vol. 4, *Stephens' Journal* (New York: AMS Press, 1970; orig. pub. 1904–16), p. 564 (hereinafter cited as *Stephens' Journal*); Sinclair Snow, "Naval Stores in Colonial Virginia," *VMHB* 72 (January 1964):75–93. In late seventeenth-century South Carolina, the felling of trees was associated with black slaves. See "Interview with James Freeman" (1712), in H. Roy Merrens, ed., *The Colonial South Carolina Scene: Contemporary Views, 1697–1774* (Columbia, SC: University of South Carolina Press, 1977), pp. 44–45.

13. "choaked": quoted in George Fenwick Jones, *The Salzburger Saga: Religious Exiles*

and Other Germans Along the Savannah (Athens, GA: University of Georgia Press, 1984), pp. 15–16.

14. "all our": John Pory, "A Letter to the Right Honble and My Singular Good Lorde," (1619) in Susan Myra Kingsbury, ed., *The Records of the Virginia Company of London*, Vol. III (Washington, DC: Government Printing Office, 1933), p. 22; Philip Alexander Bruce, *Economic History of Virginia in the Seventeenth Century* (New York: Macmillan, 1907), p. 585; Samuel Davidson to John Gilbert, April 26, 1738, *Colonial Records of the State of Georgia*, Vol. 22, Pt. 1, p. 146; Betty Wood, "James Edward Oglethorpe, Race, and Slavery: A Reassessment," in Phinizy Spalding and Harvey H. Jackson, eds., *Oglethorpe in Perspective: Georgia's Founder after Two Hundred Years* (Tuscaloosa, AL: University of Alabama Press, 1989), pp. 66–79; Betty Wood, *Slavery in Colonial Georgia, 1730–1775* (Athens, GA: University of Georgia Press, 1984); "But I . . . England": Rodney M. Baine, "Notes and Documents: Philip Thicknesse's Reminiscences of Early Georgia," *GHQ* 74 (Winter 1990):673.

15. "infinite . . . Agriculture": *Stephens' Journal*, p. 126; Betty Wood, "Thomas Stephens and the Introduction of Black Slavery in Georgia," *GHQ* 58 (Spring 1974):24–40.

16. Kevin Peter Kelly, "Economic and Social Development of Seventeenth Century Surry County, Virginia," Ph. D. thesis, University of Washington, 1972, p. 145; Morgan, *American Slavery, American Freedom*, pp. 175, 220; John A. Kinnamon, "The Public Levy in Colonial Maryland to 1689," *MHM* 53 (September 1958): 253–74.

17. "proper . . . compulsion": Barbour, ed., *Complete Works of Captain John Smith*, Vol. II, p. 185; Introduction, Stephen Innes, ed., *Work and Labor in Early America* (Chapel Hill, NC: University of North Carolina Press, 1988); "they would not": Lt. Col. Cochran (interview with Lord Egmont), Candler, ed., *Colonial Records of the State of Georgia*, Vol. 5: *Journal of the Earl of Egmont, First President of the Board of Trustees, June 14, 1738– May 25, 1744* (New York: AMS Press, 1970; orig. pub. 1904–16), p. 164 (hereinafter cited as *Journal of the Earl of Egmont*).

18. "cutting . . . Woods": Allen D. Candler, ed., *Colonial Records of the State of Georgia*, Vol. 6: *Proceedings of the President and Assistants, Oct. 12, 1741 to Oct. 30, 1754* (New York: AMS Press, 1970; orig. pub. 1904–16), p. 344 (hereinafter cited as *Colonial Records of the State of Georgia*, Vol. 6).

19. Anderson and Thomas, "Growth of Population and Labor Force"; James Horn, "Servant Emigration to the Chesapeake in the Seventeenth Century," in Thad W. Tate and David L. Ammerman, eds., *The Chesapeake in the Seventeenth Century: Essays on Anglo-American Society* (Chapel Hill, NC: University of North Carolina Press, 1979), pp. 51–95; David Galenson, *White Servitude in Colonial America: An Economic Analysis* (New York: Cambridge University Press, 1981); Peter Wood, "Changing Population of the Colonial South: An Overview by Race and Region, 1685–1790," in Peter Wood, Gregory A. Waselkov, and M. Thomas Hatley, eds., *Powhatan's Mantle: Indians in the Colonial Southeast* (Lincoln,

NE: University of Nebraska Press, 1989), pp. 35–103; Peter Wood, "Re-Counting the Past," *SE* (Summer 1988):30-37; H. Roy Merrens, ed., *The Colonial South Carolina Scene: Contemporary Views, 1697–1774* (Columbia, SC: University of South Carolina Press, 1977), p. 32; Gray and Wood, "Transition from Involuntary Servitude"; Darold D. Wax, "'New Negroes Are Always in Demand': The Slave Trade in Eighteenth-Century Georgia," *GHQ* 68 (Summer 1984):193–220.

20. Kingsbury, ed., *Records of the Virginia Company*, Vol. III, pp. 704–07.

21. Neal Salisbury, "The Indians' Old World: Native Americans and the Coming of Europeans," *WMQ* 3rd series 53 (July 1996):435–58.

22. "some neighbouring": *Stephens' Journal*, Vol. 4, p. 299; "the Archbishop's": George Fenwick Jones, *The Salzburger Saga: Religious Exiles and Other Germans Along the Savannah* (Athens, GA: University of Georgia Press, 1984), p. 23; "the disorderly": William Waller Hening, ed., *The Statutes at Large; Being a Collection of All the Laws of Virginia*, Vol. I (New York: Bartow, 1823), p. 391; "by imploying": *ibid.*, p. 457; James H. Merrell, "'The Customes of Our Countrey': Indians and Colonials in Early America," in Bailyn and Morgan, eds., *Strangers Within the Realm*, pp. 117–56; Silver, *A New Face on the Countryside*; Alfred W. Crosby, *The Columbian Exchange: Biological and Cultural Consequences of 1492* (Westport, CT: Greenwood Press, 1972). See also Alan Everitt, "Farm Labourers," in Joan Thirsk, ed., *The Agrarian History of England and Wales*, Vol. IV: *1500–1640* (Cambridge, UK: Cambridge University Press, 1967), p. 405; Susie M. Ames, *Studies of the Virginia Eastern Shore in the Seventeenth Century* (New York: Russell & Russell, 1940), pp. 58–9.

23. "Gluttonous": Barbour, ed., *Complete Works of Captain John Smith*, Vol. II, p. 213; Hening, ed., *Statutes at Large*, Vol. I, p. 525; Susie M. Ames, ed., *County Court Records of Accomack-Northampton, Virginia, 1640–1645* (Charlottesville, VA: University Press of Virginia, 1973), p. 353; Temple and Coleman, *Georgia Journeys*, p. xv.

24. Stephen R. Potter, "Early English Effects on Virginia Algonquian Exchange and Tribute in the Tidewater Potomac," in Wood, *et al.*, *Powhatan's Mantle*, pp. 151-72; "certain Doegs": "A True Narrative of the Late Rebellion in Virginia, By the Royal Commissioners, 1677," in Andrews, ed., *Narratives of the Insurrections, 1675–1690*, p. 105; *Stephens' Journal*, Vol. 4, p. 166; *ibid.*, Supp., p. 10.

25. "shall suffer": Hening, ed., *Statutes at Large*, Vol. IV, p. 104; Duncan, "Servitude and Slavery in Colonial South Carolina," pp. 1–38. See also A. W. Lauber, *Indian Slavery in Colonial Times Within the Present Limits of the United States*, Columbia University Studies in History, Economics, and Public Law, Vol. 54, no. 3 (New York: Columbia University Press, 1913); Sanford Winston, "Indian Slavery in the Carolina Region," *JNH* 19 (October 1934):431–40; William Hand Browne, ed., *Archives of Maryland*, Vol. 4 (June 1648) (Baltimore: Maryland Historical Society, 1887), p.102. On the *encomienda* system of Indian forced labor in the Spanish New World, see John Francis Bannon, ed., *Indian Labor in the Spanish Indies* (Boston: D. C. Heath, 1966); David Carrasco, *Quetzalcoatl and the Irony of Empire*

(Chicago: University of Chicago Press, 1982); Noble David Cook, *Demographic Collapse: Indian Peru, 1520–1620* (Cambridge, UK: Cambridge University Press, 1981); Nancy M. Farris, *Maya Society Under Colonial Rule* (Princeton: Princeton University Press, 1984); Charles Gibson, *The Aztecs Under Spanish Rule* (Stanford, CA: Stanford University Press, 1964).

26. Warren B. Smith, *White Servitude in Colonial South Carolina* (Columbia, SC: University of South Carolina Press, 1961), p. 63; Jon Butler, *The Huguenots in America: A Refugee People in New World Society* (Cambridge, MA: Harvard University Press, 1983), pp. 144–98; Phinizy Spalding, "Oglethorpe, William Stephens, and the Origin of Georgia Politics," in Spalding, *et al.*, eds., *Oglethorpe in Perspective*, p. 94.

27. "insolent . . . Arrival": *Colonial Records of the State of Georgia*, Vol. 6, p. 217; Abbot Emerson Smith, *Colonists in Bondage*, pp. 23, 38, 152, 162, 175; James Curtis Ballagh, *White Servitude in the Colony of Virginia: A Study of the System of Indentured Labor in the American Colonies* (Baltimore: Johns Hopkins University Press, 1895), p. 35; Rodney M. Baine, "New Perspectives on Debtors in Colonial Georgia," *GHQ* 77 (Spring 1993):1–19.

28. Silver, *A New Face on the Countryside*, pp. 139–41; Snow, "Naval Stores in Colonial Virginia, pp. 75–93; Barbour, ed., *Complete Works of Captain John Smith*, Vol. II, pp. 114, 225, 304; *Stephens' Journal*, Vol. 4, pp. 213, 310, 312; *ibid.*, Supp., pp. 25, 144, 193, 243, 248; "The Discourse of the Old Company, 1625," in Lyon Gardner Tyler, ed., *Narratives of Early Virginia, 1606–1625* (New York: Barnes and Noble, 1907), p. 435.

29. "in a . . . us": Barbour, ed., *Complete Works of Captain John Smith*, Vol. II, p. 268; "transported . . . vyniard": Hening, ed., *Statutes at Large*, Vol. I, p. 161; "Rum . . . silk": *Stephens' Journal*, Vol. 4, Supp., p. 248; "saw . . . granted," *ibid.*, p. 243. See also Temple and Coleman, *Georgia Journeys*, p. 258.

30. "I could": *Stephens' Journal*, Vol. 4, pp. 96, 378, 621. See also Lothar L. Tresp, trans. and annotator, "August, 1748 in Georgia, from the Diary of John Martin Bolzius," *GHQ* 47 (June 1963):217–18.

31. "20. and": Karen Ordahl Kupperman, "The Founding Years of Virginia—and the United States," *VMHB* 104 (Winter 1996):103–12; Craven, *White, Red, and Black*, pp. 81, 89, 91; T. H. Breen and Stephen Innes, *"Myne Owne Ground": Race and Freedom on Virginia's Eastern Shore, 1640–1646* (New York: Oxford University Press, 1980); Helen T. Catterall, ed., *Judicial Cases Concerning American Slavery and the Negro* (Washington, DC: Carnegie Institution, 1926, 1936), Vol. I, pp. 53–93; Vol. IV, pp. 1–49.

32. "List of Tithables in Northampton County, Virginia, August, 1666, Pt. I," *VMHB* 10 (October 1912):194–96; and Pt. II, *VMHB* 10 (January 1903):358–63; Main, *Tobacco Colony*, p. 128.

33. "Caine": *County Court Records of Accomack-Northampton, Virginia, 1640–1645*, p. 423; Bruce, *Economic History of Virginia*, Vol. II, pp. 57–130; McIlwaine, ed., *Minutes of the Council*, p. 45; "were . . . Task": *Stephens' Journal*, Vol. 4, Supp., p. 271; *Colonial Records of the State Of Georgia*, Vol. 6, pp. 206–10.

34. "In a newe": *Journal of the House of Burgesses, 1619–1658/9*, pp. 6–7; "young . . . children": quoted in David R. Ransome, "Wives for Virginia, 1621," *WMQ* 3rd series 48 (January 1991):3–18; "unserviceable": "Minutes of the Council and General Court, 1622–29," *VMHB* 27 (April 1919):146. The following works emphasize the utility of women in the southern colonies: Kathleen Mary Brown, *Good Wives, Nasty Wenches, and Anxious Patriarchs: Gender, Race, and Power in Colonial Virginia* (Chapel Hill, NC: University of North Carolina Press, 1996); Carr and Walsh, "The Planter's Wife." See also Mrs. Henry Lowell Cook, "Maids for Wives," *VMHB* 50 (October 1942):314.

   In evaluating the work of white women in the early years of the Chesapeake and Georgia, it is tempting to isolate a principled English gender division of labor (taking into account class and regional variations) and then to measure the allocation of tasks in the New World according to this standard. The vast majority of Englishwomen in the seventeenth century had primary responsibility for child care, clothes laundering, and food preparation; rural women in addition tended vegetable gardens, served as dairymaids, and performed other types of household industry. Nevertheless, in England during the period 1550 to 1650 in particular, expectations about men and women's work were in a state of flux; this was a time of rapid population growth, and consequently the sexual division of labor, in the fields and in workshops, was becoming increasingly specialized.

   On these themes, see Carole Shammas, "The World Women Knew: Women Workers in the North of England During the Late Seventeenth Century," in Richard Dunn and Mary Maples Dunn, ed., *The World of William Penn* (Philadelphia: University of Pennsylvania Press, 1986), pp. 99–115, and Carole Shammas, "The Domestic Environment in Early Modern England and America," *JSocH* 14 (Fall 1980):3–24; Alice Clark, *Working Life of Women in the Seventeenth Century* (London: Cass, 1968; orig. pub. 1919); D. C. Coleman, "Labour in the English Economy of the Seventeenth Century," *EHR* 2nd series 8 (April 1956):280–95; Brown, *Good Wives, Nasty Wenches and Anxious Patriarchs*, pp. 13–41; and Michael Roberts, "Sickles and Scythes: Women's Work and Men's Work at Harvest Time," *HW* 7 (Spring 1979):3–28.

35. "bravely": "Minutes of the Council and General Court of Virginia, 1622," *VMHB* 19 (April 1911):146; *Stephens' Journal*, Vol. 4, p. 151 (for a man and woman servant "assisting in bringing out of the woods" some cattle, at their master's command); Julia Cherry Spruill, *Women's Life and Work in the Southern Colonies* (New York: W.W. Norton, 1972; orig. pub. 1938); Mary Beth Norton, "The Evolution of White Women's Experience in Early America," *AHR* (June 1984):593–619.

36. "anchor": Spruill, *Women's Life and Work*, p. 9; "good . . . sarvant": *Archives of Maryland*, Vol. 53, p. 169; Mary Beth Norton, "Gender and Defamation in Seventeenth-Century Maryland," *WMQ* 44 (January 1987):3–39; and Mary Beth Norton, "Gender, Crime, and Community in Seventeenth-Century Maryland," in James Henretta, ed., *The Transformation of Early American History: Society, Authority, and Ideology* (New York: Knopf, 1991), pp. 123–50.

406 AMERICAN WORK

37. Spruill, *Women's Life and Work*, p. 10; Lois Green Carr, Russell R. Menard, and Lorena S. Walsh, *Robert Cole's World: Agriculture and Society in Early Maryland* (Chapel Hill, NC: University of North Carolina Press, 1991), p. 109; Hammond, "Leah and Rachel," pp. 290–91. See also "A Brief Description of the Province of Carolina, by Robert Horne, 1666," in Alexander S. Salley, Jr., ed., *Narratives of Early Carolina, 1650–1708* (New York: Barnes and Noble, 1953; orig. pub. 1911), p. 114; "masculine": Spruill, *Women's Life and Work*, p. 17; *County Court Records of Accomack-Northampton, Virginia, 1640–1645*, p. 25.

38. Carr, et al., *Robert Cole's World*, pp. 38–9, 51; Brown, *Good Wives, Nasty Wenches, and Anxious Patriarchs*; "occupie . . . carelesse": Hammond, "Leah and Rachel," pp. 290, 292.

39. Hammond, "Leah and Rachel," pp. 290–1; Roberts, "Sickles and Scythes"; K. D. M. Snell, "Agricultural Seasonal Unemployment, the Standard of Living, and Women's Work in the South and East, 1690–1860," *EHR*, 2nd series 34 (August 1981):407–37; "diverse . . . concealment": Hening, ed., *Statutes at Large*, Vol. II, p. 170; "List of Tithables in Northampton County, Virginia, August, 1666," *VMHB* 10 (January 1903):262; Bruce, *Economic History of Virginia*, Vol. II, pp. 40, 103; Lois Green Carr, "The Development of the Maryland Orphans' Court, 1654–1715," in Aubrey C. Land, Lois Green Carr, and Edward C. Papenfuse, eds., *Law, Society, and Politics in Early Maryland: Proceedings of the First Conference on Maryland History* (Baltimore: Johns Hopkins University Press, 1977), pp. 41–62.

40. "to make": J. Hall Pleasants, ed., *Archives of Maryland*, Vol. 49: *Proceedings of the Provincial Court of Maryland, 1663–1666* (Baltimore: Maryland Historical Society, 1932), p. 144; Kelly, "Economic and Social Development of Seventeenth-Century Surry County," p. 101; "The Axe": "The Trappanned Maiden," *VMHB* 4 (October 1896):218; "at worke": McIlwaine, *Minutes of the Council*, p. 194; "Sufficient": Robert Beverley, *The History and Present State of Virginia* (Chapel Hill, NC: University of North Carolina Press, 1947; orig. pub. 1705), p. 271. See also Carole Shammas, "Black Women's Work and the Evolution of Plantation Society in Virginia," *LH* 26 (Winter 1985):5–28; Lois Green Carr and Lorena S. Walsh, "Economic Diversification and Labor Organization in the Chesapeake, 1650–1820," in Innes, ed., *Work and Labor in Early America*, pp. 144–88.

41. "might . . . slave": Bernard C. Steiner, ed., *Archives of Maryland*, Vol. 41: *Proceedings of the Provincial Court of Maryland, 1658–1662* (Baltimore: Maryland Historical Society, 1922), p. 515; Walsh, "'Till Death Do Us Part,'" p. 144; James Horn, "Servant Emigration to the Chesapeake in the Seventeenth Century," in Tate and Ammerman, eds., *The Chesapeake in the Seventeenth Century*, p. 64; Main, *Tobacco Colony*, p. 109.

42. "to make": Joseph N. Smith and Philip A. Crowe, eds., *American Legal Records*, Vol. 9: *Court Records of Prince Georges County, Maryland, 1696–1699* (Washington, DC: American Historical Association, 1964), p. 415; Russell Menard, "Economy and Society in Early Colonial Maryland," Ph.D. thesis, University of Iowa, 1975,

p. 253; "and some": Bartlett Burleigh James and J. Franklin Jameson, eds., *Journal of Joseph Danckaerts, 1679–1680* (New York: Barnes and Noble, 1946; orig. pub. 1913), p. 133; "consider[ed]": Lothar L. Tresp, "September, 1748 in Georgia, From the Diary of John Martin Bolzius," *GHQ* 47 (September 1963):328.

43. On miscellaneous duties of women, see *Archives of Maryland*, Vol. 42, pp. 332, 480; "Will of Christopher Robinson, 1693," *VMHB* 7 (July 1899):23; *Stephens' Journal*, Vol. 4, p. 259; *County Court Records of Accomack-Northampton, Virginia, 1640–1645*, p. 129; Ames, *Studies of the Virginia Eastern Shore*, p. 129; Brown, *Good Wives, Nasty Wenches, and Anxious Patriarchs*, pp. 22–27. See also Robert W. Malcolmson, *Life and Labour in England, 1700–1780* (New York: St. Martin's Press, 1981), pp. 42, 57, 66.

44. "wher": Captain Nuce, A Letter to Sir Edwin Sandys, May 27, 1661, *Records of the Virginia Company*, Vol. III, p. 457; "useless": Hartwell, Blair, and Chilton, *The Present State of Virginia, and the College*, pp. 5–6; "the Gentlewomen": Mrs. Martha Causton to the Trustees, Savannah, Jan. 16, 1737, *Colonial Records of the State of Georgia*, Vol. 22, Pt. 1, pp. 65–6; *Stephens' Journal*, Vol. 4, Supp., p. 238. See also Jones, *Salzburger Saga*, pp. 66, 106, 117; "Letters Written by Mr. Moray, A Minister . . . ," *WMQ* 2nd series 2 (April 1922):157.

45. Malcolm Kitch, "Population and Migration in Pre-Industrial Rural England," in Brian Short, ed., *The English Rural Community: Image and Analysis* (Cambridge, UK: Cambridge University Press, 1992), p. 66; "Irish . . . little": *Archives of Maryland*, Vol. 41, p. 478, "not . . . much": p. 477; "Poor Children to Be Sent to Virginia," *VMHB* 6 (January 1899):232; Bruce, *Economic History of Virginia*, Vol. I, p. 593; Cook, "Maids for Wives," p. 311; *Court Records of Prince Georges County*, pp. 183, 188, 346.

46. Carr, "Development of Maryland Orphans' Court"; "have noe": quoted in Walsh, "'Till Death Do Us Part,'" p. 145.

47. " All . . . employment":*Journal of the Earl of Egmont*, pp. 319, 330; "Not a": quoted in Temple and Coleman, *Georgia Journeys*, p. 229; "Design . . . Chattels": *Stephens' Journal*, Vol. 4, pp. 539–40.

48. "Girle . . . them": *County Court Records of Accomack-Northampton, Virginia, 1640–1645*, p. 291; Carr, et al., *Robert Cole's World*, pp. 38, 71; *Stephens' Journal*, Vol. 4, p. 541; "Minutes of the Council and General Court," *VMHB* 21 (April 1913):140; "Children": Hammond, "Leah and Rachel," p. 296.

49. "giddy": Hammond, "Leah and Rachel," p. 394; "debauched . . . drinking": *Stephens' Journal*, p. 389; Lois Green Carr and Russell Menard, "Immigration and Opportunity: The Freedman in Early Colonial Maryland," in Tate and Ammerman, eds., *Chesapeake in the Seventeenth Century*, pp. 206–42; Russell Menard, "From Servant to Freeholder: Status Mobility and Property Accumulation in Seventeenth-Century Maryland," *WMQ*, 3rd series 30 (January 1973):37–64; Morgan, *American Slavery, American Freedom*.

50. See also "Lower Norfolk County Records, 1636–1646," *VMHB* 39 (January 1931):19; Kelly, "Economic and Social Development of Seventeenth-Century

Surry County," p. 124; Paul G. E. Clemens, *The Atlantic Economy and Colonial Maryland's Eastern Shore* (Ithaca, NY: Cornell University Press, 1980), p. 54; Allan Kulikoff, *Tobacco and Slaves: The Development of Southern Cultures in the Chesapeake, 1680–1800* (Chapel Hill, NC: University of North Carolina Press, 1986), pp. 64–77.

51. "Maid": quoted in Ballagh, *White Servitude in the Colony of Virginia*, p. 83; Kelly, "Economic and Social Development of Seventeenth-Century Surry County," p. 216; Darrett B. and Anita H. Rutman, *A Place in Time: Middlesex County, Virginia, 1650–1750* (New York: W. W. Norton, 1984), p. 176; [Nicculgutt]: *Archives of Maryland*, Vol. 49, p. 380; [Thompson]: *Archives of Maryland*, Vol. 41, pp. 494–95. See also "Minutes of the Council" (February 1625), *VMHB* 25 (July 1917):226; Hening, ed., *Statutes at Large*, Vol. II, p. 488.

52. "audacious": Hening, ed., *Statutes at Large*, Vol. I, p. 538; Raphael Semmes, *Crime and Punishment in Early Maryland* (Baltimore: Johns Hopkins University Press, 1938), pp. 80–118; "banishd": Bruce, *Economic History of Virginia*, Vol. II, pp. 111, 37; Hening, ed., *Statutes at Large*, Vol. II, p. 87; *Archives of Maryland*, Vol. 23, p. 508; *Court Records of Prince Georges County*, p. 349; Morgan, *American Slavery, American Freedom*, pp. 216–18.

53. Catterall, ed., *Judicial Cases Concerning American Slavery and the Negro*, Vol. IV (Maryland), pp. 2–3; Morgan, "British Encounters with Africans and African-Americans," pp. 171–72; Brown, *Good Wives, Nasty Wenches, and Anxious Patriarchs*, pp. 187–211.

54. "foure": "Extracts from Virginia County Records," *VMHB* 12 (April 1905):292; "a Lame": *County Court Records of Accomack-Northampton, Virginia, 1640–1645*, p. 129; "cleared . . . Hire": *Stephens' Journal*, Vol. 4, p. 468. See also *Court Records of Prince Georges County*, p. 233; "any . . . Bodyes": *Court Records of Accomack-Northampton, Virginia, 1640–1645*, p. 36.

55. Carr and Menard, "Immigration and Opportunity," pp. 214–16; "imploved . . . industry": *Archives of Maryland*, Vol. 41, p. 251; *Court Records of Prince Georges County*, p. 75. See also Clemens, *Atlantic Economy*, pp. 86–7; *Stephens' Journal*, Vol. 4, Supp., p. 48; *Archives of Maryland*, Vol. 41, p. 153.

56. "knowing . . . againe": J. Hall Pleasants, ed., *Archives of Maryland*, Vol. 54: *Proceedings of the County Courts of Kent (1648–1676), Talbot (1662–1674), Somerset (1665–1668) Counties* (Baltimore: Maryland Historical Society, 1937), p. 350; "divers": Hening, ed., *Statutes at Large*, Vol. I, p. 254. See also Daniel Meaders, "Fugitive Slaves and Indentured Servants Before 1800," Ph.D. thesis, Yale University, 1990.

57. "their . . . commerce": Hening, ed., *Statutes at Large*, Vol. II, p. 185; "Severall . . . Inhabitants": McIlwaine, ed., *Executive Journals of the Council of Colonial Virginia*, pp. 232–33, 352; "Deserting": *Court Records of Prince Georges County*, p. 430.

58. "withdraw": Hening, ed., *Statutes at Large*, Vol. 1, p. 124; "a . . . Land": *Stephens' Journal*, Vol. 4, pp. 81, 286; "doeing": *Archives of Maryland*, Vol. 41, p. 348. See also *Colonial Records of the State of Georgia*, Vol. 5, p. 192; Vol. 22, p. 105;

"Decisions of the General Court, 1626–1628," *VMHB* 4 (January 1897):250; Smith, *Colonists in Bondage*, p. 240; Morgan, *American Slavery, American Freedom*, p. 120.

59. *County Court Records of Accomack-Northampton, Virginia, 1640–1645*, pp. 129, liv; Bruce, *Economic History of Virginia*, Vol. II, pp. 13, 24; "where proper": William Stephens to Harman Verelst, *Colonial Records of the State of Georgia*, Vol. 22, p. 175; *Stephens' Journal*, Vol. 4, p. 289.

60. "to doe": Barbour, ed., *Complete Works of Captain John Smith*, Vol. II, p. 299; Morgan, *American Slavery, American Freedom*, p. 117; "were like": James Revel, "The Poor Unhappy Transported Felon's Sorrowful Account. . . ," *VMHB* 56 (April 1948): 189–94; "taken . . . Slave": *Archives of Maryland*, Vol. 41, p. 476; "stay . . . gentlemen": *County Court Records of Accomack-Northampton, Virginia, 1632–1640*, p. 120.

61. "who would": "Proceedings in York County Court," *WMQ* 11 (July 1902):34–5.

CHAPTER TWO

1. "Extreams": Allen D. Candler, comp., *Colonial Records of the State of Georgia*, Vol. 4: *Stephens' Journal* (New York: AMS Press, 1970; orig. pub. 1904), p. 300. See Phinizy Spalding, "Oglethorpe, William Stephens, and the Origin of Georgia Politics," in Phinizy Spalding and Harvey N. Jackson, eds., *Oglethorpe in Perspective: Georgia's Founder After Two Hundred Years* (Tuscaloosa, AL: University of Alabama Press, 1989), pp. 80–98; Sarah B. Gober Temple and Kenneth Coleman, *Georgia Journeys* (Athens, GA: University of Georgia Press, 1961).

2. "a work": *Stephens' Journal*, Vol. 4, p. 45; Upon . . . Water": *Colonial Records of the State of Georgia*, Vol. 22, Pt. 1, pp. 52–53; "wounded": *Stephens' Journal*, Vol. 4, p. 53; Betty Wood, "Thomas Stephens and the Introduction of Black Slavery in Georgia," *GHQ* 58 (Spring 1974):24–40.

3. "an habitual": *Stephens' Journal*, Vol. 4, p. 270; "for some": *Colonial Records of the State of Georgia*, Vol. 22, Pt. 1, p. 83; "it produced": *Stephens' Journal*, Vol. 4, p. 200.

4. "slothful": *Stephens' Journal*, Vol. 4, p. 117; "errant": *Colonial Records of the State of Georgia*, Vol. 22, Pt. 1, p. 173; "dead": *ibid.*, p. 359; "Saturday": *Stephens' Journal*, Vol. 4, p. 122; "a very": *ibid.*, pp. 248–49; "naturally . . . Provocation": *ibid.*, p. 261.

5. "proved": *Stephens' Journal*, Vol. 4, p. 51; "an egregious": *Colonial Records of the State of Georgia*, Vol. 22, Pt. 1, p. 174; Stephens' Journal, Vol. 4, p. 139; "truly": *ibid.*, p. 282; "but who": Colonial Records of the State of Georgia, Vol. 22, Pt. 1, p. 69.

6. "weak . . . Employment": *Stephens' Journal*, Vol. 4, pp. 265–66; "have often": *ibid.*, p. 263.

7. "rotten": *Colonial Records of the State of Georgia*, Vol. 22, Pt. 1, p. 173; "kept": *Stephens' Journal*, Vol. 4, p. 251; "Great": *ibid.*, Supp., p. 149.

8. "They . . . blood": Marion Tinling, ed., *The Correspondence of the Three William Byrds of Westover, Virginia, 1684–1776*, Vol. II (Charlottesville, VA: University Press of Virginia, 1977), pp. 487–88.

9. Kevin Peter Kelly, "Economic and Social Development of Seventeenth-Century Surry County, Virginia," Ph.D. thesis, University of Washington, 1972, p. 145; David Galenson, *White Servitude in Colonial America: An Economic Analysis* (New York: Cambridge University Press, 1981); Russell R. Menard, "Economy and Society in Early Colonial Maryland," Ph.D. thesis, University of Iowa, 1975; James Horn, "Servant Emigration to the Chesapeake in the Seventeenth Century," in Thad W. Tate and David L. Ammerman, eds., *The Chesapeake in the Seventeenth Century: Essays in Anglo-American Society* (Chapel Hill, NC: University of North Carolina Press, 1979):51–95. For a comparative view, see Richard S. Dunn, "Servants and Slaves: The Recruitment and Employment of Labor," in Jack P. Greene and J. R. Pole, eds., *Colonial British America: Essays in the New History of the Early Modern Era* (Baltimore: Johns Hopkins University Press, 1984), pp. 157–94.

10. "miserable": quoted in Ralph Gray and Betty Wood, "The Transition from Indentured to Involuntary Servitude in Colonial Georgia," *EEH* 13 (October 1976):358; "oblidged": Robert Paterson to Harman Verelst, Dec. 5, 1737, *Colonial Records of the State of Georgia*, Vol. 22, Pt. 1, p. 23.

11. "A Plain & Friendly Perswasive to the Inhabitants of Virginia and Maryland . . . ," *VMHB* 4 (January 1897):255; William Waller Hening, ed., *The Statues at Large: Being a Collection of all the Laws of Virginia . . .* , Vol. I (New York: Bartow, 1823), p. 539; Abbot Emerson Smith, *Colonists in Bondage: White Servitude and Convict Labor in America, 1607–1776* (Chapel Hill, NC: University of North Carolina Press, 1947); "Owen . . . Virginia": "Kidnapping Maidens, to Be Sold in Virginia," *VMHB* 6 (January 1899):229. See also Thomas Causton to Trustees, *Colonial Records of the State of Georgia*, Vol. 22, Pt. 1, p. 64; Darrett B. and Anita H. Rutman, *A Place in Time: Middlesex County, Virginia, 1650–1750* (New York: W. W. Norton, 1984), p. 131; James Davie Butler, "British Convicts Shipped to American Colonies," *AHR* 2 (October 1896):12–33. See also H. R. McIlwaine, ed., *Executive Journals of the Council of Colonial Virginia*, Vol. I (June 11, 1680–June 22, 1699) (Richmond, VA: Public Printing Office, 1925), p. 262; "Minutes of the Council and General Court," *VMHB* 24 (October 1916):342; John Hammond, "Leah and Rachel, or the Fruitful Sisters Virginia and Mary-land," in Clayton Colman Hall, ed., *Narratives of Early Maryland* (New York: Barnes and Noble, 1946; orig. pub. 1910), pp. 299, 284, 292.

12. "only hab": Hammond, "Leah and Rachel," p. 288; Menard,"Economy and Society," p. 164; Horn, "Servant Emigration to the Chesapeake," p. 59; Lois Green Carr, Russell R. Menard, and Lorena S. Walsh, *Robert Cole's World: Agriculture and Society in Early Maryland* (Chapel Hill, NC: University of North Carolina Press, 1991), p. 114; Hilary McD. Beckles, *White Servitude and Black Slavery in Barbados, 1627–1715* (Knoxville, TN: University of Tennessee Press, 1989).

13. Ann Kussmaul, *Servants in Husbandry in Early Modern England* (Cambridge, UK: Cambridge University Press, 1981); Carl Bridenbaugh, *Vexed and Troubled Englishmen, 1590–1642* (New York: Oxford University Press, 1967); Peter Bowden,

"Agricultural Prices, Farm Profits, and Rents," in Joan Thirsk, ed., *The Agrarian History of England and Wales*, Vol. IV: *1500–1640* (Cambridge, UK: Cambridge University Press, 1967), pp. 593–695; James Horn, *Adapting to a New World: English Society in the Eighteenth-Century Chesapeake* (Chapel Hill, NC: University of North Carolina Press, 1994).

14. "rather": George Alsop, "A Character of the Province of Maryland" (1666), in Hall, ed., *Narratives of Early Maryland*, p. 372; Malcolm Kitch, "Population and Migration in Pre-Industrial Rural England," in Brian Short, ed., *The English Rural Community: Image and Analysis* (Cambridge, UK: Cambridge University Press, 1992), pp. 62–84; David Souden, "'Rogues, Whores and Vagabonds'? Indentured Servant Emigrants to North America, and the Case of Mid-Seventeenth-Century Bristol," *SH* 3 (January 1978):23–41; John Wareing, "Migration to London and Transatlantic Emigration of Indentured Servants, 1683–1775," *JHG* 7 (1981):356–78; Bernard Bailyn, *Voyagers to the West: A Passage in the Peopling of America on the Eve of the Revolution* (New York: Knopf, 1986), pp. 167–85.

15. Margaret Spufford, *Contrasting Communities: English Villages in the Sixteenth and Seventeenth Centuries* (London: Cambridge University Press, 1974); Joan Thirsk, "Agricultural Conditions in England, circa 1680," in Richard S. Dunn and Mary Maples Dunn, eds., *The World of William Penn* (Philadelphia: University of Pennsylvania Press, 1986); Joan Thirsk, "English Rural Communities: Structures, Regularities and Change in the Sixteenth and Seventeenth Centuries," in Short, ed., *The English Rural Community*, pp. 44–61.

16. Ann Kussmaul, *General View of the Rural Economy of England, 1538–1840* (Cambridge, UK: Cambridge University Press, 1990); Kussmaul, *Servants in Husbandry*; David Hackett Fischer, *Albion's Seed: Four British Folkways in America* (New York: Oxford University Press, 1989); W. H. Brown, *et al.*, eds., *Archives of Maryland*, Vol. 41 (Baltimore: Maryland Historical Society, 1883–1972), p. 67.

17. Kussmaul, *Servants in Husbandry*, p. 81; Hening, ed., *Statutes at Large*, Vol. II, p. 195; Temple and Coleman, *Georgia Journeys*, p. 24; *Archives of Maryland*, Vol. 4, p. 165; "Minutes of the Executive Council," *VMHB* 25 (October 1917):344 (account of two male servants, ages twenty-three and twenty-four, convicted of "stealinge away a maide servant"; the two men had come over on the same ship, the *Bona Nova*).

18. "receved . . . waste": "Minutes of the Council and General Court, 1622–1624," *VMHB* 20 (January 1912):35; "very bad . . . drinke": *Archives of Maryland*, Vol. 41, p. 500.

19. "either": Hammond, "Leah and Rachel," p. 298; "she never . . . her": "Minutes of the Council and General Court, 1622–1624," pp. 33–35. See also Mary Beth Norton, "Gender and Defamation in Seventeenth-Century Maryland," *WMQ* 44 (January 1987):3–39; Kathleen M. Brown, *Good Wives, Nasty Wenches, and Anxious Patriarchs: Gender, Race, and Power in Colonial Virginia* (Chapel Hill, NC: University of North Carolina Press, 1996), pp. 75–106; James R. Perry, *The Formation of a Society on Virginia's Eastern Shore, 1615–1655* (Chapel Hill: University of North Carolina Press, 1990).

20. "Richard": *Archives of Maryland*, Vol. 53, p. 538.

21. "both man": *John Lawson's History of North Carolina* (Richmond, VA: Garrett & Massie, 1952), p. 2; Robert W. Malcolmson, *Life and Labour in England, 1700–1780* (New York: St. Martin's Press, 1981), pp. 75–76; Karen Ordahl Kupperman, "Fear of Hot Climates in the Anglo-American Colonial Experience," *WMQ* 3rd series 41 (April 1984):213–40; "cutting": *Colonial Records of the State of Georgia*, Vol. 6, p. 135; "Virginia Game and Field Sports," *VMHB* 7 (October 1899): 174; Alan Everitt, "Farm Labourers," in Thirsk, ed., *Agrarian History of England and Wales*, Vol. IV, pp. 426–30, 457; "loathsom": Hening, ed., *Statutes at Large*, Vol. III, p. 73. The list of spirits is from Joseph H. Smith and Philip A. Crowe, eds., *American Legal Records*, Vol. 9: *Court Records of Prince Georges County, Maryland, 1696–1699* (Washington, DC: American Historical Association, 1964), p. 156. See also James Horn, "Adapting to a New World: A Comparative Study of Local Society in England and Maryland, 1650–1700," in Lois Green Carr, Philip Morgan, and Jean Russo, eds., *Colonial Chesapeake Society* (Chapel Hill, NC: University of North Carolina Press, 1988) pp. 133–75; Farley Grubb, "Fatherless and Friendless: Factors Influencing the Flow of English Emigrant Servants," *JEH* 52 (March 1992):85–108; Carole Shammas, "The Domestic Environment in Early Modern England and America," *JSocH* 14 (Fall 1980):3–24.

22. "weake": Philip Barbour, ed., *The Complete Works of Captain John Smith*, Vol. II (Chapel Hill, NC: University of North Carolina Press, 1986), p. 190; "would": *Archives of Maryland*, Vol. 41, p. 9; Carville V. Earle, "Environment, Disease, and Mortality in Early Virginia," in Tate and Ammerman, eds., *The Chesapeake in the Early Seventeenth Century*, pp. 96–125; "so weak": *Colonial Records of the State of Georgia*, Vol. 6, p. 348.

23. Philip Alexander Bruce, *Economic History of Virginia in the Seventeenth Century* (New York: Macmillan, 1907), Vol. I, p. 444; "from working": quoted in Smith, *Colonists in Bondage*, p. 257; "useless": Lothar L. Tresp, trans., "September, 1748 in Georgia, from the Diary of John Martin Bolzius," *GHQ* 47 (September 1963):322; "almost": Hammond, "Leah and Rachel," p. 285.

24. "which made": "The Trappanned Maiden," *VMHB* 4 (October 1896):220; Carr, *et al.*, *Robert Cole's World*, p. 71; "have worn": Bartlett Burleigh James and J. Franklin Jameson, eds., *The Journal of Jasper Danckaerts, 1679–1680* (New York: Barnes and Noble, 1946; orig. pub. 1913), p. 133; "Sometimes": James Revel, "The Poor Unhappy Transported Felon's Sorrowful Account. . . ," *VMHB* 56 (April 1948):189–94; "hee": Susie M. Ames, ed., *County Court Records of Accomack-Northampton, Virginia, 1640–1645* (Charlottesville, VA: University Press of Virginia, 1973) p. 25; "why": *ibid.*, p. 246.

25. "Sitting": *Archives of Maryland*, Vol. 41, p. 26; Carr, *et al.*, *Robert Cole's World*, p. 37; "now": Barbour, ed., *Complete Works of Captain John Smith*, p. 235; David O. Percy, "Ax or Plow? Significant Colonial Landscape Alteration Rates in the Maryland and Virginia Tidewater," *AH* 66 (Spring 1992):66–74; "John have": *Archives of Maryland*, Vol. 4, p. 10; "in great": *Colonial Records of the State of Georgia*, Vol. 6, p.

62; *Stephens' Journal*, Vol. 4, p. 138; "alltogether": Susie M. Ames, ed., *County Court Records of Accomack-Northampton, Virginia, 1632–1640* (Washington, DC: American Historical Association, 1954), p. 102. See also *Archives of Maryland*, Vol. 41, p. 504; *ibid.*, Vol. 53, p. 626; *Stephens' Journal*, Vol. 4, p. 183.

26. Carr, *et al.*, *Robert Cole's World*, p. 13; "John Aubrey on Wiltshire and Herefordshire Agriculture, 1684–85," in Thirsk and Cooper, eds., *Economic Documents*, p. 181; Thirsk, "Agricultural Conditions," p. 93; Susie M. Ames, *Studies of the Virginia Eastern Shore in the Seventeenth Century* (New York: Russell & Russell, 1940), p. 43; "foreign": Bruce, *Economic History of Virginia*, Vol. I, p. 303. See also Horn, *Adapting to a New World*, pp. 60, 74, 83, 130–31, 276, 140–46.

27. "much care": Samuel Hartlib, "The Reformed Virginian Silkworm (1655)," in Force, ed., *Tracts and Other Papers*, Vol. 3, no. 13, p. 36. See for example Ames, ed., *County Court Records of Accomack-Northampton, Virginia, 1640–1645*, p. 375; "Minutes of the Council and General Court," *VMHB* 20 (April 1912):155. See also Kelly, "Economic and Social Development of Seventeenth-Century Surry County," pp. 120–49; T. H Breen, *Tobacco Culture: The Mentality of the Great Tidewater Planters on the Eve of Revolution* (Princeton: Princeton University Press, 1985), pp. 45–53; Carr, *et al.*, *Robert Cole's World*, pp. 55–66.

28. Kelly, "Economic and Social Development of Seventeenth-Century Surry County," p. 165; Morgan, *American Slavery, American Freedom*, p. 175; Everitt, "Farm Labourers," p. 413; Wesley N. Laing, "Cattle in Seventeenth–Century Virginia," *VMHB* 67 (April 1959):143–53; Ames, ed., *County Court Records of Accomack-Northampton, Virginia, 1632–1640*, p. 159; Carr, *et al.*, *Robert Cole's World*, p. 47; *Court Records of Prince Georges County*, pp. xv, 591; Silver, *A New Face on the Countryside*, pp. 175–79.

29. "their . . . privately": *Stephens' Journal*, Vol. 4, p. 109; "Carrying": *Court Records of Prince Georges County*, p. 458; Hening, ed., *Statutes at Large*, Vol. I, p. 176; "no . . . Woods": *Colonial Records of the State of Georgia*, Vol. 6, p. 184.

30. "Minutes of the Council and General Court," *VMHB* 19 (April 1911):124 (note 2); "Minutes of the Council and General Court," *VMHB* (July 1913):284–86; Hening, ed., *Statutes at Large*, Vol. I, pp. 300–01; *ibid.*, Vol. II, p. 209; *Stephens' Journal*, Vol. 4, Supp., p. 139; "Spanish": *Colonial Records of the State of Georgia*, Vol. 5, p. 99. On the murdering, kidnapping, or "entertaining" of blacks by Indians, see for example *Archives of Maryland*, Vol. 10, p. 293; Vol. 15, p. 400.

31. "There is": quoted in Kussmaul, *Servants in Husbandry*, p. 45.

32. See Robert Hughes, *The Fatal Shore* (New York: Knopf, 1987).

33. "barbarous": Hening, ed., *Statutes at Large*, Vol. II, p. 119; "tooke": "Proceedings in York County Court," *WMQ* 11 (July 1902):29; "hunge": "Minutes of the Council and General Court," *VMHB* 23 (January 1915):8; "Minutes of the Council and General Court," *VMHB* 20 (January 1912):33. See also *Archives of Maryland*, Vol. 49, p. 215.

34. "struck": *Archives of Maryland*, Vol. 41, p. 316; "naked . . . done": *Archives of Maryland*, Vol. 10, p. 535; "upp . . . her": Ames, ed. *County Court Records of Accomack-Northampton, Virginia, 1640–1645*, pp. 271–72.

35. "most . . . murthered": *County Court Records of Accomack-Northampton, Virginia, 1640–1645*, pp. 22, 26; "Deborah . . . beating": "An Assault on Charity Dallen, 1649," in Warren M. Billings, ed., *The Old Dominion in the Seventeenth Century: A Documentary History of Virginia, 1606–1689* (Chapel Hill, NC: University of North Carolina Press, 1975), p. 136; Kussmaul, *Servants in Husbandry*, p. 44; "late": Hening, ed., *Statutes at Large*, Vol. II, p. 167; "for committing": *Colonial Records of the State of Georgia*, Vol. 6, p. 14; "whore": Ames, ed., *County Court Records of Accomack-Northampton, Virginia, 1640–1645*, p. 190.

36. "great . . . hand": *Archives of Maryland*, Vol. 54, p. 224; "what": *Archives of Maryland*, Vol. 10, p. 485; "severe . . . of": *Stephens' Journal*, Vol. 4, Supp., pp. 167–68; "told": Ames, ed., *County Court Records of Accomack-Northampton, Virginia, 1640–1645*, p. 205.

37. "the . . . mistresse": Hening, ed., *Statutes at Large*, Vol. I, p. 538; "abhored . . . irksome": T. H. Breen, James H. Lewis, and Keith Schlesinger, "Motive for Murder: A Servant's Life in Virginia, 1678," *WMQ* 3rd series 40 (January 1983):111–12.

38. "with the bars": "Lower Norfolk County Records," *VMHB* 39 (January 1931):19–20; "lazing": Ames, ed., *County Court Records of Accomack-Northampton, Virginia, 1632–1640*, p. 61; Lois Green Carr and Lorena S. Walsh, "The Planter's Wife: The Experience of White Women in Seventeenth-Century Maryland," *WMQ*, 3rd series 34 (October 1977):548; Hening, ed., *Statutes at Large*, Vol. I, p. 253; "thereby": *ibid.*, p. 445. See also Ballagh, *White Servitude in the Colony of Virginia*, p. 49; Ames, *Studies of the Virginia Eastern Shore*, p. 188.

39. Hening, ed. *Statutes at Large*, Vol. II, p. 195; "utter . . . Spirits": *Colonial Records of the State of Georgia*, Vol. 22, Pt. 1, p. 164.

40. "with . . . Fowls": *Stephens' Journal*, Vol. 4, p. 256; "Overthrowe . . . Idlenes" *Records of the Virginia Company*, Vol. III, p. 226; "The Journey of Francis Louis Michel," *VMHB* 24 (January 1916):6; "The Servants' Plot of 1663," *VMHB* 15 (July 1907):38; Bruce, *Economic History of Virginia*, Vol. II, p. 30; "(who in": *Stephens' Journal*, Vol. 4, p. 267.

41. "Minutes of the Council and General Court," *VMHB* 27 (April 1919):144; "Minutes of the Council and General Court," *VMHB* 19 (July 1911):226; Rutman and Rutman, *A Place in Time*, p. 133; "hang": *Archives of Maryland*, Vol. 10, p. 539. For a comparative perspective, see Lawrence W. Towner, "'A Fondness for Freedom': Servant Protest in Puritan Society," *WMQ* 3rd series 29 (April 1962):201–19; Beckles, *White Servitude and Black Slavery in Barbados*.

42. "Occasioning . . . complaint": "A Frivolous Lawsuit, 1681," in Billings, ed., *The Old Dominion in the Seventeenth Century*, p. 144; "wth . . . her": *Archives of Maryland*, Vol. 41, p. 68.

43. "from one": *Archives of Maryland*, Vol. 41, p. 479. See also Vol. 54, p. 116; Ames, ed. *County Court Records of Accomack-Northampton, Virginia, 1640–1645*, p. 291.

44. "Neger . . . coold not": *Archives of Maryland*, Vol. 53, p. 626.

45. "We and": Revel, "The Poor Unhappy Transported Felon's Sorrowful Account,"

pp. 188–94; Ames, ed., *County Court Records of Accomack-Northampton, Virginia, 1640–1645*, pp. 42, 54.

46. "abominable": Hening, ed., *Statutes at Large*, Vol. III, p. 86; "Victor . . . elsewhere": Helen T. Catterall, ed., *Judicial Cases Concerning American Slavery and the Negro*, Vol. I (Washington, DC: Carnegie Institution, 1926), p. 77; "English": Hening, ed., *Statutes at Large*, Vol. II, p. 117; Daniel E. Meaders, "Fugitive Slaves and Indentured Servants Before 1800," Ph. D. thesis, Yale University, 1990.

47. Compare, Winthrop Jordan's discussion of what he calls white colonists' "unthinking decision" to enslave blacks. See *White Over Black: American Attitudes Toward the Negro, 1550–1812* (Chapel Hill, NC: University of North Carolina Press, 1968), pp. 44–98.

48. "How shocking": quoted in Wood, *Slavery in Colonial Georgia*, pp. 42–3.

49. "shameless": Gilbert Chinard, ed., *A Huguenot Exile in Virginia or Voyages of a Frenchman Exiled for his Religion with a Description of Virginia and Maryland* (New York: Press of the Pioneers, 1934; orig. pub. 1687), p. 120.

50. Morgan, *American Slavery, American Freedom*.

51. See for example Warren M. Billings, "The Law of Servants and Slaves in Seventeenth-Century Virginia," *VMHB* 99 (January 1991):45-62, and "The Cases of Fernando and Elizabeth Key: A Note on the Status of Blacks in Seventeenth-Century Virginia," *WMQ* 30 3rd series (July 1973):467-74; Catterall, ed., *Judicial Cases Concerning American Slavery and the Negro*, Vols. I and IV; Oscar and Mary F. Handlin, "Origins of the Southern Labor System, *WMQ* 3rd series 7 (April 1950):199-22; Kelly, "Economic and Social Development of Seventeenth-Century Surry County"; Morgan, *American Slavery, American Freedom*; T. H. Breen and Stephen Innes, *"Myne Owne Ground": Race and Freedom on Virginia's Eastern Shore, 1640-1676* (New York: Oxford University Press, 1980); T. H. Breen, "A Changing Labor Force and Race Relations in Virginia, 1660-1710," *JSocH* 7 (Fall 1973):3-25. On Georgia, see Gray and Wood, "Transition"; Darold D. Wax, "'New Negroes Are Always in Demand': The Slave Trade in Eighteenth-Century Georgia," *GHQ* 68 (Summer 1984):193-220; Betty Wood, *Slavery in Colonial Georgia, 1730-1775* (Athens, GA: University of Georgia Press, 1984).

52. "of barbarous" quoted in Meaders, "Fugitive Slaves and Indentured Servants Before 1800," p. 76; "extreme[ly] . . . weather": *Archives of Maryland*, Vol. 45, pp. 205–06; *ibid.*, Vol. 41, p. 190; "ugly": *ibid.*, p. 205. See also Gerald W. Mullin, *Flight and Rebellion: Slave Resistance in Eighteenth Century Virginia* (New York: Oxford University Press, 1972); Thomas J. Little, "The South Carolina Slave Laws Reconsidered, 1670–1700," *SCHM* 94 (April 1993):86–101.

53. "lie . . . whatsoever": Hening, ed., *Statutes at Large*, Vol. 3, p. 86; *ibid.*, pp. 447–62; Ames, *Studies of the Virginia Eastern Shore in the Seventeenth Century*, p. 99; "the riotous": "Notes from the Council and General Court Records, 1641–1659," *VMHB* 8 (July 1900):71–2; "Negro . . . Contrivances": "A Rising on the Northern Neck, 1680," in Billings, ed., *The Old Dominion in the Seventeenth Century*, p. 160;

"perhaps": *Colonial Records of the State of Georgia*, Vol. 5: *Journal of the Earl of Egmont*, p. 303.

54. "danger": *Colonial Records of the State of Georgia*, Vol. 5, p. 251; "tinge": Tinling, ed., *Correspondence of the Three William Byrds*, pp. 487–88.

CHAPTER THREE

1. Quotations from Jack P. Greene, ed., *The Diary of Colonel Landon Carter of Sabine Hall, 1752–1778*, Vol. 2 (Charlottesville, VA: University Press of Virginia, 1965), pp. 1051–52, 1054–57, 1084–85, 1109–10. See also Gary B. Nash, "Slavery, Black Resistance, and the American Revolution," *GHQ* 77 (Spring 1993):64.

2. Quotation from Greene, ed., *Diary of Colonel Landon Carter . . .* , Vol. 2, pp. 1095–96; Michael Mullin, *Africa in America: Slave Acculturation and Resistance in the American South and the British Caribbean, 1736–1831* (Urbana, IL: University of Illinois Press, 1992), pp. 88–94, 138.

3. "are by": Hugh Jones, ed., *The Present State of Virginia, From Whence Is Inferred a Short View of Maryland and North Carolina* (Chapel Hill, NC: University of North Carolina Press, 1956; orig. pub. 1724), pp. 70–71.

4. For a discussion of these ideas in comparative historical perspective, see David Brion Davis, "At the Heart of Slavery," *NYRB* 43 (Oct. 17, 1996):51–4.

5. See, for example, Philip D. Morgan, "Black Life in Eighteenth-Century Charleston," *PAH* new series 1 (1984):187–232.

6. "Letters of William Fitzhugh," *VMHB* 1 (July 1893): 30;1 (April 1894):396; "Will of William Fitzhugh," *VMHB* 2 (January 1895):277–78. See also John Donald Duncan, "Servitude and Slavery in Colonial South Carolina, 1670–1776," Ph.D. thesis, Emory University, 1972, pp. 186–88; Lois Green Carr and Lorena S. Walsh, "Economic Diversification and Labor Organization in the Chesapeake, 1650–1820," in Stephen Innes, ed., *Work and Labor in Early America* (Chapel Hill, NC: University of North Carolina Press, 1988), pp. 144–88; Paul G. E. Clemens, *The Atlantic Economy and Colonial Maryland's Eastern Shore: From Tobacco to Grain* (Ithaca, NY: Cornell University Press, 1980).

7. See Peter Way, *Common Labour: Workers and the Digging of North American Canals, 1780–1860* (Cambridge, UK: Cambridge University Press, 1993), p. 2.

8. See for example Paul Finkelman, *Slavery and the Founders: Race and Liberty in the Age of Jefferson* (Armonk, NY: M. Sharpe, 1996); David Grimsted, "Anglo-American Racism and Phillis Wheatley's 'Sable Veil,' 'Length'ned Chain,' and 'Knitted Heart,'" in Ronald Hoffman and Peter J. Albert, eds., *Women in the Age of the American Revolution* (Charlottesville, VA: University Press of Virginia, 1989), pp. 414–16; Edmund Morgan, *American Slavery, American Freedom: The Ordeal of Colonial Virginia* (New York: W. W. Norton, 1975); John Chester Miller, *The Wolf by the Ears: Thomas Jefferson and Slavery* (New York: Free Press, 1977); Judith N. Shklar, "Redeeming American Political Theory," *APSR* 85 (March 1991):3.

9. *Virginia Gazette* advertisement in Michael Mullin, ed., *American Negro Slavery: A*

Documentary History (Columbia, SC: University of South Carolina Press, 1976), p. 82.

10. See Peter H. Wood, "The Changing Population of the Colonial South: An Overview by Race and Region, 1685–1790," in Peter H. Wood, Gregory A. Waselkov, and M. Thomas Hatley, eds., *Powhatan's Mantle: Indians in the Colonial Southeast* (Lincoln, NE: University of Nebraska Press, 1989), pp. 35–103. See also Philip D. Morgan, "British Encounters with Africans and African-Americans, circa 1600–1780," in Bernard Bailyn and Philip D. Morgan, eds., *Strangers Within the Realm: Cultural Margins of the First British Empire* (Chapel Hill, NC: University of North Carolina Press, 1991), pp. 157–219.

11. For a suggestive treatment of this broader theme, see Isabel Ferguson, "County Court in Virginia, 1700–1830," *NCHR* 8 (January 1931):14–40.

12. "rangeing . . . hunting": Walter Clark, ed., *State Records of North Carolina*, Vol. XVII (1781–85) (Goldsboro: Nash Bros., 1899), p. 175; James Merrell, *The Indians' New World: Catawbas and Their Neighbors from European Contact Through the Era of Removal* (Chapel Hill, NC: University of North Carolina Press, 1989); Thomas Hatley, "Cherokee Women Farmers Hold Their Ground," in Robert D. Mitchell, ed., *Appalachian Frontier Settlement and Development in the Preindustrial Era* (Lexington, KY: University Press of Kentucky, 1991), pp. 37–51; Wood, *et al.*; eds., *Powhatan's Mantle, passim.*

13. L. Leitch Wright, Jr., *The Only Land They Knew: The Tragic Story of the American Indians in the Old South* (New York: Free Press, 1981), pp. 148–49; Theda Perdue, *Slavery and the Evolution of Cherokee Society, 1540–1866* (Knoxville, TN: University of Tennessee Press, 1979).

14. "With the": Francis L. Hawks, *History of North Carolina from 1663 to 1729* (Fayetteville, NC: E. J. Hale & Son, 1858), p. 230; " . . . to live": Ann Maury, *Memoirs of a Huguenot Family* (New York: G. P. Putnam, 1872), pp. 351–52; "well . . . delight": Jones, *The Present State of Virginia*, p. 76; "their gleaming": Mark Van Doren, ed., *The Travels of William Bartram* (New York: Facsimile Library, Barnes and Noble, 1940), p. 257.

15. "great . . . indispensable": "Journal of Diron D'Artaquiette, 1722–1723," in Newton D. Mereness, ed., *Travels in the American Colonies* (New York: Antiquarian Press, 1961), p. 21; "the land . . . yourself": "Informations Concerning the Province of North Carolina (1773)," in William K. Boyd, ed., *Some Eighteenth-Century Tracts Concerning North Carolina* (Raleigh, NC: Edwards & Broughton, 1927), pp. 441, 445; "a Negro": J. P. Brissot de Warville, *New Travels in the United States of America, 1788*, ed. by Durand Echeverria (Cambridge, MA: Harvard University Press, 1964), p. 208; Warren B. Smith, *White Servitude in Colonial South Carolina* (Columbia, SC: University of South Carolina Press, 1961), p. 35.

16. "the bears": "Virginia Game, and Field Sports," *VMHB* 7 (October 1899):174; Thomas N. Ingersoll, "Free Blacks in a Slave Society: New Orleans, 1718–1812," *WMQ*, 3rd series 48 (April 1991):173–200; Daniel H. Usner, Jr., *Indians, Settlers and Slaves in a Frontier Exchange Economy: The Lower Mississippi Valley Before 1783*

(Chapel Hill, NC: University of North Carolina Press, 1992); William S. Willis, "Divide and Rule: Red, White, and Black in the Southeast," *JNH* 48 (July 1963):157–76; J. Reuben Sheeler, "The Negro on the Virginia Frontier," *JNH* 43 (October 1958):279–97.

17. "troublesome": Janet Schaw, *Journal of a Lady of Quality; Being the Narrative of a Journey from Scotland to the West Indies, North Carolina, and Portugal . . . 1774 to 1776*, ed. by Evangeline Walker Andrews (New Haven: Yale University Press, 1934), p. 195; Peter Wood, *Black Majority: Negroes in Colonial South Carolina from 1670 Through the Stono Rebellion* (New York: Knopf, 1974); James M. Clifton, "Golden Grains of White: Rice Planting on the Lower Cape Fear," *NCHR* 50 (October 1973): 365–93.

18. Mullin, *Africa in America*, pp. 13–33; Daniel C. Littlefield, *Rice and Slaves: Ethnicity and the Slave Trade in Colonial South Carolina* (Baton Rouge, LA: Louisiana State University Press, 1981); Darold D. Wax, "Preferences for Slaves in Colonial America," *JNH* 58 (October 1973):371–401; Lorena S. Walsh, "'A Place in Time' Regained: A Fuller History of Colonial Chesapeake Slavery Through Biography," in Larry E. Hudson, Jr., ed., *Working Toward Freedom: Slave Society and Domestic Economy in the American South* (Rochester, NY: University of Rochester Press, 1994), pp. 1–32. See also Betty Wood, *Slavery in Colonial Georgia, 1730–1775* (Athens, GA: University of Georgia Press, 1984), p. 103.

19. "new . . . Soul": "Eighteenth Century Maryland as Portrayed in the 'Itinerant Observations' of Edward Kimber," *MdHM* 51 (December 1956):328; "work . . . pray": Thomas Bluett, *Some Memoirs of the Life of Job, the Son of Solomon the High Priest of Boonda in Africa . . .* [1734], in Philip D. Curtain, *et al.*, eds., *Africa Remembered: Narratives by West Africans from the Era of the Slave Trade* (Madison, WI: University of Wisconsin Press, 1967), pp. 41–2; "an Eboe . . . negro": "Extract from the Virginia Gazette 1752 and 1755," *VMHB* 25 (January 1917):19; "a fine": "Extract from the Virginia Gazette 1752 and 1755," *VMHB* 24 (October 1916): 412; Mullin, *Africa in America*.

20. "played": quoted in John Thornton, *Africa and Africans in the Making of the Atlantic World, 1400–1660* (Cambridge, UK: Cambridge University Press, 1992), pp. 226–28; "Negro Ball . . . it": *The Journal of Nicholas Cresswell, 1774–1777* (New York: Dial Press, 1924), pp. 16–17; Allan Kulikoff, *Tobacco and Slaves: The Development of Southern Cultures in the Chesapeake, 1680–1800* (Chapel Hill, NC: University of North Carolina Press, 1986), pp. 329–49; "intriguing . . . people": "Stranger" writing in *South Carolina Gazette*, in Wood, *Black Majority*, p. 343.

21. "the various uses . . . victuals": Schaw, *Journal of a Lady*, p. 176; Timothy Silver, *A New Face on the Countryside: Indians, Colonists, and Slaves in South Atlantic Forests, 1500–1800* (Cambridge, MA: Harvard University Press, 1990), p. 152; Wood, *Black Majority*, pp. 13–62; Charles Joyner, *Down by the Riverside: A South Carolina Slave Community* (Urbana, IL: University of Illinois Press, 1984), pp. 76, 71; "drawn": quoted in Thad W. Tate, *The Negro in Eighteenth-Century Williamsburg* (Charlottesville, VA: University Press of Virginia, 1965), p. 178; "Slave Resis-

tance," in Jacob Ernest Cooke, ed., *Encyclopedia of the North American Colonies*, Vol. II (New York: Charles Scribner's Sons, 1993), p. 213.

22. "sly": Henry Laurens quoted in Robert Olwell, "'A Reckoning of Accounts': Patriarchy, Market Relations, and Control on Henry Laurens's Lowcountry Plantations, 1762–1785," in Hudson, ed., *Working Toward Freedom*, p. 37; *South Carolina Gazette* quoted in Leila Sellers, *Charleston Business on the Eve of the American Revolution* (Chapel Hill, NC: University of North Carolina Press, 1934), p. 107; "Negro Quarter . . . stolen": "Travel Diary of Bishop Reichel, Mrs. Reichel, and Christian Heckewelder from Salem to Lititz, 1780," in Mereness, ed., *Travels in the American Colonies*, p. 607; Morgan, "Black Life in Eighteenth-Century Charleston," p. 195.

23. "Carter Papers," *VMHB* 7 (July 1899):64–8; Brenda E. Stevenson, *Life in Black and White: Family and Community in the Slave South* (New York: Oxford University Press, 1996), pp. 329–39; Kulikoff, *Tobacco and Slaves*, p. 386; Philip D. Morgan and Michael L. Nicholls, "Slaves in Piedmont Virginia, 1720–1790," *WMQ* 3rd series 46 (April 1989):211–51.

24 Douglas Deal, "A Constricted World: Free Blacks on Virginia's Eastern Shore, 1680–1750," in Lois Green Carr, Philip D. Morgan, and Jean B. Russo, eds., *Colonial Chesapeake Society* (Chapel Hill, NC: University of North Carolina Press, 1988), pp. 275–305; Ira Berlin, *Slaves Without Masters: The Free Negro in the Antebellum South* (New York: Vintage Books, 1974), p. 3; Kathleen M. Brown, *Good Wives, Nasty Wenches, and Anxious Patriarchs: Gender, Race and Power in Colonial Virginia* (Chapel Hill, NC: University of North Carolina Press, 1996); Michael L. Nicholls, "Passing Through This Troublesome World: Free Blacks in the Early Southside," *VMHB* 92 (January 1984):50–70.

25. "Releese": Thomas N. Ingersoll, "'Releese Us Out of this Cruell Bondegg': An Appeal from Virginia in 1723'" *WMQ* 3rd series, 51 (October 1994):781; Joan R. Gunderson, "The Double Bonds of Race and Sex: Black and White Women in a Colonial Virginia Parish," *JSouH* 52 (August 1986):371.

26. C. Robert Haywood, "Mercantilism and Colonial Slave Labor, 1700–1763," *JSouH* 23 (November 1957):454–64; Introduction, Carr, *et al.*, eds., *Colonial Chesapeake Society*, pp. 4–6; Ruth Allison Hudnut and Hayes Baker-Crothers, "Acadian Transients in South Carolina," *AHR* 43 (April 1938):500–13. See also E. Merton Coulter, "The Acadians in Georgia," *GHQ* 47 (March 1963):68–75.

27. James Davie Butler, "British Convicts Shipped to American Colonies," *AHR* 2 (October 1896):12–33; Daniel E. Meaders, "Fugitive Slaves and Indentured Servants Before 1800," Ph.D. thesis, Yale University, 1990. See also A. Roger Ekirch, "Great Britain's Secret Convict Trade to America, 1783–1784," *AHR* 89 (December 1984):1285–91; Kenneth Morgan, "The Organization of the Convict Trade to Maryland: Stevenson, Randolph & Cheston, 1768–1775," *WMQ* 3rd series 42 (January 1985):201–27.

28. "Proved . . . masters": Smith, *White Servitude in Colonial South Carolina*, Appendix II, pp. 119–27.

29. Lois Green Carr, "Diversification in the Colonial Chesapeake: Somerset County, Maryland, in Comparative Perspective," in Carr, *et al.*, eds., *Colonial Chesapeake Society*, pp. 342–48; William D. Hoyt, Jr., "The White Servants at 'Northampton': 1772–74," *MdHM* 33 (June 1938):126–33. See also Edward Miles Riley, ed., *The Journal of John Harrower, an Indentured Servant in the Colony of Virginia, 1773–76* (New York: Holt, Rinehart & Winston, 1963), pp. 166–67.

30. Wood, *Black Majority*, pp. 308–30; Harvey Wish, "American Slave Insurrections Before 1861," *JNH* 22 (July 1937):299–329; "Negro . . . him": "Extract from Virginia Gazette 1752 and 1755," *VMHB* 24 (October 1916):412; "Negroe . . . perished": "Extracts from the Virginia Gazette, 1752 and 1753," *VMHB* 25 (January 1917):13.

31. Kathleen Deagon and Darcie MacMahon, *Fort Mose: Colonial America's Black Fortress of Freedom* (Gainesville, FL: University Press of Florida, 1995); Herbert Aptheker, "Maroons Within the Present Limits of the United States," *JNH* 24 (April 1939):167–84; "Indian . . . neighborhood," quoted in James Hugo Johnston, "Documentary Evidence of the Relations of Negroes and Indians," *JNH* 14 (January 1929):32.

32. "white Indians": Rachel N. Klein, *Unification of a Slave State: The Rise of the Planter Class in the South Carolina Backcountry, 1760–1808* (Chapel Hill, NC: University of North Carolina Press, 1990), p. 51; Michel Sobel, *The World They Made Together: Black and White Values in Eighteenth-Century Virginia* (Princeton: Princeton University Press, 1987); "rusticks . . . imagine": Schaw, *Journal of a Lady*, pp. 153, 157; "divers": Virginia Assembly quoted in Fairfax Harrison, "When the Convicts Came," *VMHB* 30 (July 1922): 257.

33. "is carried": Henry Lee, "Home Manufacturers in Virginia in 1791,"*WMQ* 2nd series 2 (April 1922):140; U. B. Phillips, ed., *Plantation and Frontier, 1649–1863*, Vol. II of *A Documentary History of American Industrial Society*, ed. by John R. Commons (Cleveland: Arthur A. Clark Co., 1910), p. 315. See also Carole Shammas, "Black Women's Work and the Evolution of Plantation Society in Virginia," *LH* 26 (Winter 1985):5–28; Julia Cherry Spruill, *Women's Life and Work in the Southern Colonies* (New York: W. W. Norton, 1972; orig. pub. 1938), pp. 75–6; Gunderson, "Double Bonds of Race and Sex."

34. "an . . . pride": *Virginia Gazette* ad in Mullin, ed., *American Negro Slavery*, p. 114. See two articles in Howard B. Rock, Paul A. Gilje, and Robert Asher, eds., *American Artisans: Crafting Social Identity, 1750–1850* (Baltimore: Johns Hopkins University Press, 1995): Christine Daniels, "From Father to Son: Economic Roots of Craft Dynasties in Eighteenth Century Maryland" (pp. 3–17), and Michele K. Gillespie, "Planters in the Making: Artisanal Opportunity in Georgia, 1790–1830" (pp. 33–47).

35. Jean B. Russo, "Self-Sufficiency and Local Exchange: Free Craftsmen in the Rural Chesapeake Economy," in Carr, *et al.*, eds., *Colonial Chesapeake Society*, pp. 389–432; Christine Daniels, "'WANTED: A Blacksmith Who Understands Plantation Work': Artisans in Maryland, 1700–1810," *WMQ* 50 3rd series (October

1993):743–67; "Handycraft": quoted in Smith, *White Servitude in Colonial South Carolina*, pp. 34–5; "very wild": Charles D. Cordle, ed., "Notes and Documents: The John Tobler Manuscripts: An Account of German–Swiss Emigrants in South Carolina," *JSouH* 5 (February 1939):89; Tina H. Sheller, "Freemen, Servants, and Slaves: Artisans and the Craft Structure of Revolutionary Baltimore Town," and James Sidbury, "Slave Artisans in Richmond Virginia, 1780–1810," both in Rock, *et al.*, *American Artisans*, pp. 17–32, 48–64, respectively.

36. See for example Christine Daniels, "Gresham's Laws: Labor Management on an Early-Eighteenth-Century Chesapeake Plantation," *JSouH* 62 (May 1996): 205–37.

37. "Virginians . . . etc.": de Warville, *New Travels in the United States of America*, p. 347; "and you": Washington quoted in Calvin B. Coulter, Jr., "The Import Trade of Colonial Virginia," *WMQ* 3rd series 2 (July 1945):303.

38. Douglas Southall Freeman, *George Washington: A Biography*, Vol. 3: *Planter and Patriot* (New York: Charles Scribner's Sons, 1951), pp. 45–7, 63–7. See also Sarah S. Hughes, "Slaves for Hire: The Allocation of Black Labor in Elizabeth City County, Virginia, 1782 to 1810," *WMQ* 3rd series 35 (April 1978):260–86.

39. Willard F. Bliss, "The Rise of Tenancy in Virginia," *VMHB* 58 (October 1950):429; "workd . . . with": Donald Jackson and Dorothy Twohig, eds., *The Diaries of George Washington*, Vol. II (Charlottesville, VA: University Press of Virginia, 1976–79), pp. 164, 172, 244.

40. "both": "Letters of George Washington Bearing on the Negro," *JNH* 2 (October 1917):411.

41. "regulating . . . woods": Alan Gallay, ed., *Voices of the Old South: Eyewitness Accounts, 1528–1861* (Athens, GA: University of Georgia Press, 1994), pp. 162–67.

42. Alan D. Watson, "Impulse Toward Independence: Resistance and Rebellion Among North Carolina Slaves, 1750–1775," *JNH* 63 (Fall 1978):317–28; "impudent . . . do so": North Carolina slaveholder quoted in Jeffrey J. Crow, *The Black Experience in Revolutionary North Carolina* (Raleigh, NC: Department of Cultural Resources, Division of Archives and History, 1977), p. 35; "she will": Baltimore slaveholder quoted in Benjamin Quarles, *The Negro in the American Revolution* (Chapel Hill, NC: University of North Carolina Press, 1961), p. 126. See also Edmund Morgan, *American Slavery, American Freedom: The Ordeal of Colonial Virginia* (New York: W. W. Norton, 1975); F. Nwabueze Okoye, "Chattel Slavery as the Nightmare of the American Revolutionaries," *WMQ* 3rd series 37 (January 1980):3–29.

43. Sidney Kaplan, "The 'Domestic Insurrections' of the Declaration of Independence," *JNH* 61 (July 1976):243–55; "enemies": quoted in Sylvia Frey, *Water from the Rock: Black Resistance in a Revolutionary Age* (Princeton: Princeton University Press, 1991), p. 68.

44. "lord . . . fleet": *Virginia Gazette* (March 22, 1776) in Mullin, ed., *American Negro Slavery*, p. 121; Peter H. Wood, "'The Dream Deferred': Black Freedom Struggles on the Eve of White Independence," in Gary Y. Okihiro, ed., *In Resistance:*

Studies in African-Caribbean and Afro-American History (Amherst, MA: University of Massachusetts Press, 1986), pp. 166–87; Quarles, *Negro in the American Revolution*, pp. 199, 144; "We had": Johann Ewald quoted in Frey, *Water from the Rock*, p. 170.

45. "They ought": "Letters of George Washington Bearing on the Negro," p. 412; Luther P. Jackson, "Virginia Negro Soldiers and Seamen in the Revolutionary War" (Norfolk, VA: Guide Quality Press, 1944), pp. 13–14, 29.

46. Introduction, and Richard S. Dunn, "Black Society in the Chesapeake, 1776–1810," in Ira Berlin and Ronald Hoffman, eds., *Slavery and Freedom in the Age of the American Revolution* (Charlottesville, VA: University Press of Virginia, 1983), pp. xv–xxv, 49–82; Berlin, *Slaves Without Masters*, p. 55; Winthrop D. Jordan, *White Over Black: American Attitudes Toward the Negro, 1550–1812* (Chapel Hill, NC: University of North Carolina Press, 1968), pp. 269–314; Mary Beth Norton, "The Fate of Some Black Loyalists of the American Revolution," *JNH* 58 (October 1973):402–26.

47. Berlin, *Slaves Without Masters*, pp. 56, 47; Barbara Jeanne Fields, *Slavery and Freedom on the Middle Ground: Maryland During the Nineteenth Century* (New Haven, CT: Yale University Press, 1985), pp. 23–39.

48. "The female": J. F. D. Smyth, *A Tour in the United States of America, Containing An Account of the Present Situation of That Country*, Vol. I (Dublin: J. Perrin, 1784), pp. 118–21; Allan Kulikoff, "Uprooted Peoples: Black Migrants in the Age of the American Revolution 1790–1820," in Berlin and Hoffman, eds., *Slavery and Freedom in the Age of the American Revolution*, pp. 143–67.

49. Jacqueline Jones, "Race, Sex, and Self-Evident Truths: The Status of Slave Women During the Era of the American Revolution," in Ronald Hoffman and Peter J. Albert, eds., *Women in the Age of the American Revolution* (Charlottesville, VA: University Press of Virginia, 1989), pp. 293–337; Mamie Locke, "From Three-Fifths to Zero: Implications of the Constitution for African-American Women, 1787–1870," in Darlene Clark Hine, Wilma King, and Linda Reed, eds., *"We Specialize in the Wholly Impossible": A Reader in Black Women's History* (New York: Carlson, 1995), pp. 225–36.

50. Quotations from Paul Edwards, ed., *Equiano's Travels: His Autobiography: The Interesting Narrative of the Life of Olaudah Equiano or Gustavus Vassa the African* (Portsmouth, NH: Heinemann, 1967; orig. pub. 1789), pp. 21, 43, 99, 157.

51. Brenda Stevenson, "Distress and Discord in Virginia Slave Families, 1830–1860," in Carol Bleser, ed., *In Joy and in Sorrow: Women, Family, and Marriage in the Victorian South, 1830–1990* (New York: Oxford University Press, 1991), pp. 103–24; Ira Berlin, "Time, Space, and the Evolution of Afro-American Society in British Mainland North America," *AHR* 85 (February 1980):44–78; Allan Gally, *The Formation of a Planter Elite: Jonathan Bryan and the Southern Colonial Frontier* (Athens, GA: University of Georgia, 1989); Frey, *Water from the Rock*, p. 150; Barbara Jeanne Fields, "Slavery, Race and Ideology in the United States of America," *NLR* (May 1990):95–188; David Brion Davis, *The Problem of Slavery in the Age of*

Revolution, 1770–1823 (Ithaca, NY: Cornell University Press, 1975); Robert D. Mitchell, *Commercialization and Frontier: Perspectives on the Early Shenandoah Valley* (Charlottesville, VA: University Press of Virginia, 1977); Michael Tadman, *Speculators and Slaves: Masters, Traders and Slaves in the Old South* (Madison, WI: University of Wisconsin Press, 1989).

52. "there are": quoted in Ellen Eslinger, "The Shape of Slavery on the Kentucky Frontier, 1775–1800," *RKHS* 92 (Winter 1994):21; Neal Hammon and James Russell Harris, eds., "'In a Dangerous Situation': The Letters of Col. John Floyd, 1774–83," *RKHS* 83 (Summer 1985):217, 220.

CHAPTER FOUR

1. Winter quotations in James Phinney Baxter, ed., *Documentary History of the State of Maine*, Vol. 3: *The Trelawny Papers* (Portland, ME: Hoyt, Fogg, & Donham, 1884), pp. 25, 29, 44.
2. *Ibid.*, pp. 108, 113, 114, 164.
3. *Ibid.*, pp. 166, 465.
4. James Henretta, *The Evolution of American Society, 1700–1815: An Interdisciplinary Analysis* (New York: D. C. Heath, 1973); John J. McCusker and Russell R. Menard, *The Economy of British America, 1607–1789* (Chapel Hill, NC: University of North Carolina Press, 1985), pp. 91–116, 211–57.
5. "men . . . servants": Alden Vaughan, ed., *William Wood's New England's Prospect* (Amherst, MA: University of Massachusetts Press, 1977; orig. pub. 1634), p. 68.
6. Letter from Silvanus Davis & Others, Falmouth, July, 1689, in James Phinney Baxter, ed., *Documentary History of the State of Maine*, Vol. IX (Portland: LeFavor-Towner Co., 1907), p. 15.
7. "there is": Wood's *New England's Prospect*, p. 72.
8. Johnson quotations in J. Franklin Jameson, ed., *Johnson's Wonder-Working Providence, 1628–1651* (New York: Barnes and Noble, 1952; orig. pub. 1653), pp. 37, 113, 33, 50, 128, 34; John E. Ferling, *A Wilderness of Miseries: War and Warriors in Early America* (Westport, CT: Greenwood Press, 1980).

On the significance of the Indian threat as a source of identity for the Puritans, see Michael Zuckerman, "Identity in British America: Unease in Eden," in Nicholas P. Canny and Anthony Pagden, eds., *Colonial Identity in the Atlantic World, 1500–1800* (Princeton, NJ: Princeton University Press, 1987), pp. 135–36.
9. See Dorothy V. Jones, *License for Empire: Colonialism by Treaty in Early America* (Chicago: University of Chicago Press, 1982); Allan R. Miller and Peter Maslowski, *For the Common Defense: A Military History of the United States* (New York: Free Press, 1984); William Pencak, *War, Politics, and Revolution in Provincial Massachusetts* (Boston: Northeastern University Press, 1981).
10. "defensive": Alan Taylor, *Liberty Men and Great Proprietors: The Revolutionary Settlement and the Maine Frontier, 1760–1820* (Chapel Hill, NC: University of North Carolina Press, 1990); Thomas L. Purvis, "Origins and Patterns of Agrarian

Unrest in New Jersey, 1735–1754," *WMQ* 3rd series 39 (October 1982):600–27; Staughton Lynd, *Anti-Federalism in Dutchess County, New York: A Study of Democracy and Class Conflict in the Revolutionary Era* (Chicago: Loyola University Press, 1962); Matt B. Jones, *Vermont in the Making, 1750–1770* (Cambridge, MA: Harvard University Press, 1939); Edward Countryman, "Out of the Bounds of the Law: Northern Land Rioters in the Eighteenth Century," in Alfred T. Young, ed., *The American Revolution: Explorations in the History of American Radicalism* (DeKalb, IL: Northern Illinois University Press, 1976).

11. McCusker and Menard, *Economy of British America*, pp. 103, 203; Philip Greven, *Four Generations: Land, Population, and Family in Colonial Andover, Massachusetts* (Ithaca, NY: Cornell University Press, 1970); Bernard Bailyn, *Peopling of British North America: An Introduction* (New York: Knopf, 1986), p. 93; "Blooddy": "Second Memorial from Mr. Gray" (1725) in William A. Whitehead, ed., *Documents Relating to the Colonial History of the State of New Jersey*, Vol. V: *1720–37* (Newark: Daily Advertiser, 1882), p. 114; "annoying": Richard Partridge to the Lords of Trade, c. 1750, in Gertrude S. Kimball, ed., *The Correspondence of the Colonial Governors of Rhode Island, 1723–1745* (Boston: Houghton Mifflin, 1903), p. 113; "to watch": James MacSparran, *America Dissected, Being a Full and True Account of All the American Colonies* (1753), in Wilkins Updike, ed., *A History of the Episcopal Church in Narragansett, Rhode Island*, Vol. III (Boston: Merrymount Press, 1907), p. 21. See also Francis G. Wolett, ed., *The Diary of Ebenezer Parkman, 1703–1782* (Worcester, MA: American Antiquarian Society, 1974), p. 134.

12. "in this . . . Labour": "Petition from Pownalborough, 1764," in *Collections of the Maine Historical Society*, 2nd series, Vol. VIII, pp. 359–60; "Small": *Documentary History of the State of Maine*, Vol. IX, p. 10; "Sundery": *ibid.*, p. 13; "the Tarr": *ibid.*, p. 283. See also Jacob B. Moore, ed., *Collections of the New Hampshire Historical Society*, Vol. III (Manchester, NH: John B. Clarke, 1870; orig. pub. 1832), pp. 45–6, 53, 54, 57; Virginia DeJohn Anderson, "King Philip's Herds: Indians, Colonists, and the Problem of Livestock in Early New England," *WMQ* 3d series 51 (October 1994):601–24; James T. Lemon, *The Best Poor Man's Country: A Geographical Study of Early Southeastern Pennsylvania* (Baltimore: Johns Hopkins University Press, 1972), p. 108; Charles R. Corning, "Mr. Corning's Address (1895)," *Proceedings of the New Hampshire Historical Society*, Vol. II (Concord, NH: For the Society, 1895), pp. 138–39.

    See also Adolph B. Benson, ed., *Peter Kalm's Travels in North America*, Vol. II (New York: Dover Publications, 1937; orig. pub. 1770), p. 712; "Report of Governor Printz, 1644," J. Franklin Jameson, ed., *Original Narratives of Early American History: Narratives of Early Pennsylvania, West New Jersey, and Delaware, 1630–1707* (New York: Charles Scribner's Sons, 1912), p. 103.

13. "we Cannot": Stephen Innes, *Labor in a New Land: Economy and Society in Seventeenth-Century Springfield* (Princeton: Princeton University Press, 1983), pp. 19, 159; Taylor, *Liberty Men and Great Proprietors*.

14. Fred Anderson, *A People's Army: Massachusetts Soldiers and Society in the Seven*

Years' War (Chapel Hill, NC: University of North Carolina Press, 1984), pp. 38, 46, 81; Samuel D. McKee, Jr., *Labor in Colonial New York, 1664–1776* (Port Washington, NY: Ira J. Friedman, 1935), p. 26. See also *Documentary History of the State of Maine*, Vol. IX, p. 2.

15. Anderson, *A People's Army*, p. 168; William Pencak, "Warfare and Political Change in Mid-Eighteenth-Century Massachusetts," in Peter Marshall and Glyn Williams, eds., *The British Atlantic Empire Before the American Revolution* (London: Cass, 1980), pp. 58–9; "that . . . any thing": Gov. Hamilton of E. New Jersey to Gov. Fletcher of New York (1696), in *Documents Related to the Colonial History of New Jersey*, Vol. II: *1687–1703*, p. 115.

16. "Sick": *Documentary History of the State of Maine*, Vol. IX, p. 57; "dangerous": Charles Thornton Libby, ed., *Province and Court Records of Maine*, Vol. II: *York County Records (1672–79)* (Portland, ME: Maine Historical Society, 1928),p. 281; Vol. IV, p. 388; James Kirby Martin, "'A Most Undisciplined, Profligate Crew': Protest and Defiance in the Continental Ranks, 1776–1783," in Ronald Hoffman and Peter J. Albert, eds., *Arms and Independence: The Military Character of the American Revolution* (Charlottesville, VA: University Press of Virginia, 1984), pp. 119–41; Steven Rosswurm, "The Philadelphia Militia, 1775–1783: Active Duty and Active Radicalism," in *ibid.*, pp. 75–118.

17. "Five to": *Documentary History of the State of Maine*, Vol. IX, p. 253; "Several": *Diary of Ebenezer Parkman*, p. 82; Sharon Y. Salinger, *"To Serve Well and Faithfully": Labor and Indentured Servants in Pennsylvania, 1682–1800* (Cambridge, UK: Cambridge University Press, 1987), pp. 106–07; Darold D. Wax, "The Negro Slave Trade in Colonial Pennsylvania," Ph.D. thesis, University of Washington, 1962, pp. 46, 48.

On the demographic consequences of war, see Gary B. Nash, "The Failure of Female Factory Labor in Colonial Boston," *LH* 20 (Spring 1979):165–88; Douglas Lamar Jones, "The Strolling Poor: Transiency in Eighteenth-Century Massachusetts," *JSocH* 8 (Spring 1975):28–54; McKee, *Labor in Colonial New York*, pp. 10–11.

18. "archerie": John Russell Bartlett, ed., *Records of the Colony of Rhode Island and Providence Plantations*, Vol. I (1636–1663) (Providence, RI: A. C. Greene & Bros., 1856–65), p. 186; Roger Williams, "To the Town of Providence," c. January 1654–55 in Glenn W. LaFantasie, ed., *The Correspondence of Roger Williams*, Vol. II *(1654–1682)* (Hanover, NH: Brown University Press/University Press of New England, 1988), p. 423; "war": Jameson, ed., *Johnson's Wonder-Working Providence*, p. 100; "with stones . . . bones": Robert Roules of Marblehead, in James Axtell, ed., "The Vengeful Women of Marblehead: Robert Roules's Deposition of 1677," *WMQ* 3rd series 31 (October 1974):652; Christine Leigh Heyerman, *Commerce and Culture: The Maritime Communities of Colonial Massachusetts, 1690–1750* (New York: W. W. Norton, 1984), pp. 209–30; "she thought": "Mr. Corning's Address," p. 143.

19. "a dull": Rev. William Hubbard quoted in Axtell, "Vengeful Women of Marble-

head," p. 647; John Smith, "A Description of New England" (1616), in Peter Force, ed., *Tracts and Other Papers, Relating Principally to the Origin, Settlement and Progress of the Colonies in North America. . .* , Vol. I (New York: Peter Smith, 1647), p. 272 ("let not the meannesse of the word *Fish* distaste you, for it will afford as good gold as the mines of *Guiana* or *Tumbata*, with lesse hazard and charge, and more certaintie and facilitie. . . .")

20. See for example J. B. Walker, "Major Daniel Livermore, Citizen Soldier of the Revolution," *Proceedings of the New Hampshire Historical Society*, Vol. III *(June 1895 to 1899)* (Concord, NH: Published for the Society, 1902), p. 67.

21. Roger Williams to John Winthrop, New Providence, 1637, *Winthrop Papers*, Vol. III ((Boston: Massachusetts Historical Society, 1929), p. 436.

22. "time": Wood, *New England's Prospect*, p. 107; "they have": "New-England's Plantation, or, a Short and True Description of the Commodities and Discommodities of That Countrey," in Force, ed., *Tracts and Other Papers*, Vol. I, p. 13; "nominal . . . quarreling": Francis Daniel Pastorius, "Circumstantial Geographical Description of Pennsylvania" (1700), in Jameson, ed., *Original Narratives of Early American History*, p. 420.

23. See William Sturtevant, ed., *Handbook of North American Indians*, Vol. 15: *Northeast*, ed. by Bruce G. Trigger (Washington, DC: Smithsonian Institution Press, 1978); Carl Waldman, *Atlas of the North American Indian* (New York: Facts on File, 1985), pp. 31–32; S. F. Cook, *Indian Population of New England in the Seventeenth Century* (Berkeley: University of California Press, 1976).

24. Richard R. Johnson, "The Search for a Usable Indian: An Aspect of the Defense of Colonial New England," *JAH* 64 (December 1977):623–51; Ola Elizabeth Winslow, *John Eliot: "Apostle to the Indians"* (Boston: Houghton Mifflin, 1968); "slave": Richard VanDerBeets, ed., *Held Captive by Indians: Selected Narratives, 1642–1836* (Knoxville, TN: University of Tennessee Press, 1973), p. 34; "fell": Willam Bradford, *Of Plymouth Plantation, 1620–1647* (New York: Modern Library, 1981), p. 128. For examples of captives who referred to Indians as masters and mistresses, see VanDerBeets, ed., *Held Captive by the Indians*, p. 54 (Mary Rowlandson); p. 106 (John Gyles); p. 135 (Elizabeth Hanson). See also Perry Miller and Thomas H. Johnson, eds., *The Puritans* (New York: American Book Co., 1938), p. 533 (John Williams).

25. James Axtell, *The European and the Indian: Essays in the Ethnohistory of Colonial North America* (New York: Oxford University Press, 1981); Neal Salisbury, *Manitou and Providence: Indians, Europeans, and the Making of New England, 1500–1643* (New York: Oxford University Press, 1982); Neal Salisbury, "Red Puritans: The 'Praying Indians' of Massachusetts Bay and John Eliot," *WMQ* 3rd series 31 (January 1974):27–54; "Industrious": William S. Simmons and Cheryl L. Simmons, eds., *Old Light on Separate Ways: The Narragansett Diary of Joseph Fish, 1765–1776* (Hanover, NH: University Press of New England, 1982), p. 3.

26. "our friend": *Collections of the New Hampshire Historical Society*, Vol. III, p. 58; *Documentary History of the State of Maine*, Vol. IV, pp. 458–62; "Five Hundred": *Docu-*

ments Relating to the Colonial History of the State of New Jersey, Vol. IV: *Newspaper Extracts*, p. 310; Anderson, *A People's Army*, p. 10; Simmons and Simmons, eds., *Old Light on Separate Ways*, p. 36.

27. Douglas E. Leach, *Flintlock and Tomahawk: New England in King Philip's War* (New York: W. W. Norton, 1966), p. 154; George M. Badge, "Soldiers in King Philip's War," *NEHGR* 44 (1890):270–79, 373–81; "weary": *Documentary History of the State of Maine*, Vol. IX, p. 263; "French . . . fidelity": J. Dudley to "My Lords," Boston, 1712, in *ibid.*, p. 337; Gage and Amherst quoted in Patrick Frazier, *The Mohicans of Stockbridge* (Lincoln, NE: University of Nebraska Press, 1992), pp. 128–29.

28. Salisbury, *Manitou and Providence*, pp. 50–56; Patrick M. Malone, "Changing Military Technology Among the Indians of Southern New England, 1600–1677," *AQ* 25 (March 1973):48–63; Bruce J. Bourque and Ruth Holmes Whitehead, "Tarrentines and the Introduction of European Trade Goods in the Gulf of Maine," *Eh* 32 (1985):327–41; Calvin Martin, *Keepers of the Game: Indian-Animal Relationships and the Fur Trade* (Berkeley: University of California Press, 1978); James H. Merrell, "'The Customes of Our Countrey': Indians and Colonists in Early America," in Bernard Bailyn and Philip D. Morgan, eds., *Strangers Within the Realm: Cultural Margins of the First British Empire* (Chapel Hill, NC: University of North Carolina Press, 1991), pp. 117–56.

29. "an aversion": Carl Bridenbaugh, ed., "Patrick M'Robert's Tour Through Part of the North Provinces of America," *PMHB* 59 (1935):170; "They are": Carl Bridenbaugh, ed., *Gentleman's Progress: The Itinerarium of Dr. Alexander Hamilton, 1744* (Chapel Hill, NC: University of North Carolina Press, 1948), p. 172; "be right . . . attendance": Wood, *New England's Prospect*, p. 87; William Cronon, *Changes in the Land: Indians, Colonists, and the Ecology of New England* (New York: Hill & Wang, 1983), p. 52.

30. "lazie": Cronon, *Changes in the Land*, p. 52; "hardnesse . . . their extraordinary": *Correspondence of Roger Williams*, Vol. II, p. 590; Howard S. Russell, *Indian New England Before the Mayflower* (Hanover, NH: University Press of New England), pp. 96–103.

31. "do the": *Peter Kalm's Travels*, p. 731; Jean Marie O'Brien, "Community Dynamics in the Indian-English Town of Natick, Massachusetts, 1650–1790," Ph. D. thesis, University of Chicago, 1990, p. 100; "many familyes": *Documents Relating to the Colonial History of New Jersey*, Vol. V *(1720–1737)*, pp. 114–15.

32. "If one": Pastorius, "Circumstantial Geographical Description of Pennsylvania," p. 386; Simmons and Simmons, eds., *Old Light on Separate Ways*, p. 52; "summarily" and "I make": both quoted in Howard S. Russell, *A Long, Deep Furrow: Three Centuries of Farming in New England* (Hanover, NH: University Press of New England, 1976), pp. 188–89; Kenneth M. Morrison, "'That Art of Coyning Christians': John Eliot and the Praying Indians of Massachusetts," *Eh* 21 (Winter 1974):77–92.

33. "divers": Connecticut Statute of 1715, quoted in Bernard C. Steiner, *History of Slavery in Connecticut* (Baltimore: John Hopkins University Press, 1893), pp. 14–15; Nathaniel B. Shurtleff, ed., *Records of the Colony of New Plymouth in New*

England (New York: AMS Press; orig. pub. 1855–61), pp. 164–65; *Correspondence of Roger Williams*, Vol. II, pp. 711–12; Richard Shannon Moss, *Slavery on Long Island: A Study in Local Institutional and Early African-American Communal Life* (New York: Garland Press, 1993), pp. 10–12; Edgar J. McManus, *Law and Liberty in Early New England: Criminal Justice and Due Process, 1620–1692* (Amherst, MA: University of Massachusetts Press, 1993), p. 129.

34. "48 . . . stummach": Israel Stoughton to John Winthrop, 1637, *Winthrop Papers*, Vol. III, p. 435; *Correspondence of Roger Williams*, Vol. II, p. 109; 86–9, 97, 109–10, 122, 157–58; "1 Boy": "Indian Children Put to Service," *NEHGR* 8 (July 1854):270–73.

35. John A. Sainsbury, "Indian Labor in Early Rhode Island," *NEQ* 48 (September 1975):384; Paul R. Campbell and Glenn W. LaFantasie, "Scattered to the Winds of Heaven—Narragansett Indians, 1676–1880," *RIH* 37 (August 1978):67–75; Hamilton, *Gentleman's Progress*, p. 168; Merrell, "'The Customes of Our Countrey,'": pp. 117–56; O'Brien, "Community Dynamics in the Indian-English Town of Natick," p. 199; Daniel Vickers, "The First Whalemen of Nantucket," *WMQ* 3rd series (October 1983):560–83; Marshall J. Becker, "Hannah Freeman: An Eighteenth-Century Lenape Living and Working Among Colonial Farmers," *PMHB* 104 (April 1990):249–69; Ann Marie Plane, "Colonizing the Family: Marriage, Household, and Racial Boundaries in Southeastern New England to 1730," Ph.D. thesis, Brandeis University, 1994.

36. "lusty . . . head": "Uring's Notices of New England, 1709," *Collections of the New Hampshire Historical Society*, Vol. III, pp. 149–50.

37. "Uring's Notices," p. 144; Merrell, "'The Customes of Our Country,'" pp. 121–23.

38. Quotations from Samuel Sewall, *The Selling of Joseph*, orig. pub. in Boston, 1700, *Massachusetts Historical Society Proceedings*, series 1, vol. 7 (October 1863):161–65. See also Emory Washburn, "Slavery As It Once Prevailed in Massachusetts" (Boston: John Watson & Son, 1869), p. 23. For biographical information on Sewall, see T. B. Strandness, *Samuel Sewall: A Puritan Portrait* (East Lansing, MI: Michigan State University Press, 1967); John Frederick Martin, *Profits in the Wilderness: Entrepreneurship and the Founding of New England Towns in the Seventeenth Century* (Chapel Hill, NC: University of North Carolina Press, 1991), pp. 75–6, 78.

39. "has them": William Penn quoted in Richard R. Wright, Jr., *The Negro In Pennsylvania: A Study in Economic History* (New York: Arno Press and the New York Times, 1969; orig. pub. 1912), pp. 6–7; Richard S. Dunn, "Servants and Slaves: The Recruitment and Employment of Labor," in Jack P. Greene and J. R. Pole, eds., *Colonial British America: Essays in the New History of the Early Modern Era* (Baltimore: Johns Hopkins University Press, 1984), pp. 157–94; Moss, *Slavery on Long Island*, pp. 4, 70–3.

40. "slave societies": Philip D. Morgan, "British Encounters with Africans and African-Americans, circa 1600–1780," in Bailyn and Morgan, eds., *Strangers*

Within the Realm, p. 163; William D. Piersen, *Black Yankees: The Development of an Afro-American Subculture in Eighteenth-Century New England* (Amherst, MA: University of Massachusetts Press, 1988), p. 14; Jackson Turner Main, *Society and Economy in Colonial Connecticut* (Princeton: Princeton University Press, 1985), p. 177; Simeon F. Moss, "The Persistence of Slavery and Involuntary Servitude in a Free State (1685–1866)," *JNH* 35 (July 1950):310; McCusker and Menard, *Economy of British America*, p. 222. For a discussion of the "substantial role" played by slavery in the economy of colonial Pennsylvania and New Jersey, see Jean R. Soderlund, *Quakers and Slavery: A Divided Spirit* (Princeton: Princeton University Press, 1985).

41. Darold D. Wax, "Preferences for Slaves in Colonial America," *JNH* 58 (October 1973):371–401; "The Act": Letter from Gov. Hunter to the Lords of Trade, 1714, *Documents Relating to the Colonial History of the State of New Jersey*, Vol. IV: *1709–20*, p. 196; Darold D. Wax, "Africans on the Delaware: The Pennsylvania Slave Trade, 1759–1769," *PH* 50 (January 1983):40; "To Serve Well and Faithfully," p. 20; Gary B. Nash, "Slaves and Slaveowners in Colonial Philadelphia," *WMQ* 3rd series 30 (April 1973):226, 243–47.

42. Joyce D. Goodfriend, *Beyond the Melting Pot: Society and Culture in Colonial New York City, 1664–17* (Princeton: Princeton University Press, 1992), pp. 11–32; Gary B. Nash, "Forging Freedom: The Emancipation Experience in the Northern Seaport Cities, 1775–1820," in Ira Berlin and Ronald Hoffman, eds., *Slavery and Freedom in the Age of the American Revolution* (Charlottesville, VA: University Press of Virginia, 1983), pp. 3–48.

43. Quotations from J. Hector St. John Crèvecoeur, *Letters from An American Farmer* (New York: Fox, Duffield & Co., 1904; orig. pub. 1782), pp. 230–31; "good . . . Farming": *New Jersey Colonial Documents, Newspaper Extracts*, Vol. 12, p. 258.

44. Ira Berlin, "Time, Space and the Evolution of Afro-American Society in British Mainland North America," *AHR* 85 (February 1980):45–54; Jacqueline Jones, "Race, Sex, and Self-Evident Truths: The Status of Slave Women During the Era of the American Revolution," in Ronald Hoffman and Peter J. Albert, eds., *Women in the Age of the American Revolution* (Charlottesville, VA: University Press of Virginia, 1989), pp. 293–337; "for... Drudge": quoted in McKee, *Labor in Colonial New York*, p. 123.

45. Lorenzo Johnston Greene, *The Negro in Colonial New England, 1620–1776* (New York: Columbia University Press, 1942), pp. 111–12; "cutting": quoted in Joyce D. Goodfriend, "Burghers and Blacks: the Evolution of a Slave Society in New Amsterdam," *NYH* 59 (April 1978):129–30; Berlin, "Time, Space," p. 46; Philip S. Foner and Ronald L. Lewis, eds., *The Black Worker: A Documentary History from Colonial Times to the Present* (Philadelphia: Temple University Press, 1978), pp. 10–11.

46. Greene, *The Negro in Colonial New England*, pp. 165–68; Robert C. Twombly and Robert H. Moore, "Black Puritan: The Negro in Seventeenth-Century Massachusetts," *WMQ* 3rd series 24 (April 1967):224–42; Lawrence William Towner, "A

Good Master Well Served: A Social History of Servitude in Massachusetts, 1620–1750," Ph.D. thesis, Northwestern University, 1954, p. 280; Berlin, "Time, Place," p. 48; Alan Tully, "Patterns of Slaveholding in Colonial Pennsylvania: Chester and Lancaster Counties, 1729–1758," *JSocH* 6 (Spring 1973):284–305. On the colonial paradox that linked civility with savagery, see Bernard Bailyn, *The Peopling of British North America: An Introduction* (New York: Vintage Books, 1988), pp. 116–22; Colin G. Calloway, *The American Revolution in Indian Country: Crisis and Diversity in Native American Communities* (London: Cambridge University Press, 1995); and Bernard Bailyn, "An American Tragedy," *NYRB* (Oct. 5, 1995):14–16.

47. McKee, *Labor in Colonial New York*, pp. 151–52; Edwin Olson, "The Slave Code in Colonial New York," *JNH* 29 (April 1944):149; Jean Soderlund, "Black Women in Colonial Pennsylvania," *PMHB* 107 (January 1983):55; Greene, *The Negro in Colonial New England*, pp. 122–43.

48. "blown": "Journal of the Rev. John Pike," *Collections of the New Hampshire Historical Society*, Vol. III, p. 61; William Renwick Riddell, "The Slave in Early New York," *JNH* 13 (January 1928):66–7; Benjamin Quarles, "The Colonial Militia and Negro Manpower," *MVHR* 45 (March 1959):643–52; John Shy, *A People Numerous and Armed: Reflections on the Military Struggle for American Independence* (New York: Oxford University Press, 1976), p. 29.

49. *Records of the Colony of Rhode Island*, Vol. I (*1636–1663*), p. 162.

50. "boys": *Winthrop Papers*, Vol. III, p. 126; "multitudes": *ibid.*, p. 216.

51. "the meanest . . . hereunto": Bradford, *Of Plymouth Plantation*, pp. 226–27, 357. See also David Cressy, *Coming Over: Migration and Communication Between England and New England in the Seventeenth Century* (Cambridge, UK: Cambridge University Press, 1987), pp. 52–62.

52. Dunn, "Servants and Slaves," p. 160; Salinger, *"To Serve Well and Faithfully,"* pp. 1–3; Farley Grubb, "Redemptioner Immigration to Pennsylvania: Evidence on Contract Choice and Profitability," *JEH* 46 (June 1986):407–18; Bernard Bailyn, *Voyagers to the West: A Passage in the Peopling of America on the Eve of the Revolution* (New York: Knopf, 1986), pp. 166–89; Cheesman A. Herrick, *White Servitude in Pennsylvania: Indentured and Redemption Labor in Colony and Commonwealth* (Freeport, NY: Books for Libraries Press, 1970; orig. pub. 1926), p. 91; Sharon V. Salinger, "'Send No More Women': Female Servants in Eighteenth-Century Philadelphia," *PMHB* 107 (January 1983):29–48; Bailyn, *Voyagers to the West*, pp. 166–88; Lawrence W. Towner, "A Fondness for Freedom: Servant Protest in Puritan Society," *WMQ* 99 (April 1962):201–19.

53. "to be . . . here": Report of Governor Printz, pp. 106–07; Towner, "A Good Master Well Served," pp. 127–29, 163, 291; "considering": quoted in Butler, "British Convicts Shipped to American Colonies," pp. 12–33; Herrick, *White Servitude in Pennsylvania*, pp. 109, 121, 131, 135.

54. "we Doe": *Records of the Colony of Rhode Island*, Vol. I (*1636–1663*), p. 162; "the devil's": quoted in Towner, "Good Master Well Served," p. 154. See also *Province and County Court Records of Maine*, Vol. II, *York County Records*, p. 194.

55. Quotations from Winter in *Documentary History of the State of Maine*, Vol. III, pp. 166–68.

56. "a . . . Trade": *Colonial Documents of the State of New Jersey*, Vol. XI, *Newspaper Extracts*, p. 391; "despaired": quoted in Salinger, *"To Serve Well and Faithfully,"* p. 105. On labor resistance among northern servants, see Alexander Mackraby, "Philadelphia Society Before the Revolution," *PMHB* (1887):492; Cotton Mather, "Pillars of Salt," in Daniel E. Williams, ed., *Pillars of Salt: An Anthology of Early American Criminal Narratives* (Madison, WI: Madison House, 1993), p. 70. On runaways in general, see Susan E. Klepp and Billy G. Smith, eds., *The Infortunate: The Voyage and Adventures of William Moraley, An Indentured Servant* (University Park, PA: Pennsylvania State University Press, 1992; orig. pub. 1743), pp. 96–7. See also *Correspondence of Roger Williams*, Vol. II, p. 440, 519n; *Records of the Government and Company of the Massachusetts Bay*, Vol. IV, p. 1, pp. 326–27.

57. Meaders, "Fugitive Slaves and Indentured Servants," p. 218. Servants were often described as having a "down look": *New Jersey Colonial Documents*, Vol. XI, *Newspaper Extracts*: Henry Coulton, p. 48, and Joshua Sted, p. 81; Jonathan Prude, "Runaway Ads and the Appearance of Unfree Laborers in America, 1750–1800," *JAH* 78 (June 1991):124–29; Salinger, *"To Serve Well and Faithfully,"* p. 106.

58. Plane, "Colonizing the Family"; O'Brien, "Community Dynamics in the Indian-English Town of Natick," p. 402; Frank W. Porter III, *In Pursuit of the Past: An Anthropological and Bibliographic Guide to Maryland and Delaware* (Metuchen, NJ: Scarecrow Press, 1986), pp. 57–81; Greene, *The Negro in Colonial New England*, pp. 200–08; "both Negro": J. P. Brissot de Warville, *New Travels in the United States of America*, ed. by Durand Echeverria (Cambridge, MA: Harvard University Press, 1964; orig. pub. 1791), p. 178; Jones, "Strolling Poor," p. 47; Faith Vibert, "The SPGFP [Society for the Propagation of the Gospel in Foreign Parts], Its Work for Negroes in North America," *JNH* 18 (April 1933):183, 197, 201–02, 210; Simmons and Simmons, eds., *Old Light on Separate Ways*, p. 79.

William Penn believed that blacks and Indians might serve essentially the same function in the colonial empire. As workers and as (indirect) consumers of English goods, he noted, both groups added to the wealth of the British Empire: "consider how many thousand Blacks and Indians are also accomodated with Cloaths and many sorts of Tools and Utensils from England, and that their Labour . . . adds Wealth and People to the English Dominions": "Some Account of the Province of Pennsilvania, by William Penn, 1681," in Jameson, ed., *Original Narratives of Early American History*, p. 204.

59. Moss, *Slavery on Long Island*, p. 20; Russell, *A Long, Deep Furrow*, p. 194; Klepp and Smith, eds., *The Infortunate*, p. 87; Goodfriend, *Beyond the Melting Pot*, p. 121; "A negro . . . time": "The Journal of Madam Sarah Kemble Knight," in Miller and Johnson, eds., *The Puritans*, pp. 436–37; Wax, "Demand for Slave Labor in Colonial Pennsylvania," p. 334; "slow": de Warville, *New Travels in the United States of America*, pp. 204–05; "an Indian . . . him": *New Jersey Colonial Documents*, Vol. XI, *Newspaper Extracts*, p. 347. See also Billy G. Smith and Richard Wojtowicz, *Blacks*

Who Stole Themselves: Advertisements for Runaways in the Pennsylvania Gazette, 1728–1790 (Philadelphia: University of Pennsylvania Press, 1989).

60. Moss, *Slavery on Long Island*, p. 112; McKee, *Labor in Colonial New York*, p. 149; "all . . . require": William Renwick Riddell, "The Slave in Early New York," *JNH* 13 (January 1928):69.

61. Clarke quoted in Thomas J. Davis, *A Rumor of Revolt: The "Great Negro Plot" in Colonial New York* (New York: Free Press, 1985), p. 238; Peter Linebaugh and Marcus Rediker, "The Many-Headed Hydra: Sailors, Slaves, and the Atlantic Working Class in the Eighteenth Century," *JHS* 3 (September 1990):224–52.

62. "where . . . Thief": "Observations Concerning the Increase of Mankind, Peopling of Countries, etc." [1751], in Esmond Wright, ed., *Benjamin Franklin: His Life as He Wrote It* (Cambridge, MA: Harvard University Press, 1990), pp. 124–26; "(as every": quoted in Paul W. Conner, *Poor Richard's Politicks: Benjamin Franklin and His New American Order* (New York: Oxford University Press, 1965), p. 78; Ronald W. Clark, *Benjamin Franklin: A Biography* (New York: Random House, 1983), pp. 23–24.

63. Quoted in "Conversation on Slavery," in Verner W. Crane, ed., *Benjamin Franklin's Letters to the Press, 1758–1775* (Chapel Hill, NC: University of North Carolina Press, 1950), pp. 188–92. By 1776, Franklin had responded to the sting of British charges that white colonists were hypocritical in demanding freedom for themselves while denying it to the black people who lived among them. He began to speak out on behalf of black education and against the African slave trade, and in 1787 he became the first president of the Pennsylvania Abolition Society.

64. John Saffin, "The Negroes Character" (1701), reprinted in Lawrence W. Towner, "The Sewall-Saffin Dialogue on Slavery," *WMQ* 3rd series 21 (January 1964):48.

65. "Few can": Sewall, *Selling of Joseph*, p. 162.

CHAPTER FIVE

1. Jeremiah Asher, *An Autobiography, with Details of a Visit to England* (Philadelphia: Published by the Author, 1862), pp. 1–5.

2. "the motives . . . liberty": *ibid.*; "lonely and distressed": *ibid.*, p. 257. See also Jack Larkin, "Living and Working in a Sea of White Faces," *OSV* (Summer 1991):6–7.

3. "At the close": Bert James Loewenberg and Ruth Bogin, eds., *Black Women in Nineteenth-Century American Life: Their Words, Their Thoughts, Their Feelings* (University Park, PA: Pennsylvania State University Press, 1976), p. 80.

4. "According": "An Early Description of Pennsylvania" [Christopher Sower, 1724], *PMHB* 45 (1921):252. See also Daniel Vickers, *Farmers and Fishermen: Two Centuries of Work in Essex County, Massachusetts, 1630–1850* (Chapel Hill, NC: University of North Carolina Press, 1994), pp. 14–23; Virginia DeJohn Anderson, *New England's Generation: The Great Migration and the Formation of Society and Culture in the Seventeenth Century* (New York: Cambridge University Press, 1991); Bernard Bailyn, *The Peopling of British North America: An Introduction* (New York:

Knopf, 1986); John Frederick Martin, *Profits in the Wilderness: Entrepreneurship and the Founding of New England Towns in the Seventeenth Century* (Chapel Hill, NC: University of North Carolina Press, 1991).

See also T. H. Breen, "An Empire of Goods: The Anglicization of Colonial America, 1690–1776," *JBS* 25 (October 1986):467–99; T. H. Breen, "The Making of Things: Interpreting the Consumer Economy in the Eighteenth Century," in John Brewer and Roy Porter, eds., *Consumption and the World of Goods* (New York: Routledge, 1993), pp. 249–60; Carole Shammas, "Changes in English and Anglo-American Consumption from 1550 to 1800," in *ibid.*, pp. 177–205. For an overview, see John R. McCusker and Russell R. Menard, *The Economy of British America, 1607–1789* (Chapel Hill, NC: University of North Carolina Press, 1985).

For sources related to the dynamic growth of New England and the Middle Colonies, see William Bradford, *Of Plymouth Plantation, 1620–1647* (New York: Modern Library, 1981), pp. 266, 202–03; J. Franklin Jameson, ed., *Johnson's Wonder–Working Providence, 1628–1651* (New York: Barnes and Noble, 1910; orig. pub. 1653), p. 154; William Penn, "Some Account of Pennsilvania" (1681), in J. Franklin Jameson, ed., *Original Narratives of Early American History: Narratives of Early Pennsylvania, West New Jersey, and Delaware, 1630–1707* (New York: Charles Scribner's Sons, 1912), p. 204.

On Dutch immigrants see for example A. G. Roeber, "'The Origin of Whatever Is Not English Among Us': The Dutch-Speaking Peoples of Colonial British America," in Bernard Bailyn and Philip Morgan, eds., *Strangers Within the Realm: Cultural Margins of the First British Empire* (Chapel Hill, NC: University of North Carolina Press, 1991), pp. 220–83.

See also Stephen Innes, *Creating the Commonwealth: The Economic Culture of Puritan New England* (New York: W. W. Norton, 1995); Christine Leigh Heyrman, *Commerce and Culture: The Maritime Communities of Colonial Massachusetts, 1690–1750* (New York: W. W. Norton, 1984).

5. Carole Shammas, "Anglo-American Household Government in Comparative Perspective," *WMQ* 52 (January 1995):104–44.

6. "under": Francis G. Walett, ed., *The Diary of Ebenezer Parkman, 1703–1782. First Part: 1719–1755* (Worcester, MA: American Antiquarian Society, 1974), p. 18.

7. Parkman quotations: *ibid.*, pp. 16, 12–13, 65, 64, 82; "He that": Alden T. Vaughan, ed., *William Wood's New England's Prospect* (Amherst, MA: University of Massachusetts Press, 1977; orig. pub. 1634), p. 71; Ross W. Beales, Jr., "The Reverend Ebenezer Parkman's Farm Workers, Westborough, Massachusetts," *PAAS* 99, Pt. 1 (1989):149. See also Richard S. Dunn, "Servants and Slaves: The Recruitment and Employment of Labor," in Jack P. Greene and J. R. Pole, eds., *Colonial British America: Essays in the New History of the Early Modern Era* (Baltimore: Johns Hopkins University Press, 1984), pp. 186–88.

8. Vickers, *Farmers and Fishermen*, pp. 31–84; Laurel Thatcher Ulrich, *Good Wives: Image and Reality in the Lives of Women in Northern New England, 1650–1750* (New York: Oxford University Press, 1980), p. 37; "by her": *Documents Relating to the*

Colonial History of the State of New Jersey, Vol. XI: *Newspaper Extracts*, p. 350; Jonathan Prude, "Runaway Ads and the Appearance of Unfree Laborers in America, 1750–1800," *JAH* 78 (June 1991): 124.

9. Jeanne Boydston, *Home and Work: Housework, Wages, and the Ideology of Labor in the Early Republic* (New York: Oxford University Press, 1990); Vickers, *Farmers and Fishermen*, pp. 247–58, 313–17; Christopher Clark, *The Roots of Rural Capitalism: Western Massachusetts, 1780–1860* (Ithaca, NY: Cornell University Press, 1990), pp. 3–194; Nancy F. Cott, *The Bonds of Womanhood: "Woman's Sphere" in New England, 1780–1835* (New Haven, CT: Yale University Press, 1977).

10. Stephen Innes, *Labor in a New Land: Economy and Society in Seventeenth-Century Springfield* (Princeton: Princeton University Press, 1983).

11. Joan Jensen, *Loosening the Bonds: Mid-Atlantic Farm Women, 1750–1850* (New Haven: Yale University Press, 1986), pp. 36–37, 46; Lucy Simler, "The Landless Worker: An Index of Economic and Social Change in Chester County, Pennsylvania, 1750–1820," *PMHB* 104 (April 1990):185–86; T. H. Breen, "Back to Sweat and Toil: Suggestions for the Study of Agricultural Work in Early America," *PH* 49 (October 1982):251; Vickers, *Farmers and Fishermen*, pp. 133–34; "to cure . . . prescribed": J. Hector St. John Crèvecoeur, " Reflections on the Manners of the Americans," in Henri L. Bourdin, et al., eds., *Sketches of Eighteenth Century America: More "Letters from an American Farmer"* (New Haven: Yale University Press, 1925), pp. 70–1; Barbara E. Lacey, "The World of Hannah Heaton: The Autobiography of an Eighteenth-Century Connecticut Farm Woman," *WMQ* 45 (April 1988):287. On the work of white wives and mothers, see for example: Ulrich, *Good Wives*, p. 34; Stephanie Grauman Wolf, *As Various as Their Land: The Everyday Lives of Eighteenth-Century Americans* (New York: HarperCollins, 1993), pp. 87–99; Alice Morse Earle, *Home Life in Colonial Days* (Stockbridge, MA: Berkshire Traveller Press, 1974; orig. pub. 1898); Judith A. McGaw, Introduction, in Judith A. McGaw, ed., *Early American Technology: Making and Doing Things from the Colonial Era to 1850* (Chapel Hill, NC: University of North Carolina Press, 1994), pp. 1–15; Laurel Thatcher Ulrich, "Martha Ballard and Her Girls," in Stephen Innes, ed., *Work and Labor in Early America* (Chapel Hill, NC: University of North Carolina Press, 1988), p. 90; Rolla Milton Tryon, *Household Manufactures in the United States, 1640–1860* (Chicago: University of Chicago Press, 1917), pp. 79–80.

12. "One is": Job Orton quoted in David Hackett Fischer, *Albion's Seed: Four British Folkways in America* (New York: Knopf, 1989), p. 104.

13. "unfealing . . . distress": Frank D. Prager, ed., *The Autobiography of John Fitch* (Philadelphia: American Philosophical Society, 1976), p. 32; Richard Shannon Moss, *Slavery on Long Island: A Study in Local Institutional and Early African-American Communal Life* (New York: Garland, 1993), p. 69; Philip J. Greven, *Four Generations: Population, Land, and Family in Colonial Andover, Massachusetts* (Ithaca, NY: 1970), pp. 142–43; Dunn, "Servants and Slaves," pp. 185–86, 193, n82; Ruth Wallis Herndon, "'To Live After the Manner of an Apprentice': Public Indenture and

Social Control in Rhode Island, 1750–1800," Paper presented at the American Studies Association Conference, Boston, November 1993.

14. "being . . . them": Petition from John Marion, *et al.*, to the Right Honorable Edward Cranfield, Esq., in *Collections of the New Hampshire Historical Society*, Vol. VIII: *Provincial Records and Court Papers* (1680–92) (Concord, MA: McFarland & Jenks, 1866), p. 124; "the elderly": "A Description of Duke's County. Aug. 13th, 1807," *Collections of the Massachusetts Historical Society*, 2nd series, Vol. 3 (Boston, 1815), p. 61; Vickers, *Farmers and Fishermen*, pp. 182–86.

15. Thomas A. Hazard, ed., *Nailer Tom's Diary, Otherwise the Journal of Thomas B. Hazard of Kingstown, Rhode Island, 1778 to 1840* (Boston: Merrymount Press, 1930). See also Laurel Thatcher Ulrich, *A Midwife's Tale: The Life of Martha Ballard, Based on Her Diary, 1785–1812* (New York: Vintage Books, 1990); Bettye Hobbs Pruitt, "Self-Sufficiency and the Agricultural Economy of Eighteenth-Century Massachusetts," WMQ 3rd series 41 (July 1984):333–64; Judith A. McGaw, "'So Much Depends Upon a Red Wheelbarrow': Agricultural Tool Ownership in the Eighteenth-Century Mid-Atlantic," in McGaw, ed., *Early American Technology*, pp. 328–57.

16. Hazard, ed., *Nailer Tom's Diary*.

17. "they love": David John Jeremy, ed., *Henry Wansey and His American Journal* (Philadelphia: American Philosophical Society, 1970), p. 66.

18. Quotations from George Sheldon, "Negro Slavery in Old Deerfield," NEM (March 1893):55.

19. Lillian Ashcraft-Eason, "Freedom Among African Women Servants and Slaves in the Seventeenth-Century British Colonies," in Larry D. Eldridge, ed., *Women and Freedom in Colonial America* (New York: New York University Press, 1997), pp. 62–80; Samuel Abbott Green, "Slavery at Groton, Massachusetts, in Provincial Times" (Cambridge: John Wilson & Son), 1909; William D. Piersen, *Black Yankees: The Development of an Afro-American Subculture in Eighteenth-Century New England* (Amherst, MA: University of Massachusetts Press, 1988), pp. 42–3; Gary B. Nash, "Forging Freedom: The Emancipation Experience in the Northern Seaport Cities, 1775–1820," in Ira Berlin and Ronald Hoffman, eds., *Slavery and Freedom in the Age of the American Revolution* (Charlottesville, VA: University Press of Virginia, 1983), pp. 288, 307–10; Jerome H. Wood., Jr., "The Negro in Early Pennsylvania: The Lancaster Experience," in Elinor Miller and Eugene D. Genovese, eds., *Plantation, Town, and Country: Essays on the Local History of American Slave Society* (Urbana, IL: University of Illinois Press, 1974), pp. 451–52.

20. Lillian Ashcraft Webb, "Black Women and Religion in the Colonial Period," in Rosemary Radford Reuther and Rosemary Skinner Keller, eds., *Women and Religion in America* (New York: Harper & Row, 1983), pp. 233–59; Hubert Schmidt, "Slavery and Attitudes in Hunterdon County, New Jersey" (Flemington, NJ: Hunterdon County Historical Society, 1941), pp. 11–20; Richard D. Brown, "'Not Only Extreme Poverty, But the Worst Kind of Orphanage': Lemuel Haynes and

the Boundaries of Racial Tolerance on the Yankee Frontier, 1770–1820," *NEQ* 61 (1988):502–18

21. Joseph L. Reidy, "Negro Election Day & Black Community Life in New England, 1750–1860," *MP* 1 (Fall 1978):102–17; Melvin Wade, "'Shining in Borrowed Plumage': Affirmation of Community in the Black Coronation Festivals of New England, ca. 1750–1850," in Robert Blair St. George, ed., *Material Life in America, 1600–1860* (Boston: Northeastern University Press, 1988), pp. 171–84; Shane White, *Somewhat More Independent: The End of Slavery in New York City, 1770–1810* (Athens, GA: University of Georgia Press, 1991), pp. 95–106; James Oliver Horton and Lois E. Horton, *In Hope of Liberty: Culture, Community and Protest Among Northern Free Blacks, 1700–1860* (New York: Oxford University Press, 1997), pp. 31–6; "anxious . . . time": William J. Brown, *The Life of William J. Brown, of Providence, Rhode Island, with Personal Recollections* (Providence: Angell & Co., 1883), pp. 7–13 (the quote is on p. 13); G. S. Rowe, "Black Offenders, Criminal Courts, and Philadelphia Society in the Late Eighteenth Century," *JSocH* 22 (Summer 1989):692–95.

22. Lawrence William Towner, "A Good Master Well Served: A Social History of Servitude in Massachusetts," Ph.D. thesis, Northwestern University, 1954, pp. 127–29; James Davie Butler, "British Convicts Shipped to American Colonies," *AHR* 2 (October 1896): 14.

23. Philip Otterness, "The New York Naval Stores Project and the Transformation of the Poor Palatines," *NYH* 75 (April 1994):133–56; "by which means": quoted in Robert E. Cray, Jr., *Poverty and Poor Relief: New York City and Its Rural Environs, 1700–1830* (Philadelphia: Temple University Press, 1988), p. 43; Samuel D. McKee, Jr., *Labor in Colonial New York 1664–1776* (Port Washington, NY: I. J. Friedman, 1935), pp. 55–7; Daniel Vickers, "The First Whalemen of Nantucket," *WMQ* 3rd series 40 (October 1983):560–83.

24. Farley Grubb, "The Auction of Redemptioner Servants, Philadelphia, 1771–1804: An Economic Analysis," *JEH* 48 (September 1988):583–603; Sung Bok Kim, *Landlord and Tenant in Colonial New York: Manorial Society, 1664–1775* (Chapel Hill, NC: University of North Carolina Press, 1978). See also Staughton Lynd, *Anti-Federalism in Dutchess County, New York: A Study of Democracy and Class Conflict in the Revolutionary Era* (Chicago: Loyola University Press, 1962).

25. Edmond Dale Daniel, "Robert Hunter Morris and the Rocky Hill Copper Mine," *NJH* 92 (Spring 1974):20–3; "We have always": Charles Read quoted in Carl Raymond Woodward, *Ploughs and Politicks: Charles Read of New Jersey and His Notes on Agriculture, 1715–1774* (Philadelphia: Porcupine Press, 1974), p. 92; Innes, *Creating the Commonwealth*, pp. 237–70.

26. Extracts from the *Pennsylvania Gazette* quoted in Earle, *Home Life in Colonial Days*, pp. 292–93.
   On thieves of various kinds, see for example John Russell Bartlett, ed., *Records of the Colony of Rhode Island*, Vol. I (1636–1663) (Providence: A. C. Greene and Brothers, 1856), p. 412; "Countrie": John Endecott to John Winthrop,

Winthrop Papers, Vol. V (*1645–1649*), p. 42; Glenn W. LaFantasie, ed., *The Correspondence of Roger Williams*, Vol. II (*1654–1682*) (Hanover, NH: University Press of New England, 1988), pp. 425, 430; Bruce J. Bourque and Ruth Holmes Whitehead, "Tarrentines and the Introduction of European Trade Goods in the Gulf of Maine," *Eh* 32 (1985): 327–41. See also Joseph Smith, ed., *Colonial Justice in Western Massachusetts (1639–1702): The Pynchon Court Record* (Cambridge, MA: Harvard University Press, 1961), pp. 298–99; Rowe, "Black Offenders, Criminal Courts, and Philadelphia Society in the Late Eighteenth Century," pp. 685–712.

27. "Concealeing": Charles Thornton Libby, ed., *Province and Court Records of Maine*, Vol. II: *York County Records* (Portland, ME: Maine Historical Society, 1931), p. 499; Kenneth Scott, *Counterfeiting in Colonial America* (New York: Oxford University Press, 1957), pp. 10, 46; "sundry": Daniel E. Williams, ed., *Pillars of Salt: An Anthology of Early American Criminal Narratives* (Madison, WI: Madison House, 1993), pp. 152, 153.

28. Quotations from Williams, ed., *Pillars of Salt*, pp. 153, 154.

29. "English": *New Jersey Colonial Documents*, Vol. XL, *Newspaper Extracts* (vol. 1), p. 561 (1739); "one": *ibid.*, p. 72 (1723).

30. "Nationaly": Elizabeth Foote's Journal, October 23, 1775, quoted in Ruth Barnes Moynihan, *et al.*, *Second to None: A Documentary History of American Women*, Vol. I (Lincoln, NE: University of Nebraska Press, 1993), p. 121; Linda Kerber, *Women of the Republic: Intellect and Ideology in Revolutionary America* (Chapel Hill, NC: University of North Carolina Press, 1980); Howard B. Rock, *Artisans of the New Republic: The Tradesmen of New York City in the Age of Jefferson* (New York: New York University Press, 1979); Charles S. Olton, *Artisans for Independence: Philadelphia Mechanics and the American Revolution* (Syracuse, NY: Syracuse University Press, 1975); Steven Russwurm, *Arms, Country, and Class: The Philadelphia Militia and "Lower Sort" During the American Revolution, 1775–1783* (New Brunswick, NJ: Rutgers University Press, 1987); Gordon S. Wood, *The Radicalism of the American Revolution* (New York: Knopf, 1992); Paul A. Gilje, "Identity and Independence: The American Artisan, 1750–1850," in Howard B. Rock, *et al.*, eds., *American Artisans: Crafting Social Identity, 1750–1850* (Baltimore: Johns Hopkins University Press, 1995), pp. xi–xx.

31. "all hands": Nathaniel B. Shurtleff, ed., *Records of the Governor and Company of the Massachusetts Bay in New England*, Vol. IV, Pt. I (*1650–1660*) (Boston: William White, 1854), p. 256; Tryon, *Household Manufactures*, p. 31; Letter from Gov. Montgomerie to the Lords of Trade, November 30, 1728, *Documents Relating to the Colonial History of New Jersey*, Vol. IV (*1709–1720*) (Newark: Daily Advertiser Printing House, 1882), p. 209; "our Republican": Esther DeBerdt Reed, in Moynihan, *et al.*, *Second to None*, p. 172.

32. "sundry . . . livelihood": *New Hampshire Historical Society, Provincial Records and Court Papers*, Vol. VIII, pp. 42–3.

33. Gary B. Nash, "The Failure of Female Factory Labor in Colonial Boston," *LH* (Spring 1979):165–88.

34. John K. Alexander, *Render Them Submissive: Responses to Poverty in Philadelphia, 1760–1800* (Amherst, MA: University of Massachusetts Press, 1980), pp. 87–104; "exciting": quoted in Stephen Edward Wiberly, Jr., "Four Cities: Public Poor Relief in Urban America, 1700–1775," Ph.D. thesis, Yale University, 1975, p. 134. See also Bruce C. Daniels, *Dissent and Conformity on Narragansett Bay: The Colonial Rhode Island Town* (Middletown, CT: Wesleyan University Press, 1983), pp. 76–90.

35. Cynthia J. Shelton, *The Mills of Manayunk: Industrialization and Social Conflict in the Philadelphia Region, 1787–1837* (Baltimore: Johns Hopkins University Press, 1986), pp. ix, 15; Ronald Schultz, *The Republic of Labor: Philadelphia Artisans and the Politics of Class, 1720–1830* (New York: Oxford University Press, 1993), pp. 164–71; "A Topographical and Historical Description of Boston, 1794. By the Author of the Historical Journal of the American War," *Collections of the Massachusetts Historical Society*, Vol. III, pp. 249–83.

36. Quoted in David John Jeremy, ed., *Henry Wansey and His American Journal, 1794* (Philadelphia: American Philosophical Society, 1970), p. 83. See also Shelton, *Mills of Manayunk*, pp. 14–15; Claudia Goldin and Kenneth Sokoloff, "Women, Children, and Industrialization in the Early Republic: Evidence from the Manufacturing Censuses," *JEH* 42 (December 1982):741–44.

37. Alexander Hamilton, "Report on Manufactures, December 5, 1791," in Jacob E. Cooke, ed., *The Reports of Alexander Hamilton* (New York: Harper & Row, 1964), pp. 129–31.

38. "overstocked": Carl Bridenbaugh, ed., "Patrick M'Robert's Tour Through Part of the Provinces of America," *PMHB* 59 (1935):146; Christine Stansell, *City of Women: Sex and Class in New York, 1789–1860* (New York: Knopf, 1986), pp. 3–37; Billy G. Smith, *The "Lower Sort": Philadelphia's Laboring People, 1750–1800* (Ithaca, NY: Cornell University Press, 1990); and "Inequality in Late Colonial Philadelphia: A Note on Its Nature and Growth," *WMQ* 3rd series 41 (October 1984):629–45; Gary B. Nash, Billy G. Smith, and Dirk Hoerder, "Labor in the Era of the American Revolution: An Exchange," *LH* 24 (Summer 1983):414–54.

39. "craft": Schultz, *The Republic of Labor*, p. 105; Billy G. Smith, "The Vicissitudes of Fortune: The Careers of Laboring Men in Philadelphia, 1750–1800," in Innes, ed., *Work and Labor*, pp. 221–51; James A. Henretta, "Wealth and Social Structure," in Greene and Pole, eds., *Colonial British America: Essays in the New History of the Early Modern Era*, pp. 278–79; Richard Oestreicher, "The Counted and the Uncounted: The Occupational Structure of Early American Cities," *JSocH* 28 (Winter 1994):351–61.

40. Sharon V. Salinger, "'Send No More Women': Female Servants in Eighteenth-Century Philadelphia," *PMHB* 107 (January 1983):44; Stansell, *City of Women*, pp. 3–18; "roam'd . . . Road": Susan E. Klepp and Billy G. Smith, eds., *The Infortunate: The Voyage and Adventures of William Moraley, An Indentured Servant* (University Park, PA: Penn State University Press, 1992; orig. pub. 1743), pp. 110, 109, 128; Carole Shammas, "The Female Social Structure of Philadelphia in 1775," *PMHB*

(January 1983):69–83; Sharon V. Salinger, *"To Serve Well and Faithfully": Labor and Indentured Servants in Pennsylvania, 1682–1800* (Cambridge, UK: Cambridge University Press, 1987), p. 151.

41. Arthur Zilversmit, *The First Emancipation: The Abolition of Slavery in the North* (Chicago: University of Chicago Press, 1967); Gary B. Nash and Jean R. Soderlund, *Freedom by Degrees: Emancipation in Pennsylvania and Its Aftermath* (New York: Oxford University Press, 1991); David Grimsted, "Anglo-American Racism and Phillis Wheatley's 'Sable Veil,' 'Length'ned Chain,' and 'Knitted Heart,'" in Ronald Hoffman and Peter J. Albert, eds., *Women in the Age of the American Revolution* (Charlottesville, VA: University Press of Virginia, 1989), pp. 370–94; Robert William Fogel and Stanley L. Engerman, "Philanthropy at Bargain Prices: Notes on the Economics of Gradual Emancipation," *JLS* 3 (June 1974):377–401.

42. Zilversmit, *The First Emancipation*, pp. 189, 202; David Brion Davis, *The Problem of Slavery in the Age of Revolution, 1770–1823* (Ithaca, NY: Cornell University Press, 1975), pp. 51–4; 302–05; Joanne Pope Melish, "Owning Slaves, Disowning Slavery: Gradual Emancipation in New England, 1780–1820," Paper presented at the American Studies Association Annual Meeting, Boston, November 1993.

43. Debra L. Newman, "They Left with the British: Black Women in the Evacuation of Philadelphia, 1778," *PHe* 4 (1977):20–3; Gary B. Nash, *Forging Freedom: The Formation of Philadelphia's Black Community, 1720–1840* (Cambridge, MA: Harvard University Press, 1988); Gary B. Nash, "Forging Freedom: The Emancipation Experience in the Northern Seaport Cities, 1775–1820," in Berlin and Hoffman, eds., *Slavery and Freedom in the Age of the American Revolution*, pp. 3–48; Joseph Carvalho III, *Black Families in Hampden County, Massachusetts, 1650–1855* (Westfield, MA: New England Genealogical Society and Institute for Massachusetts Studies, 1984); Mary Beth Norton, "The Fate of Some Black Loyalists in the American Revolution," *JNH* 58 (October 1973):402–06.

44. "he . . . country": "A Tragedy of the Seventeenth and Eighteenth Centuries," *JNH* 14 (April 1929):233, 231; "Three of . . . these": Petition, in Herbert Aptheker, ed., *A Documentary History of the Negro People in the United States* (New York: Citadel Press, 1951), pp. 20–1. For other examples of late eighteenth-century free blacks kidnapped or otherwise deprived of their freedom, see Loewenberg and Bogin, eds., *Black Women in Nineteenth-Century American Life*, p. 47; Billy G. Smith and Richard Wojtowicz, "The Precarious Freedom of Blacks in the Mid-Atlantic Region: Excerpts from the *Pennsylvania Gazette, 1728–1776,*" *PMHB* 113 (April 198):341, 238; Carol Wilson, *Freedom at Risk: The Kidnapping of Free Blacks in America, 1780–1865* (Lexington, KY: University Press of Kentucky, 1994).

45. "one old": Samuel Freebody quoted in Elaine Foreman Crane, "The Black Community of Newport, Rhode Island," in Robert L. Hall, ed., *Making a Living: The Work Experience of African Americans in New England: Selected Readings* (Boston: New England Foundation for the Humanities, 1995), p. 47; Debra L. Newman,

"Black Women in the Era of the American Revolution in Pennsylvania," *JNH* 61 (July 1976):284; Carl D. Oblinger, "Alms for Oblivion: The Making of a Black Underclass in Southeastern Pennsylvania, 1780–1860," in John Bodnar, ed., *The Ethnic Experience in Pennsylvania* (Philadelphia: Bucknell University Press, 1973), pp. 94–119; Alfred M. Bingham, "Squatter Settlements of Freed Slaves in New England," *CHSB* 41 (July 1976):65–80.

46. Venture Smith, *A Narrative of the Life and Adventures of Venture, a Native of Africa, But Resident above Sixty Years in the United States of America* (New London, CT: C. Holt, 1798), p. 18.

47. *Ibid.*, pp. 30, 31.

48. W. Jeffrey Bolster, "'To Feel Like a Man': Black Seamen in the Northern States, 1800–1860," *JAH* 76 (March 1990):1173–99; Lamont D. Thomas, *Rise to be a People: A Biography of Paul Cuffe* (Urbana, IL: University of Illinois Press, 1986); Martha S. Putney, "Black Merchant Seamen of Newport, 1803–1855: A Case Study in Foreign Commerce," *JNH* 57 (April 1972):156–68; Marcus Rediker, *Between the Devil and the Deep Blue Sea: Merchant Seamen, Pirates, and the Anglo-American Maritime World, 1700–1750* (Cambridge, UK: University Press, 1987); Paul Edwards, ed., *Equiano's Travels: His Autobiography; The Interesting Narrative of the Life of Olaudah Equiano or Gustavus Vassa the African* (Portsmouth, NH: Heinemann, 1967; orig. pub. 1789).

49. James Farr, "A Slow Boat to Nowhere: The Multi-Racial Crews of the American Whaling Industry," *JNH* 68 (Spring 1983):159–70; Gaddis Smith, "Black Seamen and the Federal Courts, 1789–1860," in Timothy J. Runyan, ed., *Ships, Seafaring, and Society: Essays in Maritime History* (Detroit: Wayne State University Press, 1987), pp. 321–38; Lorin Lee Cary and Francine C. Cary, "Absolom F. Boston, His Family, and Nantucket's Black Community," *HN* 25 (Summer 1977):15–23; Lee A. Craig and Robert M. Fearn, "Discrimination and Occupational Crowding in a Competitive Industry: Evidence from the American Whaling Industry," *JEH* 53 (March 1993):123–28.

CHAPTER SIX

1. George P. Rawick, ed.., *The American Slave: A Composite Autobiography*, Vol. 7, Pt. 1 (Okla. Narrs.) (Westport, CT: Greenwood Press, 1972–79), pp. 346, 351, 345, 347, 348 (hereinafter identified by state and volume). See also Wilma King, *Stolen Childhood: Slave Youth in Nineteenth-Century America* (Bloomington, IN: Indiana University Press, 1995).

2. "will not": Frederick Law Olmsted, *The Cotton Kingdom: A Traveller's Observations on Cotton and Slavery in the American Slave States (Based Upon Three Former Volumes of Journeys and Investigations by the Same Author)*, ed. by Arthur M. Schlesinger, Sr. (New York: Modern Library, 1984), p. 87.

3. *Ibid.*, pp. 64, 147, 231.

4. *Ibid.*, pp. 346–47, 257–58, 195.

5. "that whites": James S. Buckingham, *The Slave States of America*, Vol. II (London: Fisher, Son, & Co., 1842), p. 155.

6. Eugene Genovese, *Roll, Jordan, Roll: The World the Slaves Made* (New York: Vintage Books, 1976), p. 388; "animal raisers": Charles W. Joyner, *Down by the Riverside: A South Carolina Slave Community* (Urbana, IL: University of Illinois Press, 1984), pp. 70–1; "an extra": *S.C. Narrs.*, Vol. 3, Pt. 2, p. 77; "My father": *ibid.*, Pt. 1, p. 27; "fish baskets": *ibid.*, p. 85; Philip D. Morgan, "Black Society in the Low Country, 1760–1810," in Ira Berlin and Ronald Hoffman, eds., *Slavery and Freedom in the Age of the American Revolution* (Charlottesville, VA: University Press of Virginia, 1983), p. 97. See also the essays in Ira Berlin and Philip D. Morgan, eds., *Cultivation and Culture: Labor and the Shaping of Slave Life in the Americas* (Charlottesville, VA: University Press of Virginia, 1993).

7. Michael P. Johnson, "Work, Culture and the Slave Community: Slave Occupations in the Cotton Belt in 1860," *LH* 27 (Summer 1986):325–55; Bayly E. Marks, "Skilled Blacks in Antebellum St. Mary's County, Maryland," *JSouH* 53 (November 1987):537–64; Ira Berlin and Herbert G. Gutman, "Natives and Immigrants, Free Men and Slaves: Urban Workingmen in the Antebellum South," *AHR* 88 (December 1983):1193.

8. Deborah Gray White, *Ar'n't I a Woman? Female Slaves in the Plantation South* (New York: W. W. Norton, 1985); Jacqueline Jones, *Labor of Love, Labor of Sorrow: Black Women, Work and the Family from Slavery to the Present* (New York: Basic Books, 1985), pp. 11–43; "in de . . . company": *Ala. Narrs.*, Vol. 5, Pt. 4, pp. 87–88; "My mammy": *ibid*, p. 174.

9. "wouldn'": *Miss. Narrs*, Vol. 7, p. 114; "before": *Fisk University Unwritten History of Slavery*, Vol. 18 of the Federal Writers Project Slave Narratives, p. 14; Elizabeth Fox-Genovese, *Within the Plantation Household: Black and White Women of the Old South* (Chapel Hill, NC: University of North Carolina Press, 1988); Catherine Clinton, *The Plantation Mistress: Women's World in the Old South* (New York: Pantheon, 1982); Richard Sears, "Working Like a Slave: Views of Slavery and the Status of Women in Antebellum Kentucky," *RKHS* 87 (Winter 1989):1–19.

10. "Master": *S. C. Narrs.*, Vol. 3, Pt. 2, p. 55; Joseph P. Reidy, "Obligation and Right: Patterns of Labor, Subsistence, and Exchange in the Cotton Belt of Georgia, 1790–1860," in Berlin and Morgan, eds., *Cultivation and Culture*, pp. 138–54; Larry E. Hudson, "'All That Cash': Work and Status in the Slave Quarters," in Larry E. Hudson, ed., *Working Toward Freedom: Slave Society and Domestic Economy in the American South* (Rochester, NY: University of Rochester Press, 1994), pp. 77–94; James Henry Hammond Papers, 1785–1865, *Records of Ante-Bellum Southern Plantations from the Revolution Through the Civil War*, ed. by Kenneth M. Stampp, series A, pt. 1, microfilm reel 14; Charles Lyell, *A Second Visit to the United States of North America*, Vol. I (London: John Murray, 1849), p. 264.

11. "free . . . person [s]": Canter Brown, Jr., "Race Relations in Territorial Florida, 1821–1845," *FHQ* 73 (January 1995):292–93; Joseph Conan Thompson, "Toward

a More Humane Oppression: Florida's Slave Codes, 1821–1861," *FHQ* 71 (January 1993):324–29.

12. For a discussion of these issues, see Betty Wood, *Women's Work, Men's Work: The Informal Slave Economies of Lowcountry Georgia* (Athens, GA: University of Georgia Press, 1995), and Lawrence Levine, *Black Culture and Black Consciousness: Afro-American Folk Thought From Slavery to Freedom* (New York: Oxford University Press, 1977).

13. "dairy . . . work": Testimony of Charles Jess, Savannah, March 12, 1873, in Berlin, *et al.*, eds., *Freedom: A Documentary History of Emancipation, 1861–1867*, Series I, Vol. I: *The Destruction of Slavery* (Cambridge, UK: Cambridge University Press, 1985), pp. 143–45; "so . . . themselves": Herbert Anthony Kellar, ed., *Solon Robinson: Pioneer and Agriculturalist*, Vol. II (New York: Da Capo Press, 1968), p. 296; Sidney W. Mintz and Douglas Hall, "The Origins of the Jamaican Internal Marketing System," in Sidney Mintz, ed., *Papers in Caribbean Anthropology*, no. 57 (New Haven: Yale University Press, 1960), pp. 295–96; Roderick A. McDonald, *The Economy and Material Culture of Slaves: Goods and Chattels on the Sugar Plantations of Jamaica and Louisiana* (Baton Rouge, LA: Louisiana University Press, 1993), pp. 83, 71.

14. "for a drink": Olmsted, *Cotton Kingdom*, p. 258. See also John Campbell, "As 'A Kind of Freeman'? Slaves' Market-Related Activities in the South Carolina Upcountry, 1800–1860," in Berlin and Morgan, eds., *Cultivation and Culture*, pp. 254–73; "cider": Jasper County Superior Court, "The State vs James Wilson" (1846), Box 44, doc. 4283–28, Georgia Department of Archives and History, Atlanta, Georgia. (I would like to acknowledge the research assistance of Christine Jacobson Carter in locating this and other material from the Georgia State Archives.)

15. "handkerchief . . . Walker": Jasper Superior Court, "The State vs Patsy Elliot (1832)," Box 13, doc. 4285–13, Georgia Department of Archives and History; "certain . . . time": *Vicksburg Daily Whig* (June 29, 1858) (I would like to acknowledge Jack E. Davis for this quotation). See also Jean Bradley Anderson, *Durham County: A History of Durham, County, North Carolina* (Durham, NC: Duke University Press, 1990), p. 89; Charles C. Bolton, *Poor Whites of the Antebellum South: Tenants and Laborers in Central North Carolina and Northeast Mississippi* (Durham, NC: Duke University Press, 1994), p. 58.

16. "Barnwell": quoted in Jack Kenny Williams, "White Lawbreakers in Ante-Bellum South Carolina," *JSouH* 21 (August 1955):369; "The crime": "Dunn vs. the State of Georgia," Supreme Court of the State of Georgia, Augusta, June Term, 1854, 15 Ga, p. 14; Orville Vernon Burton, *In My Father's House Are Many Mansions: Family and Community in Edgefield, South Carolina* (Chapel Hill, NC: University of North Carolina Press, 1985), pp. 75–7; "serpent . . . abolitionist": SRA-STA preamble quoted in J. William Harris, *Plain Folk and Gentry in a Slave Society: White Liberty and Black Slavery in Augusta's Hinterlands* (Middletown, CT: Wesleyan University Press, 1985), p. 60; "while": "Ricks vs the State of Georgia," Georgia Supreme Court, Savannah, January Term, 1855, 16 Ga., p. 601.

For a discussion of the significance and historiography of trafficking among slaves, see Alex Lichtenstein, "That Disposition to Theft, with Which They Have Been Branded: Moral Economy, Slave Management, and the Law," *JSocH* 21 (Spring 1988):413–40.

17. Compare for example Harris, *Plain Folk and Gentry*, pp. 94–124; Bill Cecil-Fronsman, *Common Whites: Class and Culture in Antebellum North Carolina* (Lexington, KY: University Press of Kentucky, 1992), pp. 9–30; Genovese, *Roll, Jordan, Roll*, pp. 606–09; James M. Denham, "The Florida Cracker Before the Civil War as Seen Through Travellers' Accounts," *FHQ* 72 (April 1994):453–68. See also Jacqueline Jones, *The Dispossessed: America's Underclasses from the Civil War to the Present* (New York: Basic Books, 1992), pp. 45–72.

18. Quoted from Olmsted, *Cotton Kingdom*, p. 70.

19. Michael P. Johnson and James L. Roark, *Black Masters: A Free Family of Color in the Old South* (New York: W. W. Norton, 1984); Bolton, *Poor Whites of the Antebellum South*, p. 39; Barbara Jeanne Fields, *Slavery and Freedom on the Middle Ground: Maryland During the Nineteenth Century* (New Haven: Yale University Press, 1985), pp. 73, 88; "vagabonds . . . support": Frederick Law Olmsted, *A Journey in the Back Country, 1853–1854* (New York: Schocken Books, 1970; orig. pub. 1860), p. 219.

20. Ira Berlin, *Slaves Without Masters: The Free Negro in the Antebellum South* (New York: Pantheon, 1974), pp. 174–81.

21. *Ibid.*, p. 137; Luther Porter Jackson, *Free Negro Labor and Property-Holding in Virginia, 1830–1860* (New York: Atheneum, 1969; orig. pub. 1942), pp. 34–101; Eugene D. Genovese, "The Slave States of North America," in David W. Cohen and Jack P. Greene, eds., *Neither Slave Nor Free: The Freedman of African Descent in the Slave Societies of the New World* (Baltimore: Johns Hopkins University Press, 1972), pp. 258–77.

22. Petition quoted in Brenda Stevenson, *Life in Black and White: Family and Community in the Slave South* (New York: Oxford University Press, 1996), pp. 271–72.

23. Adele Logan Alexander, *Ambiguous Lives: Free Women of Color in Rural Georgia, 1789–1879* (Fayetteville, AR: University of Arkansas Press, 1991); Marks, "Skilled Blacks in Antebellum St. Mary's County, Maryland"; Berlin, *Slaves Without Masters*, pp. 223–24; Victoria Bynum, *Unruly Women: The Politics of Social and Sexual Control in the Old South* (Chapel Hill, NC: University of North Carolina Press, 1992), pp. 79–102; Steve Baker, "Free Blacks in Antebellum Madison County," *THQ* 52 (Spring 1993):56–63.

24. "so drunk": Fred Shelley, ed., "The Journal of Ebenezer Hazard in Virginia, 1777," *VMHB* 62 (October 1954):423; Philip Africa, "Slaveholding in the Salem Community, 1771–1851," *NCHR* 54 (Summer 1957):284.

25. Steven Hahn, *The Roots of Southern Populism: Yeoman Farmers and the Transformation of the Georgia Upcountry, 1850–1890* (New York: Oxford University Press, 1983); Stephanie McCurry, *Masters of Small Worlds: Yeoman Households, Gender Relations, and the Political Culture of the Antebellum South Carolina Low Country* (New York:

Oxford University Press, 1995); Lacey K. Ford, Jr., *Origins of Southern Radicalism: The South Carolina Upcountry, 1800–1860* (New York: Oxford University Press, 1988).

26. "labourers": William Howard Russell, *My Diary North and South* (New York: Harper Brothers, 1954), p. 1; Laurence Shore, *Southern Capitalists: The Ideological Leadership of an Elite, 1832–1885* (Chapel Hill, NC: University of North Carolina Press, 1986), pp. 75–77; "who had": Olmsted, *Journey in the Back Country*, p. 211; "a big . . . labors": *Ga. Narrs.*, Vol. 12, p. 222; Michele K. Gillespie, "Planters in the Making: Artisanal Opportunity in Georgia, 1790–1830," in Howard B. Rock, et al., eds., *American Artisans: Crafting Social Identity, 1750–1850* (Baltimore: Johns Hopkins University Press, 1995), pp. 33–47.

27. Cecil-Fronsman, *Common Whites*, p. 10.

28. "I have": John Ball, Sr., quoted in Mark S. Schantz, "'A Very Serious Business': Managerial Relationships on the Ball Plantations, 1800– 1835," *SCHM* 88 (January 1987): 4 (notes Schantz, "overseers were as difficult to control as the slaves themselves" [p. 11]); Olmsted, *Cotton Kingdom*, p. 64.

29. Bolton, *Poor Whites in the Antebellum South*, pp. 44, 52, 97, 104; "we . . . morning": York quoted in Cecil-Fronsman, *Common Whites*, p. 16; "with the niggers": Olmsted, *A Journey in the Back Country*, p. 219; McCurry, *Masters of Small Worlds*, pp. 78–81; Guion Griffis Johnson, *Antebellum North Carolina: A Social History* (Chapel Hill, NC: University of North Carolina Press, 1937), p. 71.

30. Shenandoah County, Virginia, Account Books, 1799–1838, Vol. I: 1799–1838: Beckford Parish Poorhouse Accounts. *Slavery in Antebellum Southern Industries*, ed. by Charles B. Dew (Bethesda, MD: University Publications of America, 1993), microfilm reel 23. See also Burton, *In My Father's House*, p. 50.

31. "nigger . . .advantage": quoted in James F. Hopkins, *A History of the Hemp Industry in Kentucky* (Lexington, KY: University of Kentucky, 1951), pp. 4, 24–30.

32. John C. Inscoe, "Mountain Masters: Slaveholding in Western North Carolina," *NCHR* 61 (April 1984):167–69; Bolton, *Poor Whites in the Antebellum South*, pp. 15, 43; Peter Way, *Common Labour: Workers and the Digging of North American Canals, 1780–1860* (Cambridge, UK: Cambridge University Press, 1993), p. 103; Hawkins Family Papers, 1738–1865, Warren and Franklin Counties, North Carolina, folder 225, reel 19 ("Account Book, 1856") in *Antebellum Southern Industries*; Robert B. Outland III, "Slavery, Work, and the Geography of the North Carolina Naval Stores Industry, 1835–1860," *JSouH* 62 (February 1996):27–56.

33. "I have": Arthur quoted in James Hugo Johnston, "The Participation of White Men in Virginia Negro Insurrections," *JNH* 16 (April 1931):161.

34. Harris, *Plain Folk and Gentry in a Slave Society*, pp. 92–3.

35. James Henry Hammond, "Letter to an English Abolitionist, Silver Bluff (S.C.), Jan. 28, 1845, in Drew Gilpin Faust, ed., *The Ideology of Slavery: Proslavery Thought in the Antebellum South, 1830–1860* (Baton Rouge, LA: Louisiana State University Press, 1981) pp. 172, 177; "worthlessness": Hammond quoted in Harris, *Plain Folk and Gentry*, p. 67.

36. "a precarious": Hammond quoted in Burton, *In My Father's House*, p. 56; "on . . .

liquor": Miscellaneous Plantation Books, 1840–57, Silver Bluff Plantation. *Antebellum Plantation Records,* Series 1, microfilm reel 4.

37. For overviews, see Richard C. Wade, *Slavery in the Cities: The South, 1820–1860* (London: Oxford University Press, 1964); Leonard P. Curry, *The Free Black in Urban America, 1800–1850: The Shadow of the Dream* (Chicago: University of Chicago Press, 1981); Claudia Goldin, *Urban Slavery in the American South, 1820–1860: A Quantitative History* (Chicago: University of Chicago Press, 1976); Berlin, *Slaves Without Masters.*

38. "faithful": letter to the *Southern Banner* (Athens) in Ulrich B. Phillips, ed., *Plantation and Frontier,* Vol. II of *A Documentary History of American Industrial Society,* ed. by John R. Commons, *et al.* (Cleveland: Arthur H. Clark Co., 1910), p. 361. For a discussion of the different functions of slavery, see for example Barbara Jeanne Fields, *Slavery and Freedom on the Middle Ground: Maryland During the Nineteenth Century* (New Haven: Yale University Press, 1985), pp. 49–52.

39. Wade, *Slavery in the Cities,* pp. 3–27; Ira Berlin and Herbert G. Gutman, "Natives and Immigrants, Free Men and Slaves: Urban Workingmen in the Antebellum South," *AHR* 88 (December 1983):1175–1200; Fred Bateman and Thomas Weiss, *A Deplorable Scarcity: The Failure of Industry in the Slave Economy* (Chapel Hill, NC: University of North Carolina Press, 1981), pp. 90–3; Jorg Echternkamp, "Emerging Ethnicity: The German Experience in Antebellum Baltimore," *MHM* 86 (Spring 1991): 1–22.

40. Leonard Price Stavisky, "Industrialism in Ante Bellum Charleston," *JNH* 36 (July 1951):302–22; Berlin, *Slaves Without Masters,* p. 237; "slave-holding . . . mechanics": Olmsted, *The Cotton Kingdom,* pp. 231–33; Wade, *Slavery in the Cities,* pp. 28–54; Whittington B. Johnson, "Free African-American Women in Savannah: Affluence and Autonomy Amid Diversity," *GHQ* 76 (Summer 1992):260–83.

41. Christopher Silver, "A New Look at Old South Urbanization: The Irish Worker in Charleston, South Carolina, 1840–1860," in Samuel M. Hines, *et al.,* eds., *South Atlantic Urban Studies,* Vol. 3 (Charleston, SC: University of South Carolina Press, 1979), p. 160; W. Marvin Dulaney, *Black Police in America* (Bloomington, IN: Indiana University Press, 1996). See chap. 7 for a more extensive discussion of textile mills.

42. Whittington, "Free African-American Women in Savannah," pp. 260–83; Suzanne Lebsock, *The Free Women of Petersburg: Status and Culture in a Southern Town, 1784–1860* (New York: W. W. Norton, 1984), pp. 87–111; Berlin, *Slaves Without Masters,* pp. 177–81; "deliverance": H. B. Stewart, Savannah, July 17, 1848, "Documents: Letters of Negroes Addressed to the American Colonization Society," *JNH* 10 (April 1925):236; Laylon Wayne Jordan, "Police Power and Public Safety in Antebellum Charleston: The Emergence of a New Police, 1800–1860," in Hines, *et al.,* eds., *SAUS,* Vol. III, pp. 122–29; Walter J. Fraser, Jr., "The City Elite, 'Disorder,' and the Poor Children of Pre-Revolutionary Charleston," *SCHM* 84 (July 1983):167–79; Marianne Buroff Sheldon, "Black-White Relations in Richmond, Virginia, 1782–1820," *JSouH* 45 (February 1979):27–44.

43. Frederick Douglass, *My Bondage and My Freedom*, in Henry Louis Gates, ed., *Frederick Douglass: Autobiographies* (New York: Library of America, 1994), pp. 326–37; Wade, *Slavery in the Cities*, pp. 209–42; Berlin, *Slaves Without Masters*, pp. 284–315; William A. Byrne, "The Hiring of Woodson, Slave Carpenter of Savannah," *GHQ* 77 (Summer 1993):245–63; Clement Eaton, "Slave-Hiring in the Upper South: A Step Toward Freedom," *MVHR* 48 (March 1960):663–78.

44. Sheldon, "Black-White Relations in Richmond"; Stephanie Cole, "Changes for Mrs. Thornton's Arthur: Patterns of Domestic Service in Washington, D.C., 1800–1835," *SSH* 15 (Fall 1991):367–78. For historical antecedents, see Philip D. Morgan, "Black Life in Eighteenth-Century Charleston," *PAH*, new series I (1984):187–232.

45. "Tumultuous": quoted in Sheldon, "Black-White Relations in Richmond," p. 38.

46. "unnaturalness . . . master": *Daily Intelligencer*, January 9, 1860, quoted in Phillips, ed., *Plantation and Frontier*, pp. 159–60; Wade, *Slavery in the Cities*, pp. 48–54, 80–110; James Howard Brewer, "Legislation Designed to Control Slavery in Wilmington and Fayetteville," *NCHR* 30 (April 1953):155–66; John Hebron Moore, "Simon Gray, Riverman: A Slave Who Was Almost Free," *MVHR* 49 (December 1962):472–84; "patrol": Phillips, ed., *Plantation and Frontier*, p. 149; "loafing . . . kind": Address of the Mayor of New Orleans, 1813, *ibid.*, pp. 153–54; Genovese, *Roll, Jordan, Roll*, p. 559.

47. "the legions . . . board": Philip S. Foner and Ronald L. Lewis, eds., *The Black Worker: A Documentary History from Colonial Times to the Present*, Vol. I (Philadelphia: Temple University Press, 1978), p. 15; Charles Wesley, *Negro Labor in the United States, 1850–1925: A Study in Economic History* (New York: Vanguard Press, 1927), p. 79.

48. "free": quoted in Cecil-Fronsman, *Common Whites*, p. 80; "unjust": *Georgia Telegraph* (1849) quoted in Norris W. Preyer, "The Historian, the Slave, and the Ante-Bellum Textile Industry," *JNH* 46 (April 1961):80; "whose . . . government": Phillips, ed., *Plantation and Frontier*, p. 367; Silver, "A New Look at Old South Urbanization," pp. 147, 158.

49. "Rich": quoted in Wesley, *Negro Labor in the United States*, p. 71; "the right . . . yourselves": quoted in Kathleen Bruce, "Slave Labor in the Virginian Iron Industry," *WMQ* 2nd series 6 (October 1926):296–97; "It must": Anderson quoted in Charles B. Dew, *Iron Maker to the Confederacy: Joseph R. Anderson and the Tredegar Iron Works* (New York: W. W. Norton, 1994), p. 26.

CHAPTER SEVEN

1. P. G. T. Beauregard to the Chairman of a South Carolina Legislative Committee, Charleston, Dec. 10, 1863, in Ira Berlin *et al.*, eds., *Freedom: A Documentary History of Emancipation, 1861–1867*, Series 1, Vol. I. *The Destruction of Slavery* (Cambridge, UK: Cambridge University Press, 1985), pp. 715–16 (hereinafter after cited as *Destruction of Slavery*).

2. *Ibid.*

3. "there . . . etiquette": D. H. Hill, Commander of the Confederate Post of York-town, VA, June 19, 1861, in *Destruction of Slavery*, p. 685.

4. *DeBow's Review* 9 (July–December 1850):435.

5. Charles B. Dew, *Bond of Iron: Master and Slave at Buffalo Forge* (New York: W. W. Norton, 1994). See also Ronald L. Lewis, "Slave Families in Early Chesapeake Ironworks," *VMHB* 86 (April 1978):169–79.

6. Aubrey C. Land, "Economic Base and Social Structure: The Northern Chesa-peake in the Eighteenth Century," *JEH* 25 (December 1965):646–52; Fred Bate-man and Thomas Weiss, *A Deplorable Scarcity: The Failure of Industrialization in the Slave Economy* (Chapel Hill, NC: University of North Carolina Press, 1981), pp. 7, 20, 55, 84; Robert S. Starobin, *Industrial Slavery in the Old South* (New York: Oxford University Press, 1970).

7. Starobin, *Industrial Slavery in the Old South*; Joseph Clarke Robert, *The Tobacco Kingdom* (Gloucester, MA: Peter Smith, 1965; orig. pub. 1938), pp. 197–208. On the hardening of racial categories after emancipation, see for example C. Vann Woodward, *The Strange Career of Jim Crow* (New York: Oxford University Press, 1955), pp. 12–13.

8. John Edmund Stealey III, "Slavery and the West Virginia Salt Industry," *JNH* 49 (April 1974):105–31; Ronald L. Lewis, *Coal, Iron, and Slaves: Industrial Slavery in Maryland and Virginia, 1715–1865* (Westport, CT: Greenwood Press, 1979), pp. 179–214.

9. See for example Lewis, *Coal, Iron, and Slaves*, pp. 215–40; Fletcher M. Green, "Georgia's Forgotten Industry: Gold Mining," *GHQ* 19 (1935):1–19; David Williams, "Notes and Documents: African-Americans and the Georgia Gold Rush," *GHQ* 75 (Spring 1991):76–89; "1,680 spindles": Herbert Anthony Kellar, ed., *Solon Robinson, Pioneer and Agriculturist: Selected Writings*, Vol. II (New York: Da Capo Press, 1968), p. 218.

The following discussion of the antebellum textile industry is based on these sources (specific citations are included where appropriate): Bess Beatty, "Textile Labor in the North Carolina Piedmont: Mill Owner Images and Mill Worker Response, 1830–1900," *LH* 25 (Fall 1985):485–503; Richard W. Griffin and Diffee W. Standard, "The Cotton Textile Industry in Ante-Bellum North Carolina, Pt. II: An Era of Boom and Consolidation, 1830–1860," *NCHR* 34 (April 1957): 131–64; Ernest McPherson Lander, Jr., *The Textile Industry in Antebellum South Carolina* (Baton Rouge, LA: Louisiana State University Press, 1969); E. M. Lan-der, Jr., "Slave Labor in South Carolina Cotton Mills," *JNH* 38 (April 1953): 161–73; Randall M. Miller, "Daniel Pratt's Industrial Urbanism: The Cotton Mill Town in Antebellum Alabama," *AHQ* (Spring 1972):5–35; Randall M. Miller, "The Fabric of Control: Slavery in Antebellum Southern Textile Mills," *BHR* 55 (Winter 1981):471–90; Randall M. Miller, "The Cotton Mill Movement in Ante-bellum Alabama," Ph.D. thesis, Ohio State University, 1971; Broadus Mitchell, *William Gregg: Factory Master of the Old South* (Chapel Hill, NC: University of

North Carolina Press, 1928); John Hebron Moore, "Mississippi's Antebellum Textile Industry" *JMH* 16 (January 1954):81–98; Michael Shirley, "Yeoman Culture and Millworker Protest in Antebellum North Carolina," *JSouH* (August 1991):427–52; Diffee W. Standard and Richard W. Griffin, "The Cotton Textile Industry in Ante-Bellum North Carolina," Pt. I: "Origin and Growth to 1830," *NCHR* 34 (January 1957):15–35; Allen H. Stokes, Jr., "Black and White Labor and the Development of the Southern Textile Industry, 1800–1920," Ph.D. thesis, University of South Carolina, 1977; Tom E. Terrill, "Eager Hands: Labor for Southern Textiles, 1850–1860," *JEH* 36 (March 1976):84–99; and Gavin Wright, "Cheap Labor and Southern Textiles Before 1880," *JEH* 39 (September 1979):655–680.

10. Moore, "Mississippi's Ante-Bellum Textile Industry."

11. "There is . . . prejudice": James S. Buckingham, *The Slave States of America*, Vol. II (London: Fisher, Son & Co., 1842), p. 112.

12. Robinson quoted in Mitchell, *William Gregg*, p. 286, n 26. See also Kellar, ed., *Solon Robinson*, Vol. II, pp. 210–16.

13. Lander, "Slave Labor in South Carolina Cotton Mills," p. 166.

14. "never . . . seen": J. Graves quoted in *ibid.*, p. 168.

15. "A great": Freeman Hunt quoted in Griffin and Standard, "The Cotton Textile Industry in Ante-Bellum North Carolina," Pt. II, p. 155; "not only": William Gregg quoted in Mitchell, *William Gregg*, p. 63.

16. Bateman and Weiss, *A Deplorable Scarcity*, pp. 8–24; Dwight Billings, Jr., *Planters and the Making of a "New South": Class, Politics, and Development in North Carolina, 1865–1900* (Chapel Hill, NC: University of North Carolina Press, 1979), pp. 54–69; Moore, "Mississippi's Ante-Bellum Textile Industry," pp. 86–7.

17. Shirley, "Yeoman Culture and Millworker Protest in Antebellum Salem," pp. 435, 439; "Girls . . . department": James H. Taylor quoted in Mitchell, *William Gregg*, pp. 56–7. See also Orville Vernon Burton, *In My Father's House Are Many Mansions: Family and Community in Edgefield, South Carolina* (Chapel Hill, NC: University of North Carolina Press, 1985), pp. 53–7; J. William Harris, *Plain Folk and Gentry in a Slave Society: White Liberty and Black Slavery in Augusta's Hinterlands* (Middletown, CT: Wesleyan University Press, 1985), pp. 33–4.

18. Carrigan quoted in Beatty, "Textile Labor in the North Carolina Piedmont," p. 497.

19. Miller, "Daniel Pratt's Industrial Urbanism," p. 30.

20. "Cracker": Olmsted, *Cotton Kingdom*, p. 213.

21. "puts himself": William Gregg quoted in Lander, *The Textile Industry in Antebellum South Carolina*, p. 94; Shirley, "Yeoman Culture and Millworker Protest in Salem"; Beatty, "Textile Labor in the North Carolina Piedmont."

22. "render": Charles Lyell, *Second Visit to the United States*, Vol. II (New York, 1849), p. 236; "Negroes" quoted in Miller, "Fabric of Control," p. 480; Miller, "Daniel Pratt's Industrial Urbanism," p. 26; Standard and Griffin, "Cotton Textile Industry in Antebellum North Carolina," Pt. 1, p. 141; Lynda Fuller Clendenning,

"The Early Textile Industry in Maryland, 1810–1850," *MHM* 87 (Fall 1992):251–66.

23. "horrors": Alabama lawyer to the Confederate President, May 22, 1861, in Berlin, *et al.*, eds., *Destruction of Slavery*, p. 781.

24. "the sacro-sanctity": endorsement by John A. Campbell, *Destruction of Slavery*, p. 781; "If slaves": Cobb quoted in Harris, *Plain Folk and Gentry*, p. 53. For a case study, see Clarence L. Mohr, *On the Threshold of Freedom: Masters and Slaves in Civil War Georgia* (Athens, GA: University of Georgia Press, 1986).

25. "engendered": L. P. Walker to the Commander of the Confederate Army, Richmond, Aug. 28, 1861, *Destruction of Slavery*, p. 687; "seeking . . . producers": Petition from Randolph County, Alabama, to Confederate President, Wesabulga, AL, May 6, 1864, *ibid.*, pp. 757–58; "mere": John M. Gregory to the Confederate Secretary of War, Charles City Court House, VA, March 7, 1863, *ibid.*, p. 749.

26. "Soldiers": Proclamation by the Commander of the Confederate Army of the Peninsula, Lee's Farm, VA, April 11, 1862, *Destruction of Slavery*, p. 693; "Negros": John Winston to Commander of the Confederate Post of Yorktown, Yorktown, VA, June 19, 1861, *ibid.*, p. 684; "sickly": J. Bankhead Magruder to Confederate Adjutant and Inspector General, Yorktown, VA, Jan. 22, 1862, p. 689; "*One Hundred*": A. P. Hayne to the Confederate President, Charleston, SC, August 1861, *ibid.*, p. 695.

27. "had never": D. H. Hill to Commander of a Confederate Alabama Regiment, *ibid.*, p. 685.

28. "I am sure": Proclamation by the Commander of the Confederate Army of the Peninsula, April 11, 1862, *ibid.*, p. 693.

29. "Col'd": Wm Truedail to Commander of the Department of the Cumberland, Nashville, TN, March 7, 1863, *ibid.*, p. 301.

30. "Every . . . exposed": J. B. Magruder to the Confederate Secretary of War, April 29, 1862, *ibid.*, p. 694; "are . . . Sugar": R. S. Vest to the Chief Engineer of the Confederate Department of Northern Virginia, Richmond, VA, Dec. 16, 1864, *ibid*, p. 726.

31. "been appropriated": C. D. Rice to the Medical Director of the Confederate Defenses of Richmond, Dec. 13, 1862, *ibid.*, p. 703; "for the benefit": F. S. Blount to the Headquarters of the Confederate Department of Alabama, Mississippi, and East Louisiana, Mobile, AL, June 23, 1864, in *ibid.*, p. 738; "hard": Chief Engineer of the Confederate Department of Northern Virginia, Richmond, VA, December 1864, *ibid.*, p. 727; "destroyed . . . welfare": Thomas M. Jones to the Confederate Adjutant and Inspector General, Pensacola, FL, April 12, 1862, *ibid.*, p. 792.

32. "impressed": G. B. Cosby to the Confederate Commander at Gloucester Point, Williamsburg, VA, July 28, 1861, *ibid.*, p. 686; "There is": John Lenahan to the Confederate President, Lynchburg, VA, July 15, 1861, *ibid.*, p. 760; "the community": General R. A. Pryor, October, 1862, *ibid.*, p. 761.

33. "*decidedly*": Citizens of the Isle of Wight and Nansemond Counties, VA, to the Commander of the Department of North Carolina, October 1863, *ibid.*, pp.

764–65; "now wholly . . . crops": North Carolina Congressman to the Confederate Secretary of War, Enclosing a Letter from a North Carolina Farmer to the Congressman, Richmond, VA, Feb. 12, 1864, *ibid.*, pp. 765–66.

34. Virginia Millers to the Confederate Secretary of War, Lynchburg, VA, Sept. 25, 1861, *ibid.*, p. 731; "has . . . business": Wm S. Triplett, Virginia Manufacturer to the Confederate Secretary of War, Richmond, VA, April 23, 1862, *ibid.*, p. 761; "excellent": Thomas J. Kirkpatrick to the Chief of Artillery of the Confederate Army of Northern Virginia, Camp Pendleton, VA, Feb. 22, 1862, *ibid.*, p. 697; "selected . . . *hands*": John Kane to an Officer at the Richmond Arsenal, Clarksville, VA, Oct. 15, 1864, *ibid.*, p. 767.

35. "allow": D. W. Davis to the Confederate Secretary of War, Charleston, SC, Sept. 6, 1862, *ibid.*, p. 733; "fostering . . . off": Robert R. Shotwell to the Headquarters of the Confederate Department of Mississippi and East Louisiana, Jackson, MS, July 5, 1863, *ibid.*, p. 801.

36. "intelligent": John J. Werth to the Confederate Secretary of War, Richmond, VA, March 14, 1862, *ibid.*, p. 732; "stealing . . . himself": S.C. Slaveholders to the Confederate Secretary of War, Darlington District of South Carolina, March 1864, in *ibid.*, pp. 806–70.

37. J. W. Lapsley to the Confederate Secretary of War, Selma, AL, February 1864, *ibid.*, pp. 745–46; *ibid.*, p. 675.

38. "the said slaves": Charges and Testimony in the Confederate Court Martial of Five Florida Slaves, Pensacola, FL, April 6, 1862, *ibid.*, p. 785; "Traitors": Georgia Slaveholders to the Commander of the 3rd Division of the Confederate District of Georgia, Liberty County, GA, Aug. 1, 1862, *ibid.*, p. 795; "we must": "Memoranda on the Civil War," *CM* 36, new series 14 (1888): 600.

39. "working only": testimony by a South Carolina Freedman before the Southern Claims Commission, Georgetown County, SC, March 17, 1873, *ibid.*, pp. 813–14; Pension File of Henry Ellis, Co. C., 31st United States Colored Infantry, Civil War Pension Records, Record Group 15, National Archives, Washington, DC.

40. See for example Eric Foner, *Reconstruction: America's Unfinished Revolution, 1863–1877* (New York: Harper & Row, 1988).

41. Ira Berlin and Herbert Gutman, "Natives and Immigrants, Free Men and Slaves: Urban Workingmen in the Antebellum South," *AHR* 88 (December 1983): 1194; Herbert G. Gutman, *The Black Family in Slavery and Freedom, 1750–1925* (New York: Pantheon, 1976), pp. 433–60, 476–519, 623–44; Roger L. Ransom and Richard Sutch, *One Kind of Freedom: The Economic Consequences of Emancipation* (London: Cambridge University Press, 1977), pp. 228–30.

42. See for example Sharon Ann Holt, "Making Freedom Pay: Freedpeople Working for Themselves, North Carolina, 1865–1900," *JSouH* 60 (May 1994):229–62; Julie Savile, *The Work of Reconstruction: From Slave to Wage Labor in South Carolina, 1860–1870* (New York: Cambridge University Press, 1994).

43. "My father": George P. Rawick, ed., *The American Slave: A Composite Autobiography* (Westport, CT: Greenwood Press, 1972–79), Vol. 2, Pt. 2 (S. C. Narrs.), p. 38;

Banks quotations from *Okla. Narrs.*, Vol. 7, Pt. 1, p. 9; "worked . . . day": *Indiana Narrs.*, Vol. 6, Pt. 2, p. 179.

44. "delicate": Sir George Campbell, *White and Black: The Outcome of a Visit to the United States* (London: Chatto & Windus, 1879), p. 296; "We do not": Edwin DeLeon, "The New South," *Harper's New Monthly Magazine* 48 (February 1874):411.

45. Carl Schurz, *Report on the Condition of the South* (New York: Arno Press and The New York Times, 1969; orig. pub. by Congress in 1865), pp. 18, 21, 23.

46. *Ibid.*, p. 25.

CHAPTER EIGHT

1. "Hardscrabble Calendar: Report of the Trials of Oliver Cummins, Nathaniel G. Metcalf, Gilbert Humes and Arthur Farrier; Who Were Indicted. . . ." (Providence, RI, for the Purchaser, 1824), p. 16.

2. *Ibid.*, pp. 1, 19–20.

3. *Ibid.*, p. 5. On the riot and its causes, see Robert J. Cottrol, *The Afro-Yankees: Providence's Black Community in the Antebellum Era* (Westport, CT: Greenwood Press, 1982), pp. 53–5; William J. Brown, *The Life of William J. Brown of Providence, Rhode Island, with Personal Recollections* (Providence: Angell & Co., 1883), pp. 89–90.

4. See, for example, Julian Rammelkamp, "The Providence Negro Community, 1820–1842," *RIH* 7 (January 1948):29.

5. Gary Nash, *Forging Freedom: The Formation of Philadelphia's Black Community, 1720–1840* (Cambridge, MA: Harvard University Press, 1988), p. 177; Paul A. Gilje, *The Road to Mobocracy: Popular Disorder in New York City, 1763–1830* (Chapel Hill, NC: University of North Carolina Press, 1987), p. 159.

6. Truth quoted in Nell Irvin Painter, *Sojourner Truth: A Life, A Symbol* (New York: W. W. Norton, 1996), p. 126. See also Jean Fagan Yellin and John C. Van Horne, eds., *The Abolitionist Sisterhood: Women's Political Culture in Antebellum America* (Ithaca, NY: Cornell University Press, 1994); Shirley Yee, *Black Women Abolitionists: A Study in Activism, 1828–1860* (Knoxville, TN: University of Tennessee Press, 1992).

7. "burthen": Edward S. Abdy, *Journal of a Residence and Tour in the United States of North America, from April, 1833 to October, 1834* (London: John Murray, 1835), p. 331; "Letters of Governor Edward Coles Bearing on the Struggle of Freedom and Slavery in Illinois," *JNH* 3 (April 1918):158–95.

8. Eric Lott, *Love and Theft: Blackface Minstrelsy and the American Working Class* (New York: Oxford University Press, 1993); David R. Roediger, *The Wages of Whiteness: Race and the Making of the American Working Class* (London: Verso, 1991); George M. Fredrickson, *The Black Image in the White Mind: The Debate on Afro-American Character and Destiny, 1817–1914* (New York: Harper & Row, 1971), pp. 97–129; James M. McPherson, *The Abolitionist Legacy: From Reconstruction to the NAACP*

(Princeton: Princeton University Press, 1975), pp. 68–9; Reid Mitchell, *The Vacant Chair: The Northern Soldier Leaves Home* (New York: Oxford University Press, 1993), pp. 55–70.

9. The petition was reprinted in *The Liberator*, Feb. 15, 1834, and in Abdy, *Journal of a Residence and a Tour*, Vol. 3, pp. 246–47; "To the light": Jean H. Baker, *Affairs of Party: The Political Culture of Northern Democrats in the Mid-Nineteenth Century* (Ithaca, NY: Cornell University Press, 1983), p. 257.

10. *Historical Statistics of the United States, Colonial Times to 1957, A Statistical Abstract Supplement*, Vol. I (Washington, DC: Government Printing Office, 1960), p. 25; *Fifth Census: Or, Enumeration of the Inhabitants of the United States . . .* (Washington, DC: Government Printing Office, 1830), pp. 26, 27.

11. "Once": quoted in Leon Litwack, *North of Slavery*, p. 127; "The colored": Andrew T. Judson quoted in G. Smith Wormley, "Prudence Crandall," *JNH* 8 (January 1923):74; "Not satisfied": *The Liberator*, Feb. 15, 1834. According to Leonard Richards, for abolitionists black and white, "Connecticut remained the most inhospitable of the New England states," with a disproportionate share of anti-abolitionist activity during the 1830s. See Richards, *"Gentlemen of Property and Standing": Anti-Abolition Mobs in Jacksonian America* (New York: Oxford University Press, 1970), p. 40; James Oliver Horton and Lois E. Horton, *In Hope of Liberty: Culture, Community and Protest Among Northern Free Blacks, 1700–1860* (New York: Oxford University Press, 1997), pp. 213–14.

12. See the chapter "Providence, Modernization, and the Emergence of Northern Racism," in Cottrol, *The Afro-Yankees* pp. 147–64; "We dislike": James Freeman Clarke, "Present Condition of the Free Colored People of the United States," (New York: New York Anti-Slavery Society, 1859), p. 5.

13. Douglas, "[Free Blacks Must Learn Trades]" in Michael Meyer, ed., *Frederick Douglass: The Narrative and Selected Writings* (New York: Modern Library, 1984), pp. 349–50.

14. John Blassingame and John R. McKivigan, eds., *The Frederick Douglass Papers, Series One*, Vol. 3: *1855–63* (New Haven: Yale University Press, 1979), p. 71.

15. "such was": Meyer, ed., "Narrative of the Life of Frederick Douglass," p. 118.

16. "a transgressor": Blassingame and McKivigan, eds., *The Frederick Douglass Papers, Series One*, Vol. 4, pp. 232–34; "with saw . . . guest": Rosetta Douglass Sprague, "Anna Murray-Douglass—My Mother as I Recall Her," *JNH* 8 (January 1923):98. See also William S. McFeely, *Frederick Douglass* (New York: W. W. Norton, 1991).

17. "This is": The Hollingworth Family Letters, 1827–1830," in Thomas Dublin, ed., *Immigrant Voices: New Lives in America, 1773–1986* (Urbana, IL: University of Illinois Press, 1993), pp. 76–7; Bruce Laurie and Mark Schmitz, "Manufacture and Productivity: The Making of an Industrial Base, Philadelphia, 1850–1880," in Theodore Hershberg, ed., *Philadelphia: Work, Space, Family and Group Experience in the Nineteenth Century* (New York: Oxford University Press, 1981), pp. 43–92.

On deskilling, see for example Alan Dawley, *Class and Community: The Industrial Revolution in Lynn* (Cambridge, MA: Harvard University Press, 1976); Paul

Faler, *Mechanics and Manufacturers in the Early Industrial Revolution: Lynn, Massachusetts, 1800–1860* (Albany, NY: State University of New York Press, 1981). For a critique of recent labor historians' preoccupation with white male artisans and factory workers, see the Introduction to Peter Way, *Common Labour: Workers and the Digging of North American Canals, 1780–1860* (Cambridge, UK: Cambridge University Press, 1993).

18. Leonard P. Curry, *The Free Black in Urban America, 1800–1850: The Shadow of the Dream* (Chicago: University of Chicago Press, 1981), pp. 15–36.

19. Noel Ignatiev, *How the Irish Became White* (New York: Routledge, 1995), p. 115; Clarke, "Present Condition of the Free Colored People of the United States," p. 4. See also Oscar Handlin, *Boston's Immigrants* (New York: Atheneum, 1972; orig. pub. 1941), p. 252.

20. James Oliver Horton, "Shades of Color: The Mulatto in Three Antebellum Northern Communities," in James Oliver Horton, *Free People of Color: Inside the African-American Community* (Washington, D.C.: Smithsonian Institution Press, 1993), pp. 122–145; Theodore Hershberg and Henry Williams, "Mulattoes and Blacks: Intragroup Color Differences and Social Stratification in Nineteenth-Century Philadelphia," in Hershberg, ed., *Philadelphia*, pp. 392–434; Cottrol, *Afro-Yankees*, pp. 136–38; William Cheek and Aimee Lee Cheek, *John Mercer Langston and the Fight for Black Freedom, 1829–1865* (Urbana, IL: University of Illinois Press, 1989), pp. 137–43; Joseph P. Lynch, "Blacks in Springfield, 1868–1880: A Mobility Study," *HJWM* 2 (June 1979). On black women charismatic preachers, see Jean M. Humez, *Gifts of Power: The Writings of Rebecca Jackson, Black Visionary, Shaker Eldress* (Amherst, MA: University of Massachusetts Press, 1981); William L. Andrews, ed., *Sisters of the Spirit: Three Black Women's Autobiographies of the Nineteenth Century* (Bloomington, IN: Indiana University Press, 1986).

21. "Elleanor Eldridge," in Bert James Loewenberg and Ruth Bogin, eds., *Black Women in Nineteenth-Century American Life: Their Words, Their Thoughts, Their Feelings* (University Park, PA: Pennsylvania State University Press, 1976), pp. 81–3; "Memoir of Mrs. Chloe Spear, A Native of Africa, Who Was Enslaved in Childhood, and Died in Boston, January 3, 1815 . . . " (Boston: James Loring, 1832). See also Venture Smith, *A Narrative of the Life and Adventures of Venture Smith, A Native of Africa* (New London, CT: C. Holt, 1798).

22. Walter Licht, *Getting Work: Philadelphia, 1840–1950* (Cambridge, MA: Harvard University Press, 1992), pp. 45–6; Abdy, *Journal of a Residence and a Tour*, p. 185.

23. Leon Litwack, *North of Slavery: The Negro in the Free States, 1790–1860* (Chicago: University of Chicago Press, 1961), pp. 30–112; Dorothy Porter Wesley, "Integration versus Separatism: William Cooper Nell's Role in the Struggle for Equality," in Donald M. Jacobs, ed., *Courage and Conscience: Black and White Abolitionists in Boston* (Bloomington, IN: Indiana University Press, 1993), p. 220.

24. "chances": Johnson quoted in Carl D. Oblinger, "Alms for Oblivion: The Making of a Black Underclass in Southeastern Pennsylvania, 1780–1860," in John Bod-

nar, ed., *The Ethnic Experience in Pennsylvania* (Philadelphia: Bucknell University Press, 1973), p. 97.

25. Curry, *The Free Black*, pp. 15–36; Shane White, "'We Dwell in Safety and Pursue Our Honest Callings': Free Blacks in New York City, 1783–1810," *JAH* 75 (September 1988):445–70; Ira Berlin, "The Structure of the Free Negro Caste in the Antebellum United States," *JSocH* 9 (Spring 1976):297–318; "compelled": quoted in Licht, *Getting Work*, p. 31.

26. Paul A. Gilje and Howard B. Rock, "'Sweep O! Sweep O!': African-American Chimney Sweeps and Citizenship in the New Nation," *WMQ* 51 3rd series (July 1994):528–29; Laurie and Schmitz, "Manufacture and Productivity."

27. "mob . . . carman": Isaac Candler, *A Summary View of America, Comprising a Description of the Face of the Country* (London: T. Cadell, 1824), pp. 291–92; "the black": Abdy, *Journal of a Residence and a Tour*, p. 318; "there was": quoted in Curry, *The Free Black in Urban America*, p. 20.

28. Thomas C. Cochran, *Frontiers of Change: Early Industrialization in America* (New York: Oxford University Press, 1981); Thomas E. Leary, "Industrial Ecology and the Labor Process: The Redefinition of Craft in New England Textile Machinery Shops, 1820–1860," in Stephen Innes, ed., *Work and Labor in Early America* (Chapel Hill, NC: University of North Carolina Press, 1988), pp. 37–56; Judith McGaw, *Most Wonderful Machine: Mechanization and Social Change in Berkshire Paper Making, 1801–1885* (Princeton: Princeton University Press, 1987), pp. 335–74; Ronald Schultz, *The Republic of Labor: Philadelphia Artisans and the Politics of Class, 1720–1830* (New York: Oxford University Press, 1993), p. 170; Aleine Austin, *Matthew Lyon, "New Man" of the Democratic Revolution, 1749–1822* (University Park, PA: Pennsylvania State University Press, 1980), p. 37; Carroll Pursell, *The Machine in America: A Social History of Technology* (Baltimore: Johns Hopkins University Press, 1995), pp. 35–228.

29. Ignatiev, *How The Irish Became White*, p. 112; David John Jeremy, ed., *Henry Wansey and His American Journal* (Philadelphia: American Philosophical Society, 1970), p. 68; Eileen Boris, *Home to Work: Motherhood and the Politics of Industrial Homework in the United States* (Cambridge, UK: Cambridge University Press, 1994), pp. 10–12; Thomas Dublin, *Women at Work: The Transformation of Work and Community in Lowell, Massachusetts, 1826–1860* (New York: Columbia University Press, 1979); Jonathan Prude, "The Social System of Early New England Textile Mills: A Case Study, 1812–1840," in Herbert Gutman and Donald H. Bell, eds., *The New England Working Class and the New Labor History* (Urbana, IL: University of Illinois Press, 1987), pp. 90–127; Barbara M. Tucker, *Samuel Slater and the Origins of the American Textile Industry, 1790–1860* (Ithaca, NY: Cornell University Press, 1984); McGaw, *Most Wonderful Machine*, p. 293; Cottrol, *The Afro-Yankees*, p. 120. See also Herbert G. Gutman, *The Black Family in Slavery and Freedom, 1750–1925* (New York: Vintage Books, 1976), p. xviii. For another example of a "diverse" workforce consisting of immigrant men, white women, and white children, see James J. Farley, *Making Arms in the Machine Age: Philadelphia's Frank-*

ford Arsenal, 1816–1870 (University Park, PA: Pennsylvania State University Press, 1994), pp. 87–102.

30. "Anything": quoted in Edythe Quinn Caro, "'The Hills' in the Mid-Nineteenth Century: The History of a Rural Afro-American Community in Westchester County, New York" (Valhalla, NY: Westchester Historical Society, 1988), p. 21; Licht, *Getting Work*, p. 141.

31. "when respectable": *Philadelphia Morning Post* in Philip S. Foner and Ronald L. Lewis, eds., *The Black Worker: A Documentary History from Colonial Times to the Present*, Vol. II (Philadelphia: Temple University Press, 1978), p. 281; Laurie and Schmitz, "Manufacture and Productivity," pp. 54–56; Herbert G. Gutman and Ira Berlin, "Class Composition and the Development of the American Working Class," in Herbert G. Gutman, ed., *Power and Culture: Essays on the American Working Class* (New York: New Press, 1987), pp. 380–94; Bruce Laurie, Theodore Hershberg, and George Alter, "Immigrants and Industry: The Philadelphia Experience," in Hershberg, ed., *Philadelphia*, pp. 128–73; Oblinger, "Alms for Oblivion, pp. 101–03.

32. Mary Blewett, *Men, Women, and Work: Class, Gender, and Protest in the New England Shoe Industry, 1780–1910* (Urbana, IL: University of Illinois Press, 1988), pp. 113–14; Claudia Goldin and Kenneth Sokoloff, "Women, Children, and Industrialization in the Early Republic: Evidence from the Manufacturing Censuses," *JEH* 42 (December 1982):741–74; "[Free Blacks Must Learn Trades]," pp. 349–50; "that they": Philip S. Foner and George E. Walker, eds., *Proceedings of the Black State Conventions, 1840–1865*, Vol. I: *New York, Indiana, Michigan, and Ohio* (Philadelphia: Temple University Press, 1979), p. 277.

33. David Brion Davis, *The Problem of Slavery in the Age of Revolution, 1770–1823* (Ithaca, NY: Cornell University Press, 1975), pp. 241–42; "A number . . . community": "Protest Against the Conduct of Nightmen," in Howard B. Rock, ed., *The New York City Artisan, 1789–1825: A Documentary History* (Albany, NY: State University of New York Press, 1989), pp. 39–40. See also Gilje and Rock, "'Sweep O! Sweep O!'"

34. See for example Gilje, *The Road to Mobocracy*, pp. 145–201.

35. "free": "Workingmen of New Haven!" in Philip S. Foner and Herbert Shapiro, *Northern Labor and Antislavery: A Documentary History* (Westport, CT: Greenwood Press, 1994), p. 245; "Labor": "The Great Issue," *ibid.*, p. 243; Edward Magdol, *The Antislavery Rank and File: A Social Profile of the Abolitionist Constituency* (Westport, CT: Greenwood Press, 1986); Roediger, *Wages of Whiteness*.

36. "the better": Abdy, *Journal of a Residence and a Tour*, Vol. I, pp. 116–17; David O. White, "The Fugitive Blacksmith of Hartford: James W. C. Pennington," *CHSB* 49 (1984):14; "with horny . . . eloquence": Lydia Maria Child, "Letters from New York, 1843," in Judith Fetterley, ed., *Provisions: A Reader from Nineteenth-Century American Women* (Bloomington, IN: Indiana University Press, 1985), pp. 168, 176, 178; Lott, *Love and Theft*, pp. 43–44.

37. Emma Jones Lapsansky, "'Since They Got those Separate Churches': Afro-Americans and Racism in Jacksonian Philadelphia," *AQ* 32 (Spring 1980):54–

78; "the conduct . . . right": quoted in Abdy, *Journal of a Residence and a Tour*, Vol. 3, p. 318.

38. "particularly": Isaac Holmes, *An Account of the United States of America, Derived from Actual Observation* . . . (London: H. Fisher, 1823), p. 331; "rushed . . .Boston": *North Star*, Feb. 27, 1851, p. 2; Susan G. Davis, *Parades and Power: Street Theatre in Nineteenth-Century Philadelphia* (Philadelphia: Temple University Press, 1985), pp. 113–54.

39. "admonished . . . faces": A. M. Sumner quoted in Cheek and Cheek, *John Mercer Langston*, p. 61; "Many whites": Abdy, *Journal of a Residence and a Tour*, Vol. 3, p. 330. See also Shane White, *Somewhat More Independent: The End of Slavery in New York City, 1770–1810* (Athens, GA: University of Georgia Press, 1991), pp. 185–209; Linda K. Kerber, "Abolitionists and Amalgamators: The New York City Race Riots of 1834," *NYH* 48 (January 1967):28–40; Larry Tise, *Proslavery: A History of the Defense of Slavery in America, 1701–1840* (Athens, GA: University of Georgia Press, 1987), pp. 264–69.

40. "Negroes . . . negroes": quoted in *The Liberator*, Nov. 17, 1837, p. 185; Litwack, *North of Slavery*, pp. 64–112; Marvin E. Gettleman, *The Dorr Rebellion: A Study in American Radicalism, 1833–1849* (New York: Random House, 1973); Horton and Horton, *In Hope of Liberty*, pp. 167–69.

41. Lott, *Love and Theft*, p. 127; Roediger, *Wages of Whiteness*, pp. 106, 147–50.

42. Gilje, *Road to Mobocracy*, p. 1110; John Runcie, "'Hunting the Nigs' in Philadelphia: The Race Riot of August 1834," *PH* 39 (April 1972):187–218; Richards, *"Gentlemen of Property and Standing,"* pp. 115–22, 152, 174–75; Russell F. Weigley, "'A Peaceful City': Public Order in Philadelphia from Consolidation Through the Civil War," in Allen F. Davis and Mark H. Haller, eds., *The Peoples of Philadelphia: A History of Ethnic Groups and Lower-Class Life, 1790–1940* (Philadelphia: Temple University Press, 1973), pp. 155–73.

43. "although": "The Apprentice Question" in Foner and Lewis, eds., *The Black Worker*, p. 283. See also David Montgomery, *Citizen Worker: The Experience of Workers in the United States with Democracy and the Free Market During the Nineteenth Century* (Cambridge, UK: Cambridge University Press, 1993); Sean Wilentz, *Chants Democratic: New York City and the Rise of the American Working Class, 1788–1850* (New York: Oxford University Press, 1984).

44. "Race . . . slavery": Alexis de Tocqueville, *Democracy in America*, ed. by J. P. Mayer, Vol. I (Garden City, NY: Doubleday, 1969), pp. 343, 341.

CHAPTER NINE

1. Pension file of John Roberts, Company I, 102nd United States Colored Infantry, Civil War Pension Records, Record Group 15, National Archives, Washington, DC (hereinafter cited with the name of pension applicant and his regiment, RG 15, NA).

2. Pension file of George W. Patterson, Company G., 102nd USCI, RG 15, NA. The

information related to William H. Brown (Company A, 28th Regiment, USCI) is included in the Patterson file because Brown's daughter Sarah married George Patterson in 1881. After Patterson died in 1906, a dispute arose over Sarah Brown Patterson's claim to pension benefits based on her status as the daughter of one deceased veteran and the widow of another.

3. Gavin Wright, "American Agriculture and the Labor Market: What Happened to Proletarianization?" *AH* 62 (Summer 1988):182–209; Paul G. Clemons and Lucy Simler, "Rural Labor and the Farm Household in Chester County, Pennsylvania, 1750–1820," in Stephen Innes, ed., *Work and Labor in Early America* (Chapel Hill, NC: University of North Carolina Press, 1988), pp. 106–43; Jack Larkin, "'Labor is the Great Thing in Farming': The Farm Laborers of the Ward Family of Shrewsbury, Massachusetts, 1787–1860," in *PAAS* (1989):189–226.

   For an evocative fictional account of a veteran returning to his midwestern home and to his "daily fight with nature and against the injustice of his fellow-man," see Hamlin Garland, "The Return of a Private," in *Main-Travelled Roads* (New York: Harper and Brothers, 1921).

4. Jacqueline Jones, *The Dispossessed: America's Underclasses from the Civil War to the Present* (New York: Basic Books, 1992), pp. 104–26.

5. George W. Patterson Pension File, RG 15, NA; Helen T. Catterall, ed., *Judicial Cases Concerning American Slavery and the Negro*, Vol. V (Washington, DC: Carnegie Institution, 1937), pp. 31–43. See also Nicole Etcheson, *The Emerging Midwest: Upland Southerners and the Political Culture of the Old Northwest, 1787–1861* (Bloomington, IN: Indiana University Press, 1996).

6. David R. Roediger, *The Wages of Whiteness: Race and the Making of the American Working Class* (London: Verso, 1991); Noel Ignatiev, *How the Irish Became White* (New York: Routledge, 1995).

7. See for example David Brion Davis, *The Problem of Slavery in the Age of Revolution, 1770–1823* (Ithaca, NY: Cornell University Press, 1973).

8. Robert J. Steinfeld, *The Invention of Free Labor: The Employment Relation in English and American Law and Culture, 1350–1870* (Chapel Hill, NC: University of North Carolina Press, 1991), pp. 147–72; Carole Shammas, "Anglo-American Household Government in Comparative Perspective," *WMQ* 52 (January 1995):104–44; Christine Stansell, *City of Women: Sex and Class in New York, 1789–1860* (New York: Knopf, 1986), pp. 19–38; William Sanger, "Working Women of New York in 1857," in Ruth Barnes Moynihan, *et al.*, *Second to None: A Documentary History of American Women*, Vol. I (Lincoln, NE: University of Nebraska Press, 1993), p. 234; Benjamin J. Klebaner, "Pauper Auctions: The 'New England Method' of Public Poor Relief," *EIHC* 91 (July 1955):195–210; Robert E. Cray, *Poverty and Poor Relief: New York City and Its Rural Environs, 1700–1830* (Philadelphia: Temple University Press, 1988), p. 111; Lemuel Shattuck, *A History of the Town of Concord* (Boston: Russell, Odeorne & Co., 1835), pp. 218–19.

9. Ira Berlin, "The Structure of the Free Negro Caste in the Antebellum United States," *JSocH* 9 (Spring 1976): 298–99; "Life of James Mars, A Slave Born and

Sold in Connecticut, Written by Himself" (Hartford, CT: Case, Lockwood & Co., 1867); "runaway . . . distinction": Hubert Schmidt, "Slavery and Attitudes on Slavery in Hunterdon County, New Jersey" (Flemington, NJ: Hunterdon County Historical Society, 1941), p. 18; Simeon Moss, "The Persistence of Slavery and Involuntary Servitude in a Free State (1685–1866)," *JNH* 35 (July 1950):289–314.

10. David Neal Keller, "Shanghaied!" *AmH* (September 1995):66–72; Harold D. Langley, "The Negro in the Navy and Merchant Service—1789–1860," *JNH* 52 (October 1967):273–85; "disposed": "State of Delaware vs. Moses McColly, Negro," in Philip Foner and Lewis, eds., *The Black Worker: A Documentary History from Colonial Times to the Present*, Vol. I (Philadelphia: Temple University Press, 1978), pp. 95–6; Leo H. Hirsch, Jr., "The Free Negro in New York," *JNH* 16 (October 1931):440.

11. Peter Way, *Common Labour: Workers and the Digging of North American Canals, 1780–1860* (Cambridge, UK: Cambridge University Press, 1993), pp. 39, 95; Simler, "The Landless Worker," pp. 177–78; Richard B. Lyman, Jr., "'What Is Done in My Absence?' Levi Lincoln's Oakham, Massachusetts, Farm Workers, 1807–20," *PAAS* (1989), pp. 151–87; Jonathan Prude, "The Social System of Early New England Textile Mills: A Case Study, 1812–1840," in Herbert G. Gutman and Donald H. Bell, eds., *The New England Working Class and the New Labor History* (Urbana, IL: University of Illinois Press, 1987), pp. 109–12; Walter Licht, *Getting Work: Philadelphia, 1840–1950* (Cambridge, MA: Harvard University Press, 1992), p. 234; Patricia A. Cooper, *Once a Cigar Maker: Men, Women and Work Culture in American Cigar Factories, 1900–1919* (Urbana, IL: University of Illinois Press, 1987), pp. 75–93; Eileen Boris, *Home to Work: Motherhood and the Politics of Industrial Homework in the United States* (Cambridge, UK: Cambridge University Press, 1994), p. 10.

12. Lamont D. Thomas, *Rise to Be a People: A Biography of Paul Cuffee* (Urbana, IL: University of Illinois Press, 1988), p. 30; C. G. Woodson, "The Negroes of Cincinnati Prior to the Civil War," *JNH* 1 (January 1916):21; Way, *Common Labour*, pp. 2, 10–11; Grania Bolton Marcus, "A Forgotten People: Discovering the Black Experience in Suffolk County" (Mattituck, NY: Society for the Preservation of Long Island Antiquities, 1988), p. 30; David Gerber, *The Making of an American Pluralism: Buffalo, New York, 1825–1860* (Urbana, IL: University of Illinois Press, 1989), pp. 275–79; "all on an": W. M. Bohn, *Glimpses of New York City* (Charleston, SC: J. J. McCarthy, 1852), p. 126; "hard earned": Society of Friends, "A Statistical Inquiry into the Condition of the People of Color in the City and Districts of Philadelphia" (Philadelphia: Society of Friends, 1849), p. 39; Emma Jones Lapsansky, *Neighborhoods in Transition: William Penn's Dream and Urban Reality* (New York: Garland Press, 1984), p. 84.

13. Way, *Common Labour*, p. 192; Bruce Laurie, "Fire Companies and Gangs in Southwark: The 1840s," in Allen F. Davis and Mark H. Haller, eds., *The Peoples of Philadelphia: A History of Ethnic Groups and Lower-Class Life, 1790–1940* (Philadel-

phia: Temple University Press, 1973), pp. 71–88; Cynthia J. Shelton, *The Mills of Manayunk: Industrialization and Social Conflict in the Philadelphia Region, 1787–1837* (Baltimore: Johns Hopkins University Press, 1986), pp. 3–4, 74, 118; Alan Dawley, *Class and Community: The Industrial Revolution in Lynn* (Cambridge, MA: Harvard University Press, 1976); "American ladies": quoted in Mary H. Blewett, *Men, Women, and Work: Class, Gender, and Protest in the New England Shoe Industry, 1780–1910* (Urbana, IL: University of Illinois Press, 1988), p. 120; Sean Wilentz, *Chants Democratic: New York City and the Rise of the American Working Class, 1788–1850* (New York: Oxford University Press, 1984), pp. 62–3, 91–2, 238, 244; Clyde Griffen, "Workers Divided: The Effect of Craft and Ethnic Differences in Poughkeepsie, New York, 1850–1880," in Stephan Thernstrom and Richard Sennett, eds., *Nineteenth-Century Cities: Essays in the New Urban History* (New Haven: Yale University Press, 1969), pp. 49–97.

14. "all servant": Bohn, *Glimpses of New York City*, p. 134; "to . . . children": Charles Mackay, *Life and Liberty in America; Or, Sketches of a Tour in the United States and Canada (1857–58)* (London: Smith, Elder, & Co., 1859), pp. 45–7; "I . . . beautiful": Louisa May Alcott, *Work: A Story of Experience* (New York: Penguin Books, 1994; orig. pub. 1873), pp. 168, 117; Gail Parker, ed., *The Ovenbirds: American Women on Womanhood, 1820–1920* (New York: Anchor Books, 1972). See also Hasia Diner, *Erin's Daughters in America: Irish Immigrant Women in the Nineteenth Century* (Baltimore: Johns Hopkins University Press, 1983); Faye E. Dudden, *Serving Women: Household Service in Nineteenth-Century America* (Middletown, CT: Wesleyan University Press, 1983); Stansell, *City of Women*, pp. 156–61; Carol Lasser, "'The World's Dread Laugh': Sisterhood and Service in Nineteenth-Century Boston," in Gutman and Bell, eds., *The New England Working Class and the New Labor History*, pp. 72–89.

15. "for their . . . runaways": *Douglass's Monthly* (July 1859): 108–9; Daniel F. Littlefield, Jr., and Mary Ann Littlefield, "The Beams Family: Free Blacks in Indian Territory," *JNH* 61 (January 1976):16–35; James Horton, "Links to Bondage: Free Blacks and the Underground Railroad," in James Oliver Horton, *Free People of Color: Inside the African American Community* (Washington, DC: Smithsonian Institution, 1993), pp. 63–4; Carol Wilson, *Freedom at Risk: The Kidnapping of Free Blacks in America, 1780–1865* (Lexington, KY: University Press of Kentucky, 1994) (see especially chapter 5: "An Almost Sleepless Vigilance: Black Resistance to Kidnapping," pp. 103–16). See also Herbert Aptheker, ed., *A Documentary History of the Negro People in the United States*, Vol. 1: *From Colonial Times Through the Civil War* (New York: Citadel Press, 1951), pp. 334–36.

16. "in infancy": Edward S. Abdy, *Journal of a Residence and a Tour in the United States of North America* (London: John Murray, 1835), p. 174; "as if": *North Star*, April 10, 1851, p. 1; Benjamin Drew, ed., *A North-Side View of Slavery: The Refugee: Or the Narratives of Fugitive Slaves in Canada* (New York: Negro Universities Press, 1968; orig. pub. 1856).

17. "a dead": Rev. Lyman Beecher quoted in Carl F. Wittke, *The Irish in America*

(Baton Rouge, LA: Louisiana State University Press, 1956), p. 119; "thousands": William H. Herndon quoted in David Herbert Donald, *Lincoln* (New York: Simon & Schuster, 1995), p. 228; Lapsansky, *Neighborhoods in Transition*, pp. 72–3; David Montgomery, "The Shuttle and the Cross: Weavers and Artisans in the Kensington Riots of 1844," *JSocH* 5 (Summer 1972):411–46; John R. Mulkern, *The Know-Nothing Party in Massachusetts* (Boston: Northeastern University Press, 1990).

18. "Irish confetti": quoted in Roediger, *Wages of Whiteness*, p. 136.

19. "You no longer": quoted in Ignatiev, *How the Irish Became White*, p. 111; Kirby Miller, *Emigrants and Exiles: Ireland and the Irish Exodus to North America* (New York: Oxford University Press, 1985), p. 318; Robert Ernst, *Immigrant Life in New York City, 1825–1863* (Syracuse, NY: Syracuse University Press, 1994), p. 69.

20. Matilda C. F. Houstoun, *Hesperos: Or, Travels in the West . . .* (London: J. W. Parker, 1850), pp. 178–79; Dennis V. Clark, "The Philadelphia Irish: Persistent Presence," in Haller and David, eds., *Peoples of Philadelphia*, pp. 135–54; Geoffrey Blodgett, *The Gentle Reformers: Massachusetts Democrats in the Cleveland Era* (Cambridge, MA: Harvard University Press, 1966), pp. 53–5, 61–3; Dennis P. Ryan, *Beyond the Ballot Box: A Social History of the Boston Irish, 1845–1917* (E. Brunswick, NJ: Associated Universities Press, 1983).

On the significance of partisan political activity and affiliation as an element in the development of white working-class consciousness, see Amy Bridges, "Becoming American: The Working Classes in the United States Before the Civil War," in Ira Katznelson and Aristide R. Zolberg, eds., *Working-Class Formation: Nineteenth-Century Patterns in Western Europe and the United States* (Princeton: Princeton University Press, 1986), pp. 157–96.

21. "When they": "The American Colonization Society," *NEM* 2 (January 1832):17. For an extended discussion of political activism in northern African-American antebellum communities, see James Oliver Horton and Lois E. Horton, *In Hope of Liberty: Culture, Community and Protest Among Northern Free Blacks, 1700–1860* (New York: Oxford University Press, 1997), pp. 125–76.

22. Dudden, *Serving Women*, pp. 77, 222, 94, 63, 34; "She was . . . niggers": [Harriet E. Wilson], *Our Nig; Or, Sketches from the Life of a Free Black, In a Two-Story White House, North* (New York: Vintage Books, 1983; orig. pub. 1859), pp. 139, 49. See also Elise A. Guyette, "The Working Lives of African Vermonters in Census and Literature, 1790–1870," *VH* 61 (Spring 1993):69–84.

23. "How long": Marilyn Richardson, ed., *Maria W. Stewart: America's First Black Woman Political Writer: Essays and Speeches* (Bloomington, IN: Indiana University Press, 1987), p. 38; Marilyn Richardson, "'What If I Am a Woman?' Maria W. Stewart's Defense of Black Women's Political Activism," in Donald M. Jacobs., ed., *Courage and Conscience: Black and White Abolitionists in Boston* (Bloomington, IN: Indiana University Press, 1993), pp. 191–206; "position . . . globe": Martin Robison Delany, *The Condition, Elevation, Emigration, and Destiny of the Colored People in the United States, Politically Considered* (New York: Arno Press, 1968; orig. pub. 1852), p. 199.

24. *David Walker's Appeal in Four Articles* (New York: Hill & Wang, 1965; orig. pub. 1829), p. 29; "he dare": Isaac Candler, *A Summary View of America Comprising a Description of the Face of the Country* (London: T. Cadell, 1824), p. 284; "a colored": Philip S. Foner and George E. Walker, eds., *Proceedings of the Black State Conventions, 1840–1865* (Philadelphia: Temple University Press, 1978), p. 277; W. E. B. DuBois, *The Philadelphia Negro: A Social Study* (New York: Schocken Books, 1967; orig. pub. 1899), pp. 115–16; Horton and Horton, *In Hope of Liberty*, pp. 203–68.

25. "scattered": "Nancy Prince" in Bert James Loewenberg and Ruth Bogin, eds., *Black Women in Nineteenth-Century American Life: Their Words, Their Thoughts, Their Feelings* (University Park, PA: Penn State University Press, 1976), pp. 205–06; White, *Somewhat More Independent*, p. 180; G. S. Rowe, "Black Offenders, Criminal Courts, and Philadelphia Society in the Late Eighteenth Century," *JSocH* 22 (Summer 1989):685–712; Leon F. Litwack, *North of Slavery: The Negro in the Free States, 1790–1860* (Chicago: University of Chicago Press, 1961), p. 97; Curry, *The Free Black in Urban America*, pp. 112–15; Frank F. Furstenberg, Jr., Theodore Hershberg, and John Modell, "The Origins of the Female-Headed Black Family: The Impact of the Urban Experience," in Theodore Hershberg, ed., *Philadelphia: Work, Space, and Family and Group Experience in the Nineteenth Century* (New York: Oxford University Press, 1981), pp. 435–54.

26. James Oliver Horton, "Blacks in Antebellum Boston: The Migrant and the Community," in *Free People of Color*, pp. 30–37; Jeffrey Bolster, "'To Feel Like a Man': Black Seamen in the Northern States, 1800–1860," *JAH* 76 (March 1990):1173–99.

27. "When . . . exist[s]": R. H. Isabelle in Ira Berlin, Joseph P. Reidy, and Leslie S. Rowland, eds., *Freedom: A Documentary History of Emancipation, 1861–1867*. Series II: *The Black Military Experience* (Cambridge, UK: Cambridge University Press, 1982), p. 323, hereinafter cited as *Black Military Experience*; "Instead of": ibid., p. 501.

28. "I have": Capt. Oliver H. Perry quoted in Litwack, *North of Slavery*, p. 32; Joseph T. Wilson, *The Black Phalanx: A History of the Negro Soldiers of the United States in the Wars of 1775–1812, 1861–65* (Hartford, CT: American Publishing Co., 1888), pp. 79–84; White, *Somewhat More Independent*, p. 150; Horton and Horton, "Violence, Protest, and Identity," in *Free People of Color*, p. 92.

29. "compelled . . . rebels": New York Recruiting Agent to the Secretary of War, April 6, 1863, in *Black Military Experience*, pp. 89–90; "Wee": Anonymous Virginia Black Soldier to an Unidentified Washington Official, December 1865, ibid., p. 725. On the transition from slave to "free" labor overseen by northern military officials and planters, see Ira Berlin, et al., eds., *Freedom: A Documentary History of Emancipation, 1861–1867*, Series 1, vol. 3: *The Wartime Genesis of Free Labor: The Lower South* (Cambridge, UK: Cambridge University Press, 1990).

30. "I have . . . men": Samuel J. Kirkwood to General-in-Chief of the Army, Aug. 5, 1862, *Black Military Experience*, p. 85.

31. "My men": Army Engineer to the Headquarters of the Department of the South, April 3, 1863, *Black Military Experience*, p. 56. See also ibid., pp. 37–45.

32. "unjust": Commander of the Military Division of the Mississippi to a Northern Recruiter, July 30, 1864, in *Black Military Experience*, p. 110; "we cannot": White Army Surgeons to the President, February 1864, *ibid.*, p. 356; Francis A. Boyd to the Commander of the Department of Virginia and North Carolina, Jan. 5, 1865, *ibid.*, p. 351; "during": General-in-Chief of the Army to the Commander of the Department of the Tennessee, March 31, 1863, *ibid.*, p. 143; "No white": Commander of a Louisiana Black Brigade to the Headquarters of the Post of Morganzia, LA; Sept. 24, 1864, *ibid.*, p. 511. See also *ibid.*, pp. 483–87, 633–37.

33. *Black Military Experience*, pp. 406–11; "dam": Soldiers in a Louisiana Black Regiment to the Headquarters of the Department of the Gulf, March 28, 1864, *ibid.*, p. 416; "Black": Officer of a South Carolina Black Regiment to the Regimental Commander, Aug. 3, 1863, *ibid.*, p. 492; "d—d": Commander of a North Carolina Black Regiment to the Commander of a Black Brigade, Sept. 13, 1863 *ibid.*, p. 493; "Bucked": Testimony in the Court Martial of Eight Tennessee Black Soldiers, April 22, 1865, *ibid.*, p. 462. See also *ibid.*, pp. 425, 458; Donald, *Lincoln*, p. 391.

34. "such a": Thomas D. Freeman to "Dear Martha," April 25, 1864, in Brown Family Papers, Folder 1, American Antiquarian Society, Worcester, MA; "against": Order by the Commander of the Department of Virginia and North Carolina, Dec. 5, 1863, *Black Military Experience*, p. 136; *ibid.*, pp. 366, 391–95.

35. "for any": Philip S. Foner and Herbert Shapiro, eds., *Northern Labor and Anti-Slavery: A Documentary History* (Westport, CT: Greenwood Press, 1994), p. 277; "no d—d": *ibid.*, p. 278; "a large": *ibid.*, p. 275. On the last riot, see also David M. Katzman, *Before the Ghetto: Black Detroit in the Nineteenth Century* (Urbana, IL: University of Illinois Press, 1973), pp. 45–7.

36. Quotations from the Boston *Pilot* in Foner and Shapiro, eds., *Northern Labor and Anti-Slavery*, pp. 284–85.

37. *Ibid.*, Wittke, *The Irish in America*, pp. 135–49; Brian Kelly, "Ambiguous Loyalties: 'The Boston Irish, Slavery, and the American Civil War," *HJM* 24 (Summer 1996): 155–204.

38. Iver Bernstein, *The New York City Draft Riots: Their Significance in American Society and Politics in the Age of the Civil War* (New York: Oxford University Press, 1990).

39. "i think": Rachel Ann Wicker to the Governor of Massachusetts or the President, Sept. 12, 1864, *Black Military Experience*, p. 402.

40. *Ibid.*, pp. 30, 429, 435, 597–98, 769.

41. Pension file of James H. Patton, Company D. 29th Regiment, USCI, GR 15, NA.

42. Pension files of Minos Miller, Company K, 54th Regiment, USCI; Simeon Schultz, Company B, 31st Regiment, USCI; Henry Ellis, Company C, 31st Regiment, USCI, RG 15, NA.

43. *Black Military Experience*, pp. 1–34; Cindy S. Aron, *Ladies and Gentlemen of the Civil Service: Middle-Class Workers in Victorian America* (New York: Oxford, 1967), pp. 40–61; Jane E. Schultz, "The Inhospitable Hospital: Gender and Professionalism in Civil War Medicine," *Signs* 17 (Winter 1992):363–92; "shrouded . . . occupa-

tions": John Blassingame and John R. McKivigan, eds., *Frederick Douglass Papers*, Vol. 4 (New Haven: Yale University Press, 1979), p. 231.

44. "self-respect": Bernstein, *New York City Draft Riots*, p. 260; David Montgomery, *Beyond Equality: Labor and the Radical Republicans, 1862–1872* (New York: Vintage Books, 1967), pp. 458–59, 228.

45. Montgomery, *Beyond Equality*, pp. 191–92; "American": Myers quoted in William H. Harris, *The Harder We Run: Black Workers Since the Civil War* (New York: Oxford University Press, 1982), pp. 25–7. See also Philip S. Foner and Ronald Lewis, eds., *Organized Labor and the Black Worker, 1619–1973* (New York: Praeger, 1974), p. 25.

46. "profitable . . . agencies": Foner and Lewis, eds., *The Black Worker*, Vol. II, pp. 55–6; For biographical information on Cary, see the entry by Carolyn Calloway-Thomas (under Mary Ann Shadd Cary) in Darlene Clark Hine, *et al.*, eds., *Black Women in America: An Historical Encyclopedia*, Vol. I (Brooklyn, NY: Carlson, 1993), pp. 224–26. See also Thomas Dublin, *Transforming Women's Work: New England Lives in the Industrial Revolution* (Ithaca, NY: Cornell University Press, 1994).

47. "Wherever": James Finlay Weir Johnston, *Notes on North America, Agricultural, Economical, and Social* (Edinburgh and London: W. Blackwood & Sons, 1851), p. 315. See also Herbert G. Gutman, "Reconstruction in Ohio: Negroes in the Hocking Valley Coal Mines in 1873 and 1874," *LH* 3 (Fall 1962):243–64; Dennis C. Dickerson, *Out of the Crucible Black Steelworkers in Western Pennsylvania, 1875–1980* (Albany, NY: State University of New York Press, 1986), pp. 7–8.

48. See for example Dawley, *Class and Community*.

49. See for example William H. Wiggins, Jr., *O Freedom! Afro-American Emancipation Celebrations* (Knoxville, TN: University of Tennessee Press, 1987).

50. See W. E. B. DuBois, *Black Reconstruction in the United States, 1860–1880* (New York: Atheneum, 1970; orig. pub. 1935). Roediger expands upon this theme in *Wages of Whiteness*.

CHAPTER TEN

1. James P. Comer, *Maggie's American Dream: The Life and Times of a Black Family* (New York: NAL Books, 1989), pp. 149, 150, 151.

2. *Ibid.*, p. 142.

3. *Ibid.*, pp. 143, 142; "Your door": Claude McKay, "White Houses," *Selected Poems of Claude McKay* (New York: Bookman Associates, 1953), p. 78.

4. "they . . . shovel": Ronald L. Lewis, "Race and the United Mine Workers' Union in Tennessee: Selected Letters of William R. Riley, 1892–1895," *THQ* 36 (1977):528; Herbert Hill, "Myth-Making as Labor History: Herbert Gutman and the United Mine Workers of America," *IJPCS* 2 (Winter 1978):132–200. On patterns of inter-and intraregional migration during this period, see Peter Gottlieb,

Making Their Own Way: Southern Blacks' Migration to Pittsburgh, 1916–1930 (Urbana, IL: University of Illinois Press, 1987); R. R. Wright, Jr., "The Migration of Negroes to the North," *Annals* 27 (June 1906):99–116; Daniel M. Johnson and Rex R. Campbell, *Black Migration in America: A Social Demographic History* (Durham, NC: Duke University Press, 1981).

5. "stagnating": Gunnar Myrdal, *An American Dilemma: The Negro Problem and Modern Democracy*, Vol. I (New York: Harper & Row, 1944), pp. 279–303; Alex Lichtenstein, *Twice the Work of Free Labor: The Political Economy of Convict Labor in the South* (London: Verso, 1996), pp. 152–85; Rayford W. Logan, *The Negro in American Life and Thought: The Nadir, 1877–1901* (New York: Dial Press, 1954); Barbara J. Fields, "The Nineteenth Century American South: History and Theory," *PSA* 1 (April 1983):7–27; Neil R. McMillen, *Dark Journey: Black Mississippians in the Age of Jim Crow* (Urbana, IL: University of Illinois Press, 1989).

6. Jo Cavallo, "Day of the Black Jockey," *AL* 2 (Spring 1996): 22–32 ; James Weldon Johnson, *Black Manhattan* (New York: Atheneum, 1972; orig. pub. 1930), pp. 60–2; "The only": Mary White Ovington, "The Negro in the Trades Unions in New York," *Annals* 27 (June 1906):95; Elisabeth Lasch-Quinn, *Black Neighbors: Race and the Limits of Reform in the American Settlement House Movement, 1890–1945* (Chapel Hill, NC: University of North Carolina Press, 1993).

7. "may be": Charles S. Johnson, "Black Workers and the City," *Survey* (March 1, 1925):643; "the public": Alma Herbst, *The Negro in the Slaughtering and Meat-Packing Industry in Chicago* (Boston: Houghton Mifflin, 1932) p. 79; "men-": John Daniels, "Industrial Conditions Among Negro Men in Boston," *Charities* 15 (Oct. 7, 1905):35.

8. W. E. B. DuBois, *The Philadelphia Negro: A Social Study* (New York: Schocken Books, 1967; orig. pub. 1899), p. 343; "Once": Charles Johnson, "Black Workers and the City," p. 643.

9. "they had": St. Clair Drake and Horace R. Cayton, *Black Metropolis: A Study of Negro Life in a Northern City* (New York: Harcourt Brace, 1945), p. 223. See also the essays in David Montgomery, *Workers' Control in America: Studies in the History of Work, Technology, and Labor Struggles* (Cambridge, UK: Cambridge University Press, 1979).

10. Hugh B. Hammett, "Labor and Race: The Georgia Railroad Strike of 1909," *LH* 16 (Fall 1975):470–84. The quotation is on p. 479.

11. "compelled": Kelly Miller, "The Economic Handicap of the Negro in the North," *Annals* 27 (June 1906):84. For overviews, see Joe William Trotter, Jr., "Blacks in the Urban North: The 'Underclass Question' in Historical Perspective," in Michael B. Katz, ed., *The "Underclass" Debate: Views from History* (Princeton: Princeton University Press, 1993), pp. 55–84; William Harris, *The Harder We Run: Black Workers Since the Civil War* (New York: Oxford University Press, 1982); Lorenzo J. Greene and Carter G. Woodson, *The Negro Wage Earner* (Washington, DC: Association for the Study of Negro Life and History, 1930).

12. Suzanne Model, "The Ethnic Niche and the Structure of Opportunity: Immi-

grants and Minorities in New York City," in Katz, ed., *"Underclass" Debate*, pp. 161–93; Mary White Ovington, *Half a Man: The Status of the Negro in New York* (New York: Schocken Books, 1969; orig. pub. 1911), pp. 80–7; Kenneth Kusmer, *A Ghetto Takes Shape: Black Cleveland, 1870–1930* (Urbana, IL: University of Illinois Press, 1976), pp. 285–87.

13. Ray Stannard Baker, *Following the Color Line: American Negro Citizenship in the Progressive Era* (New York: Harper & Row, 1964; orig. pub. 1908), p. 135. For a historiographical overview, see Joe William Trotter, Jr., "African-American Workers: New Directions in U.S. Labor Historiography," *LH* 35 (Fall 1994): 495–523.

14. "Plenty": quoted in S. J. Kleinberg, *The Shadow of the Mills: Working-Class Families in Pittsburgh, 1870–1907* (Pittsburgh: University of Pittsburgh Press, 1989), p. 18; Lewis C. Gray, *et al.*, "Farm Ownership and Tenancy," U.S. Department of Agriculture, *Agricultural Yearbook for 1923* (Washington, DC: Government Printing Office, 1924); "'blind alley'": Charles Johnson, "Black Workers and the City," p. 643; Horace R. Cayton and George S. Mitchell, *Black Workers and the New Unions* (Westport, CT: Negro Universities Press, 1970; orig. pub. 1939), p. 19; "a motorman": Elaine Latzman Moon, ed., *Untold Tales, Unsung Heroes: An Oral History of Detroit's African-American Community, 1918–1967* (Detroit: Wayne State University Press, 1994), p. 97; Price Fishback, "Segregation in Job Hierarchies: West Virginia Coal Mining, 1906–1932," *JEH* 44 (September 1984):772; Herbst, *The Negro in the Slaughtering and Meat-Packing Industry in Chicago*, p. 69.

For other comparisons of immigrants and blacks, see Stanley Lieberson, *A Piece of the Pie: Blacks and White Immigrants Since 1880* (Berkeley: University of California Press, 1980); Theodore Hershberg, *et al.*, "A Tale of Three Cities: Blacks, Immigrants, and Opportunity in Philadelphia, 1850–1880, 1930, 1970," in Theodore Hershberg, ed., *Philadelphia: Work, Space, Family, and Group Experience in the Nineteenth Century* (New York: Oxford University Press, 1991), pp. 461–91; Lizabeth Cohen, *Making a New Deal: Industrial Workers in Chicago, 1919–1939* (New York: Cambridge University Press, 1990), pp. 1–212.

15. Sterling D. Spero and Abram L. Harris, *The Black Worker: A Study of the Negro and the Labor Movement* (New York: Columbia University Press, 1931), p. 371; Donald Dewey, "Negro Employment in Southern Industry," *JPE* 60 (August 1952):279–93; William A. Sundstrom, "The Color Line: Racial Norms and Discrimination in Urban Labor Markets, 1910–1950," *JEH* 54 (June 1994):382–96; "teach . . . men": Chicago Commission on Race Relations, *The Negro in Chicago: A Study of Race Relations and A Race Riot in 1919* (New York: Arno Press, 1968; orig. pub. 1922), p. 366.

16. "tense . . . groups": United States Department of Labor Women's Bureau, "Negro Women in Industry," Bulletin No. 20 (1922), p. 45; "Do . . . high": Arthur T. Long, "Where the Negro May Find Work in Trenton" (c. 1922), pp. 6–7, Series 4, Box 6, Folder: *Pittsburgh Courier* articles, National Urban League Papers, Library of Congress, Washington, DC; Warren C. Whatley, "Getting a Foot in

the Door: 'Learning,' State Dependence, and the Racial Integration of Firms," *JEH* 5 (March 1990):43–66.

17. "a badge": W. E. B. DuBois, *The Negro Artisan* (Atlanta: Atlanta University Press, 1902), p. 100; "awful . . . order": Helen Campbell, *Prisoners of Poverty* (Boston: Little, Brown, 1900), pp. 223, 231; "Analysis of Economic Section of Richmond, Virginia, 1928," Negro Welfare Survey Committee, Box 881, United States Women's Bureau Correspondence—Misc. Subjects and Organizations, Record Group 86, National Archives, Washington, DC.

18. "Analysis of Economic Section of Negro Welfare Survey of Richmond, Virginia, 1928," p. 15; "I never": Thordis Simonsen, ed., *You May Plow Here: The Narrative of Sara Brooks* (New York: Simon & Schuster, 1986), p. 182; "disagreeable . . . tongues": "Negro Women in Industry in Fifteen States," Women's Bureau *Bulletin* no. 70 (1929), p. 18. See also "Negro Women in South Carolina Industries," *Opportunity* (May 1924):146–47.

19. Eileen Boris, *Home to Work: Motherhood and the Politics of Industrial Homework in the United States* (Cambridge, UK: Cambridge University Press, 1994), pp. 171, 195; "imported . . . Negroes": Monroe N. Work, "The Negroes of Warsaw, Georgia," *SW* 37 (January 1908):34; Henry M. McKiven, Jr., *Iron and Steel: Class, Race and Community in Birmingham, Alabama, 1875–1920* (Chapel Hill, NC: University of North Carolina Press, 1995), p. 47; "was not": Annie Tucker quoted in Mary Ellen Curtin, "The 'Human World' of Black Women in Alabama Prisons, 1870–1890," in Virginia Bernhard, *et al.*, eds., *Hidden Histories of Women in the New South* (Columbia, MO: University of Missouri Press, 1994), p. 22.

20. "the vicious . . . them": Myrdal, *American Dilemma*, Vol. I, p. 391.

21. "employers": Charles Johnson, "Black Workers and the City," p. 643; "range . . . workmen": Emmet J. Scott, *Negro Migration During the War* (New York: Oxford University Press, 1920), pp. 114–15; Greene and Woodson, *The Negro Wage Earner*, p. 134; Jacqueline Jones, *The Dispossessed: America's Underclasses from the Civil War to the Present* (New York: Basic Books, 1992), pp. 127–66.

22. "makes": John C. Kyle (Mississippi lawyer) in *Report of the Industrial Commission on Agriculture and Agricultural Labor*, Vol. X (Washington, DC: Government Printing Office, 1901), p. 471; Walter Licht, *Getting Work: Philadelphia, 1840–1950* (Cambridge, MA: Harvard University Press, 1992), p. 133; "They can": quoted in William A. Sundstrom, "Half a Career: Discrimination and Railroad Internal Labor Markets," *IR* 29 (Fall 1990):429.

23. "one . . . workers": Francis D. Tyson, "The Negro Migrant in the North," in J. H. Dillard, ed., *Negro Migration in 1916–17* (New York: Negro Universities Press, 1969; orig. pub. 1919), p. 137. See, for example, Kenneth R. Bailey, "A Judicious Mixture: Negroes and Immigrants in the West Virginia Mines, 1880–1917," *WVH* 34 (January 1973):141–61; Patricia A. Cooper, *Once a Cigar Maker: Men, Women, and Work Culture in American Cigar Factories, 1900–1919* (Urbana, IL: University of Illinois Press, 1987).

24. George Fredrickson, *White Supremacy: A Comparative Study in American and South*

African History (New York: Oxford University Press, 1981), pp. 199–238; "altruistic": Tyson, "The Negro Migrant in the North," p. 120.

25. "There were": Charles S. Johnson, "Negroes at Work in Baltimore, Md.," *Opportunity* 1 (January 1923):14; "not . . . sell": Charles B. Spahr, "The Negro as an Industrial Factor," *The Outlook* 62 (May 6, 1899):33.

26. Whatley, "Getting a Foot in the Door"; Douglas Flamming, *Creating the Modern South: Millhands and Managers in Dalton, Georgia, 1884–1984* (Chapel Hill, NC: University of North Carolina Press, 1992), p. 109; Dolores Janiewski, "Sisters Under Their Skins: Southern Working Women, 1880–1950," in Joanne V. Hawks and Sheila L. Skemp, eds., *Sex, Race, and the Role of Women in the South: Essays* (Jackson, MS: University Press of Mississippi, 1983), p. 26; Mary Frederickson, "'I Know Which Side I'm On': Southern Women in the Labor Movement in the Twentieth Century," in Ruth Milkman, ed., *Women, Work, and Protest: A Century of U.S. Women's Labor History* (London: Routledge & Kegan Paul, 1985), pp. 156–62.

27. "If I": Chicago Commission, *The Negro in Chicago*, p. 389; "where": "Negro Women in Industry," p. 35.

28. See for example the discussion of Charles S. Johnson's study of racial discrimination among Los Angeles employers in Emory J. Tolbert, *The UNIA and Black Los Angeles: Ideology and Community in the American Garvey Movement* (Los Angeles: Center for Afro-American Studies, 1980), pp. 35–8; "We do": F. D. Welsh quoted in Spero and Harris, *The Black Worker*, pp. 222–23.

29. List quoted in Charles S. Johnson, "Negroes at Work in Baltimore, Md.," pp. 18–19.

30. August Meier and Elliott Rudwick, *Black Detroit and the Rise of the UAW* (New York: Oxford University Press, 1979), pp. 9–11; Licht, *Getting Work*; William A. Sundstrom, "Internal Labor Markets Before World War I: On-the-Job Training and Employee Promotion," *EEH* 25 (October 1988):424–45.

31. Jacquelyn Dowd Hall, *et al.*, *Like a Family: The Making of a Southern Cotton Mill World* (Chapel Hill, NC: University of North Carolina, 1987); Cathy McHugh, *Mill Family: The Labor Systems in the Southern Cotton Textile Industry, 1880–1915* (New York: Oxford University Press, 1988); Dolores E. Janiewski, *Sisterhood Denied: Race, Gender, and Class in a New South Community* (Philadelphia: Temple University Press, 1986).

32. "application . . . made": DuBois, *Philadelphia Negro*, p. 120. See also the following works by DuBois: *The Negro Artisan*; "The Negroes of Farmville, Virginia: A Social Study," *Bulletin of the Department of Labor*, no. 14 (January 1898):1–38; "Testimony of Prof. W. E. Burghardt DuBois [on Doughtery County, Georgia]" in *Report of the Industrial Commission on Education*, Vol. 15 (Washington, DC: U.S. Industrial Commission Reports, 1900–02), pp. 159–75; *The Black North in 1901: A Social Study* (New York: Arno Press, 1969; orig. pub. 1901).

33. Sharon Ann Holt, "Making Freedom Pay," Ph.D. thesis, University of Pennsylvania, p. 199; Pauli Murray, *Proud Shoes: The Story of an American Family* (New York:

Harper & Row, 1978), pp. 242–43; "taxed": Barnetta M. White, *In Search of Kith and Kin: The History of a Southern Black Family* (Baltimore: Gateway Press, 1986), p. 19; "many colored": W. T. B. Williams, "The Negro Exodus from the South," in Dillard, ed., *Negro Migration in 1916–17*, p. 105; Jones, *Dispossessed*, pp. 104–26. See also C. Vann Woodward, *Origins of the New South, 1877–1913* (Baton Rouge, LA: Louisiana State University Press, 1951).

34. "fearful": Blake McKelvey, "A Half Century of Southern Penal Exploitation," *SF* 13 (October 1934):122; Edward Ayers, *Promise of the New South: Life After Reconstruction* (New York: Oxford University Press, 1992); Jones, *Dispossessed*, pp. 127–204; Lichtenstein, *Twice the Work of Free Labor*; David Oshinsky, *"Worse Than Slavery": Parchman Farm and the Ordeal of Jim Crow Justice* (New York: Free Press, 1996).

35. "providential": Julian Reed, "The Industrial Region of Northern Alabama, Tennessee, and Georgia," *HNMM* 90 (March 1895):614; "God-given:" A. Oemler, "Truck Farming," Report of the Commissioner of Agriculture for 1885 (Washington, DC: Government Printing Office, 1885), p. 585; Richard Barry, "Slavery in the South To-Day," *CM* 42 (March 1907):488; George Otis Coalson, "The Development of the Migratory Farm Labor System in Texas, 1900–1954," Ph.D. thesis, University of Oklahoma, 1955.

36. Andrea Graziosi, "Common Laborers, Unskilled Workers, 1880–1915," *LH* 22 (Fall 1981):512–44; Joe William Trotter, Jr., *Black Milwaukee: The Making of an Industrial Proletariat, 1915–1945* (Urbana, IL: University of Illinois Press, 1985), pp. 245–63.

37. Ovington, *Half a Man*, pp. 127–37; "a low": "Employment of Colored Women in Chicago," *Crisis* 1 (January 1911):24; Thomas Cripps, *Slow Fade to Black: The Negro in American Film, 1900–1942* (New York: Oxford University Press, 1977), p. 102; James Weldon Johnson, "The Making of Harlem," *Survey* (March 1, 1925), pp. 635–36.

38. "You can": Drake and Cayton, *Black Metropolis*, pp. 494; Myrdal, *American Dilemma*, Vol. I, pp. 1268–69; Gilbert Osofsky, *Harlem: The Making of a Ghetto: Negro New York, 1890–1930* (New York: Harper & Row, 1966), pp. 146–49; Daniel Bell, "Crime as an American Way of Life: A Queer Ladder of Social Mobility," in A. B. Callow, Jr., ed., *American Urban History: An Interpretive Reader with Commentaries* (New York: Oxford University Press, 1969), pp. 274–90; Valerie Elizabeth Gold, "The Pyramid's Base and Shadows: Organized Crime, the Illicit Drug Trade, and the Black Community of New York, 1900–1965," Senior thesis, Brandeis University, 1995.

39. "the type . . . immigration": "Memorandum on Exodus of Negroes from the South," Records of Secretary William B. Wilson, File 13/65, Race Riot E. St. Louis, Illinois, 1917 (Box 205), General Records of the Department of Labor, RG 174, National Archives, Washington, DC; James R. Grossman, *Land of Hope: Chicago, Black Southerners, and the Great Migration* (Chicago: University of Chicago Press, 1989).

40. "was . . . lumber": Edw. N. Munns, "Women in Southern Lumbering Opera-

tions," *JF* 17 (February 1919):146–47; Maurine Weiner Greenwald, *Women, War, and Work: The Impact of World War I on Women Workers in the United States* (Westport, CT: Greenwood Press, 1980), pp. 20–7, 42–4, 107–15; Gottlieb, *Making Their Own Way.*

41. "The spirit": black officer quoted in Jack D. Foner, *Blacks and the Military in American History: A New Perspective* (New York: Praeger, 1974), p. 121; Arthur E. Barbeau and Florette Henri, *The Unknown Soldiers: Black American Troops in World War I* (Philadelphia: Temple University Press, 1974); Arlen Fowler, *The Black Infantry in the West, 1865–1891* (Westport, CT: Greenwood Press, 1971).

42. "Any": Moore quoted in Jeff L. Patrick, "Nothing But Slaves: The Second Kentucky Volunteer Infantry and the Spanish American War," *RKHS* 89 (Summer 1991):294; Marvin Fletcher, *The Black Soldier and Officer in the United States Army, 1891–1917* (Columbia, MO: University of Missouri Press, 1974).

43. Robert V. Haynes, *A Night of Violence: The Houston Riot of 1917* (Baton Rouge, LA: Louisiana State University Press, 1976); Bernard C. Nalty, *Strength for the Fight: A History of Black Americans in the Military* (New York: Free Press, 1989); Garna L. Christian, *Black Soldiers in Jim Crow Texas, 1899–1917* (College Station, TX: Texas A & M Press, 1995).

44. "didn't know . . . wheeling": Burniece Avery, *Walk Quietly Through the Night and Cry Softly* (Detroit: Balamp Publishing, 1977), p. 102.

45. "Greeks": T. J. Woofter, "The Negroes of Athens, Georgia," Phelps-Stokes Fellowship Studies, no. 1, *Bulletin of the University of Georgia* 14 (December 1913):27; Seth M. Scheiner, *Negro Mecca: A History of the Negro in New York City, 1865–1920* (New York: New York University Press, 1965), pp. 47–53; Gerald Gill, "Introduction to Part V: Protest and Progress, 1900–1945," in Robert L. Hall, ed., *Making a Living: The Work Experience of African Americans in New England: Selected Readings* (Boston: New England Foundation for the Humanities, 1995), p. 505; "would put": *The Crisis* 3 (January 1912):96; Ovington, *Half a Man*, p. 91; Herbert Northrup, *Organized Labor and the Negro* (New York: Harper and Brothers, 1944), pp. 17–47, 233; DuBois, *Negro Artisan.*

46. "too strenuous": *Laundry Employees* v. *Employers*, Little Rock, Arkansas, Docket no. 233, Sept. 3, 1918, Record Group 2, National War Labor Board, National Archives: reel 4, entry 5 of James R. Grossman, ed., *Black Workers in the Era of the Great Migration, 1916–1929* (Frederick, MD: University Publications of America, 1986); Carter G. Woodson, "The Negro Washerwoman, A Vanishing Figure," *JNH* 15 (July 1930):369–77; "white men's": Myrdal, *American Dilemma*, Vol. I, pp. 206, 260; Arch Fredric Blakey, *The Florida Phosphate Industry: A History of the Development and Use of a Vital Mineral* (Cambridge, MA: Harvard University Press, 1973), p. 5203; Donald T. Barnum, *The Negro in Bituminous Coal Mining*, Industrial Research Unit, Wharton School of Finance and Commerce, Report no. 14 (Philadelphia: University of Pennsylvania, 1970), p. 7; Dennis C. Dickerson, *Out of the Crucible: Black Steelworkers in Western Pennsylvania, 1875–1980* (Albany, NY: SUNY Press, 1986), p. 24. See also Carroll Pursell, *The Machine in*

America: A Social History of Technology (Baltimore: Johns Hopkins University Press, 1995); Jack Temple Kirby, *Rural Worlds Lost: The American South, 1920–1960* (Baton Rouge, LA: Louisiana State University Press, 1987); David Gartman, *Auto Slavery: The Labor Process in the American Automobile Industry, 1897–1950* (New Brunswick, NJ: Rutgers University Press, 1986), p. 183.

47. Herbst, *The Negro in the Slaughtering and Meat-Packing Industry*, pp. 31–3; Graziosi, "Common Laborers, Unskilled Workers," pp. 531–32; DuBois, *Philadelphia Negro*, pp. 129, 332 (see also the Introduction by E. Digby Baltzell to the 1967 Schocken Books edition, p. xxxvii); Licht, *Getting Work*, pp. 46, 109, 178; Gavin Wright, "*Getting Work* and Economic History," *LH* 35 (Winter 1994):100–02. See also Daniel Nelson, *Managers and Workers: Origins of the New Factory System in the United States, 1880–1920* (Madison, WI: University of Wisconsin Press, 1975).

48. Warren Whatley and Gavin Wright, "Race, Human Capital, and Labour Markets in American History," in George Grantham and Mary Mackinnon, eds., *Labour Market Evolution* (London: Routledge, 1994), pp. 279–91. See also Thomas Klug, "Employers' Strategies in the Detroit Labor Market, 1900–1929," in Nelson Lichtenstein and Stephen Meyer, eds., *On the Line: Essays in the History of Auto Work* (Urbana, IL: University of Illinois Press, 1989), pp. 42–74.

49. "keep": quoted in James E. Fickle, "Management Looks at the 'Labor Problem': The Southern Pine Industry During World War I and the Postwar Era," *JSouH* 40 (February 1974):67–8; "Rough": "Negro Women in Industry," p. 48.

50. "In work": Charles Johnson, "Black Workers and the City," p. 643; Jacqueline Jones, *Labor of Love, Labor of Sorrow: Black Women, Work and the Family from Slavery to the Present* (New York: Basic Books, 1985), pp. 178–80; Edward Meeker and James Kau, "Racial Discrimination and Occupational Attainment at the Turn of the Century," *EEH* 14 (July 1977):250–76; Drake and Cayton, *Black Metropolis*, p. 229; Miriam Cohen, *From Workshop to Office: Two Generations of Italian Women in New York City, 1900–1950* (Ithaca, NY: Cornell University Press, 1993); Sue Porter Benson, *Counter Cultures: Saleswomen, Managers, and Customers in American Department Stores, 1890–1940* (Urbana, IL: University of Illinois Press, 1986).

51. Greenwald, *Women, War, and Work*, p. 197; Herbst, *The Negro in the Slaughtering and Meat-Packing Industry*, pp. 75–80; William Leach, *Land of Desire: Merchants, Power, and the Rise of a New American Culture* (New York: Pantheon, 1993).

52. "They were": "Negro Women in Industry," p. 11; Nancy J. Weiss, *The National Urban League, 1910–1940* (New York: Oxford University Press, 1974), pp. 194–98; Moon, ed., *Untold Tales, Unsung Heroes*, pp. 33–34; "that . . . man": File no. E-38-11-C, Charles Malone, Pennsylvania Railroad, "Complaint of Discrimination Against a Colored Man on Account of His Race, 1919," Record Group 14, U.S. Railroad Administration, in Grossman, ed., *Black Workers in the Era of the Great Migration*, reel 10, entry 83; Angel Kwolek-Folland, *Engendering Business: Men and Women in the Corporate Office, 1870–1930* (Baltimore: Johns Hopkins University Press, 1994); Frank Stricker, "Affluence for Whom? Another Look at Prosperity and the Working Classes in the 1920s," *LH* (Winter 1983):5–33; Charles F. Holt,

"Who Benefited from the Prosperity of the Twenties?" *EEH* 14 (July 1977):277–89.

53. Peter J. Rachleff, *Black Labor in the South: Richmond, Virginia, 1865–1890* (Philadelphia: Temple University Press, 1984); Leon Fink, *Workingmen's Democracy: The Knights of Labor and American Politics* (Urbana, IL: University of Illinois Press, 1983); Melvyn Dubofsky, *We Shall Be All: A History of the Industrial Workers of the World* (Chicago: Quadrangle Books, 1969), pp. 192–226; Merl E. Reed, "Lumberjacks and Longshoremen: The IWW in Louisiana," *LH* 13 (Winter 1972):41–55; "wherever the union": John Stephens Durham, "The Labor Unions and the Negro," *AM* 81 (February 1898):226. See also Eric Arnesen, "Following the Color Line of Labor: Black Workers and the Labor Movement Before 1930," *RHR* 55 (Winter 1993):53–87; "Labor, Race, and the Gutman Thesis: Response to Herbert Hill," *IJPCS* 2 (Spring 1989): 361–403; Marc Karson and Ronald Radosh, "The American Federation of Labor and the Negro Worker, 1894–1949," in Julius Jacobson, ed., *The Negro and the Labor Movement* (Garden City, NY: Anchor Books, 1968), pp. 155–87.

54. Northrup, *Organized Labor and the Negro*; *Crisis* 1 (April 1911):54; "white unions": DuBois, *Negro Artisan*, pp. 115, 95; "you pay": Chicago Commission on Race Relations, *The Negro in Chicago*, p. 177.

55. Eric Arnesen, *Waterfront Workers of New Orleans: Race, Class, and Politics, 1863–1923* (New York: Oxford University Press, 1991); Elizabeth Haiken, "'The Lord Helps Those Who Help Themselves': Black Laundresses in Little Rock, Arkansas, 1917–1921," *ArHQ* 49 (Spring 1990):20–50; Daniel Letwin, "Interracial Unionism, Gender, and 'Social Equality' in the Alabama Coalfields, 1878–1908," *JSouH* 61 (August 1995):519–54.

56. Alex Lichtenstein, "Racial Conflict and Racial Solidarity in the Alabama Coal Strike of 1894: New Evidence for the Gutman-Hill Debate," *LH* 36 (Winter 1995):63–76; McKiven, *Iron and Steel*, pp. 89–90; Robert J. Norrell, "Caste in Steel: Jim Crow Careers in Birmingham, Alabama," *JAH* 73 (December 1986):669–94; Northrup, *Organized Labor and the Negro*, p. 214; Ronald Lewis, *Black Coal Miners in America: Race, Class, and Community Conflict, 1780–1980* (Lexington, KY: University Press of Kentucky, 1987), pp. 167–90.

57. "white . . . also": quoted in Spero and Harris, *The Black Worker*, p. 374; Barnum, *The Negro in Bituminous Coal Mining*, pp. 7–15; Arnesen, *Waterfront Workers*, pp. 39, 69, 250–51; Norrell, "Caste in Steel."

58. "it was": Ovington, "The Negro in the Trades Unions in New York," p. 94; Warren C. Whatley, "African-American Strikebreaking from the Civil War to the New Deal," *SSH* 17 (Winter 1993):525–58; Scheiner, *Negro Mecca*, p. 68; McKiven, *Iron and Steel*, p. 108.

59. See for example Philip S. Foner and Ronald Lewis, eds., *The Black Worker: A Documentary History from Colonial Times to the Present. Vol VI: The End of Post-War Prosperity and the Great Depression, 1920–1936* ("The Brotherhood of Sleeping Car Porters and Other Black Unions in the Train Service") (Philadelphia: Temple University Press, 1981), pp. 190–311.

60. Jack Santino, *Miles of Smiles, Years of Struggle; Stories of Black Pullman Porters* (Urbana, IL: University of Illinois Press, 1989). See also Benjamin E. Mays, "Working for the Pullman Company," in Hall, ed., *Making a Living*, pp. 524–27.

61. "I used": Ernest Ford, Jr., quoted in Santino, *Miles of Smiles, Years of Struggle*, p. 8; Jervis Anderson, *A. Philip Randolph: A Biographical Portrait* (New York: Harcourt Brace Jovanovich, 1973); Paula F. Pfeffer, *A. Philip Randolph, Pioneer of the Civil Rights Movement* (Baton Rouge, LA: Louisiana State University Press, 1990); Taylor Branch, *Parting the Waters: America in the King Years, 1954–1963* (New York: Simon & Schuster, 1988), pp. 124–25, 128–33, 135–37.

62. This is not to suggest that all black leaders North and South agreed with each other or with ordinary black people race about the specific tactics for challenging discrimination during this period. See for example Steven A. Reich, "Soldiers of Democracy: Black Texans and the Fight for Citizenship, 1917–1921," *JAH* 82 (March 1996):1478–1504; William Jordan, "'The Damnable Dilemma': African-American Accommodation and Protest During World War I," *JAH* 81 (March 1995):1562–90.

63. "When revivals": Walter L. Fleming, "The Servant Problem in a Black Belt Village," *Sewanee Review* 13 (January 1905):13; Tera Hunter, "Domination and Resistance: The Politics of Wage Household Labor in New South Atlanta," *LH* 34 (Spring–Summer 1993):205–20; Elizabeth Clark-Lewis, *Living In, Living Out: African-American Domestics in Washington, D.C., 1910–1940* (Washington, DC: Smithsonian Institution Press, 1994); "go home": Ruth Reed, "The Negro Women of Gainesville, Georgia." M.A. thesis, University of Georgia, 1920) p. 17.

64. See for example Pete Daniel, *The Shadow of Slavery: Peonage in the South, 1901–1969* (Urbana, IL: University of Illinois Press, 1972), pp. 120, 143, 144, 154, 155–57, 162–63; Walter White, Assistant Secretary, NAACP, to Robert C. Herron, Assistant U.S. District Attorney General, Aug. 30, 1920, in File 50–263, Box 10802, Department of Justice Classified Subject Files Correspondence, RG 60, National Archives.

65. "When he": John Dancy, *Sand Against the Wind: The Memoirs of John C. Dancy* (Detroit: Detroit Urban League, 1966), p. 128; "colored": Hill quoted in Weiss, *The National Urban League*, pp. 183–84; Richard W. Thomas, *Life for Us Is What We Make It: Building Black Community in Detroit, 1915–1945* (Bloomington, IN: Indiana University Press, 1992), pp. 53–60; Jesse Thomas Moore, Jr., *A Search for Equality: The National Urban League, 1910–1961* (University Park, PA: Penn State University Press, 1981); Arvarh E. Strickland, *History of the Chicago Urban League* (Urbana, IL: University of Illinois Press, 1966).

66. W. E. B. DuBois, *The Negro in Business* (New York: AMS Press, 1971; orig. pub. 1899); Darlene Clark Hine, *Black Women in White: Racial Conflict and Cooperation in the Nursing Profession, 1890–1950* (Bloomington, IN: Indiana University Press, 1989), pp. 26–62.

67. Walter B. Weare, *Black Business in the New South: A Social History of the North Car-*

olina Mutual Life Insurance Company (Urbana, IL: University of Illinois Press, 1973); Robert L. Boyd, "Demographic Change and Entrepreneurial Occupations: African Americans in Northern Cities," *AJES* 55 (April 1996):129–43; "Professor": Drake and Cayton, *Black Metropolis,* p. 474; Winthrop D. Lane, "Ambushed in the City," *Survey* (March 1, 1925):693; Howard N. Rabinowitz, *Race Relations in the Urban South, 1865–1890* (Urbana, IL: University of Illinois Press, 1980), pp. 61–96.

68. "lynching": Alfreda M. Dunster, ed., *Crusade for Justice: the Autobiography of Ida B. Wells* (Chicago: University of Chicago Press, 1971), p. 64; Paula Giddings, *When and Where I Enter: The Impact of Black Women on Race and Sex in America* (Toronto: Bantam Books, 1984), pp. 17–32; "My real": Drake and Cayton, *Black Metropolis,* p. 443; Albert S. Broussard, *Black San Francisco: The Struggle for Racial Equality in the West, 1900–1954* (Manhattan, KS: University Press of Kansas, 1993), pp. 38–58.

69. "not born . . . builders": Tanya Bolden, *The Book of African-American Women* (Holbrook, MA: Adams Media Corp., 1996), p. 131; Gilbert Osofsky, *Harlem: The Making of a Ghetto: Negro New York, 1890–1930* (New York: Harper & Row, 1986), p. 163; Elsa Barkley Brown, "Womanist Consciousness: Maggie Lena Walker and the Independent Order of Saint Luke," *Signs* 14 (Spring 1989):610–33; Judith Stein, *The World of Marcus Garvey: Race and Class in Modern Society* (Baton Rouge, LA: Louisiana State University Press, 1986). See also Harold F. Gosnell, *Negro Politicians: The Rise of Negro Politics in Chicago* (Chicago: University of Chicago Press, 1935).

70. "Oh . . . Shakespeare": Scott L. Malcolmson, "Having Their Say," *The New Yorker,* April 29 and May 6, 1996, pp. 138, 139; *The Crisis* 3 (February 1912):139; "thrift": Booker T. Washington, "A Town Owned by Negroes," *World's Work* 14 (July 1907):9125. See also Sue Armitage, "Black Women and Their Communities in Colorado," *Frontiers* 2 (1977):178–84; Glen Schwendermann, "Nicodemus: Negro Haven on the Solomon," *KHQ* 34 (Spring 1968):10–31; Mozell C. Hill, "The All-Negro Communities of Oklahoma: The Natural History of a Social Movement," *JNH* 31 (July 1946):254–68.

71. "I am . . . boy": William L. Bulkley, "The Industrial Condition of the Negro in New York City," *Annals* 27 (June 1906):131. See for example James Borchert, *Alley Life in Washington: Family, Community, Religion, and Folklife in the City, 1850–1970* (Urbana, IL: University of Illinois Press, 1980).

72. "fluxing": Tyson, "The Negro Migration in the North," p. 123. For a description of nonspecialized black labor in the upper South, see William Taylor Thom, "The Negroes of Sandy Spring, Maryland: A Social Study," *Department of Labor Bulletin* 32 (January 1901):43–102.

CHAPTER ELEVEN

1. Henry Louis Gates, Jr., *Colored People: A Memoir* (New York: Random House, 1994), pp. 8, 14, 64, 184.

2. See for example Gavin Wright, *Old South, New South: Revolutions in the Southern Economy Since the Civil War* (New York: Basic Books, 1986), pp. 264–68.; Taylor Branch, *Parting the Waters: America in the King Years, 1954–1963* (New York: Simon & Schuster, 1988).

3. "automation": Gholston quoted in Ronald Lewis, *Black Coal Miners in America: Race, Class, and Community Conflict* (Lexington, KY: University Press of Kentucky, 1987), p. 171; William H. Harris, *The Harder We Run: Black Workers Since the Civil War* (New York: Oxford University Press, 1982), pp. 131–35; Jeremy Rifkin, *The End of Work: The Decline of the Global Labor Force and the Dawn of the Post-Market Era* (New York: G. P. Putnam's Sons, 1995), pp. 69–79; John Holusha, "Squeezing the Textile Workers: Trade and Technology Force a New Wave of Job Cuts," *NYT*, Feb. 21, 1996, pp. C1, C6.

4. Jim Grayson in Studs Terkel, *Working* (New York: Avon Books, 1975), pp. 227–28.

5. Lizabeth Cohen, *Making a New Deal: Industrial Workers in Chicago, 1919–39* (Cambridge, UK: Cambridge University Press, 1990); Keith P. Griffler, *What Price Alliance? Black Radicals Confront White Labor, 1918–1938* (New York: Garland Press, 1995), pp. 165–92; Herbert Hill, "The AFL-CIO and the Black Worker: Twenty-Five Years After the Merger," *JIR* 10 (Spring 1982):5–78.

6. "would not": Bernice Anita Reed, "Accommodation Between Negro and White Employees in a West Coast Aircraft Industry, 1942–1944," *SF* 26 (October 1947):77.

7. "the available": Herbert R. Northrup, "Negroes in a War Industry: The Case of Shipbuilding," *JB* 16 (July 1943): 165; Thomas J. Sugrue, "Segmented Work, Race-Conscious Workers: Structure, Agency and Division in the CIO Era," *IRSH* 41 (1996):389–406.

8. Lois Rita Helmbold, "Downward Occupational Mobility During the Great Depression: Urban Black and White Working Class Women," *LH* 29 (Spring 1988):135–72; Mercer G. Evans, "Southern Labor Supply and Working Conditions in Industry," *Annals* 153 (January 1931):156–62; Erdmann Doane Beynon, "The Southern White Laborer Migrates to Michigan," *ASR* 3 (June 1938):338; Walter Licht, *Getting Work: Philadelphia, 1840–1956* (Cambridge, UK: Cambridge University Press, 1992), pp. 45–6.

9. Alexa B. Henderson, "FEPC and the Southern Railway Case: An Investigation into the Discriminatory Practices of Railroads During World War II," *JNH* 61 (April 1976):183; "We've": Arthur Barnes in Ann Banks, ed., *First-Person America* (New York: Vintage Books, 1980), p. 150; Laurence J. W. Hayes, *The Negro Federal Government Worker: A Study of His Classification Status in the District of Columbia, 1883–1938* (Washington, DC: Howard University, 1941), p. 105; St. Clair Drake and Horace R. Cayton, *Black Metropolis: A Study of Negro Life in a Northern City* (New York: Harcourt Brace, 1945), pp. 240, 216–17; John N. Webb, "The Migratory-Casual Worker," WPA Division of Social Research, Research Monograph VII (Washington, DC: Government Printing Office, 1937); Clinch Calkins, *Some Folks Won't Work* (New York: Harcourt Brace, 1930).

10. Mark W. Kruman, "Quotas for Blacks: The Public Works Administration and the Black Construction Worker," *LH* 16 (Winter 1975):37–51; "standing": Evelyn Macon in Banks, ed., *First-Person America*, p. 126; Annelise Orleck, *Common Sense and a Little Fire: Women and Working-Class Politics in the United States, 1900–1965* (Chapel Hill, NC: University of North Carolina Press), pp. 161–65; Alan Draper, "The New Southern Labor History Revisited: The Success of the Mine, Mill, and Smelter Workers Union in Birmingham, 1934–1938," *LH* 62 (February 1996):87–108; Richard Sterner, *The Negro's Share: A Study of Consumption, Housing, and Public Assistance* (New York: Harper and Brothers, 1943), pp. 280–85. For overviews, see Raymond Wolters, *Negroes and the Great Depression: The Problem of Economic Recovery* (Westport, CT: Greenwood Press, 1970), and Harvard Sitkoff, *A New Deal for Blacks: The Emergence of Civil Rights as a National Issue* (New York: Oxford University Press, 1978).

11. Covington and Plummer quoted in Andrew R. Keegan, "The CCC: A Successful Job Corps, 1930s Style," *AV* 1 (September–October 1986):21, 24.

12. Articles in Steve Fraser and Gary Gerstle, eds., *The Rise and Fall of the New Deal Order, 1930–1980* (Princeton: Princeton University Press, 1989); Laurence E. Norton II and Marc Linder, "Down and Out in Weslaco, Texas, and Washington, D.C.: Race-Based Discrimination Against Farm Workers Under Federal Unemployment Insurance," *UMJLR* 29 (Fall 1995–Winter 1996):177–216; Jacqueline Jones, *Labor of Love, Labor of Sorrow: Black Women, Work and the Family from Slavery to the Present* (New York: Basic Books, 1985), pp. 205–13.

13. "sometimes": Irene Nixon in Sherry Thomas, ed., *We Didn't Have Much, But We Sure Had Plenty: Stories of Rural Women* (New York: Anchor Books, 1981), p. 7; "had to": Sarah Rice, *He Included Me: The Autobiography of Sarah Rice*, ed. by Louise Westling (Athens, GA: University of Georgia Press, 1989), p. 120; "I never": "Josephine" quoted in Fran Buss Leeper, *Dignity: Lower Income Women Tell of Their Lives and Struggles* (Ann Arbor, MI: University of Michigan, 1985), p. 37; Hugh P. Brinton, "Regional Variation in Disabling Sickness Among a Group of Negro Male Railroad Employees," *SF* 20 (December 1941):264–70; Linda Leska Belgrave, "The Effects of Race Differences in Work History, Work Attitudes, Economic Resources, and Health on Women's Retirement," *ROA* 10 (September 1988):383–98. See also Linda Gordon, *Pitied But Not Entitled: Single Mothers and the History of Welfare, 1890–1935* (New York: Free Press, 1994).

14. Warren C. Whatley, "Labor for the Picking: The New Deal in the South," *JEH* 43 (December 1983):905–30; Carey McWilliams, *Ill Fares the Land: Migrants and Migratory Labor in the United States* (Boston: Little, Brown, 1942), pp. 218–19; "to . . . farms": Ernest E. Neal and Lewis W. Jones, "The Place of the Negro Farmer in the Changing Economy of the South," *RS* 15 (March 1950):41; Jones, *Labor of Love*, pp. 216–21; Harold A. Pederson, "Mechanized Agriculture and the Farm Laborer," *RS* 19 (June 1954):143–51. See also Alfred Edgar Smith, "Negro Project Workers: An Annual Report on Work Relief Matters Affecting Negro Workers

Peculiarly," p. 16, Federal Emergency Relief Administration, Works Progress Administration, RG 69, National Archives, Washington, DC.

15. "here in": Hurston quoted in Michael K. Honey, *Southern Labor and Black Civil Rights: Organizing Memphis Workers* (Urbana, IL: University of Illinois Press, 1993), p. 26; Christopher L. Tomlins, "AFL Unions in the 1930s: Their Performance in Historical Perspective," *JAH* 55 (March 1979):1021-42; Delores Janiewski, *Sisterhood Denied: Race, Gender, and Class in a New South Community* (Philadelphia: Temple University Press, 1985); Kenneth T. Jackson, "Race, Ethnicity, and Real Estate Appraisal: The Home Owners Loan Corporation and the Federal Housing Administration," *JUH* 6 (August 1980):419-52.

16. Darlene Clark Hine, "The Housewives' League of Detroit: Black Women and Economic Nationalism," in Darlene Clark Hine, *Hine Sight: Black Women and the Re-Construction of American History* (Brooklyn, NY: Carlson, 1994), pp. 129-46; Andor Skotines, "'Buy Where You Can Work': Boycotting for Jobs in African-American Baltimore," *JSocH* 27 (Summer 1994):735-63; Gary Jerome Hunter, "Don't Buy from Where You Can't Work: Black Urban Boycott Movements During the Depression, 1929-1941," Ph.D. thesis, University of Michigan, 1977; Harris, *The Harder We Run*, pp. 108-09.

17. "They . . . lacking": Nell Irvin Painter, *Narrative of Hosea Hudson: His Life as a Negro Communist in the South* (Cambridge, MA: Harvard University Press, 1979), pp. 253, 191; Orleck, *Common Sense and a Little Fire*, pp. 161–65; interview with Sylvia Woods in Alice Lynd and Staughton Lynd, eds., *Rank and File: Personal Histories by Working-Class Organizers* (Princeton: Princeton University Press, 1981), pp. 127-29; Patricia Sullivan, *Days of Hope: Race and Democracy in the New Deal Era* (Chapel Hill, NC: University of North Carolina Press, 1996); Cohen, *Making a New Deal*. See also Charles Denby, *Indignant Heart: Testimony of a Black American Worker* (London: Pluto Press, 1979), p. 89.

18. "The Negroes": Denby, *Indignant Heart*, p. 169; Steve Jefferys, "'Matters of Mutual Interest': The Unionization Process at Dodge Main, 1933-1939," in Nelson Lichtenstein and Stephen Meyer, eds., *On the Line: Essays in the History of Auto Work* (Urbana, IL: University of Illinois Press, 1989), p. 120; GM manager quoted in Ruth Milkman, "Rosie the Riveter Revisited: Management's Postwar Purge of Women Auto Workers," in Lichtenstein and Meyer, eds., *On the Line*, pp. 129-47.

19. Clarence Coe quoted in Honey, *Southern Labor and Black Civil Rights*, p. 281; Tomlins, "AFL Unions in the 1930s."

20. See juxtaposition of articles: "Vast Labor Needed," *Kansas City Times*, March 18, 1941, p. 2; "Limit Negro Air Jobs," *Kansas City Star*, March 17, 1941, all in John H. Bracey, Jr., and August Meier, eds., *Papers of the National Association for the Advancement of Colored People*, Part 13: *NAACP and Labor* (Frederick, MD: University Publications of America, 1991), reel 3, frames 213-14.

21. "One tenth": Interview with former NUL official Ann Tanneyhill, conducted by Cheryl Gilkes, in Ruth Edmonds Hill, ed., *The Black Woman Oral History Project:*

From the Arthur and Elizabeth Schlesinger Library (Westport, CT: Meckler, 1991), vol. 9, p. 234.

22. Robert C. Weaver, *Negro Labor: A National Problem* (New York: Harcourt Brace, 1946). On Weaver's career, see Harvard Sitkoff, "Robert Clifton Weaver," in Jack Salzman, *et al.*, eds., *Encyclopedia of African-American Culture and History* (New York: Macmillan, 1996), Vol. V, pp. 2795–96.

23. "would occasion": Weaver, *Negro Labor*, p. 17.

24. "that all": Rev. S. Liplin, Jr., Furniak Springs, FL, Nov. 14, 1942, in Bracey and Meier, eds., *Papers of the NAACP*, reel 4, frames 534–35; Memo to Lt. Lawrence A. Oxley from Ligon A. Wilson, State Adviser on Negro Affairs, National Youth Administration, Birmingham, March 1942, Region VII Folder, Oxley Files, Record Group 183, U.S. Employment Service Records, National Archives, Washington, DC; "looked . . . hell": Chester Himes, *If He Hollers Let Him Go* (New York: Signet, 1971; orig. pub. 1945), p. 6.

25. Dennis C. Dickerson, "Fighting on the Domestic Front: Black Steelworkers During World War II," in Charles Stephenson and Robert Asher, eds., *Life and Labor: Dimensions of American Working-Class History* (Albany, NY: SUNY Press, 1986), pp. 224–36; Tuttle quoted in Weaver, *Negro Labor*, p. 109; "We are": Louis Martin to Walter White, Detroit, October 2, 1941, in Bracey and Meier, *Papers of the NAACP*, Part 13, reel 3, frames 921–22.

26. Weaver, *Negro Labor*; Quintard Taylor, "The Great Migration: The Afro-American Communities of Seattle and Portland During the 1940s," *AW* 23 (Summer 1981):109–26. *Hearings Before the Select Committee Investigating National Defense Migration*, U.S. Congress House of Representatives Select Committee Investigating National Defense Migration, 77th Cong., 1st and 2nd sess., 1941–43, Part 33 (June 1942), pp. 12, 481, 13,016.

27. "discover": Annabel Sawyer, "The Negro Woman in National Defence," *AWJ* 2 (Summer–Fall 1941), p. 2; "Courses in Domestic Service, Fiscal Year 1943–44," Folder: Legislation Covering Domestic Workers, Box 1717, Records of the Women's Bureau, Record 86, NA; "president": "Negro Women War Workers," *Women's Bureau Bulletin* 205 (1945), pp. 8, 5; Karen Anderson, *Wartime Women: Sex Roles, Family Relations, and the Status of Women During World War II* (Westport, CT: Greenwood Press, 1981), pp. 36–42.

28. "fascist": Abraham Rubin and George J. Segal, "An Industrial Experiment," *Annals* 244 (March 1946):59; "We are": quoted in Taylor, "The Great Migration," p. 121.

29. George Lipsitz, *A Rainbow at Midnight: Labor and Culture in the 1940s* (Urbana, IL: University of Illinois Press, 1994), p. 81; Gretchen Lemke-Santangelo, *Abiding Courage: African American Migrant Women and the East Bay Community* (Chapel Hill, NC: University of North Carolina Press, 1996), pp. 130–31.

30. "The railroads": quoted in Henderson, "FEPC and the Southern Railway Case," p. 184; "were": mill manager quoted in Herbert R. Northrup and Richard L. Rowan, *Negro Employment in Southern Industry: A Study of Racial Policies in Five*

Industries (Philadelphia: University of Pennsylvania Press, 1971), p. 35; "speed": John L. Lovett quoted in Ruth Milkman, *Gender at Work: The Dynamics of Job Segregation by Sex During World War II* (Urbana, IL: University of Illinois Press, 1987), p. 54. See also Merl E. Reed, "Black Workers, Defense Industries, and Federal Agencies in Pennsylvania, 1941–5," *LH* 27 (Summer 1986):356–84; "The Employers' Viewpoint," Survey of the New York State Employment Service, Box 1387, Oxley Files, U.S. Employment Service Records, RG 183, National Archives, Washington, DC.

31. "15 Negroes": Walter White to Nicholas Fontecchio, District Director of the SWOC, April 30, 1941, in Bracey and Meier, eds., *Papers of the NAACP*, reel 1, frame 154; Minutes of the Nineteenth Meeting of the Seventh Regional Labor Supply Committtee, Birmingham, March 18, 1942, Region VII Folder, Oxley Files, RG 183, NA; "Report of Regional Labor Supply Officer for Period Ending Mar. 1, 1942," *ibid*; "would rather": John Langston Gwaltney, *Drylongso: A Self-Portrait of Black America* (New York: Random House, 1980), p. 235.

32. James E. Fickle and Donald W. Ellis, "POWs in the Piney Woods: German Prisoners of War in the Southern Labor Industry, 1943–1945," *JSouH* 56 (November 1990):695–724; Hazel Wages, "Memphis Armed Services Depot Prisoner of War Camp: 1944–1946," *THQ* 52 (Spring 1993):19–31; Kathy Rae Coker, "World War II Prisoners of War in Georgia: German Memories of Camp Gordon, 1943–1945," *GHQ* 76 (Winter 1992):837–61; C. Calvin Smith, "The Response of Arkansas to Prisoners of War and Japanese Americans in Arkansas, 1942–1945," *ArHQ* 53 (August 1994):340–66.

33. "tolerate . . . good": Reed, "Accommodation Between Negro and White Employees in a West Coast Aircraft Industry," p. 79; Alan Clive, *State of War: Michigan in World War II* (Ann Arbor, MI: University of Michigan Press, 1979), pp. 130–69; Thomas J. Sugrue, *The Origins of the Urban Crisis: A History of Inequality in Detroit, 1940–1967* (Princeton: Princeton University Press, 1996), chaps. 2 and 3.

34. Merl Reed, *Seedtime for the Modern Civil Rights Movement: The President's Committee on Fair Employment Practices, 1941–1946* (Baton Rouge, LA: Louisiana State University Press, 1991); Herbert Garfinkel, *When Negroes March: The March on Washington Movement in the Organizational Politics for FEPC* (Glencoe, IL: Free Press, 1959); Patricia L. Adams, "Fighting for Democracy in St. Louis: Civil Rights During World War II," *MHR* 80 (October 1985):58–75; Henderson, "FEPC and the Southern Railway Case"; Merl E. Reed, "FEPC and the Federal Agencies in the South," *JNH* 65 (Winter 1980):43–56; William H. Harris, "Federal Intervention in Union Discrimination: FEPC and the West Coast Shipyards During World War II," *LH* 22 (Summer 1981):325–47; Richard Polenberg, *One Nation Divisible: Class, Race, and Ethnicity in the United States Since 1938* (New York: Viking, 1980), pp. 33, 117, 121–23.

35. "refined": Dorothy K. Newman, *et al.*, *Protest, Politics, and Prosperity: Black Americans and White Institutions, 1940–75* (New York: Pantheon, 1978), pp. 33, 104; Her-

bert Northrup, *Organized Labor and the Negro* (New York: Harper and Brothers, 1944), chap. III; *To Secure These Rights: The Report of the President's Committee on Civil Rights* (New York: Simon & Schuster, 1947), p. 58.

36. "when the war": Louis Banks in Studs Terkel, *Hard Times: An Oral History of the Great Depression* (New York: Avon Books, 1970), p. 60.

37. "Camp": Gates, *Colored People*, p. 85; "Southern . . . jobs": Arnold M. Rose, "Army Policies Toward Negro Soldiers," *Annals* 244 (March 1946):90–1; Gwendolyn Midlo Hall, ed., *Love, War, and the 96th Engineers (Colored): The World War II New Guinea Diaries of Captain Hyman Samuelson* (Urbana, IL: University of Illinois Press, 1995), pp. xv–xvi; "a relatively": Stimson quoted in A. Russell Buchanan, *Black Americans in World War II* (Santa Barbara, CA: Clio Books, 1977), p. 94.

38. Buchanan, *Black Americans in World War II*, p. 11; Robert J. Jakeman, *The Divided Skies: Establishing Segregated Flight Training at Tuskegee, 1934–1942* (Tuscaloosa, AL: University of Alabama Press, 1992); "the . . . efficiency": Memorandum to the Secretary of War from William H. Hastie, Civilian Aide to the Secretary of War, January 5, 1943, in Morris J. MacGregor and Bernard C. Nalty, eds., *Blacks in the United States Air Force, Basic Documents*, Vol. V: *Black Soldiers in World War II* (Wilmington, DE: Scholarly Resources, 1977), pp. 180, 181; Bernard C. Nalty, *Strength for the Fight: A History of Black Americans in the Military* (New York: Free Press, 1986), p. 186.

39. Harold Goldstein, "The Changing Occupational Structure," *MLR* (December 1947):654–65; Mary S. Bedell, "Employment and Income of Negro Workers—1940–52," *MLR* 76 (June 1953):596–601; Constance Williams, Chief, Research Division, Women's Bureau, to Hilda Fortune, Nov. 20, 1946, Correspondence with Women's Organizations, Negro Women's Organizations, Box 849, Department of Labor, Record of the Women's Bureau, Record Group 86, National Archives, Washington, DC; "I could": quoted in "Only 1 in 73 Former Maids Returning to New York Kitchens," *Christian Science Monitor*, October 8, 1946.

40. Will Robinson in Terkel, *Working*, pp. 274–75; Newman, *et al.*, *Protest, Politics, and Prosperity*, p. 50.

41. "draped": Robin D. G. Kelley, *Race Rebels: Culture, Politics, and the Black Working Class* (New York: Free Press, 1994), p. 66. Kelley discusses this passage from *The Autobiography of Malcolm X* in his essay, "The Riddle of the Zoot: Malcolm Little and Black Cultural Politics During World War II," *ibid.*, pp. 161-81. The quotation is on p. 177.

42. "Blacks": "Standing Tall," interview with T. J. Johnson by Reginald Skinner and Jackie Collins, "Minds Stayed on Freedom: Movement Veterans Speak to Holmes County Youth," *Bloodlines*, 2 (Rural Organizing and Cultural Center of Holmes County, MS) (Spring 1990), p. 58.

43. Wright, *Old South, New South*.

44. "Handbook of Facts on Women Workers," *Women's Bureau Bulletin* no. 225 (1948), p. 22; "Handbook of Facts on Women Workers," *Women's Bureau Bulletin*

no. 255 (1954), pp. 18–20; William Chafe, *The American Woman; Her Changing Social, Economic, and Political Roles, 1920–1970* (New York: Oxford University Press, 1970), pp. 135–98.

45. James Gregory, *American Exodus: The Dustbowl Migration and Okie Culture in California* (New York: Oxford University Press, 1989); Melvin Lurie and Elton Rayack, "Racial Differences in Migration and Job Search: A Case Study," *SEJ* 33 (July 1966): 81–95; Jacqueline Jones, *The Dispossessed: America's Underclasses from the Civil War to the Present* (New York: Basic Books, 1992), pp. 205–68.

46. Kenneth L. Kusmer, "African Americans in the City Since World War II: From the Industrial to the Post-Industrial Era," *JUH* 21 (May 1995):458–504; Douglas S. Massey and Nancy A. Denton, *American Apartheid: Segregation and the Making of the Underclass* (Cambridge, UK: Cambridge University Press, 1993), pp. 17–59; Thomas J. Sugrue, "Crabgrass-Roots Politics: Race, Rights, and the Reaction against Liberalism in the Urban North, 1940–1964," *JAH* 82 (September 1995):551–78.

47. Nicholas Lemann, *The Promised Land: The Great Black Migration and How It Changed America* (New York: Knopf, 1991), pp. 1–58; Warren C. Whatley, "Southern Agrarian Labor Contracts as Impediments to Mechanization," *JEH* 47 (March 1987):45–70; Larry J. Griffin and Robert R. Korstad, "Class as Race and Gender: Making and Breaking a Labor Union in the Jim Crow South," *SSH* 19 (Winter 1995):425–53; "you . . . mines": Donald T. Barnum, *The Negro in Bituminous Coal Mining* (Philadelphia: University of Pennsylvania Wharton School of Finance and Commerce, 1970), pp. 33, 30; Lewis, *Black Coal Miners in America*, pp. 167–90.

48. Stephen Meyer, "The Persistence of Fordism: Workers and Technology in the American Automobile Industry, 1900–1960," in Lichtenstein and Meyer, eds., *On the Line*, pp. 73–99; John T. Cumbler, *A Social History of Economic Decline: Business, Politics, and Work in Trenton* (New Brunswick, NJ: Rutgers University Press, 1989).

49. Dorothy K. Newman, "The Negro's Journey to the City—Part II: The Economic Status of Negroes Today Compared with That of Immigrants at the Turn of the Century," *MLR* 88 (June 1965):644–49; Sugrue, *Origins of the Urban Crisis*, pp. 125–52.

50. See for example Theodore Hershberg, et al., "A Tale of Three Cities: Blacks, Immigrants, and Opportunity in Philadelphia, 1850–1880, 1930, 1970," in Theodore Hershberg, ed., *Philadelphia: Work, Space, Family and Group Experience in the Nineteenth Century* (New York: Oxford University Press, 1981), pp. 461–91.

51. Northrup, "Unions and Negro Employment," p. 46; "until they": Howard W. Dixon to Walter White, Miami, March 25, 1954, in Bracey and Meier, eds., *Papers of the NAACP*, reel 3, frames 669–70; Northrup and Rowan, *Negro Employment in Southern Industry*, p. 41; Sugrue, *Origins of the Urban Crisis*, pp. 95–119.

52. Interview with Florence Rice in Gerda Lerner, ed., *Black Women in White America: A Documentary History* (New York: Vintage, 1973), p. 283; Herbert Hill, "The AFL-CIO and the Black Worker." See also Honey, *Southern Labor and Black Civil Rights*, pp. 245–78.

53. Harris, *The Harder We Run*, p. 157.

54. "updated": Hugh Davis Graham, "The Origins of Affirmative Action: Civil Rights and the Regulatory State," *Annals* 523 (September 1992), p. 52; "Negro . . . whites": Alfred W. Blumrosen, "The Many Faces of Job Discrimination: A Report by the EEOC on Job Patterns for Minorities and Women in Private Industry—1966," and "The Construction Industry Problem," in *Black Employment and the Law* (New Brunswick, NJ: Rutgers University Press, 1971), pp. 121, 308. See also Michael I. Sovern, *Legal Restraints on Racial Discrimination in Employment* (New York: Twentieth Century Fund, 1966).

55. Newman, *et al.*, *Protest, Politics, and Prosperity*, pp. 111–22; Margaret Weir, *Politics and Jobs: The Boundaries of Employment Policy in the United States* (Princeton: Princeton University Press, 1992), pp. 62–98; Jill Quadagno, *The Color of Welfare: How Racism Undermined the War on Poverty* (New York: Oxford University Press, 1994).

56. Hugh Davis Graham, *Civil Rights and the Presidency: Race and Gender in American Politics, 1960–1972* (New York: Oxford University Press, 1992), pp. 102–16; J. Larry Hood, "The Nixon Administration and the Revised Philadelphia Plan for Affirmative Action: A Study in Expanding Presidential Power and Divided Government," *PresSQ* 23 (Winter 1993):145–67; John David Skrentny, *The Ironies of Affirmative Action: Politics, Culture, and Justice in America* (Chicago: University of Chicago Press, 1996), pp. 193–211.

57. William Julius Wilson, *The Truly Disadvantaged: The Inner City, the Underclass, and Public Policy* (Chicago: University of Chicago Press, 1987), pp. 109–17; Bette Woody, *Black Women in the Workplace: Impacts of Structural Change in the Economy* (Westport, CT: Greenwood Press, 1992), pp. 71–91; Jones, *Labor of Love*, pp. 301–21; Augustin Kwasi Fosu, "Occupational Mobility of Black Women, 1958–1981: The Impact of Post–1964 Antidiscrimination Measures," *ILRR* 45 (January 1992): 281–86.

58. John J. Donohue III and James Heckman, "Continuous versus Episodic Change: The Impact of Civil Rights Policy on the Economic Status of Blacks," *JEL* 29 (December 1991):1603–43; "the idea": John Foster quoted in Mary Frederickson, "Four Decades of Change: Black Workers in Southern Textiles, 1941–1981," in James Green, ed., *Workers' Struggles, Past and Present* (Philadelphia: Temple University Press, 1983), p. 74; James J. Heckman and Brook S. Payner, "Determining the Impact of Federal Antidiscrimination Policy on the Economic Status of Blacks: A Study of South Carolina," *AER* 79 (March 1989):138–77.

59. "light and": Sledge quoted in Mimi Conway, *Rise Gonna Rise: A Portrait of Textile Workers* (New York: Anchor Press, 1979), p. 109; "No Blacks Near the Top of Louisville Hotel Employment," and "Black Restaurant Workers Are Concentrated in Kitchens: A Report on Employment of Blacks and Women in the Louisville Restaurant Industry," Staff Reports 79–3 and 79–4, Kentucky Commission on Human Rights (Louisville, KY, 1979).

60. "Jobs and Housing: A Study of Employment and Housing Opportunities for

Racial Minorities in the Suburban Areas of the New York Metropolitan Region," National Committee Against Discrimination in Housing (New York, 1970); Peter K. Eisinger, "Black Employment in Municipal Jobs: The Impact of Black Political Power," APSR 76 (1982):383–87; Mack H. Jones, "Black Political Empowerment in Atlanta: Myth and Reality," Annals 439 (September 1978):90–117; Edmund J. Keller, "The Impact of Black Mayors on Urban Policy," Annals 439 (September 1978):40–52.

61. Gary Massoni, "Perspectives on Operation Breadbasket," in David J. Garrow, ed., Chicago 1966: Open Housing Marches, Summit Negotiations, and Operation Bread-basket (Brooklyn, NY: Carlson, 1989); William Julius Wilson, When Work Disappears: The World of the New Urban Poor (New York: Knopf, 1996).

62. Daniel Patrick Moynihan, The Negro Family: The Case for National Action (Washington, DC: Office of Policy Planning and Research, U.S. Department of Labor, 1965), pp. 45, 42–43; Charles C. Moskos, Jr., The American Enlisted Man: The Rank and File in Today's Military (New York: Russell Sage Foundation, 1970), pp. 108–33.

63. Gwaltney, Drylongso, p. 7; "the work" "I have": ibid., pp. 95, 67; "I don't": Terkel, Working, p. 166; "people," "Now": Gwaltney, Drylongso, pp. 173, 34.

64. "would take": Brown quoted in Marat Moore, Women in the Mines: Stories of Life and Work (New York: Twayne Publishers, 1996), p. 131; "I . . . bathroom": Brooks quoted in Conway, Rise Gonna Rise, pp. 90-91.

65. drum article quoted in James A. Gewschwender, Class, Race, and Worker Insurgency: The League of Revolutionary Black Workers (Cambridge, UK: Cambridge University Press, 1977), p. 91; Nelson Lichtenstein, "'The Man in the Middle': A Social History of Automobile Industry Foremen," in Lichtenstein and Meyer, eds., On the Line, p. 181; Dan Georgakas and Marvin Surkin, Detroit: I Do Mind Dying: A Study in Urban Revolution (New York: St. Martin's Press, 1975).

CHAPTER TWELVE

1. Ronald Smothers, "Unions Try to Push Past Workers' Fears to Sign Up Poultry Plants in the South," NYT, Jan. 30, 1996, p. A10; Barbara Goldoftas, "Inside the Slaughterhouse," SE 17 (Summer 1989):27–30; John Holsha, "First to College, Then to the Mill: Graduates are Drawn to Blue-Collar Work," NYT, Aug. 22, 1995, pp. D1, D7; "they are": David Missar quoted in Louis Uchitelle, "Union Goal of Equality Fails the Test of Time," NYT, July 9, 1995, p. A18; "race watch": Lois Benjamin, The Black Elite: Facing the Color Line in the Twilight of the Twentieth Century (Chicago: Nelson-Hall, 1991), p. 104; "what": Evelyn Lewis quoted in Patricia J. Williams, "Notes from a Small World," New Yorker, April 29 and May 6, 1996, p. 90; Lawrence M. Kahn, "The Effects of Race on Professional Football Players' Compensation," ILRR 45 (January 1992):295–310.

2. Jeff Cowie, "Rooted Workers and the Runaway Shop: A Comparative History of Capital Migration and Social Change in the United States and Mexico,

1936–1995," Ph.D. thesis, University of North Carolina Chapel Hill; Jacqueline Jones, "The Late Twentieth-Century War on the Poor: A View from Distressed Communities Throughout the Nation," *BCTWLJ* 16 (Winter 1996):1–16; Carl Husemoller Nightingale, "The Global Inner City: Towards an Historical Analysis," in Michael Katz and Thomas J. Sugrue, eds., *W. E. B DuBois and the Philadelphia Negro: A Centenary Reappraisal* (Philadelphia: University of Pennsylvania Press, 1998); "I look": Thomas Rush in Studs Terkel, *Working* (New York: Avon Books, 1972), p. 381.

3. Canty quoted in Sara Mosle, "Letter from Las Vegas: How the Maids Fought Back," *New Yorker*, Feb. 26 and Mar. 4, 1996, p. 155.

4. U.S. Department of Commerce, Bureau of the Census, *1980 Census of Population—Detailed Population Characteristics, United States Summary*, PC80-1-D1-A; Douglas S. Massey and Nancy A. Denton, *American Apartheid: Segregation and the Making of the Underclass* (Cambridge, MA: Harvard University Press, 1993), pp. 144–45.

5. Jackson quoted in Kathryn Marie Dudley, *The End of the Line: Lost Jobs, New Lives in Postindustrial America* (Chicago: University of Chicago Press, 1994), p. 145.

6. Steven A. Shull, *A Kinder, Gentler Racism? The Reagan-Bush Civil Rights Legacy* (London: M. E. Sharpe, 1993); Martin Carnoy, *Faded Dreams: The Politics and Economics of Race in America* (Cambridge, UK: Cambridge University Press, 1994). For discussions of these social indicators, see for example Andrew Hacker, *Two Nations: Black and White, Separate, Hostile, Unequal* (New York: Charles Scribner's Sons, 1992); "beneath": John E. Schwarz and Thomas J. Volgy, *The Forgotten American* (New York: W. W. Norton, 1992), p. 74; U.S. Department of Commerce, Current Population Reports, Consumer Income, "Poverty in the United States, 1991" Series P–60, no. 181 (August 1992); James A. Geschwender and Rita Carroll Seguin, "Exploding the Myth of Afro-American Progress," *Signs* 15 (Winter 1990):285–99. On the "contract at will" as an ideal basis of employer-employee relations, see Richard A. Epstein, *Forbidden Grounds: The Case Against Employment Discrimination Laws* (Cambridge, MA: Harvard University Press, 1992).

7. See Charles C. Moskos and John Sibley Butler, *All That We Can Be: Black Leadership and Racial Integration the Army Way* (New York: Basic Books, 1996). For a less sanguine view that focuses on the Army Corps of Engineers, see Bob Herbert, "Bias Intensified by Inertia," *NYT*, Jan. 24, 1997, p. A31.

8. "Black and White, Career by Career: How Younger Workers Compare" (data compiled from 1970 and 1990 censuses), *NYT*, June 19, 1995, section 4, p. 4. See also U.S. Equal Employment Opportunity Commission, "Job Patterns for Minorities and Women in Private Industry" (Government Printing Office, Office of Program Operations, 1991).

9. "Black and White, Career by Career," p. 4; Kirk Johnson, "Black Workers Bear Big Burden as Jobs in Government Dwindle," *NYT*, Feb. 2,1997, pp. A1, A36. William L. Taylor and Susan M. Less, "Affirmative Action in the 1990s: Staying

the Course," *Annals* 523 (September 1992):30–37; Gerald D. Jaynes and Robin M. Williams, Jr., eds., *A Common Destiny: Blacks and American Society* (Washington, DC: National Academy Press, 1989), pp. 269–329; Jonathan Leonard, *The Effectiveness of Equal Employment Law and Affirmative Action Regulation* (Berkeley: University of California School of Business Administration, 1985); Chuck Turner, "Sharing the Pie: The Boston Jobs Coalition," *LRR* 7 (1988):81–7.

10. "Certainly": "Working and Coexisting," *BG*, May 24, 1995, p. 24; "Have you": Sharon Collins, "Blacks on the Bubble: The Vulnerability of Black Executives in White Corporations," *SQ* 34 (1993):442.

11. "only Asians": Mike McGraw, "Cheep Labor: Programs Place Americans Low in Pecking Order," *MJ* (January–February 1996), p. 13; Karen J. Hossfeld, "Hiring Immigrant Women: Silicon Valley's 'Simple Formula,'" in Maxine Baca Zinn and Bonnie Thornton Dill, eds., *Women of Color in United States Society* (Philadelphia: Temple University Press, 1994), pp. 65, 75–6, 80–1; "lots . . . job": Steven A. Holmes, "In Iowa Town, Strains of Diversity," *NYT*, Feb. 17, 1996, p. A6; "worst": Brian MacQuarrie, "A Bitter Harvest: Maine Farm Fined $3.6 M. Over Workers' Conditions," *BG*, July 13, 1996, pp. 1, 6.

12. "They use": Eric Schlosser, "In the Strawberry Fields," *AM* (November 1995), p. 86; Jane Fritsch, "One Failed Voyage Illustrates Flow of Chinese Immigration," *NYT*, June 7, 1993, pp. A1, B5.

13. "low . . . market": The President's Commission on the Future of Worker-Management Relations (Dunlop Commission), *Fact-Finding Report* (May 1994), Bureau of National Affairs, *Daily Labor Report*, June 3, 1994, chap. 1, part 3; Stan Grossfeld, "Children of the Harvest," *BG*, April 30, 1995, pp. 74–5; Roger Waldinger, *Still the Promised City? African-Americans and New Immigrants in Postindustrial New York* (Cambridge, MA: Harvard University Press, 1996).

14. For opposing views of the immigration "crisis," see Richard Rayner, "What Immigration Crisis?" *NYT Magazine*, Jan. 7, 1996, p. 26; Peter Brimelow, *Alien Nation: Common Sense About America's Immigration Disaster* (New York: Random House, 1995); Lyn Wells, "The Cedartown Story: The Ku Klux Klan and Labor in 'The New South,'" *LRR*, pp. 69–79; Eric Bates, "Beyond Black and White," *SE* 22 (Fall 1994):10–15. In this issue of *Southern Exposure*, see also articles on various immigrant groups in the southern states.

15. Irene Nixon quoted in Sherry Thomas, *We Didn't Have Much, But We Sure Had Plenty: Stories of Rural Women* (Garden City, NY: Anchor Books, 1981), p. 12; "Alabama to Make Prisoners Break Rocks," *NYT*, June 29, 1995, p. A5. For a first-hand account, see for example Jesse F. Steiner and Roy M. Brown, *The North Carolina Chain Gang: A Study of County Convict Road Work* (Chapel Hill, NC: University of North Carolina Press, 1927).

16. Michael Tonry, *Malign Neglect—Race, Crime, and Punishment in America* (New York: Oxford University Press, 1995); "In . . . force": Christian Parenti, "Making Prisons Pay," *Nation*, Jan. 29, 1996, pp. 11–12.

17. "Long": Watkins quoted in Jon Nordheimer, "Murder a Growth in Poor, Reel-

ing Camden," *NYT*, Oct. 29, 1995, p. A38; Robert C. Smith, *Racism in the Post–Civil Rights Era: Now You See It, Now You Don't* (Albany, NY: State University of New York Press, 1995), pp. 53–75; Philippe Bourgois, *In Search of Respect: Selling Crack in El Barrio* (New York: Cambridge University Press, 1995).

18. Saskia Sassen, *The Global City: New York, London, Tokyo* (Princeton: Princeton University Press, 1991); Alejandro Portes and Alex Stepick, *City on the Edge: The Transformation of Miami* (Berkeley: University of California Press, 1993); Jacqueline Jones, *Labor of Love, Labor of Sorrow: Black Women, Work and the Family from Slavery to the Present* (New York: Basic Books, 1985), Epilogue to the 1995 edition; U.S. Department of Labor, Women's Bureau, "Facts on Working Women," no. 90–4 (June 1991); Julia Burkart, "Stronger Than Love: Louisiana's Sugar Cane Women," in Caroline Matheny Dillman, ed., *Southern Women* (New York: Hemisphere, 1988), pp. 183–89.

19. Leon Fink and Brian Greenberg, *Upheaval in the Quiet Zone: A History of Hospital Workers' Union, Local 1199* (Urbana, IL: University of Illinois Press, 1989); Ann Long, "Mississippi Still Burning," *SE* (Spring 1989): 8–29; Bob Hall, "'I Feel What Women Feel' [Donna Bazemore]" *SE* 17 (Summer 1989):31–5; James S. Cobb, *The Most Southern Place on Earth: The Mississippi Delta and the Roots of Regional Identity* (New York: Oxford University Press, 1992), pp. 330–31.

20. David M. Gordon, *Fat and Mean: The Corporate Squeeze of Working Americans and the Myth of Managerial Downsizing* (New York: Martin Kessler Books, 1996); Jon Nordheimer, "Welfare-to-Work Plans Show Success Is Difficult to Achieve," *NYT*, Sept. 1, 1996, pp. A1, A18; Joleen Kirschenman and Kathryn M. Neckerman, "'We'd Love to Hire Them, But . . . : The Meaning of Race for Employers," and Marta Tienda and Haya Stier, "Joblessness and Shiftlessness: Labor Force Activity in Chicago's Inner City," both in Christopher Jencks and Paul E. Peterson, eds., *The Urban Underclass* (Washington, DC: Brookings Institution, 1991), pp. 207, 211, 143 (the quote "I wanted" is on p. 211); Katherine S. Newman, "Working Poor: Low Wage Employment in the Lives of Harlem Youth," in J. Graber, *et al.*, eds., *Transitions Through Adolescence: Interpersonal Domains and Context* (Mahwah, NJ: Erlbaum Associates, 1996), pp. 323–44.

21. Deborah Figart, "Gender Segmentation of Craft Workers by Race in the 1970s and 1980s," *RRPE* 25 (1993):50–66; Connie Johnson's career described in Mary Lindstein Walshok, *Blue-Collar Women: Pioneers on the Male Frontier* (New York: Anchor Books, 1981), p. 130; Marat Moore, *Women in the Mines: Stories of Life and Work* (New York: Twayne, 1996).

22. Jackson quoted in Sara Ann Friedman, *Work Matters: Women Talk About Their Jobs and Their Lives* (New York: Viking, 1996), pp. 87–88.

23. "dysgenesis": Richard J. Herrnstein and Charles Murray, *The Bell Curve: Intelligence and Class Structure in American Life* (New York: Free Press, 1994); Teresa L. Amott, "Black Women and AFDC: Making Entitlement Out of Necessity," and Diana Pearce, "Welfare Is Not For Women: Why the War on Poverty Cannot Conquer the Feminization of Poverty," both in Linda Gordon, ed., *Women, The*

State and Welfare (Madison, WI: University of Wisconsin Press, 1990), pp. 28–98, 265–79; Turner quoted in Mark Robert Rank, *Living on the Edge: The Realities of Welfare in America* (New York: Columbia University Press, 1994), pp. 122–23.

24. See for example Robert B. Reich, *The Work of Nations: Preparing Ourselves for Twenty-First Century Capitalism* (New York: Vintage Books, 1991).

EPILOGUE

1. See for example the chapter entitled "Affirmative Action and the Dilemma of the 'Qualified'" in Ellis Cose, *The Rage of a Privileged Class* (New York: Harper-Collins, 1993), pp. 111–34.

2. See for example the study by Katherine S. Newman, "Working Poor: Low Wage Employment in the Lives of Harlem Youth," in J. Graber, et. al., eds., *Transitions Through Adolescence: Interpersonal Domains and Context* (Mahwah, NJ: Erlbaum Associates Publishers, 1996), pp. 323–44.

3. On this last point, see for example Roger Waldinger, *Still the Promised City? African-Americans and New Immigrants in Postindustrial New York* (Cambridge, MA: Harvard University Press, 1996), and Andres Torres, *Between Melting Pot and Mosaic: African Americans and Puerto Ricans in the New York Political Economy* (Philadelphia: Temple University Press, 1995).

4. Dinesh D'Souza, *The End of Racism: Principles for a Multiracial Society* (New York: Free Press, 1995), p. 527.

5. See, for example, Leon Dash, *Rosa Lee: A Mother and Her Family in Urban America* (New York: Basic Books, 1996); Alex Kotlowitz, *There Are No Children Here: The Story of Two Boys Growing Up in the Other America* (New York: Doubleday, 1991).

6. See for example Stephen Coate and Glenn C. Loury, "Will Affirmative-Action Policies Eliminate Negative Stereotypes?" *AER* 83 (December 1993):1220–39.

7. See for example William Julius Wilson, *When Work Disappears: The World of the New Urban Poor* (New York: Knopf, 1996), pp. 93, 197–99.

8. Bob Zelnick, *Backfire: A Reporter's Look at Affirmative Action* (Washington, DC: Regnery Publishers, 1996).

9. Ruhnke quoted in Richard Morin, "No Place for Calm and Quiet Opinions: Affirmative Action Stirs Strong Feelings—How Strong Depends a Lot on the Questions," *WP* National Weekly Edition, April 24–30, 1995, p. 34.

10. Richard Herrnstein and Charles Murray, *The Bell Curve: Intelligence and Class Structure in American Life* (New York: Free Press, 1994).

11. Antonin Scalia, "The Disease As Cure: 'In Order to Get Beyond Racism, We Must First Take Account of Race,'" *WULQ* (Winter 1979):147–60.

12. See Terry Eastland, *Ending Affirmative Action: The Case for Colorblind Justice* (New York: Basic Books, 1996); Richard Epstein, *Forbidden Grounds: The Case Against Employment Discrimination Laws* (Cambridge, MA: Harvard University Press, 1992).

13. Kevin Sack, "Atlanta Leaders See Racial Goals as Olympic Ideal," *NYT*, June 10, 1996, pp. A1, B12.

14. Claudia H. Deutsch, "Corporate Diversity, in Practice: Networks Are Created and Managers Made Accountable," *NYT*, Nov. 20, pp. D1, D20; A. Barry Rand, "Diversity in Corporate America," in George E.Curry, ed., *The Affirmative Action Debate* (Reading, MA: Addison-Wesley, 1996), pp. 65–76; Alan Wolfe, "Affirmative Action, Inc." *New Yorker*, Nov. 25, 1996, pp. 106–16.

15. Kurt Eichenwald, "The Two Faces of Texaco: The Right Policies Are on the Books, But Not Always on the Job," *NYT*, Nov. 10, 1996, Section 3 ("Money and Business"), pp. 1, 10.

16. Cose, *Rage of a Privileged Class*; Cornel West, *Race Matters* (Boston: Beacon Press, 1993); Lawrence Otis Graham, *Member of the Club: Reflections on Life in a Racially Polarized World* (New York: HarperCollins, 1995); Bruce Shapiro, "A House Divided: Racism at the State Department," *Nation*, Feb. 12, 1996, pp. 11–16.

17. "a . . . next": Smith quoted in Lois Benjamin, *The Black Elite: Facing the Color Line in the Twilight of the Twentieth Century* (Chicago: Nelson-Hall, 1991), p. 104. See also Cose, *Rage of a Privileged Class*.

18. Jill Nelson, *Volunteer Slavery: My Authentic Negro Experience* (Chicago: Noble Press, 1993), p. 62. See also Joe R. Feagin and Melvin P. Sikes, *Living with Racism: The Black Middle-Class Experience* (Boston: Beacon Press, 1994).

19. "become more": Richard Morin, "A Distorted Image of Minorities," *WP*, Oct. 8, 1995, p. A1; Elaine Tyler May, "The Radical Roots of American Studies," *AQ* 48 (June 1996):191–92. For other polls suggesting the effects of whites' perceived self-interest in relation to their view of affirmative action, see Donald R. Kinder and Lynn M. Sanders, *Divided by Color: Racial Politics and Democratic Ideals* (Chicago: University of Chicago Press, 1996), pp. 53–6.

20. Melvin L. Oliver and Thomas M. Shapiro, *Black Wealth/White Wealth: A New Perspective on Racial Inequality* (New York: Routledge, 1996), pp. 91–125; Andrew Billingsley, *Climbing Jacob's Ladder: The Enduring Legacy of African-American Families* (New York: Simon & Schuster, 1992).

21. Gary Orfield, *et al.*, *Dismantling Desegregation: The Quiet Reversal of Brown versus the Board of Education* (New York: New Press), 1996.

22. See for example David L. Kirp, John P. Dwyer, and Larry A. Rosenthal, *Our Town: Race, Housing, and the Soul of Suburbia* (New Brunswick, NJ: Rutgers University Press, 1995).

23. William Julius Wilson, *When Work Disappears: The World of the New Urban Poor* (New York: Knopf, 1996).

Selected Bibliography

Manuscript and Archival Collections

Brown Family Papers. American Antiquarian Society, Worcester, Massachusetts.

Georgia Department of Archives and History. *Superior Court Records*. Atlanta, Georgia.

National Urban League Papers. Library of Congress Manuscripts Division, Washington, DC.

United States: National Archives, Washington, DC

Record Group 15: Civil War Pension Records

Record Group 60: Department of Justice Peonage Files

Record Group 69: Works Progress Administration

Record Group 86: Department of Labor Women's Bureau

Record Group 174: General Records of the Department of Labor

Record Group 183: United States Employment Service

Microfilm Collections

Bracey, John H., Jr., and August Meier. *Papers of the National Association for the Advancement of Colored People*. Part 13. NAACP and Labor. 21 microfilm reels. Frederick, MD: University Publications of America, 1991.

Dew, Charles B. *Slavery in Antebellum Southern Industries*. Series B. Selections from the Southern Historical Collection. 38 microfilm reels. Bethesda, MD: University Publications of America, 1993.

Grossman, James R., ed. *Black Workers in the Era of the Great Migration, 1916–1929*. 25 microfilm reels. Frederick, MD: University Publications of America, 1985.

Stampp, Kenneth. *Records of Ante-Bellum Southern Plantations from the Revolution Through the Civil War*. 26 microfilm reels. Frederick, MD: University Publications of America, 1985.

PRIMARY PUBLISHED MATERIALS: BOOKS,
ARTICLES, AND PAMPHLETS

BOOKS

Abdy, Edward S. *Journal of a Residence and Tour in the United States of North America*. 3 vols. London: John Murray, 1835.

Ames, Susie M., ed. *County Court Records of Accomack-Northampton, 1632–1640*. Washington, DC: American Historical Association, 1954.

———. *County Court Records of Accomack-Northampton, Virginia, 1640–1645*. Charlottesville, VA: University Press of Virginia, 1973.

Andrews, Charles M., ed. *Narratives of the Insurrections, 1675–1690*. New York: Barnes and Noble, 1952.

Asher, Jeremiah. *An Autobiography, with Details of a Visit to England*. Philadelphia: Published by the Author, 1862.

Avery, Burniece. *Walk Quietly Through the Night and Cry Softly*. Detroit: Balamp Press, 1977.

Baker, Ray Stannard. *Following the Color Line: American Negro Citizenship in the Progressive Era*. New York: Harper & Row, 1964; orig. pub. 1908.

Banks, Ann., ed. *First-Person America*. New York: Vintage Books, 1980.

Barbour, Philip L., ed. *The Complete Works of Captain John Smith*. 3 vols. Chapel Hill: University of North Carolina Press, 1986.

Bartlett, John Russell, ed. *Records of the Colony of Rhode Island and Providence Plantations in New England*. 10 vols. Providence: 1856–65.

Baxter, James Phinney, ed. *Documentary History of the State of Maine*. 24 vols. Portland, ME: Maine Historical Society, 1869–1916.

Benson, Adolph B., ed. *Peter Kalm's Travels in North America*. 2 vols. New York: Dover Publications, 1937; orig. pub. 1770.

Berlin, Ira, *et al.*, eds. *Freedom: A Documentary History of Emancipation, 1861–1867*. Series I, Vol. 1: *The Destruction of Slavery*. Series I, Vol. 2: *The Wartime Genesis of Free Labor: The Lower South*. Series II: *The Black Military Experience*. Cambridge: Cambridge University Press, 1982–90.

Beverley, Robert. *The History and Present State of Virginia*. Chapel Hill: University of North Carolina Press, 1947; orig. pub. 1705.

Billings, Warren M., ed. *The Old Dominion in the Seventeenth Century: A Documentary History of Virginia, 1606–1689*. Chapel Hill: University of North Carolina Press, 1975.

Blassingame, John, *et al.*, eds. *The Frederick Douglass Papers*. 4 vols. New Haven: Yale University Press, 1979.

Boyd, William K., ed. *Some Eighteenth-Century Tracts Concerning North Carolina*. Raleigh: Edwards & Broughton, 1927.

Bradford, William. *Of Plymouth Plantation, 1620–1647*. New York: Modern Library, 1981; orig. pub. in full 1856.

Bridenbaugh, Carl, ed. *Gentleman's Progress: The Itinerarium of Dr. Alexander Hamilton, 1744*. Chapel Hill: University of North Carolina Press, 1948.

Brown, William J. *The Life of William J. Brown, of Providence, Rhode Island, With Personal Recollections*. Providence: Angell & Co., 1883.

Browne, William Hand, et al., eds. *Archives of Maryland*. 72 vols. Baltimore: Maryland Historical Society, 1893–1972.

Buckingham, James S. *The Slave States of America*. 2 vols. London: Fisher, Son & Co., 1842.

Calkins, Clinch. *Some Folks Won't Work*. New York: Harcourt Brace, 1930.

Campbell, George. *White and Black: The Outcome of a Visit to the United States*. London: Chatto & Windus, 1879.

Candler, Allen D., ed. *Colonial Records of the State of Georgia*. 26 vols. New York: AMS Press, 1970; orig. pub. 1904–16.

Candler, Isaac. *A Summary View of America: Comprising a Description of the Face of the Country*. London: T. Cadell, 1824.

Catterall, Helen T., ed. *Judicial Cases Concerning American Slavery and the Negro*. 5 vols. Washington, DC: Carnegie Institution, 1926–37.

Chicago Commission on Race Relations. *The Negro in Chicago: A Study of Race Relations and A Race Riot in 1919*. New York: Arno Press, 1968; orig. pub. 1922.

Chinard, Gilbert, ed. *A Huguenot Exile in Virginia or Voyages of a Frenchman Exiled for His Religion with a Description of Virginia and Maryland*. New York: Press of the Pioneers, 1934; orig. pub. 1687.

Clark, Walter, ed. *State Records of North Carolina*. 26 vols. Goldsboro, NC: Nash Bros, 1886–1907.

Comer, James P. *Maggie's American Dream: The Life and Times of a Black Family*. New York: NAL Books, 1988.

Commons, John R, et al., eds. *A Documentary History of American Industrial Society*. 10 vols. New York: Russell & Russell, 1958.

Conway, Mim. *Rise Gonna Rise: A Portrait of Textile Workers*. New York: Anchor Press, 1979.

Cooke, Jacob E., ed. *The Reports of Alexander Hamilton*. New York: Harper & Row, 1964.

Cose, Ellis. *The Rage of a Privileged Class*. New York: HarperCollins, 1993.

Crane, Verner W., ed. *Benjamin Franklin's Letters to the Press, 1758–1775*. Chapel Hill: University of North Carolina Press, 1950.

Crèvecoeur, J. Hector St. John. *Letters from an American Farmer*. New York: Fox, Duffield & Co., 1904; orig. pub. 1782.

Curtin, Philip D., ed. *Africa Remembered: Narratives by West Africans from the Era of the Slave Trade*. Madison: University of Wisconsin Press, 1967.

Dancy, John C. *Sand Against the Wind: The Memoirs of John C. Dancy*. Detroit: Detroit Urban League, 1966.

Dash, Leon. *Rosa Lee: A Mother and Her Family in Urban America*. New York: Basic Books, 1996.

David Walker's Appeal, in Four Articles, Together With a Preamble . . . New York: Hill & Wang, 1965; orig. pub. 1831.

Delany, Martin R. *The Condition, Elevation, Emigration, and Destiny of the Colored People of the United States, Politically Considered*. New York: Arno Press, 1968; orig. pub. 1852.

Denby, Charles. *Indignant Heart: Testimony of a Black American Worker*. London: Pluto Press, 1979.

Drew, Benjamin, ed. *A North-side View of Slavery. The Refugee: Or the Narratives of Fugitive Slaves in Canada*. New York: Negro Universities Press, 1969; orig. pub. 1856.

Dillard, J. H., ed. *Negro Migration in 1916–17*. New York: Negro Universities Press, 1969; orig. pub. 1919.

Dublin, Thomas, ed. *Immigrant Voices: New Lives in America, 1773–1986*. Urbana: University of Illinois Press, 1993.

DuBois, W. E. B. *The Black North in 1901: A Social Study*. New York: Arno Press, 1969; orig. pub. 1901.

———. *The Negro Artisan*. Atlanta: Atlanta University Press, 1902.

———. *The Negro in Business*. New York: AMS Press, 1971; orig. pub. 1899.

———. *The Philadelphia Negro: A Social Study*. New York: Schocken Books, 1967; orig. pub. 1899.

Dunn, Richard S., and Mary Maples Dunn, eds. *The Papers of William Penn*. Philadelphia: University of Pennsylvania Press, 1982.

Echeverria, Durand, ed. *New Travels in the United States of America, 1788* [J. P. Brissot de Warville]. Cambridge: Harvard University Press, 1964.

Eddis, William. *Letters from America*. Ed. by Aubrey C. Land. Cambridge: Harvard University Press, 1969.

Edwards, Paul, ed. *Equiano's Travels: His Autobiography: The Interesting Narrative of the Life of Olaudah Equiano or Gustavus Vassa the African*. Portsmouth, NH: Heinemann, 1967; orig. pub. 1789.

Faust, Drew Gilpin, ed. *The Ideology of Slavery: Proslavery Thought in the Antebellum South, 1830–1860*. Baton Rouge: Louisiana State University Press, 1981.

Fearon, Henry Bradshaw. *Sketches of America*. . . . London: Longman, Hurst, 1818.

Fetterley, Judith, ed. *Provisions: A Reader from Nineteenth-Century American Women*. Bloomington: Indiana University Press, 1985.

Foner, Philip S., and Ronald L. Lewis, eds., *The Black Worker: A Documentary History from Colonial Times to the Present*. 4 vols. Philadelphia: Temple University Press, 1978.

Foner, Philip S., and Herbert Shapiro, eds. *Northern Labor and Antislavery: A Documentary History*. Westport, CT: Greenwood Press, 1994.

Foner, Philip S., and George E. Walker, eds. *Proceedings of the Black State Conventions, 1840–1865*. 2 vols. Philadelphia: Temple University Press, 1979.

Force, Peter, ed. *Tracts and Other Papers, Relating Principally to the Origin, Settlement, and Progress of the Colonies in North America* . . . 4 vols. New York: Peter Smith, 1947; orig. pub. 1836.

Friedman, Sara Ann. *Work Matters: Women Talk About Their Jobs and Their Lives*. New York: Viking, 1996.

Gallay, Alan, ed. *Voices of the Old South: Eyewitness Accounts, 1528–1861*. Athens: University of Georgia Press, 1994.

Gates, Henry Louis, Jr. *Colored People: A Memoir*. New York: Random House, 1994.

Graham, Lawrence Otis. *Member of the Club: Reflections on Life in a Racially Polarized World*. New York: HarperCollins, 1995.

Greene, Jack P., ed. *The Diary of Colonel Landon Carter of Sabine Hall, 1752–1778*. 2 vols. Charlottesville: University Press of Virginia, 1965.

Gwaltney, John Langston. *Drylongso: A Self-Portrait of Black America*. New York: Random House, 1980.

Hall, Clayton Colman, ed. *Narratives of Early Maryland, 1633–1684*. New York: Barnes and Noble, 1946; orig. pub. 1910.

Hartwell, Henry, et al. *The Present State of Virginia, and the College*. Williamsburg: Colonial Williamsburg, Inc., 1940; orig. pub. 1697.

Hazard, Thomas A., ed. *Nailer Tom's Diary, Otherwise, the Journal of Thomas B. Hazard of Kingstown, Rhode Island, 1778 to 1840*. Boston: Merrymount Press, 1930.

Hening, William Waller, ed. *The Statutes at Large; Being a Collection of All the Laws of Virginia*. 13 vols. New York: Bartow, 1823.

Himes, Chester. *If He Hollers Let Him Go*. New York: Signet, 1971; orig. pub. 1945.

Holmes, Isaac. *An Account of the United States of America, Derived from Actual Observation . . .* London: H. Fisher, 1823.

Jackson, Donald, and Dorothy Twohig, eds. *The Diaries of George Washington*. 6 vols. Charlottesville: University Press of Virginia, 1976–79.

James, Bartlett Burleigh, and J. Franklin Jameson, eds. *Journal of Joseph Danckaerts, 1679–1680*. New York: Barnes and Noble, 1946; orig. pub. 1913.

Jameson, J. Franklin, ed. *Johnson's Wonder-Working Providence, 1628–1651*. New York: Barnes and Noble, 1952; orig. pub. 1653.

———. *Original Narratives of Early American History: Narratives of Early Pennsylvania, West New Jersey, and Delaware, 1630–1707*. New York: Scribner's Sons, 1912.

John Lawson's History of North Carolina. Richmond, VA: Garret & Massie, 1952.

Johnson, James Weldon. *Black Manhattan*. New York: Atheneum, 1972; orig. pub. 1930.

Jones, Hugh, ed. *The Present State of Virginia, From Whence is Inferred a Short View of Maryland and North Carolina*. Chapel Hill: University of North Carolina Press, 1956; orig. pub. 1742.

Kellar, Herbert Anthony, ed. *Solon Robinson: Pioneer and Agriculturist: Selected Writings*. 2 vols. New York: Da Capo Press, 1968.

Kimball, Gertrude S., ed. *The Correspondence of the Colonial Governors of Rhode Island, 1723–1745*. 2 vols. Boston: Houghton Mifflin, 1903.

Kingsbury, Susan Myra, ed. *The Records of the Virginia Company of London*. 4 vols. Washington, DC: Government Printing Office, 1906–35.

Klepp, Susan E., and Billy G. Smith, eds. *The Infortunate: The Voyage and Adventures of*

William Moraley, an Indentured Servant. University Park: Pennsylvania State University Press, 1992; orig. pub. 1743.

Kotlowitz, Alex. *There Are No Children Here: The Story of Two Boys Growing Up in the Other America.* New York: Doubleday, 1991.

LaFantasie, Glenn W., ed. *The Correspondence of Roger Williams.* 2 vols. Hanover, NH: Brown University Press/University Press of New England, 1988.

Leeper, Fran Buss. *Dignity: Lower Income Women Tell of Their Lives and Struggles.* Ann Arbor: University of Michigan Press, 1985.

Lerner, Gerda, ed., *Black Women in White America: A Documentary History.* New York: Vintage Books, 1973.

Libby, Charles Thornton, ed. *Province and Court Records of Maine.* 4 vols. Portland: Maine Historical Society, 1928–31.

Loewenberg, Bert James, and Ruth Bogin, eds. *Black Women in Nineteenth-Century American Life: Their Words, Their Thoughts, Their Feelings.* University Park: Pennsylvania State University Press, 1976.

Lyell, Charles, *Second Visit to the United States.* 2 vols. New York: Harper and Bros., 1849.

Lynd, Alice, and Staughton Lynd, eds. *Rank and File: Personal Histories by Working-Class Organizers.* Princeton: Princeton University Press, 1981.

MacGregor, Morris J., and Bernard C. Nalty, eds., *Blacks in the United States Armed Forces: Basic Documents.* 13 vols. Wilmington, DE: Scholarly Resources, 1977.

Mackay, Charles. *Life and Liberty in America; Or, Sketches of a Tour in the United States and Canada.* London: Smith, Elder, & Co., 1859.

McIlwaine, H. R., ed. *Minutes of the Council and General Court of Colonial Virginia.* Richmond, VA: Colonial Press, 1924.

Mereness, Newton D., ed. *Travels in the American Colonies.* New York: Antiquarian Press, 1961.

Merrens, H. Roy, ed. *The Colonial South Carolina Scene: Contemporary Views, 1697–1774.* Columbia: University of South Carolina Press, 1977.

Meyer, Michael, ed. *Frederick Douglass: The Narrative and Selected Writings.* New York: Modern Library, 1984.

Miller, Perry, and Thomas H. Johnson, eds. *The Puritans.* New York: American Book Co., 1938.

Moon, Elaine Latzman, ed. *Untold Tales, Unsung Heroes: An Oral History of Detroit's African-American Community, 1918–1967.* Detroit: Wayne State University Press, 1994.

Moore, Jacob B., ed. *Collections of the New Hampshire Historical Society.* 11 vols. Manchester, NH: John B. Clarke, 1870; orig. pub. 1824–32.

Moore, Marat. *Women in the Mines: Stories of Life and Work.* New York: Twayne Publishers, 1996.

Moynihan, Ruth Barnes, *et al.*, eds. *Second to None: A Documentary History of American Women.* 2 vols. Lincoln: University of Nebraska Press, 1993.

Mullin, Michael, ed. *American Negro Slavery: A Documentary History.* Columbia: University of South Carolina Press, 1976.

Nelson, Jill. *Volunteer Slavery: My Authentic Negro Experience*. Chicago: Noble Press, 1993.

Olmsted, Frederick Law. *A Journey in the Back Country, 1853–1854*. New York: Schocken Books, 1970; orig. pub. 1860.

———. *The Cotton Kingdom: A Traveller's Observations on Cotton and Slavery in the American Slave States* . . . New York: Modern Library, 1984.

Ovington, Mary White. *Half a Man: The Status of the Negro in New York*. New York: Schocken Books, 1969; orig. pub. 1911.

Painter, Nell Irvin. *Narrative of Hosea Hudson: His Life as a Negro Communist in the South*. Cambridge: Harvard University Press, 1979.

Prager, Frank D., ed. *The Autobiography of John Fitch*. Philadelphia: American Philosophical Society, 1976.

Rawick, George P., ed. *The American Slave: A Composite Autobiography*. 19 vols. Supp. Series I: 12 vols. Supp. Series II: 10 vols. Westport, CT: Greenwood Press, 1972–79.

Rice, Sarah. *He Included Me: The Autobiography of Sarah Rice*. Athens: University of Georgia Press, 1989.

Richardson, Marilyn, ed. *Maria W. Stewart: America's First Black Woman Political Writer: Essays and Speeches*. Bloomington: Indiana University Press, 1987.

Rock, Howard B., ed. *The New York City Artisan, 1789–1829: A Documentary History*. Albany: State University of New York Press, 1989.

Salley, Alexander S., Jr., ed. *Narratives of Early Carolina, 1650–1708*. New York: Barnes and Noble, 1953; orig. pub. 1911.

Schaw, Janet. *Journal of a Lady of Quality; Being the Narrative of a Journey from Scotland to the West Indies, North Carolina, and Portugal* . . . *1774 to 1776*. New Haven: Yale University Press, 1934.

Scott, Emmet J. *Negro Migration During the War*. New York: Arno Press, 1969; orig. pub. 1920.

Shurtleff, Nathaniel B., ed. *Records of the Governor and Company of the Massachusetts Bay in New England*. 5 vols. Boston: William White, 1854.

———. *Records of the Colony of New Plymouth in New England*. 12 vols. New York: AMS Press, 1968; orig. pub. 1857.

Simmons, William S., and Cheryl L. Simmons, eds. *Old Light on Separate Ways: The Narragansett Diary of Joseph Fish, 1765–1776*. Hanover, NH: University Press of New England, 1982.

Simonsen, Thordis, ed. *You May Plow Here: The Narrative of Sara Brooks*. New York: Simon & Schuster, 1986.

Smith, Billy G., and Richard Wojtowicz, eds. *Blacks Who Stole Themselves: Advertisements for Runaway Slaves in the "Pennsylvania Gazette," 1728–1790*. Philadelphia: University of Pennsylvania Press, 1989.

Smith, Joseph, ed. *Colonial Justice in Western Massachusetts (1639–1702): The Pynchon Court Record*. Cambridge: Harvard University Press, 1961.

Smith, Joseph H., and Philip Crowl. *Court Records of Prince Georges County, Maryland, 1696–1699*. Washington, DC: American Historical Association, 1967.

Smith, Venture. *Narrative of the Life and Adventures of Venture, a Native of Africa*. New London, CT: C. Holt, 1798.

Smyth, J. F. D. *A Tour in the United States of America*. 2 vols. Dublin: J. Perrin, 1784.

Steiner, Bernard C., ed. *Archives of Maryland*. 72 vols. Baltimore: Maryland Historical Society, 1883–1972.

Sterner, Richard. *The Negro's Share: A Study of Consumption, Housing, and Public Assistance*. New York: Harper and Bros, 1943.

Terkel, Studs. *Hard Times: An Oral History of the Great Depression*. New York: Avon Books, 1970.

———. *Working*. New York: Avon Books, 1975.

Thirsk, Joan, and J. P. Cooper, eds., *Seventeenth-Century Documents*. Oxford: Clarendon Press, 1972.

Thomas, Sherry. *We Didn't Have Much, But We Sure Had Plenty: Stories of Rural Women*. Garden City, NY: Anchor Books, 1981.

Tinling, Marion, ed. *The Correspondence of the Three William Byrds of Westover, Virginia, 1684–1776*. 2 vols. Charlottesville: University Press of Virginia, 1977.

Tocqueville, Alexis de. *Democracy in America*. 2 vols. Garden City, NY: Doubleday, 1969; orig. pub 1835.

Vaughan, Alden T., ed. *William Wood's New England Prospect*. Amherst: University of Massachusetts Press, 1977; orig. pub. 1634.

United States:

———. Department of Agriculture. *Agricultural Yearbook for 1923*. Washington, DC: Government Printing Office, 1924.

———. President's Commission on the Future of Worker-Management Relations (Dunlop Commission). *Fact-Finding Report* (May 1994), published in the Bureau of National Affairs *Daily Labor Report*, June 3, 1994.

———. President's Committee on Civil Rights. *To Secure These Rights*. New York: Simon & Schuster, 1947.

———. *Report of the Industrial Commission on Agriculture and Agricultural Labor*, Vol. X. Washington, DC: Government Printing Office, 1901.

———. House of Representatives. Select Committee Investigating National Defense Migration. *Hearings Before the Select Committee Investigating National Defense Migration*. 77th Cong., 1st and 2nd. sess., 1941–43. Parts 11–33.

VanDerBeets, Richard, ed. *Held Captive by Indians: Selected Narratives, 1642–1836*. Knoxville: University of Tennessee Press, 1973.

Van Doren, Mark, ed. *The Travels of William Bartram*. New York: Facsimilie Library, Barnes and Noble, 1940.

Virginia Historical Society Documents. *County Court Records of Accomack-Northampton, Virginia, 1640–1645*. Charlottesville: University Press of Virginia, 1973.

Walett, Francis G., ed. *The Diary of Ebenezer Parkman, 1703–1782*. Worcester, MA: American Antiquarian Society, 1974.

White, Barnetta M. *In Search of Kith and Kin: The History of a Southern Black Family*. Baltimore: Gateway Press, 1986.

Whitehead, William A., et al., eds. Documents Relating to the Colonial, Revolutionary, and Postrevolutionary History of the State of New Jersey. 42 vols. Newark: Daily Advertiser, 1880–1949.

Williams, Daniel E., ed. Pillars of Salt: An Anthology of Early American Criminal Narratives. Madison: Madison House, 1993.

The Winthrop Papers. Boston: Massachusetts Historical Society, 6 vols. 1929–92.

Woodward, Carl Raymond, ed. Ploughs and Politicks: Charles Read of New Jersey and His Notes on Agriculture, 1715–1774. Philadelphia: Porcupine Press, 1974.

Wright, Esmond, ed. Benjamin Franklin: His Life As He Wrote It. Cambridge: Harvard University Press, 1990.

ARTICLES AND PAMPHLETS

"A Plain & Friendly Perswasive to the Inhabitants of Virginia and Maryland . . ." VMHB 4 (January 1897):255–71.

"An Early Description of Pennsylvania [Chrisopher Sower, 1724]," PMHB 45 (1921):243–54.

Axtell, James, ed. "The Vengeful Women of Marblehead: Robert Roules's Deposition of 1677." WMQ 3rd series 31 (October 1974):647–52.

Baine, Rodney M. "Notes and Documents: Philip Thicknesse's Reminiscences of Early Georgia," GHQ 74 (Winter 1990):672–98.

Beynon, Erdmann Doane. "The Southern White Laborer Migrates to Michigan." ASR 3 (June 1938):353–43.

Breen, T. H., et al., eds. "Motive for Murder: A Servant's Life in Virginia, 1678," WMQ 3rd series 40 (January 1983):106–20.

Bridenbaugh, Carl, ed. "Patrick M'Robert's Tour Through Part of the North Provinces of America." PMHB 59 (1935):134–80.

"Carter Papers." VMHB 7 (July 1899):64–8.

Clarke, James Freeman. "Present Condition of the Free Colored People of the United States." New York: New York Anti-Slavery Society, 1859.

Cordle, Charles D., ed. "Notes and Documents: The John Tobler Manuscripts: An Account of German-Swiss Emigrants in South Carolina." JSouH 5 (February 1939):83–97.

Daniels, John. "Industrial Conditions Among Negro Men in Boston." Charities 15 (October 7, 1905):35–9.

DuBois, W. E. B. "The Negroes of Farmville, Virginia: A Social Study." Bulletin of the Department of Labor, no. 14 (January 1898):1–38.

Durham, John Stephens. "The Labor Unions and the Negro." AM 81 (February 1898):222–31.

"Employment of Colored Women in Chicago." Crisis 1 (January 1911):24–5.

"Extract from the Virginia Gazette 1752 and 1755." VMHB 24 (October 1916):404–16.

Hammon, Neal, and James Russell Harris, eds. "'In a Dangerous Situation': The Letters of Col. John Floyd." RKHS 83 (Summer 1985):202–36.

"Hardscrabble Calendar: Report of the Trials of Oliver Cummins, Nathaniel Metcalf, Gilbert Humes and Arthur Farrier; Who Were Indicted. . . ." Providence, RI: For the Purchaser, 1824.

Ingersoll, Thomas. "'Releese Us Out of this Cruell Bondegg': An Appeal from Virginia in 1723." WMQ 3rd series 51 (October 1994):777–82.

Johnson, Charles S. "Black Workers and the City." Survey (March 1, 1925):641–43, 718–21.

——. "Negroes at Work in Baltimore, Md." Opportunity 1 (January 1923):12–19.

Johnson, James Weldon. "The Making of Harlem." Survey (March 1, 1925):635–39.

Johnston, James Hugo. "Documentary Evidence of the Relations of Negroes and Indians." JNH 14 (January 1929):21–43.

"Letters of Governor Edward Coles Bearing on the Struggle of Freedom and Slavery in Illinois," JNH 3 (April 1918):158–95.

"Letters of Negroes Addressed to the American Colonization Society," JNH 10 (April 1925):17–54.

"Letters of William Fitzhugh." VMHB 1 (July 1893):17–55.

Lewis, Ronald L., ed. "Race and the United Mine Workers' Union in Tennessee: Selected Letters of William R. Riley, 1892–1895." THQ 36 (1977): 524–36.

"Life of James Mars, A Slave Born and Sold in Connecticut, Written by Himself." Hartford: Case, Lockwood & Co., 1867.

"Lower Norfolk County Records, 1636–1646." VMHB 39 (January 1931):1–20.

Lurie, Melvin, and Elton Rayack. "Racial Differences in Migration and Job Search: A Case Study." SEJ 33 (July 1966):81–9.

Malcomson, Scott L. "Having Their Say." The New Yorker, April 29 and May 6, 1996, pp. 138–43.

"Memoir of Mrs. Chloe Spear, a Native of Africa, Who Was Enslaved in Childhood, and Died in Boston, January 3, 1815. . . ." Boston: James Loring, 1832.

Miller, Kelly. "The Economic Handicap of the Negro in the North." Annals 27 (January–June 1906):543–50.

"Minutes of the Council and General Court of Virginia, 1622." VMHB 19 (April 1911):113–48.

National Committee Against Discrimination in Housing, Inc. "Jobs and Housing: A Study of Employment and Housing Opportunities for Racial Minorities in the Suburban Areas of the New York Metropolitan Region." New York: Published by the Committee, 1970.

"Negro Women in South Carolina Industries." Opportunity 2 (May 1924):146–47.

Northrup, Herbert. "Negroes in a War Industry: The Case of Shipbuilding." JB 16 (July 1943):160–72.

Ovington, Mary White. "The Negro in the Trades Unions in New York." Annals 27 (June 1906):551–58.

Philadelphia Society of Friends. "A Statistical Inquiry into the Condition of People of Color in the City and Districts of Philadelphia." Philadelphia: Society of Friends, 1849.

"Proceedings in York County Court." *WMQ* 1st series 11 (July 1902):28–38.

Reed, Bernice Anita. "Accommodation Between Negro and White Employees in a West Coast Aircraft Industry, 1942–1944." *SF* 26 (October 1947):76–84.

Rubin, Abraham, and George J. Segal. "An Industrial Experiment." *Annals* 244 (March 1946):57–64.

Scalia, Antonin. "The Disease as Cure: 'In Order to Get Beyond Racism, We Must First Take Account of Race.'" *WULQ* (Winter 1979):147–60.

Schlosser, Eric. "In the Strawberry Fields." *AM* 276 (November 1995):80–109.

Sewall, Samuel. "The Selling of Joseph." *MHSP*, series 1, vol. 7 (October 1863):161–65.

Sheldon, George. "Negro Slavery in Old Deerfield." *NEM* (March 1893):49–60.

Shelley, Fred, ed. "The Journal of Ebenezer Hazard in Virginia, 1777." *VMHB* 62 (October 1954):400–23.

Skinner, Reginald, and Jackie Collins. "Mr. T. C. Jackson Standing Tall." *Bloodlines* (Rural Organizing and Cultural Center) 2 (Spring 1990):55–64.

Smith, Billy G., and Richard Wojtowicz. "The Precarious Freedom of Blacks in the Mid-Atlantic Region: Excerpts from the *Pennsylvania Gazette*, 1728–1776," *PMHB* 113 (April 1989):237–64.

Sprague, Rosetta Douglass. "Anna Murray-Douglass—My Mother As I Recall Her." *JNH* 8 (January 1923):93–101.

Tresp, Lothar L. "August, 1748 in Georgia, from the Diary of John Martin Bolzius." *GHQ* 47 (June 1963):204–16.

United States: Department of Labor Women's Bureau:

———. "Changes in Women's Occupations, 1940–1950." *Bulletin* no. 253 (1954).

———. "Negro Women in Industry." *Bulletin* no. 20 (1922).

———. "Negro Women War Workers." *Bulletin* no. 205 (1945).

———. "Women's Employment in Vegetable Canneries in Delaware." *Bulletin* no. 62 (1928).

Washington, Booker T. "A Town Owned by Negroes." *World's Work* 14 (July 1907):9125–34.

Williams, Patricia J. "Notes from a Small World." *New Yorker*, April 29 and May 6, 1996, pp. 87–93.

Work, Monroe N. "The Negroes of Warsaw, Georgia." *SW* 37 (January 1908):29–40.

SECONDARY WORKS: MONOGRAPHS, ESSAY ANTHOLOGIES, ARTICLES, AND REFERENCE WORKS

MONOGRAPHS

Alexander, Adele Logan. *Ambiguous Lives: Free Women of Color in Rural Georgia, 1789–1879*. Fayetteville: University of Arkansas Press, 1991.

Alexander, John K. *Render Them Submissive: Responses to Poverty in Philadelphia, 1760–1800*. Amherst: University of Massachusetts Press, 1980.

Allen, Theodore W. *The Invention of the White Race:*. Vol I: *Racial Oppression and Social Control*. London: Verso, 1994.

Almaguer, Tomás. *Racial Fault Lines: The Historical Origins of White Supremacy in California*. Berkeley: University of California Press, 1994.

Ames, Susie M. *Studies of the Virginia Eastern Shore in the Seventeenth Century*. New York: Russell & Russell, 1940.

Anderson, Fred. *A People's Army: Massachusetts Soldiers and Society in the Seven Years' War*. Chapel Hill: University of North Carolina Press, 1984.

Anderson, Jean Bradley. *Durham County: A History of Durham County, North Carolina*. Durham: Duke University Press, 1990.

Anderson, Jervis. *A. Philip Randolph: A Biographical Portrait*. New York: Harcourt Brace Jovanovich, 1973.

Anderson, Karen. *Wartime Women: Sex Roles, Family Relations, and the Status of Women During World War II*. Westport, CT: Greenwood Press, 1981.

Anderson, Virginia DeJohn. *New England's Generation: The Great Migration and the Formation of Society and Culture in the Seventeenth Century*. New York: Cambridge University Press, 1991.

Arnesen, Eric. *Waterfront Workers of New Orleans: Race, Class, and Politics, 1863–1923*. New York: Oxford University Press, 1991.

Axtell, James. *The European and the Indian: Essays in the Ethnohistory of Colonial North America*. New York: Oxford University Press, 1981.

Bailyn, Bernard. *Voyagers to the West: A Passage in the Peopling of America on the Eve of the Revolution*. New York: Knopf, 1986.

Baker, Jean H. *Affairs of Party: The Political Culture of Northern Democrats in the Mid-Nineteenth Century*. Ithaca: Cornell University Press, 1983.

Barbeau, Arthur E., and Florette Henri. *The Unknown Soldiers: Black American Troops in World War I*. Philadelphia: Temple University Press, 1974.

Bateman, Fred, and Thomas Weiss. *A Deplorable Scarcity: The Failure of Industrialization in the Slave Economy*. Chapel Hill: University of North Carolina Press, 1981.

Beckles, Hilary McD. *White Servitude and Black Slavery in Barbados, 1627–1715*. Knoxville: University of Tennessee Press, 1989.

Benjamin, Lois. *The Black Elite: Facing the Color Line in the Twilight of the Twentieth Century*. Chicago: Nelson-Hall, 1991.

Berlin, Ira. *Slaves Without Masters: The Free Negro in the Antebellum South*. New York: Vintage Books, 1974.

Bernstein, Iver. *The New York City Draft Riots: Their Significance in American Society and Politics in the Age of the Civil War*. New York: Oxford University Press, 1990.

Billings, Dwight, Jr. *Planters and the Making of a "New South": Class, Politics, and Development in North Carolina, 1865–1900*. Chapel Hill: University of North Carolina Press, 1979.

Billingsley, Andrew. *Climbing Jacob's Ladder: The Enduring Legacy of African-American Families*. New York: Simon & Schuster, 1992.

Blakey, Arch Fredric. *The Florida Phosphate Industry: A History of the Development and Use of a Vital Mineral.* Cambridge: Harvard University Press, 1973.

Blewett, Mary. *Men, Women, and Work: Class, Gender, and Protest in the New England Shoe Industry, 1780–1910.* Urbana: University of Illinois Press, 1988.

Blumrosen, Alfred W. *Black Employment and the Law.* New Brunswick: Rutgers University Press, 1971.

Bolton, Charles C. *Poor Whites of the Antebellum South: Tenants and Laborers in Central North Carolina and Northeast Mississippi.* Durham: Duke University Press, 1994.

Borchert, James. *Alley Life in Washington: Family, Community, Religion, and Folklife in the City, 1850–1970.* Urbana: University of Illinois Press, 1980.

Boris, Eileen. *Home to Work: Motherhood and the Politics of Industrial Homework in the United States.* Cambridge: Cambridge University Press, 1994.

Boydston, Jeanne. *Home and Work: Housework, Wages, and the Ideology of Labor in the Early Republic.* New York: Oxford University Press, 1990.

Breen, T. H. *Tobacco Culture: The Mentality of the Great Tidewater Planters on the Eve of Revolution.* Princeton: Princeton University Press, 1985.

———, and Stephen Innes. *"Myne Owne Ground": Race and Freedom on Virginia's Eastern Shore, 1640–1646.* New York: Oxford University Press, 1980.

Brown, Kathleen M. *Good Wives, Nasty Wenches and Anxious Patriarchs: Gender, Race, and Power in Colonial Virginia.* Chapel Hill: University of North Carolina Press, 1996.

Bruce, Philip Alexander. *Economic History of Virginia in the Seventeeth Century.* 2 vols. New York: Macmillan, 1895.

Buchanan, A. Russell. *Black Americans in World War II.* Santa Barbara, CA: Clio Books, 1977.

Burton, Orville Vernon. *In My Father's House Are Many Mansions: Family and Community in Edgefield, South Carolina.* Chapel Hill: University of North Carolina Press, 1985.

Bynum, Victoria. *Unruly Women: The Politics of Social and Sexual Control in the Old South.* Chapel Hill: University of North Carolina Press, 1992.

Carnoy, Martin. *Faded Dreams: The Politics and Economics of Race in America.* Cambridge: Cambridge University Press, 1994.

Carr, Lois Green, Russell R. Menard, and Lorena S. Walsh. *Robert Cole's World: Agriculture and Society in Early Maryland.* Chapel Hill: University of North Carolina Press, 1991.

Cayton, Horace R., and George S. Mitchell. *Black Workers and the New Unions.* Westport, CT: Negro Universities Press, 1970; orig. pub. 1939.

Cecil-Fronsman, Bill. *Common Whites: Class and Culture in Antebellum North Carolina.* Lexington: University Press of Kentucky, 1992.

Cheek, William, and Aimee Lee Cheek. *John Mercer Langston and the Fight for Black Freedom, 1829–1865.* Urbana: University of Illinois Press, 1989.

Christian, Garna L. *Black Soldiers in Jim Crow Texas, 1899–1917.* College Station, TX: Texas A & M Press, 1995.

Clark, Ronald W. *Benjamin Franklin: A Biography.* New York: Random House, 1983.

Clark-Lewis, Elizabeth. *Living In, Living Out: African-American Domestics in Washington, D.C., 1910–1940.* Washington, DC: Smithsonian Institution Press, 1994.

Clemens, Paul G. E. *The Atlantic Economy and Colonial Maryland's Eastern Shore.* Ithaca: Cornell University Press, 1980.

Clinton, Catherine. *The Plantation Mistress: Women's World in the Old South.* New York: Pantheon, 1982.

Cobb, James S. *The Most Southern Place on Earth: The Mississippi Delta and the Roots of Regional Identity.* New York: Oxford University Press, 1992.

Cohen, Lizabeth. *Making a New Deal: Industrial Workers in Chicago, 1919–1939.* New York: Cambridge University Press, 1990.

Cott, Nancy F. *The Bonds of Womanhood: "Woman's Sphere" in New England, 1780–1835.* New Haven: Yale University Press, 1977.

Cottrol, *The Afro-Yankees: Providence's Black Community in the Antebellum Era.* Westport, CT: Greenwood Press, 1982.

Craven, Wesley Frank. *The Southern Colonies in the Seventeenth Century, 1607–1689.* Baton Rouge: Louisiana State University Press, 1949.

———. *White, Red, and Black: The Seventeenth-Century Virginian.* New York: W. W. Norton, 1971.

Cray, Robert E., Jr. *Poverty and Poor Relief: New York City and Its Rural Environs, 1700–1830.* Philadelphia: Temple University Press, 1988.

Cressy, David. *Coming Over: Migration and Communication Between England and New England in the Seventeenth Century.* Cambridge: Cambridge University Press, 1987.

Cripps, Thomas. *Slow Fade to Black: The Negro in American Film, 1900–1942.* New York: Oxford University Press, 1977.

Cronon, William. *Changes in the Land: Indians, Colonists, and the Ecology of New England.* New York: Hill & Wang, 1983.

Crosby, Alfred W. *The Columbian Exchange: Biological and Cultural Consequences of 1492.* Westport, CT: Greenwood Press, 1972.

Cumbler, John T. *A Social History of Economic Decline: Business, Politics, and Work in Trenton.* New Brunswick: Rutgers University Press, 1989.

Curry, Leonard P. *The Free Black in Urban America, 1800–1850: The Shadow of the Dream.* Chicago: University of Chicago Press, 1981.

Daniel, Pete. *The Shadow of Slavery: Peonage in the South, 1901–1969.* Urbana: University of Illinois Press, 1972.

Davis, Susan G. *Parades and Power: Street Theatre in Nineteenth-Century Philadelphia.* Philadelphia: Temple University Press, 1985.

Davis, Thomas J. *A Rumor of Revolt: The "Great Negro Plot" in Colonial New York.* New York: Free Press, 1985.

Dew, Charles B. *Bond of Iron: Master and Slave at Buffalo Forge.* New York: W. W. Norton, 1994.

Dickerson, Dennis C. *Out of the Crucible: Black Steelworkers in Western Pennsylvania, 1875–1980*. Albany: State University of New York Press, 1986.

Drake, St. Clair, and Horace R. Cayton. *Black Metropolis: A Study of Negro Life in a Northern City*. New York: Harcourt Brace, and Co., 1945.

Dublin, Thomas. *Transforming Women's Work: New England Lives in the Industrial Revolution*. Ithaca: Cornell University Press, 1994.

Dubofsky, Melvyn. *We Shall be All: A History of the Industrial Workers of the World*. Chicago: Quadrangle Books, 1969.

Dudley, Kathryn Marie. *The End of the Line: Lost Jobs, New Lives in Postindustrial America*. Chicago: University of Chicago Press, 1994.

Earle, Alice Morse. *Home Life in Colonial Days*. Stockbridge, MA: Berkshire Traveller Press, 1974; orig. pub. 1898.

Eastland, Terry. *Ending Affirmative Action: The Case for Colorblind Justice*. New York: Basic Books, 1996.

Epstein, Richard A. *Forbidden Grounds: The Case Against Employment Discrimination Laws*. Cambridge: Harvard University Press, 1992.

Ernst, Robert. *Immigrant Life in New York City, 1825–1863*. Syracuse, NY: Syracuse University Press, 1994.

Feagin, Joe R., and Melvin P. Sikes. *Living with Racism: The Black Middle-Class Experience*. Boston: Beacon Press, 1994.

Ferling, John E. *A Wilderness of Miseries: War and Warriors in Early America*. Westport, CT: Greenwood Press, 1980.

Fields, Barbara Jeanne. *Slavery and Freedom on the Middle Ground: Maryland During the Nineteenth Century*. New Haven: Yale University Press, 1985.

Fink, Leon, *Workingmen's Democracy: The Knights of Labor and American Politics*. Urbana: University of Illinois Press, 1983.

———, and Brian Greenberg. *Upheaval in the Quiet Zone: A History of Hospital Workers' Union, Local 1199*. Urbana: University of Illinois Press, 1989.

Finkelman, Paul. *Slavery and the Founders: Race and Liberty in the Age of Jefferson*. Armonk, NY: M. Sharpe, 1996.

Fischer, David Hackett. *Albion's Seed: Four British Folkways in America*. New York: Oxford University Press, 1989.

Fletcher, Marvin. *The Black Soldier and Officer in the United States Army, 1891–1917*. Columbia: University of Missouri Press, 1974.

Foner, Eric. *Reconstruction: America's Unfinished Revolution, 1863–77*. New York: Harper & Row, 1988.

Foner, Philip. *Organized Labor and the Black Worker, 1619–1973*. New York: Praeger, 1974.

Fox-Genovese, Elizabeth. *Within the Plantation Household: Black and White Women of the Old South*. Chapel Hill: University of North Carolina Press, 1988.

Fredrickson, George M. *The Black Image in the White Mind: The Debate on Afro-American Character and Destiny, 1817–1914*. New York: Harper & Row, 1971.

———. *White Supremacy: A Comparative Study in American and South African History*. New York: Oxford University Press, 1981.

Frey, Sylvia. *Water from the Rock: Black Resistance in a Revolutionary Age.* Princeton: Princeton University Press, 1991.

Galenson, David. *White Servitude in Colonial America: An Economic Analysis.* New York: Cambridge University Press, 1981.

Genovese, Eugene. *Roll, Jordan, Roll: The World the Slaves Made.* New York: Vintage Books, 1976.

Gerber, David. *The Making of an American Pluralism: Buffalo, New York, 1825–1860.* Urbana: University of Illinois Press, 1989.

Geschwender, James A. *Class, Race, and Worker Insurgency: The League of Revolutionary Black Workers.* Cambridge: Cambridge University Press, 1977.

Giddings, Paula. *When and Where I Enter: The Impact of Black Women on Race and Sex in America.* Toronto: Bantam Books, 1984.

Gilje, Paul. *The Road to Mobocracy: Popular Disorder in New York City, 1763–1834.* Chapel Hill: University of North Carolina Press, 1987.

Goldin, Claudia. *Urban Slavery in the American South, 1820–1860: A Quantitative History.* Chicago: University of Chicago Press, 1976.

Goodfriend, Joyce D. *Before the Melting Pot: Society and Culture in Colonial New York City, 1664–1730.* Princeton: Princeton University Press, 1992.

Gordon, David M. *Fat and Mean: The Corporate Squeeze of Working Americans and the Myth of Managerial "Downsizing."* New York: Martin Kessler Books, 1996.

Gordon, Linda. *Pitied But Not Entitled: Single Mothers and the History of Welfare, 1890–1935.* New York: Free Press, 1994.

Gosnell, Harold F. *Negro Politicians: The Rise of Negro Politics in Chicago.* Chicago: University of Chicago Press, 1967; orig. pub. 1935.

Gottlieb, Peter. *Making Their Own Way: Southern Blacks' Migration to Pittsburgh, 1916–1930.* Urbana: University of Illinois Press, 1987.

Graham, Hugh Davis. *Civil Rights and the Presidency: Race and Gender in American Politics, 1960–1972.* New York: Oxford University Press, 1992.

Greene, Jack P. *Pursuits of Happiness: The Social Development of Early Modern British Colonies and the Formation of American Culture.* Chapel Hill: University of North Carolina Press, 1988.

Greene, Lorenzo Johnston. *The Negro in Colonial New England, 1620–1776.* New York: Columbia University Press, 1942.

———, and Carter G. Woodson. *The Negro Wage Earner.* Washington, DC: Association for the Study of Negro Life and History, 1930.

Greenwald, Maurine Weiner. *Women, War, and Work: The Impact of World War I on Women Workers in the United States.* Westport, CT: Greenwood Press, 1980.

Griffler, Keith P. *What Price Alliance: Black Radicals Confront White Labor, 1918–1938.* New York: Garland, 1995.

Grossman, James R. *Land of Hope: Chicago, Black Southerners, and the Great Migration.* Chicago: University of Chicago Press, 1989.

Gutman, Herbert G. *The Black Family in Slavery and Freedom, 1750–1925.* New York: Pantheon, 1976.

———— (edited by Ira Berlin). *Power and Culture: Essays on the American Working Class.* New York: Pantheon, 1987.

Hacker, Andrew. *Two Nations: Black and White, Separate, Hostile, Unequal.* New York: Charles Scribner's Sons, 1992.

Hahn, Steven. *The Roots of Southern Populism: Yeoman Farmers and the Transformation of the Georgia Upcountry, 1850–1890.* New York: Oxford University Press, 1983.

Harris, J. William. *Plain Folk and Gentry in a Slave Society: White Liberty and Black Slavery in Augusta's Hinterlands.* Middletown, CT: Wesleyan University Press, 1985.

Harris, William H. *The Harder We Run: Black Workers Since the Civil War.* New York: Oxford University Press, 1982.

Hayes, Laurence J. W. *The Negro Federal Government Worker: A Study of His Classification Status in the District of Columbia, 1883–1938.* Washington, DC: Howard University Press, 1941.

Haynes, Robert V. *A Night of Violence: The Houston Riot of 1917.* Baton Rouge: Louisiana State University Press, 1976.

Hazard, Caroline. *Thomas Hazard, Son of Robt, Call'd College Tom: A Study of Life in Narragansett in the XVIIIth Century.* Boston: Houghton Mifflin, 1893.

Herbst, Alma. *The Negro in the Slaughtering and Meat-Packing Industry in Chicago.* Boston: Houghton Mifflin, 1932.

Herrick, Cheesman A. *White Servitude in Pennsylvania: Indentured and Redemption Labor in Colony and Commonwealth.* Freeport, NY: Books for Libraries Press, 1970; orig. pub. 1926.

Hine, Darlene Clark. *Black Women in White: Racial Conflict and Cooperation in the Nursing Profession, 1890–1950.* Bloomington: Indiana University Press, 1989.

Honey, Michael K. *Southern Labor and Black Civil Rights: Organizing Memphis Workers.* Urbana: University of Illinois Press, 1993.

Horn, James. *Adapting to a New World: English Society in the Eighteenth-Century Chesapeake.* Chapel Hill: University of North Carolina Press, 1994.

Horton, James Oliver. *Free People of Color: Inside the African-American Community.* Washington, DC: Smithsonian Institution Press, 1993.

————, and Lois E. Horton. *In Hope of Liberty: Culture, Community and Protest Among Northern Free Blacks, 1700–1860.* New York: Oxford University Press, 1997.

Ignatiev, Noel. *How the Irish Became White.* New York: Routledge, 1995.

Innes, Stephen. *Labor in a New Land: Economy and Society in Seventeenth-Century Springfield.* Princeton: Princeton University Press, 1983.

————. *Creating the Commonwealth: The Economic Culture of Puritan New England.* New York: W. W. Norton, 1995.

Jackson, Luther Porter. *Free Negro Labor and Property-Holding in Virginia, 1830–1860.* New York: Atheneum, 1969; orig. pub. 1942.

Janiewski, Dolores E. *Sisterhood Denied: Race, Gender, and Class in a New South Community.* Philadelphia: Temple University Press, 1986.

Johnson, Daniel M., and Rex R. Campbell. *Black Migration in America: A Social Demographic History.* Durham: Duke University Press, 1981.

Johnson, Michael P., and James L. Roark. *Black Masters: A Free Family of Color in the Old South.* New York: W. W. Norton, 1984.

Jones, George Fenwick. *The Salzburger Saga: Religious Exiles and Other Germans Along the Savannah.* Athens: University of Georgia Press, 1984.

Jones, Jacqueline. *The Dispossessed: America's Underclasses from the Civil War to the Present.* New York: Basic Books, 1992.

—— *Labor of Love, Labor of Sorrow: Black Women, Work and the Family from Slavery to the Present.* New York: Basic Books, 1985.

Jordan, Winthrop. *White Over Black: American Attitudes Toward the Negro, 1550–1812.* Chapel Hill: University of North Carolina Press, 1968.

Joyner, Charles. *Down by the Riverside: A South Carolina Slave Community.* Urbana: University of Illinois Press, 1984.

Katzman, David M. *Before the Ghetto: Black Detroit in the Nineteenth Century.* Urbana: University of Illinois Press, 1973.

Kelley, Robin D. G. *Race Rebels: Culture, Politics and the Black Working Class.* New York: Free Press, 1994.

Kirby, Jack Temple. *Rural Worlds Lost: The American South, 1920–1960.* Baton Rouge: Louisiana State University Press, 1987.

Kirp, David L., et al. *Our Town: Race, Housing, and the Soul of Suburbia.* New Brunswick, NJ: Rutgers University Press, 1995.

Kleinberg, S. J. *The Shadow of the Mills: Working-Class Families in Pittsburgh, 1870–1907.* Pittsburgh: University of Pittsburgh Press, 1989.

Kulikoff, Allan. *Tobacco and Slaves: The Development of Southern Cultures in the Chesapeake, 1680–1800.* Chapel Hill: University of North Carolina Press, 1986.

Kupperman, Karen Ordahl, *Settling With the Indians: The Meeting of English and Indian Cultures in America, 1580–1640.* Totowa, NJ: Rowman & Littlefield, 1980.

Kusmer, Kenneth. *A Ghetto Takes Shape: Black Cleveland, 1870–1930.* Urbana: University of Illinois Press, 1976.

Lander, Ernest McPherson, Jr. *The Textile Industry in Antebellum South Carolina.* Baton Rouge: Louisiana State University Press, 1969.

Lapsansky, Emma Jones. *Neighborhoods in Transition: William Penn's Dream and Urban Reality.* New York: Garland Press, 1994.

Lauber, Almon W. *Indian Slavery in Colonial Times Within the Present Limits of the United States.* New York: Columbia University Press, 1913.

Lebsock, Suzanne. *The Free Women of Petersburg: Status and Culture in a Southern Town, 1784–1860.* New York: W. W. Norton, 1984.

Lemke-Santangelo, Gretchen. *Abiding Courage: African American Migrant Women and the East Bay Community.* Chapel Hill: University of North Carolina Press, 1996.

Lewis, Ronald. *Black Coal Miners in America: Race, Class, and Community Conflict, 1780–1980.* Lexington: University Press of Kentucky, 1987.

Licht, Walter. *Getting Work: Philadelphia, 1840–1950.* Cambridge: Harvard University Press, 1992.

Lichtenstein, Alex. *Twice the Work of Free Labor: The Political Economy of Convict Labor in the New South.* London: Verso, 1996.

Lieberson, Stanley. *A Piece of the Pie: Blacks and White Immigrants Since 1880.* Berkeley: University of California Press, 1980.

Lipsitz, George. *A Rainbow at Midnight: Labor and Culture in the 1940s.* Urbana: University of Illinois Press, 1994.

Littlefield, Daniel C. *Rice and Slaves: Ethnicity and the Slave Trade in Colonial South Carolina.* Baton Rouge: Louisiana State University Press, 1981.

Litwack, Leon. *North of Slavery: The Negro in the Free States, 1790–1860.* Chicago: University of Chicago Press, 1961.

———. *Been in the Storm So Long: The Aftermath of Slavery.* New York: Vintage Books, 1979.

Lott, Eric. *Love and Theft: Blackface Minstrelsy and the American Working Class.* New York: Oxford University Press, 1993.

Massey, Douglas S., and Nancy A. Denton. *American Apartheid: Segregation and the Making of the Underclass.* Cambridge: Harvard University Press, 1993.

McCurry, Stephanie. *Masters of Small Worlds: Yeoman Households, Gender Relations, and the Political Culture of the Antebellum South Carolina Low Country.* New York: Oxford University Press, 1995.

McCusker, John J., and Russell R. Menard. *The Economy of British America, 1607–1789.* Chapel Hill: University of North Carolina Press, 1985.

McDonald, Roderick A. *The Economy and Material Culture of Slaves: Goods and Chattels on the Sugar Plantations of Jamaica and Louisiana.* Baton Rouge: Louisiana State University Press, 1993.

McFeely, William S. *Frederick Douglass.* New York: W. W. Norton, 1991.

McGaw, Judith. *Most Wonderful Machine: Mechanization and Social Change in Berkshire Paper Making, 1801–1885.* Princeton: Princeton University Press, 1987.

McKee, Samuel D., Jr. *Labor in Colonial New York, 1664–1776.* Port Washington, NY: Ira J. Friedman, 1935.

McKiven, Henry M., Jr. *Iron and Steel: Class, Race, and Community in Birmingham, Alabama, 1875–1920.* Chapel Hill: University of North Carolina Press, 1995.

McMillen, Neil R. *Dark Journey: Black Mississippians in the Age of Jim Crow.* Urbana: University of Illinois Press, 1989.

Meier, August, and Elliott Rudwick. *Black Detroit and the Rise of the UAW.* New York: Oxford University Press, 1979.

Merrell, James. H. *The Indians' New World: Catawbas and Their Neighbors from European Contact Through the Era of Removal.* Chapel Hill: University of North Carolina Press, 1989.

Mitchell, Broadus. *William Gregg: Factory Master of the Old South.* Chapel Hill: University of North Carolina Press, 1928.

Mitchell, Robert D. *Commercialization and Frontier: Perspectives on the Early Shenandoah Valley.* Charlottesville: University Press of Virginia, 1977.

Mohr, Clarence. *On the Threshold of Freedom: Masters and Slaves in Civil War Georgia.* Athens: University of Georgia Press, 1986.

Montgomery, David. *Citizen Worker: The Experience of Workers in the United States with Democracy and the Free Market During the Nineteenth Century.* Cambridge: Cambridge University Press, 1993.

———. *Workers' Control in America: Studies in the History of Work, Technology, and Labor Struggles.* Cambridge: Cambridge University Press, 1979.

Morgan, Edmund S. *American Slavery, American Freedom: The Ordeal of Colonial Virginia.* New York: W. W. Norton, 1975.

Moskos, Charles C., Jr. *The American Enlisted Man: The Rank and File in Today's Military.* New York: Russell Sage Foundation, 1970.

———, and John Sibley Butler. *All That We Can Be: Black Leadership and Racial Integration the Army Way.* New York: Basic Books, 1996.

Moss, Richard Shannon. *Slavery on Long Island: A Study in Local Institutional and Early African-American Communal Life.* New York: Garland Press, 1993.

Mullin, Gerald. *Flight and Rebellion: Slave Resistance in Eighteenth-Century Virginia.* New York: Oxford University Press, 1972.

Mullin, Michael. *Africa in America: Slave Acculturation and Resistance in the American South and the British Caribbean, 1736–1831.* Urbana: University of Illinois Press, 1992.

Myrdal, Gunnar. *An American Dilemma: The Negro Problem and American Democracy.* 2 vols. New York: Harper & Row, 1944.

Nalty, Bernard C. *Strength for the Fight: A History of Black Americans in the Military.* New York: Free Press, 1986.

Nash, Gary B. *Forging Freedom: The Formation of Philadelphia's Black Community, 1720–1840.* Cambridge: Harvard University Press, 1988.

———, and Jean R. Soderlund. *Freedom by Degrees: Emancipation in Pennsylvania and Its Aftermath.* New York: Oxford University Press, 1991.

Nelson, Daniel. *Managers and Workers: Origins of the New Factory System in the United States, 1880–1920.* Madison: University of Wisconsin Press, 1975.

Newman, Dorothy, *et al. Protest, Politics, and Prosperity: Black Americans and White Institutions, 1940–1975.* New York: Pantheon, 1978.

Northrup, Herbert. *Organized Labor and the Negro.* New York: Harper and Bros, 1944.

———, and Richard L. Rowan. *Negro Employment in Southern Industry: A Study of Racial Policies in Five Industries.* Philadelphia: University of Pennsylvania Press, 1971.

Oliver, Melvin L., and Thomas M. Shapiro. *Black Wealth/White Wealth: A New Perspective on Racial Inequality.* New York: Routledge, 1995.

Orfield, Gary, *et al. Dismantling Desegregation: The Quiet Reversal of Brown v. the Board of Education.* New York: New Press, 1996.

Oshinsky, David. *"Worse Than Slavery": Parchman Farm and the Ordeal of Jim Crow Justice.* New York: Free Press, 1996.

Osofsky, Gilbert. *Harlem: The Making of a Ghetto: Negro New York, 1890–1930.* New York: Harper & Row, 1966.

Painter, Nell Irvin. *Sojourner Truth: A Life, A Symbol.* New York: W. W. Norton, 1996.

Perry, James R. *The Formation of a Society on Virginia's Eastern Shore, 1615–1655.* Chapel Hill: University of North Carolina Press, 1990.

Piersen, William D. *Black Yankees: The Development of an Afro-American Subculture in Eighteenth-Century New England.* Amherst: University of Massachusetts Press, 1988.

Pursell, Carroll. *The Machine in America: A Social History of Technology.* Baltimore: Johns Hopkins University Press, 1995.

Quarles, Benjamin. *The Negro in the American Revolution.* Chapel Hill: University of North Carolina Press, 1961.

Rabinowitz, Howard N. *Race Relations in the Urban South, 1865–1890.* Urbana: University of Illinois Press, 1980.

Rachleff, Peter J. *Black Labor in the South: Richmond, Virginia, 1865–1890.* Philadelphia: Temple University Press, 1984.

Rank, Mark Robert. *Living on the Edge: The Realities of Welfare in America.* New York: Columbia University Press, 1994.

Ransom, Roger L., and Richard Sutch. *One Kind of Freedom: The Economic Consequences of Emancipation.* London: Cambridge University Press, 1977.

Rediker, Marcus. *Between the Devil and the Deep Blue Sea: Merchant Seamen, Pirates, and the Anglo-American Maritime World, 1700–1750.* Cambridge: Cambridge University Press, 1987.

Reed, Merl. *Seedtime for the Modern Civil Rights Movement: The President's Committee on Fair Employment Practice, 1941–1946.* Baton Rouge: Louisiana State University Press, 1991.

Richards, Leonard L. *Gentlemen of Property and Standing: Anti-Abolition Mobs in Jacksonian America.* New York: Oxford University Press, 1970.

Roediger, David R., *The Wages of Whiteness: Race and the Making of the American Working Class.* London: Verso, 1991.

Russell, Howard S. *A Long, Deep Furrow: Three Centuries of Farming in New England.* Hanover, NH: University Press of New England, 1976.

Rutman, Darrett B., and Anita H. Rutman. *A Place in Time: Middlesex County, Virginia, 1650–1750.* New York: W. W. Norton, 1984.

Salisbury, Neal. *Manitou and Providence: Indians, Europeans, and the Making of New England, 1500–1643.* New York: Oxford University Press, 1982.

Salinger, Sharon Y. *"To Serve Well and Faithfully": Labor and Indentured Servants in Pennsylvania, 1682–1800.* Cambridge: Cambridge University Press, 1987.

Santino, Jack. *Miles of Smiles, Years of Struggle: Stories of Black Pullman Porters.* Urbana: University of Illinois Press, 1989.

Sassen, Saskia. *The Global City: New York, London, Tokyo.* Princeton: Princeton University Press, 1991.

Saxton, Alexander. *The Indispensable Enemy: Labor and the Anti-Chinese Movement in California.* Berkeley: University of California Press, 1971.

Scheiner, Seth M. *Negro Mecca: A History of the Negro in New York City, 1865–1920.* New York: New York University Press, 1965.

Schultz, Ronald. *The Republic of Labor: Philadelphia Artisans and the Politics of Class, 1720–1830.* New York: Oxford University Press, 1993.

Schwarz, John E., and Thomas J. Volgy. *The Forgotten American.* New York: W. W. Norton, 1992.

Shelton, Cynthia J. *The Mills of Manayunk: Industrialization and Social Conflict in the Philadelphia Region, 1787–1837.* Baltimore: Johns Hopkins University Press, 1986.

Shull, Steven A. *A Kinder, Gentler Racism? The Reagan-Bush Civil Rights Legacy.* London: M. E. Sharpe, 1993.

Shy, John. *A People Numerous and Armed: Reflections on the Military Struggle for American Independence.* New York: Oxford University Press, 1976.

Silver, Timothy. *A New Face on the Countryside: Indians, Colonists, and Slaves in South Atlantic Forests, 1500–1800.* Cambridge: Cambridge University Press, 1990.

Sitkoff, Harvard. *A New Deal for Blacks: The Emergence of Civil Rights as a National Issue.* New York: Oxford University Press, 1978.

Smith, Abbot Emerson. *Colonists in Bondage: White Servitude and Convict Labor in America, 1607–1776.* Chapel Hill: University of North Carolina Press, 1947.

Smith, Billy G. *The "Lower Sort": Philadelphia's Laboring People, 1750–1800.* Ithaca: Cornell University Press, 1990.

Smith, Warren B. *White Servitude in Colonial South Carolina.* Columbia: University of South Carolina Press, 1961.

Sobel, Michel. *The World They Made Together: Black and White Values in Eighteenth-Century Virginia.* Princeton: Princeton University Press, 1987.

Soderlund, Jean R. *Quakers and Slavery: A Divided Spirit.* Princeton: Princeton University Press, 1985.

Sovern, Michael I. *Legal Restraints on Racial Discrimination in Employment.* New York: Twentieth Century Fund, 1966.

Spear, Allan H. *Black Chicago: The Making of a Negro Ghetto, 1890–1920.* Chicago: University of Chicago Press, 1967.

Spero, Sterling D., and Abram L. Harris. *The Black Worker: A Study of the Negro and the Labor Movement.* New York: Columbia University Press, 1931.

Spruill, Julia Cherry. *Women's Life and Work in the Southern Colonies.* New York: W. W. Norton, 1972; orig. pub. 1938.

Stansell, Christine. *City of Women: Sex and Class in New York, 1789–1860.* New York: Knopf, 1986.

Starobin, Robert S. *Industrial Slavery in the Old South.* New York: Oxford University Press, 1970.

Steiner, Bernard C. *History of Slavery in Connecticut.* Baltimore: Johns Hopkins University Press, 1893.

Steinfeld, Robert J. *The Invention of Free Labor: The Employment Relation in English and American Law and Culture, 1350–1870.* Chapel Hill: University of North Carolina Press, 1991.

Stevenson, Brenda E. *Life in Black and White: Family and Community in the Slave South.* New York: Oxford University Press, 1996.

Strickland, Arvarh E. *History of the Chicago Urban League.* Urbana: University of Illinois Press, 1966.

Sugrue, Thomas J. *The Origins of the Urban Crisis: A History of Inequality in Detroit, 1940–1967.* Princeton: Princeton University Press, 1996.

Tate, Thad W. *The Negro in Eighteenth-Century Williamsburg.* Charlottesville: University Press of Virginia, 1965.

Thomas, Lamont D. *Rise to Be a People: A Biography of Paul Cuffee.* Urbana: University of Illinois Press, 1986.

Thomas, Richard W. *Life for Us Is What We Make It: Building Black Community in Detroit, 1915–1945.* Bloomington: Indiana University Press, 1992.

Tolbert, Emory J. *The UNIA and Black Los Angeles: Ideology and Community in the American Garvey Movement.* Los Angeles: Center for Afro-American Studies, 1980.

Tonroy, Michael. *Malign Neglect—Race, Crime, and Punishment in America.* New York: Oxford University Press, 1995.

Trotter, Joe William, Jr. *Black Milwaukee: The Making of an Industrial Proletariat, 1915–1945.* Urbana: University of Illinois Press, 1985.

———. *Coal, Class, and Color: Blacks in Southern West Virginia, 1915–32.* Urbana: University of Illinois Press, 1990.

Usner, Daniel H., Jr. *Indians, Settlers, and Slaves in a Frontier Exchange Economy: The Lower Mississippi Valley Before 1783.* Chapel Hill: University of North Carolina Press, 1992.

Vickers, Daniel. *Farmers and Fishermen: Two Centuries of Work in Essex County, Massachusetts, 1630–1850.* Chapel Hill: University of North Carolina Press, 1994.

Wade, Richard C. *Slavery in the Cities: The South, 1820–1860.* New York: Oxford University Press, 1964.

Waldinger, Roger. *Still the Promised City?: African-Americans and New Immigrants in Postindustrial New York.* Cambridge: Harvard Univerity Press, 1996.

Walshok, Mary Lindenstein. *Blue Collar Women: Pioneers on the Male Frontier.* Garden City, NY: Anchor Books, 1981.

Way, Peter. *Common Labour: Workers and the Digging of North American Canals, 1780–1860.* Cambridge: Cambridge University Press, 1993.

Weir, Margaret. *Politics and Jobs: The Boundaries of Employment Policy in the United States.* Princeton: Princeton University Press, 1992.

Weiss, Nancy J. *The National Urban League, 1910–1940.* New York: Oxford University Press, 1974.

Wesley, Charles H. *Negro Labor in the United States, 1850–1925: A Study in American Economic History.* New York: Vanguard Press, 1927.

West, Cornel. *Race Matters.* Boston: Beacon Press, 1993.

White, Deborah Gray. *Ar'n't I a Woman? Female Slaves in the Plantation South.* New York: W. W. Norton, 1985.

White, Shane. *Somewhat More Independent: The End of Slavery in New York City, 1770–1810.* Athens: University of Georgia Press, 1991.

Wilson, William Julius. *The Truly Disadvantaged: The Inner City, the Underclass, and Public Policy*. Chicago: University of Chicago Press, 1987.

———. *When Work Disappears: The World of the New Urban Poor*. New York: Knopf, 1996.

Wittke, Carl F. *The Irish in America*. Baton Rouge: Louisiana State University Press, 1956.

Wood, Betty. *Slavery in Colonial Georgia, 1730–1775*. Athens: University of Georgia Press, 1984.

———. *Women's Work, Men's Work: The Informal Slave Economies of Lowcountry Georgia*. Athens: University of Georgia Press, 1995.

Wood, Gordon S. *The Radicalism of the American Revolution*. New York: Knopf, 1992.

Wood, Peter. *Black Majority: Negroes in Colonial South Carolina from 1670 Through the Stono Rebellion*. New York: Knopf, 1974.

Woodward, C. Vann. *Origins of the New South, 1877–1913*. Baton Rouge: Louisiana State University Press, 1951.

———. *The Strange Career of Jim Crow*. New York: Oxford University Press, 1955.

Woody, Bette. *Black Women in the Workplace: Impacts of Structural Change in the Economy*. Westport, CT: Greenwood Press, 1992.

Wright, Gavin. *Old South, New South: Revolutions in the Southern Economy Since the Civil War*. New York: Basic Books, 1986.

Yee, Shirley. *Black Women Abolitionists: A Study in Activism, 1828–1860*. Knoxville: University of Tennessee Press, 1992.

Zilversmit, Arthur. *The First Emancipation: The Abolition of Slavery in the North*. Chicago: University of Chicago Press, 1967.

ESSAY ANTHOLOGIES

Andrews, K. R., N. P. Canny, and P. E. H. Hair., eds. *The Westward Enterprise: English Activities in Ireland, the Atlantic, and America, 1480–1650*. Detroit: Wayne State University Press, 1979.

Bailyn, Bernard, and Philip D. Morgan, eds. *Strangers Within the Realm: Cultural Margins of the First British Empire*. Chapel Hill: University of North Carolina Press, 1991.

Berlin, Ira, and Ronald Hoffman, eds. *Slavery and Freedom in the Age of the American Revolution*. Charlottesville: University Press of Virginia, 1983.

Berlin, Ira, and Philip D. Morgan, eds. *Cultivation and Culture: Labor and the Shaping of Slave Life in the Americas*. Charlottesville: University Press of Virginia, 1993.

Bernhard, Virginia, et al., eds. *Hidden Histories of Women in the New South*. Columbia: University of Missouri Press, 1994.

Bleser, Carol, ed. *In Joy and in Sorrow: Women, Family and Marriage in the Victorian South, 1830–1990*. New York: Oxford University Press, 1991.

Bodnar, John, ed. *The Ethnic Experience in Pennsylvania*. Philadelphia: Bucknell University Press, 1973.

Brewer, John, and Roy Porter, eds. *Consumption and the World of Goods*. New York: Routledge, 1993.

Callow, A. B., Jr., ed. *American Urban History: An Interpretive Reader with Commentaries*. New York: Oxford University Press, 1969.

Canny, Nicholas P., and Anthony Pagden, eds. *Colonial Identity in the Atlantic World, 1500–1800*. Princeton: Princeton University Press, 1987.

Carr, Lois Green, Philip D. Morgan, and Jean B. Russo, eds. *Colonial Chesapeake Society*. Chapel Hill: University of North Carolina Press, 1988.

Cohen, David W., and Jack P. Greene, eds. *Neither Slave Nor Free: The Freedman of African Descent in the Slave Societies of the New World*. Baltimore: Johns Hopkins University Press, 1972.

Curry, George E., ed. *The Affirmative Action Debate*. Reading, MA: Addison-Wesley, 1996.

Davis, Allen F., and Mark H. Haller, eds. *The Peoples of Philadelphia: A History of Ethnic Groups and Lower-Class Life, 1790–1940*. Philadelphia: Temple University Press, 1973.

Dillman, Caroline Matheny, ed. *Southern Women*. New York: Hemisphere, 1988.

Dunn, Richard S., and Mary Maples Dunn, eds. *The World of William Penn*. Philadelphia: University of Pennsylvania Press, 1986.

Fraser, Steve, and Gary Gerstle, eds. *The Rise and Fall of the New Deal Order, 1930–1980*. Princeton: Princeton University Press, 1989.

Friedman, Jean *et al.*, eds. *Sex, Race, and the Role of Women in the South: Essays*. Jackson: University Press of Mississippi, 1983.

Gordon, Linda, ed. *Women, the State and Welfare*. Madison: University of Wisconsin Press, 1990.

Graber, J, *et al.*, eds. *Transitions Through Adolescence: Interpersonal Domains and Context*. Mahwah, NJ: Erlbaum Associates, 1996.

Green, James R., ed. *Workers' Struggles, Past and Present*. Philadelphia: Temple University Press, 1983.

Greene, Jack P., and J. R. Pole, eds. *Colonial British America: Essays in the New History of the Early Modern Era*. Baltimore: Johns Hopkins University Press, 1984.

Gutman, Herbert G., and Donald H. Bell, eds. *The New England Working Class and the New Labor History*. Urbana: University of Illinois Press, 1987.

Hall, Robert L., ed. *Making a Living: The Work Experience of African Americans in New England: Selected Readings*. Boston: New England Foundation for the Humanities, 1995.

Hawks, Joanne V., and Sheila L. Skemp, eds. *Sex, Race, and the Role of Women in the South: Essays*. Jackson: University Press of Mississippi, 1983.

Henretta, James, *et al.*, eds. *The Transformation of Early American History: Society, Authority, and Ideology*. New York: Knopf, 1991.

Hershberg, Theodore, ed. *Philadelphia: Work, Space, Family and Group Experience in the Nineteenth Century*. New York: Oxford University Press, 1981.

Hine, Darlene Clark. *Hine Sight: Black Women and the Re-Construction of American History*. New York: Carlson, 1994.

————. *Speak Truth to Power: Black Professional Class in United States History.* New York: Carlson, 1996.

————, Wilma King, and Linda Reed, eds. *"We Specialize in the Wholly Impossible": A Reader in Black Women's History.* New York: Carlson, 1995.

Hoffman, Ronald, and Peter J. Albert, eds. *Women in the Age of the American Revolution.* Charlottesville: University Press of Virginia, 1989.

————. *Arms and Independence: The Military Character of the American Revolution.* Charlottesville: University Press of Virginia, 1984.

Hudson, Larry E., Jr., ed. *Working Toward Freedom: Slave Society and Domestic Economy in the American South.* Rochester, NY: University of Rochester Press, 1994.

Innes, Stephen, ed. *Work and Labor in Early America.* Chapel Hill: University of North Carolina Press, 1988.

Jacobs, Donald M., ed. *Courage and Conscience: Black and White Abolitionists in Boston.* Bloomington: Indiana University Press, 1993.

Jaynes, Gerald D., and Robin M. Williams, Jr., eds. *A Common Destiny: Blacks and American Society.* Washington, DC: National Academy Press, 1989.

Jencks, Christopher, and Paul E. Peterson, eds. *The Urban Underclass.* Washington, DC: Brookings Institution, 1991.

Katz, Michael, B., ed. *The "Underclass" Debate: Views from History.* Princeton: Princeton University Press, 1993.

Katz, Michael, and Thomas J. Sugrue, eds. *W. E. B. DuBois and "The Philadelphia Negro": A Centenary Reappraisal.* Philadelphia: University of Pennsylvania Press, 1998.

Katznelson, Ira, and Aristide R. Zolberg, eds. *Working-Class Formation: Nineteenth-Century Patterns in Western Europe and the United States.* Princeton: Princeton University Press, 1986.

Land, Aubrey C., Lois Green Carr, and Edward C. Papenfuse, eds. *Law, Society, and Politics in Early Maryland: Proceedings of the First Conference on Maryland History.* Baltimore: Johns Hopkins University Press, 1977.

Lichtenstein, Nelson, and Stephen Meyer, ed. *On the Line: Essays in the History of Auto Work.* Urbana: University of Illinois Press, 1989.

McGaw, Judith A., ed. *Early American Technology: Making and Doing Things from the Colonial Era to 1850.* Chapel Hill: University of North Carolina Press, 1994.

Milkman, Ruth, ed. *Women, Work and Protest: A Century of U.S. Women's Labor History.* London: Routledge & Kegan Paul, 1985.

Miller, Elinor, and Eugene D. Genovese, eds. *Plantation, Town, and Country: Essays on the Local History of American Slave Society.* Urbana: University of Illinois Press, 1974.

Okihiro, Gary Y., ed. *In Resistance: Studies in African, Caribbean and Afro-American History.* Amherst: University of Massachusetts Press, 1986.

Quinn, David B., ed. *Early Maryland in a Wider World.* Detroit: Wayne State University Press, 1982.

Reuther, Rosemary Radford, and Rosemary Skinner Keller, eds. *Women and Religion in America.* San Francisco: Harper & Row, 1983.

Rock, Howard B., Paul A. Gilje, and Robert Asher, eds. *American Artisans: Crafting Social Identity, 1750–1850.* Baltimore: Johns Hopkins University Press, 1995.

Runyan, Timothy J., ed. *Ships, Seafaring, and Society: Essays in Maritime History.* Detroit: Wayne State University Press, 1987.

Spalding, Phinizy, and Harvey H. Jackson, eds. *Oglethorpe in Perspective: Georgia's Founder After Two Hundred Years.* Tuscaloosa: University of Alabama Press, 1989.

Stephenson, Charles, and Robert Asher, eds., *Life and Labor: Dimensions of American Working-Class History.* Albany: State University of New York Press, 1986.

Tate, Thad W., and David L. Ammerman, eds. *The Chesapeake in the Seventeenth Century: Essays on Anglo-American Society.* Chapel Hill: University of North Carolina Press, 1979.

Thernstrom, Stephan, and Richard Sennett, eds. *Nineteenth-Century Cities: Essays in the New Urban History.* New Haven: Yale University Press, 1969.

Wood, Peter H., Gregory A. Waselkov, and M. Thomas Hatley, eds. *Powhatan's Mantle: Indians in the Colonial Southeast.* Lincoln: University of Nebraska Press, 1989.

Yellin, Jean Fagan, and John C. Van Horne, eds. *The Abolitionist Sisterhood: Women's Political Culture in Antebellum America.* Ithaca: Cornell University Press, 1994.

Zinn, Maxine Baca, and Bonnie Thornton Dill, eds., *Women of Color in United States Society.* Philadelphia: Temple University Press, 1994.

ARTICLES AND PAMPHLETS

Adams, Patricia L. "Fighting for Democracy in St. Louis: Civil Rights During World War II." *MHR* 80 (October 1985):58–75.

Africa, Philip. "Slaveholding in the Salem Community, 1771–1851." *NCHR* 54 (Summer 1957):271–307.

Anderson, Terry L., and Robert Paul Thomas. "The Growth of Population and Labor Force in the 17th-Century Chesapeake." *EEH* 15 (July 1978):290–312.

Anderson, Virginia DeJohn. "King Philip's Herds: Indians, Colonists, and the Problem of Livestock in Early New England." *WMQ* 3rd series 51 (October 1994):601–24.

Aptheker, Herbert. "Maroons Within the Present Limits of the United States." *JNH* 24 (April 1939):167–84.

Armitage, Sue. "Black Women and Their Communities in Colorado." *Frontiers* 2 (1977):178–84.

Arnesen, Eric. "Following the Color Line of Labor: Black Workers and the Labor Movement Before 1930." *RHR* 55 (Winter 1993):53–87.

Badge, George M. "Soldiers in King Philip's War." *NEHGR* 44 (1890):270–79.

Bailey, Kenneth R. "A Judicious Mixture: Negroes and Immigrants in the West Virginia Mines, 1880–1917." *WVH* 34 (January 1973):141–61.

Bailyn, Bernard. "An American Tragedy." *NRYB* (October 5, 1995):14–16.

Baine, Rodney M. "New Perspectives on Debtors in Colonial Georgia." *GHQ* 77 (Spring 1993):1–19.

Baker, Steve. "Free Blacks in Antebellum Madison County." *THQ* 52 (Spring 1993):56–63.

Bates, Eric. "Beyond Black and White." *SE* 22 (Fall 1994):10–15.

Beatty, Bess. "Textile Labor in the North Carolina Piedmont: Mill Owner Images and Mill Worker Response, 1830–1900." *LH* 25 (Fall 1985):485–503.

Becker, Marshall J. "Hannah Freeman: An Eighteenth-Century Lenape Living and Working Among Colonial Farmers." *PMHB* 104 (April 1990):249–69.

Berlin, Ira. "Time, Space, and the Evolution of Afro-American Society in British Mainland North America." *AHR* 85 (February 1980):44–78.

———. "Structure of the Free Negro Caste in the Antebellum United States." *LH* 9 (Spring 1976):297–318.

———, and Herbert G. Gutman. "Natives and Immigrants, Free Men and Slaves: Urban Workingmen in the Antebellum South." *AHR* 88 (December 1983):1175–1200.

Bernhard, Virginia. "'Men, Women, and Children' at Jamestown: Population and Gender in Early Virginia, 1607–1610." *JSouH* 58 (November 1992):599–618.

Billings, Warren M. "The Law of Servants and Slaves in Seventeenth-Century Virginia." *VMHB* 99 (January 1991):45–62.

Bliss, Willard F. "The Rise of Tenancy in Virginia." *VMHB* 58 (October 1950):427–41.

Bolster, W. Jeffrey. "'To Feel Like a Man': Black Seamen in the Northern States, 1800–1860." *JAH* 76 (March 1990):1173–99.

Bourque, Bruce J., and Ruth Holmes Whitehead. "Tarrantines and the Introduction of European Trade Goods in the Gulf of Maine." *Eh* 32 (1985):327–41.

Boyd, Robert L. "Demographic Change and Entrepreneurial Occupations: African American in Northern Cities." *AJES* 55 (April 1996):129–43.

Breen, T. H. "A Changing Labor Force and Race Relations in Virginia 1660–1710." *JSocH* 7 (Fall 1973):3–25.

———. "An Empire of Goods: The Anglicization of Colonial America, 1690–1776." *JBS* 25 (October 1986):467–99.

———. "Back to Sweat and Toil: Suggestions for the Study of Agricultural Work in Early America." *PH* 49 (October 1982):241–58.

Brewer, James Howard. "Legislation Designed to Control Slavery in Wilmington and Fayetteville." *NCHR* 30 (April 1953):155–66.

Brown, Elsa Barkley. "Womanist Consciousness: Maggie Lena Walker and the Independent Order of Saint Luke." *Signs* 14 (Spring 1989):610–33.

Brown, Richard D. "'Not Only Extreme Poverty, But the Worst Kind of Orphanage': Lemuel Haynes and the Boundaries of Racial Tolerance on the Yankee Frontier, 1770–1820." *NEQ* 61 (1988):502–18.

Bruce, Kathleen. "Slave Labor in the Virginian Iron Industry." *WMQ* 2nd series 6 (October 1926):289–302.

Butler, James Davie. "British Convicts Shipped to American Colonies." *AHR* 2 (October 1896):12–33.

Byrne, William A. "The Hiring of Woodson, Slave Carpenter of Savannah." *GHQ* 77 (Summer 1993):245–63.

Campbell, Paul R., and Glenn W. LaFantasie. "Scattered to the Winds of Heaven—Narragansett Indians, 1676–1880." *RIH* 37 (August 1978):67–75.

Caro, Edythe Quinn. "'The Hills' in the Mid-Nineteenth Century: The History of a Rural Afro-American Community in Westchester County, New York." Valhalla, NY: Westchester Historical Society, 1988.

Carr, Lois Green, and Lorena S. Walsh. "The Planter's Wife: The Experience of White Women in Seventeenth-Century Maryland." *WMQ* 3rd series 34 (October 1977):542–71.

Cary, Lorin Lee, and Francine C. Cary. "Absolom F. Boston, His Family, and Nantucket's Black Community." *HN* 25 (Summer 1977):15–23.

Cashin, Joan. "Black Families in the Old Northwest." *JER* 15 (Fall 1995):449–75.

Cavallo, Jo. "Day of the Black Jockey." *AL* 2 (Spring 1996):22–32.

Cheyney, Edward P. "Some English Conditions Surrounding the Settlement of Virginia." *AHR* 12 (April 1907):507–28.

Clendenning, Lynda Fuller. "The Early Textile Industry in Maryland, 1810–1850." *MdHM* 87 (Fall 1992):251–66.

Clifton, James M. "Golden Grains of White: Rice Planting on the Lower Cape Fear." *NCHR* 50 (October 1973):365–93.

Cole, Stephanie. "Changes for Mrs. Thornton's Arthur: Patterns of Domestic Service in Washington, DC, 1800–1835." *SSH* 15 (Fall 1991):367–79.

Coulter, E. Merton. "The Acadians in Georgia." *GHQ* 47 (March 1963):68–75.

Daniel, Edmond Dale. "Robert Hunter Morris and the Rocky Hill Copper Mine." *NJH* 92 (Spring 1974):13–32.

Daniels, Christine. "Gresham's Laws: Labor Management on an Early-Eighteenth-Century Chesapeake Plantation." *JSouH* 62 (May 1996):205–37.

————. "'WANTED: A Blacksmith who understands Plantation Work': Artisans in Maryland, 1700–1810." *WMQ* 3rd series 50 (October 1993):743–67.

Dawley, Alan, and Joe William Trotter, Jr. "African-American Workers: New Directions in United States Labor Historiography." *LH* 35 (Fall 1994):486–94.

Donohue, John J. III, and James Heckman. "Continuous versus Episodic Change: The Impact of Civil Rights Policy on the Economic Status of Blacks." *JEL* 29 (December 1991):1603–43.

Draper, Alan. "The New Southern Labor History Revisited: The Success of the Mine, Mill, and Smelter Workers Union in Birmingham, 1934–1938." *LH* 62 (February 1966):87–108.

Eaton, Clement. "Slave-Hiring in the Upper South: A Step Toward Freedom." *MVHR* 48 (March 1960):663–78.

Eisinger, Peter K. "Black Employment in Municipal Jobs: The Impact of Black Political Power." *APSR* 76 (June 1982):380–92.

Ekirch, A. Roger. "Great Britain's Secret Convict Trade to America, 1783–1784." *AHR* 89 (December 1984):1285–91.

Eslinger, Ellen. "The Shape of Slavery on the Kentucky Frontier, 1775–1800." *RKHS* 92 (Winter 1994):1–23.

Farr, James. "A Slow Boat to Nowhere: The Multi-Racial Crews of the American Whaling Industry." *JNH* 68 (Spring 1983):159–70.

Ferguson, Isabel. "County Court in Virginia, 1700–1830." *NCHR* 8 (January 1931):14–40.

Fickle, James E. "Management Looks at the 'Labor Problem': The Southern Pine Industry During World War I and the Postwar Era." *JSouH* 40 (February 1974):61–76.

Fields, Barbara Jeanne. "The Nineteenth Century American South: History and Theory." *PSA* 1 (April 1983):7–27.

——. "Slavery, Race and Ideology in the United States of America." *NLR* (May 1990):95–118.

Figart, Deborah. "Gender Segmentation of Craft Workers by Race in the 1970s and 1980s." *RRPE* 25 (1993):50–66.

Fishback, Price. "Segregation in Job Hierarchies: West Virginia Coal Mining, 1906–1932." *JEH* 44 (September 1984):755–74.

Fogel, Robert William, and Stanley L. Engerman. "Philanthropy at Bargain Prices: Notes on the Economics of Gradual Emancipation." *JLS* 3 (June 1974):377–401.

Fosu, Augustin Kwasi. "Occupational Mobility of Black Women, 1958–1981: The Impact of Post–1964 Antidiscrimination Measures." *ILRR* 45 (January 1992):281–86.

Fraser, Walter J., Jr. "The City Elite, 'Disorder,' and the Poor Children of Pre-Revolutionary Charleston." *SCHM* 84 (July 1983):167–79.

Geschwender, James A., and Rita Carroll Seguin. "Exploding the Myth of Afro-American Progress." *Signs* 15 (Winter 1990):285–99.

Gilje, Paul A., and Howard B. Rock. "'Sweep O! Sweep O!' African-American Chimney Sweeps and Citizenship in the New Nation." *WMQ* 3rd series 51 (July 1994):507–38.

Goldin, Claudia, and Kenneth Sokoloff. "Women, Children, and Industrialization in the Early Republic: Evidence from the Manufacturing Censuses." *JEH* 42 (December 1982):741–74.

Goldoftas, Barbara. "Inside the Slaughterhouse." *SE* 17 (Summer 1989):27–30.

Goodfriend, Joyce D. "Burghers and Blacks: The Evolution of a Slave Society in New Amsterdam." *NYH* 59 (April 1978):125–44.

Gray, Ralph, and Betty Wood. "The Transition from Indentured to Involuntary Servitude in Colonial Georgia." *EEH* 13 (October 1976):353–70.

Graziosi, Andrea. "Common Laborers, Unskilled Workers, 1880–1915." *LH* 22 (Fall 1981):512–44.

Green, Fletcher M. "Georgia's Forgotten Industry: Gold Mining." *GHQ* 19 (1935):1–19.

Green, Samuel Abbott. "Slavery at Groton, Massachusetts, in Provincial Times." Cambridge: John Wilson & Son, 1909.

Greene, Lorenzo J. "Some Observations on the Black Regiment of Rhode Island in the American Revolution." *JNH* 37 (April 1952):142–72.

Griffin, Richard W. "The Origins of the Industrial Revolution in Georgia: Cotton Textiles, 1810–1865." *GHQ* 42 (December 1948):355–75.

————, and Diffee W. Standard. "The Cotton Textile Industry in Ante-Bellum North Carolina. Pt II: An Era of Boom and Consolidation, 1830–1860." *NCHR* 34 (April 1957):131–64.

Grubb, Farley. "The Auction of Redemptioner Servants, Philadelphia, 1771–1804: An Economic Analysis." *JEH* 48 (September 1988):583–603.

————. "Fatherless and Friendless: Factors Influencing the Flow of English Emigrant Servants." *JEH* 52 (March 1992):85–108.

————. "Immigrant Servant Labor: Their Occupational and Geographic Distribution in the Late Eighteenth Century Mid-Atlantic Economy." *SSH* 9 (Summer 1995):259–75.

————. "Redemptioner Immigration to Pennsylvania: Evidence on Contract Choice and Profitability." *JEH* 46 (June 1986):407–18.

Gunderson, Joan R. "The Double Bonds of Race and Sex: Black and White Women in a Colonial Virginia Parish." *JSouH* 52 (August 1986):351–72

Guyette, Elise A. "The Working Lives of African Vermonters in Census and Literature, 1790–1870." *VH* 61 (Spring 1993):69–84.

Haiken, Elizabeth. "'The Lord Helps Those Who Help Themselves': Black Laundresses in Little Rock, Arkansas, 1917–1921." *ArHQ* 49 (Spring 1990):20–50.

Hammett, Hugh B. "Labor and Race: The Georgia Railroad Strike of 1909." *LH* 16 (Fall 1975):470–84.

Handlin, Oscar, and Mary F. Handlin. "Origins of the Southern Labor System." *WMQ* 3rd series 7 (April 1950):199–22.

Harris, William H. "Federal Intervention in Union Discrimination: FEPC and the West Coast Shipyards During World War II." *LH* 22 (Summer 1981):325–47.

Haywood, C. Robert. "Mercantilism and Colonial Slave Labor, 1700–1763." *JSouH* 23 (November 1957):454–64.

Helmbold, Lois Rita. "Downward Occupational Mobility During the Great Depression: Urban Black and White Working Class Women." *LH* 29 (Spring 1988):135–72.

Heckman, James J., and Brook S. Payner. "Determining the Impact of Federal Antidiscrimination Policy on the Economic Status of Blacks: A Study of South Carolina." *AER* 79 (March 1989):138–77.

Henderson, Alexa B. "FEPC and the Southern Railway Case: An Investigation into the Discriminatory Practices of Railroads During World War II." *JNH* 61 (April 1976):173–87.

Hill, Herbert. "The AFL-CIO and the Black Worker: Twenty-Five Years After the Merger." *JIR* 10 (Spring 1982):5–78.

————. "Myth-Making as Labor History: Herbert Gutman and the United Mine Workers of America." *IJPCS* 2 (Winter 1978):132–200.

————. "No Harvest for the Reaper: The Story of the Migratory Agricultural Worker in the United States." New York: National Association for the Advancement of Colored People, n.d.

Hill, Mozell C. "The All-Negro Communities of Oklahoma: The Natural History of a Social Movement." *JNH* 31 (July 1946):254–68.

Holt, Sharon Ann. "Making Freedom Pay: Freedpeople Working for Themselves, North Carolina, 1865–1900." *JSouH* 60 (May 1994):229–62.

Hood, J. Larry. "The Nixon Administration and the Revised Philadelphia Plan for Affirmative Action: A Study in Expanding Presidential Power and Divided Government." *PresSQ* 23 (Winter 1993):1145–67.

Hoyt, William D., Jr. "The White Servants at 'Northampton,' 1772–74." *MHM* 33 (June 1938):126–33.

Hudnut, Ruth Allison, and Hayes Baker-Crothers. "Acadian Transients in South Carolina." *AHR* 43 (April 1938):500–13.

Hughes, Sarah S. "Slaves for Hire: The Allocation of Black Labor in Elizabeth City County, Virginia, 1782–1810." *WMQ* 3rd series 35 (April 1978):260–86.

Hunter, Tera. "Domination and Resistance: The Politics of Wage Household Labor in New South Atlanta." *LH* 34 (Spring–Summer 1993):205–20.

Inscoe, John C. "Mountain Masters: Slaveholding in Western North Carolina." *NCHR* 61 (April 1984):143–73.

Jackson, Luther P. "Virginia Negro Soldiers and Seamen in the Revolutionary War." Norfolk: Guide Quality Press, 1944.

Johnson, Michael P. "Work, Culture and the Slave Community: Slave Occupations in the Cotton Belt in 1860." *LH* 27 (Summer 1986):325–55.

Johnson, Richard R. "The Search for a Usable Indian: An Aspect of the Defense of Colonial New England." *JAH* 64 (December 1977):623–51.

Johnson, Wittington B. "Free African-American Women in Savannah, 1800–1860: Affluence and Autonomy Amid Adversity." *GHQ* 76 (Summer 1992):260–83.

Johnston, James Hugo. "The Participation of White Men in Virginia Negro Insurrections." *JNH* 16 (April 1931):158–67.

Jones, Douglas Lamar. "The Strolling Poor: Transiency in Eighteenth-Century Massachusetts." *JSocH* 8 (Spring 1975):28–54.

Jones, Jacqueline. "The Late Twentieth Century War on the Poor: A View from Distressed Communities Throughout the Nation." *BCTWLJ* 16 (Winter 1996):1–16.

Jones, Mack H. "Black Political Empowerment in Atlanta: Myth and Reality." *Annals* 439 (September 1978):90–117.

Kaplan, Sidney. "The 'Domestic Insurrections' of the Declarations of Independence." *JNH* 61 (July 1976):243–55.

Klebaner, Benjamin J. "Pauper Auctions: The 'New England Method' of Public Poor Relief." *EIHC* 91 (July 1955):195–210.

Kruman, Mark W. "Quotas for Blacks: The Public Works Administration and the Black Construction Worker." *LH* 16 (Winter 1975):37–49.

Kupperman, Karen Ordahl. "Apathy and Death in Early Jamestown." *JAH* 46 (June 1979):24–40.

———. "Fear of Hot Climates in the Anglo-American Colonial Experience." *WMQ* 3rd series 41 (April 1984):213–40.

———. "The Founding Years of Virginia—and the United States." *VMHB* 104 (Winter 1996):103–12.

Kusmer, Kenneth L. "African Americans in the City Since World War II: From the Industrial to the Post-Industrial Era." *JUH* 21 (May 1995):458–504.

Lacey, Barbara E. "The World of Hannah Heaton: The Autobiography of an Eighteenth-Century Connecticut Farm Woman." *WMQ* 45 (April 1988):280–304.

Lander, E. M., Jr. "Slave Labor in South Carolina Cotton Mills." *JNH* 38 (April 1953):161–73.

Lapsansky, Emma Jones. "'Since They Got Those Separate Churches': Afro-Americans and Racism in Jacksonian Philadelphia." *AQ* 32 (Spring 1980):54–78.

Larkin, Jack. "Living and Working in a Sea of White Faces." *OSV* (Summer 1991):6–7.

Letwin, Daniel. "Interracial Unionism, Gender, and 'Social Equality' in the Alabama Coal Fields, 1878–1908." *JSouH* 61 (August 1995):519–54.

Lewis, Ronald L. "Slave Families at Early Chesapeake Ironworks." *VMHB* 86 (April 1978):169–79.

———. "Slavery on Chesapeake Iron Plantations Before the American Revolution." *JNH* 59 (July 1974):242–53.

Lichtenstein, Alex. "Racial Conflict and Racial Solidarity in the Alabama Coal Strike of 1894: New Evidence for the Gutman-Hill Debate." *LH* 36 (Winter 1995):63–76.

———. "That Disposition to Theft, with Which They Have Been Branded: Moral Economy, Slave Management, and the Law." *JSocH* 21 (Spring 1988):413–40.

Linebaugh, Peter, and Marcus Rediker. "The Many-Headed Hydra: Sailors, Slaves, and the Atlantic Working Class in the Eighteenth Century." *JHS* 3 (September 1990):224–52.

Little, Thomas J. "The South Carolina Slave Laws Reconsidered, 1670–1700." *SCHM* 94 (April 1993):86–101.

Littlefield, Daniel F., and Mary Ann Littlefield. "The Beams Family: Free Blacks in Indian Territory." *JNH* 61 (January 1976):16–35.

Malone, Patrick M. "Changing Military Technology Among the Indians of Southern New England, 1600–1677." *AQ* 25 (March 1973):48–63.

Marcus, Grania Bolton. "A Forgotten People: Discovering the Black Experience in Suffolk County." Mattituck, NY: Society for the Preservation of Long Island Antiquities, 1988.

May, Elaine Tyler. "The Radical Roots of American Studies." *AQ* 48 (June 1996):179–200.

Meeker, Edward, and James Kau. "Racial Discrimination and Occupational Attainment at the Turn of the Century." *EEH* 14 (July 1977):250–76.

Menard, Russell R. "From Servant to Freeholder: Status Mobility and Property Accumulation in Seventeenth-Century Maryland." *WMQ* 3rd series 30 (January 1973):37–64.

Merrell, James H. "Some Thoughts on Colonial Historians and American Indians." *WMQ* 3rd series 46 (January 1989):94–119.

Miller, Randall M. "Daniel Pratt's Industrial Urbanism: The Cotton Mill Town in Antebellum Alabama." *AHQ* (Spring 1972):5–35.

———. "The Fabric of Control: Slavery in Antebellum Southern Textile Mills." *BHR* 55 (Winter 1981):471–90.

Montgomery, David. "The Shuttle and the Cross: Weavers and Artisans in the Kensington Riots of 1844." *JSocH* 5 (Summer 1972):411–46.

Moore, John Hebron. "Mississippi's Antebellum Textile Industry." *JMH* 16 (April 1954):81–98.

———. "Simon Gray, Riverman: A Slave Who Was Almost Free." *MVHR* 49 (December 1962):472–84.

Morgan, Philip D. "Black Life in Eighteenth-Century Charleston." *PAH* new series 1 (1984):187–232.

———, and Michael L. Nicholls. "Slaves in Piedmont Virginia." *WMQ* 3rd series 46 (April 1989):211–51.

Morrison, Kenneth M. "'That Art of Coyning Christians': John Eliot and the Praying Indians of Massachusetts." *Eh* 21 (Winter 1974):77–92.

Moss, Simeon F. "The Persistence of Slavery and Involuntary Servitude in a Free State (1685–1866)." *JNH* 35 (July 1950):289–314.

Munns, Edw. N. "Women in Southern Lumbering Operations." *JF* 17 (February 1919):144–49.

Nash, Gary B. "The Failure of Female Factory Labor in Colonial Boston." *LH* (Spring 1979):165–88.

———, et al. "Labor in the Era of the American Revolution: An Exchange." *LH* 24 (Summer 1983):414–54.

———. "Slave and Slaveowners in Colonial Philadelphia." *WMQ* 3rd series 30 (April 1973):223–56.

———. "Slavery, Black Resistance, and the American Revolution." *GHQ* 77 (Spring 1993):62–70.

Newman, Debra. "Black Women in the Era of the American Revolution in Pennsylvania." *JNH* 61 (July 1976):278–89.

———. "They Left with the British: Black Women in the Evacuation of Philadelphia, 1778." *PHe* 4 (1977):2–23.

Nicholls, Michael L. "Passing Through This Troublesome World: Free Blacks in the Early Southside." *VMHB* 92 (January 1984):50–70.

Norrell, Robert J. "Caste in Steel: Jim Crow Careers in Birmingham, Alabama." *JAH* 73 (December 1986):669–94.

Norton, Laurence E. II, and Marc Linder. "Down and Out in Weslaco, Texas, and Washington, D.C.: Race-Based Discrimination Against Farm Workers Under Federal Unemployment Insurance." *UMJLR* 29 (Fall 1995–Winter 1996):177–216.

Norton, Mary Beth. "The Evolution of White Women's Experience in Early America." *AHR* (June 1984):593–619.

———. "The Fate of Some Black Loyalists of the American Revolution." *JNH* 58 (October 1973):402–26.

Oestreicher, Richard. "The Counted and the Uncounted: The Occupational Structure of Early American Cities." *JSocH* 28 (Winter 1994):351–61.

Okoye, F. Nwabueze. "Chattel Slavery as the Nightmare of the American Revolutionaries." *WMQ* 3rd series 37 (January 1980):3–29.

Olson, Edwin. "The Slave Code in Colonial New York." *JNH* 29 (April 1944): 147–65.

Otterness, Philip. "The New York Naval Stores Project and the Transformation of the Poor Palantines, 1710–1712." *NYH* 75 (April 1994):133–56.

Outland, Robert B. III. "Slavery, Work, and the Geography of the North Carolina Naval Stores Industry, 1835–1860." *JSouH* 62 (February 1996):27–56.

Parenti, Christian. "Making Prison Pay: Business Finds the Cheapest Labor of All." *Nation* 262 (January 29, 1996):11–14.

Patrick, Jeff L. "Nothing But Slaves: The Second Kentucky Volunteer Infantry and the Spanish American War." *RKHS* 89 (Summer 1991):287–99.

Pedersen, Harold A. "Mechanized Agriculture and the Farm Laborer." *RS* 15 (March 1950):143–51.

Percy, David O. "Ax or Plow? Significant Colonial Landscape Alteration Rates in the Maryland and Virginia Tidewater." *AH* 66 (Spring 1992):66–74.

Pidgeon, Mary Elizabeth. "Women Workers and Recent Economic Change." *MLR* 65 (December 1947):666–71.

Preyer, Norris W. "The Historian, the Slave, and the Ante-Bellum Textile Industry." *JNH* 46 (April 1961):67–82.

Prude, Jonathan. "Runaway Ads and the Appearance of Unfree Laborers in America, 1750–1800." *JAH* 78 (June 1991):124–59.

Pruitt, Bettye Hobbs. "Self-Sufficiency and the Agricultural Economy of Eighteenth-Century Massachusetts." *WMQ* 3rd series 41 (July 1984):333–64.

Purvis, Thomas L. "Origins and Patterns of Agrarian Unrest in New Jersey, 1735–1754." *WMQ* 3rd series 39 (October 1982):600–27.

Quarles, Benjamin. "The Colonial Militia and Negro Manpower." *MVHR* 45 (March 1959):643–52.

Rammelkamp, Julian. "The Providence Negro Community, 1820–1842." *RIH* 7 (January 1948):20–33.

Ransome, David R. "Wives for Virginia, 1621." *WMQ* 3rd series 48 (January 1991):3–18.

Reed, Merl E. "Black Workers, Defense Industries, and Federal Agencies in Pennsylvania, 1941–5." *LH* 27 (Summer 1986):356–84.

———. "FEPC and the Federal Agencies in the South." *JNH* 65 (Winter 1980):43–56.

——— "Lumberjacks and Longshoremen: The IWW in Louisiana." *LH* 13 (Winter 1972):41–55.

Reidy, Joseph L. "Negro Election Day & Black Community Life in New England, 1750–1860." *MP* 1 (Fall 1978)):102–17.

Rowe, G. S. "Black Offenders, Criminal Courts, and Philadelphia Society in the Late Eighteenth Century." *JSocH* 22 (Summer 1989):685–712.

Runcie, John. "'Hunting the Nigs' in Philadelphia: The Race Riot of August 1934." *PH* 39 (April 1972):187–218.

Sainsbury, John A. "Indian Labor in Early Rhode Island." *NEQ* 48 (September 1975):378–93.

Salinger, Sharon V. "'Send No More Women': Female Servants in Eighteenth-Century Philadelphia." *PMHB* 107 (January 1983):29–48.

Salisbury, Neal. "The Indians' Old World: Native Americans and the Coming of Europeans." *WMQ* 3rd series 53 (July 1996):435–58.

———. "Red Puritans: The 'Praying Indians' of Masschusetts Bay and John Eliot." *WMQ* 3rd series 31 (January 1974):27–54.

Schantz, Mark S. "'A Very Serious Business': Managerial Relationships on the Ball Plantations, 1800–1835." *SCHM* 88 (January 1987):1–22.

Schmidt, Hubert. "Slavery and Attitudes on Slavery in Hunterdon County, New Jersey." Flemington, NJ: Hunterdon County Historical Society, 1941.

Schultz, Jane E. "The Inhospitable Hospital: Gender and Professionalism in Civil War Medicine." *Signs* 17 (Winter 1992):363–92.

Schwendermann, Glen. "Nicodemus: Negro Haven on the Solomon." *KHQ* 34 (Spring 1968):10–31.

Shammas, Carole. "Anglo-American Household Government in Comparative Perspective." *WMQ* 52 (January 1995):104–44.

———. "Black Women's Work and the Evolution of Plantation Society in Virginia." *LH* 26 (Winter 1985):5–28.

———. "The Domestic Environment in Early Modern England and America." *JSocH* 14 (Fall 1980):3–24.

———. "The Female Social Structure of Philadelphia in 1775." *PMHB* 107 (January 1983):69–83.

Sheeler, J. Reuben. "The Negro on the Virginia Frontier." *JNH* 43 (October 1958):279–97.

Sheldon, Marianne Buroff. "Black-White Relations in Richmond, Virginia, 1782–1820." *JSouH* 45 (February 1979):27–44.

Shirley, Michael. "Yeoman Culture and Millworker Protest in Antebellum Salem, North Carolina." *JSouH* 57 (August 1991):427–52.

Simler, Lucy. "The Landless Worker: An Index of Economic and Social Change in Chester County, Pennsylvania, 1750–1820." *PMHB* 104 (April 1990):163–99.

Skotines, Andor. "'Buy Where You Can Work': Boycotting for Jobs in African-American Baltimore." *JSocH* 27 (Summer 1994):735–63.

Smith, Alonzo, and Quintard Taylor. "Racial Discrimination in the Workplace: A Study of Two West Coast Cities During the 1940s." *JES* 8 (Spring 1980): 35–54.

Snow, Sinclair. "Naval Stores in Colonial Virginia." *VMHB* 72 (January 1964):75–93.

Soderlund, Jean. "Black Women in Colonial Pennsylvania." *PMHB* 107 (January 1983):49–68.

Souden, David. "'Rogues, Whores and Vagabonds'? Indentured Servant Emigrants to North America, and the Case of Mid-Seventeenth Century Bristol," *SH* 3 (January 1978):23–41.

Standard, Diffee W., and Richard W. Griffin. "The Cotton Textile Industry in Ante-Bellum North Carolina. Pt. I: Origin and Growth to 1830." *NCHR* 34 (January 1957):15–35.

Stavisky, Leonard Price. "Industrialism in Ante Bellum Charleston." *JNH* 36 (July 1951):302–22.

Stealey, John Edmund III. "Slavery and the West Virginia Salt Industry." *JNH* 49 (April 1974):105–31.

Sugrue, Thomas J. "Crabgrass-Roots Politics: Race, Rights, and the Reaction Against Liberalism in the Urban North, 1940–1964." *JAH* 82 (September 1995):551–78.

———. "Segmented Work, Race-Conscious Workers: Structure, Agency and Division in the CIO Era." *IRSH* 41 (1996):389–406.

Sundstrom, William A. "The Color Line: Racial Norms and Discrimination in Urban Labor Markets, 1910–1950." *JEH* 54 (June 1994):382–96.

———. "Half a Career: Discrimination and Railroad Internal Labor Markets." *IR* 29 (Fall 1990):423–40.

———. "Internal Labor Markets Before World War I: On-the-Job Training and Employee Promotion." *EEH* 25 (October 1988):424–45.

Taylor, Quintard. "The Great Migration: The Afro-American Communities of Seattle and Portland During the 1940s." *AW* 23 (Summer 1981):109–26.

Terrill, Tom E. "Eager Hands: Labor for Southern Textiles, 1850–1860." *JEH* 36 (March 1976):84–99.

Thom, William Taylor. "The Negroes of Sandy Spring, Maryland: A Social Study." *Department of Labor Bulletin* 32 (January 1901):43–102.

Thompson, Joseph Conan. "Toward a More Humane Oppression: Florida's Slave Codes, 1821–1861." *FHQ* 71 (January 1993):324–38.

Tomlins, Christopher L. "AFL Unions in the 1930s: Their Performance in Historical Perspective." *JAH* 55 (March 1979):1021–42.

Towner, Lawrence W. "'A Fondness for Freedom': Servant Protest in Puritan Society." *WMQ* 3rd series 29 (April 1962):201–19.

———. "The Sewall-Saffin Dialogue on Slavery." *WMQ* 3rd series 21 (January 1964):40–52.

Tully, Alan. "Patterns of Slaveholding in Colonial Pennsylvania: Chester and Lancaster Counties, 1729–1758." *JSocH* 6 (Spring 1973):284–305.

Twombly, Robert C., and Robert H. Moore. "Black Puritans: The Negro in Seventeenth-Century Massachusetts." *WMQ* 3rd series 24 (April 1967):224–42.

Vickers, Daniel. "The First Whalemen of Nantucket." *WMQ* 3rd series 40 (October 1983):560–83.

Wareing, John, "Migration to London and Transatlantic Emigration of Indentured Servants, 1683–1775." *JHG* 7 (1981):356–78.

Washburn, Emory. "Slavery As It Once Prevailed in Massachusetts." Boston: John Wilson & Son, 1869.

Watson, Alan D. "Impulse Toward Independence: Resistance and Rebellion Among North Carolina Slaves, 1750–1775." *JNH* 63 (Fall 1978):317–28.

Wax, Darold D. "Africans on the Delaware: The Pennsylvania Slave Trade, 1759–1765." *PH* 50 (January 1983):38–49.

———. "Demand for Slave Labor in Colonial Pennsylvania." *PH* 34 (October 1967):331–45.

———. "'New Negroes Are Always in Demand': The Slave Trade in Eighteenth-Century Georgia." *GHQ* 68 (Summer 1984):193–220.

———. "Preferences for Slaves in Colonial America." *JNH* 58 (October 1973):371–401.

Whatley, Warren C. "African-American Strikebreaking from the Civil War to the New Deal." *SSH* 17 (Winter 1993):525–58.

———. "Getting a Foot in the Door: 'Learning,' State Dependence, and the Racial Integration of Firms." *JEH* 5 (March 1990):43–66.

White, David O. "The Fugitive Blacksmith of Hartford: James W. C. Pennington." *CHSB* 49 (1984):5–31.

Williams, David. "Notes and Documents: Georgia's Forgotten Miners: African-Americans and the Georgia Gold Rush." *GHQ* 75 (Spring 1991):76–89.

Willis, William S. "Divide and Rule: Red, White and Black in the Southeast." *JNH* 48 (July 1963):157–76.

Winston, Sanford. "Indian Slavery in the Carolina Region." *JNH* 19 (October 1934):431–40.

Wish, Harvey. "American Slave Insurrections Before 1861." *JNH* 22 (July 1937):299–320.

Wood, Betty. "Thomas Stephens and the Introduction of Black Slavery in Georgia." *GHQ* 58 (Spring 1974):24–40.

Wood, Gordon. "Inventing American Capitalism." *NYRB* (June 9, 1994):44–49.

Woodson, Carter G. "The Negroes of Cincinnati Prior to the Civil War," *JNH* 1 (January 1916):431–40.

———. "The Negro Washerwoman, A Vanishing Figure." *JNH* 15 (July 1930):269–77.

Woofter, T. J. "The Negroes of Athens, Georgia." Phelps-Stokes Fellowship Studies, no. 1, *Bulletin of the University of Georgia* 14 (December 1913).

Wormley, G. Smith. "Prudence Crandall." *JNH* 8 (January 1923):72–8.

Wright, Gavin. "American Agriculture and the Labor Market: What Happened to Proletarianization?" *AH* 62 (Summer 1988):182–209.

———. "Cheap Labor and Southern Textiles Before 1880." *JEH* 39 (September 1979):655–680.

UNPUBLISHED THESES AND TYPESCRIPTS

Coalson, George Otis. "The Development of the Migratory Farm Labor System in Texas, 1900–1954." Ph.D. thesis, University of Oklahoma, 1955.

Cowie, Jeff. "Rooted Workers and the Runaway Shop: A Comparative History of

Capital Migration and Social Change in the United States and Mexico, 1936–1995." Ph.D. thesis, University of North Carolina–Chapel Hill, 1996.

Duncan, John Donald. "Servitude and Slavery in Colonial South Carolina, 1670–1776." Ph.D. thesis, Emory University, 1972.

Herndon, Ruth Wallis. "Governing the Affairs of the Town: Continuity and Change in Rhode Island, 1750–1800." Ph.D. thesis, American University, 1993.

Holt, Sharon Ann. "Making Freedom Pay." Ph.D. thesis, University of Pennsylvania, 1995.

Kelly, Kevin Peter. "Economic and Social Development of Seventeenth-Century Surry County, Virginia." Ph.D. thesis, University of Washington, 1972.

Meaders, Daniel. "Fugitive Slaves and Indentured Servants Before 1800." Ph.D. thesis, Yale University, 1990.

Melish, Joanne Pope. "Disowning Slavery: Gradual Emancipation and the Cultural Construction of 'Race' in New England, 1780–1860." Ph.D. thesis, Brown University, 1996.

Menard, Russell R. "Economy and Society in Early Colonial Maryland." Ph.D. thesis, University of Iowa, 1975.

Miller, Randall M. "The Cotton Mill Movement in Antebellum Alabama." Ph.D. thesis, Ohio State University, 1971.

O'Brien, Jean Marie. "Community Dynamics in the Indian-English Town of Natick, Massachusetts, 1650–1790." Ph.D. thesis, University of Chicago, 1990.

Plane, Ann Marie. "Colonizing the Family: Marriage, Household, and Racial Boundaries in Southeastern New England to 1730." Ph.D. thesis, Brandeis University, 1994.

Reed, Ruth. "The Negro Women of Gainesville, Georgia." M.A. thesis, University of Georgia, 1920.

Stokes, Allen H., Jr. "Black and White Labor and the Development of the Southern Textile Industry, 1800–1920." Ph.D. thesis, University of South Carolina, 1977.

Towner, Lawrence William. "A Good Master Well Served: A Social History of Servitude in Massachusetts, 1620–1750." Ph.D. thesis, Northwestern University, 1954.

Wax, Darold D. "The Negro Slave Trade in Colonial Pennsylvania." Ph.D. thesis, University of Washington, 1962.

Wiberly, Edward Jr. "Four Cities: Public Poor Relief in Urban America, 1700–1775." Ph.D. thesis, Yale University, 1975.

REFERENCE WORKS

Cooke, Jacob Ernest, ed. *Encyclopedia of the North American Colonies*. 3 vols. New York: Charles Scribner's Sons, 1993.

Hine, Darlene Clark, Elsa Barkley Brown, and Rosalyn Terborg-Penn, eds. *Black Women in America: An Historical Encyclopedia*. 2 vols. New York: Carlson, 1993.

Murphy, Larry G., J. Gordon Melton, and Gary L. Ward, eds. *Encyclopedia of African American Religions*. New York: Garland, 1993.

Salzman, Jack, David Lionel Smith, and Cornel Wet, eds. *Encyclopedia of African-American Culture and History*. 4 vols. New York: Macmillan Library Reference USA, 1996.

Sturtevant, William, *et al.*, eds. *Handbook of North American Indians*. 6 vols. Washington, DC: Smithsonian Institution Press, 1978– .

INDEX

Page numbers in *italics* refer to illustrations.

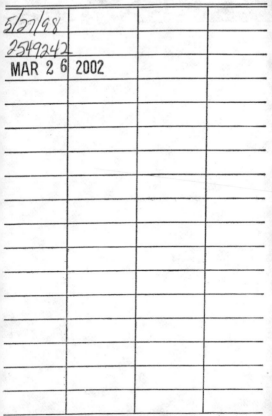

DATE DUE

5/27/98			
2549242			
MAR 2 6 2002			